ZAGAT
2013

Los Angeles/
So. California
Restaurants

SENIOR CONSULTING EDITOR
Merrill Shindler

LOS ANGELES EDITORS
John Bergano, Melissa Brandzel, Gillian Ferguson,
Grace Jidoun and Helen Sillett

ORANGE COUNTY EDITORS
Cynthia Furey and Gretchen Kurz

STAFF EDITOR
Michelle Golden

Published and distributed by
Zagat Survey, LLC
76 Ninth Avenue
New York, NY 10011
T: 212.977.6000
E: losangeles@zagat.com
plus.google.com/local

ACKNOWLEDGMENTS

We're grateful to our local editors, Merrill Shindler, an ABC radio commentator, food writer, critic and a Zagat editor for more than 25 years; John Bergano, a freelance writer, restaurant critic and food blogger; Melissa Brandzel, a freelance writer and cookbook editor; Gillian Ferguson, a food blogger and producer of KCRW's Good Food; Grace Jidoun, a food writer and cookbook editor; Helen Sillett, a freelance writer and editor; Cynthia Furey, a writer and editor; and Gretchen Kurz, a Zagat editor for more than 16 years and dining critic for *Orange Coast* magazine. We also sincerely thank the thousands of people who participated in this survey – this guide is really "theirs."

We also thank Simon Butler, Karen Hudes, Nikki Pierce, Jamie Selzer and Stefanie Tuder, as well as the following members of our staff: Caitlin Miehl (editor), Brian Albert, Sean Beachell, Maryanne Bertollo, Reni Chin, Larry Cohn, Nicole Diaz, Kelly Dobkin, Jeff Freier, Alison Gainor, Matthew Hamm, Justin Hartung, Marc Henson, Ryutaro Ishikane, Natalie Lebert, Mike Liao, Vivian Ma, James Mulcahy, Polina Paley, Emil Ross, Amanda Spurlock, Chris Walsh, Jacqueline Wasilczyk, Sharon Yates, Anna Zappia and Kyle Zolner.

ABOUT ZAGAT

In 1979, we asked friends to rate and review restaurants purely for fun. The term "user-generated content" had yet to be coined. That hobby grew into Zagat Survey; 33 years later, we have loyal surveyors around the globe and our content now includes nightlife, shopping, tourist attractions, golf and more. Along the way, we evolved from being a print publisher to a digital content provider. We also produce marketing tools for a wide range of corporate clients, and you can find us on Google+ and just about any other social media network.

Our reviews are based on public opinion surveys. The ratings reflect the average scores given by the survey participants who voted on each establishment. The text is based on quotes from, or paraphrasings of, the surveyors' comments. Phone numbers, addresses and other factual data were correct to the best of our knowledge when published in this guide.

JOIN IN: To improve our guides, we solicit your comments – positive or negative; it's vital that we hear your opinions. Just contact us at **nina-tim@zagat.com.** We also invite you to share your opinions at plus.google.com/local.

© 2012 Zagat Survey, LLC
ISBN-13: 978-1-60478-516-6
ISBN-10: 1-60478-516-0
Printed in the
United States of America

Contents

Ratings & Symbols

Zagat Top Spot	Name	Symbols		Cuisine	Zagat Ratings			
					FOOD	DECOR	SERVICE	COST

Area, Address & Contact

Ƶ Tim & Nina's ◐ *Asian*

▽ 23 | 9 | 13 | $15

Hollywood | 346 Sunset Blvd. (1st St.) | 213-555-2570 | www.zagat.com

Review, surveyor comments in quotes

"Trend"-spotters hail this "high-concept" production on Sunset offering "fantastic" Asian-deli fare that includes "tantalizing tongue sushi" slathered in "to-die-for hijiki coleslaw"; decor that "hasn't changed since Cecil B. DeMille" was a regular and "reeeal New Yawk-style" service don't seem to deter "agents", "stars" and "working gals" hooked on the "delicious sake-celery soda-tinis."

Ratings

Food, Decor & **Service** are rated on a 30-point scale.

26 – 30   extraordinary to perfection

21 – 25   very good to excellent

16 – 20   good to very good

11 – 15   fair to good

0 – 10   poor to fair

▽   low response | less reliable

Cost

The price of dinner with a drink and tip; lunch is usually 25% to 30% less. For unrated **newcomers,** the price range is as follows:

I $25 and below   E $41 to $65

M $26 to $40   VE $66 or above

Symbols

Ƶ   highest ratings, popularity and importance

◐   serves after 11 PM

Ƶ M   closed on Sunday or Monday

⊘   no credit cards accepted

Maps

Index maps show restaurants with the highest Food ratings in those areas.

About This Survey

- 2,082 restaurants covered
- 18,450 surveyors
- 93 notable openings
- Top Rated: **Urasawa** (Food), **Sir Winston's** (Decor), **Providence** (Service), **101 Coffee Shop** (Popularity), **Cheesecake Factory** (Most Popular Chain), **In-N-Out Burger** (Bang for the Buck)
- No. 1 Newcomer: **Ink**

SURVEY STATS: Los Angeles surveyors report eating out an average of 3.5 times per week, significantly more than their counterparts in New York (3.0) and San Francisco (2.9) . . . 31% say they're spending more per meal, 56% say the same and only 13% say less . . . Favorite cuisines: Italian (26%), American (15%) and Japanese (15%) . . . 46% book via phone, 43% use the Internet . . . Surveyors rank the top LA dining neighborhoods as West Hollywood, Beverly Hills and Santa Monica . . . 43% occasionally patronize one of the city's many food trucks, but only 19% make it a point to follow favorites via social media . . . Service remains dining-out's top drawback (cited by 61%) followed by noise (18%), driving/parking (7%) and prices (6%) . . . Angelenos tip an average of 18.7%, compared to a national average of 19.3% . . . On a 30-point scale, Los Angeles rates 26 for culinary diversity, 23 for creativity and 17 for table availability and hospitality.

HOT NEIGHBORHOODS: Beverly Hills (**BierBeisl, Bouchon Bakery, Caulfield's, Larder at Maple Drive, Livello**); Santa Monica (**The Charleston, Mercado, Milo & Olive, Tar & Roses, Ushuaia**); West Hollywood (**A1 Cucina, The Churchill, PaliKitchen**); West LA (**Freddy Smalls, Gottsui, Morinoya, Plan Check**)

BIG-NAME OPENINGS: Govind Armstrong (**Post & Beam**); Josef Centeno (**Baco Mercat**); Roy Choi (**Sunny Spot**); Alain Giraud (**Maison Giraud**); Suzanne Goin (**Larder at Maple Drive**); Andre Guerrero (**Little Bear, Maximiliano**); Thomas Keller (**Bouchon Bakery**); Andrew Kirschner (**Tar & Roses**); Josie Le Balch (**Next Door by Josie**); Wolfgang Puck (**Wolfgang Puck at Hotel Bel-Air**); Jet Tila (**The Charleston**); Ricardo Zarate (**Mo-Chica**)

TRENDS: Exotic sandwiches (**Baco Mercat, Bouchon Bakery, Fundamental LA, Mendocino Farms**); gastropubs (**Larry's, Little Bear, The Pikey**); booze-focused boîtes (**Freddy Smalls, Hot's Kitchen, Next Door by Josie, Post & Beam**); pizza (**Crust Pizza Bar, 800 Degrees, Milo & Olive, Settebello**)

TOUGH TICKETS: Baco Mercat, Mercato di Vetro, Milo & Olive, Mo-Chica, Tar & Roses

Los Angeles, CA   Merrill Shindler
October 22, 2012

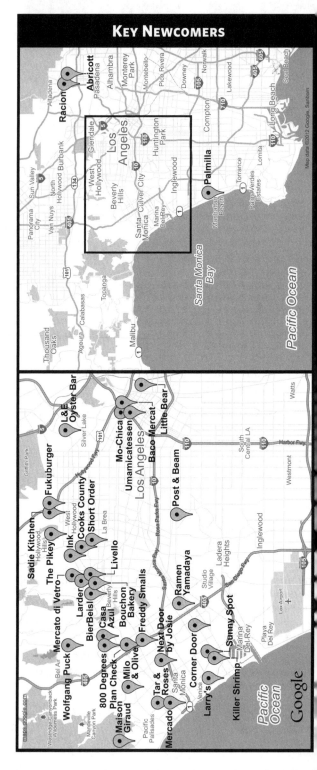

KEY NEWCOMERS

Racion
Abricott
Pasadena
Altadena

Los Angeles
Glendale
West Hollywood
Beverly Hills
Culver City
Santa Monica
Marina Del Rey
Inglewood
Huntington Park
Compton
Torrance
Palmilla
Manhattan Beach

Santa Monica Bay

Pacific Ocean

Map data ©2012 Google, Sanborn

L&E Oyster Bar
Mo-Chica
Umamicatessen
Baco Mercat
Little Bear
Fukuburger
Sadie Kitchen
The Pikey
Ink
Cooks County
Short Order
Livello
Mercato di Vetro
Larder
BierBeisl
Casa Azul
Bouchon Bakery
Freddy Smalls
Next Door by Josie
Ramen Yamadaya
Post & Beam
Wolfgang Puck
800 Degrees
Plan Check
Milo & Olive
Maison Giraud
Tar & Roses
Corner Door
Sunny Spot
Mercado
Larry's
Killer Shrimp

Los Angeles

Griffin Park
Silver Lake
Hollywood
West Hollywood
La Brea
Beverly Hills
Studio Village
Ladera Heights
Inglewood
Santa Monica
Venice
Marina Del Rey
Playa Del Rey
Lax Airport

Pacific Ocean

Google

maps.google.com

Key Newcomers

Our editors' picks among this year's arrivals. See full list at p. 28.

BIG NAMES

Baco Mercat
Bouchon Bakery
Ink
Maison Giraud
Mercato di Vetro
Mo-Chica
Plan Check
Post & Beam
Short Order
Sunny Spot
Tar & Roses
Umamicatessen
Wolfgang Puck at Hotel Bel-Air

SCENES

Baco Mercat
Cooks County
Corner Door
800 Degrees
Freddy Smalls
Ink
Killer Shrimp
Pikey
Sadie Kitchen
Short Order
Tar & Roses

FARM-TO-TABLE

Larder at Maple Drive
Larry's
Mercado
Next Door by Josie
Post & Beam

STRIKING SPACES

Plan Check
Post & Beam
Umamicatessen
Wolfgang Puck at Hotel Bel-Air

NEIGHBORHOOD STARS

Abricott
BierBeisl
Casa Azul
L&E Oyster Bar
Palmilla
Racion

ON THE RUN

Bouchon Bakery
800 Degrees
Larry's
Milo & Olive

BARGAIN BITES

Baco Mercat
Fukuburger
Ramen Yamadaya
Short Order
Umamicatessen

MIXOLOGY MECCAS

Freddy Smalls
Ink
Livello
Mercato di Vetro
Next Door by Josie's
Pikey
Tar & Roses

PROJECTS ON TAP

Word has it that über-chef Jean-Georges Vongerichten has been scouting for a Los Angeles location for his NYC hit **ABC Kitchen.** Walter Manzke is pushing ahead with the French-inspired **République** Downtown, while Eric Greenspan puts the finishing touches on his grilled-cheese restaurant adjacent to his **Foundry on Melrose.** Later this year Gordon Ramsay will debut **The Fat Cow** in The Grove. Joining him nearby at the Farmers Market will be Neal Fraser with artisanal weenies at **Fritzi Dog.** Michael Cardenas (**Lazy Ox**) and his chef, Perfecto Rocher, are planning a 2013 debut for their paella-focused **Taberna Arros y Vi** in Santa Monica. Other anticipated openings are **Bar Amá,** Josef Centeno's ode to Tex-Mex Downtown, David Myers' modern Cal in Century City and **Connie & Ted's,** a New England–style seafood shack in West Hollywood from Michael Cimarusti of **Providence.**

Most Popular

A full list is plotted on the map at the back of this book.

1 101 Coffee Shop | *Diner*

2 Spago | *Californian*

3 101 Noodle Express | *Chinese*

4 Angelini Osteria | *Italian*

5 Brent's Deli | *Deli*

6 Bazaar/José Andrés | *Spanish*

7 Cafe Bizou | *French*

8 Mélisse | *Amer./French*

9 Bouchon | *French*

10 Osteria Mozza | *Italian*

11 Pizzeria Mozza | *Pizza*

12 Lawry's Prime Rib | *Steak*

13 Mastro's Steak | *Steak*

14 Providence | *Amer./Seafood*

15 Lucques | *Californian/Med.*

16 Apple Pan | *American*

17 A.O.C. | *Californian/Med.*

18 Roscoe's Chicken | *Soul Food*

19 Joe's | *Californian/French*

20 Gjelina | *American*

21 Hatfield's | *American*

22 Porto's Bakery | *Bakery/Cuban*

23 Animal | *American*

24 Bottega Louie | *Italian*

25 Sugarfish | *Japanese*

26 26 Beach | *Californian*

27 Matsuhisa | *Japanese*

28 17th Street Cafe | *Californian*

29 Din Tai Fung | *Chinese*

30 Campanile | *Californian/Med.*

31 Water Grill | *Seafood*

32 Philippe/Original | *Sandwiches*

33 800 Degrees | *Pizza*

34 Chinois on Main | *Asian/French*

35 Barney's Beanery | *Eclectic*

36 555 East | *Steak*

37 Drago Centro | *Italian*

38 Bay Cities Deli | *Deli*

39 Stonefire Grill | *BBQ*

40 Valentino | *Italian*

Many of the above restaurants are among the Los Angeles area's most expensive, but if popularity were calibrated to price, a number of other restaurants would surely join their ranks. To illustrate this, we have added two lists comprising 80 Best Buys on page 16.

MOST POPULAR CHAINS

1 Cheesecake Factory | *American*

2 In-N-Out | *Burgers*

3 BJ's | *Pub Food*

4 Elephant Bar | *Asian*

5 California Pizza | *Pizza*

6 Wood Ranch BBQ | *BBQ*

7 Black Angus | *Steak*

8 Chipotle | *Mexican*

9 Outback | *Steak*

10 Acapulco | *Mexican*

Top Food

28 Urasawa | *Japanese*
Michael's/Naples | *Italian*
Asanebo | *Japanese*
Sushi Zo | *Japanese*
Mélisse | *American/French*
Piccolo | *Italian*
Matsuhisa | *Japanese*
Echigo | *Japanese*
Providence | *American/Seafood*
Angelini Osteria | *Italian*
Michael's Pizzeria | *Pizza*
Hamasaku | *Japanese*
Kiwami | *Japanese*
M.B. Post | *American*
Bashan | *American*

27 Lucques | *Californian/Med.*
Sushi Masu | *Japanese*
Bazaar/José Andrés | *Spanish*
Cut | *Steak*
Nobu Malibu | *Japanese*
Spago | *Californian*
Katsu-ya | *Japanese*
Mosto Enoteca | *Italian*
Jitlada | *Thai*
Bludso's BBQ | *BBQ*
Leila's | *Californian*

Brandywine | *Continental*
Shiro | *French/Japanese*
Saam/The Bazaar | *Eclectic*
Osteria Mozza | *Italian*
Hatfield's | *American*
Babita | *Mexican*
Water Grill | *Seafood*
Ado/Casa Ado | *Cal./Italian*
Pizzeria Mozza | *Pizza*
Omino Sushi | *Japanese*
Hirozen | *Japanese*
Animal | *American*
Alfredo's | *Mexican*
Patina | *American/Californian*
Gjelina Take Away | *American*
Suzanne's Cuisine | *Fr./Italian*
Katana | *Japanese*
Chinois on Main | *Asian/French*
Café 14 | *Continental*
Brother Sushi | *Japanese*
Cicada* | *Californian/Italian*
Hot's Kitchen* | *Eclectic*
Mori Sushi* | *Japanese*
Nanbankan* | *Japanese*
Sushi Sasabune* | *Japanese*
Belvedere* | *American*

BY CUISINE

AMERICAN (NEW)

28 Mélisse
Providence
M.B. Post
Bashan
27 Hatfield's

AMERICAN (TRAD.)

26 Farmshop
25 Salt's Cure
Grill on the Alley
Clementine
Griddle Cafe*
Martha's 22nd St. Grill*

ASIAN/ASIAN FUSION

27 Chinois on Main
26 LudoBites
25 Crustacean
Gina Lee's
Spice Table

BAKERIES

26 Porto's Bakery
25 Clementine
Euro Pane*
24 Joan's on Third
Susina Bakery

BARBECUE

27 Bludso's BBQ
Woody's BBQ
26 Phillips BBQ
Naples Rib Co.
25 Rattler's BBQ

BURGERS

26 Golden State
In-N-Out
25 Tommy's
Back Abbey
25 Degrees

Excludes places with low votes; * indicates a tie with restaurant above

CALIFORNIAN

27 Lucques
Spago
Leila's
Patina
Ado

CARIBBEAN/CUBAN

26 Porto's Bakery
24 Asia de Cuba
23 Versailles
22 Cha Cha Chicken
Cha Cha Cha

CHINESE

27 Newport Seafood
26 Din Tai Fung
Sea Harbour
WP24
25 Duck House

CONTINENTAL

27 Brandywine
Café 14
26 Dal Rae
Sir Winston's
25 Fins

DELIS

26 Brent's Deli
Bay Cities Deli
Langer's Deli
24 Pico Kosher Deli
23 Lascari's Deli

DIM SUM

26 Sea Harbour
24 Elite
Panda Inn
23 Ocean Seafood
22 Bao Dim Sum

DINERS

25 Original Pancake
23 Cora's Coffee
101 Coffee Shop
Nickel Diner
Uncle Bill's

ECLECTIC

27 Saam/The Bazaar
Hot's Kitchen
26 Chez Mélange
Ink
Depot

FRENCH

28 Mélisse
27 Shiro
Suzanne's Cuisine
Maison Akira
26 JiRaffe

GREEK

25 Petros
24 George's Greek
23 Papa Cristo's
Le Petit Greek
Great Greek

INDIAN

26 Addi's Tandoor
24 Bombay Palace
Bollywood Cafe
Nawab of India
Anarbagh

ITALIAN

28 Michael's/Naples
Piccolo
Angelini Osteria
27 Mosto Enoteca
Osteria Mozza

JAPANESE

28 Urasawa
Asanebo
Sushi Zo
Matsuhisa
Echigo

KOREAN

25 Park's BBQ
Soot Bull Jeep
24 Chego!
ChoSun Galbee
22 Kyochon

MEDITERRANEAN

27 Lucques
Cleo
Christine
26 Campanile
A.O.C.

MEXICAN

27 Babita
Alfredo's
26 El Tepeyac
Mucho Ultima
25 Yuca's

MIDDLE EASTERN

26 Raffi's Place
25 Open Sesame
Carnival
Alwazir Chicken
Carousel

PIZZA

28 Michael's Pizzeria
27 Pizzeria Mozza
Vito's
26 Gjelina
Buono's

SEAFOOD

28 Providence
27 Water Grill
26 Santa Monica Seafood
25 Boiling Crab
Mailbu Seafood

SMALL PLATES

28 M.B. Post
27 Bazaar/José Andrés
Leila's
Cleo
26 A.O.C.

SOUL/SOUTHERN

25 Johnny Rebs'
M & M Soul Food
24 Les Sisters
Lucille's BBQ
Roscoe's Chicken

SOUTH AMERICAN

26 Mario's Peruvian
25 Fogo de Chão
Picca
24 Carlitos Gardel
Mo-Chica

STEAKHOUSES

27 Cut
Mastro's Steak
Ruth's Chris
26 Morton's Steak
Lawry's Prime Rib

THAI

27 Jitlada
24 Ayara Thai
Cholada
Saladang
23 Palms Thai

VEGETARIAN

25 Native Foods
24 Cafe Gratitude
Mohawk Bend
23 Real Food Daily
Veggie Grill

VIETNAMESE

26 Pho So 1
25 Crustacean
Golden Deli
24 Pho 79
23 Red Medicine

BY SPECIAL FEATURE

BREAKFAST

26 Julienne
25 Clementine
Griddle Cafe*
Martha's 22nd St.*
Original Pancake*

BRUNCH

27 Belvedere
26 Saddle Peak
Joe's
Campanile
A.O.C.

BUSINESS DINING

28 Mélisse
Providence
27 Cut
Hatfield's
Water Grill

FOOD TRUCKS

26 Grill 'Em All Truck
Kogi Korean BBQ
25 Buttermilk Truck
24 LudoTruck
Border Grill Truck

HOTEL DINING

27 Bazaar/José Andrés (SLS)
Cut (Beverly Wilshire)
Belvedere (Peninsula)
Cleo (Redbury)
26 Mar'sel (Terranea)

LATE DINING

27 Pizzeria Mozza
26 Gjelina
Tasting Kitchen
In-N-Out
25 Lazy Ox

LUNCH

NEWCOMERS (RATED)

PEOPLE-WATCHING

POWER SCENES

TRENDY

WINNING WINE LISTS

BY LOCATION

BEVERLY BOULEVARD

BEVERLY HILLS

BRENTWOOD

CHINATOWN

DOWNTOWN

FAIRFAX

HOLLYWOOD

LA BREA

LONG BEACH

LOS FELIZ/ SILVER LAKE

MALIBU

27 Nobu Malibu
26 Savory
25 Malibu Seafood
24 Fish Grill
   Cholada

MELROSE

27 Hatfield's
25 Red O
24 Foundry on Melrose
   Carlitos Gardel
   Tomato Pie

PASADENA AREA

27 Shiro
   Maison Akira
   Ruth's Chris
26 Parkway Grill
   Bistro 45

SAN FERNANDO VALL.

28 Asanebo
   Kiwami
   Bashan
27 Katsu-ya
   Brandywine

SAN GABRIEL VALL.

27 Babita
   Newport Seafood
26 Sea Harbour
   Dal Rae
   California Grill

SANTA MONICA

28 Mélisse
27 Chinois on Main
26 Bay Cities Deli

   JiRaffe
   Sugarfish

SOUTH BAY

28 M.B. Post
27 Hot's Kitchen
   Woody's BBQ
   Christine
26 Chef Melba's

THIRD STREET

26 A.O.C.
   Izaka-ya by Katsu-ya
25 Locanda Veneta
   Son of a Gun
24 Olio Pizzeria & Cafe

VENICE

28 Piccolo
27 Ado
   Gjelina Take Away
26 Joe's
   Gjelina

WEST HOLLYWOOD

27 Lucques
   Katana
26 Ink
   Nobu LA
   Mozza to Go

WEST LA

28 Sushi Zo
   Echigo
   Hamasaku
27 Sushi Masu
   Mori Sushi
   Nanbankan*
   Sushi Sasabune*

Top Decor

<u>28</u> Sir Winston's
Mar'sel
Cicada
Saddle Peak
Bazaar/José Andrés

<u>27</u> Belvedere
Yamashiro
Royce
Penthouse
Getty Center
Katana
Perch
Geoffrey's
Mohawk Bend
Raphael*
Red O
RockSugar
WP24
Inn of the Seventh Ray
Takami*

Cliff's Edge
Sky Room
Crustacean
Culina

<u>26</u> Michael's Restaurant
Strand House
Providence
Saam/The Bazaar
Dar Maghreb
Craft
Fig & Olive
One Pico
Mélisse
Patina
Asia de Cuba
Polo Lounge
Raymond
Bistro Garden/Coldwater
Parkway Grill
Bahooka

OUTDOORS

Alcove
Belvedere
Biergarten at The Standard
Cafe Pinot
Culina
Eveleigh

Gjelina
Joe's
Lucques
Michael's Restaurant
Ray's & Stark Bar
Wilshire

ROMANCE

Bazaar/José Andrés
Brandywine
Cliff's Edge
Il Cielo
Lucques

Mar'sel
Mélisse
Michael's Restaurant
Perch
Valentino

ROOMS

Getty Center
Hatfield's
Mélisse
Parkway Grill
Polo Lounge

Red Medicine
RockSugar
Saam/The Bazaar
Spice Table
Tavern

VIEWS

Asia de Cuba
Baleen
BLT Steak
Cafe Del Rey
Katana

Lobster
Penthouse
Saddle Peak Lodge
WP24
Yamashiro

Top Service

<u>28</u> Providence
Shiro

<u>27</u> Mélisse
Belvedere
Patina
Urasawa

<u>26</u> Piccolo
Lawry's Prime Rib
Sam's by the Beach
Alfredo's
Tuscany
Brandywine
Hatfield's
Saam/The Bazaar
Valentino
Saddle Peak
Michael's/Naples
Royce
Sir Winston's
Bashan

Spago
Cut
Ruth's Chris
Culina
Water Grill
Mastro's Steak
Lucques
Angelino Cafe
Mosto Enoteca
Craig's
Michael's Restaurant
Marino
Morton's Steak
Chez Mélange
Christine
Rustico

<u>25</u> Grill on the Alley
WP24
Hostaria del Piccolo
Larsen's Steak

Best Buys

In order of rating.

1. In-N-Out
2. Wienerschnitzel
3. Lee's Sandwiches
4. Tommy's
5. Chipotle
6. Habit Burger
7. Yuca's
8. Fab Hot Dogs
9. Berlin Currywurst
10. Tito's Tacos
11. Portillo's Hot Dogs
12. Cook's Tortas
13. Carney's Express
14. Wahoo's Fish Taco
15. Cafe Rio
16. Best Fish Taco
17. El Gallo Giro
18. Burrito King
19. Dog Haus
20. King Taco
21. Five Guys
22. Poquito Más
23. Farmer Boy's
24. Chili John's
25. Chronic Tacos
26. Papaya King
27. Pho Show
28. Pink's Chili Dogs
29. Pho So 1
30. Tops
31. Slaw Dogs
32. Super Mex
33. Porto's Bakery
34. Hakata
35. Spitz
36. Samosa House
37. Astro Burger
38. El Tepeyac
39. Philippe/Original
40. Mendocino Farms

BEST BUYS: OTHER GOOD VALUES

Alejo's
Apple Pan
Artisan Cheese
Baby Blues BBQ
Bay Cities Deli
BCD Tofu
Beer Belly
Bludso's BBQ
Blue Cow Kitchen
Bouchon Bakery
CaCao
Cafe Gratitude
Cal. Chicken Cafe
Chego!
Cook's Tortas
Counter
Daikokuya
Dr. Hogly Wogly's
Eden Burger Bar
800 Degrees

Euro Pane
exEat
Golden Deli
Hole in the Wall
JR's BBQ
Lamonica's Pizza
Let's Be Frank
Mohawk Bend
Native Foods
Oinkster
101 Noodle
Ramen Yamadaya
Reddi Chick
Shamshiri Grill
Stella Rossa
Umami Burger
Veggie Grill
Village Pizzeria
Wurstküche
Zankou Chicken

LOS ANGELES
OTHER USEFUL LISTS*

Special Features 18
Cuisines 41
Locations 58

LOCATION MAPS

Hollywood | Melrose 79
Downtown 80
Marina del Rey | Santa Monica | Venice 81
Pasadena 82

---

* These lists include low vote places that do not qualify for top lists.

Special Features

Listings cover the best in each category and include names, locations and Food ratings. Multi-location restaurants' features may vary by branch.

BREAKFAST

(See also Hotel Dining)

Julienne | **San Marino**	26
Farmshop | **Santa Monica**	26
NEW Milo & Olive | **Santa Monica**	25
Buttermilk | **Location Varies**	25
Clementine | **Century City**	25
Griddle Cafe | **Hollywood**	25
Martha's 22nd St. | **Hermosa Bch**	25
Original Pancake | **Redondo Bch**	25
Tavern | **Brentwood**	24
Olio/Cafe | **Third St**	24
Cajun Kitchen | **Ventura**	24
NEW Maison Giraud | **Pacific Palisades**	24
Susina | **Beverly Blvd**	24
3 Square | **Venice**	24
French Crêpe Co. | **multi.**	23
Huckleberry | **Santa Monica**	23
Sweet Lady Jane | **Melrose**	23
Auntie Em's | **Eagle Rock**	23
Cora's | **Santa Monica**	23
Cecconi's | **W Hollywood**	23
Barney Greengrass | **Beverly Hills**	23
Square One | **E Hollywood**	23
Nickel Diner | **Downtown**	23
Uncle Bill's | **Manhattan Bch**	23
Doughboys | **Third St**	22
Hugo's | **multi.**	22
Art's | **Studio City**	22
BLD | **Beverly Blvd**	22
Alcove | **Los Feliz**	21
Marston's | **Pasadena**	21
Café Laurent | **Culver City**	21
Lemon Moon | **West LA**	21
Ruby's | **multi.**	21
Maxwell's | **Venice**	20
Jinky's | **multi.**	20
La Dijonaise | **Culver City**	20
John O'Groats | **Rancho Pk**	20
Farm/Bev. Hills | **Beverly Hills**	19
Marmalade | **multi.**	19
Patrick's | **Santa Monica**	19
Fred 62 | **Los Feliz**	19
Overland Cafe | **Culver City**	19
Du-par's | **Fairfax**	18

Mel's Drive-In | **Hollywood**	18
NEW Larder at Maple Dr. | **Beverly Hills**	-

BRUNCH

Belvedere | **Beverly Hills**	27
Saddle Peak | **Calabasas**	26
Joe's | **Venice**	26
Campanile | **La Brea**	26
A.O.C. | **Third St**	26
Gjelina | **Venice**	26
Tasting Kitchen | **Venice**	26
Farmshop | **Santa Monica**	26
Salt's Cure | **Hollywood**	25
NEW Cooks County | **Beverly Blvd**	25
Raymond | **Pasadena**	25
Bouchon | **Beverly Hills**	25
Blu Jam | **Mid-City**	25
Tavern | **Brentwood**	24
Grub | **Hollywood**	24
NEW Larry's | **Venice**	24
Cafe Verde | **Pasadena**	24
Canelé | **Atwater Vill**	24
Comme Ça | **W Hollywood**	24
3 Square | **Venice**	24
One Pico | **Santa Monica**	24
26 Beach | **Venice**	24
Ocean Seafood | **Chinatown**	23
Bottega Louie | **Downtown**	23
Fig | **Santa Monica**	23
Little Dom's/Deli | **Los Feliz**	23
Ammo | **Hollywood**	23
Nickel Diner | **Downtown**	23
Porta Via | **Beverly Hills**	22
Dusty's | **Silver Lake**	22
Polo | **Beverly Hills**	22
McCormick/Schmick | **El Segundo**	22
Whist | **Santa Monica**	22
Hugo's | **multi.**	22
NEW Abigaile | **Hermosa Bch**	22
Firefly Bistro | **S Pasadena**	21
Cliff's Edge | **Silver Lake**	21
House Café | **Beverly Blvd**	21
Napa Valley | **Westwood**	19
Lilly's | **Venice**	19

Twohey's | **Alhambra** 19
Jer-ne | **Marina del Rey** 19

BUFFET

(Check availability)
Maison Akira | **Pasadena** 27
Bombay Palace | **Beverly Hills** 24
Nawab | **Santa Monica** 24
Ocean Tava | **Redondo Bch** 24
Panda Inn | **multi.** 24
Kravings | **Tarzana** 23
Tanzore | **Beverly Hills** 23
India's Tandoori | **multi.** 23
Castaway | **Burbank** 22
Chakra | **Beverly Hills** 22
Wahib's | **Alhambra** 22
Smoke Hse. | **Burbank** 22
O-Nami | **Torrance** 21
All India | **West LA** 21
El Torito Grill | **Torrance** 21
Inn/Seventh Ray | **Topanga** 21
Walter's | **Claremont** 21
El Torito | **multi.** 21
Picanha | **Burbank** 21
Frida | **Glendale** 20
Salt Creek | **Valencia** 20
Mijares | **Pasadena** 20
Burger Continental | **Pasadena** 18

BUSINESS DINING

Mélisse | **Santa Monica** 28
Providence | **Hollywood** 28
Lucques | **W Hollywood** 27
Cut | **Beverly Hills** 27
Spago | **Beverly Hills** 27
Hatfield's | **Melrose** 27
Water Grill | **Downtown** 27
Patina | **Downtown** 27
Belvedere | **Beverly Hills** 27
Cicada | **Downtown** 27
Ruth's Chris | **multi.** 27
Mistral | **Sherman Oaks** 26
Campanile | **La Brea** 26
Morton's | **multi.** 26
Nobu | **W Hollywood** 26
Valentino | **Santa Monica** 26
BLT Steak | **W Hollywood** 26
Mar'sel | **Rancho Palos Verdes** 26
WP24 | **Downtown** 26
Bistro 45 | **Pasadena** 26
Rivera | **Downtown** 26
Drago Centro | **Downtown** 26

555 East | **Long Bch** 26
Safire | **Camarillo** 26
Josie | **Santa Monica** 26
Madeo | **W Hollywood** 26
Arroyo | **Pasadena** 26
Craft | **Century City** 25
Fleming's | **multi.** 25
Grill on Alley | **Beverly Hills** 25
Rustic Canyon | **Santa Monica** 25
Celestino | **Pasadena** 25
Michael's Rest. | **Santa Monica** 25
NEW Wolfgang Puck/Hotel Bel-Air | **Bel-Air** 25
Il Grano | **West LA** 25
Bouchon | **Beverly Hills** 25
Jar | **Beverly Blvd.** 25
Petros | **Manhattan Bch** 25
STK | **W Hollywood** 25
Roy's | **Downtown** 25
Grill on Hollywood/Alley | **Hollywood** 24
Culina | **Beverly Hills** 24
Wolfgang's | **Beverly Hills** 24
Taylor's | **multi.** 24
Chaya | **Downtown** 24
Gordon Ramsay | **W Hollywood** 24
La Botte | **Santa Monica** 24
Scarpetta | **Beverly Hills** 24
Nick & Stef's | **Downtown** 24
One Pico | **Santa Monica** 24
Cheval Blanc | **Pasadena** 24
Fig & Olive | **Melrose** 23
Dan Tana's | **W Hollywood** 23
Nic's | **Beverly Hills** 23
Checkers | **Downtown** 23
Wilshire | **Santa Monica** 23
Coast | **Santa Monica** 23
Barney Greengrass | **Beverly Hills** 23
Catch | **Santa Monica** 23
Wolfgang Puck B&G | **Downtown** 23
Westside Tav. | **West LA** 23
Polo | **Beverly Hills** 22
Paul Martin's | **El Segundo** 22
Blvd | **Beverly Hills** 22
Kincaid's | **Redondo Bch** 22
Peppone | **Brentwood** 22
Il Moro | **West LA** 22
L.A. Market | **Downtown** 21
Ombra | **Studio City** 21
NEW Caulfield's | **Beverly Hills** -
NEW FigOly | **Downtown** -
NEW Towne | **Downtown** -

CELEBRITY CHEFS

José Andrés
- Tres/José Andrés | **Beverly Hills** — 29
- Bazaar by José Andrés | **Beverly Hills** — 27
- Saam/The Bazaar | **Beverly Hills** — 27

Gino Angelini
- Angelini | **Beverly Blvd** — 28

Govind Armstrong
- NEW Post & Beam | **Mid-City** — 26

Mario Batali
- Osteria Mozza | **Hollywood** — 27
- Pizzeria Mozza | **Hollywood** — 27

Rick Bayless
- Red O | **Melrose** — 25

Josef Centeno
- NEW Baco Mercat | **Downtown** — 26

Roy Choi
- Kogi | **Location Varies** — 26
- Chego! | **Palms** — 24
- A-Frame | **Culver City** — 23
- NEW Sunny Spot | **Marina del Rey** — 22

Michael Cimarusti
- Providence | **Hollywood** — 28

Josiah Citrin
- Mélisse | **Santa Monica** — 28
- Lemon Moon | **West LA** — 21

Tom Colicchio
- Craft | **Century City** — 25

Brendan Collins
- NEW Larry's | **Venice** — 24
- Waterloo & City | **Culver City** — 24

Scott Conant
- Scarpetta | **Beverly Hills** — 24

Celestino Drago
- Drago Centro | **Downtown** — 26

Todd English
- Beso | **Hollywood** — 19

Susan Feniger
- Street | **Hollywood** — 25
- Border Grill | **Santa Monica** — 22

Ben Ford
- Ford's | **Culver City** — 21

Neal Fraser
- BLD | **Beverly Blvd** — 22
- NEW Strand House | **Manhattan Bch** — 21
- Cole's | **Downtown** — 17

Alain Giraud
- NEW Maison Giraud | **Pacific Palisades** — 24

Suzanne Goin
- Lucques | **W Hollywood** — 27
- A.O.C. | **Third St** — 26
- Tavern | **Brentwood** — 24
- NEW Larder at Maple Dr. | **Beverly Hills** — -

Andre Guerrero
- NEW Maximiliano | **Highland Pk** — 25
- Oinkster | **Eagle Rock** — 22
- NEW Little Bear | **Downtown** — 18

Ilan Hall
- Gorbals | **Downtown** — 22

Thomas Keller
- NEW Bouchon Bakery | **Beverly Hills** — 26
- Bouchon | **Beverly Hills** — 25
- Bar Bouchon | **Beverly Hills** — 24

Ludo Lefebvre
- LudoBites | **Location Varies** — 26
- LudoTruck | **Location Varies** — 24

David LeFevre
- M.B. Post | **Manhattan Bch** — 28

David Lentz
- Hungry Cat | **Santa Monica** — 24

Bruce Marder
- Capo | **Santa Monica** — 26
- Cora's | **Santa Monica** — 23
- House Café | **Beverly Blvd** — 21

Nobu Matsuhisa
- Matsuhisa | **Beverly Hills** — 28
- Nobu | **Malibu** — 27
- Nobu | **W Hollywood** — 26

Joe Miller
- Joe's | **Venice** — 26
- Bar Pintxo | **Santa Monica** — 22

David Myers
- Comme Ça | **W Hollywood** — 24

Mark Peel
- Campanile | **La Brea** — 26

Wolfgang Puck
- Cut | **Beverly Hills** — 27
- Spago | **Beverly Hills** — 27
- Chinois | **Santa Monica** — 27
- WP24 | **Downtown** — 26
- NEW Wolfgang Puck/ Hotel Bel-Air | **Bel-Air** — 25

Wolfgang Puck B&G | **Downtown** 23

Wolfgang Puck Express/Bistro | **multi.** 21

Gordon Ramsay

Gordon Ramsay | **W Hollywood** 24

Akasha Richmond

Akasha | **Culver City** 22

Stefan Richter

Stefan's/L.A. Farm | **Santa Monica** 22

Hans Röckenwagner

3 Square | **Venice** 24

Röckenwagner | **Santa Monica** 20

Richard Sandoval

Zengo | **Santa Monica** 23

John Sedlar

Rivera | **Downtown** 26

Playa | **Beverly Blvd** 25

Jimmy Shaw

Lotería! | **multi.** 23

Paul Shoemaker

Savory | **Malibu** 26

Nancy Silverton

Osteria Mozza | **Hollywood** 27

Pizzeria Mozza | **Hollywood** 27

NEW Short Order | **Fairfax** 18

Kerry Simon

L.A. Market | **Downtown** 21

Simon LA | **W Hollywood** 21

Jet Tila

NEW Charleston | **Santa Monica** -

Michael Voltaggio

Ink | **W Hollywood** 26

Roy Yamaguchi

Roy's | **multi.** 25

Sang Yoon

Lukshon | **Culver City** 25

Father's Office | **multi.** 24

Ricardo Zarate

Picca | **Century City** 25

NEW Mo-Chica | **Downtown** 24

CHILD-FRIENDLY

(Alternatives to the usual fast-food places; * children's menu available)

Din Tai Fung | **Arcadia** 26

Brent's Deli | **multi.** 26

Langer's | **Downtown** 26

Carnival* | **Sherman Oaks** 25

NEW 800 Degrees* | **Westwood** 25

Martha's 22nd St.* | **Hermosa Bch** 25

Les Sisters* | **Chatsworth** 25

Caffé Delfini | **Santa Monica** 24

Wood Ranch* | **multi.** 24

Lucille's* | **multi.** 24

Panda Inn | **multi.** 24

Abbot's | **multi.** 24

22nd St. Landing* | **San Pedro** 24

Casa Bianca | **Eagle Rock** 23

Palms Thai | **E Hollywood** 23

Apple Pan | **West LA** 23

Pizzicotto | **Brentwood** 23

Cheesecake Factory* | **multi.** 23

Zankou | **multi.** 23

Umami* | **multi.** 23

Feast/East | **West LA** 23

Cal. Chicken* | **multi.** 23

Poquito Más* | **multi.** 23

Le Petit Greek | **Hancock Pk** 23

Versailles | **multi.** 23

Big Mama's* | **Pasadena** 23

Chart House* | **multi.** 23

Bluewater* | **Redondo Bch** 23

Mulberry St. Pizzeria | **multi.** 23

Robin's* | **Pasadena** 23

BJ's* | **multi.** 23

Farfalla/Vinoteca | **Los Feliz** 23

Original Roadhse. Grill* | **Whittier** 23

Ribs USA* | **Burbank** 23

Pitfire* | **multi.** 23

Dish* | **La Cañada Flintridge** 23

Lotería!* | **multi.** 23

Fabiolus | **Hollywood** 22

Fritto Misto* | **multi.** 22

Cha Cha Chicken | **Santa Monica** 22

Caffe Pinguini | **Playa del Rey** 22

A'float Sushi | **Pasadena** 22

Mi Piace | **Pasadena** 22

Mama D's* | **Manhattan Bch** 22

Johnnie's Pastrami* | **Culver City** 22

Cal. Pizza Kitchen* | **multi.** 22

P.F. Chang's* | **multi.** 22

Pie 'N Burger* | **Pasadena** 22

Carney's | **multi.** 22

Il Forno Caldo | **Beverly Hills** 22

Barney's* | **Santa Monica** 22

BLD | **Beverly Blvd** 22

Amici | **multi.** 22

Enterprise Fish* | **Santa Monica** 21

Bravo* | **Santa Monica** 21

Marston's* | **Pasadena** 21

Gaucho*	Brentwood	21	Josie	Santa Monica	26
Paco's Tacos*	Westchester	21	NEW Milo & Olive	Santa Monica	25
Black Cat	Fairfax	21	Clementine	Century City	25
Counter*	Santa Monica	21	Bouchon	Beverly Hills	25
Ruby's*	multi.	21	La Crêperie Café	Long Bch	24
El Torito*	multi.	21	Joan's on Third Cafe	Third St	24
17th St. Cafe*	Santa Monica	21	Susina	Beverly Blvd	24
La Grande Orange*	Pasadena	21	French Crêpe Co.	multi.	23
Five Guys*	multi.	21	Melting Pot	multi.	23
Maxwell's*	Venice	20	Bottega Louie	Downtown	23
Thai Dishes	multi.	20	Huckleberry	Santa Monica	23
Hop Woo	West LA	20	Cheesecake Factory	multi.	23
Duke's*	Malibu	20	Sweet Lady Jane	Melrose	23
Jody Maroni's	multi.	20	Auntie Em's	Eagle Rock	23
Johnnie's NY	Downtown	20	Jin Patisserie	Venice	23
Jinky's*	multi.	20	Nickel Diner	Downtown	23
Stanley's	Sherman Oaks	20	Akasha	Culver City	22
Louise's*	Pasadena	20	Doughboys	Third St	22
Maria's*	multi.	20	Mi Piace	Pasadena	22
John O'Groats*	Rancho Pk	20	Urth	multi.	22
Miceli's*	Hollywood	20	Le Pain Quotidien	multi.	22
La Salsa*	multi.	19	Alcove	Los Feliz	21
Hop Li	multi.	19	L.A. Market	Downtown	21
Kay 'n Dave's*	multi.	19	Phoenix	Alhambra	21
Mo's*	Burbank	19	17th St. Cafe	Santa Monica	21
Babalu	Santa Monica	19	Simon LA	W Hollywood	21
Gladstone's*	Pacific Palisades	18	Cafe Montana	Santa Monica	21
Burger Continental*	Pasadena	18	Jack n' Jill's	Santa Monica	20
El Coyote*	Beverly Blvd	17	Farm/Bev. Hills	multi.	19
Fromin's*	Santa Monica	17	Babalu	Santa Monica	19

DANCING

Watermark on Main	Ventura	24
Cafe Fiore	Ventura	23
El Pollo Inka	Gardena	22
Padri	Agoura Hills	22
Wahib's	Alhambra	22
Smoke Hse.	Burbank	22
Monsoon	Santa Monica	21
Whale & Ale	San Pedro	21
Buffalo Club	Santa Monica	19
Rush St.	Culver City	18

DESSERT SPECIALISTS

Providence	Hollywood	28
Spago	Beverly Hills	27
Campanile	La Brea	26
NEW Bouchon Bakery	Beverly Hills	26
Forage	Silver Lake	26
Porto's	multi.	26

DINING AT THE BAR

M.B. Post	Manhattan Bch	28
Lucques	W Hollywood	27
Osteria Mozza	Hollywood	27
Water Grill	Downtown	27
Pizzeria Mozza	Hollywood	27
Parkway Grill	Pasadena	26
Joe's	Venice	26
Campanile	La Brea	26
A.O.C.	Third St	26
Gjelina	Venice	26
Rivera	Downtown	26
Drago Centro	Downtown	26
Lazy Ox	Little Tokyo	25
Stella Rossa	Santa Monica	25
Lukshon	Culver City	25
Bouchon	Beverly Hills	25
Jar	Beverly Blvd.	25
Playa	Beverly Blvd	25
Roy's	multi.	25

Church/State | **Downtown** 24

Hungry Cat | **Hollywood** 24

Houston's | **multi.** 24

Waterloo & City | **Culver City** 24

Father's Office | **multi.** 24

Chaya | **Downtown** 24

Brentwood | **Brentwood** 24

AKA Bistro | **Pasadena** 23

Westside Tav. | **West LA** 23

Firefly | **Studio City** 22

ENTERTAINMENT

(Call for days and times of
performances)

Mastro's | **Beverly Hills** 27

Parkway Grill | **Pasadena** 26

Arroyo | **Pasadena** 26

Carousel | **Glendale** 25

Sky Room | **Long Bch** 25

Fins | **Westlake Vill** 25

Carlitos Gardel | **Melrose** 24

Bandera | **West LA** 24

Lucille's | **Long Bch** 24

One Pico | **Santa Monica** 24

Papa Cristo's | **Mid-City** 23

Galletto | **Westlake Vill** 23

Alegria | **Long Bch** 23

Great Greek | **Sherman Oaks** 23

Parker's | **Long Bch** 23

Vibrato Grill | **Bel-Air** 23

Catch | **Santa Monica** 23

Antonio's | **Melrose** 22

El Pollo Inka | **multi.** 22

Polo | **Beverly Hills** 22

Padri | **Agoura Hills** 22

Geisha Hse. | **Hollywood** 22

Dar Maghreb | **Hollywood** 22

Moonshadows | **Malibu** 21

Buffalo Club | **Santa Monica** 19

FIREPLACES

Mélisse | **Santa Monica** 28

Lucques | **W Hollywood** 27

Suzanne's | **Ojai** 27

Mastro's | **Thousand Oaks** 27

Maison Akira | **Pasadena** 27

Saddle Peak | **Calabasas** 26

Parkway Grill | **Pasadena** 26

Capo | **Santa Monica** 26

Lawry's Prime | **Beverly Hills** 26

Dal Rae | **Pico Rivera** 26

Mar'sel | **Rancho Palos Verdes** 26

Buono's | **Long Bch** 26

Larchmont Grill | **Hollywood** 26

Safire | **Camarillo** 26

Josie | **Santa Monica** 26

Arroyo | **Pasadena** 26

NEW Mercato di Vetro | 26
W Hollywood

Michael's Rest. | **Santa Monica** 25

71 Palm | **Ventura** 25

Derby | **Arcadia** 25

NEW Wolfgang Puck/ 25
Hotel Bel-Air | **Bel-Air**

Raymond | **Pasadena** 25

Koi | **W Hollywood** 25

Watermark on Main | **Ventura** 24

Culina | **Beverly Hills** 24

Houston's | **multi.** 24

Baleen | **Redondo Bch** 24

Bar | Kitchen | **Downtown** 24

Waterloo & City | **Culver City** 24

Cafe Del Rey | **Marina del Rey** 24

Panda Inn | **Ontario** 24

Little Door | **Third St** 24

One Pico | **Santa Monica** 24

Cafe Fiore | **Ventura** 23

Cafe Firenze | **Moorpark** 23

A & W Seafood | **Northridge** 23

Dan Tana's | **W Hollywood** 23

Zin | **Westlake Vill** 23

Il Cielo | **Beverly Hills** 23

Tam O'Shanter | **Atwater Vill** 23

Chart House | **multi.** 23

Bluewater | **Redondo Bch** 23

Osteria La Buca | **Hollywood** 23

Vibrato Grill | **Bel-Air** 23

Catch | **Santa Monica** 23

Stinking Rose | **Beverly Hills** 23

Ca' del Sole | **N Hollywood** 23

Wolfgang Puck B&G | **Downtown** 23

Pitfire | **West LA** 23

Dish | **La Cañada Flintridge** 23

Old Tony's | **Redondo Bch** 23

Zengo | **Santa Monica** 23

Taverna Tony | **Malibu** 22

Reel Inn | **Malibu** 22

Ivy | **W Hollywood** 22

Marrakesh | **Studio City** 22

Monty's | **Woodland Hills** 22

Tanino | **Westwood** 22

Clearman's | **San Gabriel** 22

Original Red Onion | 22
Rolling Hills Estates

Il Fornaio | **multi.**	22
R+D Kitchen | **Santa Monica**	22
Padri | **Agoura Hills**	22
Beckham Grill | **Pasadena**	22
Guido's | **West LA**	22
NEW Haven | **Pasadena**	22
McCormick/Schmick | **Pasadena**	22
Admiral Risty | **Rancho Palos Verdes**	22
Penthouse | **Santa Monica**	22
31Ten | **Santa Monica**	22
Taste | **Pacific Palisades**	22
Geisha Hse. | **Hollywood**	22
Off Vine | **Hollywood**	22
Smoke Hse. | **Burbank**	22
NEW Abigaile | **Hermosa Bch**	22
Amalfi | **La Brea**	22
Inn/Seventh Ray | **Topanga**	21
Vertical Wine | **Pasadena**	21
Mediterraneo | **Westlake Vill**	21
Rive Gauche | **Sherman Oaks**	21
Bistro Gdn. | **Studio City**	21
Dominick's | **W Hollywood**	21
James' | **Venice**	21
Walter's | **Claremont**	21
Taix | **Echo Pk**	21
Whale & Ale | **San Pedro**	21
El Torito | **Long Bch**	21
La Boheme | **W Hollywood**	21
Eveleigh | **W Hollywood**	21
Larchmont Bungalow | **Hancock Pk**	21
Il Covo | **W Hollywood**	21
Home | **multi.**	20
Salt Creek | **El Segundo**	20
Casa Vega | **Sherman Oaks**	20
Buggy Whip | **Westchester**	20
El Cholo | **multi.**	20
Gonpachi | **Torrance**	20
Napa Valley | **Westwood**	19
Hamburger Hamlet | **Pasadena**	19
Abbey | **W Hollywood**	19
Paradise Cove | **Malibu**	19
Jer-ne | **Marina del Rey**	19
Ye Olde King's | **Santa Monica**	18
Literati | **West LA**	18
Perch | **Downtown**	18
Barney's Beanery | **Westwood**	17
El Coyote | **Beverly Blvd**	17
NEW Outpost | **Hollywood**	-
Tom Bergin's | **Mid-City**	-
NEW Towne | **Downtown**	-

FOOD TRUCKS

Grill 'Em All | **Location Varies**	26
Kogi | **Location Varies**	26
Buttermilk | **Location Varies**	25
Baby's/Burgers | **Location Varies**	24
LudoTruck | **Location Varies**	24
Border Grill Truck | **Location Varies**	24
Grilled Cheese Truck | **Location Varies**	24
Lobsta Truck | **Location Varies**	23
Frysmith | **Location Varies**	23
Lomo Arigato | **Location Varies**	22
Flying Pig | **Location Varies**	22
Nom Nom | **Location Varies**	21
Let's Be Frank | **Culver City**	19

GREEN/LOCAL/ ORGANIC

Mélisse | **Santa Monica**	28
Providence | **Hollywood**	28
Bashan | **Montrose**	28
Lucques | **W Hollywood**	27
Hatfield's | **Melrose**	27
Animal | **Fairfax**	27
Joe's | **Venice**	26
Golden State | **Fairfax**	26
Savory | **Malibu**	26
Forage | **Silver Lake**	26
Farmshop | **Santa Monica**	26
Lazy Ox | **Little Tokyo**	25
Salt's Cure | **Hollywood**	25
Rustic Canyon | **Santa Monica**	25
Michael's Rest. | **Santa Monica**	25
Eva | **Beverly Blvd**	25
Son of a Gun | **Third St**	25
Jar | **Beverly Blvd.**	25
Native Foods | **Westwood**	25
Cube Cafe | **La Brea**	25
Elf Café | **Echo Pk**	25
Playa | **Beverly Blvd**	25
Tavern | **Brentwood**	24
Hungry Cat | **Hollywood**	24
Waterloo & City | **Culver City**	24
Axe | **Venice**	24
Bloom | **Mid-City**	24
Cabbage Patch | **multi.**	23
Real Food | **multi.**	23
Huckleberry | **Santa Monica**	23
Tender Greens | **multi.**	23
Fig | **Santa Monica**	23
True Food | **Santa Monica**	23
Ammo | **Hollywood**	23

Simmzy's | **Manhattan Bch**	23
Square One | **E Hollywood**	23
Akasha | **Culver City**	22
M Café | **multi.**	22
Urth | **multi.**	22
Le Pain Quotidien | **multi.**	22
Vegan Glory | **Beverly Blvd**	22
Greenleaf | **multi.**	22
A Votre Sante | **Brentwood**	21
Inn/Seventh Ray | **Topanga**	21
Blue Hen | **Eagle Rock**	21
M Street | **Santa Monica**	21
Farm Stand | **El Segundo**	21
Larchmont Bungalow | **Hancock Pk**	21
Literati | **West LA**	18

HISTORIC PLACES

(Year opened; * building)

1900 | Saddle Peak* | **Calabasas**	26
1900 | Raymond* | **Pasadena**	25
1902 | L'Opera* | **Long Bch**	25
1902 | redwhite+bluezz* | **Pasadena**	23
1906 | Pete's* | **Downtown**	21
1907 | Watermark on Main* | **Ventura**	24
1908 | Philippe/Original | **Chinatown**	24
1908 | Anacapa Brewing* | **Ventura**	23
1908 | Off Vine* | **Hollywood**	22
1908 | Cole's* | **Downtown**	17
1910 | Via Veneto* | **Santa Monica**	26
1910 | 71 Palm* | **Ventura**	25
1910 | Warszawa* | **Santa Monica**	23
1911 | Pitfire* | **Downtown**	23
1912 | Polo* | **Beverly Hills**	22
1912 | Engine Co. 28* | **Downtown**	20
1914 | Yamashiro* | **Hollywood**	22
1916 | Alcove* | **Los Feliz**	21
1917 | Enterprise Fish* | **Santa Monica**	21
1919 | Musso & Frank* | **Hollywood**	23
1920 | Salt's Cure* | **Hollywood**	25
1920 | La Paella* | **Beverly Hills**	23
1920 | Clafoutis | **W Hollywood**	22
1920 | Haven* | **Pasadena**	22
1920 | Mijares | **Pasadena**	20
1920 | Barney's Beanery | **W Hollywood**	17
1920 | Farm/Bev. Hills* | **Beverly Hills**	19

1922 | Derby* | **Arcadia**	25
1922 | Tam O'Shanter | **Atwater Vill**	23
1923 | Wood & Vine* | **Hollywood**	23
1923 | Farfalla/Vinoteca* | **Los Feliz**	23
1923 | El Cholo | **Mid-City**	20
1924 | Grub* | **Hollywood**	24
1924 | Canter's | **Fairfax**	21
1924 | Original Pantry | **Downtown**	20
1925 | Bay Cities | **Santa Monica**	26
1925 | Palm* | **Downtown**	25
1925 | Church/State* | **Downtown**	24
1925 | Taste* | **W Hollywood**	22
1926 | Sky Room* | **Long Bch**	25
1927 | Far Niente* | **Glendale**	24
1927 | Taix | **Echo Pk**	21
1927 | Pig 'n Whistle* | **Hollywood**	19
1928 | Cafe Stella* | **Silver Lake**	22
1929 | Campanile* | **La Brea**	26
1929 | Tanino* | **Westwood**	22
1930 | Brighton Coffee | **Beverly Hills**	20
1931 | Lucques* | **W Hollywood**	27
1931 | El Coyote | **Beverly Blvd**	17
1933 | Michael's Rest.* | **Santa Monica**	25
1933 | Sidecar* | **Ventura**	23
1934 | Luggage Room* | **Pasadena**	23
1934 | Galley* | **Santa Monica**	20
1935 | Stand* | **Westwood**	19
1936 | Sir Winston's* | **Long Bch**	26
1938 | Lawry's Prime | **Beverly Hills**	26
1938 | Du-par's | **multi.**	18
1939 | Bistro 45* | **Pasadena**	26
1939 | Pink's Dogs | **La Brea**	23
1939 | Luna Park* | **La Brea**	21
1939 | Traxx* | **Downtown**	21
1939 | Formosa | **W Hollywood**	16
1940 | Tommy's* | **Downtown**	25
1940 | Il Cielo | **Beverly Hills**	23
1945 | Nate 'n Al | **Beverly Hills**	20
1946 | Chili John's | **Burbank**	24
1946 | Uncle Bill's | **Manhattan Bch**	23
1946 | Smoke Hse. | **Burbank**	22
1946 | Paradise Cove* | **Malibu**	19
1946 | Billingsley's | **West LA**	17
1954 | Angelini* | **Beverly Blvd**	28
1955 | El Tepeyac | **East LA**	26
1955 | Casa Bianca | **Eagle Rock**	23
1955 | Trader Vic's | **Beverly Hills**	19
1956 | Antonio's | **Melrose**	22

HOTEL DINING

Thompson Beverly Hills
  NEW Caulfield's | **Beverly Hills** ⌐

Viceroy Santa Monica
  Whist | **Santa Monica**   22

W Hollywood Hotel
  Delphine | **Hollywood**   22

LATE DINING

(Weekday closing hour)

Bazaar by José Andrés | varies | 27
  Beverly Hills

Pizzeria Mozza | 12 AM | 27
  Hollywood

NEW Freddy Smalls | varies | 26
  West LA

NEW Tsujita LA | varies | 26
  West LA

Gjelina | varies | **Venice**   26
In-N-Out | varies | **multi.**   26
Lazy Ox | 12 AM | **Little Tokyo**   25
Stella Rossa | varies | 25
  Santa Monica

Alwazir Chicken | 12 AM | 25
  Hollywood

NEW 800 Degrees | 2 AM | 25
  Westwood

Tommy's | 24 hrs. | **Downtown**   25
Park's BBQ | 1 AM | **Koreatown**   25
Back Abbey | 12 AM | **Claremont**   25
Pho Café | 12 AM | **Silver Lake**   25
Katsuya | varies | **Hollywood**   25
Bar Hayama | 11:15 PM | 25
  West LA

Le Petit Bistro | 12 AM | 25
  W Hollywood

Iroha | 12 AM | **Studio City**   25
King Taco | varies | **multi.**   24
NEW Larry's | varies | **Venice**   24
NEW Fukuburger | 12 AM | 24
  Hollywood

25 Degrees | 1:30 AM | 24
  Hollywood

NEW Mo-Chica | 12 AM | 24
  Downtown

Black Market | 2 AM | **Studio City**   24
Joe's Pizza | varies | **multi.**   24
Daikokuya | 12 AM | **multi.**   24
Honda-Ya | 1 AM | **Little Tokyo**   24
Waterloo & City | 12 AM | 24
  Culver City

Father's Office | varies | 24
  Santa Monica

Lamonica's | varies | **Westwood**   24
Wurstküche | 12 AM, 2 AM | 24
  multi.

Roscoe's | varies | **multi.**   24
Brentwood | 12 AM | 24
  Brentwood

101 Noodle | 1 AM | **Alhambra**   23
Casa Bianca | varies | **Eagle Rock**   23
Fishbar | varies | **Manhattan Bch**   23
Palms Thai | 12 AM | **E Hollywood**   23
Sanamluang Cafe | 3:30,   23
  3:30 AM | **multi.**

Apple Pan | 12 AM | **West LA**   23
Zankou | 11:45 PM | **E Hollywood**   23
Umami | 1 AM | **N Hollywood**   23
Red Medicine | 2 AM | **Beverly Hills** 23
Z Pizza | varies | **W Hollywood**   23
Dan Tana's | 1 AM | **W Hollywood**   23
Nic's | varies | **Beverly Hills**   23
Ago | 12 AM | **W Hollywood**   23
Poquito Más | varies | **Studio City**   23
Hudson Hse. | varies | **Redondo Bch**   23
BJ's | varies | **multi.**   23
Cecconi's | varies | **W Hollywood**   23
101 Coffee | 3 AM | **Hollywood**   23
Bossa Nova | varies | **multi.**   23
Boneyard | 2 AM | **Sherman Oaks**   23
Pink's Dogs | 2 AM | **La Brea**   23
NEW Umamicatessen | 12 AM | 23
  Downtown

Farfalla/Vinoteca | 12 AM | 23
  Glendale

Caffe Roma | varies | **Beverly Hills** 23
New Capital Seafood | 1 AM | 23
  San Gabriel

Kyochon | 12 AM | **Koreatown**   22
Astro Burger | varies | **Hollywood**   22
Misfit | varies | **Santa Monica**   22
Polo | 1:30 AM | **Beverly Hills**   22
Yard House | varies | **multi.**   22
BCD Tofu | varies | **multi.**   22
El Gallo Giro | 24 hrs. | 22
  Huntington Pk

Johnnie's Pastrami | varies | 22
  Culver City

NEW Haven | 1 AM | **Pasadena**   22
Bowery | 2 AM | **Hollywood**   22
Full House | 3 AM | **Chinatown**   22
Gorbals | 12 AM | **Downtown**   22
Carney's | varies | **W Hollywood**   22
Geisha Hse. | 12 AM | **Hollywood**   22
Wokcano | varies | **multi.**   22
Burrito King | 3 AM | **Echo Pk**   22
Firefly | 12 AM | **Studio City**   22
Lazy Dog | 12 AM | **Valencia**   22
Lares | 1 AM | **Santa Monica**   22

Hummus Bar | 1 AM | **Tarzana**	22
El Compadre | varies | **Echo Pk**	22
Fat Dog | 1 AM | **multi.**	22
Alcove | 12 AM | **Los Feliz**	21
Bravo | 1:30 AM | **Santa Monica**	21
Sam Woo | 12 AM | **multi.**	21
Vertical Wine | varies | **Pasadena**	21
Sushi Dan | varies | **Hollywood**	21
Toi | 4 AM | **W Hollywood**	21
Dominick's | 12:45 AM | **W Hollywood**	21
Pho Show | 2 AM | **Culver City**	21
Federal Bar | 1 AM | **N Hollywood**	21
Canter's | 24 hrs. | **Fairfax**	21
Manhattan Beach BrewCo | 1 AM | **Manhattan Bch**	21
Phoenix | 1 AM | **multi.**	21
NEW Killer Shrimp | 12 AM | **Marina del Rey**	21
Pete's | 2 AM | **Downtown**	21
Kitchen 24 | 24 hrs. | **multi.**	21
Eveleigh | varies | **W Hollywood**	21
Auld Dubliner | varies | **Long Bch**	21
Nate 'n Al | 1 AM | **LAX**	20
Swingers | varies | **multi.**	20
Hop Woo | varies | **Chinatown**	20
Casa Vega | 1 AM | **Sherman Oaks**	20
Wienerschnitzel | 24 hr. | **Diamond Bar**	20
Gaby's | varies | **Palms**	20
Kate Mantilini | varies | **Beverly Hills**	20
Original Pantry | 24 hrs. | **Downtown**	20
Wirtshaus | 12 AM | **La Brea**	20
Trader Vic's | varies | **Beverly Hills**	19
Hop Li | 1 AM | **Arcadia**	19
Greenblatt's | 1:30 AM | **Hollywood**	19
Buffalo Club | 2 AM | **Santa Monica**	19
Abbey | 2 AM | **W Hollywood**	19
NEW Plan Check | varies | **West LA**	19
Restaurant/Standard | 24 hrs. | **multi.**	19
BottleRock | varies | **multi.**	19
Fred 62 | 24 hrs. | **Los Feliz**	19
Pig 'n Whistle | 1:30 AM | **Hollywood**	19
Tea Station | varies | **multi.**	19
Noodle World | 1 AM | **Alhambra**	19

Baja Sharkeez | 1:30 AM | **Hermosa Bch**	18
NEW Little Bear | 2 AM | **Downtown**	18
Pink Taco | 2 AM | **W Hollywood**	18
Papaya King | 3 AM | **Hollywood**	18
Hamburger Mary's | 2 AM | **Long Bch**	18
Jerry's Deli | varies | **multi.**	18
Baja Cantina | 2 AM | **Marina del Rey**	18
Du-par's | 24 hrs. | **multi.**	18
Mel's Drive-In | varies | **multi.**	18
Perch | varies | **Downtown**	18
Barney's Beanery | varies | **multi.**	17
NEW The Churchill | varies | **W Hollywood**	17
Formosa | varies | **W Hollywood**	16
NEW Ba Restaurant | 12 AM | **Highland Pk**	–
NEW BierBeisl | varies | **Beverly Hills**	–
NEW Biergarten/Standard | 2 AM | **Downtown**	–
NEW Bow & Truss | 2 AM | **N Hollywood**	–
NEW Corner Door | varies | **Culver City**	–
NEW Duplex on Third | 1 AM | **W Hollywood**	–
NEW Eat.Drink.Americano | varies | **Downtown**	–
NEW Eden Burger Bar | 12 AM | **Glendale**	–
NEW Gottsui | 12 AM | **West LA**	–
NEW Lago d'Argento | 12 AM | **Silver Lake**	–
NEW Outpost | 2 AM | **Hollywood**	–
NEW Pikey | 2 AM | **Hollywood**	–
NEW Tatsu Ramen | 2 AM | **West LA**	–
The Parish | 2 AM | **Downtown**	–
Tom Bergin's | 2 AM | **Mid-City**	–
NEW Wolfslair | 2 AM | **Hollywood**	–

NEWCOMERS

Freddy Smalls | **West LA**	26
Tsujita LA | **West LA**	26
Post & Beam | **Mid-City**	26
Ink | **W Hollywood**	26
Bouchon Bakery | **Beverly Hills**	26
Baco Mercat | **Downtown**	26

Mercato di Vetro	**W Hollywood**	26
Maximiliano	**Highland Pk**	25
Milo & Olive	**Santa Monica**	25
800 Degrees	**Westwood**	25
Cooks County	**Beverly Blvd**	25
Wolfgang Puck/Hotel Bel-Air	**Bel-Air**	25
Next Door/Josie	**Santa Monica**	25
Larry's	**Venice**	24
Fukuburger	**Hollywood**	24
Maison Giraud	**Pacific Palisades**	24
Mo-Chica	**Downtown**	24
A1 Cucina	**W Hollywood**	24
Settebello	**Pasadena**	24
Tar & Roses	**Santa Monica**	23
Ramen Yamadaya	**Culver City**	23
Blue Cow Kitchen	**Downtown**	23
Umamicatessen	**Downtown**	23
Lab Brewing Co.	**Agoura Hills**	22
Haven	**Pasadena**	22
Abigaile	**Hermosa Bch**	22
Sunny Spot	**Marina del Rey**	22
Abricott	**Pasadena**	22
Casa Azul	**Westwood**	21
Strand House	**Manhattan Bch**	21
Killer Shrimp	**Marina del Rey**	21
Plan Check	**West LA**	19
Little Bear	**Downtown**	18
Manna	**Downtown**	18
Short Order	**Fairfax**	18
The Churchill	**W Hollywood**	17
Ba Restaurant	**Highland Pk**	–
Bashi	**Rancho Palos Verdes**	–
BierBeisl	**Beverly Hills**	–
Biergarten/Standard	**Downtown**	–
Black Hogg	**Silver Lake**	–
Boardwalk/Burgers	**Hermosa Bch**	–
Bosc	**Hollywood**	–
Bow & Truss	**N Hollywood**	–
Bugatta	**Melrose**	–
Caulfield's	**Beverly Hills**	–
Charleston	**Santa Monica**	–
Corner Door	**Culver City**	–
Crust	**Studio City**	–
Duplex on Third	**W Hollywood**	–
Eat.Drink.Americano	**Downtown**	–
Eden Burger Bar	**Glendale**	–
exEat/Eatalian	**Gardena**	–
FigOly	**Downtown**	–
Gottsui	**West LA**	–
Gusto	**Third St**	–

Hannosuke	**Mar Vista**	–
Industriel	**Downtown**	–
Killer Cafe	**Marina del Rey**	–
Lago d'Argento	**Silver Lake**	–
L&E Oyster Bar	**Silver Lake**	–
Larder at Maple Dr.	**Beverly Hills**	–
Limani Taverna	**San Pedro**	–
Livello	**Beverly Hills**	–
Mercado	**Santa Monica**	–
Morinoya	**West LA**	–
Nong La	**West LA**	–
One Eyed Gypsy	**Downtown**	–
Osteria Drago	**W Hollywood**	–
Outpost	**Hollywood**	–
Palikitchen	**W Hollywood**	–
Palmilla	**Hermosa Bch**	–
Pikey	**Hollywood**	–
P'tit Soleil	**Westwood**	–
Racion	**Pasadena**	–
Sadie Kitchen	**Hollywood**	–
Seoul House/Tofu	**West LA**	–
Soleto Trattoria	**Downtown**	–
Tatsu Ramen	**West LA**	–
Tortilla Republic	**W Hollywood**	–
Towne	**Downtown**	–
Ushuaia	**Santa Monica**	–
Wolfslair	**Hollywood**	–

OUTDOOR DINING

Lucques	**W Hollywood**	27
Spago	**Beverly Hills**	27
Katana	**W Hollywood**	27
Belvedere	**Beverly Hills**	27
Saddle Peak	**Calabasas**	26
Joe's	**Venice**	26
Gjelina	**Venice**	26
Safire	**Camarillo**	26
Michael's Rest.	**Santa Monica**	25
Martha's 22nd St.	**Hermosa Bch**	25
Koi	**W Hollywood**	25
Fins	**Westlake Vill**	25
Culina	**Beverly Hills**	24
Cafe Pinot	**Downtown**	24
Ray's/Stark Bar	**Mid-Wilshire**	24
Hungry Cat	**Hollywood**	24
Locanda/Lago	**Santa Monica**	24
Asia de Cuba	**W Hollywood**	24
Little Door	**Third St**	24
Il Cielo	**Beverly Hills**	23
Cora's	**Santa Monica**	23
Pink's Dogs	**La Brea**	23

Wilshire | **Santa Monica**	23	Cicada | **Downtown**	27
Barney Greengrass | **Beverly Hills**	23	Mastro's | **Beverly Hills**	27
Ca' del Sole | **N Hollywood**	23	Ruth's Chris | **Beverly Hills**	27
Lotería! | **Fairfax**	23	Parkway Grill | **Pasadena**	26
Reel Inn | **Malibu**	22	Campanile | **La Brea**	26
Ivy | **W Hollywood**	22	A.O.C. | **Third St**	26
Mediterraneo | **Hermosa Bch**	22	Morton's | **multi.**	26
Mi Piace | **Pasadena**	22	Lawry's Prime | **Beverly Hills**	26
Geoffrey's | **Malibu**	22	Depot | **Torrance**	26
Off Vine | **Hollywood**	22	Valentino | **Santa Monica**	26
Firefly | **Studio City**	22	Dal Rae | **Pico Rivera**	26
Barney's | **multi.**	22	Fleming's | **El Segundo**	25
Ivy/Shore | **Santa Monica**	22	Michael's Rest. | **Santa Monica**	25
Cafe Med | **W Hollywood**	22	Giorgio Baldi | **Santa Monica**	25
BLD | **Beverly Blvd**	22	Palm | **multi.**	25
Il Moro | **West LA**	22	Spice Table | **Little Tokyo**	25
Alcove | **Los Feliz**	21	L'Opera | **Long Bch**	25
Bravo | **Santa Monica**	21	Cafe Pinot | **Downtown**	24
Firefly Bistro | **S Pasadena**	21	Tavern | **Brentwood**	24
Inn/Seventh Ray | **Topanga**	21	Cafe Del Rey | **Marina del Rey**	24
Mediterraneo | **Westlake Vill**	21	Little Door | **Third St**	24
Café Santorini | **Pasadena**	21	Nick & Stef's | **Downtown**	24
Rose Cafe | **Venice**	21	One Pico | **Santa Monica**	24
Dominick's | **W Hollywood**	21	Enoteca Drago | **Beverly Hills**	23
James' | **Venice**	21	Getty Ctr. | **Brentwood**	23
Cliff's Edge | **Silver Lake**	21	Red Medicine | **Beverly Hills**	23
China Grill | **Manhattan Bch**	21	Il Cielo | **Beverly Hills**	23
Ford's | **Culver City**	21	Chart House | **Redondo Bch**	23
Eveleigh | **W Hollywood**	21	Checkers | **Downtown**	23
Moonshadows | **Malibu**	21	Vibrato Grill | **Bel-Air**	23
Acapulco | **San Pedro**	20	King's Fish | **Long Bch**	23
Gumbo Pot | **Fairfax**	20	Ca' del Sole | **N Hollywood**	23
Shack | **multi.**	20	Cafe Bizou | **multi.**	23
Farm/Bev. Hills | **Beverly Hills**	19	RockSugar | **Century City**	22
Lilly's | **Venice**	19	Castaway | **Burbank**	22
Restaurant/Standard | **W Hollywood**	19	Antonio's | **Melrose**	22
		Tanino | **Westwood**	22
Gladstone's | **Pacific Palisades**	18	Polo | **Beverly Hills**	22
Burger Continental | **Pasadena**	18	Maggiano's | **multi.**	22
NEW Biergarten/Standard | **Downtown**	–	Il Fornaio | **multi.**	22
		McCormick/Schmick | **multi.**	22
		Geisha Hse. | **Hollywood**	22

PARTIES/ PRIVATE ROOMS

(Restaurants charge less at off times; call for capacity)

Mélisse | **Santa Monica**	28	Off Vine | **Hollywood**	22
Matsuhisa | **Beverly Hills**	28	Dar Maghreb | **Hollywood**	22
Spago | **Beverly Hills**	27	Il Moro | **West LA**	22
Saam/The Bazaar | **Beverly Hills**	27	Inn/Seventh Ray | **Topanga**	21
Hatfield's | **Melrose**	27	Canal Club | **Venice**	21
Katana | **W Hollywood**	27	Monsoon | **Santa Monica**	21
Belvedere | **Beverly Hills**	27	Bistro Gdn. | **Studio City**	21
		James' | **Venice**	21
		Ca'Brea | **La Brea**	21

McKenna's | **Long Bch** | 21
Simon LA | **W Hollywood** | 21
Duke's | **Malibu** | 20
El Cholo | **Santa Monica** | 20
Morels French Steak | **Fairfax** | 20
Kendall's | **Downtown** | 20
Napa Valley | **Westwood** | 19
Buffalo Club | **Santa Monica** | 19
Gladstone's | **Pacific Palisades** | 18

PEOPLE-WATCHING

Bazaar by José Andrés | **Beverly Hills** | 27
Cut | **Beverly Hills** | 27
Nobu | **Malibu** | 27
Spago | **Beverly Hills** | 27
Osteria Mozza | **Hollywood** | 27
Ado/Casa Ado | **Marina del Rey** | 27
Pizzeria Mozza | **Hollywood** | 27
Animal | **Fairfax** | 27
Katana | **W Hollywood** | 27
Mastro's | **Beverly Hills** | 27
NEW Freddy Smalls | **West LA** | 26
Ink | **W Hollywood** | 26
Gjelina | **Venice** | 26
NEW Baco Mercat | **Downtown** | 26
Rivera | **Downtown** | 26
Madeo | **W Hollywood** | 26
Mucho Ultima | **Manhattan Bch** | 26
Craft | **Century City** | 25
Grill on Alley | **Beverly Hills** | 25
Rustic Canyon | **Santa Monica** | 25
NEW Wolfgang Puck/ Hotel Bel-Air | **Bel-Air** | 25
Katsuya | **multi.** | 25
Son of a Gun | **Third St** | 25
Koi | **W Hollywood** | 25
Palm | **W Hollywood** | 25
Spice Table | **Little Tokyo** | 25
Red O | **Melrose** | 25
Petros | **Manhattan Bch** | 25
STK | **W Hollywood** | 25
Church/State | **Downtown** | 24
Culina | **Beverly Hills** | 24
Mr. Chow | **Beverly Hills** | 24
Ray's/Stark Bar | **Mid-Wilshire** | 24
NEW Larry's | **Venice** | 24
NEW Mo-Chica | **Downtown** | 24
Black Market | **Studio City** | 24
Asia de Cuba | **W Hollywood** | 24
Tripel | **Playa del Rey** | 24
Chaya | **W Hollywood** | 24

Little Door | **Third St** | 24
Scarpetta | **Beverly Hills** | 24
Brentwood | **Brentwood** | 24
Wood & Vine | **Hollywood** | 23
Chaya | **Venice** | 23
Sushi Roku | **multi.** | 23
Little Dom's/Deli | **Los Feliz** | 23
Cecconi's | **W Hollywood** | 23
NEW Umamicatessen | **Downtown** | 23
Barney Greengrass | **Beverly Hills** | 23
Ivy | **W Hollywood** | 22
RockSugar | **Century City** | 22
Misfit | **Santa Monica** | 22
Penthouse | **Santa Monica** | 22
Geisha Hse. | **Hollywood** | 22
Le Pain Quotidien | **multi.** | 22
NEW Sunny Spot | **Marina del Rey** | 22
NEW Strand House | **Manhattan Bch** | 21
Nate 'n Al | **Beverly Hills** | 20
Abbey | **W Hollywood** | 19
Restaurant/Standard | **W Hollywood** | 19
Charlie's | **Malibu** | 18
NEW Short Order | **Fairfax** | 18
Perch | **Downtown** | 18
NEW Bashi | **Rancho Palos Verdes** | -
NEW Biergarten/Standard | **Downtown** | -
NEW Black Hogg | **Silver Lake** | -
NEW Bow & Truss | **N Hollywood** | -
NEW Crust | **Studio City** | -
NEW Mercado | **Santa Monica** | -
NEW Osteria Drago | **W Hollywood** | -
NEW Pikey | **Hollywood** | -
NEW Sadie Kitchen | **Hollywood** | -
NEW Soleto Trattoria | **Downtown** | -
The Parish | **Downtown** | -
Tom Bergin's | **Mid-City** | -
NEW Tortilla Republic | **W Hollywood** | -
NEW Towne | **Downtown** | -

POWER SCENES

Matsuhisa | **Beverly Hills** | 28
Providence | **Hollywood** | 28
Angelini | **Beverly Blvd** | 28
Cut | **Beverly Hills** | 27
Spago | **Beverly Hills** | 27

Osteria Mozza | **Hollywood**	27
Water Grill | **Downtown**	27
Pizzeria Mozza | **Hollywood**	27
Patina | **Downtown**	27
Belvedere | **Beverly Hills**	27
Vincenti | **Brentwood**	27
Mastro's | **Beverly Hills**	27
Cleo | **Hollywood**	27
A.O.C. | **Third St**	26
Ink | **W Hollywood**	26
Morton's | **multi.**	26
Nobu | **W Hollywood**	26
Valentino | **Santa Monica**	26
BLT Steak | **W Hollywood**	26
Rivera | **Downtown**	26
Drago Centro | **Downtown**	26
Toscana | **Brentwood**	26
Craft | **Century City**	25
NEW Wolfgang Puck/ Hotel Bel-Air | **Bel-Air**	25
Bouchon | **Beverly Hills**	25
Katsuya | **multi.**	25
Palm | **W Hollywood**	25
STK | **W Hollywood**	25
Grill on Hollywood/Alley | **Hollywood**	24
Culina | **Beverly Hills**	24
Tavern | **Brentwood**	24
Hungry Cat | **Santa Monica**	24
Craig's | **W Hollywood**	24
Bar Bouchon | **Beverly Hills**	24
Chaya | **Downtown**	24
Gordon Ramsay | **W Hollywood**	24
Scarpetta | **Beverly Hills**	24
Comme Ça | **W Hollywood**	24
Bar Toscana | **Brentwood**	24
Nick & Stef's | **Downtown**	24
Red Medicine | **Beverly Hills**	23
Dan Tana's | **W Hollywood**	23
Ago | **W Hollywood**	23
Cecconi's | **W Hollywood**	23
Wilshire | **Santa Monica**	23
Barney Greengrass | **Beverly Hills**	23
Akasha | **Culver City**	22
Polo | **Beverly Hills**	22
NEW Strand House | **Manhattan Bch**	21
Il Covo | **W Hollywood**	21
NEW FigOly | **Downtown**	–
NEW Livello | **Beverly Hills**	–
NEW Osteria Drago | **W Hollywood**	–

Tom Bergin's | **Mid-City**	–
NEW Towne | **Downtown**	–

QUIET CONVERSATION

Tres/José Andrés | **Beverly Hills**	29
Tierra Sur/Herzog | **Oxnard**	28
Mélisse | **Santa Monica**	28
Providence | **Hollywood**	28
Saam/The Bazaar | **Beverly Hills**	27
Hatfield's | **Melrose**	27
Ado/Casa Ado | **Marina del Rey**	27
Café 14 | **Agoura Hills**	27
Belvedere | **Beverly Hills**	27
NEW Bouchon Bakery | **Beverly Hills**	26
Valentino | **Santa Monica**	26
Mar'sel | **Rancho Palos Verdes**	26
Marino | **Hollywood**	26
Madeo | **W Hollywood**	26
Michael's Rest. | **Santa Monica**	25
71 Palm | **Ventura**	25
NEW Wolfgang Puck/ Hotel Bel-Air | **Bel-Air**	25
Il Grano | **West LA**	25
Raymond | **Pasadena**	25
Bouchon | **Beverly Hills**	25
Upstairs 2 | **West LA**	24
Culina | **Beverly Hills**	24
Wolfgang's | **Beverly Hills**	24
Ray's/Stark Bar | **Mid-Wilshire**	24
Noir | **Pasadena**	24
Gordon Ramsay | **W Hollywood**	24
La Botte | **Santa Monica**	24
Cafe Fiore | **Ventura**	23
Fuego/Maya | **Long Bch**	23
Vito | **Santa Monica**	23
Checkers | **Downtown**	23
Coast | **Santa Monica**	23
Sidecar | **Ventura**	23
Dusty's | **Silver Lake**	22
Polo | **Beverly Hills**	22
Blossom | **Downtown**	22
Bottle Inn | **Hermosa Bch**	22
Blvd | **Beverly Hills**	22
Enzo/Angela | **West LA**	22
Le Pain Quotidien | **multi.**	22
Momed | **Beverly Hills**	22
Villetta | **Santa Monica**	21
Ombra | **Studio City**	21
Oliva | **Sherman Oaks**	21

NEW Bashi | **Rancho Palos Verdes** ⌐‐¹

NEW FigOly | **Downtown** ⌐‐¹

NEW Livello | **Beverly Hills** ⌐‐¹

RAW BARS

Water Grill	**Downtown**	27
Joe's	**Venice**	26
Santa Monica Seafood	**Santa Monica**	26
Sky Room	**Long Bch**	25
Lobster	**Santa Monica**	25
Ocean Ave.	**Santa Monica**	24
Hungry Cat	**multi.**	24
Delmonico's	**Encino**	24
Comme Ça	**W Hollywood**	24
BP Oysterette	**Santa Monica**	23
Gulfstream	**Century City**	23
Brophy Bros.	**Ventura**	23
Bluewater	**Redondo Bch**	23
King's Fish	**multi.**	23
Armstrong's	**Catalina Is.**	23
Coast	**Santa Monica**	23
Canal Club	**Venice**	21
McKenna's	**Long Bch**	21
Neptune's Net	**Malibu**	20
Kendall's	**Downtown**	20
NEW L&E Oyster Bar	**Silver Lake**	⌐‐¹

ROMANTIC PLACES

Tres/José Andrés	**Beverly Hills**	29
Michael's/Naples	**Long Bch**	28
Tierra Sur/Herzog	**Oxnard**	28
Mélisse	**Santa Monica**	28
Piccolo	**Venice**	28
Providence	**Hollywood**	28
Lucques	**W Hollywood**	27
Bazaar by José Andrés	**Beverly Hills**	27
Spago	**Beverly Hills**	27
Brandywine	**Woodland Hills**	27
Hatfield's	**Melrose**	27
Ado/Casa Ado	**Marina del Rey**	27
Patina	**Downtown**	27
Belvedere	**Beverly Hills**	27
Cleo	**Hollywood**	27
Saddle Peak	**Calabasas**	26
NEW Bouchon Bakery	**Beverly Hills**	26
Le Chêne	**Saugus**	26
Capo	**Santa Monica**	26
Valentino	**Santa Monica**	26

Mar'sel	**Rancho Palos Verdes**	26
Bistro 45	**Pasadena**	26
Sir Winston's	**Long Bch**	26
Rivera	**Downtown**	26
Drago Centro	**Downtown**	26
Josie	**Santa Monica**	26
Craft	**Century City**	25
Michael's Rest.	**Santa Monica**	25
71 Palm	**Ventura**	25
Pace	**Laurel Canyon**	25
NEW Wolfgang Puck/ Hotel Bel-Air	**Bel-Air**	25
Raymond	**Pasadena**	25
Bouchon	**Beverly Hills**	25
Sky Room	**Long Bch**	25
Culina	**Beverly Hills**	24
Ray's/Stark Bar	**Mid-Wilshire**	24
Baleen	**Redondo Bch**	24
Cafe Del Rey	**Marina del Rey**	24
Gordon Ramsay	**W Hollywood**	24
La Botte	**Santa Monica**	24
Little Door	**Third St**	24
Meet/Bistro	**Culver City**	24
Comme Ça	**W Hollywood**	24
Brentwood	**Brentwood**	24
Cafe Fiore	**Ventura**	23
Getty Ctr.	**Brentwood**	23
Fig & Olive	**Melrose**	23
Il Cielo	**Beverly Hills**	23
Fuego/Maya	**Long Bch**	23
Ozumo	**Santa Monica**	23
Vito	**Santa Monica**	23
Checkers	**Downtown**	23
Caffe Roma	**Beverly Hills**	23
Catch	**Santa Monica**	23
Via Alloro	**Beverly Hills**	22
Yamashiro	**Hollywood**	22
Geoffrey's	**Malibu**	22
Blvd	**Beverly Hills**	22
Penthouse	**Santa Monica**	22
Inn/Seventh Ray	**Topanga**	21
Noé	**Downtown**	21
Vertical Wine	**Pasadena**	21
Villetta	**Santa Monica**	21
Dominick's	**W Hollywood**	21
Bistro/Gare	**S Pasadena**	21
Cliff's Edge	**Silver Lake**	21
NEW Strand House	**Manhattan Bch**	21
Café Laurent	**Culver City**	21
La Boheme	**W Hollywood**	21
Ombra	**Studio City**	21

Il Covo	**W Hollywood**	21
Villa Blanca	**Beverly Hills**	19
Jer-ne	**Marina del Rey**	19
Charlie's	**Malibu**	18
Perch	**Downtown**	18
NEW Ba Restaurant	**Highland Pk**	–
NEW Bashi	**Rancho Palos Verdes**	–
NEW Biergarten/Standard	**Downtown**	–
NEW Duplex on Third	**W Hollywood**	–
NEW FigOly	**Downtown**	–
NEW Livello	**Beverly Hills**	–
NEW Osteria Drago	**W Hollywood**	–
NEW Sadie Kitchen	**Hollywood**	–
NEW Soleto Trattoria	**Downtown**	–
NEW Towne	**Downtown**	–

SINGLES SCENES

Pizzeria Mozza	**Hollywood**	27
Parkway Grill	**Pasadena**	26
NEW Freddy Smalls	**West LA**	26
Safire	**Camarillo**	26
Mucho Ultima	**Manhattan Bch**	26
Rustic Canyon	**Santa Monica**	25
Hama	**Venice**	25
Katsuya	**multi.**	25
Koi	**W Hollywood**	25
Bouzy	**Redondo Bch**	25
STK	**W Hollywood**	25
Boa	**W Hollywood**	24
Ocean Ave.	**Santa Monica**	24
NEW Larry's	**Venice**	24
25 Degrees	**Hollywood**	24
Father's Office	**multi.**	24
Chaya	**W Hollywood**	24
Comme Ça	**W Hollywood**	24
Wood & Vine	**Hollywood**	23
Chaya	**Venice**	23
Sushi Roku	**multi.**	23
Hudson Hse.	**Redondo Bch**	23
Cecconi's	**W Hollywood**	23
NEW Umamicatessen	**Downtown**	23
Caffe Roma	**Beverly Hills**	23
Wolfgang Puck B&G	**Downtown**	23
Rock'n Fish	**Manhattan Bch**	22
1321 Downtown	**Torrance**	22
Border Grill	**Santa Monica**	22

Corkbar	**Downtown**	22
NEW Haven	**Pasadena**	22
Bowery	**Hollywood**	22
Penthouse	**Santa Monica**	22
Geisha Hse.	**Hollywood**	22
Blue Dog	**Sherman Oaks**	21
NEW Casa Azul	**Westwood**	21
Canal Club	**Venice**	21
Dominick's	**W Hollywood**	21
James'	**Venice**	21
Primitivo	**Venice**	21
Ford's	**Culver City**	21
Kitchen 24	**Hollywood**	21
Simon LA	**W Hollywood**	21
City Tavern	**Culver City**	20
Abbey	**W Hollywood**	19
Restaurant/Standard	**W Hollywood**	19
The Rockefeller	**Hermosa Bch**	19
Rush St.	**Culver City**	18
NEW Biergarten/Standard	**Downtown**	–
NEW Mercado	**Santa Monica**	–
NEW Pikey	**Hollywood**	–
NEW Sadie Kitchen	**Hollywood**	–
NEW Soleto Trattoria	**Downtown**	–
The Parish	**Downtown**	–
NEW Towne	**Downtown**	–

SPECIAL OCCASIONS

Tres/José Andrés	**Beverly Hills**	29
Tierra Sur/Herzog	**Oxnard**	28
Matsuhisa	**Beverly Hills**	28
Providence	**Hollywood**	28
Bazaar by José Andrés	**Beverly Hills**	27
Cut	**Beverly Hills**	27
Spago	**Beverly Hills**	27
Saam/The Bazaar	**Beverly Hills**	27
Osteria Mozza	**Hollywood**	27
Hatfield's	**Melrose**	27
Water Grill	**Downtown**	27
Ado/Casa Ado	**Marina del Rey**	27
Patina	**Downtown**	27
Chinois	**Santa Monica**	27
Belvedere	**Beverly Hills**	27
Cicada	**Downtown**	27
Mastro's	**Beverly Hills**	27
Saddle Peak	**Calabasas**	26
Tuscany	**Westlake Vill**	26
Ink	**W Hollywood**	26
Nobu	**W Hollywood**	26

Valentino	**Santa Monica**	26
Mar'sel	**Rancho Palos Verdes**	26
Bistro 45	**Pasadena**	26
Drago Centro	**Downtown**	26
Marino	**Hollywood**	26
Josie	**Santa Monica**	26
Craft	**Century City**	25
Fleming's	**multi.**	25
NEW Wolfgang Puck/ Hotel Bel-Air	**Bel-Air**	25
Bouchon	**Beverly Hills**	25
Palm	**W Hollywood**	25
Jar	**Beverly Blvd.**	25
Petros	**Manhattan Bch**	25
Roy's	**multi.**	25
Culina	**Beverly Hills**	24
Wolfgang's	**Beverly Hills**	24
Gordon Ramsay	**W Hollywood**	24
Scarpetta	**Beverly Hills**	24
Comme Ça	**W Hollywood**	24
Cecconi's	**W Hollywood**	23
Noé	**Downtown**	21
NEW Strand House	**Manhattan Bch**	21
NEW Bashi	**Rancho Palos Verdes**	–
NEW FigOly	**Downtown**	–
NEW Morinoya	**West LA**	–
NEW Soleto Trattoria	**Downtown**	–
NEW Ushuaia	**Santa Monica**	–

STARGAZING

Nishimura	**W Hollywood**	29
Urasawa	**Beverly Hills**	28
Matsuhisa	**Beverly Hills**	28
Hamasaku	**West LA**	28
M.B. Post	**Manhattan Bch**	28
Cut	**Beverly Hills**	27
Nobu	**Malibu**	27
Spago	**Beverly Hills**	27
Osteria Mozza	**Hollywood**	27
Pizzeria Mozza	**Hollywood**	27
Savory	**Malibu**	26
Nobu	**W Hollywood**	26
BLT Steak	**W Hollywood**	26
Madeo	**W Hollywood**	26
Craft	**Century City**	25
Grill on Alley	**Beverly Hills**	25
Giorgio Baldi	**Santa Monica**	25
Griddle Cafe	**Hollywood**	25
Katsuya	**multi.**	25
Koi	**W Hollywood**	25

Boa	**multi.**	24
Culina	**Beverly Hills**	24
Mr. Chow	**Beverly Hills**	24
Tavern	**Brentwood**	24
Black Market	**Studio City**	24
Craig's	**W Hollywood**	24
Tra Di Noi	**Malibu**	24
Bar Toscana	**Brentwood**	24
Brentwood	**Brentwood**	24
Fig & Olive	**Melrose**	23
Dan Tana's	**W Hollywood**	23
Sushi Roku	**multi.**	23
Cecconi's	**W Hollywood**	23
Taverna Tony	**Malibu**	22
Ivy	**W Hollywood**	22
Misfit	**Santa Monica**	22
Polo	**Beverly Hills**	22
Sotto	**Century City**	22
Ivy/Shore	**Santa Monica**	22
Café Habana	**Malibu**	21
Eveleigh	**W Hollywood**	21

TRANSPORTING EXPERIENCES

Urasawa	**Beverly Hills**	28
Bazaar by José Andrés	**Beverly Hills**	27
Cicada	**Downtown**	27
Campanile	**La Brea**	26
Michael's Rest.	**Santa Monica**	25
Crustacean	**Beverly Hills**	25
Little Door	**Third St**	24
Comme Ça	**W Hollywood**	24
Musso & Frank	**Hollywood**	23
Vibrato Grill	**Bel-Air**	23
Barney Greengrass	**Beverly Hills**	23
Marrakesh	**Studio City**	22
RockSugar	**Century City**	22
Yamashiro	**Hollywood**	22
Dar Maghreb	**Hollywood**	22
Inn/Seventh Ray	**Topanga**	21
La Boheme	**W Hollywood**	21

TRENDY

Bazaar by José Andrés	**Beverly Hills**	27
Cut	**Beverly Hills**	27
Nobu	**Malibu**	27
Katsu-ya	**multi.**	27
Osteria Mozza	**Hollywood**	27
Ado/Casa Ado	**Marina del Rey**	27
Pizzeria Mozza	**Hollywood**	27

Animal | **Fairfax**	27
Katana | **W Hollywood**	27
Mastro's | **Beverly Hills**	27
NEW Freddy Smalls | **West LA**	26
Ink | **W Hollywood**	26
Nobu | **W Hollywood**	26
Gjelina | **Venice**	26
Tasting Kitchen | **Venice**	26
Kogi | **Location Varies**	26
LudoBites | **Location Varies**	26
NEW Baco Mercat | **Downtown**	26
Mucho Ultima | **Manhattan Bch**	26
Craft | **Century City**	25
Street | **Hollywood**	25
Lazy Ox | **Little Tokyo**	25
NEW 800 Degrees | **Westwood**	25
NEW Wolfgang Puck/ Hotel Bel-Air | **Bel-Air**	25
Lukshon | **Culver City**	25
Hama | **Venice**	25
Bouchon | **Beverly Hills**	25
Katsuya | **multi.**	25
Son of a Gun | **Third St**	25
Koi | **W Hollywood**	25
Spice Table | **Little Tokyo**	25
Red O | **Melrose**	25
Jar | **Beverly Blvd.**	25
Playa | **Beverly Blvd**	25
Tavern | **Brentwood**	24
Hungry Cat | **multi.**	24
NEW Larry's | **Venice**	24
NEW Mo-Chica | **Downtown**	24
Mohawk Bend | **Echo Pk**	24
Asia de Cuba | **W Hollywood**	24
Father's Office | **Culver City**	24
Bar Bouchon | **Beverly Hills**	24
Wurstküche | **Downtown**	24
Tin Roof | **Manhattan Bch**	24
Tripel | **Playa del Rey**	24
Little Door | **Third St**	24
Scarpetta | **Beverly Hills**	24
Bar Toscana | **Brentwood**	24
LudoTruck | **Location Varies**	24
Musha | **Pasadena**	23
NEW Tar & Roses | **Santa Monica**	23
Wood & Vine | **Hollywood**	23
Ago | **W Hollywood**	23
Chaya | **Venice**	23
Sushi Roku | **multi.**	23
Cecconi's | **W Hollywood**	23
NEW Umamicatessen | **Downtown**	23

A-Frame | **Culver City**	23
Akasha | **Culver City**	22
Misfit | **Santa Monica**	22
Rock'n Fish | **Manhattan Bch**	22
Aburiya Toranoko | **Downtown**	22
Gorbals | **Downtown**	22
Penthouse | **Santa Monica**	22
Whist | **Santa Monica**	22
NEW Strand House | **Manhattan Bch**	21
Kitchen 24 | **Hollywood**	21
Eveleigh | **W Hollywood**	21
Il Covo | **W Hollywood**	21
City Tavern | **Culver City**	20
NEW Plan Check | **West LA**	19
Papaya King | **Hollywood**	18
NEW Short Order | **Fairfax**	18
NEW The Churchill | **W Hollywood**	17
Cole's | **Downtown**	17
NEW Biergarten/Standard | **Downtown**	–
NEW Black Hogg | **Silver Lake**	–
NEW Bow & Truss | **N Hollywood**	–
NEW Corner Door | **Culver City**	–
NEW Mercado | **Santa Monica**	–
NEW Sadie Kitchen | **Hollywood**	–
NEW Soleto Trattoria | **Downtown**	–
The Parish | **Downtown**	–
NEW Towne | **Downtown**	–

VIEWS

Katana | **W Hollywood**	27
Saddle Peak | **Calabasas**	26
Savory | **Malibu**	26
Rustico | **Westlake Vill**	26
Hostaria/Piccolo | **Santa Monica**	26
Sam's/Beach | **Santa Monica**	26
BLT Steak | **W Hollywood**	26
Mar'sel | **Rancho Palos Verdes**	26
WP24 | **Downtown**	26
Sir Winston's | **Long Bch**	26
Salt's Cure | **Hollywood**	25
71 Palm | **Ventura**	25
Raymond | **Pasadena**	25
Malibu Seafood | **Malibu**	25
Sky Room | **Long Bch**	25
Lobster | **Santa Monica**	25
Boa | **Santa Monica**	24
Royce | **Pasadena**	24
Ray's/Stark Bar | **Mid-Wilshire**	24

Baleen | **Redondo Bch**	24	Patrick's | **Santa Monica**	19
Ocean Tava | **Redondo Bch**	24	Paradise Cove | **Malibu**	19
Asia de Cuba | **W Hollywood**	24	Jer-ne | **Marina del Rey**	19
Cafe Del Rey | **Marina del Rey**	24	Charlie's | **Malibu**	18
Meet/Bistro | **Culver City**	24	Gladstone's | **multi.**	18
22nd St. Landing | **San Pedro**	24	Baja Cantina | **Marina del Rey**	18
One Pico | **Santa Monica**	24	🆕 FigOly | **Downtown**	-
Getty Ctr. | **Brentwood**	23		

Cheesecake Factory | **Redondo Bch**	23		

VISITORS ON EXPENSE ACCOUNT

🆕 Blue Cow Kitchen | **Downtown**	23	Tres/José Andrés | **Beverly Hills**	29
Brophy Bros. | **Ventura**	23	Tierra Sur/Herzog | **Oxnard**	28
Fuego/Maya | **Long Bch**	23	Mélisse | **Santa Monica**	28
Chart House | **multi.**	23	Matsuhisa | **Beverly Hills**	28
Luggage Room | **Pasadena**	23	Providence | **Hollywood**	28
Parker's | **Long Bch**	23	Lucques | **W Hollywood**	27
Talésai/Night | **W Hollywood**	23	Bazaar by José Andrés | **Beverly Hills**	27
Armstrong's | **Catalina Is.**	23	Cut | **Beverly Hills**	27
Coast | **Santa Monica**	23	Nobu | **Malibu**	27
Catch | **Santa Monica**	23	Shiro | **S Pasadena**	27
Old Tony's | **Redondo Bch**	23	Saam/The Bazaar | **Beverly Hills**	27
Zengo | **Santa Monica**	23	Osteria Mozza | **Hollywood**	27
Taverna Tony | **Malibu**	22	Hatfield's | **Melrose**	27
Reel Inn | **Malibu**	22	Water Grill | **Downtown**	27
Boccaccio's | **Westlake Vill**	22	Patina | **Downtown**	27
Bocca | **Encino**	22	Chinois | **Santa Monica**	27
Yamashiro | **Hollywood**	22	Belvedere | **Beverly Hills**	27
Geoffrey's | **Malibu**	22	Cicada | **Downtown**	27
Guido's | **Malibu**	22	Mastro's | **Beverly Hills**	27
Go Burger | **Hollywood**	22	Saddle Peak | **Calabasas**	26
Admiral Risty | **Rancho Palos Verdes**	22	Parkway Grill | **Pasadena**	26
Penthouse | **Santa Monica**	22	Joe's | **Venice**	26
Wahib's | **Alhambra**	22	Campanile | **La Brea**	26
Kincaid's | **Redondo Bch**	22	A.O.C. | **Third St**	26
Ivy/Shore | **Santa Monica**	22	JiRaffe | **Santa Monica**	26
M Street | **Santa Monica**	21	Ink | **W Hollywood**	26
Madame Chou Chou | **Santa Monica**	21	Morton's | **multi.**	26
McKenna's | **Long Bch**	21	Nobu | **W Hollywood**	26
🆕 Strand House | **Manhattan Bch**	21	Capo | **Santa Monica**	26
Rosa Mexicano | **W Hollywood**	21	Valentino | **Santa Monica**	26
Ruby's | **multi.**	21	BLT Steak | **W Hollywood**	26
El Torito | **Marina del Rey**	21	Mar'sel | **Rancho Palos Verdes**	26
Typhoon | **Santa Monica**	21	Rivera | **Downtown**	26
Cheebo | **Hollywood**	21	Drago Centro | **Downtown**	26
Moonshadows | **Malibu**	21	Josie | **Santa Monica**	26
Belmont Brewing | **Long Bch**	21	Arroyo | **Pasadena**	26
Duke's | **Malibu**	20	Craft | **Century City**	25
Jinky's | **Agoura Hills**	20	Fleming's | **Downtown**	25
		Fogo de Chão | **Beverly Hills**	25
		Celestino | **Pasadena**	25
		Michael's Rest. | **Santa Monica**	25

Crustacean	**Beverly Hills**	25
NEW Wolfgang Puck/ Hotel Bel-Air	**Bel-Air**	25
Raymond	**Pasadena**	25
Bouchon	**Beverly Hills**	25
Palm	**W Hollywood**	25
Red O	**Melrose**	25
L'Opera	**Long Bch**	25
Jar	**Beverly Blvd.**	25
Petros	**Manhattan Bch**	25
STK	**W Hollywood**	25
Lobster	**Santa Monica**	25
Playa	**Beverly Blvd**	25
Roy's	**multi.**	25
Grill on Hollywood/Alley	**Hollywood**	24
Boa	**W Hollywood**	24
Culina	**Beverly Hills**	24
Mr. Chow	**Beverly Hills**	24
Wolfgang's	**Beverly Hills**	24
Tavern	**Brentwood**	24
Bar Bouchon	**Beverly Hills**	24
Chaya	**W Hollywood**	24
Chaya	**Downtown**	24
Gordon Ramsay	**W Hollywood**	24
Scarpetta	**Beverly Hills**	24
Comme Ça	**W Hollywood**	24
Nick & Stef's	**Downtown**	24
One Pico	**Santa Monica**	24
Fig & Olive	**Melrose**	23
Nic's	**Beverly Hills**	23
Ago	**W Hollywood**	23
Sushi Roku	**multi.**	23
Cecconi's	**W Hollywood**	23
Checkers	**Downtown**	23
Wilshire	**Santa Monica**	23
Catch	**Santa Monica**	23
Zengo	**Santa Monica**	23
Ivy	**W Hollywood**	22
Polo	**Beverly Hills**	22
Geoffrey's	**Malibu**	22
Blvd	**Beverly Hills**	22
Geisha Hse.	**Hollywood**	22
Ivy/Shore	**Santa Monica**	22
Dominick's	**W Hollywood**	21
NEW Strand House	**Manhattan Bch**	21
Ombra	**Studio City**	21
Il Covo	**W Hollywood**	21
Beso	**Hollywood**	19
Buffalo Club	**Santa Monica**	19
Jer-ne	**Marina del Rey**	19

NEW Bashi	**Rancho Palos Verdes**	–
NEW FigOly	**Downtown**	–
NEW Livello	**Beverly Hills**	–
NEW Osteria Drago	**W Hollywood**	–
NEW Towne	**Downtown**	–

WATERSIDE

Nobu	**Malibu**	27
Mar'sel	**Rancho Palos Verdes**	26
Sir Winston's	**Long Bch**	26
Martha's 22nd St.	**Hermosa Bch**	25
Lobster	**Santa Monica**	25
Boa	**Santa Monica**	24
Baleen	**Redondo Bch**	24
Cafe Del Rey	**Marina del Rey**	24
22nd St. Landing	**San Pedro**	24
One Pico	**Santa Monica**	24
Cheesecake Factory	**Redondo Bch**	23
Brophy Bros.	**Ventura**	23
Zin	**Westlake Vill**	23
Fuego/Maya	**Long Bch**	23
Chart House	**multi.**	23
Bluewater	**Redondo Bch**	23
Parker's	**Long Bch**	23
Armstrong's	**Catalina Is.**	23
Coast	**Santa Monica**	23
Catch	**Santa Monica**	23
Boccaccio's	**Westlake Vill**	22
Yard House	**Long Bch**	22
Geoffrey's	**Malibu**	22
Guido's	**Malibu**	22
Kincaid's	**Redondo Bch**	22
Ivy/Shore	**Santa Monica**	22
Good Stuff	**Hermosa Bch**	21
Mediterraneo	**Westlake Vill**	21
McKenna's	**Long Bch**	21
Ruby's	**Redondo Bch**	21
NEW Killer Shrimp	**Marina del Rey**	21
Moonshadows	**Malibu**	21
Belmont Brewing	**Long Bch**	21
Neptune's Net	**Malibu**	20
Duke's	**Malibu**	20
Jody Maroni's	**Venice**	20
Paradise Cove	**Malibu**	19
Jer-ne	**Marina del Rey**	19
Gladstone's	**multi.**	18

WINE BARS

Leila's	**Oak Pk**	27
A.O.C.	**Third St**	26

Valentino | **Santa Monica**	26
Fleming's | **multi.**	25
Rustic Canyon | **Santa Monica**	25
Michael's Rest. | **Santa Monica**	25
Cube Cafe | **La Brea**	25
Upstairs 2 | **West LA**	24
Petrossian | **W Hollywood**	24
Hungry Cat | **Hollywood**	24
NEW Larry's | **Venice**	24
25 Degrees | **Hollywood**	24
Noir | **Pasadena**	24
Bar Toscana | **Brentwood**	24
Enoteca Drago | **Beverly Hills**	23
Corkbar | **Downtown**	22
Lazy Dog | **Thousand Oaks**	22
Bar Pintxo | **Santa Monica**	22
Vertical Wine | **Pasadena**	21
Monsieur Marcel | **Fairfax**	21
Bistro/Gare | **S Pasadena**	21
Primitivo | **Venice**	21
Lilly's | **Venice**	19
BottleRock | **Culver City**	19
NEW Little Bear | **Downtown**	18
First & Hope | **Downtown**	18
NEW Ba Restaurant | **Highland Pk**	-

WINNING WINE LISTS

Tres/José Andrés | **Beverly Hills**	29
Tierra Sur/Herzog | **Oxnard**	28
Mélisse | **Santa Monica**	28
Lucques | **W Hollywood**	27
Bazaar by José Andrés | **Beverly Hills**	27
Cut | **Beverly Hills**	27
Spago | **Beverly Hills**	27
Mosto | **Marina del Rey**	27
Saam/The Bazaar | **Beverly Hills**	27
Water Grill | **Downtown**	27
Patina | **Downtown**	27
Chinois | **Santa Monica**	27
Cleo | **Hollywood**	27
Parkway Grill | **Pasadena**	26
Campanile | **La Brea**	26
Chez Mélange | **Redondo Bch**	26
A.O.C. | **Third St**	26
JiRaffe | **Santa Monica**	26
Ink | **W Hollywood**	26
Nobu | **W Hollywood**	26
Valentino | **Santa Monica**	26

BLT Steak | **W Hollywood**	26
Mar'sel | **Rancho Palos Verdes**	26
Bistro 45 | **Pasadena**	26
Rivera | **Downtown**	26
Drago Centro | **Downtown**	26
555 East | **Long Bch**	26
Safire | **Camarillo**	26
Arroyo | **Pasadena**	26
Craft | **Century City**	25
Street | **Hollywood**	25
Fleming's | **multi.**	25
Grill on Alley | **Beverly Hills**	25
Michael's Rest. | **Santa Monica**	25
NEW Wolfgang Puck/ Hotel Bel-Air | **Bel-Air**	25
Raymond | **Pasadena**	25
Bouchon | **Beverly Hills**	25
Larsen's | **Encino**	25
Bouzy | **Redondo Bch**	25
Red O | **Melrose**	25
STK | **W Hollywood**	25
Playa | **Beverly Blvd**	25
Roy's | **Downtown**	25
Boa | **Santa Monica**	24
Foundry/Melrose | **Melrose**	24
Upstairs 2 | **West LA**	24
E. Baldi | **Beverly Hills**	24
Culina | **Beverly Hills**	24
Cafe Pinot | **Downtown**	24
Ocean Ave. | **Santa Monica**	24
Wolfgang's | **Beverly Hills**	24
Tavern | **Brentwood**	24
Hungry Cat | **Santa Monica**	24
Baleen | **Redondo Bch**	24
Noir | **Pasadena**	24
Cafe Del Rey | **Marina del Rey**	24
Bar Bouchon | **Beverly Hills**	24
Tin Roof | **Manhattan Bch**	24
Chaya | **Downtown**	24
Gordon Ramsay | **W Hollywood**	24
La Botte | **Santa Monica**	24
Scarpetta | **Beverly Hills**	24
Comme Ça | **W Hollywood**	24
Bar Toscana | **Brentwood**	24
Nick & Stef's | **Downtown**	24
NEW Tar & Roses | **Santa Monica**	23
Fig & Olive | **Melrose**	23
Bistro Provence | **Burbank**	23
Ago | **W Hollywood**	23
Cecconi's | **W Hollywood**	23
Wilshire | **Santa Monica**	23

Kravings | **Tarzana**	23
King's Fish | **Calabasas**	23
redwhite+bluezz | **Pasadena**	23
Westside Tav. | **West LA**	23
Via Alloro | **Beverly Hills**	22
Akasha | **Culver City**	22
Delphine | **Hollywood**	22
Paul Martin's | **El Segundo**	22
Corkbar | **Downtown**	22
Blvd | **Beverly Hills**	22
Gorbals | **Downtown**	22
Taste | **W Hollywood**	22
Peppone | **Brentwood**	22
Il Moro | **West LA**	22
Vertical Wine | **Pasadena**	21
Fraîche | **Santa Monica**	21

NEW Strand House | **Manhattan Bch**	21
Primitivo | **Venice**	21
Ombra | **Studio City**	21
Eveleigh | **W Hollywood**	21
Simon LA | **W Hollywood**	21
Kendall's | **Downtown**	21
Napa Valley | **Westwood**	20
Ugo/Café | **Culver City**	19
Jer-ne | **Marina del Rey**	19
NEW FigOly | **Downtown**	19
NEW Livello | **Beverly Hills**	-
NEW Osteria Drago | **W Hollywood**	-
NEW Soleto Trattoria | **Downtown**	-
NEW Towne | **Downtown**	-

Cuisines

Includes names, locations and Food ratings.

AFGHAN

Azeen's	**Pasadena**	27
Walter's	**Claremont**	21

AMERICAN

Mélisse	**Santa Monica**	28
Providence	**Hollywood**	28
M.B. Post	**Manhattan Bch**	28
Bashan	**Montrose**	28
Hatfield's	**Melrose**	27
Animal	**Fairfax**	27
Patina	**Downtown**	27
Gjelina Take Away	**Venice**	27
Belvedere	**Beverly Hills**	27
Saddle Peak	**Calabasas**	26
NEW Freddy Smalls	**West LA**	26
JiRaffe	**Santa Monica**	26
NEW Post & Beam	**Mid-City**	26
Savory	**Malibu**	26
Ink	**W Hollywood**	26
Gjelina	**Venice**	26
Farmshop	**Santa Monica**	26
Larchmont Grill	**Hollywood**	26
Safire	**Camarillo**	26
Josie	**Santa Monica**	26
In-N-Out	**multi.**	26
Craft	**Century City**	25
Salt's Cure	**Hollywood**	25
NEW Milo & Olive	**Santa Monica**	25
Buttermilk	**Location Varies**	25
Grill on Alley	**Beverly Hills**	25
Darren's	**Manhattan Bch**	25
71 Palm	**Ventura**	25
Clementine	**Century City**	25
Griddle Cafe	**Hollywood**	25
Martha's 22nd St.	**Hermosa Bch**	25
Original Pancake	**Redondo Bch**	25
Park	**Echo Pk**	25
NEW Next Door/Josie	**Santa Monica**	25
Blair's	**Silver Lake**	25
Blu Jam	**Mid-City**	25
Bouzy	**Redondo Bch**	25
Sky Room	**Long Bch**	25
Raphael	**Studio City**	25
Jar	**Beverly Blvd.**	25
Grill on Hollywood/Alley	**multi.**	24
Foundry/Melrose	**Melrose**	24

Watermark on Main	**Ventura**	24
Nook	**West LA**	24
Royce	**Pasadena**	24
Wolfgang's	**Beverly Hills**	24
Chili John's	**Burbank**	24
Food	**Rancho Pk**	24
Grub	**Hollywood**	24
NEW Larry's	**Venice**	24
Houston's	**multi.**	24
Baleen	**Redondo Bch**	24
Cafe Gratitude	**multi.**	24
Bar	Kitchen	**Downtown**	24
NEW Fukuburger	**Hollywood**	24
Tinga	**La Brea**	24
Joan's on Third Cafe	**Third St**	24
Bandera	**West LA**	24
208 Rodeo	**Beverly Hills**	24
Cafe Verde	**Pasadena**	24
Think Bistro	**San Pedro**	24
Wood Ranch	**multi.**	24
Craig's	**W Hollywood**	24
Father's Office	**multi.**	24
Tin Roof	**Manhattan Bch**	24
Alondra Hot Wings	**multi.**	24
Buffalo Fire Dept.	**Torrance**	24
Tops	**Pasadena**	24
Bloom	**Mid-City**	24
Brentwood	**Brentwood**	24
Grilled Cheese Truck	**Location Varies**	24
Bru's Wiffle	**Santa Monica**	24
NEW Tar & Roses	**Santa Monica**	23
Fundamental LA	**Westwood**	23
Think Café	**San Pedro**	23
Apple Pan	**West LA**	23
Huckleberry	**Santa Monica**	23
Habit Burger	**multi.**	23
Cheesecake Factory	**multi.**	23
Tender Greens	**multi.**	23
Wood & Vine	**Hollywood**	23
NEW Blue Cow Kitchen	**Downtown**	23
AKA Bistro	**Pasadena**	23
Nic's	**Beverly Hills**	23
Zin	**Westlake Vill**	23
Lulu's Cafe	**W Hollywood**	23
Auntie Em's	**Eagle Rock**	23
Fig	**Santa Monica**	23

Frysmith	**Location Varies**	23
Hudson Hse.	**Redondo Bch**	23
BJ's	**multi.**	23
Cora's	**Santa Monica**	23
Musso & Frank	**Hollywood**	23
101 Coffee	**Hollywood**	23
Farmer Boy's	**Downtown**	23
Wilshire	**Santa Monica**	23
Vibrato Grill	**Bel-Air**	23
redwhite+bluezz	**Pasadena**	23
Simmzy's	**multi.**	23
Square One	**E Hollywood**	23
Nickel Diner	**Downtown**	23
Anacapa Brewing	**Ventura**	23
Sidecar	**Ventura**	23
Uncle Bill's	**Manhattan Bch**	23
Dish	**La Cañada Flintridge**	23
Caffe Opera	**Monrovia**	23
More Than Waffles	**Encino**	23
Oinkster	**Eagle Rock**	22
Akasha	**Culver City**	22
Doughboys	**Third St**	22
Lulu's	**Van Nuys**	22
NEW Lab Brewing Co.	**Agoura Hills**	22
Astro Burger	**W Hollywood**	22
Smitty's	**Pasadena**	22
Dusty's	**Silver Lake**	22
Clearman's	**San Gabriel**	22
Yard House	**multi.**	22
Paul Martin's	**El Segundo**	22
1321 Downtown	**Torrance**	22
R+D Kitchen	**Santa Monica**	22
Beckham Grill	**Pasadena**	22
Mi Piace	**Pasadena**	22
Spark	**Studio City**	22
NEW Haven	**Pasadena**	22
Bowery	**Hollywood**	22
Penthouse	**Santa Monica**	22
Taste	**multi.**	22
Lawry's Carvery	**Downtown**	22
Off Vine	**Hollywood**	22
Six	**multi.**	22
Firefly	**Studio City**	22
South Beverly Grill	**Beverly Hills**	22
Vermont	**Los Feliz**	22
NEW Abigaile	**Hermosa Bch**	22
Eat Well	**multi.**	22
Coral Cafe	**Burbank**	22
BLD	**Beverly Blvd**	22
Green St.	**Pasadena**	22

Greenleaf	**multi.**	22
Fat Dog	**multi.**	22
Alcove	**Los Feliz**	21
Marston's	**multi.**	21
Blue Dog	**Sherman Oaks**	21
Beckers Bakery	**Manhattan Bch**	21
Firefly Bistro	**S Pasadena**	21
Traxx	**Downtown**	21
L.A. Market	**Downtown**	21
Blue Plate	**Santa Monica**	21
Granville Cafe	**multi.**	21
Noé	**Downtown**	21
Good Stuff	**multi.**	21
M Street	**Santa Monica**	21
Upper West	**Santa Monica**	21
James'	**Venice**	21
Daily Grill	**multi.**	21
Black Cat	**Fairfax**	21
NEW Strand House	**Manhattan Bch**	21
Gaffey St. Diner	**San Pedro**	21
Federal Bar	**N Hollywood**	21
Manhattan Beach BrewCo	**Manhattan Bch**	21
Waffle	**Hollywood**	21
Luna Park	**La Brea**	21
Hof's Hut	**multi.**	21
Ruby's	**multi.**	21
Yamato	**Brentwood**	21
Valley Inn Rest.	**Sherman Oaks**	21
Ford's	**Culver City**	21
Mike & Anne's	**S Pasadena**	21
Frisco's	**multi.**	21
Pete's	**Downtown**	21
Kitchen 24	**multi.**	21
Eveleigh	**W Hollywood**	21
Billy's	**multi.**	21
Simon LA	**W Hollywood**	21
Larchmont Bungalow	**Hancock Pk**	21
Moonshadows	**Malibu**	21
Truxton's	**Westchester**	21
Palomino	**Westwood**	21
Belmont Brewing	**Long Bch**	21
Ocean Pk. Omelette	**Santa Monica**	20
Maxwell's	**Venice**	20
Engine Co. 28	**Downtown**	20
Swingers	**multi.**	20
Wienerschnitzel	**Burbank**	20
Jinky's	**multi.**	20
Kate Mantilini	**multi.**	20

Huckleberry	**Santa Monica**	23
Sweet Lady Jane	**multi.**	23
Jin Patisserie	**Venice**	23
Baker	**Woodland Hills**	23
La Provence	**multi.**	22
Doughboys	**Third St**	22
King's Hawaiian	**Torrance**	22
Le Pain Quotidien	**multi.**	22
Champagne	**West LA**	22
Beckers Bakery	**Manhattan Bch**	21
17th St. Cafe	**Santa Monica**	21
Jack n' Jill's	**multi.**	20
Röckenwagner	**Santa Monica**	20
Breadbar	**Century City**	18

BARBECUE

Bludso's BBQ	**Compton**	27
Woody's BBQ	**multi.**	27
Phillips BBQ	**multi.**	26
Naples Rib Co.	**Long Bch**	26
Rattler's BBQ	**Santa Clarita**	25
Beachwood BBQ	**Long Bch**	25
Johnny Rebs'	**multi.**	25
JR's	**Culver City**	25
Road to Seoul	**Mid-City**	24
Wood Ranch	**multi.**	24
Lucille's	**multi.**	24
Smoke City	**Van Nuys**	24
Dr. Hogly Wogly's	**Van Nuys**	24
Big Mama's	**Pasadena**	23
Robin's	**Pasadena**	23
Boneyard	**Sherman Oaks**	23
Stonefire	**multi.**	23
Ribs USA	**Burbank**	23
Oinkster	**Eagle Rock**	22
Baby Blues	**multi.**	22
Zeke's	**Montrose**	21
Gus's	**S Pasadena**	20
Reddi Chick	**Santa Monica**	20

BELGIAN

Wurstküche	**Downtown**	24
Le Pain Quotidien	**multi.**	22
NEW Little Bear	**Downtown**	18

BRAZILIAN

Fogo de Chão	**Beverly Hills**	25
Green Field	**multi.**	23
Galletto	**Westlake Vill**	23
Bossa Nova	**multi.**	23
Kravings	**Tarzana**	23
Café Brasil	**multi.**	22
Picanha	**Burbank**	21

BRITISH

Waterloo & City	**Culver City**	24
Whale & Ale	**San Pedro**	21
Ye Olde King's	**Santa Monica**	18
The Parish	**Downtown**	-

BURGERS

Golden State	**Fairfax**	26
Grill 'Em All	**Location Varies**	26
In-N-Out	**multi.**	26
Rustic Canyon	**Santa Monica**	25
Tommy's	**Downtown**	25
Back Abbey	**Claremont**	25
King's Burgers	**Northridge**	24
Hungry Cat	**multi.**	24
Baby's/Burgers	**Location Varies**	24
25 Degrees	**Hollywood**	24
Hole in the Wall	**multi.**	24
Father's Office	**multi.**	24
Buffalo Fire Dept.	**Torrance**	24
Comme Ça	**W Hollywood**	24
26 Beach	**Venice**	24
Apple Pan	**West LA**	23
Habit Burger	**multi.**	23
Umami	**multi.**	23
Farmer Boy's	**Downtown**	23
Oinkster	**Eagle Rock**	22
Astro Burger	**multi.**	22
Clearman's	**San Gabriel**	22
Go Burger	**Hollywood**	22
Bowery	**Hollywood**	22
Pie 'N Burger	**Pasadena**	22
Barney's	**multi.**	22
Blue Dog	**Sherman Oaks**	21
Counter	**multi.**	21
Five Guys	**multi.**	21
Wienerschnitzel	**Diamond Bar**	20
Shack	**multi.**	20
Hamburger Hamlet	**Sherman Oaks**	19
Mo's	**Burbank**	19
Burger Continental	**Pasadena**	18
Hamburger Mary's	**W Hollywood**	18
NEW Short Order	**Fairfax**	18
NEW Boardwalk/Burgers	**Hermosa Bch**	-
NEW Eden Burger Bar	**Glendale**	-

CAJUN

Boiling Crab	**multi.**	25
Cajun Kitchen	**Ventura**	24
Uncle Darrow's	**Marina del Rey**	21
Gumbo Pot	**Fairfax**	20

CALIFORNIAN

Lucques | **W Hollywood**	27
Spago | **Beverly Hills**	27
Leila's | **Oak Pk**	27
Ado/Casa Ado | **Venice**	27
Patina | **Downtown**	27
Cicada | **Downtown**	27
Chef Melba's | **Hermosa Bch**	26
Parkway Grill | **Pasadena**	26
Joe's | **Venice**	26
Campanile | **La Brea**	26
A.O.C. | **Third St**	26
Forage | **Silver Lake**	26
Sam's/Beach | **Santa Monica**	26
Mar'sel | **Rancho Palos Verdes**	26
Bistro 45 | **Pasadena**	26
Farmshop | **Santa Monica**	26
Sir Winston's | **Long Bch**	26
California Grill | **Whittier**	26
NEW Milo & Olive | **Santa Monica**	25
Rustic Canyon | **Santa Monica**	25
Darren's | **Manhattan Bch**	25
Michael's Rest. | **Santa Monica**	25
NEW Cooks County | **Beverly Blvd**	25
NEW Wolfgang Puck/ Hotel Bel-Air | **Bel-Air**	25
Raymond | **Pasadena**	25
Eva | **Beverly Blvd**	25
Gina Lee's | **Redondo Bch**	25
Native Foods | **Westwood**	25
Cafe Pinot | **Downtown**	24
Tavern | **Brentwood**	24
Green St. Tavern | **Pasadena**	24
Cafe Del Rey | **Marina del Rey**	24
Axe | **Venice**	24
Gordon Ramsay | **W Hollywood**	24
Bloom | **Mid-City**	24
One Pico | **Santa Monica**	24
26 Beach | **Venice**	24
Getty Ctr. | **Brentwood**	23
Cabbage Patch | **multi.**	23
Checkers | **Downtown**	23
Ammo | **Hollywood**	23
Coast | **Santa Monica**	23
Catch | **Santa Monica**	23
Food + Lab | **multi.**	23
Wolfgang Puck B&G | **Downtown**	23
Westside Tav. | **West LA**	23
Cuvée | **multi.**	23
Ivy | **W Hollywood**	22
Cafe Cordiale | **Sherman Oaks**	22
Castaway | **Burbank**	22
LAMILL | **Silver Lake**	22
Porta Via | **Beverly Hills**	22
Polo | **Beverly Hills**	22
Yamashiro | **Hollywood**	22
Geoffrey's | **Malibu**	22
Blvd | **Beverly Hills**	22
Lemonade | **multi.**	22
Whist | **Santa Monica**	22
Off Vine | **Hollywood**	22
Hugo's | **multi.**	22
Ivy/Shore | **Santa Monica**	22
Caioti Pizza | **Studio City**	22
Inn/Seventh Ray | **Topanga**	21
L.A. Market | **Downtown**	21
Canal Club | **Venice**	21
Xiomara | **Hollywood**	21
Rose Cafe | **Venice**	21
Cliff's Edge | **Silver Lake**	21
Lemon Moon | **West LA**	21
17th St. Cafe | **Santa Monica**	21
Milky Way | **Pico-Robertson**	21
La Boheme | **W Hollywood**	21
Cafe Montana | **Santa Monica**	21
La Grande Orange | **Pasadena**	21
Wolfgang Puck Express/Bistro | **multi.**	21
Basix | **W Hollywood**	20
Stanley's | **Sherman Oaks**	20
Louise's | **multi.**	20
Röckenwagner | **Santa Monica**	20
Napa Valley | **Westwood**	19
Babalu | **Santa Monica**	19
Marmalade | **Westlake Vill**	19
Literati | **West LA**	18
NEW FigOly | **Downtown**	-

CANADIAN

Soleil | **Westwood**	21

CARIBBEAN

Prado | **Hancock Pk**	23
Cha Cha Chicken | **Santa Monica**	22
Cha Cha Cha | **Silver Lake**	22
Bamboo | **Culver City**	22
NEW Sunny Spot | **Marina del Rey**	22

CHINESE

(* dim sum specialist)

Newport Seafood | **multi.**	27
Din Tai Fung | **Arcadia**	26
Sea Harbour* | **Rosemead**	26

WP24	**Downtown**	26
Duck Hse.	**Monterey Pk**	25
Mr. Chow	**Beverly Hills**	24
Elite*	**Monterey Pk**	24
888 Seafood	**Rosemead**	24
New Moon	**multi.**	24
Panda Inn*	**multi.**	24
Ocean Seafood*	**Chinatown**	23
101 Noodle	**multi.**	23
Bamboo Cuisine	**Sherman Oaks**	23
A & W Seafood	**Northridge**	23
Capital Seafood	**Monterey Pk**	23
City Wok	**Studio City**	23
Yang Chow	**multi.**	23
Mandarin	**multi.**	22
Bao*	**Beverly Blvd**	22
Ocean Star*	**Monterey Pk**	22
Sea Empress*	**Gardena**	22
W's China	**Redondo Bch**	22
Full House	**Chinatown**	22
P.F. Chang's	**multi.**	22
Xi'an	**Beverly Hills**	22
Empress Pavilion*	**Chinatown**	21
Sam Woo	**multi.**	21
NBC Seafood*	**Monterey Pk**	21
Golden Dragon	**Chinatown**	21
Chi Dynasty	**multi.**	21
China Grill	**Manhattan Bch**	21
Phoenix	**multi.**	20
CBS Seafood*	**Chinatown**	20
Hop Woo	**multi.**	19

COFFEEHOUSES

Black Dog Coffee	**Mid-City**	22
LAMILL	**Silver Lake**	22
Urth	**multi.**	22
Caffe Luxxe	**multi.**	21
Literati	**West LA**	18

CONTINENTAL

Brandywine	**Woodland Hills**	27
Café 14	**Agoura Hills**	27
Dal Rae	**Pico Rivera**	26
Sir Winston's	**Long Bch**	26
Fins	**Westlake Vill**	25
Boccaccio's	**Westlake Vill**	22
Polo	**Beverly Hills**	22
Bistro Gdn.	**Studio City**	21
Pig 'n Whistle	**Hollywood**	19

CREOLE

Harold & Belle's	**Mid-City**	25
Uncle Darrow's	**Marina del Rey**	21

CRÊPES

La Crêperie Café	**Long Bch**	24
French Crêpe Co.	**multi.**	23
Crème de la Crêpe	**multi.**	23
Café Laurent	**Culver City**	21

CUBAN

Porto's	**multi.**	26
Asia de Cuba	**W Hollywood**	24
Versailles	**multi.**	23
Café Habana	**Malibu**	21

DELIS

Brent's Deli	**multi.**	26
Bay Cities	**Santa Monica**	26
Langer's	**Downtown**	26
Pico Kosher Deli	**Century City**	24
Lascari's Deli	**Whittier**	23
Little Dom's/Deli	**Los Feliz**	23
Barney Greengrass	**Beverly Hills**	23
Art's	**Studio City**	22
La Bottega Marino	**multi.**	21
Canter's	**Fairfax**	21
Billy's	**multi.**	21
Nate 'n Al	**multi.**	20
Factor's	**Pico-Robertson**	20
Greenblatt's	**Hollywood**	19
Jerry's Deli	**multi.**	18
Fromin's	**Santa Monica**	17
Roll 'n Rye	**Culver City**	17
Junior's	**West LA**	16

DINER

Original Pancake	**Redondo Bch**	25
Cora's	**Santa Monica**	23
101 Coffee	**Hollywood**	23
Nickel Diner	**Downtown**	23
Uncle Bill's	**Manhattan Bch**	23
Johnnie's Pastrami	**Culver City**	22
Pie 'N Burger	**Pasadena**	22
Eat Well	**multi.**	22
Ruby's	**multi.**	21
Ocean Pk. Omelette	**Santa Monica**	20
Swingers	**multi.**	20
Kate Mantilini	**multi.**	20
Original Pantry	**Downtown**	20
Brighton Coffee	**Beverly Hills**	20

Hamburger Hamlet	**multi.**	19
Patrick's	**Santa Monica**	19
Fred 62	**Los Feliz**	19
Dinah's	**Westchester**	19
Hamburger Mary's	**multi.**	18
Du-par's	**multi.**	18

EASTERN EUROPEAN

Aroma	**West LA**	21

ECLECTIC

Tres/José Andrés	**Beverly Hills**	29
Saam/The Bazaar	**Beverly Hills**	27
Hot's Kitchen	**Hermosa Bch**	27
Chez Mélange	**Redondo Bch**	26
Ink	**W Hollywood**	26
Depot	**Torrance**	26
Street	**Hollywood**	25
Lazy Ox	**Little Tokyo**	25
Native Foods	**Westwood**	25
Noir	**Pasadena**	24
Black Market	**Studio City**	24
Mohawk Bend	**Echo Pk**	24
Tripel	**Playa del Rey**	24
LudoTruck	**Location Varies**	24
Think Café	**San Pedro**	23
Cheesecake Factory	**Pasadena**	23
Boneyard	**Sherman Oaks**	23
NEW Umamicatessen	**Downtown**	23
A-Frame	**Culver City**	23
Caffe Opera	**Monrovia**	23
Cafe Cordiale	**Sherman Oaks**	22
NEW Lab Brewing Co.	**Agoura Hills**	22
Misfit	**Santa Monica**	22
Wahoo's Fish Taco	**Santa Clarita**	22
Plate 38	**Pasadena**	22
Olive/Thyme	**Burbank**	22
Corkbar	**Downtown**	22
Gorbals	**Downtown**	22
31Ten	**Santa Monica**	22
Lazy Dog	**multi.**	22
Beer Belly	**Koreatown**	22
Stefan's/L.A. Farm	**Santa Monica**	22
NEW Sunny Spot	**Marina del Rey**	22
NEW Abricott	**Pasadena**	22
Vertical Wine	**Pasadena**	21
Canal Club	**Venice**	21
Farm Stand	**El Segundo**	21
Walter's	**Claremont**	21
Grand Lux	**Beverly Hills**	21

Hof's Hut	**multi.**	21
House Café	**Beverly Blvd**	21
Home	**multi.**	20
La Salsa	**Malibu**	19
Restaurant/Standard	**multi.**	19
American Farmhouse	**Manhattan Bch**	19
Overland Cafe	**Culver City**	19
Literati	**West LA**	18
Barney's Beanery	**multi.**	17
NEW Bosc	**Hollywood**	-
NEW Bugatta	**Melrose**	-
NEW Charleston	**Santa Monica**	-
NEW Larder at Maple Dr.	**Beverly Hills**	-
NEW One Eyed Gypsy	**Downtown**	-

ETHIOPIAN

Nyala	**Mid-Wilshire**	25

EUROPEAN

Euro Pane	**Pasadena**	25
Blu Jam	**Mid-City**	25
Green St. Tavern	**Pasadena**	24
Wurstküche	**Venice**	24
2117	**West LA**	23
Gorbals	**Downtown**	22
Eveleigh	**W Hollywood**	21
BottleRock	**multi.**	19

FONDUE

Melting Pot	**multi.**	23

FRENCH

Mélisse	**Santa Monica**	28
Shiro	**S Pasadena**	27
Suzanne's	**Ojai**	27
Chinois	**Santa Monica**	27
Maison Akira	**Pasadena**	27
Joe's	**Venice**	26
JiRaffe	**Santa Monica**	26
Le Chêne	**Saugus**	26
LudoBites	**Location Varies**	26
71 Palm	**Ventura**	25
Petrossian	**W Hollywood**	24
Cafe Pinot	**Downtown**	24
Le Sanglier	**Tarzana**	24
NEW Maison Giraud	**Pacific Palisades**	24
Think Bistro	**San Pedro**	24
Chaya	**W Hollywood**	24
Chaya	**Downtown**	24

Gordon Ramsay	**W Hollywood**	24
Aimee's Bistro	**Redondo Bch**	24
French Crêpe Co.	**multi.**	23
Wood & Vine	**Hollywood**	23
Fig	**Santa Monica**	23
Chaya	**Venice**	23
Crème de la Crêpe	**Culver City**	23
La Provence	**multi.**	22
Delphine	**Hollywood**	22
Dusty's	**Silver Lake**	22
Clafoutis	**W Hollywood**	22
Champagne	**multi.**	22
Soleil	**Westwood**	21
L'Epicerie	**Culver City**	21
Madame Chou Chou	**Santa Monica**	21
Fraîche	**Santa Monica**	21
Café Laurent	**Culver City**	21
Taix	**Echo Pk**	21
Morels French Steak	**Fairfax**	20
Kendall's	**Downtown**	20
La Frite	**multi.**	19
Perch	**Downtown**	18
NEW Ba Restaurant	**Highland Pk**	-
NEW Industriel	**Downtown**	-

FRENCH (BISTRO)

Café Beaujolais	**Eagle Rock**	26
Mistral	**Sherman Oaks**	26
NEW Bouchon Bakery	**Beverly Hills**	26
Julienne	**San Marino**	26
Bouchon	**Beverly Hills**	25
Le Petit Bistro	**W Hollywood**	25
Church/State	**Downtown**	24
La Crêperie Café	**Long Bch**	24
Le Petit Cafe	**Santa Monica**	24
Café Pierre	**Manhattan Bch**	24
Bar Bouchon	**Beverly Hills**	24
Meet/Bistro	**Culver City**	24
Le Petit Rest.	**Sherman Oaks**	24
Cheval Blanc	**Pasadena**	24
Figaro	**Los Feliz**	23
Bistro Provence	**Burbank**	23
Cafe Bizou	**multi.**	23
Cafe Stella	**Silver Lake**	22
Rive Gauche	**Sherman Oaks**	21
Monsieur Marcel	**multi.**	21
Bistro/Gare	**S Pasadena**	21
La Dijonaise	**Culver City**	20
Lilly's	**Venice**	19

GASTROPUB

Back Abbey	American	**Claremont**	25
Bouzy	Amer.	**Redondo Bch**	25
NEW Larry's	Amer.	**Venice**	24
Black Market	Eclectic	**Studio City**	24
Waterloo & City	British	**Culver City**	24
Father's Office	Amer.	**multi.**	24
AKA Bistro	Amer.	**Pasadena**	23
Hudson Hse.	Amer.	**Redondo Bch**	23
Anacapa Brewing	Eclectic	**Ventura**	23
Misfit	Eclectic	**Santa Monica**	22
R+D Kitchen	Amer.	**Santa Monica**	22
Beer Belly	Eclectic	**Koreatown**	22
Fat Dog	Amer.	**W Hollywood**	22
Federal Bar	Amer.	**N Hollywood**	21
The Rockefeller	Amer.	**Hermosa Bch**	19
NEW The Churchill	Amer.	**W Hollywood**	17

GERMAN

Brats Brothers	**Sherman Oaks**	24
Wurstküche	**Downtown**	24
Berlin Currywurst	**Silver Lake**	24
Wirtshaus	**La Brea**	20
NEW Biergarten/Standard	**Downtown**	-
NEW Wolfslair	**Hollywood**	-

GREEK

Petros	**Manhattan Bch**	25
George's Greek	**multi.**	24
Papa Cristo's	**Mid-City**	23
Le Petit Greek	**Hancock Pk**	23
Great Greek	**Sherman Oaks**	23
Taverna Tony	**Malibu**	22
NEW Limani Taverna	**San Pedro**	-

HAWAIIAN

Roy's	**multi.**	25
King's Hawaiian	**Torrance**	22
Rutts	**Culver City**	22
Back Home	**multi.**	20
Loft	**multi.**	20

HOT DOGS

Golden State	**Fairfax**	26
Tommy's	**Downtown**	25

Portillo's | **Moreno Valley**	25
Berlin Currywurst | **Silver Lake**	24
Fab Hot Dogs | **Reseda**	24
Pink's Dogs | **La Brea**	23
Slaw Dogs | **multi.**	22
Carney's | **multi.**	22
Dog Haus | **Pasadena**	21
Jody Maroni's | **multi.**	20
Wienerschnitzel | **multi.**	20
Wirtshaus | **La Brea**	20
Let's Be Frank | **Culver City**	19
Stand | **multi.**	19
Papaya King | **Hollywood**	18

INDIAN

Addi's | **Redondo Bch**	26
Bombay Palace | **Beverly Hills**	24
Bollywood | **Studio City**	24
Nawab | **Santa Monica**	24
Ocean Tava | **Redondo Bch**	24
Anarbagh | **Woodland Hills**	24
Agra/Indian Kitchen | **multi.**	23
Clay Oven | **Sherman Oaks**	23
Tanzore | **Beverly Hills**	23
Agra Cafe | **Silver Lake**	23
India's Tandoori | **multi.**	23
Bombay Cafe | **West LA**	22
Annapurna | **Culver City**	22
Akbar | **multi.**	22
Chakra | **Beverly Hills**	22
Flavor of India | **multi.**	22
Taste of India | **multi.**	22
Jaipur | **West LA**	22
All India | **multi.**	21
Samosa Hse. | **Culver City**	21

IRISH

Auld Dubliner | **Long Bch**	21
Tom Bergin's | **Mid-City**	–

ITALIAN

(N=Northern; S=Southern)

Michael's/Naples | **Long Bch**	28
Piccolo | N | **Venice**	28
Oliverio | **Beverly Hills**	28
Angelini | **Beverly Blvd**	28
Mosto | **Marina del Rey**	27
Osteria Mozza | **Hollywood**	27
Ado/Casa Ado | **multi.**	27
Pizzeria Mozza | **Hollywood**	27
Suzanne's | **Ojai**	27
Cicada | N | **Downtown**	27

Vincenti | **Brentwood**	27
Vito's | **Beverly Hills**	27
Tuscany | **Westlake Vill**	26
Bay Cities | **Santa Monica**	26
Palmeri | S | **Brentwood**	26
La Vecchia | **Santa Monica**	26
Il Pastaio | **Beverly Hills**	26
Rustico | **Westlake Vill**	26
Capo | **Santa Monica**	26
Hostaria/Piccolo | **Santa Monica**	26
Valentino | **Santa Monica**	26
Via Veneto | **Santa Monica**	26
Drago Centro | **Downtown**	26
Marino | **Hollywood**	26
Osteria Latini | **Brentwood**	26
Toscana | N | **Brentwood**	26
Madeo | N | **W Hollywood**	26
🆕 Mercato di Vetro | **W Hollywood**	26
Pecorino | **Brentwood**	25
Café Piccolo | N | **Long Bch**	25
🆕 Maximiliano | **Highland Pk**	25
Locanda Veneta | N | **Third St**	25
Celestino | **Pasadena**	25
🆕 800 Degrees | S | **Westwood**	25
Panzanella | S | **Sherman Oaks**	25
Pace | **Laurel Canyon**	25
Prosecco | N | **Toluca Lake**	25
Giorgio Baldi | **Santa Monica**	25
Riviera | **Calabasas**	25
Il Grano | **West LA**	25
Barbrix | **Silver Lake**	25
Colori Kitchen | **Downtown**	25
La Parolaccia | **multi.**	25
Osteria Mamma | N | **Hollywood**	25
Eatalian | **Gardena**	25
Locanda Positano | **Marina del Rey**	25
L'Opera | N | **Long Bch**	25
Divino | **Brentwood**	25
Cube Cafe | **La Brea**	25
La Pergola | **Sherman Oaks**	25
Casa Nostra | **Pacific Palisades**	24
Amarone | N | **W Hollywood**	24
Il Piccolino | **W Hollywood**	24
Da Pasquale | S | **Beverly Hills**	24
E. Baldi | N | **Beverly Hills**	24
Far Niente | N | **Glendale**	24
Culina | **Beverly Hills**	24
Olio/Cafe | **Third St**	24
Caffé Delfini | **Santa Monica**	24
Piccolo Paradiso | **Beverly Hills**	24

Spaghetti Eddie's | **Glendora**	24
Pastina | S | **West LA**	24
Locanda/Lago | N | **Santa Monica**	24
Cafe Verde | **Pasadena**	24
NEW A1 Cucina | **W Hollywood**	24
NEW Settebello | **Pasadena**	24
Vince's Spaghetti | **Ontario**	24
Boccali's | **Ojai**	24
Tra Di Noi | **Malibu**	24
Tutti Mangia | **Claremont**	24
Aroma | **Silver Lake**	24
La Botte | **Santa Monica**	24
Scarpetta | **Beverly Hills**	24
Il Tiramisù | N | **Sherman Oaks**	24
La Dolce Vita | **Beverly Hills**	24
Bar Toscana | **Brentwood**	24
Angelino Cafe | **Mid-City**	24
Cafe Fiore | S | **Ventura**	23
Enoteca Drago | **Beverly Hills**	23
Cafe Firenze | N | **Moorpark**	23
Casa Bianca | **Eagle Rock**	23
Terroni | S | **Beverly Blvd**	23
Bottega Louie | **Downtown**	23
Pizzicotto | **Brentwood**	23
Galletto | **Westlake Vill**	23
Dan Tana's | **W Hollywood**	23
Nonna | **W Hollywood**	23
Modo Mio | **Pacific Palisades**	23
La Bruschetta | **Westwood**	23
Sor Tino | **Brentwood**	23
Il Cielo | N | **Beverly Hills**	23
Ago | N | **W Hollywood**	23
Luggage Room | **Pasadena**	23
Vito | **Santa Monica**	23
Gale's | N | **Pasadena**	23
Little Dom's/Deli | **Los Feliz**	23
Brunello | **Culver City**	23
Mulberry St. Pizzeria | **multi.**	23
Adagio | N | **Woodland Hills**	23
Cecconi's | N | **W Hollywood**	23
Frascati | N | **Rolling Hills Estates**	23
Il Forno | N | **Santa Monica**	23
Farfalla/Vinoteca | **multi.**	23
Osteria La Buca | N | **Hollywood**	23
Caffe Roma | **Beverly Hills**	23
Palermo | **Los Feliz**	23
Fabrocini's | **Mid-City**	23
Obika | **multi.**	23
Grissini | **Agoura Hills**	23
Stinking Rose | **Beverly Hills**	23
Ca' del Sole | N | **N Hollywood**	23

Pitfire | **multi.**	23
Il Tramezzino | **multi.**	23
Old Tony's | **Redondo Bch**	23
Fabiolus | N | **Hollywood**	22
Via Alloro | **Beverly Hills**	22
Alessio/Bistro | **multi.**	22
Mama Terano | **Rolling Hills Estates**	22
Tanino | S | **Westwood**	22
Fritto Misto | **multi.**	22
C & O | **Marina del Rey**	22
Clafoutis | **W Hollywood**	22
Alejo's | **multi.**	22
Maggiano's | **multi.**	22
Caffe Pinguini | **Playa del Rey**	22
Il Fornaio | **multi.**	22
Padri | **Agoura Hills**	22
Sotto | S | **Century City**	22
Mi Piace | **Pasadena**	22
Panini Cafe | **multi.**	22
Guido's | N | **multi.**	22
Mama D's | **Manhattan Bch**	22
Bottle Inn | **Hermosa Bch**	22
Enzo/Angela | **West LA**	22
Giovanni | **Woodland Hills**	22
Cal. Pizza Kitchen | **Downtown**	22
Barone's | **Van Nuys**	22
Vivoli | **multi.**	22
Peppone | **Brentwood**	22
Il Forno Caldo | **Beverly Hills**	22
Amalfi | **La Brea**	22
La Scala | **multi.**	22
Lamppost Pizza | **multi.**	22
Ivy/Shore | **Santa Monica**	22
Cafe Med | **W Hollywood**	22
Amici | **multi.**	22
Firenze | **N Hollywood**	22
Il Moro | **West LA**	22
Bravo | **Santa Monica**	21
Villetta | **Santa Monica**	21
Fraîche | **Santa Monica**	21
Dominick's | **W Hollywood**	21
Spumoni | **multi.**	21
Ca'Brea | N | **La Brea**	21
La Bottega Marino | **multi.**	21
Cliff's Edge | **Silver Lake**	21
Zane's | **Hermosa Bch**	21
Pasta Pomodoro | **multi.**	21
Matteo's | **West LA**	21
Ombra | **Studio City**	21
Cheebo | **Hollywood**	21

Trastevere | **multi.**	21
Oliva | N | **Sherman Oaks**	21
Il Covo | **W Hollywood**	21
Basix | **W Hollywood**	20
Coral Tree | **Century City**	20
Sisley | **multi.**	20
Louise's | **multi.**	20
Maria's | **multi.**	20
Miceli's | **multi.**	20
Toscanova | **multi.**	19
Ugo/Café | **multi.**	19
Rosti | N | **multi.**	18
NEW exEat/Eatalian | **Gardena**	⌐
NEW FigOly | **Downtown**	⌐
NEW Gusto | **Third St**	⌐
NEW Livello | **Beverly Hills**	⌐
NEW Osteria Drago | **W Hollywood**	⌐
NEW Soleto Trattoria | **Downtown**	⌐
Trattoria Neapolis | **Pasadena**	⌐

JAPANESE

(* sushi specialist)

Nishimura* | **W Hollywood**	29
Urasawa* | **Beverly Hills**	28
Asanebo* | **Studio City**	28
Sushi Zo* | **West LA**	28
Matsuhisa* | **Beverly Hills**	28
Echigo* | **West LA**	28
Hamasaku* | **West LA**	28
Kiwami | **Studio City**	28
Sushi Masu* | **West LA**	27
Nobu | **Malibu**	27
Katsu-ya* | **multi.**	27
Sushi Sushi* | **Beverly Hills**	27
Shiro | **S Pasadena**	27
Omino* | **Chatsworth**	27
Hirozen* | **Beverly Blvd.**	27
Katana* | **W Hollywood**	27
Brother Sushi* | **Woodland Hills**	27
Mori Sushi* | **West LA**	27
Nanbankan | **West LA**	27
Sushi Sasabune/Sushi-Don* | **multi.**	27
Takao* | **Brentwood**	27
Maison Akira | **Pasadena**	27
Irori | **Marina del Rey**	26
NEW Tsujita LA | **West LA**	26
Sushi Gen* | **Little Tokyo**	26
K-Zo* | **Culver City**	26
Sugarfish* | **multi.**	26
Nobu | **W Hollywood**	26

Izaka-ya/Katsu-ya | **multi.**	26
Ahi* | **Studio City**	26
Hakata | **Gardena**	25
R23* | **Downtown**	25
N/Naka | **Palms**	25
Musashi | **Northridge**	25
Boss Sushi* | **Beverly Hills**	25
Hama* | **Venice**	25
Katsuya* | **multi.**	25
Koi* | **W Hollywood**	25
Shin-Sen-Gumi Yakitori | **multi.**	25
Bar Hayama | **West LA**	25
Iroha* | **Studio City**	25
Banzai* | **Calabasas**	25
King's Burgers* | **Northridge**	24
Takami* | **Downtown**	24
U-Zen* | **West LA**	24
NEW Fukuburger | **Hollywood**	24
Daikokuya | **multi.**	24
Honda-Ya | **Little Tokyo**	24
Hide* | **West LA**	24
Ramen Jinya | **multi.**	24
Noshi Sushi | **Koreatown**	24
Taiko* | **Brentwood**	24
Santouka Ramen | **multi.**	24
Musha | **multi.**	23
Gin Sushi | **Pasadena**	23
B.A.D. SUSHI | **West LA**	23
Ramen Yamadaya | **multi.**	23
Yen* | **multi.**	23
Yabu* | **multi.**	23
Chaya | **Venice**	23
Ozumo | **Santa Monica**	23
Sushi Roku* | **multi.**	23
Shabu Shabu | **Little Tokyo**	23
Asakuma* | **multi.**	23
Teru Sushi* | **Studio City**	23
RA Sushi* | **Torrance**	23
Furaibo | **West LA**	23
Hirosuke* | **Encino**	23
Lomo Arigato | **Location Varies**	22
Zip Fusion* | **Downtown**	22
Wabi-Sabi* | **Venice**	22
A'float Sushi | **Pasadena**	22
Kabuki* | **multi.**	22
Aburiya Toranoko | **Downtown**	22
Crazy Fish | **Beverly Hills**	22
Asaka* | **multi.**	22
Geisha Hse.* | **Hollywood**	22
Gyu-Kaku | **multi.**	22
Torafuku* | **West LA**	22

O-Nami*	Torrance	21
Sushi Dan*	Hollywood	21
Asahi	West LA	21
Hurry Curry	West LA	21
Ramenya	West LA	21
Yamato	multi.	21
Octopus*	multi.	20
Gonpachi	Torrance	20
Fat Spoon	Little Tokyo	18
NEW Gottsui	West LA	-
NEW Hannosuke	Mar Vista	-
NEW Morinoya	West LA	-
NEW Tatsu Ramen	West LA	-

KOREAN

(* barbecue specialist)

Kogi	Location Varies	26
Genwa	Koreatown	25
Park's BBQ*	Koreatown	25
Soot Bull Jeep*	Koreatown	25
Chego!	Palms	24
Ahn Joo	Glendale	24
Road to Seoul	Mid-City	24
ChoSun Galbee*	Koreatown	24
Kyochon	Koreatown	22
BCD Tofu	multi.	22
Tofu Ya*	West LA	21
NEW Manna*	Downtown	18
NEW Seoul House/Tofu	West LA	-

KOSHER/ KOSHER-STYLE

Tierra Sur/Herzog	Oxnard	28
Fish Grill	multi.	24
Real Food	multi.	23
Bocca	Encino	22
Milky Way	Pico-Robertson	21

LEBANESE

Marouch	E Hollywood	29
Open Sesame	multi.	25
Carnival	Sherman Oaks	25
Sunnin	Westwood	24
Alcazar	Encino	21

MEDITERRANEAN

Tierra Sur/Herzog	Oxnard	28
Lucques	W Hollywood	27
Cleo	Hollywood	27
Christine	Torrance	27
Campanile	La Brea	26

A.O.C.	Third St	26
Tasting Kitchen	Venice	26
Sam's/Beach	Santa Monica	26
Open Sesame	Long Bch	25
Rustic Canyon	Santa Monica	25
NEW Wolfgang Puck/ Hotel Bel-Air	Bel-Air	25
Barbrix	Silver Lake	25
Elf Café	Echo Pk	25
Zazou	Redondo Bch	24
Upstairs 2	West LA	24
Tavern	Brentwood	24
Ray's/Stark Bar	Mid-Wilshire	24
Cafe Del Rey	Marina del Rey	24
Mezze	W Hollywood	24
Little Door	Third St	24
Canelé	Atwater Vill	24
One Pico	Santa Monica	24
Cabbage Patch	multi.	23
Fig & Olive	Melrose	23
Zankou	multi.	23
Emle's	Northridge	23
Kravings	Tarzana	23
Falafel Palace	Northridge	23
Mediterraneo	Hermosa Bch	22
Delphine	Hollywood	22
Panini Cafe	multi.	22
Momed	Beverly Hills	22
Mediterraneo	Westlake Vill	21
Café Santorini	Pasadena	21
Lemon Moon	West LA	21
Primitivo	Venice	21
Palomino	Westwood	21
Gaby's	multi.	20
Villa Blanca	Beverly Hills	19

MEXICAN

Babita	San Gabriel	27
Alfredo's	Lomita	27
El Tepeyac	East LA	26
Kogi	Location Varies	26
NEW Baco Mercat	Downtown	26
Mucho Ultima	Manhattan Bch	26
Yuca's	Los Feliz	25
Cook's Tortas	Monterey Pk	25
Chichen Itza	Downtown	25
Red O	Melrose	25
CaCao	Eagle Rock	25
Alegria/Sunset	Silver Lake	24
Guelaguetza	multi.	24
Yxta	Downtown	24
King Taco	multi.	24

Latest openings, menus, photos and more on plus.google.com/local

Chego! | **Palms** 24
Tinga | **La Brea** 24
Las Fuentes | **Reseda** 24
Los Arroyos | **Camarillo** 24
Tlapazola | **multi.** 24
La Paz | **Calabasas** 24
La Cabanita | **Montrose** 24
Border Grill Truck | **Location Varies** 24
Casa Sanchez | **West LA** 23
Super Mex | **multi.** 23
Chipotle | **multi.** 23
Poquito Más | **multi.** 23
Fuego/Maya | **Long Bch** 23
Monte Alban | **West LA** 23
Gloria's Cafe | **Culver City** 23
La Serenata | **multi.** 23
Tito's Tacos | **Culver City** 23
Malo | **Silver Lake** 23
Los Toros | **Chatsworth** 23
Lotería! | **multi.** 23
Café Rio | **multi.** 23
El Portal | **Pasadena** 22
Ortega 120 | **Redondo Bch** 22
Sol y Luna | **Tarzana** 22
Antonio's | **Melrose** 22
Wahoo's Fish Taco | **multi.** 22
Lupe's | **Thousand Oaks** 22
El Gallo Giro | **multi.** 22
Original Red Onion | 22
  Rolling Hills Estates
Border Grill | **multi.** 22
Best Fish Taco | **Los Feliz** 22
Burrito King | **Echo Pk** 22
Avila's El Ranchito | **multi.** 22
Coral Cafe | **Burbank** 22
Lares | **Santa Monica** 22
El Compadre | **Echo Pk** 22
El Tarasco | **Venice** 22
El Torito Grill | **multi.** 21
NEW Casa Azul | **Westwood** 21
Paco's Tacos | **multi.** 21
Chronic Tacos | **multi.** 21
Café Habana | **Malibu** 21
Rosa Mexicano | **multi.** 21
El Torito | **multi.** 21
Barragan's | **multi.** 21
Ernie's | **N Hollywood** 21
Frisco's | **Rowland Hts** 21
Acapulco | **multi.** 20
Frida | **multi.** 20
Adobe Cantina | **Agoura Hills** 20

Casa Vega | **Sherman Oaks** 20
Mijares | **Pasadena** 20
El Cholo | **multi.** 20
La Salsa | **multi.** 19
Casablanca | **Venice** 19
Kay 'n Dave's | **multi.** 19
Baja Sharkeez | **multi.** 18
Pink Taco | **multi.** 18
Baja Cantina | **Marina del Rey** 18
El Coyote | **Beverly Blvd** 17
NEW Mercado | **Santa Monica** -
NEW Palmilla | **Hermosa Bch** -
NEW Tortilla Republic | -
  W Hollywood

MIDDLE EASTERN

NEW Baco Mercat | **Downtown** 26
Raffi's Place | **Glendale** 26
Alwazir Chicken | **Hollywood** 25
Carousel | **multi.** 25
Pita Kitchen | **Sherman Oaks** 24
Falafel Palace | **Northridge** 23
Wahib's | **Alhambra** 22
Hummus Bar | **Tarzana** 22
Itzik Hagadol | **Encino** 21
Falafel King | **multi.** 18
Burger Continental | **Pasadena** 18

MONGOLIAN

Big Wok | **Manhattan Bch** 22

MOROCCAN

Babouch | **San Pedro** 26
Tagine | **Beverly Hills** 24
Marrakesh | **Studio City** 22
Dar Maghreb | **Hollywood** 22

NEW ENGLAND

Lobsta Truck | **Location Varies** 23

NOODLE SHOPS

NEW Tsujita LA | **West LA** 26
Pho So 1 | **multi.** 26
Hakata | **Gardena** 25
Golden Deli | **San Gabriel** 25
Pho Café | **Silver Lake** 25
Daikokuya | **multi.** 24
Pho 79 | **Alhambra** 24
Ramen Jinya | **multi.** 24
Santouka Ramen | **multi.** 24
101 Noodle | **multi.** 23
Ramen Yamadaya | **multi.** 23

Mandarin	**multi.**	22
Blossom	**multi.**	22
9021Pho	**multi.**	22
Absolutely Pho	**multi.**	22
Blue Hen	**Eagle Rock**	21
Asahi	**West LA**	21
Pho Show	**Culver City**	21
Ramenya	**West LA**	21
Noodle World	**multi.**	19
NEW Nong La	**West LA**	-
NEW Tatsu Ramen	**West LA**	-

NUEVO LATINO

Alegria	**Long Bch**	23

PACIFIC RIM

Christine	**Torrance**	27
Flying Pig	**Location Varies**	22
Duke's	**Malibu**	20

PAN-LATIN

Rivera	**Downtown**	26
Playa	**Beverly Blvd**	25
Fuego/Maya	**Long Bch**	23
Beso	**Hollywood**	19

PERSIAN

Shamshiri Grill	**Westwood**	24
Shaherzad	**Westwood**	23
Javan	**West LA**	22

PERUVIAN

Mario's Peruvian	**Hollywood**	26
Picca	**Century City**	25
NEW Mo-Chica	**Downtown**	24
El Rocoto	**multi.**	23
Los Balcones/Peru	**Hollywood**	23
Lomo Arigato	**Location Varies**	22
El Pollo Inka	**multi.**	22

PIZZA

Michael's Pizzeria	**Long Bch**	28
Pizzeria Mozza	**Hollywood**	27
Vito's	**Beverly Hills**	27
Mozza to Go	**W Hollywood**	26
Gjelina	**Venice**	26
Buono's	**Long Bch**	26
Village Pizzeria	**multi.**	25
NEW Milo & Olive	**Santa Monica**	25
Stella Rossa	**Santa Monica**	25
NEW 800 Degrees	**Westwood**	25
Pace	**Laurel Canyon**	25
Olio/Cafe	**Third St**	24
Beach Pizza	**multi.**	24

Zelo Pizzeria	**Arcadia**	24
Joe's Pizza	**multi.**	24
Lamonica's	**Westwood**	24
Masa	**Echo Pk**	24
Abbot's	**multi.**	24
Tomato Pie	**multi.**	24
Casa Bianca	**Eagle Rock**	23
Terroni	**Beverly Blvd**	23
Bottega Louie	**Downtown**	23
Z Pizza	**multi.**	23
Valentino's	**Manhattan Bch**	23
Luggage Room	**Pasadena**	23
Little Dom's/Deli	**Los Feliz**	23
Mulberry St. Pizzeria	**multi.**	23
BJ's	**multi.**	23
Farfalla/Vinoteca	**Los Feliz**	23
Pitfire	**multi.**	23
Extreme Pizza	**multi.**	22
Sotto	**Century City**	22
Cal. Pizza Kitchen	**multi.**	22
Barone's	**Van Nuys**	22
Lamppost Pizza	**multi.**	22
Caioti Pizza	**Studio City**	22
Bravo	**Santa Monica**	21
La Bottega Marino	**multi.**	21
Sammy's/Pizza	**El Segundo**	21
Cheebo	**Hollywood**	21
Johnnie's NY	**multi.**	20
NEW Crust	**Studio City**	-
NEW Soleto Trattoria	**Downtown**	-

POLISH

Warszawa	**Santa Monica**	23

POLYNESIAN

Bahooka	**Rosemead**	21
Trader Vic's	**multi.**	19

PUB FOOD

Heroes/Legends	**Claremont**	23
BJ's	**multi.**	23
Westside Tav.	**West LA**	23
Whale & Ale	**San Pedro**	21
Auld Dubliner	**Long Bch**	21
Gordon Biersch	**Burbank**	19
Ye Olde King's	**Santa Monica**	18
NEW Pikey	**Hollywood**	-
Tom Bergin's	**Mid-City**	-

QUÉBÉCOIS

NEW P'tit Soleil	**Westwood**	-

SALVADORAN

Gloria's Cafe | **Culver City** 23

SANDWICHES

(See also Delis)

Brent's Deli	**multi.**	26
Bay Cities	**Santa Monica**	26
Langer's	**Downtown**	26
Porto's	**multi.**	26
NEW Baco Mercat	**Downtown**	26
Cook's Tortas	**Monterey Pk**	25
Artisan	**Studio City**	25
Clementine	**Century City**	25
Mendocino Farms	**multi.**	25
Thyme Café	**Santa Monica**	25
Food	**Rancho Pk**	24
Label's Table	**Century City**	24
Philippe/Original	**Chinatown**	24
3 Square	**Venice**	24
Grilled Cheese Truck	**Location Varies**	24
Fundamental LA	**Westwood**	23
Huckleberry	**Santa Monica**	23
NEW Blue Cow Kitchen	**Downtown**	23
Little Dom's/Deli	**Los Feliz**	23
Barney Greengrass	**Beverly Hills**	23
Food + Lab	**multi.**	23
Baker	**Woodland Hills**	23
Il Tramezzino	**multi.**	23
Porta Via	**Beverly Hills**	22
Milk	**Mid-City**	22
Johnnie's Pastrami	**Culver City**	22
Lawry's Carvery	**Downtown**	22
Burrito King	**Echo Pk**	22
Art's	**Studio City**	22
Il Forno Caldo	**Beverly Hills**	22
Homeboy Diner	**Downtown**	21
Lemon Moon	**West LA**	21
Canter's	**Fairfax**	21
Lee's Sandwiches	**multi.**	21
Nate 'n Al	**multi.**	20
Coral Tree	**multi.**	20
Factor's	**Pico-Robertson**	20
Cafe Surfas	**Culver City**	19
Breadbar	**Century City**	18
Cole's	**Downtown**	17
Fromin's	**Santa Monica**	17
Roll 'n Rye	**Culver City**	17
NEW Eden Burger Bar	**Glendale**	–

SCOTTISH

Tam O'Shanter | **Atwater Vill** 23

SEAFOOD

Providence	**Hollywood**	28
Water Grill	**Downtown**	27
Newport Seafood	**multi.**	27
Sea Harbour	**Rosemead**	26
Santa Monica Seafood	**Santa Monica**	26
Boiling Crab	**multi.**	25
Malibu Seafood	**Malibu**	25
Son of a Gun	**Third St**	25
Palm	**multi.**	25
Lobster	**Santa Monica**	25
Fins	**Westlake Vill**	25
Fish King	**Glendale**	25
Ocean Ave.	**Santa Monica**	24
Hungry Cat	**multi.**	24
Baleen	**Redondo Bch**	24
Lure Fish Hse.	**Camarillo**	24
888 Seafood	**Rosemead**	24
Fish Grill	**multi.**	24
Crab Pot	**Long Bch**	24
Delmonico's	**Encino**	24
22nd St. Landing	**San Pedro**	24
One Pico	**Santa Monica**	24
BP Oysterette	**Santa Monica**	23
Lobsta Truck	**Location Varies**	23
Ocean Seafood	**Chinatown**	23
Fishbar	**Manhattan Bch**	23
Gulfstream	**Century City**	23
A & W Seafood	**Northridge**	23
Brophy Bros.	**Ventura**	23
Chart House	**multi.**	23
Capital Seafood	**Monterey Pk**	23
Bluewater	**Redondo Bch**	23
Parker's	**Long Bch**	23
King's Fish	**multi.**	23
Armstrong's	**Catalina Is.**	23
New Capital Seafood	**San Gabriel**	23
La Serenata	**multi.**	23
Coast	**Santa Monica**	23
Catch	**Santa Monica**	23
Old Tony's	**Redondo Bch**	23
Reel Inn	**Malibu**	22
Rock'n Fish	**multi.**	22
Wahoo's Fish Taco	**multi.**	22
Holdren's	**Thousand Oaks**	22
McCormick/Schmick	**multi.**	22
Admiral Risty	**Rancho Palos Verdes**	22

Full House | **Chinatown**	22
Kincaid's | **Redondo Bch**	22
Enterprise Fish | **Santa Monica**	21
NBC Seafood | **Monterey Pk**	21
McKenna's | **Long Bch**	21
NEW Killer Shrimp | **Marina del Rey**	21
CBS Seafood | **Chinatown**	20
Neptune's Net | **Malibu**	20
Duke's | **Malibu**	20
Buggy Whip | **Westchester**	20
Galley | **Santa Monica**	20
Hop Li | **multi.**	19
Paradise Cove | **Malibu**	19
Charlie's | **Malibu**	18
Gladstone's | **multi.**	18
NEW L&E Oyster Bar | **Silver Lake**	-

SINGAPOREAN

Spice Table | **Little Tokyo**	25

SMALL PLATES

(See also Spanish tapas specialist)

M.B. Post | Amer. | **Manhattan Bch**	28
Bazaar by José Andrés | Spanish | **Beverly Hills**	27
Leila's | Cal. | **Oak Pk**	27
Cleo | Med. | **Hollywood**	27
A.O.C. | Cal./French | **Third St**	26
K-Zo | Japanese | **Culver City**	26
Izaka-ya/Katsu-ya | Japanese | **multi.**	26
Gjelina | Amer. | **Venice**	26
Street | Eclectic | **Hollywood**	25
Lazy Ox | Eclectic | **Little Tokyo**	25
Rustic Canyon | Med. | **Santa Monica**	25
Bar Hayama | Japanese | **West LA**	25
Cube Cafe | Italian | **La Brea**	25
Playa | Latin | **Beverly Blvd**	25
Upstairs 2 | Med. | **West LA**	24
Noir | Eclectic | **Pasadena**	24
Bar Bouchon | French | **Beverly Hills**	24
Mezze | Med. | **W Hollywood**	24
Musha | Japanese | **multi.**	23
Enoteca Drago | Italian | **Beverly Hills**	23
2117 | Asian/Euro. | **West LA**	23
Talésai/Night | Thai | **W Hollywood**	23

Zengo | Asian/Nuevo Latino | **Santa Monica**	23
Mediterraneo | Med. | **Hermosa Bch**	22
Corkbar | Eclectic | **Downtown**	22
Gorbals | Eclectic | **Downtown**	22
Vertical Wine | Eclectic/Med. | **Pasadena**	21
Primitivo | Med. | **Venice**	21
BottleRock | Euro. | **multi.**	19

SOUL FOOD

M & M Soul Food | **Carson**	25
Roscoe's | **multi.**	24
Big Mama's | **Pasadena**	23

SOUTHERN

Johnny Rebs' | **multi.**	25
Les Sisters | **Chatsworth**	25
Lucille's | **multi.**	24

SOUTHWESTERN

Bandera | **West LA**	24
Coyote Cantina | **Redondo Bch**	22
Foxy's | **Glendale**	21
Jinky's | **multi.**	20

SPANISH

(* tapas specialist)

Bazaar by José Andrés | **Beverly Hills**	27
La Paella* | **Beverly Hills**	23
Bar Pintxo* | **Santa Monica**	22
NEW Bow & Truss | **N Hollywood**	-
NEW Racion | **Pasadena**	-

STEAKHOUSES

Cut | **Beverly Hills**	27
Mastro's | **multi.**	27
Ruth's Chris | **multi.**	27
Morton's | **multi.**	26
Lawry's Prime | **Beverly Hills**	26
BLT Steak | **W Hollywood**	26
555 East | **Long Bch**	26
Arroyo | **Pasadena**	26
Fleming's | **multi.**	25
Grill on Alley | **Beverly Hills**	25
Fogo de Chão | **Beverly Hills**	25
Capital Grille | **Beverly Hills**	25
Derby | **Arcadia**	25
Larsen's | **Encino**	25
Palm | **multi.**	25

Jar | **Beverly Blvd.** 25
STK | **W Hollywood** 25
Boa | **multi.** 24
Wolfgang's | **Beverly Hills** 24
Carlitos Gardel | **Melrose** 24
Taylor's | **multi.** 24
1810 Rest. | **Pasadena** 24
Nick & Stef's | **Downtown** 24
Outback | **multi.** 23
Chart House | **multi.** 23
Lala's | **Studio City** 23
Kravings | **Tarzana** 23
Vibrato Grill | **Bel-Air** 23
Black Angus | **multi.** 23
Malbec | **multi.** 23
Original Roadhse. Grill | **multi.** 23
Damon's | **Glendale** 23
Monty's | **Woodland Hills** 22
Rock'n Fish | **multi.** 22
Beckham Grill | **Pasadena** 22
Bocca | **Encino** 22
Holdren's | **Thousand Oaks** 22
Smoke Hse. | **Burbank** 22
Kincaid's | **Redondo Bch** 22
Gaucho | **multi.** 21
McKenna's | **Long Bch** 21
Zane's | **Hermosa Bch** 21
Salt Creek | **multi.** 20
Buggy Whip | **Westchester** 20
Morels French Steak | **Fairfax** 20
Chez Jay | **Santa Monica** 20
Galley | **Santa Monica** 20
Charlie's | **Malibu** 18
Billingsley's | **West LA** 17
Tom Bergin's | **Mid-City** ⌐

TAIWANESE

Tea Station | **multi.** 19

TEAHOUSE

Tea Station | **multi.** 19

TEX-MEX

Marix | **multi.** 17

THAI

Jitlada | **E Hollywood** 27
Ayara Thai | **Westchester** 24
Cholada | **multi.** 24
Saladang | **Pasadena** 24
Palms Thai | **E Hollywood** 23

Sanamluang Cafe | **multi.** 23
Talésai/Night | **multi.** 23
Bangkok West | **Santa Monica** 23
Chan Dara | **multi.** 23
Tuk Tuk | **Pico-Robertson** 22
Chadaka | **Burbank** 22
Toi | **W Hollywood** 21
Natalee | **multi.** 21
Buddha's Belly | **multi.** 21
Thai Dishes | **multi.** 20

TURKISH

Spitz | **multi.** 23

VEGETARIAN

(* vegan)
Zephyr | **Long Bch** 25
Native Foods* | **multi.** 25
Elf Café | **Echo Pk** 25
Cafe Gratitude* | **multi.** 24
Mohawk Bend* | **Echo Pk** 24
Real Food* | **multi.** 23
Veggie Grill* | **multi.** 23
True Food | **Santa Monica** 23
M Café* | **multi.** 22
Follow Your Heart | **Canoga Pk** 22
Urth* | **multi.** 22
Vegan Glory* | **Beverly Blvd** 22
A Votre Sante | **Brentwood** 21
Flore* | **Silver Lake** 21

VIETNAMESE

Benley | **Long Bch** 28
Pho So 1 | **multi.** 26
Crustacean | **Beverly Hills** 25
Golden Deli | **San Gabriel** 25
Pho Café | **Silver Lake** 25
Spice Table | **Little Tokyo** 25
Pho 79 | **Alhambra** 24
Good Girl | **Highland Pk** 24
Red Medicine | **Beverly Hills** 23
Gingergrass | **Silver Lake** 23
Blossom | **multi.** 22
9021Pho | **multi.** 22
Absolutely Pho | **multi.** 22
Blue Hen | **Eagle Rock** 21
Nom Nom | **Location Varies** 21
Pho Show | **Culver City** 21
Buddha's Belly | **multi.** 21
NEW Nong La | **West LA** ⌐

Locations

Includes names, cuisines and Food ratings.

LA Central

ATWATER VILLAGE

Canelé	*Med.*	24
Tam O'Shanter	*Scottish*	23
Acapulco	*Mex.*	20

BEVERLY BLVD.

(bet. La Brea & La Cienega; see map on back of gatefold)

Angelini	*Italian*	28
Hirozen	*Japanese*	27
NEW Cooks County	*Cal.*	25
Eva	*Cal.*	25
Jar	*Amer.*	25
Playa	*Latin*	25
Fish Grill	*Seafood*	24
Susina	*Bakery*	24
Terroni	*Italian*	23
Obika	*Italian*	23
Bao	*Chinese*	22
Vegan Glory	*Vegan*	22
BLD	*Amer.*	22
Buddha's Belly	*Asian*	21
House Café	*Eclectic*	21
Swingers	*Diner*	20
El Coyote	*Mex.*	17

CHINATOWN

King Taco	*Mex.*	24
Philippe/Original	*Sandwiches*	24
Ocean Seafood	*Chinese/Seafood*	23
Yang Chow	*Chinese*	23
Full House	*Chinese/Seafood*	22
Empress Pavilion	*Chinese*	21
Sam Woo	*Chinese*	21
Golden Dragon	*Chinese*	21
Homegirl Café	*Amer./Mex.*	21
CBS Seafood	*Seafood*	20
Hop Woo	*Chinese*	20
Hop Li	*Chinese/Seafood*	19

DOWNTOWN

(see map on page 80)

Water Grill	*Seafood*	27
Patina	*Amer./Cal.*	27
Cicada	*Cal./Italian*	27
Sugarfish	*Japanese*	26
Morton's	*Steak*	26
Langer's	*Deli*	26
NEW Baco Mercat	*Sandwiches*	26
WP24	*Chinese*	26
Rivera	*Pan-Latin*	26
Drago Centro	*Italian*	26
Fleming's	*Steak*	25
R23	*Japanese*	25
Tommy's	*Burgers/Hot Dogs*	25
Colori Kitchen	*Italian*	25
Mendocino Farms	*Sandwiches*	25
Katsuya	*Japanese*	25
Palm	*Steak*	25
Chichen Itza	*Mex.*	25
Roy's	*Hawaiian*	25
Church/State	*French*	24
Takami	*Japanese*	24
Cafe Pinot	*Cal./French*	24
Yxta	*Mex.*	24
King Taco	*Mex.*	24
Bar	Kitchen	*Amer.*	24
NEW Mo-Chica	*Peruvian*	24
New Moon	*Chinese*	24
Wurstküche	*Euro.*	24
Chaya	*Asian/French*	24
Nick & Stef's	*Steak*	24
Cabbage Patch	*Cal./Med.*	23
Bottega Louie	*Italian*	23
NEW Blue Cow Kitchen	*Amer./Eclectic*	23
Farmer Boy's	*Burgers*	23
Checkers	*Cal.*	23
NEW Umamicatessen	*Eclectic*	23
Nickel Diner	*Diner*	23
Wolfgang Puck B&G	*Cal.*	23
Pitfire	*Pizza*	23
Zip Fusion	*Japanese/Korean*	22
Rock'n Fish	*Seafood*	22
Yard House	*Amer.*	22
El Gallo Giro	*Mex.*	22
Blossom	*Viet.*	22
Border Grill	*Mex.*	22
Panini Cafe	*Italian/Med.*	22
Urth	*Amer.*	22
Corkbar	*Eclectic*	22
Aburiya Toranoko	*Japanese*	22
McCormick/Schmick	*Seafood*	22
Lemonade	*Cal.*	22

Gorbals	*Eclectic*	22
Cal. Pizza Kitchen	*Pizza*	22
Lawry's Carvery	*Amer.*	22
Wokcano	*Asian*	22
Traxx	*Amer.*	21
L.A. Market	*Cal.*	21
Noé	*Amer.*	21
Daily Grill	*Amer.*	21
Homeboy Diner	*Sandwiches*	21
Rosa Mexicano	*Mex.*	21
Pete's	*Amer.*	21
Engine Co. 28	*Amer.*	20
Octopus	*Japanese*	20
Johnnie's NY	*Pizza*	20
El Cholo	*Mex.*	20
Original Pantry	*Diner*	20
Maria's	*Italian*	20
Kendall's	*French*	20
Trader Vic's	*Polynesian*	19
La Salsa	*Mex.*	19
Farm/Bev. Hills	*Amer.*	19
Restaurant/Standard	*Eclectic*	19
BottleRock	*Euro.*	19
NEW Little Bear	*Belgian*	18
NEW Manna	*Korean*	18
First & Hope	*Amer.*	18
Perch	*French*	18
Cole's	*Sandwiches*	17
NEW Biergarten/Standard	*German*	-
NEW Eat.Drink.Americano	*Amer.*	-
NEW FigOly	*Cal./Italian*	-
NEW Industriel	*French*	-
Kitchen Faire	*Amer.*	-
NEW One Eyed Gypsy	*Eclectic*	-
NEW Soleto Trattoria	*Italian*	-
The Parish	*British*	-
NEW Towne	*Amer.*	-

EAST HOLLYWOOD

Marouch	*Lebanese*	29
Jitlada	*Thai*	27
Carousel	*Mideast.*	25
Palms Thai	*Thai*	23
Sanamluang Cafe	*Thai*	23
Zankou	*Med.*	23
Square One	*Amer.*	23

ECHO PARK

Park	*Amer.*	25
Elf Café	*Med./Veg.*	25

Mohawk Bend	*Eclectic*	24
Masa	*Pizza*	24
Burrito King	*Mex.*	22
El Compadre	*Mex.*	22
Taix	*French*	21
Barragan's	*Mex.*	21

FAIRFAX

Animal	*Amer.*	27
Golden State	*Burgers*	26
Mendocino Farms	*Sandwiches*	25
Wood Ranch	*BBQ*	24
French Crêpe Co.	*French*	23
Cheesecake Factory	*Amer.*	23
Veggie Grill	*Vegan*	23
Umami	*Burgers*	23
Chipotle	*Mex.*	23
Lotería!	*Mex.*	23
Maggiano's	*Italian*	22
Monsieur Marcel	*French*	21
Black Cat	*Amer.*	21
Canter's	*Deli*	21
Gumbo Pot	*Cajun*	20
Morels French Steak	*French/Steak*	20
Marmalade	*Amer.*	19
NEW Short Order	*Burgers*	18
Du-par's	*Diner*	18

HANCOCK PARK/ LARCHMONT VILLAGE

Village Pizzeria	*Pizza*	25
Cafe Gratitude	*Amer.*	24
Z Pizza	*Pizza*	23
Le Petit Greek	*Greek*	23
Prado	*Carib.*	23
Chan Dara	*Thai*	23
Wahoo's Fish Taco	*Mex./Seafood*	22
La Bottega Marino	*Italian*	21
Larchmont Bungalow	*Amer.*	21
Louise's	*Cal./Italian*	20

HIGHLAND PARK

NEW Maximiliano	*Italian*	25
Good Girl	*Viet.*	24
NEW Ba Restaurant	*French*	-

HOLLYWOOD

(see map on page 79)

Providence	*Amer./Seafood*	28
Osteria Mozza	*Italian*	27

Pizzeria Mozza	*Pizza*	27
Cleo	*Med.*	27
Larchmont Grill	*Amer.*	26
Marino	*Italian*	26
In-N-Out	*Burgers*	26
Mario's Peruvian	*Peruvian*	26
Village Pizzeria	*Pizza*	25
Street	*Eclectic*	25
Salt's Cure	*Amer.*	25
Alwazir Chicken	*Mideast.*	25
Griddle Cafe	*Amer.*	25
Osteria Mamma	*Italian*	25
Katsuya	*Japanese*	25
Grill on Hollywood/Alley	*Amer.*	24
Hungry Cat	*Seafood*	24
Grub	*Amer.*	24
NEW Fukuburger	*Burgers*	24
25 Degrees	*Burgers*	24
Joe's Pizza	*Pizza*	24
Roscoe's	*Soul Food*	24
French Crêpe Co.	*French*	23
Tender Greens	*Amer.*	23
Wood & Vine	*Amer./French*	23
Umami	*Burgers*	23
Cal. Chicken	*Amer.*	23
Musso & Frank	*Amer.*	23
101 Coffee	*Diner*	23
Bossa Nova	*Brazilian*	23
Osteria La Buca	*Italian*	23
Ammo	*Cal.*	23
Chan Dara	*Thai*	23
Lotería!	*Mex.*	23
Los Balcones/Peru	*Peruvian*	23
Fabiolus	*Italian*	22
Astro Burger	*Burgers*	22
Delphine	*French/Med.*	22
Yamashiro	*Asian/Cal.*	22
Kabuki	*Japanese*	22
Go Burger	*Burgers*	22
Bowery	*Amer.*	22
Cal. Pizza Kitchen	*Pizza*	22
Geisha Hse.	*Japanese*	22
Off Vine	*Cal.*	22
Dar Maghreb	*Moroccan*	22
Sushi Dan	*Japanese*	21
Xiomara	*Cal.*	21
Waffle	*Amer.*	21
Cheebo	*Italian*	21
Kitchen 24	*Amer.*	21
Trastevere	*Italian*	21
Miceli's	*Italian*	20

Greenblatt's	*Deli*	19
Beso	*Pan-Latin*	19
Pig 'n Whistle	*Continental*	19
Papaya King	*Hot Dogs*	18
Mel's Drive-In	*Amer.*	18
NEW Bosc	*Eclectic*	-
NEW Outpost	*Amer.*	-
NEW Pikey	*Pub*	-
NEW Sadie Kitchen	*Amer.*	-
NEW Wolfslair	*German*	-

HUNTINGTON PARK

El Gallo Giro	*Mex.*	22
Avila's El Ranchito	*Mex.*	22

KOREATOWN

Genwa	*Korean*	25
Boiling Crab	*Cajun/Seafood*	25
Park's BBQ	*Korean*	25
Soot Bull Jeep	*Korean*	25
Guelaguetza	*Mex.*	24
ChoSun Galbee	*Korean*	24
Noshi Sushi	*Japanese*	24
Taylor's	*Steak*	24
Kyochon	*Korean*	22
BCD Tofu	*Korean*	22
Beer Belly	*Eclectic*	22

LA BREA

Campanile	*Cal./Med.*	26
Cube Cafe	*Italian*	25
Tinga	*Mex.*	24
Pink's Dogs	*Hot Dogs*	23
Amalfi	*Italian*	22
Ca'Brea	*Italian*	21
Luna Park	*Amer.*	21
Wirtshaus	*German*	20

LAUREL CANYON

Pace	*Italian*	25

LEIMERT PARK

Phillips BBQ	*BBQ*	26

LINCOLN HEIGHTS

King Taco	*Mex.*	24

LITTLE TOKYO

Sushi Gen	*Japanese*	26
Lazy Ox	*Eclectic*	25
Spice Table	*Asian*	25
Daikokuya	*Japanese*	24

Honda-Ya	*Japanese*	24
Yen	*Japanese*	23
Spitz	*Turkish*	23
Shabu Shabu	*Japanese*	23
Fat Spoon	*Japanese*	18

LOS FELIZ

Yuca's	*Mex.*	25
Figaro	*French*	23
Little Dom's/Deli	*Italian*	23
Farfalla/Vinoteca	*Italian*	23
Palermo	*Italian*	23
Best Fish Taco	*Mex.*	22
Vermont	*Amer.*	22
Alcove	*Amer.*	21
Chi Dynasty	*Chinese*	21
Acapulco	*Mex.*	20
Home	*Eclectic*	20
Louise's	*Cal./Italian*	20
Fred 62	*Diner*	19

MELROSE

(see map on page 79)

Hatfield's	*Amer.*	27
Red O	*Mex.*	25
Foundry/Melrose	*Amer.*	24
Carlitos Gardel	*Argent./Steak*	24
Tomato Pie	*Pizza*	24
Fig & Olive	*Med.*	23
Sweet Lady Jane	*Bakery*	23
Antonio's	*Mex.*	22
M Café	*Veg.*	22
Frida		20
NEW Bugatta	*Eclectic*	-

MID-CITY

Woody's BBQ	*BBQ*	27
NEW Post & Beam	*Amer.*	26
Phillips BBQ	*BBQ*	26
Harold & Belle's	*Creole*	25
Blu Jam	*Amer./Euro.*	25
King Taco	*Mex.*	24
Road to Seoul	*Korean/BBQ*	24
Roscoe's	*Soul Food*	24
Bloom	*Cal.*	24
Angelino Cafe	*Italian*	24
Papa Cristo's	*Greek*	23
Versailles	*Cuban*	23
Fabrocini's	*Italian*	23
Black Dog Coffee	*Coffee*	22
Milk	*Sandwiches*	22

El Cholo	*Mex.*	20
Tom Bergin's	*Irish*	-

MID-WILSHIRE

Nyala	*Ethiopian*	25
Ray's/Stark Bar	*Med.*	24
Umami	*Burgers*	23
India's Tandoori	*Indian*	23
Counter	*Burgers*	21
Johnnie's NY	*Pizza*	20

PICO-ROBERTSON

Fish Grill	*Seafood*	24
Yen	*Japanese*	23
Tuk Tuk	*Thai*	22
Milky Way	*Cal./Kosher*	21
Factor's	*Deli*	20
Hop Li	*Chinese/Seafood*	19

SILVER LAKE

Forage	*Cal.*	26
Barbrix	*Italian/Med.*	25
Blair's	*Amer.*	25
Pho Café	*Viet.*	25
Alegria/Sunset	*Mex.*	24
Aroma	*Italian*	24
Berlin Currywurst	*German*	24
Tomato Pie	*Pizza*	24
Gingergrass	*Viet.*	23
Agra Cafe	*Indian*	23
Malo	*Mex.*	23
Food + Lab	*Cal.*	23
LAMILL	*Cal.*	22
Dusty's	*Amer./French*	22
Blossom	*Viet.*	22
Cafe Stella	*French*	22
Cha Cha Cha	*Carib.*	22
Cliff's Edge	*Cal./Italian*	21
Flore	*Vegan*	21
Home	*Eclectic*	20
NEW Black Hogg	*Amer.*	-
NEW Lago d'Argento	*Italian*	-
NEW L&E Oyster Bar	*Seafood*	-

THIRD STREET

(bet. La Brea & Robertson; see map on back of gatefold)

A.O.C.	*Cal./Med.*	26
Izaka-ya/Katsu-ya	*Japanese*	26
Locanda Veneta	*Italian*	25
Son of a Gun	*Seafood*	25
Olio/Cafe	*Italian*	24

LOS ANGELES

LOCATIONS

Joan's on Third Cafe | *American* 24
Little Door | *Med.* 24
Sushi Roku | *Japanese* 23
Doughboys | *Amer.* 22
Toast | *Amer.* 19
NEW Gusto | *Italian* -

WEST HOLLYWOOD
(see map on back of gatefold)
Nishimura | *Japanese* 29
Lucques | *Cal./Med.* 27
Katana | *Japanese* 27
Ink | *Amer./Eclectic* 26
Nobu | *Japanese* 26
Mozza to Go | *Pizza* 26
BLT Steak | *Steak* 26
Madeo | *Italian* 26
NEW Mercato di Vetro | *Italian* 26
Mendocino Farms | *Sandwiches* 25
Koi | *Japanese* 25
Palm | *Steak* 25
Le Petit Bistro | *French* 25
STK | *Steak* 25
Boa | *Steak* 24
Amarone | *Italian* 24
Il Piccolino | *Italian* 24
Petrossian | *French* 24
Joe's Pizza | *Pizza* 24
Hole in the Wall | *Burgers* 24
Craig's | *Amer.* 24
NEW A1 Cucina | *Italian* 24
Asia de Cuba | *Asian/Cuban* 24
Mezze | *Med.* 24
Chaya | *Asian/French* 24
Gordon Ramsay | *Cal./French* 24
Comme Ça | *French* 24
Real Food | *Vegan* 23
Veggie Grill | *Vegan* 23
Tender Greens | *Amer.* 23
Z Pizza | *Pizza* 23
Yabu | *Japanese* 23
Dan Tana's | *Italian* 23
Nonna | *Italian* 23
Lulu's Cafe | *Amer.* 23
Ago | *Italian* 23
Poquito Más | *Mex.* 23
Agra/Indian Kitchen | *Indian* 23
Lala's | *Argent./Steak* 23
Cecconi's | *Italian* 23
Talésai/Night | *Thai* 23
Bossa Nova | *Brazilian* 23
Food + Lab | *Cal.* 23

Pitfire | *Pizza* 23
Cuvée | *Cal.* 23
Ivy | *Cal.* 22
Baby Blues | *BBQ* 22
Astro Burger | *Burgers* 22
Clafoutis | *French/Italian* 22
Flavor of India | *Indian* 22
Urth | *Amer.* 22
Lemonade | *Cal.* 22
Taste | *Amer.* 22
Carney's | *Hot Dogs* 22
Absolutely Pho | *Viet.* 22
Wokcano | *Asian* 22
Vivoli | *Italian* 22
Hugo's | *Cal.* 22
Le Pain Quotidien | *Bakery* 22
Eat Well | *Amer.* 22
Cafe Med | *Italian* 22
Fat Dog | *Amer.* 22
Toi | *Thai* 21
Dominick's | *Italian* 21
Counter | *Burgers* 21
Pasta Pomodoro | *Italian* 21
Rosa Mexicano | *Mex.* 21
La Boheme | *Cal.* 21
Kitchen 24 | *Amer.* 21
Eveleigh | *Amer./Euro.* 21
Simon LA | *Amer.* 21
Il Covo | *Italian* 21
Basix | *Cal./Italian* 20
Chin Chin | *Asian* 20
Abbey | *Amer.* 19
Restaurant/Standard | *Eclectic* 19
Pink Taco | *Mex.* 18
Hamburger Mary's | *Diner* 18
Kings Rd. | *Amer.* 18
Jerry's Deli | *Deli* 18
Mel's Drive-In | *Amer.* 18
Barney's Beanery | *Eclectic* 17
NEW The Churchill | *Amer.* 17
Marix | *Tex-Mex* 17
Formosa | *Asian* 16
NEW Duplex on Third | *Amer.* -
NEW Osteria Drago | *Italian* -
NEW Palikitchen | *Amer.* -
NEW Tortilla Republic | *Mex.* -

LA East

BOYLE HEIGHTS
King Taco | *Mex.* 24
La Serenata | *Mex./Seafood* 23

EAST LA

El Tepeyac	*Mex.*	26
King Taco	*Mex.*	24
El Gallo Giro	*Mex.*	22

HACIENDA HEIGHTS

| Daikokuya | *Japanese* | 24 |
| Tea Station | *Taiwanese/Tea* | 19 |

NORWALK

| Habit Burger | *Burgers* | 23 |
| Outback | *Steak* | 23 |

LA South

ARTESIA

| Lee's Sandwiches | *Sandwiches* | 21 |
| Tea Station | *Taiwanese/Tea* | 19 |

BELLFLOWER

| Johnny Rebs' | *BBQ* | 25 |

CARSON

M & M Soul Food	*Soul Food*	25
Five Guys	*Burgers*	21
Back Home	*Hawaiian*	20
Johnnie's NY	*Pizza*	20

CERRITOS

Wood Ranch	*BBQ*	24
Lucille's	*BBQ*	24
El Rocoto	*Peruvian*	23
BJ's	*Pub*	23
BCD Tofu	*Korean*	22
Sam Woo	*Chinese*	21
Chronic Tacos	*Mex.*	21
Five Guys	*Burgers*	21
Loft	*Hawaiian*	20

COMPTON

| Bludso's BBQ | *BBQ* | 27 |

HAWTHORNE

| Chipotle | *Mex.* | 23 |
| India's Tandoori | *Indian* | 23 |

LAKEWOOD

George's Greek	*Greek*	24
Super Mex	*Mex.*	23
Outback	*Steak*	23
Chipotle	*Mex.*	23
Black Angus	*Steak*	23

Café Rio	*Mex.*	23
Elephant Bar	*Asian*	22
El Torito	*Mex.*	21

LAWNDALE

| El Pollo Inka | *Peruvian* | 22 |

LOMITA

| Alfredo's | *Mex.* | 27 |

LYNWOOD

| Guelaguetza | *Mex.* | 24 |
| El Gallo Giro | *Mex.* | 22 |

PALOS VERDES PENINSULA/ ROLLING HILLS

Mar'sel	*Cal.*	26
Frascati	*Italian*	23
Mama Terano	*Italian*	22
Original Red Onion	*Mex.*	22
Admiral Risty	*Seafood*	22
Asaka	*Japanese*	22
Ruby's	*Diner*	21
Marmalade	*Amer.*	19
NEW Bashi	*Asian*	-

SOUTH GATE/ PARAMOUNT

| Alondra Hot Wings | *Amer.* | 24 |

LA West

BEL-AIR

| NEW Wolfgang Puck/ Hotel Bel-Air | *Cal./Med.* | 25 |
| Vibrato Grill | *Amer./Steak* | 23 |

BEVERLY HILLS

(see map on back of gatefold)

Tres/José Andrés	*Eclectic*	29
Urasawa	*Japanese*	28
Oliverio	*Italian*	28
Matsuhisa	*Japanese*	28
Bazaar by José Andrés	*Spanish*	27
Cut	*Steak*	27
Spago	*Cal.*	27
Sushi Sushi	*Japanese*	27
Saam/The Bazaar	*Eclectic*	27
Belvedere	*Amer.*	27
Vito's	*Pizza*	27
Mastro's	*Steak*	27

Restaurant	Rating
Ruth's Chris	*Steak*	27
Morton's	*Steak*	26
NEW Bouchon Bakery	*Bakery*	26
Il Pastaio	*Italian*	26
Lawry's Prime	*Steak*	26
Grill on Alley	*Amer.*	25
Fogo de Chão	*Brazilian/Steak*	25
Crustacean	*Asian/Viet.*	25
Capital Grille	*Steak*	25
Boss Sushi	*Japanese*	25
Bouchon	*French*	25
Bombay Palace	*Indian*	24
Tagine	*Moroccan*	24
Da Pasquale	*Italian*	24
E. Baldi	*Italian*	24
Culina	*Italian*	24
Mr. Chow	*Chinese*	24
Wolfgang's	*Steak*	24
Piccolo Paradiso	*Italian*	24
208 Rodeo	*Amer.*	24
Bar Bouchon	*French*	24
Scarpetta	*Italian*	24
La Dolce Vita	*Italian*	24
Enoteca Drago	*Italian*	23
Cabbage Patch	*Cal./Med.*	23
La Paella	*Spanish*	23
Cheesecake Factory	*Amer.*	23
Red Medicine	*Viet.*	23
Chipotle	*Mex.*	23
Nic's	*Amer.*	23
Il Cielo	*Italian*	23
Mulberry St. Pizzeria	*Pizza*	23
Talésai/Night	*Thai*	23
Asakuma	*Japanese*	23
Tanzore	*Indian*	23
Caffe Roma	*Italian*	23
Barney Greengrass	*Deli*	23
Stinking Rose	*Italian*	23
Il Tramezzino	*Italian*	23
La Provence	*French*	22
Via Alloro	*Italian*	22
M Café	*Veg.*	22
Porta Via	*Cal.*	22
Polo	*Cal./Continental*	22
Il Fornaio	*Italian*	22
Chakra	*Indian*	22
Panini Cafe	*Italian/Med.*	22
Urth	*Amer.*	22
Blvd	*Cal.*	22
McCormick/Schmick	*Seafood*	22
Cal. Pizza Kitchen	*Pizza*	22

Restaurant	Rating
Crazy Fish	*Japanese*	22
P.F. Chang's	*Chinese*	22
9021Pho	*Viet.*	22
Gyu-Kaku	*Japanese*	22
South Beverly Grill	*Amer.*	22
Le Pain Quotidien	*Bakery*	22
Il Forno Caldo	*Italian*	22
La Scala	*Italian*	22
Greenleaf	*Amer.*	22
Amici	*Italian*	22
Xi'an	*Chinese*	22
Champagne	*French*	22
Momed	*Med.*	22
El Torito Grill	*Mex.*	21
Grand Lux	*Eclectic*	21
Natalee	*Thai*	21
Nate 'n Al	*Deli*	20
Frida	*Mex.*	20
Kate Mantilini	*Amer.*	20
Jack n' Jill's	*Amer.*	20
Brighton Coffee	*Diner*	20
Chin Chin	*Asian*	20
Trader Vic's	*Polynesian*	19
Farm/Bev. Hills	*Amer.*	19
Villa Blanca	*Med.*	19
NEW BierBeisl	*Austrian*	-
NEW Caulfield's	*Amer.*	-
NEW Larder at Maple Dr.	*Eclectic*	-
NEW Livello	*Eclectic*	-

BRENTWOOD

Restaurant	Rating
Vincenti	*Italian*	27
Takao	*Japanese*	27
Sugarfish	*Japanese*	26
Palmeri	*Italian*	26
Osteria Latini	*Italian*	26
Toscana	*Italian*	26
Pecorino	*Italian*	25
Katsuya	*Japanese*	25
Divino	*Italian*	25
Tavern	*Cal./Med.*	24
Fish Grill	*Seafood*	24
Taiko	*Japanese*	24
Bar Toscana	*Italian*	24
Brentwood	*Amer.*	24
Getty Ctr.	*Cal.*	23
Pizzicotto	*Italian*	23
Cheesecake Factory	*Amer.*	23
Yen	*Japanese*	23
Sor Tino	*Italian*	23
La Provence	*French*	22

Peppone | *Italian* 22
Le Pain Quotidien | *Bakery* 22
Barney's | *Burgers* 22
La Scala | *Italian* 22
Amici | *Italian* 22
A Votre Sante | *Health* 21
Gaucho | *Argent./Steak* 21
Caffe Luxxe | *Coffee* 21
Spumoni | *Italian* 21
Daily Grill | *Amer.* 21
Yamato | *Japanese* 21
Coral Tree | *Sandwiches* 20
Maria's | *Italian* 20
Chin Chin | *Asian* 20
La Salsa | *Mex.* 19

CENTURY CITY

Craft | *Amer.* 25
Picca | *Japanese/Peruvian* 25
Clementine | *Amer.* 25
Pico Kosher Deli | *Deli* 24
Label's Table | *Sandwiches* 24
Gulfstream | *Amer./Seafood* 23
Obika | *Italian* 23
Cuvée | *Cal.* 23
RockSugar | *Asian* 22
Sotto | *Pizza* 22
Greenleaf | *Amer.* 22
Counter | *Burgers* 21
Johnnie's NY | *Pizza* 20
Coral Tree | *Sandwiches* 20
Toscanova | *Italian* 19
Take a Bao | *Asian* 19
Stand | *Hot Dogs* 19
Breadbar | *Bakery* 18
Pink Taco | *Mex.* 18

CULVER CITY

K-Zo | *Japanese* 26
In-N-Out | *Burgers* 26
Lukshon | *Asian* 25
Native Foods | *Vegan* 25
JR's | *BBQ* 25
Lucille's | *BBQ* 24
Waterloo & City | *British* 24
Father's Office | *Amer.* 24
Meet/Bistro | *French* 24
101 Noodle | *Chinese* 23
NEW Ramen Yamadaya | *Japanese* 23
Tender Greens | *Amer.* 23
Empanada's Place | *Argent.* 23

Brunello | *Italian* 23
Gloria's Cafe | *Mex./Salvadoran* 23
Crème de la Crêpe | *Crêpes* 23
Tara's Himalayan | *Asian* 23
A-Frame | *Eclectic* 23
Tito's Tacos | *Mex.* 23
Pitfire | *Pizza* 23
Akasha | *Amer.* 22
Annapurna | *Indian* 22
Extreme Pizza | *Pizza* 22
Johnnie's Pastrami | *Diner* 22
Café Brasil | *Brazilian* 22
Rutts | *Hawaiian* 22
Bamboo | *Carib.* 22
L'Epicerie | *French* 21
Pho Show | *Viet.* 21
Café Laurent | *French* 21
Samosa Hse. | *Indian* 21
Ford's | *Amer.* 21
Five Guys | *Burgers* 21
Gaby's | *Med.* 20
La Dijonaise | *French* 20
City Tavern | *Amer.* 20
Cafe Surfas | *Amer.* 19
Ugo/Café | *Italian* 19
Kay 'n Dave's | *Mex.* 19
BottleRock | *Euro.* 19
Let's Be Frank | *Hot Dogs* 19
Overland Cafe | *Eclectic* 19
Rush St. | *Amer.* 18
Roll 'n Rye | *Deli* 17
NEW Corner Door | *Amer.* –

MALIBU

Nobu | *Japanese* 27
Savory | *Amer.* 26
Malibu Seafood | *Seafood* 25
Fish Grill | *Seafood* 24
Cholada | *Thai* 24
Tra Di Noi | *Italian* 24
Chart House | *Seafood/Steak* 23
Taverna Tony | *Greek* 22
Reel Inn | *Seafood* 22
Geoffrey's | *Cal.* 22
Guido's | *Italian* 22
Café Habana | *Cuban/Mex.* 21
Moonshadows | *Amer.* 21
Thai Dishes | *Thai* 20
Neptune's Net | *Seafood* 20
Duke's | *Pac. Rim* 20
La Salsa | *Mex.* 19

Marmalade | *Amer.*   19
Paradise Cove | *Amer./Seafood*   19
Charlie's | *Steak*   18

MARINA DEL REY

(see map on page 81)

Mosto | *Italian*   27
Ado/Casa Ado | *Cal./Italian*   27
Irori | *Japanese*   26
Sugarfish | *Japanese*   26
Mendocino Farms | *Sandwiches*   25
Locanda Positano | *Italian*   25
Beach Pizza | *Pizza*   24
Cafe Del Rey | *Cal./Med.*   24
Cheesecake Factory | *Amer.*   23
Chipotle | *Mex.*   23
Chart House | *Seafood/Steak*   23
C & O | *Italian*   22
Akbar | *Indian*   22
Alejo's | *Italian*   22
NEW Sunny Spot | *Eclectic*   22
Uncle Darrow's | *Cajun/Creole*   21
Counter | *Burgers*   21
El Torito | *Mex.*   21
NEW Killer Shrimp | *Seafood*   21
Gaby's | *Med.*   20
Jer-ne | *Amer.*   19
Jerry's Deli | *Deli*   18
Baja Cantina | *Mex.*   18
NEW Killer Cafe | *Amer.*   -

MAR VISTA

Santouka Ramen | *Japanese*   24
Paco's Tacos | *Mex.*   21
NEW Hannosuke | *Japanese*   -

PACIFIC PALISADES

Sushi Sasabune/Sushi-Don | 27
  Japanese
Casa Nostra | *Italian*   24
NEW Maison Giraud | *French*   24
Modo Mio | *Italian*   23
Taste | *Amer.*   22
Pearl Dragon | *Asian*   21
Kay 'n Dave's | *Mex.*   19
Gladstone's | *Seafood*   18

PALMS

In-N-Out | *Burgers*   26
N/Naka | *Japanese*   25
Chego! | *Korean/Mex.*   24
Versailles | *Cuban*   23
Café Brasil | *Brazilian*   22

Champagne | *French*   22
Natalee | *Thai*   21
Gaby's | *Med.*   20

PLAYA DEL REY

Tripel | *Eclectic*   24
Caffe Pinguini | *Italian*   22
Shack | *Burgers*   20

RANCHO PARK

Food | *Amer.*   24
Six | *Amer.*   22
John O'Groats | *Amer.*   20

SANTA MONICA

(see map on page 81)

Mélisse | *Amer./French*   28
Chinois | *Asian/French*   27
Bay Cities | *Deli*   26
JiRaffe | *Amer./French*   26
Sugarfish | *Japanese*   26
La Vecchia | *Italian*   26
Capo | *Italian*   26
Hostaria/Piccolo | *Italian*   26
Valentino | *Italian*   26
Sam's/Beach | *Cal./Med.*   26
Santa Monica Seafood | *Seafood*   26
Farmshop | *Amer.*   26
Via Veneto | *Italian*   26
Josie | *Amer.*   26
NEW Milo & Olive | *Amer.*   25
Stella Rossa | *Pizza*   25
Rustic Canyon | *Cal./Med.*   25
Michael's Rest. | *Cal.*   25
Giorgio Baldi | *Italian*   25
Thyme Café | *Sandwiches*   25
NEW Next Door/Josie | *Amer.*   25
Native Foods | *Vegan*   25
Lobster | *Seafood*   25
Boa | *Steak*   24
Ocean Ave. | *Seafood*   24
Hungry Cat | *Seafood*   24
Caffé Delfini | *Italian*   24
Le Petit Cafe | *French*   24
Nawab | *Indian*   24
Houston's | *Amer.*   24
Locanda/Lago | *Italian*   24
Joe's Pizza | *Pizza*   24
Father's Office | *Amer.*   24
La Botte | *Italian*   24
Abbot's | *Pizza*   24
Bru's Wiffle | *Amer.*   24
One Pico | *Med.*   24

BP Oysterette	*Seafood*	23
Musha	*Japanese*	23
NEW Tar & Roses	*Eclectic*	23
Real Food	*Vegan*	23
Huckleberry	*Amer.*	23
Veggie Grill	*Vegan*	23
Umami	*Burgers*	23
Sweet Lady Jane	*Bakery*	23
Cal. Chicken	*Amer.*	23
Poquito Más	*Mex.*	23
Fig	*Amer./French*	23
True Food	*Health*	23
Ozumo	*Japanese*	23
Vito	*Italian*	23
Sushi Roku	*Japanese*	23
Cora's	*Diner*	23
Il Forno	*Italian*	23
Wilshire	*Amer.*	23
Bangkok West	*Thai*	23
Warszawa	*Polish*	23
Coast	*Cal./Seafood*	23
Catch	*Seafood*	23
Lotería!	*Mex.*	23
Cafe Bizou	*French*	23
Zengo	*Asian/Nuevo Latino*	23
Fritto Misto	*Italian*	22
Cha Cha Chicken	*Carib.*	22
Misfit	*Eclectic*	22
Wahoo's Fish Taco	*Mex./Seafood*	22
Akbar	*Indian*	22
Il Fornaio	*Italian*	22
R+D Kitchen	*Amer.*	22
Border Grill	*Mex.*	22
Urth	*Amer.*	22
Penthouse	*Amer.*	22
31Ten	*Eclectic*	22
Cal. Pizza Kitchen	*Pizza*	22
P.F. Chang's	*Chinese*	22
Wokcano	*Asian*	22
Whist	*Cal.*	22
Le Pain Quotidien	*Bakery*	22
Barney's	*Burgers*	22
Ivy/Shore	*Cal.*	22
Bar Pintxo	*Spanish*	22
Stefan's/L.A. Farm	*Eclectic*	22
Lares	*Mex.*	22
Enterprise Fish	*Seafood*	21
Bravo	*Italian/Pizza*	21
Blue Plate	*Amer.*	21
M Street	*Amer.*	21

Monsoon	*Asian*	21
Villetta	*Italian*	21
Madame Chou Chou	*French*	21
Fraîche	*French/Italian*	21
Monsieur Marcel	*French*	21
Caffe Luxxe	*Coffee*	21
Upper West	*Amer.*	21
Spumoni	*Italian*	21
Daily Grill	*Amer.*	21
Counter	*Burgers*	21
El Torito	*Mex.*	21
17th St. Cafe	*Cal.*	21
Typhoon	*Asian*	21
Buddha's Belly	*Asian*	21
Trastevere	*Italian*	21
Cafe Montana	*Cal.*	21
Wolfgang Puck Express/Bistro	*Cal.*	21
Ocean Pk. Omelette	*Amer.*	20
Thai Dishes	*Thai*	20
Swingers	*Diner*	20
Frida	*Mex.*	20
Johnnie's NY	*Pizza*	20
Jinky's	*Diner*	20
El Cholo	*Mex.*	20
Reddi Chick	*BBQ*	20
Jack n' Jill's	*Amer.*	20
Louise's	*Cal./Italian*	20
Chez Jay	*Steak*	20
Röckenwagner	*Bakery*	20
Shack	*Burgers*	20
Galley	*Seafood/Steak*	20
La Salsa	*Mex.*	19
Ugo/Café	*Italian*	19
Buffalo Club	*Amer.*	19
Kay 'n Dave's	*Mex.*	19
Babalu	*Cal.*	19
Marmalade	*Amer.*	19
Patrick's	*Diner*	19
Falafel King	*Mideast.*	18
Rosti	*Italian*	18
Ye Olde King's	*Pub*	18
Barney's Beanery	*Eclectic*	17
Marix	*Tex-Mex*	17
Fromin's	*Deli*	17
NEW Charleston	*Eclectic*	-
NEW Mercado	*Mex.*	-
NEW Ushuaia	*Argent./Steak*	-

TOPANGA

Inn/Seventh Ray	*Cal.*	21

VENICE

(see map on page 81)

Piccolo	*Italian*	28
Ado/Casa Ado	*Cal./Italian*	27
Gjelina Take Away	*Amer.*	27
Joe's	*Cal./French*	26
Gjelina	*Amer.*	26
Tasting Kitchen	*Med.*	26
Hama	*Japanese*	25
NEW Larry's	*Amer.*	24
Café Gratitude	*Amer.*	24
Tlapazola	*Mex.*	24
Wurstküche	*Euro.*	24
Axe	*Cal.*	24
Abbot's	*Pizza*	24
3 Square	*Sandwiches*	24
26 Beach	*Cal.*	24
Cal. Chicken	*Amer.*	23
Agra/Indian Kitchen	*Indian*	23
Chaya	*Asian/French*	23
Jin Patisserie	*Bakery*	23
Asakuma	*Japanese*	23
Baby Blues	*BBQ*	22
Wabi-Sabi	*Japanese*	22
Lemonade	*Cal.*	22
El Tarasco	*Mex.*	22
Canal Club	*Cal./Eclectic*	21
Rose Cafe	*Cal.*	21
James'	*Amer.*	21
Primitivo	*Med.*	21
Maxwell's	*Diner*	20
Jody Maroni's	*Hot Dogs*	20
Johnnie's NY	*Pizza*	20
Casablanca	*Mex.*	19
Lilly's	*French*	19

WEST LA

Sushi Zo	*Japanese*	28
Echigo	*Japanese*	28
Hamasaku	*Japanese*	28
Sushi Masu	*Japanese*	27
Mori Sushi	*Japanese*	27
Nanbankan	*Japanese*	27
Sushi Sasabune/Sushi-Don	*Japanese*	27
NEW Freddy Smalls	*Amer.*	26
NEW Tsujita LA	*Japanese*	26
Il Grano	*Italian*	25
Bar Hayama	*Japanese*	25
Upstairs 2	*Med.*	24
Nook	*Amer.*	24
U-Zen	*Japanese*	24

Pastina	*Italian*	24
Bandera	*SW*	24
Hole in Wall	*Burgers*	24
Hide	*Japanese*	24
Tlapazola	*Mex.*	24
Ramen Jinya	*Japanese*	24
B.A.D. SUSHI	*Japanese*	23
Cabbage Patch	*Cal./Med.*	23
Casa Sanchez	*Mex.*	23
Apple Pan	*Amer.*	23
Zankou	*Med.*	23
2117	*Asian/Euro.*	23
Yabu	*Japanese*	23
Feast/East	*Asian*	23
Cal. Chicken	*Amer.*	23
Poquito Más	*Mex.*	23
Monte Alban	*Mex.*	23
Bossa Nova	*Brazilian*	23
Asakuma	*Japanese*	23
La Serenata	*Mex./Seafood*	23
Furaibo	*Japanese*	23
Chan Dara	*Thai*	23
Pitfire	*Pizza*	23
India's Tandoori	*Indian*	23
Westside Tav.	*Cal.*	23
Bombay Cafe	*Indian*	22
Javan	*Persian*	22
Guido's	*Italian*	22
Enzo/Angela	*Italian*	22
Gyu-Kaku	*Japanese*	22
Jaipur	*Indian*	22
Torafuku	*Japanese*	22
Champagne	*French*	22
Il Moro	*Italian*	22
All India	*Indian*	21
Good Stuff	*Amer.*	21
Asahi	*Japanese*	21
Aroma	*E Euro.*	21
Hurry Curry	*Japanese*	21
La Bottega Marino	*Italian*	21
Lemon Moon	*Cal./Med.*	21
Ramenya	*Japanese*	21
Tofu Ya	*Korean*	21
Matteo's	*Italian*	21
Hop Woo	*Chinese*	20
Johnnie's NY	*Pizza*	20
Louise's	*Cal./Italian*	20
Maria's	*Italian*	20
Hop Li	*Chinese/Seafood*	19
NEW Plan Check	*Amer.*	19
Literati	*Cal./Eclectic*	18

Billingsley's | *Steak* 17
Junior's | *Deli* 16
NEW Gottsui | *Japanese* —
NEW Morinoya | *Japanese* —
NEW Nong La | *Viet.* —
NEW Seoul House/Tofu | *Korean* —
NEW Tatsu Ramen | *Japanese* —

WESTWOOD

In-N-Out | *Burgers* 26
NEW 800 Degrees | *Pizza* 25
Native Foods | *Vegan* 25
Shamshiri Grill | *Persian* 24
Lamonica's | *Pizza* 24
Sunnin | *Lebanese* 24
Fundamental LA | *Sanwiches* 23
Ramen Yamadaya | *Japanese* 23
La Bruschetta | *Italian* 23
BJ's | *Pub* 23
Shaherzad | *Persian* 23
Tanino | *Italian* 22
Extreme Pizza | *Pizza* 22
Panini Cafe | *Italian/Med.* 22
Cal. Pizza Kitchen | *Pizza* 22
Le Pain Quotidien | *Bakery* 22
NEW Casa Azul | *Mex.* 21
Soleil | *Canadian/French* 21
Palomino | *Amer.* 21
Acapulco | *Mex.* 20
Napa Valley | *Cal.* 19
Noodle World | *Asian* 19
Stand | *Hot Dogs* 19
Falafel King | *Mideast.* 18
Jerry's Deli | *Deli* 18
Barney's Beanery | *Eclectic* 17
NEW P'tit Soleil | *Quebecois* —

South Bay

CATALINA ISLAND

Armstrong's | *Seafood* 23

DOWNEY

Porto's | *Bakery/Cuban* 26
Elephant Bar | *Asian* 22
Acapulco | *Mex.* 20

EL SEGUNDO

Fleming's | *Steak* 25
Habit Burger | *Burgers* 23
Veggie Grill | *Vegan* 23
Z Pizza | *Pizza* 23

Chipotle | *Mex.* 23
Paul Martin's | *Amer.* 22
McCormick/Schmick | *Seafood* 22
P.F. Chang's | *Chinese* 22
Good Stuff | *Amer.* 21
Farm Stand | *Eclectic* 21
Counter | *Burgers* 21
Sammy's/Pizza | *Pizza* 21
Salt Creek | *Steak* 20
Marmalade | *Amer.* 19

GARDENA

Pho So 1 | *Viet.* 26
Hakata | *Japanese* 25
Eatalian | *Italian* 25
Shin-Sen-Gumi Yakitori | *Japanese* 25
El Rocoto | *Peruvian* 23
El Pollo Inka | *Peruvian* 22
Sea Empress | *Chinese* 22
Tea Station | *Taiwanese/Tea* 19
NEW exEat/Eatalian | *Italian* —

HERMOSA BEACH

Hot's Kitchen | *Eclectic* 27
Chef Melba's | *Cal.* 26
Martha's 22nd St. | *Amer.* 25
Umami | *Burgers* 23
Crème de la Crêpe | *Crêpes* 23
Mediterraneo | *Med.* 22
Fritto Misto | *Italian* 22
El Pollo Inka | *Peruvian* 22
Akbar | *Indian* 22
Bottle Inn | *Italian* 22
NEW Abigaile | *Amer.* 22
Good Stuff | *Amer.* 21
Zane's | *Italian/Steak* 21
Counter | *Burgers* 21
The Rockefeller | *Amer.* 19
Baja Sharkeez | *Mex.* 18
NEW Boardwalk/Burgers | *Burgers* —
NEW Palmilla | *Mex.* —

INGLEWOOD

Woody's BBQ | *BBQ* 27
Phillips BBQ | *BBQ* 26
Thai Dishes | *Thai* 20

LAX

Daily Grill | *Amer.* 21
Ruby's | *Diner* 21

Wolfgang Puck Express/Bistro | Cal. | 21
Nate 'n Al | Deli | 20
Thai Dishes | Thai | 20
El Cholo | Mex. | 20

LONG BEACH

Michael's/Naples | Italian | 28
Benley | Viet. | 28
Michael's Pizzeria | Pizza | 28
Naples Rib Co. | BBQ | 26
Sir Winston's | Cal./Continental | 26
Buono's | Pizza | 26
555 East | Steak | 26
Café Piccolo | Italian | 25
Open Sesame | Lebanese | 25
La Parolaccia | Italian | 25
Beachwood BBQ | BBQ | 25
Johnny Rebs' | BBQ | 25
Sky Room | Amer. | 25
L'Opera | Italian | 25
Zephyr | Veg. | 25
La Crêperie Café | French | 24
Lucille's | BBQ | 24
Crab Pot | Seafood | 24
Alondra Hot Wings | Amer. | 24
George's Greek | Greek | 24
Roscoe's | Soul Food | 24
Green Field | Brazilian | 23
Yen | Japanese | 23
Super Mex | Mex. | 23
Z Pizza | Pizza | 23
Fuego/Maya | Mex./Pan-Latin | 23
Alegria | Nuevo Latino | 23
BJ's | Pub | 23
Crème de la Crêpe | Crêpes | 23
Parker's | Seafood | 23
King's Fish | Seafood | 23
Original Roadhse. Grill | Steak | 23
Simmzy's | Amer. | 23
Wahoo's Fish Taco | Mex./Seafood | 22
Extreme Pizza | Pizza | 22
Yard House | Amer. | 22
P.F. Chang's | Chinese | 22
Wokcano | Asian | 22
Avila's El Ranchito | Mex. | 22
Gaucho | Argent./Steak | 21
Chronic Tacos | Mex. | 21
McKenna's | Seafood/Steak | 21
Lee's Sandwiches | Sandwiches | 21
Hof's Hut | Amer./Eclectic | 21
Ruby's | Diner | 21

El Torito | Mex. | 21
Frisco's | Amer. | 21
Auld Dubliner | Pub | 21
Belmont Brewing | Amer. | 21
Acapulco | Mex. | 20
Octopus | Japanese | 20
Gladstone's | Seafood | 18
Hamburger Mary's | Diner | 18

MANHATTAN BEACH

M.B. Post | Amer. | 28
Izaka-ya/Katsu-ya | Japanese | 26
Mucho Ultima | Mex. | 26
Open Sesame | Lebanese | 25
Darren's | Cal. | 25
Petros | Greek | 25
Beach Pizza | Pizza | 24
Houston's | Amer. | 24
Café Pierre | French | 24
Tin Roof | Amer. | 24
Fishbar | Seafood | 23
Valentino's | Pizza | 23
Versailles | Cuban | 23
Crème de la Crêpe | Crêpes | 23
Simmzy's | Amer. | 23
Uncle Bill's | Diner | 23
Café Rio | Mex. | 23
Big Wok | Mongolian | 22
Rock'n Fish | Seafood | 22
Wahoo's Fish Taco | Mex./Seafood | 22
Il Fornaio | Italian | 22
Mama D's | Italian | 22
Le Pain Quotidien | Bakery | 22
Beckers Bakery | Bakery/Deli | 21
NEW Strand House | Amer. | 21
Pasta Pomodoro | Italian | 21
China Grill | Chinese | 21
Manhattan Beach BrewCo | Amer. | 21
El Torito | Mex. | 21
Back Home | Hawaiian | 20
Thai Dishes | Thai | 20
American Farmhouse | Amer./Eclectic | 19
Baja Sharkeez | Mex. | 18

REDONDO BEACH

Chez Mélange | Eclectic | 26
Addi's | Indian | 26
Original Pancake | Amer. | 25
Gina Lee's | Asian/Cal. | 25
Bouzy | Amer. | 25
Zazou | Med. | 24

Baleen | *Amer.*	24
Ocean Tava | *Indian*	24
Aimee's Bistro | *French*	24
Cheesecake Factory | *Amer.*	23
Chart House | *Seafood/Steak*	23
Bluewater | *Seafood*	23
Hudson Hse. | *Amer.*	23
Crème de la Crêpe | *Crêpes*	23
Old Tony's | *Italian/Seafood*	23
Ortega 120 | *Mex.*	22
Coyote Cantina | *SW*	22
W's China | *Chinese*	22
Asaka | *Japanese*	22
Kincaid's | *Seafood/Steak*	22
Good Stuff | *Amer.*	21
Chronic Tacos | *Mex.*	21
Ruby's | *Diner*	21
El Torito | *Mex.*	21

SAN PEDRO

Babouch | *Moroccan*	26
Think Bistro | *Amer./French*	24
22nd St. Landing | *Seafood*	24
Think Café | *Amer./Eclectic*	23
Gaffey St. Diner | *Diner*	21
Whale & Ale | *Pub*	21
Acapulco | *Mex.*	20
NEW Limani Taverna | *Greek*	-

TORRANCE

Christine | *Med./Pac. Rim*	27
Depot | *Eclectic*	26
Lucille's | *BBQ*	24
Buffalo Fire Dept. | *Amer.*	24
Santouka Ramen | *Japanese*	24
Musha | *Japanese*	23
Ramen Yamadaya | *Japanese*	23
Melting Pot | *Fondue*	23
Veggie Grill | *Vegan*	23
Outback | *Steak*	23
Chipotle | *Mex.*	23
Black Angus | *Steak*	23
RA Sushi | *Japanese*	23
King's Hawaiian | *Hawaiian*	22
El Pollo Inka | *Peruvian*	22
Wahoo's Fish Taco | *Mex./Seafood*	22
BCD Tofu | *Korean*	22
1321 Downtown | *Amer.*	22
P.F. Chang's | *Chinese*	22
Gyu-Kaku | *Japanese*	22
Lazy Dog | *Eclectic*	22

Lamppost Pizza | *Pizza*	22
Elephant Bar | *Asian*	22
O-Nami | *Japanese*	21
El Torito Grill | *Mex.*	21
Hof's Hut | *Amer./Eclectic*	21
El Torito | *Mex.*	21
Billy's | *Deli*	21
Loft | *Hawaiian*	20
Gonpachi | *Japanese*	20

WESTCHESTER

In-N-Out | *Burgers*	26
Ayara Thai | *Thai*	24
Alejo's | *Italian*	22
Kabuki | *Japanese*	22
Paco's Tacos | *Mex.*	21
Truxton's | *Amer.*	21
Buggy Whip | *Seafood/Steak*	20
Dinah's | *Diner*	19

Inland Empire

MORENO VALLEY

Portillo's | *Hot Dogs*	25
BJ's | *Pub*	23

ONTARIO

Vince's Spaghetti | *Italian*	24
Panda Inn | *Chinese*	24
Black Angus | *Steak*	23

Pasadena & Environs

ARCADIA

Din Tai Fung | *Chinese*	26
Derby | *Steak*	25
Zelo Pizzeria | *Pizza*	24
Wood Ranch | *BBQ*	24
Daikokuya | *Japanese*	24
101 Noodle | *Chinese*	23
Cheesecake Factory | *Amer.*	23
Outback | *Steak*	23
BJ's | *Pub*	23
Phoenix | *Chinese*	21
Hop Li | *Chinese/Seafood*	19

EAGLE ROCK

Café Beaujolais | *French*	26
CaCao | *Mex.*	25
Casa Bianca | *Pizza*	23
Auntie Em's | *Amer.*	23
Spitz | *Turkish*	23

LOS ANGELES

LOCATIONS

Oinkster | *BBQ* 22
Blue Hen | *Viet.* 21

LA CAÑADA FLINTRIDGE

Taylor's | *Steak* 24
Dish | *Amer.* 23

MONROVIA

Caffe Opera | *Amer./Eclectic* 23

PASADENA

(see map on page 82)
Azeen's | *Afghan* 27
Maison Akira | *French/Japanese* 27
Ruth's Chris | *Steak* 27
Parkway Grill | *Cal.* 26
Bistro 45 | *Cal.* 26
Arroyo | *Steak* 26
Celestino | *Italian* 25
Euro Pane | *Bakery* 25
Raymond | *Cal.* 25
Roy's | *Hawaiian* 25
Royce | *Amer.* 24
Houston's | *Amer.* 24
Noir | *Eclectic* 24
Cafe Verde | *Amer./Italian* 24
Green St. Tavern | *Cal.* 24
NEW Settebello | *Pizza* 24
Saladang | *Thai* 24
Panda Inn | *Chinese* 24
1810 Rest. | *Argent./Steak* 24
Tops | *Amer.* 24
Roscoe's | *Soul Food* 24
Cheval Blanc | *French* 24
Musha | *Japanese* 23
Gin Sushi | *Japanese* 23
Real Food | *Vegan* 23
Melting Pot | *Fondue* 23
Cheesecake Factory | *Amer.* 23
Zankou | *Med.* 23
Tender Greens | *Amer.* 23
Chipotle | *Mex.* 23
AKA Bistro | *Amer.* 23
Big Mama's | *BBQ/Soul Food* 23
Luggage Room | *Pizza* 23
Sushi Roku | *Japanese* 23
Gale's | *Italian* 23
Robin's | *BBQ* 23
Crème de la Crêpe | *Crêpes* 23
Yang Chow | *Chinese* 23
redwhite+bluezz | *Amer.* 23

Malbec | *Argent./Steak* 23
Stonefire | *BBQ* 23
Cafe Bizou | *French* 23
El Portal | *Mex.* 22
Smitty's | *Amer.* 22
Wahoo's Fish Taco | *Mex./Seafood* 22
Akbar | *Indian* 22
Yard House | *Amer.* 22
Slaw Dogs | *Hot Dogs* 22
Plate 38 | *Eclectic* 22
Il Fornaio | *Italian* 22
Beckham Grill | *Amer.* 22
A'float Sushi | *Japanese* 22
Mi Piace | *Cal./Italian* 22
Kabuki | *Japanese* 22
NEW Haven | *Amer.* 22
McCormick/Schmick | *Seafood* 22
Cal. Pizza Kitchen | *Pizza* 22
P.F. Chang's | *Chinese* 22
Pie 'N Burger | *Diner* 22
Wokcano | *Asian* 22
Gyu-Kaku | *Japanese* 22
Le Pain Quotidien | *Bakery* 22
Green St. | *Amer.* 22
NEW Abricott | *Eclectic* 22
Marston's | *Amer.* 21
All India | *Indian* 21
Vertical Wine | *Eclectic/Med.* 21
Café Santorini | *Med.* 21
Dog Haus | *Hot Dogs* 21
Lee's Sandwiches | *Sandwiches* 21
El Torito | *Mex.* 21
La Grande Orange | *Cal.* 21
Mijares | *Mex.* 20
El Cholo | *Mex.* 20
Louise's | *Cal./Italian* 20
Maria's | *Italian* 20
Hamburger Hamlet | *Diner* 19
Noodle World | *Asian* 19
Burger Continental | *Mideast.* 18
Barney's Beanery | *Eclectic* 17
NEW Racion | *Spanish* -
Trattoria Neapolis | *Italian* -

SAN MARINO

Julienne | *French* 26
Noodle World | *Asian* 19

SOUTH PASADENA

Shiro | *French/Japanese* 27
Firefly Bistro | *Amer.* 21

Bistro/Gare | *French* 21
Mike & Anne's | *Amer.* 21
Phoenix | *Chinese* 21
Gus's | *BBQ* 20

San Fernando Valley & Burbank

BURBANK

Morton's | *Steak* 26
Porto's | *Bakery/Cuban* 26
Chili John's | *Amer.* 24
French Crêpe Co. | *French* 23
Bistro Provence | *French* 23
Habit Burger | *Burgers* 23
Zankou | *Med.* 23
Outback | *Steak* 23
Z Pizza | *Pizza* 23
Chipotle | *Mex.* 23
Poquito Más | *Mex.* 23
BJ's | *Pub* 23
Black Angus | *Steak* 23
Ribs USA | *BBQ* 23
Castaway | *Cal.* 22
Wahoo's Fish Taco | *Mex./Seafood* 22
Chadaka | *Thai* 22
Flavor of India | *Indian* 22
Olive/Thyme | *Eclectic* 22
Kabuki | *Japanese* 22
Cal. Pizza Kitchen | *Pizza* 22
P.F. Chang's | *Chinese* 22
Wokcano | *Asian* 22
Smoke Hse. | *Steak* 22
Coral Cafe | *Amer./Mex.* 22
Elephant Bar | *Asian* 22
Granville Cafe | *Amer.* 21
Daily Grill | *Amer.* 21
Picanha | *Brazilian* 21
Barragan's | *Mex.* 21
Octopus | *Japanese* 20
Wienerschnitzel | *Burgers/Hot Dogs* 20
Mo's | *Amer.* 19
Gordon Biersch | *Pub* 19
Barney's Beanery | *Eclectic* 17

CALABASAS

Saddle Peak | *Amer.* 26
Riviera | *Italian* 25
Banzai | *Japanese* 25
La Paz | *Mex.* 24
King's Fish | *Seafood* 23

Toscanova | *Italian* 19
Marmalade | *Amer.* 19
Rosti | *Italian* 18

CANOGA PARK

Yang Chow | *Chinese* 23
Follow Your Heart | *Veg.* 22
Gyu-Kaku | *Japanese* 22

CHATSWORTH

Omino | *Japanese* 27
Les Sisters | *Southern* 25
Poquito Más | *Mex.* 23
Stonefire | *BBQ* 23
Los Toros | *Mex.* 23

ENCINO

Katsu-ya | *Japanese* 27
Larsen's | *Steak* 25
Delmonico's | *Seafood* 24
Habit Burger | *Burgers* 23
Cal. Chicken | *Amer.* 23
Versailles | *Cuban* 23
Mulberry St. Pizzeria | *Pizza* 23
Farfalla/Vinoteca | *Italian* 23
Hirosuke | *Japanese* 23
More Than Waffles | *Amer.* 23
Bocca | *Steak* 22
Absolutely Pho | *Viet.* 22
Alcazar | *Lebanese* 21
Itzik Hagadol | *Israeli* 21
Octopus | *Japanese* 20
Coral Tree | *Sandwiches* 20
Maria's | *Italian* 20
John O'Groats | *Amer.* 20
Stand | *Hot Dogs* 19
Rosti | *Italian* 18
Jerry's Deli 18

GLENDALE

Porto's | *Bakery/Cuban* 26
Raffi's Place | *Mideast.* 26
Carousel | *Mideast.* 25
Katsuya | *Japanese* 25
Fish King | *Seafood* 25
Far Niente | *Italian* 24
Ahn Joo | *Korean* 24
Panda Inn | *Chinese* 24
Habit Burger | *Burgers* 23
Zankou | *Med.* 23
Farfalla/Vinoteca | *Italian* 23
Damon's | *Steak* 23

Eat Well	*Amer.*	22	Acapulco	*Mex.*	20
Amici	*Italian*	22	Maria's	*Italian*	20
Granville Cafe	*Amer.*	21		
Chi Dynasty	*Chinese*	21	**PANORAMA CITY**	
Foxy's	*SW*	21	El Gallo Giro	*Mex.*	22
Barragan's	*Mex.*	21		
Billy's	*Deli*	21	**RESEDA**	
Acapulco	*Mex.*	20	Pho So 1	*Viet.*	26
Octopus	*Japanese*	20	Las Fuentes	*Mex.*	24
Frida	*Mex.*	20	Fab Hot Dogs	*Hot Dogs*	24
Johnnie's NY	*Pizza*	20	BCD Tofu	*Korean*	22

MONTROSE

Bashan | *Amer.* — 28
New Moon | *Chinese* — 24
La Cabanita | *Mex.* — 24
Fat Dog | *Amer.* — 22
Zeke's | *BBQ* — 21

NORTH HOLLYWOOD

In-N-Out | *Burgers* — 26
Sanamluang Cafe | *Thai* — 23
Zankou | *Med.* — 23
Umami | *Burgers* — 23
Poquito Más | *Mex.* — 23
Ca' del Sole | *Italian* — 23
Pitfire | *Pizza* — 23
Firenze | *Italian* — 22
Counter | *Burgers* — 21
Federal Bar | *Amer.* — 21
Ernie's | *Mex.* — 21
NEW Bow & Truss | *Spanish* — –

NORTHRIDGE

Hot's Cantina | *Eclectic* — 27
Brent's Deli | *Deli* — 26
Musashi | *Japanese* — 25
King's Burgers | *Burgers* — 24
Wood Ranch | *BBQ* — 24
Habit Burger | *Burgers* — 23
Emle's | *Med.* — 23
Outback | *Steak* — 23
Z Pizza | *Pizza* — 23
A & W Seafood |
  Chinese/Seafood — 23
Cal. Chicken | *Amer.* — 23
Falafel Palace |
  Med./Mideast. — 23
Black Angus | *Steak* — 23
Alessio/Bistro | *Italian* — 22
Mandarin | *Chinese* — 22

Acapulco | *Mex.* — 20
Maria's | *Italian* — 20

PANORAMA CITY

El Gallo Giro | *Mex.* — 22

RESEDA

Pho So 1 | *Viet.* — 26
Las Fuentes | *Mex.* — 24
Fab Hot Dogs | *Hot Dogs* — 24
BCD Tofu | *Korean* — 22

SAN FERNANDO

El Gallo Giro | *Mex.* — 22

SHERMAN OAKS

Mistral | *French* — 26
In-N-Out | *Burgers* — 26
Carnival | *Lebanese* — 25
Panzanella | *Italian* — 25
La Pergola | *Italian* — 25
Pita Kitchen | *Mideast.* — 24
Brats Brothers | *German* — 24
Il Tiramisù | *Italian* — 24
Le Petit Rest. | *French* — 24
Bamboo Cuisine | *Chinese* — 23
Ramen Yamadaya | *Japanese* — 23
Habit Burger | *Burgers* — 23
Cheesecake Factory | *Amer.* — 23
Poquito Más | *Mex.* — 23
Mulberry St. Pizzeria | *Pizza* — 23
Great Greek | *Greek* — 23
Boneyard | *BBQ/Eclectic* — 23
Clay Oven | *Indian* — 23
Cafe Bizou | *French* — 23
Cafe Cordiale | *Cal./Eclectic* — 22
Taste of India | *Indian* — 22
P.F. Chang's | *Chinese* — 22
Gyu-Kaku | *Japanese* — 22
Barney's | *Burgers* — 22
Blue Dog | *Amer.* — 21
El Torito Grill | *Mex.* — 21
Rive Gauche | *French* — 21
Spumoni | *Italian* — 21
El Torito | *Mex.* — 21
Valley Inn Rest. | *Amer.* — 21
Oliva | *Italian* — 21
Casa Vega | *Mex.* — 20
Jinky's | *Diner* — 20
Stanley's | *Cal.* — 20
Sisley | *Italian* — 20
Maria's | *Italian* — 20

Hamburger Hamlet	*Diner*	19
La Frite	*French*	19
Marmalade	*Amer.*	19
Mel's Drive-In	*Amer.*	18

STUDIO CITY

Asanebo	*Japanese*	28
Kiwami	*Japanese*	28
Katsu-ya	*Japanese*	27
Ahi	*Japanese*	26
In-N-Out	*Burgers*	26
Artisan	*Cheese/Sandwiches*	25
Raphael	*Amer.*	25
Iroha	*Japanese*	25
Bollywood	*Indian*	24
Black Market	*Eclectic*	24
Ramen Jinya	*Japanese*	24
Yen	*Japanese*	23
Poquito Más	*Mex.*	23
Lala's	*Argent./Steak*	23
City Wok	*Chinese*	23
Talésai/Night	*Thai*	23
Teru Sushi	*Japanese*	23
Il Tramezzino	*Italian*	23
Lotería!	*Mex.*	23
Marrakesh	*Moroccan*	22
Spark	*Amer.*	22
Cal. Pizza Kitchen	*Pizza*	22
Carney's	*Hot Dogs*	22
Six	*Amer.*	22
Hugo's	*Cal.*	22
Art's	*Deli*	22
Firefly	*Amer.*	22
Le Pain Quotidien	*Bakery*	22
Caioti Pizza	*Pizza*	22
Bistro Gdn.	*Continental*	21
Daily Grill	*Amer.*	21
Chi Dynasty	*Chinese*	21
Counter	*Burgers*	21
Ombra	*Italian*	21
Jinky's	*Diner*	20
Chin Chin	*Asian*	20
Take a Bao	*Asian*	19
Kings Rd.	*Amer.*	18
Du-par's	*Diner*	18
NEW Crust	*Pizza*	-

SUN VALLEY/ TUJUNGA

Acapulco	*Mex.*	20

TARZANA

Le Sanglier	*French*	24
Zankou	*Med.*	23
Kravings	*Brazilian*	23
Il Tramezzino	*Italian*	23
Sol y Luna	*Mex.*	22
Hummus Bar	*Mideast.*	22

TOLUCA LAKE

Prosecco	*Italian*	25
Malbec	*Argent./Steak*	23

UNIVERSAL CITY

Wolfgang Puck Express/Bistro	*Cal.*	21
Jody Maroni's	*Hot Dogs*	20
Miceli's	*Italian*	20

VAN NUYS

Pho So 1	*Viet.*	26
In-N-Out	*Burgers*	26
Smoke City	*BBQ*	24
Dr. Hogly Wogly's	*BBQ*	24
Zankou	*Med.*	23
Lulu's	*Amer.*	22
Barone's	*Italian/Pizza*	22
Sam Woo	*Chinese*	21

WEST HILLS

Stonefire	*BBQ*	23
Alessio/Bistro	*Italian*	22

WOODLAND HILLS

Brandywine	*Continental*	27
Brother Sushi	*Japanese*	27
Ruth's Chris	*Steak*	27
Morton's	*Steak*	26
In-N-Out	*Burgers*	26
Fleming's	*Steak*	25
Roy's	*Hawaiian*	25
Label's Table	*Sandwiches*	24
Anarbagh	*Indian*	24
Habit Burger	*Burgers*	23
Cheesecake Factory	*Amer.*	23
Cal. Chicken	*Amer.*	23
Poquito Más	*Mex.*	23
Adagio	*Italian*	23
BJ's	*Pub*	23
Baker	*Bakery/Sandwiches*	23
Monty's	*Steak*	22
Maggiano's	*Italian*	22
Slaw Dogs	*Hot Dogs*	22

Panini Cafe	Italian/Med.	22
Kabuki	Japanese	22
Taste of India	Indian	22
Giovanni	Italian	22
P.F. Chang's	Chinese	22
Asaka	Japanese	22
Ruby's	Diner	21
Kate Mantilini	Amer.	20
Maria's	Italian	20
La Frite	French	19
Stand	Hot Dogs	19
Jerry's Deli	Deli	18

San Gabriel Valley

ALHAMBRA

Boiling Crab	Cajun/Seafood	25
Pho 79	Viet.	24
Alondra Hot Wings	Amer.	24
101 Noodle	Chinese	23
Wahib's	Mideast.	22
Sam Woo	Chinese	21
Lee's Sandwiches	Sandwiches	21
Phoenix	Chinese	21
Tea Station	Taiwanese/Tea	19
Noodle World	Asian	19
Twohey's	Amer.	19

BALDWIN PARK

King Taco	Mex.	24

CITY OF INDUSTRY

Honda-Ya	Japanese	24
Outback	Steak	23

CLAREMONT

La Parolaccia	Italian	25
Back Abbey	Burgers	25
Tutti Mangia	Italian	24
Heroes/Legends	Pub	23
Walter's	Eclectic	21

COVINA/ WEST COVINA

Green Field	Brazilian	23
Outback	Steak	23
BJ's	Pub	23
Elephant Bar	Asian	22
Chronic Tacos	Mex.	21
Lee's Sandwiches	Sandwiches	21
El Torito	Mex.	21

DIAMOND BAR

Wienerschnitzel	Burgers/Hot Dogs	20

DUARTE

Slaw Dogs	Hot Dogs	22

EL MONTE

King Taco	Mex.	24
Lamppost Pizza	Pizza	22

GLENDORA

Spaghetti Eddie's	Italian	24

LA VERNE

Habit Burger	Burgers	23

MONTCLAIR

Acapulco	Mex.	20

MONTEBELLO

Alondra Hot Wings	Amer.	24
Zankou	Med.	23
Astro Burger	Burgers	22

MONTEREY PARK

Duck Hse.	Chinese	25
Cook's Tortas	Mex.	25
Shin-Sen-Gumi Yakitori	Japanese	25
Elite	Chinese	24
Daikokuya	Japanese	24
Capital Seafood	Chinese/Seafood	23
Mandarin	Chinese	22
Ocean Star	Chinese	22
NBC Seafood	Chinese/Seafood	21
Lee's Sandwiches	Sandwiches	21

PICO RIVERA

Dal Rae	Continental	26

ROSEMEAD

Sea Harbour	Chinese/Seafood	26
888 Seafood	Chinese/Seafood	24
Bahooka	Polynesian	21
Lee's Sandwiches	Sandwiches	21

ROWLAND HEIGHTS

Newport Seafood	Chinese/Seafood	27
Boiling Crab	Cajun/Seafood	25
BCD Tofu	Korean	22
Lee's Sandwiches	Sandwiches	21
Frisco's	Amer.	21
Tea Station	Taiwanese/Tea	19

SAN GABRIEL

Babita	*Mex.*	27
Newport Seafood	*Chinese/Seafood*	27
Golden Deli	*Viet.*	25
New Capital Seafood	*Seafood*	23
Clearman's	*Amer.*	22
Sam Woo	*Chinese*	21
Phoenix	*Chinese*	21
Tea Station	*Taiwanese/Tea*	19

TEMPLE CITY

Tea Station	*Taiwanese/Tea*	19

WHITTIER

California Grill	*Cal.*	26
Lascari's Deli	*Deli*	23
Black Angus	*Steak*	23
Original Roadhse. Grill	*Steak*	23
Ruby's	*Diner*	21

Conejo/Simi Valley/ Oxnard/Ventura & Environs

AGOURA HILLS/ OAK PARK

Leila's	*Cal.*	27
Café 14	*Continental*	27
Wood Ranch	*BBQ*	24
Grissini	*Italian*	23
NEW Lab Brewing Co.	*Amer./Eclectic*	22
Padri	*Italian*	22
Yamato	*Japanese*	21
Adobe Cantina	*Mex.*	20
Jinky's	*Diner*	20
Maria's	*Italian*	20

CAMARILLO

Safire	*Amer.*	26
Lure Fish Hse.	*Seafood*	24
Wood Ranch	*BBQ*	24
Los Arroyos	*Mex.*	24

MOORPARK

Wood Ranch	*BBQ*	24
Cafe Firenze	*Italian*	23
Lamppost Pizza	*Pizza*	22

OJAI

Suzanne's	*French/Italian*	27
Boccali's	*Italian*	24

OXNARD

Tierra Sur/Herzog	*Kosher/Med.*	28
Café Rio	*Mex.*	23
Du-par's	*Diner*	18

SIMI VALLEY

Pho So 1	*Viet.*	26
Elephant Bar	*Asian*	22

THOUSAND OAKS

Mastro's	*Steak*	27
Grill on Hollywood/Alley	*Amer.*	24
Cholada	*Thai*	24
Cheesecake Factory	*Amer.*	23
Outback	*Steak*	23
Z Pizza	*Pizza*	23
Stonefire	*BBQ*	23
Lupe's	*Mex.*	22
Holdren's	*Seafood/Steak*	22
P.F. Chang's	*Chinese*	22
Lazy Dog	*Eclectic*	22
Buddha's Belly	*Asian*	21

VENTURA

71 Palm	*Amer./French*	25
Watermark on Main	*Amer.*	24
Cajun Kitchen	*Cajun*	24
Wood Ranch	*BBQ*	24
Cafe Fiore	*Italian*	23
Brophy Bros.	*Seafood*	23
Anacapa Brewing	*Amer.*	23
Sidecar	*Amer.*	23

WESTLAKE VILLAGE

Brent's Deli	*Deli*	26
Tuscany	*Italian*	26
Rustico	*Italian*	26
Fins	*Continental/Seafood*	25
Melting Pot	*Fondue*	23
Galletto	*Brazilian/Italian*	23
Zin	*Amer.*	23
BJ's	*Pub*	23
Farfalla/Vinoteca	*Italian*	23
Lotería!	*Mex.*	23
Boccaccio's	*Continental*	22
9021Pho	*Viet.*	22
Vivoli	*Italian*	22
Lamppost Pizza	*Pizza*	22
Mediterraneo	*Med.*	21
Counter	*Burgers*	21
Marmalade	*Amer.*	19

Santa Clarita Valley & Environs

SANTA CLARITA

Rattler's BBQ | *BBQ*   25
Wahoo's Fish Taco | *Mex./Seafood* 22
Wokcano | *Asian*   22
Lamppost Pizza | *Pizza*   22

SAUGUS/NEWHALL

Le Chêne | *French*   26
Wood Ranch | *BBQ*   24
Chronic Tacos | *Mex.*   21

STEVENSON RANCH

Spumoni | *Italian*   21

VALENCIA

New Moon | *Chinese*   24
Habit Burger | *Burgers*   23
Outback | *Steak*   23
Z Pizza | *Pizza*   23
BJ's | *Pub*   23
Stonefire | *BBQ*   23
Lazy Dog | *Eclectic*   22
Marston's | *Amer.*   21
Thai Dishes | *Thai*   20
Salt Creek | *Steak*   20
Sisley | *Italian*   20

Pomona & East

POMONA

Joey's | *BBQ*   26

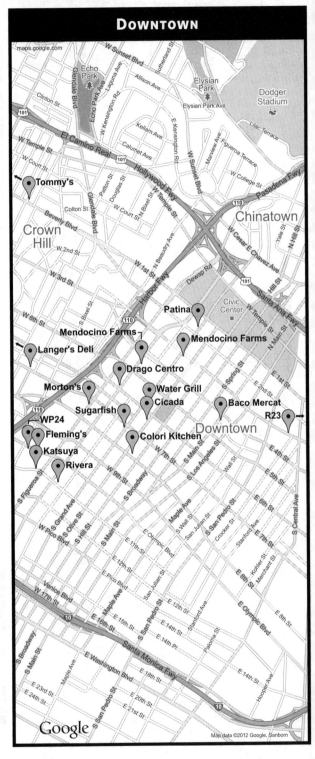

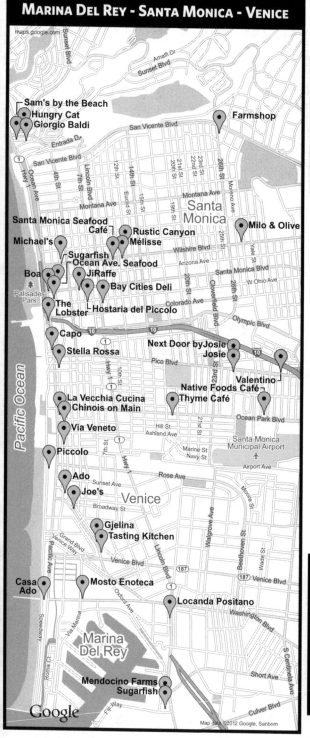

MARINA DEL REY - SANTA MONICA - VENICE

maps.google.com

Sunset Blvd
Sunset Blvd
Amalfi Dr

Sam's by the Beach
Hungry Cat
Giorgio Baldi

Farmshop

San Vicente Blvd
Entrada Dr
San Vicente Blvd
Moreno Ave

Ocean Ave
4th St
7th St
Lincoln Blvd
12th St
14th St
15th St
Euclid St
19th St
20th St
21st St
22nd St
23d St
26th St

Montana Ave
Montana Ave

Santa Monica

Santa Monica Seafood Café
Rustic Canyon
Mélisse
Milo & Olive

25th St
Yale St

Michael's
Sugarfish
Ocean Ave. Seafood
Boa
JiRaffe
Bay Cities Deli

Wilshire Blvd
Arizona Ave
Santa Monica Blvd
W Ohio Ave
20th St
26th St
Cloverfield Blvd

Palisades Park
The Lobster
Hostaria del Piccolo

Colorado Ave
Olympic Blvd

Capo

Next Door by Josie
Josie

Stella Rossa

Pico Blvd
10th St
Hwy 1
23rd St

Valentino

Native Foods Café
Thyme Café

La Vecchia Cucina
Chinois on Main

Ocean Park Blvd

Via Veneto

Hill St
Ashland Ave
21st St

Piccolo

Santa Monica Municipal Airport
Airport Ave

Pacific Ocean

Marine St
Navy St
7th St
Hwy 1

Ado
Joe's

Sunset Ave
Broadway St

Venice

Rose Ave
Moore St
Walgrove Ave
Beethoven St
Wade St

Gjelina
Tasting Kitchen

Grand Blvd
Venice Way
Venice Blvd
Lincoln Blvd
187
187 Venice Blvd

Casa Ado

Mosto Enoteca

Pacific Ave
Oxford Ave

Locanda Positano

Washington Blvd

Speedway
Via Marina

Marina Del Rey

S Centinela Ave
Short Ave

Mendocino Farms
Sugarfish

Roma Ct
Fiji Way
Culver Blvd

Google

Map data ©2012 Google, Sanborn

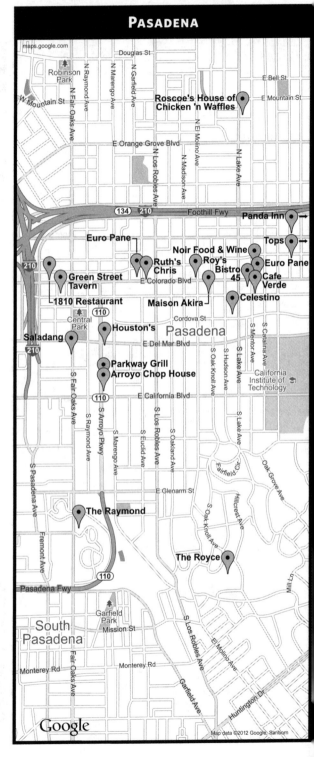

PASADENA

Robinson Park

Roscoe's House of
Chicken 'n Waffles

Panda Inn →

Tops →

Euro Pane

Noir Food & Wine

Ruth's
Chris

Roy's
Bistro
45

Euro Pane

Cafe
Verde

Celestino

Green Street
Tavern

1810 Restaurant

Maison Akira

Saladang

Houston's

Pasadena

Parkway Grill
Arroyo Chop House

California
Institute of
Technology

The Raymond

The Royce

South
Pasadena

Google

Map data ©2012 Google, Sanborn

LOS ANGELES
RESTAURANT
DIRECTORY

A & W Seafood *Chinese/Seafood* `23` `17` `20` `$22`
Northridge | 9306 Reseda Blvd. (Prairie St.) | 818-882-6668
Avoiding a "long haul" to points east, San Fernando Valley denizens turn to this Chinese seafooder in Northridge for "appealing" dim sum at "affordable" prices; decor is "average" and service varies, but visiting is a "joy" nonetheless – even if it's "not quite up to the San Gabriel Valley standard", most are thrilled to remain "west of the 405."

The Abbey ● *American* `19` `23` `19` `$33`
West Hollywood | 692 N. Robertson Blvd. (bet. Melrose Ave. & Santa Monica Blvd.) | 310-289-8410 | www.abbeyfoodandbar.com
"WeHo boys and their gal pals" fill up this sprawling "mostly gay" lounge to sip "froofy cocktails that pack a serious punch" in a "Gothic-Roman" indoor-outdoor space decked out with fireplaces and cabanas; although there's "modern", midpriced New American nibbles and a "laid-back" Sunday brunch proffered by "cute waiters", most "go for the scene."

Abbot's Pizza *Pizza* `24` `12` `19` `$15`
Culver City | 4410 Sepulveda Blvd. (Braddock Dr.) | 310-398-9000
Santa Monica | 1811 Pico Blvd. (18th St.) | 310-314-2777
Venice | 1407 Abbot Kinney Blvd. (California Ave.) | 310-396-7334
www.abbotspizzaco.com
"Ex–New Yorkers" sing the praises of the "excellent", "chewy-crust" 'za at this "funky" pizzeria trio also featuring "idiosyncratic" creations like "delicious" salad-topped and bagel-crusted pies; service nets mixed reviews, and "with precious little seating" in the "utilitarian" settings, many find takeout or delivery "much more tolerable."

NEW Abigaile *American* ▽ `22` `21` `22` `$43`
Hermosa Beach | 1301 Manhattan Ave. (bet. 14th St. & Pier Ave.) | 310-999-3508 | www.abigailerestaurant.com
Though it "hasn't been open long", Hermosa locals "foresee a great future" for this newcomer presenting an "inventive" American menu (at a slightly upscale price range) backed by house-brewed craft beers; the "edgy, cool" and "loud" interior is graffiti-ed as a nod to the setting's former life as a Black Flag rehearsal space, while "gorgeous views" deepen the atmosphere.

NEW Abricott *Eclectic* ▽ `22` `19` `22` `$20`
Pasadena | 238 S. Lake Ave. (E. Del Mar Blvd.) | 626-796-1613 | www.abricott.com
Internationalists welcome the "surprising" Eclectic menu bringing together Thai, Vietnamese and French (pho, grilled seafood, croque-monsieur with frites) at this morning-to-night Pasadenan set in an "arty, relaxed" space lined with books; "large servings" for "reasonable prices" are deemed an "unbelievable value" and the mood is "friendly", leading early backers to "hope it stays forever."

Absolutely Phobulous *Vietnamese* `22` `14` `19` `$17`
West Hollywood | 350 N. La Cienega Blvd. (Oakwood Ave.) | 310-360-3930
Encino | 15928 Ventura Blvd. (bet. Gaviota & Gloria Aves.) | 818-788-3560 Ⓢ
www.abpho.com
"If you can't make it" to Little Saigon, this "cheap, cheerful" Vietnamese pair in Encino and West Hollywood "will do", serving up bowls of

"straightforward" pho plus "huge, fresh" spring rolls – all deemed "authentic enough"; service gets mixed marks and the "plain" decor is just "one step up from a diner", but "no one cares when slurping up" the soups.

Aburiya Toranoko *Japanese*   22 | 20 | 21 | $39

Downtown | 243 S. San Pedro St. (2nd St.) | 213-621-9500 | www.toranokola.com

"Novel" small plates by chef Hisa Kawabe (ex Nobu) offer "something different" at this "festive, communal" izakaya in "gentrified" Little Tokyo, right next door to sib Lazy Ox Canteen; "urban hipsters" "approve" of the "edgy", "tattoo"-inspired decor and "creative" cocktails, even though the "budget-friendly" bites can turn "expensive" if you fill up.

Acapulco *Mexican*   20 | 20 | 21 | $23

Atwater Village | 3280 Glendale Blvd. (Atwater Ave.) | 323-663-8275
Los Feliz | 4444 Sunset Blvd. (bet. Fountain & Virgil Aves.) | 323-665-5751 Ⓢ Ⓜ
Westwood | 1109 Glendon Ave. (Kinross Ave.) | 310-208-3884
Downey | 9021 E. Firestone Blvd. (Lakewood Blvd.) | 562-923-4656
Long Beach | Marina Pacifica Mall | 6270 E. PCH (E 2nd St.) | 562-596-3371
San Pedro | 750 Sampson Way (S. Harbor Blvd.) | 310-548-6800
Glendale | 722 N. Pacific Ave. (Burchett St.) | 818-246-8175
Northridge | 9400 Reseda Blvd. (Vincennes St.) | 818-349-4584
Sun Valley | 8431 Sunland Blvd. (Roscoe Blvd.) | 818-767-4240
Montclair | 9405 Monte Vista Ave. (Palo Verde St) | 909-621-3955
www.acapulcorestaurants.com
Additional locations throughout Southern California

The margaritas take you "back to spring break in Cabo" at this "festive" Mexican chain putting out *"gigante"*, "traditional" plates for "cheap"; critics call the fare "forgettable" ("where's the spice?"), but "fast", "courteous" service makes it a "reliable" place for "family or groups of all ages."

Adagio Ⓜ *Italian*   23 | 17 | 24 | $38

Woodland Hills | 22841 Ventura Blvd. (Fallbrook Ave.) | 818-225-0533

"Gracious" owner Claudio Gontier "makes it a joy to visit" this Woodland Hills "classic" turning out "consistently good", "uncomplicated" Northern Italian; while a few note the "old standby" could use "some freshening up", its "personal" service coupled with "more-than-fair" tabs have kept neighborhood customers "coming back for years"; P.S. "reservations advised", especially on the weekends.

Addi's Tandoor *Indian*   26 | 19 | 24 | $29

Redondo Beach | 800 Torrance Blvd. (bet. PCH & Prospect Ave.) | 310-540-1616 | www.addistandoor.com

"Exceptional" "Goan-influenced" cuisine goes "as spicy as you like" at this Redondo Beach Indian whose "cut-above" cooking and "inviting", "professional" service come with a bill that's "pricier" than the norm but "well worth it"; the fairly "spare" yet "comfortable" strip-mall space is often packed with "loyal patrons", so reservations are recommended.

	FOOD	DECOR	SERVICE	COST

Admiral Risty *Seafood*

22 **21** **23** **$42**

Rancho Palos Verdes | Golden Cove Shopping Ctr. |
31250 Palos Verdes Dr. W. (Hawthorne Blvd.) | 310-377-0050 |
www.admiral-risty.com

The "beautiful" ocean views "go on and on" at this '60s "stalwart" in
Palos Verdes serving "well-prepared, basic" seafood along with "perfect" martinis in a "newly restyled" nautical setting overseen by an
"experienced, genuine" crew; so while the "dazzling" sunsets tend to
trump the surf 'n' turf, backers point out "it's been there since the beginning of time so they must be doing something right"; P.S. frequent
live music at the bar adds to the atmosphere.

☑ Ado *Californian/Italian*

27 **21** **23** **$54**

Venice | 796 Main St. (Abbot Kinney Blvd.) | 310-399-9010 |
www.adovenice.com

☑ NEW Casa Ado *Californian/Italian*

Marina del Rey | 12 Washington Blvd. (Speedway) | 310-577-2589 |
www.casaado.com

Out of an "unassuming little yellow cottage", this Venice "gem" (with
a larger outpost in Marina del Rey) delivers "luscious" Cal-Italian
fare – including a "melt-in-your-mouth" beet pasta with quail ragu
that's the stuff of "dreams" – to a "trendy" clientele; though "crowded"
tables are a drawback, the candlelit setting is otherwise "romantic"
and the "charming" staff "greets you like friends", so it's a "special"
(and "expensive") "treat."

Adobe Cantina *Mexican*

20 **19** **21** **$25**

Agoura Hills | 29100 Agoura Rd. (Cornell Rd.) | 818-991-3474

With a pretty patio "tucked among the trees", this Agoura Hills Mexican
is an "unusually lovely" alfresco setting for "lingering" over "awesome"
margaritas; the staff encourages a "friendly", "relaxed" vibe, and while
most find the food "good" but "nothing fancy" (or particularly "authentic"), the "large portions" and "reasonable" prices are pleasers.

A'float Sushi *Japanese*

22 **20** **20** **$24**

Pasadena | 87 E. Colorado Blvd. (N. Raymond Ave.) |
626-792-9779

"The conveyor belt is water" at this kaiten sushi spot in Pasadena where
diners "snatch" "precious cargo" from floating boats, and "are charged
by the color and number of plates" they take; sure, it's a little "gimmicky" and the "decent" cuts are "not the highest quality" around, but
the "price is right" and it's an "entertaining" night out, especially for
"groups"; P.S. for the "freshest" catch, "go when it's busy."

A-Frame *Eclectic*

23 **18** **21** **$34**

Culver City | 12565 W. Washington Blvd. (Neosho Ave.) | 310-398-7700 |
www.aframela.com

"Bold", "original" dishes by "genius" Roy Choi (of Kogi truck fame) deliver an "homage to LA's immigrant flavors" at this Culver City Eclectic
set in a "stylish" "repurposed IHOP" done up à la "Dick Van Dyke's vacation lodge"; "spectacular" cocktails, "helpful" service and a fire-
warmed patio lend extra appeal, and while some could do without the
"waits", "noise" and "awkward" seating at communal tables, others
take the opportunity to "meet fellow foodies."

	FOOD	DECOR	SERVICE	COST

Ago ● *Italian* | 23 | 22 | 22 | $58 |

West Hollywood | 8478 Melrose Ave. (La Cienega Blvd.) | 323-655-6333 |
www.agorestaurant.com

"The people-watching alone" scores points at this West Hollywood
"showbiz hangout" co-owned by Robert De Niro, where luminaries
"turn heads" on the tiled patio, often overshadowing the "excellent" Tuscan food by Agostino Sciandri; observers say the "accommodating" service is even more so "if you're a known entity" and
bills seem "too expensive for what you get", but after brushing shoul-
ders with the A-list in "lovely" environs, most feel they "totally got
their money's worth."

Agra Cafe *Indian* | 23 | 15 | 19 | $20 |

Silver Lake | 4325 W. Sunset Blvd. (Fountain Ave.) | 323-665-7818 |
www.agracafe.com

Tucked in amongst a "liquor store and tae kwon do studio", this "secluded" Silver Laker plates "consistent", "correctly spiced" Indian fare
that makes for "bargain" meals; service can vary, but most find it "A-ok"
and call the "online ordering" a plus.

Agra Indian Kitchen *Indian* | 23 | 16 | 21 | $22 |

Venice | 2553 Lincoln Blvd. (Harrison Ave.) | 310-827-0050 |
www.agraindiankitchen.com

Indian Kitchen *Indian*

West Hollywood | 8165 Santa Monica Blvd. (Crescent Heights Blvd.) |
323-656-9000 | www.theindiankitchenca.com

These "serviceable" sibs in Venice and West Hollywood deliver "simple" "homey" Indian fare that's "easy on the pocketbook"; the settings
may be modest, but "just remember, you're there for the food."

Ahi Sushi *Japanese* | 26 | 21 | 23 | $33 |

Studio City | 12915 Ventura Blvd. (Coldwater Canyon Ave.) | 818-981-0277 |
www.ahisushi.com

At this "welcoming" Japanese in Studio City, chefs prepare a "wonderful assortment" of "quality" fish (some on a new crudo menu) in a "casual" setting with a "fresh feel" and small bamboo-lined patio; though
there's lots of high-profile "competition" along "sushi row", it's an "enjoyable" "local" option where you're "treated like family" and the "lunch
special is the bomb."

Ahn Joo *Korean* | ∇ 24 | 16 | 22 | I |
(fka Ahn Joo Truck)

Glendale | Americana at Brand | 668 Americana Way (Brand Blvd.) |
818-242-3793 | www.ahnjoo.com

"Spicy, pickley" flavors mingle at this former food truck, now a snack-
food stand in The Americana at Brand devising inexpensive "twists on
Korean pub food" including an "amazing play" on nachos made with
deep-fried rice cakes and kimchi salsa; some find the product "mediocre", but most insist the "awesome" combinations "all tie together"
in an "interesting" package.

Aimee's Bistro 🄯Ⓜ *French* | 24 | 18 | 23 | $37 |

Redondo Beach | 800 S. PCH (Knob Hill Ave.) | 310-316-1081
Guests "get a kiss on both cheeks" from "always attentive", "very
French" owner-host Aimee Mizrahi, whose Redondo Beach bistro pre-

	FOOD	DECOR	SERVICE	COST

pares "homestyle cooking" like coq au vin and duck confit with a "magic touch"; critics contend the kitchen's performance is a bit "uneven", but live performances on Fridays and Saturdays perk up the strip-mall setting, and longtime loyalists swear it's a South Bay "sleeper."

AKA Bistro *American*   23 | 23 | 23 | $37

Pasadena | One Colorado | 41 Hugus Alley (Fair Oaks Ave.) | 626-564-8111 | www.akabistro.com

Set in an "old-school brick courtyard away from the street" in Old Pasadena's One Colorado Plaza, this "easy" New American from Robert Simon (Bistro 45) delivers "high-quality" gastropub grub backed by a "winning wine list" in a "hip", yet "relaxing" setting with a "beautiful" patio; an "eager-to-please" staff and moderate pricing make it a "top choice for the neighborhood."

Akasha *American*   22 | 22 | 21 | $38

Culver City | 9543 Culver Blvd. (Washington Blvd.) | 310-845-1700 | www.akasharestaurant.com

"Modern takes on market-driven cuisine" fill the menu at Akasha Richmond's Culver City New American serving food that's "wonderful" without being too "far out", alongside biodynamic wines, "fancy elixirs" and "coffee snob–approved" java; the "cool space" plays host to a "lively" "scene", resulting in sometimes "earsplitting" noise, but loyalists "like the energy" – "ho-hum service" and somewhat "pricey" tabs notwithstanding; P.S. "hit up the on-site bakery for some treats to go."

Akbar Cuisine of India *Indian*   22 | 17 | 20 | $28

Marina del Rey | 3115 Washington Blvd. (Yale Ave.) | 310-574-0666

Santa Monica | 2627 Wilshire Blvd. (bet. Princeton & 26th Sts.) | 310-586-7469

Hermosa Beach | 1101 Aviation Blvd. (Prospect Ave.) | 310-937-3800

Pasadena | 44 N. Fair Oaks Ave. (Union St.) | 626-577-9916 www.akbarcuisineofindia.com

"Rich, complex flavors" skew to "the spicy side" but can be "adjusted to your liking" at this "stellar" Indian quartet where "a mix of traditional and modern dishes" and "delicious" naan are set down by "pleasant" servers; the ambiance varies by location but prices are eminently "reasonable" and regulars insist it "never disappoints."

Alcazar *Lebanese*   21 | 19 | 18 | $34

Encino | 17239 Ventura Blvd. (Louise Ave.) | 818-789-0991 | www.al-cazar.com

"Praiseworthy Middle Eastern food" awaits at this Encino Lebanese where "wonderful meze" and kebabs are served by a "friendly, accommodating" team in "lushly decorated surroundings" with a garden patio; weekends are especially festive thanks to hookah service and "delightful" live music and belly-dancing performances.

Alcove ◗ *American*   21 | 22 | 18 | $21

Los Feliz | 1929 Hillhurst Ave. (Franklin Ave.) | 323-644-0100 | www.alcovecafe.com

Los Feliz hipsters fill up the "amazing sun-drenched patio" at this "adorable" bungalow boasting "tasty" American eats, "jet-fuel" coffee and "indulgent" desserts "so picture-perfect you feel lustful just looking at them"; true, the "self-service ordering" system can get "a little crazy", but it's perennially "popular" so clearly no one minds too much.

Alegria *Nuevo Latino*   23 | 22 | 22 | $32

Long Beach | 115 Pine Ave. (bet. B'way & 1st St.) | 562-436-3388 | www.alegriacocinalatina.com

A "wonderful variety" of Nuevo Latino dishes turns up at this Downtown Long Beacher, where highly "drinkable" sangria fuels the "party atmosphere" amid mosaic-adorned surroundings; flamenco dancers and salsa lessons provide "evening entertainment" some nights, so though some gripe that the "food could be better", for a "fun" atmosphere, this "is the place to go."

Alegria on Sunset ☒ *Mexican*   24 | 16 | 21 | $21

Silver Lake | 3510 W. Sunset Blvd. (Golden Gate Ave.) | 323-913-1422 | www.alegriaonsunset.com

It's "like eating in your mother's kitchen (if your mother was Mexican)" at this "cute" neighborhood standby in a "random strip mall in Silver Lake" serving "unique" regional fare like "superb mole" that's "comforting and consistent"; the digs are colorful, and although it's "small and crowded, that doesn't hurt the food"; P.S. there's no alcohol, but don't miss the "amazing" fresh-fruit elixirs muddled with herbs.

Alejo's *Italian*   22 | 12 | 20 | $22

Westchester | 8343 Lincoln Blvd. (84th St.) | 310-670-6677 | www.alejoswestchester.com

Alejo's Presto Trattoria *Italian*

Marina del Rey | 4002 Lincoln Blvd. (Washington Blvd.) | 310-822-0095

"Garlic, garlic everywhere" "keeps vampires at bay" at these "neighborhood staples" in Marina del Rey and Westchester doling out "huge portions" of "homey" Italian fare; true, the "stripped-down" settings are "not the greatest", but the mood is "exuberant" and bills are "small", so "good luck getting in"; P.S. Marina del Rey is BYO, while Westchester pours beer and wine.

Alessio Bistro *Italian*   22 | 20 | 22 | $36

West Hills | Platt Vill. | 6428 Platt Ave. (Victory Blvd.) | 818-710-0270 | www.alessiobistro.com

Bistro Alessio *Italian*

Northridge | 9725 Reseda Blvd. (Superior St.) | 818-709-8393 | www.bistroalessio.com

Tucked away in the "sleepy" North Valley suburbs, this separately owned pair of "neighborhood" Italians are "reliable" venues for "tasty", well-priced fare; there's "more noise and bustle" due to weekend live music at the West Hills locale, but in general both branches offer a "relaxing" vibe, and though service garners mixed reviews, most agree they're "local favorites."

Alfredo's *Mexican*   27 | 20 | 26 | $20

Lomita | 2372 PCH (Pennsylvania Ave.) | 310-784-0393 | www.alfredosrestaurant.com

This Lomita Mexican "satisfies cravings" with a broad menu of "perfectly cooked" traditional dishes plus some less common Yucatáninfluence specialties; the "atmosphere is a little cold", but prices are "fair" so most insist "you have to try it."

All India Cafe *Indian*
21 | 16 | 19 | $22

West LA | Santa Monica Plaza | 12113 Santa Monica Blvd. (Bundy Dr.) | 310-442-5250

Pasadena | 39 S. Fair Oaks Ave. (bet. Colorado Blvd. & Green St.) | 626-440-0309

www.allindiacafe.com

The menu's chock-"full of variety" at this "brightly decorated" Indian trio in Pasadena, West LA and Santa Barbara serving "consistently good" if "not spectacular" cuisine alongside some "interesting" uncommon dishes like Frankie rolls; "friendly" servers and "decent" prices help offset the "slow" pace of things as well as "crowds" and "noise."

Alondra Hot Wings *American*
24 | 20 | 21 | $19

Paramount | 8411 Alondra Blvd. (Indiana Ave.) | 562-531-4200

Long Beach | 245 Pine Ave. (W. 3rd St.) | 562-437-2103

Alhambra | 515 W. Main St. (bet. Atlantic Blvd. & 5th St.) | 626-576-7119

Montebello | 616 W. Whittier Blvd. (6th St.) | 323-722-2731

www.alondrawings.com

Expect "finger-lickin' good" hot wings in "an array of flavors" – including an "atomic" version so spicy customers are required to sign a waiver – at this American quartet that also appeases "wing-haters" with burgers, beer and deep-fried Twinkies for dessert; the "nothing-fancy" digs are done up with "mobster"-themed photos, while TVs lead to an especially "lively" mood "when there's a game on."

Alwazir Chicken ● *Mideastern*
25 | 12 | 20 | $14

Hollywood | 6051 Hollywood Blvd. (Gower St.) | 323-856-0660 | www.alwazirchicken.com

"Juicy" rotisserie chicken is "made just right" and served up with a "garlicky" sauce ("mmmm") at this Hollywood Middle Easterner whose kebabs and falafel make a "quick", "convenient" bite; calling decor "simple" is putting it mildly, but prices are "shockingly cheap" and "flavor is the priority" anyhow.

Amalfi *Italian*
22 | 21 | 21 | $37

La Brea | 143 N. La Brea Ave. (bet. Beverly Blvd. & 1st St.) | 323-938-2504 | www.amalfiristorante.com

"Reliable, if not thrilling" is the word on this La Brea "neighborhood Italian" plying pizzas and pastas (including a noteworthy pumpkin ravioli with short rib) in a cozy setting and also playing host to a lively bar scene and comedy acts in the upstairs lounge; even if a few feel it's "nothing to run back for", it's deemed a "solid", midrange choice if you're seeing a show.

Amarone Kitchen & Wine ⊠ *Italian*
24 | 16 | 22 | $60

West Hollywood | 8868 W. Sunset Blvd. (San Vicente Blvd.) | 310-652-2233 | www.amaronela.com

Although it's "not much from the outside", inside this "warm, cozy" West Hollywood Italian awaits "exceptional" "bliss"-inducing pastas delivered by a "charming" staff; tabs can be "costly", but the "dark, intimate" setting is made for "dates", and acolytes insist it's "as close to Italy as it gets in LA."

	FOOD	DECOR	SERVICE	COST

American Farmhouse Tavern *American/Eclectic*   19 | 17 | 19 | $29

Manhattan Beach | 924 N. Sepulveda Blvd. (10th St.) | 310-376-8044 | www.americanfarmhousetavern.com

"Hearty", "homestyle" cooking – from "darn good cuts of meat" to buttermilk fried chicken – pulls patrons to this Manhattan Beach American-Eclectic where the "modern, polished" setting walks the line between "family-friendly" and "refined enough" for "adult" gatherings; plentiful "draft beers" and accessible pricing are added allures, and though some think it's "still working out the kinks", most attest it's a neighborhood "hit."

Amici *Italian*   22 | 19 | 22 | $44

Beverly Hills | Beverly Terrace Hotel | 469 N. Doheny Dr. (Santa Monica Blvd.) | 310-858-0271 | www.tamici.com
Brentwood | 2538 San Vicente Blvd. (26th St.) | 310-260-4900 | www.amicibrentwood.com
Glendale | Americana at Brand | 783 Americana Way (bet. Brand Blvd. & Central Ave.) | 818-502-1220 | www.amicila.com

Locals "in the know" like these "warm, welcoming" separately owned trattorias where "accommodating" servers "aim to please" and the "classic Italian" cuisine is "tasty", if "not especially exciting"; the Beverly Terrace Hotel branch has a "sweet" patio, while the Brentwood outpost feels "fancier", and outside tables at the new Americana at Brand branch in Glendale provide a prime vantage point for "watching the action go by."

Ammo *Californian*   23 | 19 | 22 | $46

Hollywood | 1155 N. Highland Ave. (bet. Fountain Ave. & Santa Monica Blvd.) | 323-871-2666 | www.ammocafe.com

A "favorite" among "industry" types, this "hip" Hollywood Californian plates "marvelous" "market"-driven fare that "leaves you feeling healthy" in a "chic, well-weathered" setting offering a "good chance at a celebrity sighting"; "special" cocktails and cool music are further boosts, and though a few are irked by "too expensive" bills, most put it on their "must-return list"; P.S. "brunch is tops."

Anacapa Brewing Co. *American*   23 | 21 | 22 | $22

Ventura | 472 E. Main St. (California St.) | 805-643-2337 | www.anacapabrewing.com

"It's really all about the beer" at this Ventura gastropub brewing up its own "tasty" ales and lagers on-site to accompany a menu of "standard" pub selections of "above-average" quality; the "noisy", "relaxed" atmosphere "has a local feel" and is staffed by a "friendly" crew, so it hits the mark for a "quick bite", a "date" or hanging "at the bar" with a group.

Anarbagh *Indian*   24 | 20 | 23 | $28

Woodland Hills | 22721 Ventura Blvd. (Ponce Ave.) | 818-224-3929 | www.anarbaghindiancuisinewoodlandhills.com

"Standing out" among other San Fernando Valley Indians, this "authentic" "gem" in Woodland Hills delivers "flavorful, high-quality" dishes with "panache", including "oh-so-tasty vegetarian" options; even if the setting's understated and it's a "bit of a drive", the "attentive" staff "always offers a warm greeting" and "you get a lot for your money" too.

☑ Angelini Osteria Ⓜ Italian

28 | 19 | 24 | $54

Beverly Boulevard | 7313 Beverly Blvd. (bet. N. Fuller Ave. & N. Poinsettia Pl.) | 323-297-0070 | www.angeliniosteria.com

"Every dish and nibble is a heavenly experience" at this "superb" Italian on Beverly Boulevard famed for chef-owner Gino Angelini's "incredible", "rustic" cooking including "pitch-perfect" pastas, "fabulous" roasted meats and "delectable" branzino baked whole in a salt crust; "budget-busting" tabs and a "constant din" in the "claustrophobic" room are drawbacks, and opinions are split on service, but most agree the "spectacular food wins out."

Angelino Cafe Italian

24 | 18 | 26 | $33

Mid-City | 8735 W. Third St. (S. Robertson Blvd.) | 310-246-1177 | www.cafeangelino.com

Boasting the cozy "atmosphere of a small kitchen in Italy", this "reliable" Mid-City "standby" appeals to "neighborhood" types with a "family-friendly" vibe and "wholesome" cooking like pastas and "cracker-thin" pizzas; prices are low and digs are "comfortable" enough, so consensus is "you can't go wrong."

☑ Animal American

27 | 18 | 23 | $51

Fairfax | 435 N. Fairfax Ave. (Oakwood Ave.) | 323-782-9225 | www.animalrestaurant.com

"If it moos, oinks, baas, clucks, coos or swims you'll find it" at this "brilliantly creative" Fairfax New American where Jon Shook and Vinny Dotolo "rock the kitchen" with a "wild selection" of "insanely rich, over-the-top" "ironic snout-to-tail" creations that leave even "unashamed" carnivores "in a meat coma"; yes, it's "a little expensive" and can be "loud" in the "sparse" "no-frills" space, but it's a "must-try" "cutting-edge" "foodie experience."

Annapurna Indian

22 | 15 | 20 | $16

Culver City | 10200 Venice Blvd. (Vinton Ave.) | 310-204-5500 | www.annapurnacuisine.com

This all-vegetarian Culver City curry house "stands out" for an "impressive variety" of "tasty" dosas and other South Indian specialties "toward the healthful side" at affordable rates; some say service "gets bogged down" when they're busy, but plain digs are "enlivened" by TVs "streaming Bollywood videos" and "excellent value" on the lunch buffet is an additional asset.

Antonio's Ⓜ Mexican

22 | 20 | 23 | $28

Melrose | 7470 Melrose Ave. (bet. Fairfax & La Brea Aves.) | 323-658-9060 | www.antoniosonmelrose.com

"Charming" owner Antonio Gutierrez always "greets patrons at the door" of this "iconic" Melrose Mexican that's been a "tradition" for "gourmet" grub and "well-mixed" margaritas for over 50 years; a few find the food's "not what it used to be", but the vibe's "like visiting an old friend", and that's how the many regulars like it.

☑ A.O.C. Californian/Mediterranean

26 | 22 | 24 | $54

Third Street | 8022 W. Third St. (bet. Crescent Heights Blvd. & Fairfax Ave.) | 323-653-6359 | www.aocwinebar.com

"Now this is bar food" boast guests "impressed" by the "sumptuous" small plates – including "exceptional" charcuterie and cheese – that "continue to amaze" at this "sophisticated" Third Street "standout" by Suzanne Goin (Lucques, Tavern), where "inspiring" Cal-Med cooking, a "vast", "superb" wine list and "knowledgeable" service come together in "understated" surroundings; the clientele is "stylish" and "convivial", so never mind the "high prices" – the back patio "in summer is what LA is all about."

🆕 A1 Cucina Italiana *Italian*

24 | 22 | 24 | $35

West Hollywood | 107 N. Robertson Blvd. (Alden Dr.) | 310-657-1345

Pasta reminiscent of "Rome" and other "fab" Italiana make a promising start at this "nice makeover" of Giacomino Drago's Il Buco in WeHo, now boasting a contemporary brown-meets-orange color scheme with a Vespa in the front as the finishing touch; "generous" plates and "responsive" service are further pluses, leading locals to declare it a new neighborhood "find."

🅉 Apple Pan ●Ⓜ⇴ *American*

23 | 13 | 21 | $14

West LA | 10801 W. Pico Blvd. (bet. Glendon Ave. & Westwood Blvd.) | 310-475-3585

A "true Los Angeles treasure" that "never seems to change", this circa-1947 West LA "legend" delivers "simple, amazing" hickory burgers that fans call "the platonic ideal" alongside "old-fashioned" pies tendered by a "swift", "no-nonsense" staff that "works with military precision"; "be prepared to jockey for a seat" at the U-shaped counter, but it's all part of a "nostalgic" experience that's "a must for any visitor"; P.S. cash only.

Armstrong's Fish Market & Seafood Restaurant *Seafood*

23 | 20 | 20 | $31

Catalina Island | 306 Crescent Ave. (Whitney Ave.) | Avalon | 310-510-0113 | www.armstrongseafood.com

A Catalina "tradition", this "noisy" venue "packs" 'em in with "well-prepared" seafood that is "amply portioned" and "moderately priced" in a "quaint", "nautically themed" setting; it also boasts "lovely" views of Avalon Bay, which make long "waits" "well worth it", and it's especially "recommended for tourists."

Aroma Ⓜ *Italian*

24 | 19 | 21 | $28

Silver Lake | 2903 W. Sunset Blvd. (Silver Lake Blvd.) | 323-644-2833 | www.aromaatsunset.com

"The location in a strip mall is a little odd, but the food makes up for it" at this "quaint, charming" Silver Lake "treasure" delivering "delicious", "top-quality" Italian fare from ex-Valentino chef Edin Marroquin; "personal" service and relatively modest pricing make it a "great find."

Aroma Café *Eastern European*

21 | 18 | 19 | $22

West LA | Rancho Park Plaza | 2530 Overland Ave. (Cushdon Aves.) | 310-836-2919 | www.aromacafe-la.com

"Savory", "carb-filled" "cuisine from the Adriatic" lures lovers of Eastern-European fare to this "casual", "reasonably priced" cafe in West LA, where the expat crowd "sits for hours" over "fab desserts" and "addictive" Turkish coffee; those put off by the parking lot views and sometimes "slow" service can check out the mini "Euro market" for grab 'n' go cheeses and other delicacies.

Arroyo Chop House *Steak*

| 26 | 24 | 24 | $61 |

Pasadena | 536 S. Arroyo Pkwy. (California Blvd.) | 626-577-7463 |
www.arroyochophouse.com

"High-class without being stuffy", this "Pasadena tradition" from the
Smith Brothers (Parkway Grill) draws devout carnivores with "cooked-
to-perfection" steaks in a "clubby" setting complete with "mood lighting", "large leather booths" and "stiff drinks"; "professional" servers
"make you feel like a king", helping to justify the "expensive" tabs.

Artisan Cheese
Gallery *Cheese/Sandwiches*

| 25 | 15 | 19 | $20 |

Studio City | 12023 Ventura Blvd. (Laurel Canyon Blvd.) | 818-505-0207 |
www.artisancheesegallery.com

"Fantastic" sandwiches and a "bountiful" array of all the "rare" cheeses
known to man and mouse "delight" *fromage* fans at this upmarket
shop/cafe, a "wonderful find in Studio City"; the "knowledgeable"
staff "indulges every customer" with free nibbles, so "be prepared to
wait" at the "crowded" counter.

Art's Deli *Deli*

| 22 | 13 | 20 | $22 |

Studio City | 12224 Ventura Blvd. (bet. Laurelgrove & Vantage Aves.) |
818-762-1221 | www.artsdeli.com

On the Studio City scene since 1957, this "no-nonsense", family-run
deli doles out the obligatory "sky-high" sandwiches that staunch supporters swear are "better than bubbe's"; "old-fashioned" booths and
"fast", "snappy" waitresses lend it a bit of "NY style", though critics
kvetch it's "a little too pricey for what you get."

Asahi Ramen ⊄ *Japanese*

| 21 | 11 | 19 | $14 |

West LA | 2027 Sawtelle Blvd. (bet. La Grange & Mississippi Aves.) |
310-479-2231 | www.asahiramen.com

"Excellent", "filling" Japanese ramen in "steaming hot broth" "hits the
spot" at this "tiny storefront" in West LA's Little Osaka, where the
"cheap, huge portions" of food come fast and furious thanks to "light-
ning service"; just bring cash and "be prepared for a wait", since the
line often "spills out onto Sawtelle."

Asaka *Japanese*

| 22 | 20 | 20 | $27 |

Rancho Palos Verdes | Golden Cove Shopping Ctr. |
31208 Palos Verdes Dr. W. (Hawthorne Blvd.) | 310-377-5999
Redondo Beach | 1870 S. Elena Ave. (Palos Verdes Blvd.) |
310-373-5999
Woodland Hills | 6020 Canoga Ave. (Oxnard St.) | 818-888-2234
www.asakausa.com

Handy for locals, these Japanese joints present "fresh", "tasty" sushi
and "reasonably priced" rolls that are "good for everyday meals";
though service is uneven and the "mini-mall" decor "ordinary in the
extreme", the Rancho Palos Verdes branch ups the ante with "spectacular" ocean views from a "spacious" outdoor deck.

Asakuma *Japanese*

| 23 | 17 | 20 | $35 |

Beverly Hills | 141 S. Robertson Blvd. (bet. Charleville & Wilshire Blvds.) |
310-659-1092
Venice | Hoyt Plaza | 2805 Abbot Kinney Blvd. (Washington Blvd.) |
310-577-7999

(continued)

Asakuma

West LA | 11769 Santa Monica Blvd. (bet. Granville & Stoner Aves.) | 310-473-8990
www.asakuma.com

Offering a "rare" option for Angelenos, these "wonderful", separately owned Japanese restaurants focus on delivery to satisfy sushi "cravings"; even if the settings are "not really set up for a dine-in experience", when you're "too lazy to leave your living room" they're "worth the price."

Z Asanebo M *Japanese* 28 18 25 $84

Studio City | 11941 Ventura Blvd. (bet. Carpenter & Radford Aves.) | 818-760-3348 | www.asanebo-restaurant.com

"Go with the omakase" and have a "sublime" time at Tetsuya Nakao's Studio City Japanese, a "shining star" on sushi row where fish fanatics pay "flown-in-from-Japan" prices for "mind-boggling" results; forget "ridiculous novelty rolls", it's unadorned all around, from the "incredibly fresh" cuts to the "low-key" staff and "unassuming" setting, yet "always a total delight."

Asia de Cuba *Asian/Cuban* 24 26 21 $63

West Hollywood | Mondrian Hotel | 8440 W. Sunset Blvd. (bet. La Cienega Blvd. & Olive Dr.) | 323-848-6000 | www.chinagrillmanagement.com

"Well-done" Asian-Cuban fusion cuisine is made to "share with friends" at this "sleek" Philippe Starck–designed "people-watching place" in West Hollywood's Mondrian Hotel, where the "stunning" setting extends from the "young, attractive" clientele to the "fabulous" views of the city ; for most, the "over-the-top" atmosphere still thrills, the somewhat "iffy" service and "overpriced" tabs not so much.

Astro Burger ⇏ *Burgers* 22 15 20 $14

Hollywood | 5601 Melrose Ave. (Gower St.) | 323-469-1924 | www.astroburger.com ◐
West Hollywood | 7475 Santa Monica Blvd. (Gardner St.) | 323-874-8041 ◐
Montebello | 3421 W. Beverly Blvd. (Bradshawe Ave.) | 323-724-3995

Fans find an "old-fashioned burger joint with a twist" at this trio of "greasy spoons" slinging "juicy" patties, "heaps of fries", "amazing veggie burgers" and "all sorts" of Greek-inspired fare; it's "quick" and "cheap" with a "colorful" clientele, plus the WeHo branch is an "easy late-night choice."

Auld Dubliner ◐ *Pub Food* 21 21 20 $23

Long Beach | Pike at Rainbow Harbor | 71 S. Pine Ave. (W. Ocean Blvd. & W. Shoreline Dr.) | 562-437-8300 | www.aulddubliner.com

"Hear an Irish band" and grab a "proper pint of Guinness" at this imported pub "replica" in Long Beach serving "hearty" staples like fish 'n' chips and bangers 'n' mash; while some critics call the cooking and service just "ok", it's still always "shoulder-to-shoulder" on the weekends and "you may have to fight your way to the bar."

Auntie Em's Kitchen *American*

23 | 16 | 20 | $18

Eagle Rock | 4616 Eagle Rock Blvd. (Corliss St.) | 323-255-0800 |
www.auntieemskitchen.com

"Arty locals line up" for this "funky" inexpensive "Eagle Rock institution" dishing out "creative", locally sourced American "comfort food",
including "swell" breakfasts, "phenomenal" sandwiches and "top-notch"
cupcakes; the vibe is "friendly and upbeat", but be ready to roll with a
"divey-cafe" atmosphere.

Avila's El Ranchito *Mexican*

22 | 19 | 21 | $22

Huntington Park | 6703 Santa Fe Ave. (Mortimer St.) | 323-585-5055 |
www.el-ranchito.com

Long Beach | 5345 Long Beach Blvd. (Plymouth St.) | 562-428-7348 |
www.avilaselranchito.com

"Tantalizing tacos", burritos and other "homestyle" Mexican eats fuel
the "fiesta" at these "popular" Huntington Park and Long Beach chain
links boasting a "casual" "cantina" atmosphere perfect for "relaxing and
chilling" with friends or family; offering "reasonably fast" service and "affordable" tabs, it's thrived since the '60s and "keeps gaining converts."

A Votre Sante *Health Food*

21 | 16 | 20 | $25

Brentwood | 13016 San Vicente Blvd. (26th St.) | 310-451-1813 |
www.avotresantela.com

"Those who want to live to 120" – including "San Vicente runners",
"bikers" and "yoga maidens" – hit up this veg-friendly Brentwood
health-fooder for "generous portions" of "beautiful", "satisfying" fare
with "all the right foodie/eco values"; "basic but homey" and "not too
fussy" or expensive, it benefits from a "nice attitude" and "neighborhood vibe" that's "hard to beat."

Axe *Californian*

24 | 19 | 19 | $36

Venice | 1009 Abbot Kinney Blvd. (B'way St.) | 310-664-9787 |
www.axerestaurant.com

Employing "excellent" organic and local ingredients on a "well-edited"
menu, this Venice "gem" (pronounced "ah-shay") nails the "clean,
vegetarian-conscious" Californian genre in an airy "minimalist" setting
with a "charming" garden out back; though a few complain of "attitude"
and "uncomfortable" seating, most of the "eclectic clientele" is "happy
to have it back" after a fire; P.S. brunch only Mondays and Tuesdays.

Ayara Thai *Thai*

24 | 18 | 22 | $21

Westchester | 6245 W. 87th St. (La Tijera Blvd.) | 310-410-8848 |
www.ayarathaicuisine.com

Setting the "local" standard for "what Thai should be", this "family-
owned" Westchester "favorite" "near LAX" "consistently" turns out
"excellent", "authentic" Siamese that's "sometimes so hot it brings
tears to your eyes" ("watch out"); "attentive" service and "reasonable
prices" are further reasons "everyone loves" it.

Azeen's Afghani Restaurant *Afghan*

∇ 27 | 21 | 25 | $26

Pasadena | 110 E. Union St. (Arroyo Pkwy.) | 626-683-3310 |
www.azeensafghanirestaurant.com

Pasadenans explore the "amazing goodness" of affordable, "home-
cooked" Afghan cuisine – including "some of the best kebabs
anywhere" – at this "small" "charmer" on the edge of Old Town; "ex-

quisite flavors" and a staff as "welcoming" as "family" keep the faithful "going back" for more.

Babalu *Californian*   19 | 16 | 17 | $25

Santa Monica | 1002 Montana Ave. (10th St.) | 310-395-2500 | www.babalu.info

"Dessert should be your first course" declare sweet tooths at this Santa Monica spot known for "decadent pies" and cakes from the in-house bakery and "satisfying" Cal cuisine spiked with "Caribbean flair"; dissenters dis the "cramped" seating and "erratic" service, but between the "relaxed vibe", tropical decor and sidewalk tables it remains "popular."

✪ Babita Mexicuisine ⊠ Ⓜ *Mexican*   27 | 15 | 25 | $44

San Gabriel | 1823 S. San Gabriel Blvd. (Norwood Pl.) | 626-288-7265 | www.babita-mexicuisine.com

Hidden behind a "plain" San Gabriel facade, this "unexpected" "culinary treasure" leaves adventurous eaters "blown away" by the "creative" "gourmet Mexican" cuisine "lovingly crafted" by chef-owner Roberto Berrelleza, who "relishes educating diners about the unusual menu"; it's a "high-end" excursion that may spark "sticker shock", but most maintain it's "worth the trip."

Babouch Moroccan Ⓜ *Moroccan*   26 | 25 | 24 | $40

San Pedro | 810 S. Gaffey St. (bet. W. 8th & W. 9th Sts.) | 310-831-0246 | www.babouchrestaurant.com

Tricked out like an "Arabian prince's palace", this veteran San Pedro Moroccan is an "exotic" "experience" with its "sumptuous" Bedouin decor, "delish" eats and "entertaining" belly dancers and tarot readers; "the meal will take some time" and the "low tables" "could be more comfortable", but it's still a hit for "a great night out" with a group.

Baby Blues BBQ *BBQ*   22 | 15 | 19 | $26

West Hollywood | 7953 Santa Monica Blvd. (Hayworth Ave.) | 323-656-1277 | www.babyblueswh.com
Venice | 444 Lincoln Blvd. (Rose Ave.) | 310-396-7675 | www.babybluesvenice.com

"Chow down" on a "belly-busting meal" of "total man food" at this "legit" Venice BBQ joint and its marginally "fancier" West Hollywood spin-off, "four-napkin" purveyors of "killer", "Fred Flintstone-esque" ribs; they're known for "long waits" and "whistle-stop decor" relieved by "eye-candy" servers, and while the tabs may run "high for a hole-in-the-wall", you'll "roll yourself" out, baby.

Baby's Badass Burgers ⌘ *Burgers*   ∇ 24 | 17 | 22 | $16

Location varies; see website | 877-962-2297 | www.babysbadassburgers.com
"Seriously awesome burgers" "plus a cute staff equals dining heaven" at this hot pink–hued food truck, where the 'Burger Babes' shtick – namely the crew of "lively", "pretty" ladies – doesn't overshadow some "of the best" patties in town; flirty menu monikers like She's Smokin', Cougar and The Perfect 10 further a "fun" bite that's "amazing for its price."

Back Abbey ◐ ⊠ *Burgers*   25 | 20 | 19 | $24

Claremont | 128 Oberlin Ave. (1st St.) | 909-625-2642 | www.thebackabbey.com

"Decadent" burgers and "wicked fries" "cooked in duck fat" put this "lively" Claremont gastropub on the culinary map, and the "huge selection" of "rare, tasty" Belgian brews poured by "personable" 'tenders have "local" backers "quite enamored"; the "rustic", Mission-style dining room "can get a bit cramped", so "plan on an early start" to snag "patio" seating – and "call a cab" home.

Back Home in Lahaina *Hawaiian*

20 | 18 | 20 | $19

Carson | 519 E. Carson St. (Grace Ave.) | 310-835-4014
Manhattan Beach | 916 N. Sepulveda Blvd. (9th St.) | 310-374-0111
www.backhomeinlahaina.com

"Epic" fried chicken, long rice and other "ono" grinds are "uniformly fattening", but they'll "send you straight back to the Islands" at this "authentic" "taste of Hawaii" in Carson and Manhattan Beach; some snipe at the "slow" service and "half-hearted decor", but given the "good value" they "serve their purpose well."

NEW Baco Mercat ⬧ *Sandwiches*

26 | 20 | 21 | $33

Downtown | 408 S. Main St. (4th St.) | 213-687-8808 |
www.bacomercat.com

"Creative" chef-owner Josef Centeno (ex Lazy Ox Canteen) "must have made some sort of pact with the devil to create" the "ridiculously delicious" bäco, an "intense" "sandwich-taco fusion" that's the signature of this "dang original" Downtown newcomer; the "beautifully executed" Mex-Mideastern dishes and "hip but not off-putting" vibes draw a clientele that spans the spectrum from "suits and ties to tats and jeans."

B.A.D. SUSHI *Japanese*

23 | 18 | 22 | $29

West LA | 11617 Santa Monica Blvd. (Federal Ave.) | 310-479-4910 |
www.badsushi.net

"Don't let the name fool you" at this West LA Japanese, which area devotees deem "anything but bad" (the name stands for 'best and delicious') thanks to the sushi samurais cutting up "creative rolls"; "quick", "friendly service" offsets the nondescript decor, and yen-watchers confirm the prices are pretty "good."

Bahooka *Polynesian*

21 | 26 | 22 | $28

Rosemead | 4501 Rosemead Blvd. (Lower Azusa Rd.) | 626-285-1241 |
www.bahooka.com

"One of the few" "vintage tiki watering holes" in the Southland, Rosemead's "old-school Polynesian" "monument" features "fish tanks overlooking private booths" in a "labyrinthine" space (Rufus, the infamous "carrot-eating" paku, is still afloat); throw in the "requisite flaming" "tropical drinks", and even some say if the "food is ordinary", hooked habitués "just want to stay on this island forever."

Baja Cantina ◐ *Mexican*

18 | 18 | 19 | $25

Marina del Rey | 311 Washington Blvd. (Pacific Ave.) | 310-821-2252 |
www.bajacantina.com

"Enthusiastic" staffers slinging "strong drinks" and "decent" "bar food" boost the "party atmosphere" at this Marina del Rey Mexican just "blocks from the beach" that's open till 2 AM daily; with water views and twin patios, it's almost "too busy" "with the locals" – "for a good reason."

Baja Sharkeez *Mexican*

18 | 18 | 16 | $21

Hermosa Beach | 52 Pier Ave. (bet. Beach Dr. & Hermosa Ave.) |
310-318-0004 ◐

(continued)

Baja Sharkeez

Manhattan Beach | 3600 Highland Ave. (36th St.) | 310-545-8811
www.sharkeez.net

The "frat-party" "rowdies" and "happy-hour" deals deliver an *uno-dos*
punch at these "Mexican dive bars" in Hermosa and Manhattan Beach,
where the "cost depends upon your level of drinking"; foodwise they're
just "ok", but if you "grab a few friends" and wear your "team jersey on
game night, you won't be alone."

The Baker *Bakery/Sandwiches*

23 | 16 | 20 | $18

Woodland Hills | 21600 Ventura Blvd. (bet. Baza & De Roja Aves.) |
818-340-1987 | www.thebakerbread.com

"Don't let the plain storefront fool you", this low-key bakery/cafe in a
Woodland Hills strip mall is "a go-to" for "excellent" artisan breads
and "yummy" breakfasts and lunch items and "homemade soups"
at sensible prices; there's often "a line to get in", but locals insist
it's "worth it."

Baleen Los Angeles *American*

24 | 25 | 24 | $43

Redondo Beach | Portofino Hotel & Yacht Club | 260 Portofino Way
(Harbor Dr.) | 310-372-1202 | www.hotelportofino.com

A "lovely", "soft"-lit dining room overlooking "beautiful" King Harbor
and the marina sets a "cozy" scene for "well-prepared", seafood-
centric dishes at this "quiet" Redondo Beach New American nestled in
the Portofino Hotel & Yacht Club; per usual for a resort eatery, one can
expect "discreet service" and tabs "on the pricey side."

Bamboo *Caribbean*

22 | 17 | 21 | $26

Culver City | 10835 Venice Blvd. (bet. Overland Ave. & Sepulveda Blvd.) |
310-287-0668 | www.bamboorestaurant.net

For "lovers of exotic spices", the "down-home Caribbean food" is "da
bomb" at this "casual" Culver City joint, a "neighborhood staple" also
favored for its "no-attitude" service; the decor's decidedly "nothing
fancy", but a few "yummy" mojitos on the bamboo-bordered patio will
"transport you to the islands" ("well, almost").

Bamboo Cuisine *Chinese*

23 | 19 | 21 | $26

Sherman Oaks | 14010 Ventura Blvd. (bet. Costello & Murietta Aves.) |
818-788-0202 | www.bamboocuisine.com

"Crowded for a reason", this "relaxed" Sherman Oaks "standby" ranks
among "the best Chinese in the Valley" for "solid" chow ferried by "efficient servers" to tables with "lazy Suzans" where parties can "share
family-style"; between the "dependable quality" and fair prices, the
"locals love it" whether to "eat in or take out."

Bandera *Southwestern*

24 | 22 | 22 | $37

West LA | 11700 Wilshire Blvd. (Barrington Ave.) | 310-477-3524 |
www.hillstone.com

Like a "sexy" version of Houston's, this West LA chain spin-off is a
"consistent" "winner" for "solid" Southwestern-American fare according to "well-heeled" "grown-ups" who applaud the "attentive" service
and "attractive" environs replete with "leather booths", "live jazz" and
a "hoppin'" "singles bar"; while it's "not cheap", all that "scenery"
draws "crowds like a movie opening."

Bangkok West *Thai*

23 | 21 | 23 | $26

Santa Monica | 606 Santa Monica Blvd. (6th St.) | 310-395-9658 | www.bangkokwestthaicuisine.com

"Upscalish" airs and an "expansive menu" of "wonderful" "standards" take things "up a notch from your typical Thai" at this "reliable" Santa Monican "conveniently located" near The Promenade; the "attentive service" and "white tablecloths" justify tabs that skew "a bit pricier" than its "local" rivals.

Banzai Sushi *Japanese*

25 | 17 | 21 | $37

Calabasas | 23508 Calabasas Rd. (Valley Circle Blvd.) | 818-222-5800 | www.banzaisushi.com

The "surprising quality" of its "consistently fresh and delicious" rolls bolsters the rep of this informal Calabasas Japanese among area sushiphiles; add a "friendly" feel, "reasonable prices" and a shady patio, and it's an "excellent choice" when that raw-fish "craving" strikes.

Bao Dim Sum House *Chinese*

22 | 22 | 22 | $27

Beverly Boulevard | 8256 Beverly Blvd. (Sweetzer Ave.) | 323-655-6556 | www.baodimsum.com

"Bao wow!" bay fans of the "melt-in-your-mouth" dumplings and other "tasty" (albeit "not totally authentic") "dim sum classics" at this Beverly Boulevard Chinese, a "rare find" for folks who "don't want to drive to Monterey Park"; the "made-to-order" menu and "contemporary" milieu may explain why it's "spendy" for its kind.

Bar | Kitchen ●◻ *American*

24 | 24 | 20 | $36

Downtown | O Hotel | 819 S. Flower St. (bet. 8th & 9th Sts.) | 213-623-9904 | www.barandkitchenla.com

Downtown's boutique O Hotel berths this "charming" bar/eatery in "funky" neo-rustic digs, where "creative" American grub ("really wonderful small plates" included) is matched with craft beers, small-production wines and "incredible" custom cocktails; hedgers suggest "it's still coming into its own", "but the scene and food make up for" any misgivings.

Bar Bouchon *French*

24 | 24 | 22 | $40

Beverly Hills | 235 N. Cañon Dr. (bet. Dayton Way & Wilshire Blvd.) | 310-271-9910 | www.bouchonbistro.com

This "easily accessible" "cafe version" of Thomas Keller's Beverly Hills bistro upstairs will leave you "dreaming of Paris" with a small-plates lineup of "scrumptious" French dishes and "swell cocktails" served at an "elegant" zinc bar or on a "wonderfully civilized veranda for alfresco dining"; "service is variable", but the bills are low given the chef's pedigree, and "happy-hour prices are excellent."

Barbrix *Italian/Mediterranean*

25 | 20 | 22 | $41

Silver Lake | 2442 Hyperion Ave. (Tracy St.) | 323-662-2442 | www.barbrix.com

"Small plates are where it's at" for "foodies in Silver Lake" who flock to this "inventive" Med-Italian "gem", which matches its "sensational" bites with a "smart wine list" that won't "break the bank"; the "intimate" dining room's often "hopping" with a "convivial" crowd, but the service stays "well informed" and there's a bar and "cute patio" to handle any overflow.

	FOOD	DECOR	SERVICE	COST

NEW Ba Restaurant ⬤ Ⓜ *French* — — — M

Highland Park | 5100 York Blvd. (Ave. 51) | 323-739-6243 |
www.restaurantba.com

This Highland Park French brings a touch of European elegance to a
working-class neighborhood, with an open kitchen turning out classic,
moderately priced Gallic fare and seasonally inspired, globally flavored specials; the husband-and-wife team behind the sun-drenched
restaurant goes for a baroque punk-rock vibe, with pastel-pink walls
offset by black framework.

Bar Hayama ⬤ *Japanese* 25 24 23 $46

West LA | 1803 Sawtelle Blvd. (Nebraska Ave.) | 310-235-2000 |
www.bar-hayama.com

"Dining by the light" of a "gorgeous" fire pit is a "romantic" *hai* point at
this "excellent" West LA Japanese, where chef-owner Toshi Sugiura's
"talented" team turns out "fresh", "inventive" sushi and small plates
paired with an "interesting sake list" until 1 AM most nights; the
"knowledgeable staff" and smooth "modern" decor keep the feel
"comfortable" "inside or out."

Barney Greengrass *Deli* 23 19 19 $32

Beverly Hills | Barneys New York | 9570 Wilshire Blvd. (bet. Camden &
Peck Drs.) | 310-777-5877

"Ladies and agents who lunch" hit this Jewish "deli gone chic" atop
Barneys for "first-rate" smoked fish, bagels and other "nosh" essen-
tials worthy of the NYC original; while the prices are almost as "exag-
gerated" as they are downstairs, the terrace's "beautiful views" ("famous
faces" included) are a "treat when you feel like splurging."

Barney's Beanery ⬤ *Eclectic* 17 19 18 $21

West Hollywood | 8447 Santa Monica Blvd. (bet. Holloway & Olive Drs.) |
323-654-2287

Santa Monica | Third St. Promenade | 1351 Third St. Promenade
(Santa Monica Blvd.) | 310-656-5777 Ⓢ

Westwood | 1037 Broxton Ave. (Weyburn Ave.) | 310-443-7777

Pasadena | 99 E. Colorado Blvd. (N. Arroyo Pkwy.) | 626-405-9777

Burbank | 250 N. First St. (E. Palm Ave.) | 818-524-2912
www.barneysbeanery.com

The "legendary" WeHo roadhouse oozes "rock 'n' roll history", while
the "raucous" spin-offs – "kitschy theme-park versions of the original" –
capture the "platonic ideal of a college hangout", with "beer and
grease" ("a billion ways to have potato skins") and "more TVs than
Best Buy"; service is "hit-or-miss" and the "vast" Eclectic menu is "mediocre", but "who comes here for the food" anyway?

Barney's Gourmet Hamburgers *Burgers* 22 13 19 $17

Brentwood | 11660 San Vicente Blvd. (bet. Barrington & Darlington Aves.) |
310-447-6000

Santa Monica | Brentwood Country Mart | 225 26th St. (San Vicente Blvd.) |
310-899-0133

Sherman Oaks | Westfield Fashion Sq. | 14006 Riverside Dr.
(Woodman Ave.) | 818-808-0680
www.barneyshamburgers.com

"Variety" brings burger buffs to this SF-based trio, which furnish
"juicy, cooked-to-order" beef, fowl and veggie patties "styled a zillion

different ways" plus "super" fries (and even noteworthy salads, "but why bother?"); they're "informal joints" and service is uneven, but for an "affordable" feed this is a "good bet"; P.S. the Brentwood Country Mart site is alfresco.

Barone's *Italian/Pizza*
22 | 17 | 20 | $25

Van Nuys | 13726 Oxnard St. (Woodman Ave.) | 818-782-6004 | www.baronesfamousitalian.com

"They don't cut corners" when it comes to flavor at this '40s-era Van Nuys "institution", an "old-timey red-sauce" Italian with retro "red vinyl booths" and weekend live combos that's famed for its "divine" "rectangular pizza"; with its fair prices and "been-there-for-years" staff, as a "longtime family favorite" it's "in a class by itself."

Bar Pintxo *Spanish*
22 | 17 | 19 | $34

Santa Monica | 109 Santa Monica Blvd. (Ocean Ave.) | 310-458-2012 | www.barpintxo.com

Ever a "lively" scene, this pint-sized Santa Monica Spaniard from Joe Miller (Joe's) has supporters "squeezed" in to graze on "scrumptious" "traditional tapas", "addictive" sangria and by-the-glass wines courtesy of "personable" staffers; *sí*, it's a "tight space" and the checks run "pricey", but "go with fun in mind" and it's "like you're in Barcelona."

Barragan's *Mexican*
21 | 17 | 20 | $22

Echo Park | 1538 W. Sunset Blvd. (Echo Park Ave.) | 213-250-4256 Ⓢ Ⓜ
Burbank | 730 N. Victory Blvd. (W. Chandler Blvd.) | 818-848-2325
Glendale | 814 S. Central Ave (bet. W. Garfield Ave. & W. Windsor Rd.) | 213-250-4256
www.barragansrestaurants.com

Though "the name sounds like an Irish pub", locals seeking "standard Mexican fare" for not too many pesos turn to this "reliable neighborhood" trio for "solid" eats in "old-style" environs; maybe "they could use a little sprucing", but the staffers are "courteous" "and quick" – "and you don't leave hungry."

Bar Toscana Ⓢ *Italian*
24 | 24 | 23 | $43

Brentwood | 11633 San Vicente Blvd. (Darlington Ave.) | 310-826-0028 | www.bartoscana.com

Milan-style nibbling in sleek digs has "trendy" "locals" touting this "Brentwood watering hole" alongside Toscana, where the "wonderful" stuzzichini (small plates) are almost overshadowed by the "meticulously crafted cocktails" and "attractive" waiters "with Italian accents"; given the "upscale pickup scene" featuring "the future housewives of Brentwood", needless to say the tabs "aren't cheap."

🄏 Bashan Ⓜ *American*
28 | 21 | 26 | $57

Montrose | 3459 N. Verdugo Rd. (bet. Ocean View & Sunview Blvds.) | 818-541-1532 | www.bashanrestaurant.com

A "culinary highlight of the 818", chef/co-owner Nadav Bashan's "fabulous" "sleeper" in Montrose "hews to seasonal fare", offering "creative, exceptional" New American cuisine with "caring" service in a "small", "tasteful" setting decorated with grass wallpaper and Danish fixtures; though some would prefer more space, most agree the "expensive" tabs are "worth every bit."

	FOOD	DECOR	SERVICE	COST

NEW Bashi *Asian* — — — E

Rancho Palos Verdes | Terranea Resort | 100 Terranea Way
(Palos Verdes Dr. S.) | 310-265-2800 | www.terranea.com
Sitting pretty on the edge of the Pacific in the Terranea Resort in Palos
Verdes, this pricey Pan-Asian combines an ocean view with fusiony
small plates from the other side of the sea; the wood-heavy dining
room screens Japanese art films on the wall, but most diners opt to sit
alfresco in the heated patio and watch the fog roll in.

Basix Cafe *Californian/Italian* 20 17 19 $24

West Hollywood | 8333 Santa Monica Blvd. (Flores St.) | 323-848-2460 |
www.basixcafe.com
Living up to its name, this WeHo "neighborhood joint" "gets the job
done" with "well-made", "uncomplicated" Cal-Italian eats (especially
for brunch or breakfast) at a "decent" price; despite occasional "service with a snicker", most find it "welcoming" with a "lively, diverse
crowd" and "excellent" outdoor people-watching, adding a bit of
"Hollywood charm and chatter."

Bay Cities Deli ⓜ *Deli* 26 11 16 $14

Santa Monica | 1517 Lincoln Blvd. (bet. B'way & Colorado Ave.) |
310-395-8279 | www.bcdeli.com
"The rock star of Italian delis", this "Santa Monica institution" is beloved for its "life-changing" Godmother sub with the works and other
"delish" sammies on "fabulous", "freshly baked" bread, plus "unique
imported gourmet goodies that can't be found elsewhere"; parking
can feel "like driving in a demolition derby", and in spite of an "efficient" counter staff, "half of LA is lined up for a fix" – so "do yourself a
favor" and order online for faster pickup.

⛛ The Bazaar by José Andrés ⓞ *Spanish* 27 28 25 $83

Beverly Hills | SLS at Beverly Hills | 465 S. La Cienega Blvd. (Clifton Way) |
310-246-5555 | www.thebazaar.com
"Go with an open mind and be dazzled" by this "crazy gourmet circus"
in the SLS Hotel from "mad genius" José Andrés that will leave you
"giddy" thanks to "mind-blowingly delicious" Spanish-inspired small
plates and cocktails "that look like they were made in chemistry
class", all presented with "extra care"; just prepare for "sensory
overload" when it comes to the "noisy", "luxe" Philippe Starck–designed
space (including a "whimsical" patisserie), and "make sure your wallet can take it."

BCD Tofu House *Korean* 22 14 17 $16

Koreatown | 3575 Wilshire Blvd. (Kingsley Ave.) |
213-382-6677 ⓞ
Koreatown | 869 S. Western Ave. (bet. 8th & 9th Sts.) | 213-380-3807 ⓞ
Cerritos | 11818 South St. (Pioneer Blvd.) | 562-809-8098
Torrance | 1607 Sepulveda Blvd. (Western Ave.) | 310-534-3480
Reseda | 18044 Saticoy St. (Lindley Ave.) | 818-342-3535 ⓞ
Rowland Heights | Yes Plaza | 1731 Fullerton Rd. (Colima Rd.) |
626-964-7073 ⓞ
www.bcdtofu.com
"Warning: the spicy soft tofu is extremely habit-forming" at this "late-
night" mini-chain meting out big bowls of "delicious" "piping-hot tofu
soup", bibimbop and other "Seoul-style" comfort food; the decor is

nothing to speak of and the "hard-working" staff is often "harried" ("you have to practically trip someone to get the check"), but "cheap" and "satisfying" trump all.

Beach Pizza *Pizza*
24 | 13 | 19 | $21

Marina del Rey | 8601 Lincoln Blvd. (Manchester Ave.) | 310-827-2000

Manhattan Beach | 3301 Highland Ave. (33rd Pl.) | 310-546-5401 | www.eatbeachpizza.com

Known for some of the "best pizza in the South Bay", this longtime local duo in Manhattan Beach and Marina del Rey makes its pies "just a little crispy" with "lots of topping options" (such as shrimp scampi), sided with "amazing" salads; you can "spot the beach" from the rustic, brick-house digs in Manhattan Beach, but many make it a "favorite for takeout."

Beachwood BBQ Ⓜ *BBQ*
25 | 19 | 22 | $23

Long Beach | 210 E. Third St. (Long Beach Blvd.) | 562-436-4020 | www.beachwoodbbq.com

Both the clientele and atmosphere are "buzzing" at this midcentury-style Long Beach BBQ "winner" where a "knowledgeable" staff pours a "fantastic array" of affordable "craft beers", some "brewed on premises", to go with "melt-in-your-mouth", "dry-rub" 'cue and sides with a "new twist"; it's "almost always crowded", but then "all good things are worth the wait, right?"

Beckers Bakery & Deli Ⓜ *Bakery/Deli*
21 | 13 | 18 | $14

Manhattan Beach | 1025 Manhattan Ave. (10th Pl.) | 310-372-3214 | www.beckersbakeryanddeli.com

This "pleasant", '40s-era Manhattan Beach bakery and deli, with its "huge", "old-fashioned" sandwiches and "crowd-pleasing" sweets ("note the colorful surfboard cookies"), proves a cupcake "doesn't have to cost four bucks to taste fantastic"; it's a standard counter-service spot, so many opt to "grab something delicious" and "take it down to the beach."

Beckham Grill *American*
22 | 22 | 23 | $33

Pasadena | 77 W. Walnut St. (Fair Oaks Ave.) | 626-796-3399 | www.beckhamgrill.com

The digs say "English pub" (red telephone box, "old English taxi out front"), but the food takes a Traditional American tack at this "throwback" Pasadena steakhouse specializing in prime rib and other "solid" comfort classics at "value" pricing; the staff is "on the ball" and the "bar doesn't stint", so even if some find it "just fair", it's still a "dependable" "standby", particularly for the "over-65" set.

Beer Belly *Eclectic*
▽ 22 | 21 | 18 | $26

Koreatown | 532 S. Western Ave. (bet. W. 5th & W. 6th Sts.) | 213-387-2337 | www.beerbellyla.com

"It ain't just beer that rounds off your belly here" – the "offbeat" Eclectic grub (like "crazy good" duck-fat fries) is also "worth adding to your waistline" at this modestly priced gastropub in an "unsuspecting" Koreatown location; "waiting in line to order" can be a drag, but the "unique" urban-industrial space with concrete floors, mahogany walls and steel tables is a "cool" place to "hang"; P.S. closed Tuesdays.

	FOOD	DECOR	SERVICE	COST

Belmont Brewing Co. *American*

| | 21 | 21 | 21 | $26 |

Long Beach | 25 39th Pl. (E. Ocean Blvd.) | 562-433-3891 | www.belmontbrewing.com

From its "awesome" "berth by the beach", this "long-running" brew-pub (one of SoCal's first) at Long Beach's Belmont Pier pairs "filling" American fare with an "excellent" list of "quality" "housemade" suds; "casual", "friendly" and "reasonably priced", it corners a "young crowd" vying to "soak up the California sun" on the "hard-to-top" patio.

☑ The Belvedere *American*

| | 27 | 27 | 27 | $72 |

Beverly Hills | Peninsula Beverly Hills | 9882 S. Santa Monica Blvd. (Wilshire Blvd.) | 310-788-2306 | www.peninsula.com

Very "refined", this "elegant throwback" in the Peninsula Hotel "never fails to please" with James Overbaugh's "sophisticated", "fabulous" New American cuisine, including high tea and one of "the most sumptuous power breakfasts on the West coast"; you can expect to be "treated like royalty" in the "intimate", "nestled-away" dining room, so even if it's "a bit stuffy" for some, for most there's "nothing negative except the price."

Benley Vietnamese Kitchen ☒ *Vietnamese*

| | ▽ 28 | 14 | 25 | $26 |

Long Beach | 8191 E. Wardlow Rd. (Norwalk Blvd.) | 562-596-8130

Banh vivants savor the "fresh", "exquisite" Vietnamese dishes – "perpetually well prepared and flavorful" – at this low-cost Long Beach "phenomenon" "tucked in an unassuming strip mall"; while the "intimate" digs aren't the "Ritz-Carlton", it's "charming" enough with a "wonderful, efficient" staff.

Berlin Currywurst *German*

| | 24 | 17 | 25 | $13 |

Silver Lake | 3827 W. Sunset Blvd. (Hyperion Ave.) | 323-663-1989 | www.berlincurrywurst.com

Offering a "new take on German street food", this "first-rate" Silver Laker delivers "the best" of the wurst, with a "shockingly affordable" menu of "snappy" sausage and "spicy" sauces to "make your own currywurst" (matched with "great fries"); the "delightful young" Berliners who run the joint and a "hip", "minimalist"-industrial backdrop temper any complaints about "limited seating."

Beso ☒ *Pan-Latin*

| | 19 | 24 | 19 | $53 |

Hollywood | 6350 Hollywood Blvd. (Ivar Ave.) | 323-467-7991 | www.besohollywood.com

With a "fabulous" "Hollywood atmosphere" beneath the exposed beams and chandeliers, it's no wonder "pretty people" "pack the bar" of Eva Longoria and chef Todd English's Pan-Latin "hot spot"; though critics call the "expensive" menu "lackluster" (apart from "lovely presentations") and service gets "so-so" marks, most concede "it's a place to be seen, not a foodie haven."

Best Fish Taco in Ensenada *Mexican*

| | 22 | 10 | 16 | $10 |

Los Feliz | 1650 Hillhurst Ave. (Prospect Ave.) | 323-466-5552 | www.bestfishtacoinensenada.com

The tiny menu "rocks" at this "funky" Los Feliz Mex turning out "fresh, tasty" Baja-style shrimp and fish tacos "in a flash", topped by salsas "ranging from sweet to 'get the fire extinguisher'"; with a "no-frills", "beach-bum" setting and "relaxing" patio, it's a "favorite" "budget bite in the neighborhood"; P.S. ask for the underground menu.

	FOOD	DECOR	SERVICE	COST

NEW BierBeisl ●☒ Austrian — — — M

Beverly Hills | 9669 Santa Monica Blvd. (Bedford Dr.) | 310-271-7274 | www.bierbeisl-la.com

"Terrific Austrian food" is the draw at this moderately priced, "late-night" Beverly Hills newcomer from Patina alum Bernhard Mairinger, whose menu includes three types of schnitzel – turkey, veal and pork – along with rotating sausage-and-beer pairings; the "relaxed" woodsy setting has a long communal stammtisch table and even a schnapps bar, leading fans to declare "watch out, Puck!"

NEW Biergarten at The Standard ● German — — — I

Downtown | The Standard Downtown LA | 550 S. Flower St. (W. 6th St.) | 213-892-8080 | www.standardhotels.com

There's no shortage of irony at this modern beer garden serving up classic German sausages, big pretzels and brews from the roof of The Standard Downtown; basking in "magnificent views", youthful, "über-trendy" guests line up at a wood-shingled booth to buy tickets for each meal, then park at the communal picnic tables or play foosball while waitresses in dirndl-themed T-shirts wielding hefty steins drive home the campy theme.

Big Mama's Rib Shack Ⓜ BBQ/Soul Food — 23 15 21 $24

Pasadena | 1453 N. Lake Ave. (Rio Grande St.) | 626-797-1792 | www.bigmamas-ribshack.com

"Classic soul food" is alive and well at this "welcoming" family-owned Pasadena eatery that brings together "excellent" BBQ ribs, fried chicken and sides with "live blues" on Tuesday and Saturday nights; the room is on the "shabby" side, but most agree "you come here for the food and not the looks."

Big Wok Mongolian BBQ Mongolian — 22 12 19 $16

Manhattan Beach | 250 N. Sepulveda Blvd. (2nd St.) | 310-798-1155

"Small but mighty", this "busy" Mongolian barbecue in Manhattan Beach comes through with a "tasty" array of meat, vegetables and "spicy" sauces that you select and see "cooked to order" on "giant, scorching hot stones"; the room is "spare", but it's "fast" and "cheap", and kids will flip for the "wok experience."

Billingsley's Steak — 17 13 20 $27

West LA | 11326 W. Pico Blvd. (Sawtelle Blvd.) | 310-477-1426 | www.billingsleysrestaurant.com

Though it's no longer owned by the family of June Cleaver (Barbara Billingsley), this "nostalgic" West LA "institution" will still "transport you to 1956 when red Naugahyde was the rage" and "hearty family fare" consisted of steaks, martinis and "all the cheese toast you could muster"; early birds dig the waitresses who "talk your ears off", as well as the "modest" tabs.

Billy's Deli — 21 14 19 $21

Torrance | 5160 W. 190th St. (Anza Ave.) | 310-371-0168
Glendale | 216 N. Orange St. (Wilson Ave.) | 818-246-1689
www.billysdeli.com

"When you need a deli fix", this "New York-style" duo in Glendale and Torrance does the trick with "traditional", "heaped-high" corned beef sandwiches and "large, inexpensive breakfasts", plus burgers and other American eats, set down by "personality-plus" waitresses; the "'40s" decor in the original Glendale locale may look "aged", but that's just part of the "charm."

Bistro de la Gare ◼ French   21 | 18 | 19 | $38

South Pasadena | 921 Meridian Ave. (bet. El Centro & Mission Sts.) | 626-799-8828 | www.bistrodelagare.com

This "casual" "little French bistro" next to the South Pas Gold Line is a "world unto itself", turning out a "tight menu" of "well-executed" fare amid "comfortable" old-world surroundings (complete with antique mahogany bar); though the "friendly Frenchmen" sometimes provide uneven service, "moderate" prices enhance the "value."

Bistro 45 ◼ Californian   26 | 24 | 25 | $52

Pasadena | 45 S. Mentor Ave. (bet. Colorado Blvd. & Green St.) | 626-795-2478 | www.bistro45.com

"Winning in every regard", this Californian tucked down a quiet side street in Pasadena offers a "refined" yet "innovative" menu abetted by a "stupendous" wine list and "thoughtful" service; it may be "expensive" for the area, but with "beautiful" restyled art deco surroundings, it's still a "favorite" for "a special night out."

Bistro Garden at Coldwater Continental   21 | 26 | 23 | $49

Studio City | 12950 Ventura Blvd. (Coldwater Canyon Ave.) | 818-501-0202 | www.bistrogarden.com

An "airy" "winter garden" with light streaming through "gorgeous casement windows" makes for "elegant" dining at this "pricey" Studio City locale, one of the "last bastions" in the Valley for "tasteful" Continental fare with "attentive" service (as well as live piano at dinner); some say the food "comes in second to the ambiance", but an "older crowd" still counts it as a "special place to celebrate."

Bistro Provence ◧ French   23 | 18 | 23 | $39

Burbank | Lakeside Ctr. | 345 N. Pass Ave. (Rte. 134) | 818-840-9050 | www.bistroprovenceburbank.com

"One of the hidden treasures in Burbank" muse mavens of this "unassuming" strip-mall bistro specializing in "high-quality", "beautifully prepared" Southern French cooking that's particularly "affordable" for weekday lunches; the "tiny" space leaves almost "no room for decor", but a "personable" crew lends it lots of "warmth."

BJ's Pub Food   23 | 22 | 22 | $24

Cerritos | 11101 183rd St. (Studebaker Rd.) | 562-467-0850 | www.bjsrestaurants.com ◑

Westwood | 939 Broxton Ave. (bet. Le Conte & Weyburn Aves.) | 310-209-7475 | www.bjsbrewhouse.com ◑

Long Beach | 5258 E. Second St. (bet. Covina & Laverne Aves.) | 562-439-8181 | www.bjsbrewhouse.com

Moreno Valley | 22920 Centerpoint Dr. (Frederick St.) | 951-571-9370 | www.bjsrestaurants.com ◑

Arcadia | 400 E. Huntington Dr. (bet. 5th & 2nd Aves.) | 626-462-1494 | www.bjsrestaurants.com ◑

Burbank | 107 S. First St. (Angeleno Ave.) | 818-557-0881 | www.bjsbrewhouse.com

(continued)

(continued)

BJ's

Woodland Hills | 6424 Canoga Ave. (bet. Erwin St. & Victory Blvd.) | 818-340-1748 | www.bjsbrewhouse.com

West Covina | Eastland Shopping Ctr. | 2917 E. Eastland Center Dr. (N. Baranca St.) | 626-858-0054 | www.bjsrestaurants.com ●

Westlake Village | 3955 E. Thousand Oaks Blvd. (Westlake Blvd.) | 805-497-9393 | www.bjsrestaurants.com ●

Valencia | Valencia Town Ctr. | 24320 Town Center Dr. (McBean Pkwy.) | 661-288-1299 | www.bjsrestaurants.com

Additional locations throughout Southern California

"Can you say 'Pizookie'" ask fans of this "reasonable", family-friendly American chain, which offers "manhole-cover-thick" deep-dish pizzas, "seasonal" brewskis and other "decent" pub fare in a "raucous" sports-bar environment; true, contrarians may point to "variable" service, but if you're going to "watch the game", "who cares?"

Black Angus *Steak* | 23 | 21 | 22 | $34 |

Lakewood | 5000 Candlewood St. (Clarke Ave.) | 562-531-6921

Torrance | 3405 W. Carson St. (Madrona Ave.) | 310-370-1523

Ontario | 3640 Porsche Way (N. Haven Ave.) | 909-944-6882

Burbank | 235 S. First St. (E. Tujunga Ave.) | 818-848-8880

Northridge | 9145 Corbin Ave. (Nordhoff Pl.) | 818-701-1600

Whittier | 15500 Whittier Blvd. (Cullen St.) | 562-947-2200

www.blackangus.com

A "safe bet" for "budget-conscious" carnivores, this chain delivers "dependably delicious" steaks and "fancy drinks" at "reasonable" rates, especially if you keep an eye out for "coupons aplenty"; servers get you in and out "fast", although a few find it "feels like herding cattle", while others insist the "homey" "country" decor could use an "update."

Black Cat Bakery *American* | 21 | 18 | 21 | $17 |

Fairfax | 519 S. Fairfax Ave. (bet. Maryland Dr. & W. 5th St.) | 323-932-1500 | www.blackcatla.com

"Belly up" to the counter to order at this little American cafe on Fairfax supplying a "pleasing" menu of inexpensive breakfast and lunch "staples" – including "fantastic" housemade pastries and breads – jazzed up with a few "intriguing" surprises (like farro bibimbop); even if full table service "would be nice", its "quirky" "neighborhood" appeal is good enough for most; P.S. open till 6 PM.

Black Dog Coffee *Coffeehouse* | 22 | 16 | 20 | $13 |

Mid-City | 5657 Wilshire Blvd. (Hauser Blvd.) | 323-933-1976 | www.blackdogcoffee.com

LACMA-goers and local office workers refuel at this "wonderful little" Mid-City coffeehouse dispensing "outstanding daily soups", "packed sandwiches with flair" and "custom hot dogs" – not to mention "great coffee"; set in a simple storefront with "personable" service, it's a "good bet" for "grabbing a quick bite" or "snacks for meetings", and "makes your everyday pickup lunch special."

NEW Black Hogg Ⓜ *American* | - | - | - | M |

Silver Lake | 2852 W. Sunset Blvd. (Silver Lake Blvd.) | 323-953-2820 | www.blackhogg.com

This storefront New American sits on a Silver Lake block where it offers a midpriced menu with oysters in spicy pickle juice, roasted marrow bones with an heirloom carrot salad and toast spread with uni; the space is cleanly functional, with blond-wood tables, chairs covered with black fabric and lots of mirrors on the wall to give the illusion of space.

Black Market Liquor Bar ● *Eclectic* | 24 | 23 | 22 | $39

Studio City | 11915 Ventura Blvd. (Carpenter Ave.) | 818-446-2533 | www.blackmarketliquorbar.com

"Antonia Lofaso's *Top Chef* talents shine" at this late-night gastropub in Studio City, turning out an Eclectic mix of "fantastic" market-driven small plates designed to go with the "innovative" stylings of "stellar mix-ologists"; the "casual" room's "curved brick ceiling and candlelight help set a romantic atmosphere" and the staff "works as a team", but "be prepared for a loud crowd", a "long wait" and somewhat "pricey" bites.

Blair's *American* | 25 | 21 | 23 | $42

Silver Lake | 2903 Rowena Ave. (bet. Glendale Blvd. & Hyperion Ave.) | 323-660-1882 | www.blairsrestaurant.com

This "lovely" Silver Laker wins hearts with its "phenomenal" short ribs, mac 'n' cheese and other "chilly-evening" New American dishes "prepared with care" and served by a "casual but professional" staff in a "calm" setting warmed up with terra-cotta tones; slightly upscale yet "fairly priced", it's an "unexpected gem" for the neighborhood.

BLD *American* | 22 | 19 | 20 | $34

Beverly Boulevard | 7450 Beverly Blvd. (Vista St.) | 323-930-9744 | www.bldrestaurant.com

"All hail" chef Neal Fraser who "spruces up old staples" in "thoughtful" ways at this "decently priced" New American on Beverly Boulevard, famous for "amazing blueberry ricotta pancakes" at its "dandy", "crowded" brunch (it's "secretly fantastic for lunch and dinner too, without all the chaos"); the staff lends a "pleasant" air to the "bright, open" space, which is a bit "austere" but "cool without being pretentious."

Bloom Cafe *Californian* | 24 | 17 | 20 | $20

Mid-City | 5544 W. Pico Blvd. (Sierra Bonita Ave.) | 323-934-6900 | www.bloomcafe.com

"Conscious eaters" say "yes, please!" to the "healthful, delicious twists" on traditional eats at this "cute", all-day Cal-American BYO in Mid-City; with a "laid-back" vibe and "friendly" service, plus colorful digs and "reasonable prices", it's a "darn-good neighborhood cafe."

Blossom *Vietnamese* | 22 | 12 | 19 | $17

Downtown | 426 S. Main St. (Winston St.) | 213-623-1973 ⊠
NEW **Silver Lake** | 4019 W. Sunset Blvd. (Sanborn Ave.) | 323-953-8345
www.blossomrestaurant.com

Pho phans hankering for "healthy" Vietnamese head to this super-"chill" duo in Downtown and Silver Lake for the "dependable" signature soup and other "fresh", "flavorful" Saigon standards, along with a "surprisingly sophisticated" wine list; expect "fast" service and a "funky, modern" vibe in a casual setting – though without "sky-high prices."

BLT Steak ⊠Ⓜ *Steak* | 26 | 24 | 23 | $68

West Hollywood | Sunset Plaza | 8720 W. Sunset Blvd. (Sunset Plaza Dr.) | 310-360-1950 | www.bltsteak.com

At this "glam" West Hollywood chophouse, a "high-powered" clientele straight "out of central casting" tucks into "terrific" steaks and "interesting" sides (like the "fab" signature popovers) in a sleek, "well-designed" setting presided over by a "gracious" team; the "classy" package is certainly worthy of a "special occasion", just "watch out for sticker shock when you get the bill."

☑ Bludso's BBQ Ⓜ *BBQ*   27 | 9 | 20 | $22

Compton | 811 S. Long Beach Blvd. (Alondra Blvd.) | 310-637-1342 | www.bludsosbbqandcatering.com

The Texas-style barbecue is "lip-smackin' good" at this budget-friendly Compton pit stop, which cooks up meats "so tender you want to weep" (the brisket is "off the charts"), plus desserts such as red-velvet cake; the "sweet, helpful" staff obliges, but with only limited counter seats available, regulars suggest "taking it home and pigging out."

NEW Blue Cow Kitchen ☒ *American/Eclectic*   ▽ 23 | 22 | 23 | $26

Downtown | Two California Plaza | 350 S. Grand Ave. (3rd St.) | 213-621-2249 | www.bluecowkitchen.com

A "unique concept" in the Downtown area, this midpriced New American–Eclectic from the Mendocino Farms folks proffers "stand-out" sandwiches, small plates and retro cocktails with "trendy" twists (think "to-die-for" short-rib French dip) in a quirky, wood-and-chalkboard–bedecked setting; props also go to happy-hour deals and a staff who "checks on you" – making habitués coo "what an experience!"

Blue Dog Beer Tavern *American*   21 | 20 | 20 | $19

Sherman Oaks | 4524 Saugus Ave. (Greenleaf St.) | 818-990-2583 | www.bluedogbeertavern.com

"Creative" specialty burgers and other American grub, plus an "endless" selection of craft brews, make this inexpensive dog-themed tavern in Sherman Oaks a neighborhood "winner"; cat-ankerous sorts may feel the wood-walled setting, equipped with flat-screen TVs, can get "loud", but a "comfy", Fido-friendly patio and "helpful" staff keep such barks at bay.

Blue Hen *Vietnamese*   ▽ 21 | 16 | 19 | $18

Eagle Rock | 1743 Colorado Blvd. (Argus Dr.) | 323-982-9900 | www.eatatbluehen.com

This "no-nonsense" eatery in an Eagle Rock strip mall produces "fresh" twists on Vietnamese classics – using local, organic ingredients in its banh mi and "addictive" spring rolls; maybe it's "not the best", but for an inexpensive, takeout-ready spot, it's just "what you want."

Blue Plate *American*   21 | 16 | 19 | $24

Santa Monica | 1415 Montana Ave. (bet. 14th &15th Sts.) | 310-260-8877 | www.blueplatesantamonica.com

For a "little of everything", locals visit this Santa Monica "neighborhood haunt", where "simple" American "comfort food" is served by a "friendly" crew in a bright, "beachy" atmosphere; some say the "cramped" digs "can get noisy", but the outdoor seating and mild prices provide regulars with enough "fuel" for area shopping.

Bluewater Grill *Seafood*   23 | 21 | 22 | $36

Redondo Beach | King Harbor Marina | 665 N. Harbor Dr. (Beryl St.) | 310-318-3474 | www.bluewatergrill.com

Waterfront dining with a harbor view is a "pleasure" at this "affordable" seafood chainlet's Redondo Beach outpost, where locals "set their hooks" for a "broad" selection of "well-prepared" traditional fish dishes; the "friendly" service and "relaxing" nautical-themed ambiance also charm, and if culinary adventurers say it'll "leave you blue", most feel it's "reliable."

Blu Jam *American/European*   25 | 19 | 23 | $23

Mid-City | 7371 Melrose Ave. (bet. Fuller & Martle Aves.) | 323-951-9191 | www.blujamcafe.com

"Popular with weekend brunchers", this Mid-City "gem" delivers "creative" American-European "comfort food" (the "crunchy French toast is a must-try") with a local-ingredient focus throughout the day; the "super-nice" staff navigates the "cozy" digs well, and though patrons point out "crowds", they generally agree it's "worth the wait."

The Blvd *Californian*   22 | 24 | 23 | $57

Beverly Hills | Beverly Wilshire | 9500 Wilshire Blvd. (Rodeo Dr.) | 310-385-3901 | www.fourseasons.com

"Glam up to be part of the ladies who lunch" at this "lovely" hotel dining room inside the Beverly Wilshire hosting premium "people-watching" in a "beautiful" art deco setting; service is generally "professional", but many find the Californian menu "pricey for what you get", although drinks at the bar is a less-expensive option.

Boa *Steak*   24 | 25 | 23 | $66

West Hollywood | 9200 Sunset Blvd. (Doheny Dr.) | 310-278-2050
Santa Monica | 101 Santa Monica Blvd. (Ocean Ave.) | 310-899-4466
www.boasteak.com

"Feel like a rock star" at this "swanky" Santa Monica and WeHo steakhouse duo, where a "showbiz clientele" laps up the "energetic scene" ("the paparazzi is constantly stationed outside") and "sexy" contemporary ambiance while nibbling "melt-in-your-mouth" meats ferried by "considerate" servers; detractors decry "wallet-emptying" prices and "loud" settings, but to stargazers they're still the "coolest steakhouses in town."

🆕 Boardwalk Fresh   - | - | - | I
Burgers & Fries *Burgers*

Hermosa Beach | 1031 Hermosa Ave. (bet. 11th Ct. & 11th St.) | 310-318-0533 | www.boardwalkfreshburgersandfries.com

The taste of Ocean City, Maryland, comes to Hermosa Beach with this fast-growing, wallet-friendly burger-and-fry chain, which handmakes fresh patties daily and fries potatoes multiple times to achieve the ideal crunchy-crisp texture; the brightly lit, all-glass space, just a block from the pier, is perfect for people-watching while drinking the 'coldest beer in town' – yes, there's a thermometer to ensure that bottles stay crisp at 29.3 degrees.

Bocca *Steak*   22 | 22 | 22 | $36

Encino | 16610 Ventura Blvd. (bet. Petit & Rubio Aves.) | 818-905-5855 | www.boccasteakhouse.com

Kosher steak is the hook at this Encino chophouse, which draws noshers for its broad range of "imaginative" dishes – dispensed with commensurate service (and prices); the patio-outfitted setting and regular live music are attractions too, and as "one of the few" of its genre in the area, it may well merit a "try."

Boccaccio's *Continental*

| 22 | 23 | 22 | $40 |

Westlake Village | 32123 Lindero Canyon Rd. (Lakeview Canyon Rd.) | 818-889-8300 | www.boccacciosonthelake.com

A "drop-dead beautiful" waterside view makes this longtime Westlake Villager optimal for "romantic sunset dinners", which fete diners with "consistently good" Continental cuisine delivered by a "courteous" staff; while detractors assert "you're there for the atmosphere, not the food", regulars note it hits the spot for "special-occasion" dining that's "not very pricey."

Boccali's ⊅ *Italian*

| 24 | 19 | 23 | $27 |

Ojai | 3277 Ojai-Santa Paula Rd. (Reeves Rd.) | 805-646-6116 | www.boccalis.com

"Just-picked freshness" is the calling card of this family-owned Ojai Italian, which uses ingredients from the Boccali farm for "delightful" pizzas, pastas and other standards, paired with wine from its own vineyard; "accommodating" service, moderate prices and a "wonderful", "rustic" setting make it a local "favorite"; P.S. cash and checks only.

Boiling Crab *Cajun/Seafood*

| 25 | 18 | 19 | $28 |

Koreatown | 3377 Wilshire Blvd. (Alexandria Ave.) | 213-389-2722
Alhambra | 33 W. Main St. (bet. 1st St. & Garfield Ave.) | 626-300-5898
Alhambra | 742 W. Valley Blvd. (bet. 7th & 8th Sts.) | 626-576-9368
Rowland Heights | 18902 Gale Ave. (Nogales St.) | 626-964-9300
www.theboilingcrab.com

"Wear a bib" and "get your hands dirty" at this midpriced Cajun-seafood chain where diners dig into "spicy", "magically seasoned" crabs, shrimp and crawfish in a casual "seasidey" setting; some gripe about "waits" and merely "ok" service, but to fans, the food "makes up for everything."

Bollywood Cafe *Indian*

| 24 | 16 | 22 | $23 |

Studio City | 11101 Ventura Blvd. (Vineland Ave.) | 818-508-8400 | www.bollywoodcafela.com

Regulars call this Studio City Indian "a cut above" with "authentic" cooking "with the perfect amount of heat" and plenty of vegetarian options; perhaps the modest setting lacks the pizzazz of the real Bollywood, but "courteous service" and "low prices" make up for it and there's always "fast delivery."

Bombay Cafe *Indian*

| 22 | 15 | 19 | $33 |

West LA | 12021 W. Pico Blvd. (Bundy Dr.) | 310-473-3388 | www.bombaycafe-la.com

After all these years, this West LA Indian still produces "high-quality", "spicy" "street food" ("no tired steam table here") alongside other traditional dishes, plus cocktails such as ginger margaritas – furnished by a "knowledgeable" staff in a "casual" yellow-and-blue setting; a few knock the "upscale prices", but it's certainly "worth going for a Mumbai fix."

Bombay Palace *Indian*

| 24 | 23 | 24 | $39 |

Beverly Hills | 8690 Wilshire Blvd. (bet. Hamel & Willaman Drs.) | 310-659-9944 | www.bombaypalace.com

"Classy and elegant" describes this Beverly Hills Indian, a "tried-and-true" mainstay since 1984 for "celestial", "authentic" fare (including a lunchtime buffet) offered in an upscale space with statues and "dramatic lighting"; allies appreciate the "gracious" servers too, and though some call prices "a little high", "you're paying for the complete package."

Boneyard Bistro ● *BBQ/Eclectic*

| 23 | 17 | 21 | $34 |

Sherman Oaks | 13539 Ventura Blvd. (Woodman Ave.) | 818-906-7427 | www.boneyardbistro.com

"So much more than a BBQ place", this "down-home-meets-Downtown" Sherman Oaks eatery regales diners with both "top-notch" slow-smoked meats and "amazing" Eclectic bistro fare, plus a "dizzying" array of beers; critics call it "pricey" for the genre, but a "knowledge-able" staff and "upscale" environs with a patio help keep it on 'cue.

Border Grill *Mexican*

| 22 | 19 | 20 | $36 |

Downtown | Union Bank Tower | 445 S. Figueroa St. (5th St.) | 213-486-5171
Santa Monica | 1445 Fourth St. (bet. B'way & Santa Monica Blvd.) | 310-451-1655
www.bordergrill.com

Celeb chef-owners Susan Feniger and Mary Sue Milliken are "still the queens" of "smart", "upper-end" "modern Mexican" cuisine made "with flair" as evidenced by these "high-energy" cantinas that's "worth checking out for the happy hour" alone; service is "well informed" and the vibe is "lively", so even if your "taste buds might tremble" from the noise", after a few "spicy margaritas", how can you not "love it"? - "mas tamales por favor."

Border Grill Truck *Mexican*

| 24 | 16 | 21 | $12 |

Location varies; see website | 213-542-1102 | www.bordergrill.com

"Somehow the Border Grill is even better on a truck" say champions of this cheap "moveable feast" from the Two Hot Tamales, who inject an extra dose of "whimsy" into their "tasty" Mexican cuisine (ceviche in a cone and churro bites are "faves"); it's manned by a "personable" staff (Susan Feniger included), so regulars are more than happy "to make a run for the Border."

NEW Bosc ⧄Ⓜ *Eclectic*

| - | - | - | M |

Hollywood | 724 Vine St. (bet. Camerford Ave. & Laneway Access) | 323-962-6369 | www.bosconvine.com

What was long home to Lou in Hollywood is now this Eclectic gastro-pub built around a small batch-centric wine and artisanal beer list, but with the addition of a larger, midpriced menu that changes seasonally (though Lou's beloved 'pig candy' remains a constant); the space, hidden in a nondescript mini-mall, is dominated by hanging fabrics, blazing candles and a long communal table.

Bossa Nova ● *Brazilian*

| 23 | 17 | 20 | $24 |

Hollywood | 7181 W. Sunset Blvd. (Formosa Ave.) | 323-436-7999
West Hollywood | 685 N. Robertson Blvd. (bet. Melrose Ave. & Santa Monica Blvd.) | 310-657-5070
West LA | 10982 W. Pico Blvd. (bet. Greenfield & Veteran Aves.) | 310-441-0404
www.bossafood.com

You get "lots of meat" for the money at this "casual" Brazilian trio, where the "massive" menu runs from "tasty" South American standards to steaks and salads; diners cite "slow" (though "friendly") service and "ridiculously packed" digs, but weekend late hours, plus take-out and delivery options, sate night owls and "value"-hunters.

Boss Sushi *Japanese*
25 | 17 | 23 | $39

Beverly Hills | 270A S. La Cienega Blvd. (Gregory Way) | 310-659-5612 | www.bosssushi.com

Carving up "fresh, tasty" fish for relatively little yen (including a "value" lunch menu), this "low-key" Beverly Hills Japanese manned by chef-owner Tom Sagara – the eponymous sushi "Boss" – showcases an array of "imaginative" rolls, served by a "friendly" staff; meanwhile, the modern decor suits the fin fare well, so don't be surprised if you "find yourself coming back."

Bottega Louie *Italian*
23 | 23 | 21 | $35

Downtown | 700 S. Grand Ave. (7th St.) | 213-802-1470 | www.bottegalouie.com

Exuding a "New York vibe", this "ultrachic" Downtown Italian restaurant and gourmet market is perpetually "mobbed" for its "high-style" (yet "low-priced") Italian fare, including "fabulous" pizzas and "top-notch" desserts; amid "sky-high ceilings" and "marble everywhere", the "energetic" staff comes through, though be prepared for "shatter-the-sound-barrier" acoustics and a no-reservations policy that can spur "waits."

Bottle Inn *Italian*
22 | 19 | 23 | $36

Hermosa Beach | 26 22nd St. (bet. Beach Dr. & Hermosa Ave.) | 310-376-9595 | www.thebottleinn.com

For "special" nights, "you can't go wrong" with this "hideaway" near the ocean, an "old-fashioned" Hermosa Beach "favorite" known for its "friendly" service and "lovely" classic-Italian cuisine since 1974; coupled with choices from the "superb" wine list, it may not be the cheapest meal, but its "cozy" ambiance works wonders – especially if you dine in the "romantic" wine cellar.

BottleRock ❶ *European*
19 | 19 | 21 | $29

Downtown | Met Lofts | 1050 S. Flower St. (11 St.) | 213-747-1100
Culver City | 3847 Main St. (bet. Culver & Venice Blvds.) | 310-836-9463
www.bottlerock.net

Oenophiles relish these "informal" wine-bar twins, where a "knowledgeable" staff "helps you discover" new bottles while providing affordable, "gourmet" European munchies; that's manna for "couples and singles" alike, who dig the happy hours and modern spaces at the Staples Center–convenient Downtown location (with a full kitchen) and Culver City (best for little bites).

❷ Bouchon *French*
25 | 25 | 25 | $63

Beverly Hills | 235 N. Cañon Dr. (bet. Dayton Way & Wilshire Blvd.) | 310-271-9910 | www.bouchonbistro.com

"*Vive Bouchon!*" gush *admirateurs* of Thomas Keller's "inviting", celeb-frequented Beverly Hills bistro – sib to the Yountville original – where "superbly trained" servers deliver "sublime", "meticulously prepared" French classics to industry "bigwigs" (and mere mortals) in a "bright" room that's like "Paris without the long flight"; while some "aren't dazzled", most feel for "special occasions", it's "money well spent", and you don't "have to drive to the wine country" to indulge.

NEW Bouchon Bakery *Bakery*

| 26 | 19 | 22 | $19 |

Beverly Hills | 235 N. Cañon Dr. (bet. Dayton Way & Wilshire Blvd.) | 310-271-9910 | www.bouchonbakery.com

An "informal glimpse" into Thomas Keller's world, this "fabulous" Beverly Hills French bakery in the Bouchon bistro lobby "wows" with "fantastic" breads, pastries and sandwiches costing relatively little dough; it's a to-go kiosk, so the setting's "casual" (though service is of typical Keller quality), but for fans, it's one of the "best secrets in town."

Bouzy Gastropub at Chez Mélange *American*

| 25 | 21 | 24 | $30 |

Redondo Beach | 1611 S. Catalina Ave. (bet. Aves. H & I) | 310-540-1222 | www.chezmelange.com

"Always filled with energy", this "foodie paradise" gastropub in Chez Mélange's front room draws Redondo Beach denizens with "inventive", midpriced New American fare, partnered with "creative cocktails" and microbrews; "friendly" service and a "comfortable", dimly lit setting, plus "top-notch" happy hours, offer a prime venue to "get your booze on."

NEW Bow & Truss ◑ *Spanish*

| – | – | – | M |

North Hollywood | 11122 Magnolia Blvd. (bet. Blakeslee Ave. & Lankershim Blvd.) | 818-985-8787 | www.bowandtruss.com

This North Hollywood Spanish taverna serves midpriced tapas, tacos and large plates, plus wines and artisanal beers; the handsome space is built inside of a former auto body shop, with high-beamed ceilings, bare-brick walls and a dramatic bar with LED lighting that glows from within, along with a sheltered outdoor patio.

Bowery ◑ *American*

| 22 | 21 | 21 | $26 |

Hollywood | 6268 W. Sunset Blvd. (bet. Argyle Ave. & Vine St.) | 323-465-3400 | www.theboweryhollywood.com

A "little slice of New York" in Hollywood, this American near the ArcLight is a popular late-night spot for its "awesome" trademark burger, complemented by a "sophisticated" wine list and intriguing beer selection; its "hip" clientele also likes the "surprisingly good" service and "decent prices", making the small subway-tiled room a "go-to" destination.

BP Oysterette *Seafood*

| 23 | 18 | 20 | $37 |

Santa Monica | 1355 Ocean Ave. (Santa Monica Blvd.) | 310-576-3474 | www.blueplatesantamonica.com

"You'd think you're on the East Coast" at this "little" "Cape Cod–meets–Santa Monica" eatery, a local Ocean Avenue fave for "excellent" "simply prepared" seafood (think clams, lobster rolls and "slurp-worthy" oysters) and wines; other perks are "pleasant" service and "casual", "seafood-shack" digs with water views – mitigating some diners' complaints about pricing that "ain't cheap."

☑ Brandywine ⌧ *Continental*

| 27 | 20 | 26 | $65 |

Woodland Hills | 22757 Ventura Blvd. (Fallbrook Ave.) | 818-225-9114

"Heaven", for many diners, is this Woodland Hills "jewel", a "special-occasion" spot run by a "dynamic" husband-and-wife team that proffers "incredible" Continental cuisine – written on a chalkboard menu – while treating you like a "guest" in an "intimate" space; some find the French country decor "fussy" and prices "steep", but for "quiet", "classy" dinners, it "doesn't get much better."

Brats Brothers *German*   24 | 15 | 20 | $16

Sherman Oaks | 13355 Ventura Blvd. (Dixie Canyon Ave.) | 818-986-4020 | www.bratsbrothers.com

"You'll want to oompah" – "especially on nights with the accordion player" – after trying the "tasty" brats at this "inviting" Sherman Oaks German known for its "exotic" game varieties and mini beer barrels for the table; throw in "wonderful" *fräuleins* in full dress, "kitschy" Bavarian-style decor and "cheap" tabs, and diners admit the *brüder* "do it right."

Bravo Cucina *Italian/Pizza*   21 | 15 | 18 | $23

Santa Monica | Third St. Promenade | 1319 Third St. Promenade (Arizona Ave.) | 310-394-0374

Bravo Pizzeria ⏺ *Italian/Pizza*

Santa Monica | 2400D Main St. (Hollister Ave.) | 310-392-7466 www.bravosantamonica.com

These "reliable" spots on Santa Monica's Third Street Promenade and Main Street offer "solid" Italian fare such as pastas, Gotham-style pizzas and cannoli flown in from New York; providing "quick" service, modest tabs and casual settings with "people-watching"–capable patios, they "do the job" – especially for "big groups."

Breadbar *Bakery*   18 | 15 | 17 | $22

Century City | Westfield Century City Shopping Ctr. | 10250 Santa Monica Blvd. (bet. Ave. of the Stars & Century Park W.) | 310-277-3770 | www.breadbar.net

The "carbs are worth it" at this casual Century City American bakery that purveys "comforting" breads, along with "well-prepared" sandwiches and salads; the modern decor and "convenient" location make it suitable for brunch, lunch or a "bite after shopping", but crumb bums snicker at "indifferent" service and "overpriced" eats, noting it's "not worth traveling to."

🄳 Brent's Deli *Deli*   26 | 16 | 23 | $23

Northridge | 19565 Parthenia St. (bet. Corbin & Shirley Aves.) | 818-886-5679 **Westlake Village** | 2799 Townsgate Rd. (Westlake Blvd.) | 805-557-1882 www.brentsdeli.com

"The air is redolent with corned beef, stuffed cabbage" and other "quintessential" "NYC" eats at this "old-school" Northridge deli and "more luxurious" Westlake Village spin-off, where the "delish" "mile-high sandwiches" on "crusty rye" are "worth the schlep"; it's not inexpensive, but the "staff's a hoot" and "hefty portions" make for a "good value" – "bring an extra stomach."

The Brentwood ⏺ *American*   24 | 22 | 23 | $49

Brentwood | 148 S. Barrington Ave. (Sunset Blvd.) | 310-476-3511 | www.brentwoodrestaurant.com

"Well-heeled Westsiders" and "industry" folks frequent this "cozy, little" Brentwood watering hole to "soak up worthy libations" with "wonderfully prepared" New American cuisine "served with care and personality"; the "denlike atmosphere" with black leather booths and dim lighting is "perfect for canoodling" – just "make sure your credit card has plenty of room for the tab."

Brighton Coffee Shop *Diner*

20	11	20	$17

Beverly Hills | 9600 Brighton Way (N. Camden Dr.) | 310-276-7732

"What a coffee shop should be", this "refreshingly genuine" Beverly Hills diner has been slinging "solid" American "comfort food" (the tuna and meatloaf sandwiches draw raves) since 1930; nostalgists laud the "old-fashioned" vibe, fostered by servers who "aim to please", a vintage setting and prices that "can't be beat" – there's a reason it's "been there forever."

Brophy Bros. Restaurant & Clam Bar *Seafood*

23	19	21	$29

Ventura | 1559 Spinnaker Dr. (Harbor Blvd.) | 805-639-0865 | www.brophybros.com

"The fish hop from the water to your plate" at these "casual" Santa Barbara and Ventura seafooders, where diners devour "fresh" fare and Bloody Marys while watching "seagulls begging" amid a "happening" harborside atmosphere; "friendly" service, "postcard sunsets" and "cheap" tabs are yours if you can handle the "wait" to get in.

☑ Brother Sushi 🖩Ⓜ *Japanese*

27	15	21	$43

Woodland Hills | 21418 Ventura Blvd. (bet. Canoga & De Roja Aves.) | 818-992-1284

"Don't blink or you might miss" this "tiny" Japanese in Woodland Hills, "still primo" after all these years for "fantastic" sushi and rolls, proffered in a setting where you "always feel welcome"; belt-tighteners say it's "not cheap", but it's often hopping, as regulars know "you get what you pay for."

Brunello Trattoria *Italian*

23	16	23	$31

Culver City | 6001 Washington Blvd. (La Cienega Blvd.) | 310-280-3856 | www.brunello-trattoria.com

The "secret" may be out on this "charming" "mom-and-pop" trattoria – nestled in Culver City's art-gallery district – where "delightful" pastas, "fresh" breads and other "tastes-like-Italy" fare regale diners at "reasonable" prices; "warm", "accommodating" servers and a "homey", picture-filled room where it's "easy to chat" round out the setting, making it just the right mix for a "neighborhood" spot.

Bru's Wiffle Ⓜ *American*

24	16	21	$18

Santa Monica | 2408 Wilshire Blvd. (24th St.) | 310-453-2787 | www.bruswiffle.com

They seemingly "will put anything on a waffle" at this inexpensive Santa Monica American, where this once-humble breakfast staple reaches "epic" heights with combos such as pizza and curry-chicken salad; "sweet" service and a kid-friendly atmosphere prevail, but because it's "popular", insiders suggest "arriving early" to avoid any "bru-haha"-induced "waits."

Buddha's Belly *Asian*

21	19	21	$26

Beverly Boulevard | 7475 Beverly Blvd. (N. Gardner St.) | 323-931-8588
Santa Monica | 205 Broadway (2nd St.) | 310-458-2500
NEW Thousand Oaks | 446 W. Hillcrest Dr. (McCloud Ave.) | 805-557-1212
www.bbfood.com

"Meditate" on the "love" generated by this "trendy" Pan-Asian trio, which provides "nourishing", "satisfying" eats, plus soju and sake cocktails, in a casual environment that's "full of energy"; "courteous" service and "reasonable prices" are welcome, and while bellyachers carp about "noise" and a "lack of authenticity", overall it "hits the mark."

Buffalo Club ●🅕 *American* 19 | 21 | 19 | $58

Santa Monica | 1520 Olympic Blvd. (bet. 14th & 16th Sts.) | 310-450-8600 | www.thebuffaloclub.com

"Hidden" in an "industrial" section of Santa Monica is this "clublike" American spot, where a "dark" art deco–style dining room and "enchanting" patio attract LA "bigwigs" intrigued by the "solid" "comfort-food" and small-plates menus; "welcoming" service also charms, and while a few dismiss "expensive", just-"ok" fare, late hours and a suitable "scene" compensate.

Buffalo Fire Department 🅕 *American* 24 | 21 | 23 | $24

Torrance | 1261 Cabrillo Ave. (Torrance Blvd.) | 310-320-2332 | www.buffalofiredepartment.com

For "juicy", "over-the-top" patties ("mac 'n' cheese burger, need I say more?") and spicy wings, try this "casual", mildly priced Torrance American from chef-owner and Buffalo, NY, native Michael Shafer of Depot across the street; "spot-on" service and a "vibrant" firehouse decor help spark the "kid-friendly" atmosphere, making it a local "favorite."

🆕 Bugatta 🅕 *Eclectic* - | - | - | M

Melrose | 7174 Melrose Ave. (N. Formosa Ave.) | 323-964-9494 | www.bugatta.com

The name of this Melrose District entry sounds Italian, but the mid-priced menu is Eclectic with touches of Vietnamese and Thai, and offerings ranging from sushi rolls to bruschetta to skewers; the elegantly edgy space features polished parquet floors, banquettes with green-blue leather and an L-shaped bar that glitters with small lights.

Buggy Whip *Seafood/Steak* 20 | 17 | 21 | $41

Westchester | 7420 La Tijera Blvd. (W. 74th St.) | 310-645-7131 | www.thebuggywhip.com

"Old-school class" lives on at this Westchester "treasure", a circa-1952 chophouse where a "charming" staff delivers "ample" portions of "satisfying" prime rib and seafood, plus "wonderful" Green Goddess dressing, in a "clubby", "dimly lit" setting; though a minority calls it "tired" and "expensive" (unless you opt for the early-bird menu), the "days-gone-by" atmosphere spurs loyalists to "settle into a leather booth" and enjoy.

Buono's *Pizza* 26 | 19 | 22 | $23

Long Beach | 250 W. Ocean Blvd. (bet. S. Pine Ave. & Queens Way) | 562-432-2211 | www.buonospizza.com

The "awesomely delicious" thick-crust pizza will "win you over" at this "casual" piemaking trio, local faves for their "varied" (and "filling") Italian selections provided at "little cost"; "excellent" service and "homey" environs round it all out, but ultimately, it's the food that makes regulars feel like "eating there every day."

Burger Continental *Mideastern* 18 | 12 | 18 | $19

Pasadena | 535 S. Lake Ave. (California Blvd.) | 626-792-6634 | www.burgercontinentalpasadena.com

"It's not just burgers" being proffered at this Pasadena "institution" known for its "varied", "cheap" menu of Middle Eastern dishes and suitable suds, distributed by an "attentive" staff; its Cal-Techie clientele also fancies the "pleasant" covered patio and regular belly dancing, and though some huff about "quantity over quality", it's certainly a "unique" experience.

Burrito King ●⊅ *Mexican*   22 | 12 | 20 | $12

Echo Park | 2109 W. Sunset Blvd. (Alvarado St.) | 213-484-9859
Eastsiders get their "grub" on "whether it's 2 AM or 2 PM" at this "fab" longtime Mexican eatery in Echo Park, which cooks up "huge", "budget"-priced burritos and other "authentic" *comida* that satisfy serious "cravings"; it's a "simple" taco-stand setting, and there's only sidewalk seating, but "quick" service sees that hungry *estómagos* are filled "fast."

Buttermilk Truck ⊠⊅ *American*   25 | 14 | 20 | $12

Location varies; see website | www.buttermilktruck.com
"Religiously" followed by truckoholics, this "motorized culinary studio of the gods" proffers "decadent" red velvet pancakes and "moist" chicken and waffles, plus breakfast sandwiches and other American bites to legions of loyal fans; regulars say it's "not for the diet-conscious" and warn of "painfully slow" "waits", but for an inexpensive "guilty pleasure", it's the stuff "dreams" are made of.

Cabbage Patch ⊠ *Californian/Mediterranean*   23 | 16 | 21 | $17

Downtown | 520 W. Sixth St. (bet. S. Grand Ave. & S. Olive St.) | 213-489-4489 | www.cabbagepatchla.com
Beverly Hills | 214 S. Beverly Dr. (Charleville Blvd.) | 310-550-8655 | www.cabbagepatchbh.com
West LA | 12531 Beatrice St. (bet. Grosvenor Blvd. & Westlawn Ave.) | 310-305-1547 | www.cabbagepatchbh.com
At this trio of "wholesome" "lunch alternatives", a talented kitchen turns out "healthy" twists on "tradition" with an inexpensive Cal-Med menu of "slammin'" rice bowls and slaw, plus Niman Ranch meats and sustainable fish – all served in "casual" settings; the afternoon crowd also likes the "friendly" staff, and you can always "order to go."

Ca'Brea *Italian*   21 | 20 | 21 | $43

La Brea | 346 S. La Brea Ave. (bet. 3rd & 4th Sts.) | 323-938-2863 | www.cabrearestaurant.com
"Quality still rules" at this "unassuming" La Brea Northern Italian, a local "standby" for "solid", "old-school" standards dispensed by an "attentive" staff in a "cozy", painting-adorned space; a few thrifty types grimace at "pricey" fare, but the fact that it's often "crowded" speaks for itself.

CaCao Mexicatessen Ⓜ *Mexican*   25 | 16 | 17 | $19

Eagle Rock | 1576 Colorado Blvd. (Townsend Ave.) | 323-478-2791 | www.cacaodeli.com
No longer Eagle Rock's "best little secret", this taqueria produces "top-notch" Mexican eats ("duck tacos, are you kidding?") and "fantastic" weekly specials to a diverse crowd that likes the "cute" decor and commensurate service; pricing's "reasonable", and you can also buy spices, grains and its signature hot chocolate at the on-site deli; P.S. an expansion should allow for more space, along with beer and wine.

	FOOD	DECOR	SERVICE	COST

Ca' del Sole *Italian*

23 | 22 | 23 | $41

North Hollywood | 4100 Cahuenga Blvd. (Lankershim Blvd.) |
818-985-4669 | www.cadelsole.com

"Playing home to the heavy-hitters of the Valley media circuit", this
"charming" North Hollywood Venetian, modeled after a country
inn, blends "beautifully executed" Northern Italian cuisine (and a
700-bottle wine list) with "prompt" service, making it *perfetto* for
"business-lunchers"; couple that with a "divine" plant-filled patio, and
it's a "great value."

Café Beaujolais Ⓜ *French*

26 | 19 | 24 | $36

Eagle Rock | 1712 Colorado Blvd. (bet. La Roda Ave. & Mt. Royal Dr.) |
323-255-5111

C'est toujours Paris at this "moderately priced" Eagle Rock bistro,
where the "incredible", traditional French fare is served by "dreamy"
waiters who are nearly as "authentic" as the food; *bien sûr*, the "convivial", poster-adorned setting adds to the feeling that you're in the
City of Light, leading *admirateurs* to say it's "not to be missed."

🅩 Cafe Bizou *French*

23 | 19 | 22 | $33

Santa Monica | 2450 Colorado Ave. (26th St.) | 310-453-8500 🅑
Pasadena | 91 N. Raymond Ave. (Holly St.) | 626-792-9923
Sherman Oaks | 14016 Ventura Blvd. (bet. Costello & Murietta Aves.) |
818-788-3536
www.cafebizou.com

It's "not expensive but feels like it" at this "upbeat" bistro three-
some that's "always crazy busy" with "loyal customers" who "love"
the "delightful" French food, "festive" atmosphere and "courteous" service; while a few surveyors find it too "ordinary", it remains a "safe choice" for "date night" and "celebrating something
special", plus the "fantastic" $2 corkage makes it a BYO "bargain";
P.S. "make a reservation."

Café Brasil *Brazilian*

22 | 16 | 18 | $19

Culver City | 11736 W. Washington Blvd. (McLaughlin Ave.) |
310-391-1216
Palms | 10831 Venice Blvd. (Westwood Blvd.) | 310-837-8957
www.cafe-brasil.com

Regulars "leave full" after downing the "tasty" grilled meats, "heavenly" juices and other "inexpensive" staples purveyed at these
"cheerful" Culver City and Palms Brazilians, where the "funky",
"beach-shacky" ambiance (complete with outdoor seating) accen-
tuates the "charm"; the "friendly" staff makes the counter-style
service manageable, and enthusiasts have no qualms about labeling
them a "winner."

Cafe Cordiale *Californian/Eclectic*

22 | 21 | 23 | $31

Sherman Oaks | 14015 Ventura Blvd. (bet. Hazeltine Ave. & Colbath Ave.) |
818-789-1985 | www.cafecordiale.com

A "welcoming" atmosphere, plus "outstanding" live music six
nights a week, is the calling card of this Sherman Oaks Cal-Eclectic, a
"neighborhood institution" for its "consistent" fare, "no-pressure"
service and late hours; mix in a "pleasant", patio-outfitted setting
and "affordable" prices, and it's an "underrated" "treat" for devotees
old and new.

	FOOD	DECOR	SERVICE	COST

Cafe Del Rey *Californian/Mediterranean* | 24 | 24 | 22 | $49 |

Marina del Rey | 4451 Admiralty Way (bet. Bali Way & Via Marina) | 310-823-6395 | www.cafedelreymarina.com

An "exception to the rule" concerning typical waterside restaurants, this "high-class" Marina del Rey Cal-Med features "stunning" harbor views that are as "wonderful" as the food – no small feat, considering the scope of the "innovative" menu; moreover, the "romantic" ambiance, "personable" staff and "chichi" crowd assuage tabs some deem "pricey"; P.S. the bar is "excellent" for apps, especially in winter when the fireplace is going.

Cafe Fiore *Italian* | 23 | 22 | 22 | $38 |

Ventura | 66 S. California St. (bet. Main & Santa Clara Sts.) | 805-653-1266 | www.fiorerestaurant.net

"Delicious" Southern Italian accompanied by a martini lounge with live music sets the scene at this midpriced neighborhood "hangout" in Old Town Ventura, favored by locals for its "intimate", patio-enhanced trattoria decor and concomitant service; savants advise "getting reservations", citing the "noisy", "busy" environs, but that won't stop advocates from itching to "go again."

Cafe Firenze Ⓜ *Italian* | 23 | 22 | 20 | $40 |

Moorpark | Mission Bell Plaza | 563 W. Los Angeles Ave. (bet. Park Ln. & Shasta Ave.) | 805-532-0048 | www.cafefirenze.net

Locals "love" Fabio Viviani, the former *Top Chef*-er and "face" of this mildly priced Moorpark "gem", which supplies "memorable" Northern Italian food (including pastas and thin-crust pizzas) to a charmed crowd; the "lovely" space – featuring an open kitchen and patio – compensates for what cynics call "variable" service, but an unwavering attribute is FV himself, who'll often "take a moment to greet" starstruck guests.

🅩 Café 14 Ⓜ *Continental* | 27 | 22 | 25 | $51 |

Agoura Hills | Reyes Adobe Plaza | 30315 Canwood St. (Reyes Adobe Rd.) | 818-991-9560 | www.cafe-14.com

Nestled in an Agoura Hills strip mall just off the 101, this "wonderful little hideaway" delights diners with "sophisticated" Continental cuisine served by a staff that treats you like "royalty"; with its muted, upscale ambiance, "cozy" patio and "neighborhood feel", it's an "extraordinary" dining experience – and it carries price points to match.

Cafe Gratitude *American* | 24 | 20 | 21 | $25 |

Hancock Park | 639 N. Larchmont Blvd. (Melrose Ave.) | 323-580-6383
Venice | 512 Rose Ave. (bet. 5th & Rennie Aves.) | 424-231-8000
www.cafegratitudela.com

There's "vegan magic" in this American chainlet's "innovative" organic cuisine, characterized by "exceptional" green-oriented dishes; a "sweet" staff oversees the modern, airy digs with an "amazing" patio, and if a minority pooh-poohs the "hippie" sensibility, there's still plenty to be "grateful" for – including the sensible prices.

Café Habana *Cuban/Mexican* | 21 | 22 | 18 | $31 |

Malibu | Malibu Lumber Yard | 3939 Cross Creek Rd. (PCH) | 310-317-0300 | www.habana-malibu.com

The "cheese-covered, char-grilled corn" is a "new addiction" of "Malibu locals" who "meet and eat" at this "flavorful" Cuban-Mex, an NYC im-

FOOD DECOR SERVICE COST

port by impresario Rande Gerber, sporting a "pleasant patio" with a huge Shepard Fairey mural; service is free of the "typical 'tude" and prices are down-to-earth as well, but it's still "TMZ-central for star sightings."

Café Laurent *French*
21 | 17 | 18 | $20

Culver City | 4243 Overland Ave. (Barman Ave.) | 310-558-8622 | www.cafelaurent.com

"Sit on the patio and make believe you're in France" at this Culver City bistro dishing up crêpes, omelets and other "delicious" French fare that's a "favorite" for brunch; the interior's "a bit cramped", but regulars report that "faster service" and "expanded hours" (it's now open for dinner Tuesday–Saturday) have "renewed the old gal."

Cafe Med *Italian*
22 | 20 | 22 | $37

West Hollywood | Sunset Plaza | 8615 W. Sunset Blvd. (Sunset Plaza Dr.) | 310-652-0445

"Pizza and people-watching from the patio facing Sunset" make a winning combo at this "easy, no-attitude" West Hollywood Italian, a "chillout" spot where "the occasional celebrity can be found just hanging with friends"; it's "reasonable", so even if most go for the "prime location", they're satisfied with the "consistent" cooking too.

Cafe Montana *Californian*
21 | 18 | 20 | $32

Santa Monica | 1534 Montana Ave. (16th St.) | 310-829-3990 | www.cafemontana.net

Attracting "ladies who lunch" since 1984, this "cute", "convivial" locale in Santa Monica succeeds with "spot-on" Cal fare ranging from "nice salads" to "huge", "amazing" desserts for "reasonable" tabs; given the "accommodating" service and a "sunny" setting with glass walls overlooking Montana Avenue, it's a "comfortable neighborhood" stop; P.S. "try the Lithuanian meat dumplings."

Café Piccolo *Italian*
25 | 24 | 24 | $37

Long Beach | 3222 E. Broadway (bet. Coronado & Obispo Aves.) | 562-438-1316 | www.cafepiccolo.com

It's all about the "enchanting" "garden atmosphere" at this "romantic" Long Beach oasis featuring fountains, a waterfall and "cozy" firepits on the patio to complement "scrumptious" Northern Italian food; add in "unbeatable" service and moderate tabs, and it's "popular for dates, special occasions" and simply as a "go-to" "any day of the week."

Café Pierre *French*
24 | 20 | 23 | $47

Manhattan Beach | 317 Manhattan Beach Blvd. (bet. Highland Ave. & Morningside Dr.) | 310-545-5252 | www.cafepierre.com

Bringing "a bit of Paris to Manhattan Beach" for 35 years, this "old neighborhood favorite" by chef-owner Guy Gabriele is still a "solid performer" when it comes to "excellent" French bistro fare and "great service"; the "tight, noisy" quarters don't diminish the "quality at a reasonable price", though some regulars feel the menu "could use a change of pace"; P.S. check out the $35 prix fixe Sunday–Wednesday.

Cafe Pinot *Californian/French*
24 | 25 | 23 | $51

Downtown | 700 W. Fifth St. (Flower St.) | 213-239-6500 | www.cafepinot.com

Diners "delight" to this "Downtown hideaway" from Joachim Splichal providing "wonderful upscale Cal-French" dishes and "very good"

	FOOD	DECOR	SERVICE	COST

wines that fit the "pre-theater" bill (plus servers are adept in "getting you out in time" for the show); most distinctively, the "tranquil" patio "overlooking the gardens" of the Central Library "adds a magical element" that makes it "worth the price tag."

Café Rio *Mexican*

| 23 | 17 | 21 | $13 |

Manhattan Beach | 1800 Rosecrans Ave. (bet. N. Aviation Blvd. & Redondo Ave.) | 424-456-3800
Oxnard | 1831 N. Rose Ave. (Gonzales Rd.) | 805-288-3250
Lakewood | 5021 Lakewood Blvd. (bet. Del Amo Blvd. & Hardwick St.) | 562-616-6700
www.caferio.com

The pork barbacoa is "unreal" and the healthy options "loaded with flavor" at this "fast-casual" chain where a "cheerful" staff sets down "fresh Mex" (including handmade tortillas) inspired by the Rio Grande Valley region; it has a "family atmosphere" with "fun decor", plus it's worth braving the "long lines" for Taco Tuesday – one of the "best deals in town."

Café Santorini *Mediterranean*

| 21 | 21 | 20 | $36 |

Pasadena | 64 W. Union St. (bet. De Lacey & Fair Oaks Aves.) | 626-564-4200 | www.cafesantorini.com

A "beautiful" rooftop balcony "tucked away from the hustle and bustle" of Old Town Pasadena "adds to the allure" of this "refreshing" Med specializing in "simple", "affordable" seafood, pizza and mezes; service gets mixed marks, but with the iPic Theater just steps away, it's "quite popular on weekend nights" with showgoers.

Cafe Stella *French*

| 22 | 22 | 17 | $40 |

Silver Lake | 3932 W. Sunset Blvd. (bet. Hyperion & Sanborn Aves.) | 323-666-0265 | www.cafestella.com

A savvy "Silver Lake clientele" gathers on the "romantic" patio for "satisfying" "everyday bistro" fare at this "convivial" French boîte "hidden away" in the Sunset Junction; still, some dissenters are "disappointed" by "surly" service and feel it's "a little overpriced for the neighborhood."

Cafe Surfas *American*

| 19 | 10 | 14 | $16 |

Culver City | 8777 Washington Blvd. (National Blvd.) | 310-558-1458 | www.cafesurfas.com

Westsiders "ogling the aisles" of Culver City's "restaurant supply emporium" "staunch their cravings" at this cafe specializing in "tasty" panini made with "top-quality meats and cheeses", along with salads and breakfast sandwiches; it's "lunchroom" looks are basic, service can be "slow" and some feel the food "should be better" at such a "gourmet" hub, but most say it works for a "shopping break."

Cafe Verde *American/Italian*

| 24 | 17 | 22 | $29 |

Pasadena | 961 E. Green St. (Mentor Ave.) | 626-356-9811 | www.cafeverdepasadena.com

A "loyal following" "squeezes" into this "unique" sidewalk cafe in Pasadena for "excellent", "creatively prepared" American-Italian fare, plus some Latin twists at breakfast; while "claustrophobes" would balk at the "cramped" interior (and a "parade of pedestrians bumping your chair" outside), it's still has its "charms", boosted by modest prices and an "attentive" staff.

	FOOD	DECOR	SERVICE	COST

Caffé Delfini *Italian* | 24 | 18 | 22 | $46

Santa Monica | 147 W. Channel Rd. (PCH) | 310-459-8823 |
www.caffedelfini.com

Oozing "Italian charm", this upscale, dinner-only "gem" in the Santa Monica Canyon delivers "on-the-money" pasta and seafood with a little "stargazing" on the side; diners differ over whether the simple candelit room is "cozy" or "crammed", but loyalists just "love" it.

Caffe Luxxe *Coffeehouse* | 21 | 18 | 19 | $12

Brentwood | 11975 San Vicente Blvd. (bet. Montana & Saltiar Aves.) |
310-394-2222
Santa Monica | Brentwood Country Mart | 225 26th St.
(bet. Brentwood Terr. & San Vicente Blvd.) | 310-394-2222
Santa Monica | 925 Montana Ave. (bet. Lincoln Blvd. & 7th St.) |
310-394-2222
www.caffeluxxe.com

"No need to go to Italy", the "espresso jockeys" at these Euro-style coffeehouses know how to fashion "strong, rich" caffeinated creations (with "artistic foam toppings") at equally rich prices; there are "great pastries" and sandwiches too, and while you may not nab a spot to "work on your screenplay", "it's all about" the "top-notch" java here.

Caffe Opera *American/Eclectic* | 23 | 22 | 23 | $34

Monrovia | 402 S. Myrtle Ave. (E. Lime Ave.) | 626-305-0094 |
www.operamonrovia.com

This "tasty" American-Eclectic strikes the right chord with Monrovia locals, bringing a meaty menu – including coffee bean–crusted rib-eye – to Old Town business lunchers and others for a "surprisingly low price"; strong service and a "relaxing", "date"-friendly dining room with big windows overlooking the main drag are additional high notes.

Caffe Pinguini Ⓜ *Italian* | 22 | 20 | 21 | $42

Playa del Rey | 6935 Pacific Ave. (Culver Blvd.) | 310-306-0117 |
www.caffepinguini.com

Both a "trusted neighborhood fixture" and "seaside escape", this "fairly priced" Playa del Rey Italian offering "delicious" fare and "classy" service provides a "romantic" prelude to a "walk on the beach"; given its "quiet trattoria ambiance" enhanced by Roman-style frescoes and a heated patio, guests wonder how it's "continued to stay a well-kept secret."

Caffe Roma ◗ *Italian* | 23 | 21 | 21 | $39

Beverly Hills | 350 N. Cañon Dr. (Brighton Way) | 310-274-7834 |
www.cafferomabeverlyhills.com

Beverly Hills' "old guard" are livin' "la dolce vita" at this *"tutto Italiano"* cafe by Agostino Sciandri (Ago) where the "extraordinary people-watching" often upstages the "reliable" food ("rocking" salads and pizzas) at moderate to high prices; "happy hour is beyond happy", and nighttime touches like silent black-and-white flicks, live music and DJ sets amp up the "amazing scene."

Caioti Pizza Cafe *Pizza* | 22 | 11 | 16 | $22

Studio City | 4346 Tujunga Ave. (Moorpark St.) | 818-761-3588 |
www.caiotipizzacafe.com

Seekers of the "original" California pizza feed their fancy at this Studio City cafe from Spago's first pizza chef, the late Ed LaDou, that still

	FOOD	DECOR	SERVICE	COST

turns out a "variety" of "awesome" pies and famous salads in casual quarters; a few critics "expect more" given the pedigree, and service is hit-or-miss, but it's an economical choice that many "wish" were in their neighborhood; P.S. no alcohol, no BYO.

Cajun Kitchen *Cajun*
24 | 16 | 22 | $16

Ventura | 301 E. Main St. (Palm St.) | 805-643-7701
Hashing out meals "just like mom makes", these dollarwise, multisite Cajuns satisfy "cornbread cravings" and other deep needs for "spicy", "quickly served" N'Awlins grub; some say there's "nothing fancy" about the "diner-style" ambiance or patio seating, so you may opt for takeout.

California Chicken Cafe *American*
23 | 13 | 20 | $14

Hollywood | 6805 Melrose Ave. (Mansfield Ave.) | 323-935-5877 Ⓢ
Santa Monica | 2401 Wilshire Blvd. (24th St.) | 310-453-0477 Ⓢ
Venice | 424 Lincoln Blvd. (bet. Flower & Sunset Aves.) | 310-392-3500
West LA | 2005 Westwood Blvd. (La Grange Ave.) | 310-446-1933 Ⓢ
Encino | 15601 Ventura Blvd. (bet. Firmament & Haskell Aves.) | 818-789-8056 Ⓢ
Northridge | University Plaza | 18445 Nordhoff St. (Reseda Blvd.) | 818-700-9977 Ⓢ
Woodland Hills | 22333 Ventura Blvd. (Shoup Ave.) | 818-716-6170
www.californiachickencafe.com
"Juicy chicken hot off the rotisserie" is key to this "remarkably consistent" American chain offering a "healthy fast-food alternative" with a "bargain" menu of "extra-large, fresh" salads (Chinese chicken "lives up to the hype"), wraps and veggie sides; the "plain" surroundings become a "zoo" at "peak times", but at least the "efficient" counter staff gets you in and out "quickly."

California Grill *Californian*
26 | 22 | 24 | $21

Whittier | 6751 Painter Ave. (Philadelphia St.) | 562-907-7017 | www.californiagrill.biz
A "hidden gem" in Whittier, this "casual" Californian serves "excellent" breakfasts and other "good, satisfying", affordable eats (burgers, pastas, Mex selections) with "caring" hospitality; it's a "cozy place to take the family" or an "after-work" group for "relaxing" patio dining, and regulars appreciate that it bolsters the community with "plenty of local support."

California Pizza Kitchen *Pizza*
22 | 19 | 21 | $23

Downtown | Wells Fargo Ctr. | 330 S. Hope St. (bet. 3rd & 4th Sts.) | 213-626-2616
Downtown | Ronald Tutor Student Campus Ctr. | 3607 Trousdale Pkwy. (34th St.) | 213-821-3482
Hollywood | Hollywood & Highland Ctr. | 6801 Hollywood Blvd. (Highland Ave.) | 323-460-2080
Beverly Hills | Beverly Ctr. | 121 N. La Cienega Blvd. (bet. Beverly Blvd. & 3rd St.) | 310-854-6555
Beverly Hills | 207 S. Beverly Dr. (Charleville Blvd.) | 310-275-1101
Santa Monica | 210 Wilshire Blvd. (bet. 2nd & 3rd Sts.) | 310-393-9335
Westwood | Westwood Vill. | 1001 Broxton Ave. (bet. Kinross & Weyburn Aves.) | 310-209-9197
Pasadena | Plaza Las Fuentes | 99 N. Los Robles Ave. (Union St.) | 626-585-9020

(continued)

(continued)
California Pizza Kitchen
Burbank | 601 N. San Fernando Blvd. (Cypress Ave.) | 818-972-2589
Studio City | 12265 Ventura Blvd. (Laurelgrove Ave.) | 818-505-6437
www.cpk.com
Additional locations throughout Southern California

"Before all the gourmet pizzas, there was CPK" say longtimers of this "steady" pie chain specializing in "tasty" "nontraditional toppings" (like BBQ chicken) and "scrumptious" salads; it's "light and colorful" with an "easy atmosphere" and "pleasant" service that "works well for families", and if some say the menu "verges on boring after lo these many years", many feel it's "predictable in a good way."

Campanile *Californian/Mediterranean*   26 | 25 | 25 | $57
La Brea | 624 S. La Brea Ave. (bet. 6th St. & Wilshire Blvd.) |
323-938-1447 | www.campanilerestaurant.com

"Top-notch in every way" – from the "artful", market-driven Cal-Med dishes by "trend-defying" chef-owner Mark Peel, to the "fabulous" wine list, to the "elegant" "historic" setting and "professional" staff – this La Brea "classic" "continues to shine year after year"; though many reserve it for a "special-occasion splurge", the ever-popular Grilled Cheese Night on Thursdays makes for a "less pricey evening."

Canal Club *Californian/Eclectic*   ∇ 21 | 21 | 20 | $38
Venice | 2025 Pacific Ave. (N. Venice Blvd.) | 310-823-3878 |
www.canalclubvenice.com

Done up in "dark, sexy" style by local artists, this "hoppin'" Cal-Eclectic bro to James' Beach offers a diverse (some say "random") dinner menu of grilled meats and "especially tasty" sushi to go with its "Venice vibe"; a "well-stocked bar", "no-stress happy hour" and staff that "adds to the fun" are a boon for "young eaters and drinkers" who say it's "all good."

C & O Cucina *Italian*   22 | 19 | 22 | $27
Marina del Rey | 3016 Washington Blvd. (bet. Abbot Kinney Blvd. & PCH) | 310-301-7278 | www.cocucina.com
C & O Trattoria *Italian*
Marina del Rey | 31 Washington Blvd. (Pacific Ave.) | 310-823-9491 | www.cotrattoria.com

"An endless supply" of "scrumptious" garlic knots "just keep on coming" at this "kitschy" midpriced Italian duo in Marina del Rey, where "gargantuan" helpings of "familiar, well-prepared" pastas are set down by "friendly" opera-singing waiters; "rousing renditions of *That's Amore* occur hourly" and the "pitchers of wine" keep flowing, so even if it's "totally a madhouse" with perpetual "waits", most still find it all a lot of "fun."

Canelé Ⓜ *Mediterranean*   24 | 17 | 21 | $39
Atwater Village | 3219 Glendale Blvd. (bet. Brunswick & Edenhurst Aves.) |
323-666-7133 | www.canele-la.com

Chef/co-owner Corina Weibel (ex Lucques) "lets the ingredients shine" in her "terrific", "fresh-from-the-farmers-market" Med fare at this "homey" Atwater Villager with moderate prices, "attentive" service and an "intimate", "bohemian" feel; "beautifully prepared" brunches and "lovely" canelé pastries as a takeaway are added allures, so while it does get "busy", it's "just what you'd want in a neighborhood bistro."

	FOOD	DECOR	SERVICE	COST

Canter's ● *Deli* | 21 | 12 | 18 | $22

Fairfax | 419 N. Fairfax Ave. (bet. Oakwood & Rosewood Aves.) | 323-651-2030 | www.cantersdeli.com

"Towering", "delish" deli sandwiches, "kitschy" "throwback" decor and "motherly" waitresses "who tell you what to eat" are all part of the "tradition" at this 24/7 family-owned Fairfax "legend", a "longtime hangout for Hollywood notables"; sure, critics say its "bakery is better than the food", but it's still "an experience to remember" – and "one of the few delis with a full bar" and live music in the famous Kibitz Room.

The Capital Grille *Steak* | 25 | 25 | 25 | $63

Beverly Hills | Beverly Ctr. | 8614 Beverly Blvd. (La Cienega Blvd.) | 310-358-0650 | www.thecapitalgrille.com

While it's part of a "high-end" steakhouse chain, this "elegant, clubby" Beverly Center outpost feels like the "one and only one", with a "beautifully designed" space setting the stage for "excellent prime" cuts "presented with care"; a "heavy" check is part of the package, but the "well-heeled" clientele agrees it's a "class act" all around.

Capital Seafood *Chinese/Seafood* | 23 | 18 | 18 | $23

Monterey Park | 755 W. Garvey Ave. (N. Atlantic Blvd.) | 626-282-3318

Dim sum seekers "highly recommend" the "Hong Kong fare in the heart of Monterey Park" at this Chinese seafooder where carts deliver "very good" dumplings and other morsels for "value" prices; the "large" space does get "noisy", but "you won't have a bad meal if you don't mind the crowds."

Capo 🖼️Ⓜ️ *Italian* | 26 | 23 | 24 | $79

Santa Monica | 1810 Ocean Ave. (Vicente Terr.) | 310-394-5550 | www.caporestaurant.com

An "intimate" locale for "tremendous" dining, this Santa Monica Italian by Bruce Marder is dubbed the "*capo di tutti capi*" for its "exquisitely grilled meats" and other "superlative" fare backed by an "amazing wine list" and "solid" service; its "Tuscan-villa" decor with an "open hearth" provides the "romance" factor big-time, but even ardent supporters are less than enamored with the "astronomical prices."

Carlitos Gardel *Argentinean/Steak* | 24 | 19 | 25 | $47

Melrose | 7963 Melrose Ave. (bet. Edinburgh & Hayworth Aves.) | 323-655-0891 | www.carlitosgardel.com

It feels like the "Buenos Aires of the '50s" at this "charming" Melrose Argentinean "attracting expats" and locals alike with "mouthwatering" grass-fed steaks "as big as the table" and other upscale "*comida excelente*"; with its "dark, romantic" digs, carefully curated wine cellar and "top-notch" service overseen by a "dedicated family", it's a "real" find – "all that's missing is the tango."

Carney's Express *Hot Dogs* | 22 | 18 | 18 | $12

West Hollywood | 8351 W. Sunset Blvd. (bet. Kings Rd. & Sweetzer Ave.) | 323-654-8300 ●

Studio City | 12601 Ventura Blvd. (bet. Coldwater Canyon & Whitsett Aves.) | 818-761-8300

www.carneytrain.com

"Get on that train" and "forget your diet" at these "classic" hot dog joints housed in vintage railcars dishing up "fat, flavorful" franks, burgers and fries topped with "gobs of chili"; it's an order-at-the-counter setup, "but the line goes quickly" and "best of all, the price is right."

Carnival *Lebanese* | 25 | 12 | 19 | $22 |

Sherman Oaks | 4356 Woodman Ave. (bet. Moorpark St. & Ventura Blvd.) | 818-784-3469 | www.carnivalrest.com

"Heavenly" hummus, "great kebabs" and "fabulous fluffy rice" star at this "real-deal" Lebanese in Sherman Oaks that's frequently "as busy as a Beirut market", but "worth the wait"; it's also a "great value", despite sometimes "so-so service" and a "no-atmosphere" storefront setting.

Carousel Ⓜ *Mideastern* | 25 | 17 | 22 | $31 |

East Hollywood | High Plaza | 5112 Hollywood Blvd. (bet. Normandie Ave. & Winona Blvd.) | 323-660-8060
Glendale | 304 N. Brand Blvd. (California Ave.) | 818-246-7775
www.carouselrestaurant.com

"Prepare to eat" and then "roll out" of this "authentic" Middle Eastern duo doling out "huge" platters of Lebanese-Armenian fare "for vegetarians and meat lovers" alike (one "tasty" meze platter "could be dinner on its own"); East Hollywood is a "no-frills, but friendly" setup, while weekend belly dancers in Glendale create a "wonderfully exotic atmosphere", and the occasional Kardashian sighting is icing on the cake.

NEW Casa Azul Cantina *Mexican* | ▽ 21 | 24 | 21 | $32 |

Westwood | 10853 Lindbrook Dr. (Triverton Ave.) | 310-209-0666
This "cool" Westwood newcomer from the folks behind Frida is a find for "high-end Mexican with a gourmet touch" proffered by an "attentive" team; it's named after Frida Kahlo's home, and the decor pays tribute with "colorful murals" and a "beautiful" blue-lit bar that's a "perfect setting to bring a date, or meet one."

Casa Bianca ●Ⓢ Ⓜ 🗶 *Pizza* | 23 | 15 | 18 | $19 |

Eagle Rock | 1650 Colorado Blvd. (bet. Mt. Royal Dr. & Vincent Ave.) | 323-256-9617 | www.casabiancapizza.com

"Thin-crust heaven" awaits those who brave the "lines" at this cash-only Eagle Rock pizza "icon" famed for its "sweet homemade sausage" ("the only topping you need") and "classic" 1950s setting reminiscent of "an Italian grandma's dining room" but with "smiling" waitresses; critics call the "buzz" "overrated", but diehards deem it "the best", thanks in part to the "great prices."

Casablanca *Mexican* | 19 | 18 | 20 | $27 |

Venice | 220 Lincoln Blvd. (Rose Ave.) | 310-392-5751 | www.casablancacatering.com

"Around forever", this "funky" Humphrey Bogart–themed Mexican puts Venice locals in a "fiesta mood" with its "warm, handmade tortillas", "famous" calamari steak and "stiff margaritas" made from a "roaming" tequila cart; don't question, just kick back to "live Spanish guitar" and "ponder" the "strange mishmash" of Mexican food and "floor-to-ceiling movie memorabilia."

Casa Nostra *Italian* | 24 | 22 | 25 | $39 |

Pacific Palisades | 1515 Palisades Dr. (Vereda De La Montura) | 310-454-8889 | www.casanostraristorantela.com
This Italian "gem" "hidden away in the Pacific Palisades Highlands" excels in "personal service" and "excellent" "simply prepared" cuisine

that's "a cut above"; it's "family"-friendly early on, and then offers more "sophisticated" dining later in the evening, making it "one of the few civilized spots" around with "reasonable" prices – *"grazie for that!"*

Casa Sanchez *Mexican*
23 | 24 | 23 | $32

West LA | 4500 S. Centinela Ave. (Short Ave.) | 310-397-9999 | www.casa-sanchez.com

"Olé!" cheer amigos of this "vast" West LA hacienda hosting "top-notch" mariachi to complement "delicious" Mexican cuisine that "goes beyond burritos"; with "helpful professionals" manning a "beautiful" dining room, it's a "wow"-worthy spot that's "great for groups" or "special evenings" at a "reasonable price" – after all, "you've got dinner and entertainment all wrapped up in one."

Casa Vega ● *Mexican*
20 | 18 | 20 | $26

Sherman Oaks | 13301 Ventura Blvd. (Fulton & Nagle Aves.) | 818-788-4868 | www.casavega.com

A "very-happy happy hour" complete with "knock-your-socks-off margaritas" keeps Valleyites (and "celebs") coming to this "dark", "moody" "'50s throwback" in Sherman Oaks serving "solid" "gringo Mex" grub; yes, there's often a "ridiculous wait" to get in, but it's one of the few locals open till 1 AM, so "have another margarita and get over it."

Castaway *Californian*
22 | 25 | 22 | $41

Burbank | 1250 E. Harvard Rd. (Sunset Canyon Dr.) | 818-848-6691 | www.castawayrestaurant.com

It's all about the "magnificent views" that "get better as the evening darkens" at these hilltop Californians in Burbank and San Bernardino best enjoyed for "romantic" cocktails by the fire pits or at the "delightful Sunday brunch"; "fine service" is a plus, but remember it's a "perennial prom night" and "wedding favorite", which means special-occasion tabs.

Catch *Seafood*
23 | 26 | 25 | $52

Santa Monica | Hotel Casa Del Mar | 1910 Ocean Way (Pico Blvd.) | 310-581-7714 | www.hotelcasadelmar.com

For "elegant" dining with "outstanding" ocean views, Santa Monicans surface at this "high-class" Californian inside the Hotel Casa del Mar plying "excellent" local seafood in modern, leather-appointed digs; "splendid service" plus live music filtering in from the "happening" lounge add up to a "a thoroughly wonderful experience" – "with prices to match."

NEW Caulfield's *American*
- | - | - | E

Beverly Hills | Thompson Beverly Hills | 9360 Wilshire Blvd. (Crescent Dr.) | 310-388-6860 | www.caulfieldsbeverlyhills.com

The West Coast outpost of the stylish Thompson Hotel chain is now home to a New American (named for, yes, Holden – as in *Catcher in the Rye*) offering a pricey menu of burrata, beef short ribs and the inevitable upscale burger; its glass-walled setting sparkles with the lights of Beverly Hills, and there's a large clock over the mixology-heavy bar that's mysteriously set to New York time.

CBS Seafood *Seafood*
20 | 10 | 13 | $21

Chinatown | 700 N. Spring St. (Ord St.) | 213-617-2323

The carts keep on rolling at this "authentic Hong Kong–style" dim sum palace in Chinatown, where you can sample a "good variety" of "standard" morsels and seafood dishes on the cheap; it's "not the fanciest" place, to say the least, and the service score speaks for itself, but the fare is "solid" and an "extensive" to-go menu is a bonus.

Cecconi's ● Italian
23 | 25 | 23 | $59

West Hollywood | 8764 Melrose Ave. (Robertson Blvd.) | 310-432-2000 | www.cecconiswesthollywood.com

A "gorgeous crowd" convenes at this "posh" WeHo Italian – a "London transplant" in the former Morton's space – decked out in blue leather with patterned floors and chandeliers lending a "Rome-in-the-mid-'60s feel"; the "expensive" Venetian cuisine and "endearing" staff are equally "fabulous", and if you "go for brunch on the patio, you'll feel like a movie star."

Celestino Italian
25 | 20 | 24 | $43

Pasadena | 141 S. Lake Ave. (bet. Cordova & Green Sts.) | 626-795-4006 | www.celestinopasadena.com

One of Pasadena's more "sophisticated" Italians, this "wonderful local" from the Drago Brothers delivers "amazing fresh pastas" and other "dependably delicious" fare at the "right price"; expect "charming" service from "actual Italian waiters" and "noisy", "informal" digs with a patio providing a quieter atmosphere.

Cha Cha Cha Caribbean
22 | 19 | 19 | $24

Silver Lake | 656 N. Virgil Ave. (bet. Clinton St. & Melrose Ave.) | 323-664-7723 | www.theoriginalchachacha.com

This "funky" "colorful" "Silver Lake icon" still satisfies that "Caribbean urge" after 27 years with "tasty" platters of "spicy" jerk chicken and "delish" sangria in a pleasantly "tacky" setting; some bemoan the "so-so service", but "the value is good" – it's so "filling", you "won't be able to cha cha cha out the door."

Cha Cha Chicken Caribbean
22 | 18 | 19 | $16

Santa Monica | 1906 Ocean Ave. (Pico Blvd.) | 310-581-1684 | www.chachachicken.com

"Spicy" Caribbean staples like jerk chicken are accompanied by "amazing fruit juices" at this "funky" open-air "shack" in Santa Monica that "looks like an island-style cabana with mismatched tables and chairs" and "vibrant, colorful" decor; it's counter service only, but food arrives "quickly" and BYO abets the "bang-for-the-buck" prices.

Chadaka Thai
22 | 22 | 21 | $27

Burbank | 310 N. San Fernando Blvd. (bet. Magnolia Blvd. & Palm Ave.) | 818-848-8520 | www.chadaka.com

"Small and chic", this "upscale" Burbank Thai has locals "hopelessly addicted" to well-priced staples like pad Thai, chicken satay and yellow curry; reports on service are mixed, and diehards declare it "isn't the most authentic", but a "unique" wine list and full bar make it a "best-kept secret" for a "fancy-pants" meal that won't break the bank.

Chakra Indian
22 | 23 | 21 | $35

Beverly Hills | 151 S. Doheny Dr. (bet. Charleville Blvd. & Wilshire Blvd.) | 310-246-3999 | www.chakracuisine.com

Diners find "toothsome", "well-prepared" subcontinental cuisine and a "lovely" atmosphere with a full bar at this "upscale" Indian in Beverly Hills appealing to "vegetarians and carnivores" alike; a few find it "too expensive" for the genre, although the "divine lunch buffet" is a less costly option.

Champagne *French*

$\boxed{22}$ $\boxed{17}$ $\boxed{18}$ $\boxed{\$22}$

Beverly Hills | 200 S. Beverly Dr. (Charleville Blvd.) | 310-271-4556
Palms | 11709 National Blvd. (Stoner Ave.) | 310-231-9700
West LA | 2202 Sawtelle Blvd. (W. Olympic Blvd.) | 310-268-9444
www.champagnebakery.com

"Handy" for breakfast, this "French-style" fast-casual chain is also an "easy" option for sandwiches, salads and an array of pastries proclaimed "an assault on the waistline"; it's mostly self-service, and loyalists claim it's "lost its fizz" in recent years, though it still works for a low-cost bite.

Chan Dara *Thai*

$\boxed{23}$ $\boxed{18}$ $\boxed{21}$ $\boxed{\$29}$

Hancock Park | 310 N. Larchmont Blvd. (bet. Beverly Blvd. & Rosewood Ave.) | 323-467-1052
West LA | 11940 W. Pico Blvd. (Bundy Dr.) | 310-479-4461
www.chandararestaurants.com

Chan Darae *Thai*

Hollywood | 1511 N. Cahuenga Blvd. (Sunset Blvd.) | 323-464-8585 | www.chan-darae.com

The "smokin' hot waitresses" almost upstage the "tasty" fare at these Thai sibs offering "lots to choose from" in a menu that "runs a fine line between authentic and accessible"; although it's sometimes "a scene" with a "higher-end" atmosphere, tabs are still easy on the wallet.

NEW The Charleston *Eclectic*

$\boxed{-}$ $\boxed{-}$ $\boxed{-}$ $\boxed{M}$

Santa Monica | 2460 Wilshire Blvd. (25th St.) | 310-828-2115 | www.charlestonla.com

This buzzy Westside 'gastrolounge' offers a wide-ranging cocktail menu with fresh fruits and juices, and upscale Eclectic comfort food (short rib tacos with Korean salsa, smoked mac 'n' cheese) from Vegas expat Jet Tila; the dangling chandelier lights and leather booths, combined with live entertainment on a small stage in the center of the restaurant, may mark the start of a new wave of Hollywood-style eateries in the neighborhood.

Charlie's *Steak*

$\boxed{18}$ $\boxed{18}$ $\boxed{17}$ $\boxed{\$44}$

Malibu | 22821 PCH (Sweetwater Canyon Dr.) | 310-456-3132 | www.charliesmalibu.com

Seemingly "the only steakhouse for miles", this loungey Malibu meatery is designed for "chilling with some wine" and cocktails along with chops and seafood; still, given complaints about "average food" and "not-so-hot" service (unless "you're a star"), many feel it's "too expensive for what you get."

Chart House *Seafood/Steak*

$\boxed{23}$ $\boxed{24}$ $\boxed{23}$ $\boxed{\$46}$

Malibu | 18412 PCH (S. Topanga Canyon Blvd.) | 310-454-9321
Marina del Rey | 13950 Panay Way (Via Marina) | 310-822-4144
Redondo Beach | 231 Yacht Club Way (Harbor Dr.) | 310-372-3464
www.chart-house.com

"Gorgeous" waterside views provide a backdrop for "special dinners" at these "lovely" chain links offering "satisfying" seafood and steaks accompanied by "dependable" service; while some say the "expensive" fare doesn't leave them "overly impressed", those who "sit by the window" are wowed enough to remember the "wonderful location."

Chaya Brasserie *Asian/French*

| 24 | 23 | 23 | $52 |

West Hollywood | 8741 Alden Dr. (Robertson Blvd.) | 310-859-8833 |
www.thechaya.com

"Still going strong", this "timeless" West Hollywood Asian-French
pulls a "beautiful" crowd with "consistently innovative" dishes, "excellent" service and a "lovely" "Zen"-like interior that feels "trendy, but
isn't a hassle to get into"; it's "not cheap", but consensus is "you can
wear a blindfold and still pick something good to eat."

Chaya Downtown *Asian/French*

| 24 | 24 | 23 | $50 |

Downtown | City Nat'l Plaza | 525 S. Flower St. (bet. 5th & 6th Sts.) |
213-236-9577 | www.thechaya.com

This "classy" Downtown eatery in the Chaya empire is a "favorite" for
business lunches and pre-theater dining thanks to its "creative, delicious" Asian-French fusion fare and "terrific cocktails" served by a
"brisk, professional" staff in a "stylish", "sophisticated" setting; some
say prices are "best suited for an expense account", or try a seat at the
"happening" bar for nibbles and drinks at happy hour.

Chaya Venice *Asian/French*

| 23 | 22 | 21 | $43 |

Venice | 110 Navy St. (Main St.) | 310-396-1179 |
www.thechaya.com

"Still hot after all these years", this perpetually "packed" Venice canteen attracts lots of "pretty people" with "wonderfully fresh" sushi and
"consistently delicious" Asian-French fare served by a "sophisticated"
staff; there's also a "cool bar scene" – just "go early if you value your
eardrums", and take advantage of the "epic" happy hour.

Checkers Downtown *Californian*

| 23 | 23 | 22 | $51 |

Downtown | Hilton Checkers | 535 S. Grand Ave. (bet. 5th & 6th Sts.) |
213-891-0519 | www.hiltoncheckers.com

The place to go for a "civilized business breakfast meeting" or pre-
theater dining, this "quiet" Californian in the Hilton Checkers Downtown
serves all "the usual suspects" with "excellent" execution; while it's
expensive, the setting's "refined" and service is "thoughtful", so most
are "never disappointed."

Cheebo *Italian*

| 21 | 17 | 19 | $27 |

Hollywood | 7533 W. Sunset Blvd. (bet. Gardner St. & Sierra Bonita Ave.) |
323-850-7070 | www.cheebo.com

A "neighborhood" crowd counts on this "buzzy" Hollywood joint featuring a "wide-ranging", "healthy", mostly organic Italian menu and
"tasty" pizza sold by the slab; some say it's "pricier than you might
think", but with an unpretentious bright-orange setting and affable
service, it's "always busy"; it also works well for takeout.

☑ Cheesecake Factory *American*

| 23 | 22 | 22 | $28 |

Fairfax | The Grove | 189 The Grove Dr. (bet. Beverly Blvd. & 3rd St.) |
323-634-0511
Beverly Hills | 364 N. Beverly Dr. (Brighton Way) | 310-278-7270
Brentwood | 11647 San Vicente Blvd. (bet. Barrington & Darlington Aves.) |
310-826-7111
Marina del Rey | 4142 Via Marina (Panay Way) | 310-306-3344
Redondo Beach | 605 N. Harbor Dr. (Marina Way) | 310-376-0466
Arcadia | 400 S. Baldwin Ave. (W. Huntington Dr.) | 626-447-2800

(continued)

Cheesecake Factory

Pasadena | 2 W. Colorado Blvd. (Fair Oaks Ave.) | 626-584-6000
Sherman Oaks | Sherman Oaks Galleria | 15301 Ventura Blvd.
(Sepulveda Blvd.) | 818-906-0700
Woodland Hills | Warner Ctr. | 6324 Canoga Ave. (bet. Erwin St. &
Victory Blvd.) | 818-883-9900
Thousand Oaks | Thousand Oaks Mall | 442 W. Hillcrest Dr. (McCloud Ave.) |
805-371-9705
www.thecheesecakefactory.com
Additional locations throughout Southern California

"Eat dessert first" say fans of the "innovative cheesecake flavors" at
this "energetic" concept – LA's Most Popular chain – known for its
"overwhelming" menu of "reliable" American eats served in "gigantic"
portions, "big enough to split" for the best value; the columned rooms
are "interesting" and the service "prompt", but be ready for some
"hustle-bustle" since there are "long lines" at peak hours; P.S. calorie-
counters call the "new lighter fare" a "welcome addition."

Chef Melba's Bistro Ⓜ *Californian*   26 | 16 | 23 | $45

Hermosa Beach | 1501 Hermosa Ave. (15th St.) | 310-376-2084 |
www.chefmelbasbistro.com

A "small place with big taste", this Hermosa Beach bistro is a "top
pick" thanks to the "delicious", "lovingly prepared" Cal cuisine cooked
up by chef Melba herself in an open kitchen; never mind the "nondescript" setting, the mood is "warm and welcoming" and "the best part
is the shockingly affordable price."

Chego! ❶ⓏⓂ *Korean/Mexican*   24 | 12 | 16 | $15

Palms | 3300 Overland Ave. (Rose Ave.) | 310-287-0337 |
www.eatchego.com

This "trendy" mini-mall sibling of Kogi provides a permanent
Palms home for Roy Choi's "clever", "intensely flavored" Korean-
Mex street-food concoctions like the "unforgettable" pork belly
bowl; the counter-serve setting is frequently "busy" and "noisy",
but "amazing" prices make up for it; P.S. you can BYO from the liquor
store next door.

Cheval Blanc Bistro Ⓜ *French*   24 | 23 | 23 | $45

Pasadena | 41 S. De Lacey Ave. (Colorado Blvd.) | 626-577-4141 |
www.chevalblancbistro.com

It's like "Paris in Pasadena" at this Old Town French from the Smith
Brothers, earning a "thumbs-up" for its "enjoyable" menu elevated by
specialty cocktails and an "epic" wine list in a "quiet" space whose
centerpiece is a 100-year-old mahogany bar; midrange pricing is a
plus, and although a few find fault with "inconsistent" food and service, most leave "satisfied."

Chez Jay *Steak*   20 | 18 | 20 | $33

Santa Monica | 1657 Ocean Ave. (Colorado Ave.) | 310-395-1741 |
www.chezjays.com

"An oldie but goodie", this circa-1959 Santa Monica "dive" is a "sentimental favorite" for "decent" steaks that "won't break the bank" helped
along by "stiff drinks" in a "kitschy" setting with red-checkered tablecloths and sawdust on the floor; most "don't go for the food", but "if

you want to experience a little bit of Hollywood history by the beach, then this is the place."

Chez Mélange *Eclectic*
26 | 22 | 26 | $45

Redondo Beach | 1611 S. Catalina Ave. (bet. Aves. H & I) | 310-540-1222 | www.chezmelange.com

"As reliable as ever", this Redondo Beach "local favorite" continues to be "ahead of the curve" with an "imaginative" Eclectic menu that "shines with local, seasonal ingredients" and an "A+ wine list"; with "gracious" service and a "lovely" setting, most find it a "delightful experience that pleases the palate but doesn't hurt the wallet"; P.S. the Trust the Chef prix fixe dinners are "a bargain and delicious."

Chichen Itza *Mexican*
25 | 11 | 18 | $17

Downtown | Mercado La Paloma | 3655 S. Grand Ave. (bet. 35th & 37th Sts.) | 213-741-1075 | www.chichenitzarestaurant.com

"*Que sabroso!*" say fans of the "startlingly unique" Yucatecan cuisine like cochinita pibil and other "amazing", "authentic" items that "have legitimate wow factor" at this "no-frills" Mexican in Downtown's Mercado La Paloma; it's counter service only, but the staff is "helpful" with recommendations, and it's one of the "best bets around USC for sure."

Chi Dynasty *Chinese*
21 | 20 | 20 | $28

Los Feliz | Los Feliz Plaza | 1813 Hillhurst Ave. (bet. Melbourne & Russell Aves.) | 323-667-3388

NEW **Glendale** | Americana at Brand | 769 Americana Way (bet. Brand Blvd. & Central Ave.) | 818-500-9888

Studio City | 12229 Ventura Blvd. (Lauren Canyon Blvd.) | 818-753-5300 www.chidynasty.com

Locals "love the Chinese chicken salad" and other "fresh, flavorful" (if "inauthentic") eats at this chainlet manned by a "pleasant" staff; the menu is a "tad pricier than your average take-out" joint, but the ambiance is a step up too, with a "dark", contemporary look that "makes you want to drink mai tais all night."

Chili John's ☒ *American*
24 | 13 | 22 | $14

Burbank | 2018 W. Burbank Blvd. (N. Keystone St.) | 818-846-3611

A "throwback to the lunch counters of the '40s", this Burbank old-timer is crammed with a "dedicated clientele" digging into "tasty" chili "served every which way" and "yummy" icebox pies; the dinerlike space with a horseshoe-shaped counter is utterly "no-frills", but that's all part of the "charm"; P.S. closed in July.

China Grill *Chinese*
21 | 18 | 19 | $31

Manhattan Beach | Manhattan Vill. | 3282 N. Sepulveda Blvd. (bet. Marine & Rosecrans Aves.) | 310-546-7284 | www.chinagrillbistro.com

"Modern" Chinese cuisine is presented with a "tasty" California twist at this "reliable" option in Manhattan Beach cherished for its signature orange chicken and "addictive wonton chips"; the service and contemporary setting are nothing to write home about, but midrange prices and a "great" selection mean there's "something for everyone."

Chin Chin *Asian*
20 | 17 | 19 | $25

West Hollywood | Sunset Plaza | 8618 W. Sunset Blvd. (Sunset Plaza Dr.) | 310-652-1818

Beverly Hills | 206 S. Beverly Dr. (Charleville Blvd.) | 310-248-5252

(continued)
Chin Chin
Brentwood | San Vincente Plaza | 11740 San Vicente Blvd. (Gorham Ave.) | 310-826-2525
Studio City | 12215 Ventura Blvd. (Woodley Ave.) | 818-985-9090
www.chinchin.com

It's all about the "addictive" Chinese chicken salad at this 1980s-era chainlet offering Asian fare that's "not terribly genuine, but still damn tasty" (chocolate-dipped fortune cookies anyone?) and "well priced" too; even if decor "needs a face-lift", "generous portions" and a "courteous" staff make for a pleasantly "predictable" experience; it's also "good for takeout."

☑ Chinois on Main *Asian/French*   27 | 21 | 24 | $64
Santa Monica | 2709 Main St. (Hill St.) | 310-392-9025 | www.wolfgangpuck.com

"Still smokin' after all these years", Wolfgang Puck's "one-of-a-kind", "high-priced" Asian-French destination in Santa Monica delivers "delectable" dishes like curried lobster and sizzling catfish via "superior" servers; "you can see lots of stars" in the "cramped, noisy" dining room, so even if some say "it still looks like 1983 in there", most consider it an "LA classic."

Chipotle *Mexican*   23 | 17 | 21 | $11
Fairfax | The Grove at Farmers Mkt. | 110 S. Fairfax Ave. (bet. Beverly Blvd. & 3rd St.) | 323-857-0608
Hawthorne | 5330 W. Rosecrans Ave. (bet. Hindry & Isis Aves.) | 310-297-0850
Lakewood | 5310 Lakewood Blvd. (Candlewood St.) | 562-790-8786
Beverly Hills | Beverly Ctr. | 121 N. La Cienega Blvd. (W. 3rd St.) | 310-855-0371
Beverly Hills | 244 S. Beverly Dr. (Gregory Way) | 310-273-8265
Marina del Rey | 4718 Admiralty Way (Mindanao Way) | 310-821-0059
El Segundo | 307 N. Sepulveda Blvd. (Grand Ave.) | 310-426-1437
Torrance | Torrance Crossroads | 24631 Crenshaw Blvd. (Skypark Dr.) | 310-530-0690
Pasadena | Hastings Ranch Shopping Ctr. | 3409 E. Foothill Blvd. (N. Halstead St.) | 626-351-6017
Burbank | Burbank Town Ctr. | 135 E. Palm Ave. (N. 1st St.) | 818-842-0622
www.chipotle.com
Additional locations throughout Southern California

"Filling" "build-your-own" burritos assembled from "fresh, mostly organic" ingredients keep the lines "long" at this "cheerful" "fast-casual" Mexican chain; not everyone digs the "assembly-line vibe" or "generic" modern decor, but at least "the price is right."

Cholada *Thai*   24 | 12 | 18 | $23
Malibu | 18763 PCH (Topanga Canyon Blvd.) | 310-317-0025
Thousand Oaks | 1724 E. Thousand Oaks Blvd. (Erbes Rd.) | 805-557-0899
www.choladathaicuisine.com

"Soak in the salty sea breeze" at this "funky" Thai "beach shack" nestled on PCH in Malibu, where "wonderfully authentic" "mouthwatering" fare makes a "true believer" out of many; the bills are low, so the only downside is that "service is so efficient, you may be out the door in 30 minutes"; P.S. the newer Thousand Oaks location is less of a charmer.

	FOOD	DECOR	SERVICE	COST

ChoSun Galbee *Korean* | 24 | 19 | 20 | $37 |

Koreatown | 3330 W. Olympic Blvd. (Manhattan Pl.) |
323-734-3330

This "upscale", elegant" Korean "impresses" guests with "tender, flavorful" grill-your-own meats of "excellent quality" and "good wines" in
a "lovely" modern milieu that's "rare for K-town"; service is "attentive"
and a patio is a plus, so the only drawback is the "premium pricing."

Christine ⊠ *Mediterranean/Pacific Rim* | 27 | 20 | 26 | $44 |

Torrance | Hillside Vill. | 24530 Hawthorne Blvd. (Via Valmonte) |
310-373-1952 | www.restaurantchristine.com

"Charming" is the word for this "adorable, little" "local favorite" in
Torrance where the "warm personality and creativity" of chef-owner
Christine Brown is reflected in her "wonderful", "constantly evolving"
Med–Pacific Rim menu; true, it's a touch "expensive", but an "atten-
tive staff makes sure your dining experience is a pleasant one."

Chronic Tacos Cantina *Mexican* | 21 | 16 | 20 | $13 |

Cerritos | 11308 South St. (Gridley Rd.) | 562-809-8226 |
www.chroniccantina.com
Long Beach | 3870 E. Ocean Blvd. (E. Livingston Dr.) | 562-438-2714 |
www.chroniccantina.com
Long Beach | 5525 E. Stearns St. (Bellflower Rd.) | 562-493-2211 |
www.chroniccantina.com
Long Beach | 6602 E. PCH (Channel Dr.) | 562-430-8200 |
www.chroniccantina.com ⊅
Redondo Beach | 306 S. PCH (Torrance Blvd.) | 310-316-8226 |
www.chroniccantina.com
West Covina | Westfield West Covina Mall | 112 Plaza Dr. (Garvey Ave. S.) |
626-960-1221 | www.eatchronictacos.com
West Covina | 2260 S. Azusa Ave. (Amar Rd.) | 626-964-8000 |
www.chroniccantina.com
Saugus | 27665 Bouquet Canyon Rd. (Haskell Canyon Rd.) | 661-296-6900 |
www.chroniccantina.com

You'll find everyone from "surfers to stuffy bankers" at this "justifiably
famous" chain of "gringo"-Mex joints where you select your own
"fresh", "flavorful" fillings and watch as tacos and burritos are "made
to order"; counter service comes "with a smile", and some sites boast
full bars, but for many "it's just a cool place to eat and go."

Church & State *French* | 24 | 21 | 20 | $47 |

Downtown | 1850 Industrial St. (Mateo St.) | 213-405-1434 |
www.churchandstatebistro.com

Evoking both "SoHo and Paris", this "cool" bistro on an "industrial"
stretch Downtown is a "find" for "delectable" French fare ("the
housemade charcuterie is mandatory") and "excellent drinks" in a
"hip", if "ear-achingly noisy", space; some say it's "pricey" and service can be "slow", but on the whole "church and state never went
together so well."

NEW The Churchill ◗ *American* | ▽ 17 | 20 | 15 | $35 |

West Hollywood | Orlando Hotel | 8384 W. Third St. (S. Orlando Ave.) |
323-655-8384 | www.the-churchill.com

It "looks like a pub" but "feels like a club" at this "sceney" two-story
WeHo gastropub newcomer that's "ridiculously packed at night" with
"young professionals chitchatting and networking" who ignore the

"unapologetically slow" service and slightly high tabs; some say the food's "tasty" enough, but the consensus is it's more about the "swell" cocktails and "excellent" beer selection than the "mediocre" eats.

☑ Cicada ☒ *Californian/Italian*

27 | 28 | 25 | $59

Downtown | 617 S. Olive St. (bet. 6th & 7th Sts.) | 213-488-9488 | www.cicadarestaurant.com

"Old-school glamour" is alive and well at this "exquisite" art deco Downtowner boasting 30-ft. ceilings, a grand staircase and swing dancing on Sunday nights; it's "pricey", but it follows through with "fabulous" Cal-Italian fare and "wonderful" service, so "you can't beat" it for a "special" night; P.S. hours vary if it's booked for an event, so call ahead.

City Tavern *American*

20 | 21 | 19 | $29

Culver City | 9739 Culver Blvd. (Duquesne Ave.) | 310-838-9739 | www.citytavernculvercity.com

"If you love beer" you'll certainly appreciate the self-serve taps at the tables (a "fun gimmick") and the selection of ever-changing local brews at this rustic-chic Culver City tavern; a "limited menu" of "inventive", well-priced American comfort food pleases, but service is erratic and some find the "frat-boy" crowd a little hard to handle.

City Wok *Chinese*

23 | 15 | 22 | $17

Studio City | 10949 Ventura Blvd. (Vineland Ave.) | 818-506-4050 | www.citywok.com

"From the kung pao shrimp to the wonton soup, it's all good" profess neighborhood fans of this "bustling" Studio City Chinese churning out "fast, flavorful" takes on all the "classics"; as long as you "don't have haute cuisine expectations", you won't be disappointed by the strip-mall ambiance, but those in the know prefer takeout.

Clafoutis *French/Italian*

22 | 20 | 21 | $36

West Hollywood | Sunset Plaza | 8630 W. Sunset Blvd. (Sunset Plaza Dr.) | 310-659-5233 | www.leclafoutis.fr

For some of the "best people-watching" on the Sunset Strip, snag a seat outside at this "casual" cafe in Sunset Plaza smack-dab "in the center of all the action" where "you never know who you'll see sitting next to you"; decent service and a "reasonably priced" French-Italian menu appeal to the "Euro" clientele, and if some say there's "better fare elsewhere", at least you can't beat the scene.

Clay Oven *Indian*

23 | 17 | 19 | $26

Sherman Oaks | 14611 Ventura Blvd. (Van Nuys Blvd.) | 818-995-1777 | www.myindiancuisine.com

The "sumptuous" lunch buffet is the "best deal" at this Sherman Oaks Indian offering "solid", "well-prepared" fare in a selection that "changes daily"; although reviews on service are mixed, prices are reasonable and the patio is a plus.

Clearman's Galley *American*

22 | 20 | 20 | $21

San Gabriel | 7215 N. Rosemead Blvd. (Huntington Dr.) | 626-286-1484 | www.clearmansrestaurants.com

Known to locals as "the boat", this San Gabriel American "throwback" is known for its signature cheese bread, red-cabbage salad and "sloppy chili burgers" served in way-"casual" digs; "wall-to-wall TVs" and a "good beer selection" mean "on game days it gets pretty full", although some still gripe about the prices.

Clementine ☒ *American* | 25 | 13 | 17 | $20 |

Century City | 1751 Ensley Ave. (Santa Monica Blvd.) | 310-552-1080 | www.clementineonline.com

"Simply adorable", this "tiny, little" Century City cafe is a find for "delish" sandwiches and salads, plus "wonderful" "artisan-style" pastries and breads; counter service is "kind", but the vibe is "hectic" thanks to "scarce" parking and "cramped", "crowded" quarters, so many prefer takeout; P.S "don't miss" the special grilled cheese menu in April.

Cleo *Mediterranean* | 27 | 25 | 22 | $50 |

Hollywood | Redbury Hotel | 1717 Vine St. (Hollywood Blvd.) | 323-962-1711 | www.cleorestaurant.com

"A see-and-be-seen scene" permeates this "terminally hip", "gorgeous" destination in Sam Nazarian's Redbury Hotel, where "expertly prepared" Mediterranean small plates, a "solid wine list" and "fun" cocktails "raise the bar" for Hollywood nightlife; a "knowledgeable" staff is a plus, but the bill adds up quickly and the partylike atmosphere makes it "incredibly loud."

Cliff's Edge *Californian/Italian* | 21 | 27 | 20 | $39 |

Silver Lake | 3626 W. Sunset Blvd. (Edgecliffe Dr.) | 323-666-6116 | www.cliffsedgecafe.com

"Lingering alfresco is what it's all about" at this Silver Lake charmer – a "surprising oasis" in an "unassuming strip mall" – boasting a "magical" patio shaded by trees that works for brunch or "when you have a date you want to impress"; it's not inexpensive, but service is solid and the Cal-Italian menu (kale salad, Cornish hen) is "enjoyable" too.

Coast *Californian/Seafood* | 23 | 25 | 23 | $43 |

Santa Monica | Shutters on the Beach | 1 Pico Blvd. (Ocean Ave.) | 310-587-1707 | www.coastsantamonica.com

"As close as you can get to the beach" without being sand-bound, this "expensive" Santa Monica Californian at Shutters hotel (with a spin-off in Santa Barbara) regales diners with "wonderful" ocean views from its waterside patio; some say the "competent" seafood may not match the ambiance, but service is "excellent" and to most it's a "class act."

Cole's *Sandwiches* | 17 | 19 | 15 | $20 |

Downtown | 118 E. Sixth St. (bet. S. Los Angeles & S. Main Sts.) | 213-622-4090 | www.colesfrenchdip.com

A dose of "old-fashioned goodness", this circa-1908 Downtown "classic" "feels like a trip back in time" with "fair" French dips made with beef and lamb served in an "atmospheric" setting; critics claim it's "expensive" and "used to be better", so its biggest asset may be the hidden speakeasy in back – The Varnish – known for its crafty mixologists, "designer" cocktails and "hipster" crowd.

Colori Kitchen ☒ *Italian* | 25 | 15 | 20 | $29 |

Downtown | 429 W. Eighth St. (bet. S. Hill & S. Olive Sts.) | 213-622-5950 | www.colorikitchen.com

Regulars worry that "the secret is out" about this "cozy", "mom-and-pop" Downtown Italian featuring "hearty", "authentic" fare like "wonderful" pastas at affordable rates helped along by a BYO policy; the setting's rather "basic", but locals don't seem to mind – "in a glitzier location, reservations would be a must."

Comme Ça *French*

24 | 22 | 22 | $49

West Hollywood | 8479 Melrose Ave. (La Cienega Blvd.) | 323-782-1104 | www.commecarestaurant.com

Feel transported to "Paris in a flash" at this "beloved" West Hollywood brasserie where "Oscar winners and wannabes" tuck into "fabulous", "authentic" eats and "wonderful cheeses" plus a "phenomenal" burger in a "swank" setting; with "creative cocktails" and a "good-looking" staff, it makes for a "delightful", if "pricey", experience – now if only they could "turn down the volume."

NEW Cooks County *Californian*

25 | 20 | 24 | $41

Beverly Boulevard | 8009 Beverly Blvd. (bet. N. Edinburgh & N. Laurel Aves.) | 323-653-8009 | www.cookscountyrestaurant.com

"It feels like an urban farmhouse" at this market-driven entry on Beverly Boulevard, where regulars report "you can't go wrong" with the "imaginative" Californian fare offered all day at "reasonable" rates; a "lovely staff" brings "lots of smiles" to the *"très* informal" setting, and despite some quibbles about noise and tight seating, most dub it truly "stress-free dining."

Cook's Tortas *Mexican*

25 | 15 | 21 | $12

Monterey Park | 1944 S. Atlantic Blvd. (bet. Brightwood St. & Floral Dr.) | 323-278-3536 | www.cookstortas.com

"The definition of a hidden gem", this Monterey Park Mexican sandwich shop purveys "the platonic ideal of tortas" crafted with "flavorful" meats and "fresh" "homemade" bread, in "imaginative" combinations; "long lines" can be the norm in the deli-style space, but "fast, friendly" service keeps the crowds moving and prices won't break the bank; P.S. don't forget the agua frescas!

Coral Cafe ● *American/Mexican*

22 | 14 | 22 | $15

Burbank | 3321 W. Burbank Blvd. (N. Lima St.) | 818-566-9725 | www.coralcafe.com

"At any hour of the day" you'll find "locals and studio folks" at this "quintessential" Burbank diner serving "reliable" American-Mexican coffee-shop grub, from waffles to huevos rancheros; "it's a dive, but a good one", with affable staff and "reasonable" prices, plus it's open 24/7 – "what more could you want?"

Coral Tree Café *Sandwiches*

20 | 17 | 18 | $18

Brentwood | 11645 San Vicente Blvd. (bet. Barrington & Darlington Aves.) | 310-979-8733

Encino | 17499 Ventura Blvd. (Encino Ave.) | 818-789-8733

Coral Tree Express *Sandwiches*

Century City | Westfield Century City Shopping Ctr. | 10250 Santa Monica Blvd. (bet. Ave. of the Stars & Century Park W.) | 310-553-8733
www.coraltreecafe.com

Neighborhood types rely on these "comfy" cafes for "healthy" "dependable" sandwiches, salads and pastries crafted from organic ingredients, and "decent coffee"; decor is a "mixed bag", but free WiFi helps, and most find "friendliness trumps its few flaws."

	FOOD	DECOR	SERVICE	COST

Cora's Coffee Shoppe *Diner*

| 23 | 16 | 18 | $22 |

Santa Monica | 1802 Ocean Ave. (bet. Colorado Ave. & Pico Blvd.) | 310-451-9562 | www.corascoffee.com

Locals love this "cool breakfast spot" in Santa Monica slinging "gourmet coffee-shop" grub "geared for foodies" and offered till 3 PM daily; service is "efficient", and it boasts a "cute" covered patio, but it's often "so crowded" that it's "tough to get a seat."

Corkbar *Eclectic*

| 22 | 22 | 22 | $38 |

Downtown | 403 W. 12th St. (Grand Ave.) | 213-746-0050 | www.corkbar.com

A "fantastic" selection of nearly 70 wines by the glass paired with "solid" Eclectic nibbles (like fish tacos and grilled cheese) makes this "minimalist" Downtown bar a "cool" hangout after work or before a game at Staples Center; "wonderful" happy-hour deals draw "noisy" crowds, so snag a seat near the outdoor fire pit for more elbow room.

NEW Corner Door ● *American*

| - | - | - | M |

Culver City | 12477 W. Washington Blvd. (Wasatch Ave.) | 310-313-5810 | www.thecornerdoorla.com

The door is indeed in the corner of this Culver City New American offering a moderately priced menu of farm-to-table pub fare and creative cocktails (plus beer and wine); the spacious bare-brick and polished wood-lined interior and brightly lit bar are a welcome addition to the burgeoning Westside Restaurant Row.

The Counter *Burgers*

| 21 | 15 | 18 | $19 |

Mid-Wilshire | 5779 Wilshire Blvd. (S. Curson Ave.) | 323-932-8900
West Hollywood | 7919 Sunset Blvd. (bet. Fairfax & Hayworth Aves.) | 323-436-3844
NEW Century City | Westfield Century City Shopping Ctr. | 10250 Santa Monica Blvd. (bet. Ave. of the Stars & Century Park W.) | 310-282-8888
Marina del Rey | 4786 Admiralty Way (Fiji Way) | 310-827-8600
Santa Monica | 2901 Ocean Park Blvd. (bet. 29th & 30th Sts.) | 310-399-8383
El Segundo | Plaza El Segundo | 700 S. Allied Way (Rosecrans Ave.) | 310-524-9967
NEW Hermosa Beach | 719 Pier Ave. (PCH) | 310-374-1511
North Hollywood | 10123 Riverside Dr. (Talofa Ave.) | 818-509-1881
Studio City | 12117 Ventura Blvd. (Laurel Canyon Blvd.) | 818-980-0004
Westlake Village | 30990 Russell Ranch Rd. (Lindero Canyon Rd.) | 818-889-0080
www.thecounterburger.com
Additional locations throughout Southern California

There's a "smorgasbord" of "exotic toppings" to go with the "juicy, well-seasoned" patties at this "cute" "build-your-own" burger chain also offering "awesome sweet potato fries", "old-fashioned milkshakes" (available spiked) and craft brews "served with a smile"; even if it's "costly" and the "utilitarian", "industrial-chic" interiors can be "too loud", most "love the concept."

Coyote Cantina *Southwestern*

| 22 | 22 | 23 | $25 |

Redondo Beach | King Harbor Marina | 531 N. PCH (Beryl St.) | 310-376-1066 | www.coyotecantina.net

The mood is always "friendly" at this "happening" joint in Redondo Beach, where "tasty" Southwestern fare is matched with over 100 "top-notch" tequilas in colorful strip-mall quarters; "fairly reasonable" prices seal the deal, but "get there early" because it's "always packed."

Crab Pot *Seafood*   24 | 21 | 22 | $40

Long Beach | 215 N. Marina Dr. (Marina Dr.) | 562-430-0272 | www.crabpotlongbeach.com

The specialty at this mariner-themed Long Beach seafood chainlet is a mound of steamed crustaceans piled on butcher paper for diners to "navigate" with only a mallet and a bib; "hammering away at the crab" is "loud" and "a bit messy", and some balk at the "premium" price, but "lovely" sunset views and "fast, friendly" service make it "worth every penny."

Craft ✉ *American*   25 | 26 | 25 | $70

Century City | 10100 Constellation Blvd. (bet. Ave. of the Stars & Century Park E.) | 310-279-4180 | www.craftrestaurant.com

"Everything is on point" at celeb chef Tom Colicchio's "sophisticated" enclave (and unofficial CAA commissary) in Century City, from the "refined", "farm-fresh" American cuisine offered family-style to the "impeccable" service and "architecturally perfect" setting encased in glass; the pricing is made for an "expense account", or opt for the lower-priced Craftbar menu available on the patio or in the bar.

Craig's *American*   24 | 25 | 26 | $57

West Hollywood | 8826 Melrose Ave. (Doheny Dr.) | 310-276-1900 | www.craigs.la

"Lots of celebs" are drawn to this pricey West Hollywood "'in' place" from Craig Susser (ex maitre d' at Dan Tana's) set in "clubby" digs with deco touches; although the upmarket American comfort fare like honey-truffle fried chicken is mostly "delicious", the real draw is the "gracious" service that "treats everyone like a regular", and "you can't go wrong" with a "star sighting or two."

Crazy Fish *Japanese*   22 | 13 | 17 | $29

Beverly Hills | 9105 W. Olympic Blvd. (S. Doheny Dr.) | 310-550-8547

"Monster-size" "fried, battered and cream-cheesed" sushi rolls "for the masses" turn up at this Beverly Hills Japanese boasting solid "bang for the buck"; the service and setting are strictly "no frills", but it's still often "crowded" and "waits" are the norm.

Crème De La Crêpe *Crêpes*   23 | 18 | 21 | $21

Culver City | 6000 Sepulveda Blvd. (W. Slauson Ave.) | 310-391-8818

Hermosa Beach | 424 Pier Ave. (Valley Dr.) | 310-937-2822

Long Beach | 400 E. First St. (Elm Ave. & N. Frontena Ct.) | 562-437-2222

Manhattan Beach | 1140 Highland Ave. (Center Pl.) | 310-546-9900

Redondo Beach | 1708 Catalina Ave. (Del Norte Ave.) | 310-540-8811

Pasadena | 36 W. Colorado Blvd. (Mills Pl.) | 626-844-0007 www.cremedelacrepe.com

"A taste of France" on a "budget", this "charming" chain puts out "every kind of crêpe imaginable" along with "yummy lattes" and more substantial fare for dinner; the ambiance is "cute" and service is "pleasant", making it a "good value" for a "casual" bite.

	FOOD	DECOR	SERVICE	COST

Crustacean *Asian/Vietnamese*

| 25 | 27 | 23 | $63 |

Beverly Hills | 9646 Little Santa Monica Blvd. (Bedford Dr.) | 310-205-8990 | www.houseofan.com

It's all about the "sublime" garlic noodles and "last meal–worthy" cracked crab at this "posh" Vietnamese-Asian fusion restaurant that's equally "memorable" for its "exotic" "faux-rainforest setting" with a koi pond underfoot; a few find the "glitzy" atmosphere "stuck in the '90s", and warn that you should expect to pay "Beverly Hills prices"

NEW Crust Pizza Bar *Pizza*

| – | – | – | I |

Studio City | 11928 Ventura Blvd. (bet. Carpenter & Radford Aves.) | 818-980-0008 | www.crust.com

This Studio City newcomer is the first American outpost of an affordable Australian chain serving pizzas (Neapolitan or deep-dish) with toppings that range from the familiar to Aussie favorites like garlic prawn and peri-peri chicken; it's all served in a modern red-and-black space with low tables and a design-your-own-pizza bar.

Cube Cafe ●M *Italian*

| 25 | 18 | 22 | $41 |

La Brea | 615 N. La Brea Ave. (Clinton St.) | 323-939-1148 | www.EatAtCube.com

"A foodie favorite", this "adorable, little" La Brea Italian packs a big punch with "imaginative" small plates, "outstanding pastas" and "well-chosen" cheeses and salumi all at "reasonable" prices; add in an "unpretentious" atmosphere and "knowledgeable" service, and it's "satisfying" all around.

Culina Modern Italian *Italian*

| 24 | 27 | 26 | $65 |

Beverly Hills | Four Seasons Beverly Hills | 300 S. Doheny Dr. (Burton Way) | 310-860-4000 | www.culinarestaurant.com

The celeb-heavy Four Seasons Beverly Hills is home to this "elegant", "grown-up" hideaway offering "delicious" Italian dishes with a "fresh, local spin" – plus a "fantastic crudo bar" – backed by an "awesome wine list with hard-to-find gems"; prices are a "splurge", but insiders insist the service is "gracious and unpretentious", and sitting on the patio near the fire pit is a "pleasure."

☑ Cut Ⓢ *Steak*

| 27 | 25 | 26 | $102 |

Beverly Hills | Beverly Wilshire | 9500 Wilshire Blvd. (Rodeo Dr.) | 310-276-8500 | www.wolfgangpuck.com

"The apex of meatdom", Wolfgang Puck's "innovative, extravagant" take on the classic steakhouse in Beverly Hills "hits it out of the park" with "sublime cuts" and "divine" sides offered in a "sleek, modern", "star-studded" setting; it follows through with "exceptional" service, but you may "need to take out a loan" to foot the bill; P.S. a limited menu is available in the no-reservations Sidebar.

Cuvée *Californian*

| 23 | 18 | 19 | $21 |

West Hollywood | 145 N. Robertson Blvd. (bet. Beverly Blvd. & Burton Way) | 310-271-4333

Century City | 2000 Ave. of the Stars (Constellation Blvd.) | 310-277-3303 Ⓢ www.mycuvee.com

When you need a "quick, healthy bite" these "reliable" Cal cafes in Century City and West Hollywood do the trick with an "enormous selection" of "beautifully prepared" sandwiches, salads and smoothies;

prices are "fair" for the location and service is "fast and friendly", plus there's outdoor seating for those who want to linger.

Daikokuya *Japanese*　　24 | 13 | 16 | $15

Little Tokyo | 327 E. First St. (Judge John Aiso St.) | 213-626-1680 ●⊄
Hacienda Heights | 15827 E. Gale Ave. (bet. Hacienda Blvd. & Olympus Ave.) | 626-968-0810
Arcadia | 1220 S. Golden W. Ave. (W. Duarte Rd.) | 626-254-0127 ⊄
Monterey Park | 111 N. Atlantic Blvd. (Garvey Ave.) | 626-570-1930 ●
www.daikoku-ten.com

"Warm, bouncy noodles" and "rich", "flavorful broth" "make all the difference" for the "superior ramen" at this affordable chainlet of Japanese "greasy spoons"; there's "minimal service, little capacity and long lines", but "is it worth it? absolutely."

Daily Grill *American*　　21 | 19 | 21 | $32

Downtown | Pegasus Apartments | 612 S. Flower St. (bet. 6th St. & Wilshire Blvd.) | 213-622-4500
Brentwood | Brentwood Gdns. | 11677 San Vicente Blvd. (bet. Barrington & Darlington Aves.) | 310-442-0044
Santa Monica | Yahoo! Ctr. | 2501 Colorado Ave. (bet. Cloverfield Blvd. & 26th St.) | 310-309-2170 ⊠
LAX | LA Int'l Airport, TBIT | 1 World Way (Sepulveda Blvd.) | 310-215-5180
Burbank | Burbank Marriott | 2500 Hollywood Way (Empire Ave.) | 818-840-6464
Studio City | Laurel Promenade | 12050 Ventura Blvd. (Laurel Canyon Blvd.) | 818-769-6336
www.dailygrill.com

Customers "count on" "generous portions" of "homespun" American fare (like "gotta-try" chicken pot pie) that's "prepared well" and "served with a smile" at this "comfortable", "popular" chain; though a few feel it's priced "a buck or two higher than the food merits", most find it a "reasonable", "reliable" choice.

Dal Rae *Continental*　　26 | 21 | 25 | $53

Pico Rivera | 9023 E. Washington Blvd. (Rosemead Blvd.) | 562-949-2444 | www.dalrae.com

"Dress to the nines" and "step back in time" for a trip to this "expensive" Pico Rivera "icon" delivering "top-shelf", "old-school" Continental fare; service is "outstanding" in the dim wood-and-leather setting with a piano bar, making it "one of the last of its kind."

Damon's Steakhouse *Steak*　　23 | 20 | 23 | $33

Glendale | 317 N. Brand Blvd. (bet. W. California Ave. & W. Lexington Dr.) | 818-507-1510 | www.damonsglendale.com

If you like "kitschy", head to this "nifty" 75-year-old tiki bar and "Polynesian"-themed steakhouse in Glendale delivering "good" cuts and "strong" mai tais in a delightfully "dated" setting among fake palms; no, "it's not gourmet", but a "friendly" vibe and "decent prices" earn it a "steady following."

Dan Tana's ● *Italian*　　23 | 20 | 23 | $62

West Hollywood | 9071 Santa Monica Blvd. (Doheny Dr.) | 310-275-9444 | www.dantanasrestaurant.com

There's "never a dull moment" at this "legendary" late-night "hideaway" in West Hollywood, where a "celeb"-studded crowd comes for "perfect martinis" and "pricey" "old-fashioned" Italian fare in "dark", "clubby" digs that take you "back to the '50s"; "waits" are the norm and "unless you're George Clooney, good luck getting a reservation", but once you nab a table, consensus is it's "still fabulous."

Da Pasquale 🗷 *Italian* | 24 | 18 | 23 | $38 |

Beverly Hills | 9749 Little Santa Monica Blvd. (bet. Linden & Roxbury Drs.) | 310-859-3884 | www.dapasqualecaffe.com
This "charming" Beverly Hills "mom-and-pop" Italian is a standby for "simple" "unpretentious" fare like "homemade pastas" and "hearty", "rustic" mains; "good-value" pricing, "quaint", "cozy" surroundings and a "welcoming" staff further the "warm" mood.

Dar Maghreb *Moroccan* | 22 | 26 | 23 | $49 |

Hollywood | 7651 W. Sunset Blvd. (Stanley Ave.) | 323-876-7651 | www.darmaghrebrestaurant.com
"Hollywood glamour" and "Moroccan delights" come together at this "unique" "palace" that "transports you to a different world" with "wonderfully tiled" decor and an "authentic" seven-course feast that's "a real indulgent treat"; if you "have a yen for the exotic" it's "fun for groups", and even if a handful of critics call it a "shadow of its former self", "the belly dancers keep you distracted enough."

Darren's 🗷 *Californian* | 25 | 21 | 24 | $53 |

Manhattan Beach | 1141 Manhattan Ave. (Manhattan Beach Blvd.) | 310-802-1973 | www.darrensrestaurant.com
Chef-owner Darren Weiss' Manhattan Beach "respite" "keeps things interesting" with "fabulous" "upscale" Californian–New American cuisine set down in "stylish, comfortable" quarters; service is "attentive, but not overly so", and with a "happening bar scene" later on, fans "couldn't ask for more."

Delmonico's Lobster House *Seafood* | 24 | 22 | 23 | $49 |

Encino | 16358 Ventura Blvd. (Noeline Ave.) | 818-986-0777 | www.delmonicossteakandlobsterhouse.com
An "old standby", this Encino seafooder delivers "reliable" surf 'n' turf and an "excellent brunch" in a mahogany-trimmed room with private booths ("a nice touch"); it's "a bit pricey" and a minority are "under-whelmed" by the food, but service is "polite" and it remains a "special-occasion" mainstay nonetheless.

Delphine *French/Mediterranean* | 22 | 21 | 22 | $43 |

Hollywood | W Hollywood Hotel | 6250 Hollywood Blvd. (Vine St.) | 323-798-1355 | www.restaurantdelphine.com
This "sleek, chic" bistro in the W Hollywood Hotel is a find for "artful" French-Med dishes and "drinks with a kick" "served with just the right amount of attitude"; its proximity to the Pantages ("right across the street") also makes it a "cool" change of pace for theatergoers, even if some call it "underwhelming, except for prices."

The Depot 🗷 *Eclectic* | 26 | 23 | 25 | $40 |

Torrance | 1250 Cabrillo Ave. (Torrance Blvd.) | 310-787-7501 | www.depotrestaurant.com
"Witty" chef-owner Michael Shafer "entertains the palate" with "imaginative", "exceptional" Eclectic cuisine at this "tried-and-true" Torrance "favorite"; it's "a little high-priced" for the area, but pays off

with an "attractive", inviting" setting in an old train depot and "gracious" service that makes it well suited to "special celebrations."

The Derby *Steak*
25 **25** **25** **$46**

Arcadia | 233 E. Huntington Dr. (bet. Gateway Dr. & 2nd Ave.) | 626-447-2430 | www.thederbyarcadia.com

"Place your bets on this winner" cheer fans of this Arcadia steakhouse near Santa Anita Park that's been a "top-of-the-line" "post-race tradition" since 1938 for "classic" chops and seafood; "attentive service" and a "charming" "old-school" atmosphere with equestrian mementos make it "memorable", and "you may even see a famous jockey or two."

Dinah's Family Restaurant *Diner*
19 **12** **20** **$17**

Westchester | 6521 S. Sepulveda Blvd. (W. Centinela Ave.) | 310-645-0456 | www.dinahsrestaurant.com

"It ain't fancy" but this "old-fashioned" diner from 1959 with "retro" red-vinyl booths is "the place to go" for "tender, juicy" fried chicken and "breakfast all day" including "endless" varieties of pancakes; tabs are cheap, "waitresses call you hon" and proximity to LAX makes it a "must-stop" before the airport for many.

Din Tai Fung *Chinese*
26 **17** **18** **$22**

Arcadia | 1088 S. Baldwin Ave. (Arcadia Ave.) | 626-446-8588
Arcadia | 1108 S. Baldwin Ave. (bet. Arcadia Ave. & Duarte Rd.) | 626-574-7068
www.dintaifungusa.com

The "crazy-delicious" Shanghai soup dumplings – like "tender little clouds in your mouth" – are the specialty at these ultra-"popular" Chinese twins in Arcadia delivering the "dim sum of your dreams" for "cheap"; it's "a madhouse during lunch", but a "precise" staff keeps things "running like a well-oiled machine", and "no matter how much you grumble during the wait, after your first round, you'll be euphoric."

Dish *American*
23 **18** **21** **$21**

La Cañada Flintridge | 734 Foothill Blvd. (Hobbs Dr.) | 818-790-5355 | www.dishbreakfastlunchanddinner.com

La Cañada Flintridge locals "cozy up" at this "homey" "kid-friendly" American serving "approachable" all-day fare at "modest" rates in a "pleasant", "countrylike" setting; the staff is "well-intentioned", but regulars report "slow" service during peak hours.

Divino *Italian*
25 **19** **23** **$43**

Brentwood | 11714 Barrington Ct. (Barrington Ave.) | 310-472-0886 | www.divinobrentwood.com

A "best-kept secret" in Brentwood, this "neighborhood" "trattoria" "consistently delivers" "outstanding" Italian eats and "warm, personal service" in "inviting", "elegant" environs; it's a bit "expensive" and you have to have a high tolerance for "sardinelike" seating at peak hours, though most agree it gets "better every year."

Dog Haus *Hot Dogs*
21 **15** **19** **$12**

Pasadena | 105 N. Hill Ave. (E. Union St.) | 626-577-4287 | www.doghausdogs.com

Pasadena's entry in the burgeoning weenie scene is this shiny little number that "brings hot dogs to a whole new level" with "haute versions" of "unusual", elaborately topped franks served up on King's

Hawaiian bread, plus burgers and tater tots; "fast, friendly" service keeps the "long lines" moving, and low prices keep fans "hooked."

Dominick's ❶ *Italian*　　21 | 22 | 21 | $40

West Hollywood | 8715 Beverly Blvd. (bet. Robertson & San Vicente Blvds.) | 310-652-2335 | www.dominicksrestaurant.com

An "upbeat" young crowd convenes on the "wonderful, Tuscan-style patio" of this longtime West Hollywood Italian also lauded for its "strong drinks" and "inexpensive" red-sauce fare that's a "throwback to the old days"; late hours are a perk, but for many the real draw is the $15 three-course Sunday night dinner – "one of the best deals in town."

Doughboys *American*　　22 | 16 | 18 | $19

Third Street | 8136 W. Third St. (Crescent Heights Blvd.) | 323-852-1020 | www.doughboyscafe.com

"Famous for its red-velvet cake", this casual Third Street American eatery and bakery is also beloved for its "inventive" breakfast items ("who else has PB&J pancakes?") and other "stick-to-your-ribs", "hangover"-curing fare served all day; some say service is "not the best", but prices are low and "the food makes up for it"; P.S. watch out for "crazy lines at brunch."

Drago Centro *Italian*　　26 | 26 | 24 | $59

Downtown | City Nat'l Plaza | 525 S. Flower St. (bet. 5th & 6th Sts.) | 213-228-8998 | www.dragocentro.com

"Everything is fabulous" – from the "exquisite" Italian fare and "world-class wine list" to the "on-point" service – at this "coolly glamorous" Downtown destination from Celestino Drago; many find the prices and the noise level a bit on the "high" side, but on the whole, it's all so "pleasant" that "one almost hates to leave"; P.S. happy hour is a steal.

Dr. Hogly Wogly's BBQ *BBQ*　　24 | 9 | 20 | $23

Van Nuys | 8136 Sepulveda Blvd. (bet. Lanark St. & Roscoe Blvd.) | 818-780-6701 | www.hoglywogly.com

"Get extra napkins" for the "epic portions" of "juicy, meaty", "irresistible" BBQ at this "oldie but goodie" in Van Nuys offering solid "bang for the buck"; parking is tough and "there's no decor" to speak of, "but you go for the 'cue and don't worry about the rest."

Duck House *Chinese*　　25 | 19 | 20 | $31

Monterey Park | 501 S. Atlantic Blvd. (Harding Ave.) | 626-284-3227 | www.duckshouse.com

"Tender" Peking duck is "served just the way it's done in China", carved tableside with "super-crispy skin" and "thin, tortillalike" pancakes at this Monterey Park one-dish-wonder also offering "traditional" banquet-style fare; reasonable tabs and comfortable environs make it "excellent for groups"; P.S. duck must be ordered in advance, so call ahead.

Duke's *Pacific Rim*　　20 | 23 | 21 | $36

Malibu | 21150 PCH (Las Flores Canyon Rd.) | 310-317-0777 | www.dukesmalibu.com

"Surfers and sun-drenched families" swarm this oceanfront hangout in Malibu, where "front-row" views of the Pacific and a "fun" island vibe makes it feel "like vacation"; critics claim service can be "MIA" and the Pacific Rim menu doesn't always "hit the mark" ("especially given the price"), but "where else can you see a sunset with frolicking dolphins while you sip your wine?"

Du-par's ● *Diner* 18 | 13 | 18 | $19

Fairfax | Farmers Mkt. | 6333 W. Third St. (S. Fairfax Ave.) | 323-933-8446

Studio City | Studio City Plaza | 12036 Ventura Blvd. (Laurel Canyon Blvd.) | 818-766-4437

Oxnard | 2420 E. Vineyard Ave. (bet. Hwy. 101 & Oxnard Blvd.) | 805-983-2232
www.dupars.com

"Trek down memory lane" at this chainlet of "classic coffee shops" where "the menu, the ambiance and the waitresses" all "bring you back to the '50s"; it's "nothing fancy, but always reliable" with "yummy" pancakes, pies and other affordable grub served late into the night, though some loyalists lament it's "not what it used to be."

NEW Duplex on Third ● *American* - | - | - | M

West Hollywood | 8722 W. Third St. (bet. George Burns Rd. & Robertson Blvd.) | 310-276-6223 | www.duplexonthird.com
Situated directly across from Cedars-Sinai in West Hollywood, this midpriced New American has a sprawling three-squares farm-to-table menu with something for everyone, plus a mixology-based bar where medicos kick back after a long shift; the two-story space in a century-old residence has been rebuilt to look like a home once again, with sofas and armchairs in the lounge, bookcases and patchwork rugs in the dining room and a cute patio in the back.

Dusty's *American/French* 22 | 22 | 21 | $27

Silver Lake | 3200 W. Sunset Blvd. (Descanso Dr.) | 323-906-1018 | www.dustysbistro.com
Hipsters "shake off the grogginess after a late night out" at this "neighborhood" American-French bistro boasting "cool art" and a "laid-back" feel that's "perfect for Silver Lake"; baskets of fresh breads and homemade jams at brunch are appreciated and service is "super-sweet", but some "wish they were more adventurous" with the dinner menu.

Eatalian ⊠ *Italian* 25 | 15 | 19 | $24

Gardena | 15500 S. Broadway (Redondo Beach Blvd.) | 310-532-8880 | www.eataliancafe.com
"Move over, Mario" say enthusiasts of this "fabulous" "diamond-in-the-rough" Gardena Italian, where the "thin-crust" pizzas, "fresh pastas", and "otherworldly" gelato "transport" you to Italy at "bargain prices"; there's no alcohol, and perhaps the "industrial" space is "not conducive to leisurely dining", but the eating alone is "worth the trip."

NEW Eat.Drink.Americano ●Ⓜ *American* - | - | - | M

Downtown | 923 E. Third St. (bet. Garey St. & Santa Fe Ave.) | 213-620-0781 | www.eatdrinkamericano.com
This Arts District Gastropub offers a multicultural menu of midpriced plates ranging from steak tartare with mustard ice cream to soft-shell crab with pickled seaweed, plus plenty of craft beers; the exposed-brick and wood interior comes complete with a zinc bar, vintage bottle dryer and a dazzling assortment of oddball sconces and chandeliers.

| | FOOD | DECOR | SERVICE | COST |

Eat Well Cafe *American*

22 | 16 | 19 | $15

West Hollywood | 8252 Santa Monica Blvd. (N. Harper Ave.) | 323-656-1383

Glendale | 1013 S. Brand Blvd. (Chevy Chase Dr.) | 818-243-5928

It's all about "breakfast" at these "bright" retro diners in Glendale and WeHo dishing out "no-frills", "homestyle" American grub at "super-cheap" rates; service can sometimes be "nonexistant", but it's generally a "fun place to connect with friends over a chili burger."

E. Baldi 🅂 Ⓜ *Italian*

24 | 18 | 20 | $63

Beverly Hills | 375 N. Cañon Dr. (bet. Brighton & Dayton Ways) | 310-248-2633 | www.ebaldi.com

"Studio execs", "agents with their newly minted starlets" and other "heavy-hitters" come to dine at this compact Beverly Hills Northern Italian from Giorgio Baldi's son Edoardo known for "sophisticated, superb" cuisine set down in a "tight", "noisy" setting; the bills are "enormous" and you can expect "lots of attitude" given the "see-and-be-seen" scene.

🄴 Echigo 🅂 *Japanese*

28 | 10 | 21 | $58

West LA | 12217 Santa Monica Blvd. (Amherst Ave.) | 310-820-9787

"Purists" praise this "traditional" West LA Japanese specializing in simple, "ultrafresh", "tender" fish "harmoniously" paired with "warm, vinegary rice" at prices that are moderate for the genre; just overlook the strip-mall decor, grab a seat at the bar and "go for the omakase"; P.S. the lunch set is one of the "best deals in town."

NEW Eden Burger Bar ● *Burgers*

- | - | - | M

Glendale | 333 N. Verdugo Rd. (Chevy Chase Dr.) | 818-552-2212 | www.edenburgerbar.com

The half-pounders at this upscale Glendale burger specialist are made with a house blend of dry-aged beef, though the meat gets topped with so many accoutrements (jalapeño-cured bacon, pastrami slices, wild mushroom sauce), you might not taste it; the ultramod black-and-white dining room is filled with the sort of curvilinear chairs more often found in salons than burger joints.

1810 Restaurant *Argentinean/Steak*

24 | 21 | 22 | $32

Pasadena | 121 W. Colorado Blvd. (bet. De Lacey & Pasadena Aves.) | 626-795-5658 | www.1810restaurant.com

"Tender" "marinated meats" cooked "exactly as asked" are the headliners at this Argentinean steakhouse in Old Town Pasadena, where a "helpful" staff is happy to "guide you through the menu"; carnivores also "love" the "cool ambiance" (dark wood, high ceilings, brick walls), outdoor patio and reasonable pricing, so most insist they'll "be back."

888 Seafood *Chinese/Seafood*

24 | 20 | 20 | $34

Rosemead | 8450 Valley Blvd. (Delta St.) | 626-573-1888

"Dim sum on weekends is the main event" at this Rosemead Chinese where a "wonderful selection" of "well-prepared" seafood dumplings, buns and other "delights" are circulated on rolling carts in a pleasant, "not-too-fancy" dining room; the "place can get mobbed" (and fills up for wedding banquets), but it's good for groups and "family dining", and the cost is "fair."

	FOOD	DECOR	SERVICE	COST

NEW 800 Degrees Pizzeria ❶ *Pizza*   25 | 19 | 21 | $17

Westwood | 10889 Lindbrook Dr. (bet. Glendon Ave. & Westwood Blvd.) |
424-239-5010 | www.800degreespizza.com

"Pizza in a flash, designed by you" earns "800% approval" at this "brilliant" Westwood newcomer from the Umami Burger team that's "burning it up" topping Neapolitan pies with "incredible" ingredients, then firing them for "just the right amount of chew and char" ("ask for it well done"); it's tough to nab a table in the "minimalist" space, but "insanely low" costs help keep lines "winding out the door at all hours"; P.S. the "futuristic soda machine" is a hit too.

El Cholo Cafe *Mexican*   20 | 20 | 21 | $25

Mid-City | 1121 S. Western Ave. (W. 11th St.) | 323-734-2773
Santa Monica | 1025 Wilshire Blvd. (bet. 10th & 11th Sts.) | 310-899-1106
www.elcholo.com

El Cholo Cantina *Mexican*

LAX | LA Int'l Airport, Terminal 5 | 209 World Way (Sepulveda Blvd.) |
310-417-1910 | www.elcholo.com

El Cholo Downtown *Mexican*

Downtown | 1037 S. Flower St. (bet. 11th St. & Olympic Blvd.) |
213-746-7750 | www.elcholo.com

El Cholo Pasadena *Mexican*

Pasadena | Paseo Colorado | 260 E. Colorado Blvd. (bet. Los Robles & Marengo Aves.) | 626-795-5800 | www.elcholopasadena.com

An "LA original", this Mid-City mainstay from 1923 and its offshoots "hasn't changed much over the years" with "straightforward" "Cali-Mex" grub (with standout green-corn tamales) that's either "decent" or "delicious" "depending on how many margaritas you drink"; although some suggest it's "living on its long history", the "old-world" decor is "charming", costumed servers "pleasant" and, on the whole, "it just oozes fun."

El Compadre ❶ *Mexican*   22 | 20 | 23 | $27

Echo Park | 1449 W. Sunset Blvd. (Sutherland St.) | 213-250-4505 |
www.elcompadrerestaurant.com

"Flaming margaritas" are all the rage at this "reliable" Echo Park spot serving up "consistently good", "affordable" Mexican fare; though the "throwback" setting is "always packed", listening to live "mariachi music" helps pass the time while you wait for a table.

El Coyote Cafe *Mexican*   17 | 17 | 20 | $21

Beverly Boulevard | 7312 Beverly Blvd. (bet. N. Fuller Ave. & N. Poinsettia Pl.) | 323-939-2255 | www.elcoyotecafe.com

With over-the-top decor that's "right out of an old Carmen Miranda movie", this "LA institution" on Beverly Boulevard still offers a "festive atmosphere after 80 years in business"; the Mexican "comfort food" is "nothing special", but it's "nice for the price" and served by a "staff as cool as a margarita."

Elephant Bar *Asian*   22 | 23 | 21 | $27

Lakewood | 4634 Candlewood St. (Graywood Ave.) | 562-529-3200
Downey | 12002 Lakewood Blvd. (Gary Rd.) | 562-803-9910
Torrance | 21227 Hawthorne Blvd. (Torrance Blvd.) | 310-543-5595
Burbank | 110 N. First St. (E. Orange Grove Ave.) | 818-842-1334
(continued)

(continued)

Elephant Bar

West Covina | 200 S. Vincent Ave. (Lakes Dr.) | 626-918-3400
Simi Valley | 1825 Madera Rd. (McCoy Pl.) | 805-584-9119
www.elephantbar.com

"Come for happy hour, stay for the food" at these "popular" outlets that are "yuppie central" and "fun for kids" too with "unique" Asian eats deemed "pretty good for a chain", "tasty drinks" and "exotic" "safari" decor; a few find the food and atmosphere a bit "corporate", but at least prices "won't break the bank"

Elf Café ☒☞ *Mediterranean/Vegetarian* ∇ 25 | 18 | 22 | $26

Echo Park | 2135 W. Sunset Blvd. (Alvarado St.) | 213-484-6829 | www.elfcafe.com

"Vegetarians rejoice" over the "well-crafted", "soul-soothing" dishes at this "hipster" Echo Park Mediterranean offering a variety of "savory" vegan choices for a moderate price; it packs "lots of tables in a small space" ("reservations are a must") but the nonetheless "charming" locale remains a "pure joy" for many.

El Gallo Giro *Mexican* 22 | 14 | 17 | $12

Downtown | 701 E. Jefferson Blvd. (S. San Pedro St.) | 323-233-3623
Huntington Park | 7148 Pacific Blvd. (E. Florence Ave.) | 323-585-4433 ●
East LA | 5686 E. Whittier Blvd. (S. Gerhart Ave.) | 323-726-1246
Lynwood | 3180 E. Imperial Hwy. (Long Beach Blvd.) | 310-667-4670
Panorama City | 8309 Van Nuys Blvd. (Roscoe Blvd.) | 818-891-5533
San Fernando | 315 Mission Blvd. (Pico St.) | 818-361-9570
www.gallogiro.com

"Repeat customers" crave the "authentic" eats made "fresh on the premises" at this Mexican chainlet; though the decor is "nothing to write home about", those willing to endure "long lines" at peak hours can get a taste of the "real thing" on a "tight budget."

Elite Restaurant *Chinese* 24 | 15 | 16 | $24

Monterey Park | 700 S. Atlantic Blvd. (El Portal Pl.) | 626-282-9998 | www.elitechineserestaurant.com

"Dim sum is all the rage" – served "hot to the table, not from carts" – at this "upscale Cantonese-style" Monterey Park Chinese featuring a "super" menu with a nod to the "adventurous eater"; just be prepared for a wait "if you arrive at 11 AM", followed by a likely "rushed" meal in the "standard-issue" surrounds.

El Pollo Inka *Peruvian* 22 | 15 | 19 | $18

Lawndale | Lawndale Plaza | 15400 Hawthorne Blvd. (154th St.) | 310-676-6665
Gardena | Gateway Plaza | 1425 W. Artesia Blvd. (Normandie Ave.) | 310-516-7378
Hermosa Beach | 1100 PCH (Aviation Blvd.) | 310-372-1433
Torrance | 23705 Hawthorne Blvd. (PCH) | 310-373-0062
www.elpolloinka.com

"Terrific" rotisserie chicken with "out-of-this-world" green sauce makes for a "zesty" combo at this "quick" Peruvian mini-chain serving "high-quality" fare in "not fancy, but upbeat" settings; it's a "real value for the money", and weekend entertainment at some locales is a bonus.

	FOOD	DECOR	SERVICE	COST

El Portal *Mexican* — 22 | 19 | 23 | $23

Pasadena | 695 E. Green St. (bet. S. El Molino & S. Oak Knoll Aves.) | 626-795-8553 | www.elportalrestaurant.com

"Yucatan-style" specialties and other "well-prepared" fare that's "not your typical Mexican" go for a "solid value" at this "convivial, comfortable" Pasadenan with a "pretty outdoor patio"; live music on the weekends and "quality" tequilas and margaritas "tailored to your taste" (there's a "delicious skinny" version) round out the "relaxing" vibe.

El Rocoto *Peruvian* — ▽ 23 | 16 | 22 | $21

Cerritos | 11433 South St. (Gridley Rd.) | 562-924-1919
Gardena | 1356 W. Artesia Blvd. (S. Normandie Ave.) | 310-768-8768
www.elrocoto.com

Locals "love" the "excellent Peruvian" at this "wonderful neighborhood" duo in Cerritos and Gardena proffering "tasty" specialties and sauces with a "kick"; "reasonable prices", strong service and simple but "pleasant" decor round out the "solid" meal.

El Tarasco *Mexican* — 22 | 10 | 18 | $16

Venice | 109 Washington Blvd. (Pacific Ave.) | 310-306-8552
This "classic hole-in-the-wall" in Venice dishes out "pretty darned authentic" Mexican eats, including "fresh chips and salsa" and carnitas tacos that committed customers "crave"; though some would like to see a "better eye" on upkeep, it's a "fun lunch counter" to indulge in some good "greasy" grub.

El Tepeyac *Mexican* — 26 | 14 | 22 | $15

East LA | 812 N. Evergreen Ave. (bet. Blanchard & Winter Sts.) | 323-267-8668

Since 1955, owner Manuel Rojas has been welcoming customers "with a big smile" and often a "shot of tequila" at his "homey", "heartwarming" East LA Mexican "landmark" where diners endure "long lines" for "delicious", "gargantuan" Hollenbeck burritos (a "true eating challenge"), "top" guacamole and other "real home-cooked" dishes that make it one of the city's "best buys"; while some may be "put off by the location", fans insist "it has never been a problem."

El Torito *Mexican* — 21 | 20 | 21 | $24

Lakewood | 5242 Lakewood Blvd. (Candlewood St.) | 562-531-7460
Marina del Rey | 13715 Fiji Way (Lincoln Blvd.) | 310-823-8941
Santa Monica | 3360 Ocean Park Blvd. (Centinela Ave.) | 310-450-8665
Long Beach | 6605 PCH (bet. 2nd St. & Westminster Ave.) | 562-594-6917
Manhattan Beach | 600 N. Sepulveda Blvd. (Tennyson St.) | 310-318-8500
Redondo Beach | Fisherman's Wharf | 100G Fisherman's Wharf (Catalina Ave.) | 310-376-0547
Torrance | 23225 Hawthorne Blvd. (Lomita Blvd.) | 310-378-0331
Pasadena | 3333 E. Foothill Blvd. (Sierra Madre Villa Ave.) | 626-351-8995
Sherman Oaks | 14433½ Ventura Blvd. (Van Nuys Blvd.) | 818-990-5860
West Covina | 3133 E. Garvey Ave. N. (S. Barranca St.) | 626-966-7516
www.eltorito.com
Additional locations throughout Southern California

You can "relax, meet friends and not bust the budget" at this "cheerful" but "cookie-cutter" Mexican chain that pleases with an "amazing happy hour", Sunday brunch buffet and generally "prompt" service; it's "reliable" and "family-friendly", but "don't expect authenticity."

El Torito Grill *Mexican*

21 | 20 | 21 | $26

Beverly Hills | 9595 Wilshire Blvd. (Camden Dr.) | 310-550-1599
Torrance | 21321 Hawthorne Blvd. (Torrance Blvd.) | 310-543-1896
Sherman Oaks | Sherman Oaks Galleria | 15301 Ventura Blvd.
(Sepulveda Blvd.) | 818-907-7172
www.etgrill.com

"Big parties" dig into Mexican with a "fancy twist" at these "semi-upscale" sibs to El Torito, serving "hot" tortillas, "guacamole made at your table" and other "well-prepared" eats on an "updated" menu; the "huge" margaritas and "low tabs" also appeal, so they're a prime choice to "meet the gang after work."

Emle's *Mediterranean*

23 | 16 | 23 | $19

Northridge | 9250 Reseda Blvd. (bet. Dearborn & Prairie Sts.) |
818-772-2203 | www.emlesrestaurant.com

"What a find" say fans of this "small" Mediterranean in Northridge, known for its "nice range" of food, "decadent" French toast and "terrific" early-bird specials, all in portions that are nothing short of "redonkulous"; the decor is ordinary, but it "isn't too expensive" and the staff "treats you like relatives."

Empanada's Place ⊉ *Argentinean*

23 | 14 | 18 | $14

Culver City | 3811 Sawtelle Blvd. (Venice Blvd.) | 310-391-0888 |
www.empanadasplace.com

Known for making a "mean empanada", this "quick" Culver City Argentinean serves "crispy hot pockets of goodness" packed with an "impressive variety" of "tasty" vegetarian and meat fillings; basic decor is offset by prices "so cheap you can try everything on the menu"; P.S. it's cash only and BYO.

Empress Pavilion *Chinese*

21 | 15 | 16 | $23

Chinatown | Bamboo Plaza | 988 N. Hill St. (Bamboo Ln.) | 213-617-9898 |
www.empresspavilion.com

"An oldie but a goodie for Chinese food", this "dim sum mother ship" in Chinatown occupies an "enormous space" with a "low-rent coffee-shop" vibe and "women in a hurry" pushing carts with a "dizzying array" of "fresh", "inexpensive" offerings that add up to a "feast"; while some claim the kitchen's "seen better days", it still gets "super-crowded" for lunch and "early on the weekends."

Engine Co. No. 28 *American*

20 | 23 | 21 | $38

Downtown | 644 S. Figueroa St. (bet. 7th St. & Wilshire Blvd.) |
213-624-6996 | www.engineco.com

Housed in a restored "vintage" fire station Downtown, this "cozy but upscale" American offers "reliable" "gourmet comfort food" in a "charming" atmosphere; though service can "fluctuate" and some feel it's "overpriced", others say it's just right for a "business lunch" or "pre-concert" dinner, made extra-convenient with a free shuttle to the Music and Staples Centers.

Enoteca Drago *Italian*

23 | 21 | 23 | $50

Beverly Hills | 410 N. Cañon Dr. (bet. Brighton Way & Santa Monica Blvd.) |
310-786-8236 | www.celestinodrago.com

Celestino Drago (Il Pastaio, Drago) attracts an atypical Beverly Hills crowd to his "elegant", "old-world-style" Italian providing an "interesting wine list" and "enjoyable" large and small plates "better than mama ever made"; it's "less hectic" than others and dishes are "served with a smile", though some claim it's "nothing extraordinary" for the price.

Enterprise Fish Co. Seafood | 21 | 19 | 20 | $35 |

Santa Monica | 174 Kinney St. (Main St.) | 310-392-8366 | www.enterprisefishco.com

The lobster special (Monday–Thursday) is "one heck of a deal", as is the "affordable" happy hour at these "lively" Santa Barbara and Santa Monica sibs delivering a variety of "simply grilled", "straightforward" seafood; the "nautical" decor is "exactly what you'd expect" and the staff "attentive and lighthearted" as it tends to the "noisy" crowd.

Enzo & Angela Ⓢ Italian | 22 | 17 | 24 | $38 |

West LA | 11701 Wilshire Blvd. (Barrington Ave.) | 310-477-3880 | www.enzoandangela.com

Servers treat you "as if you're their long-lost cousin" at this "visit to Italy" in West LA presenting a "remarkable" roster of "unusual dishes as well as the standards", all "prepared from the heart"; some are put off by the "expensive" specials and cite a "sort of sterile" ambiance, though fans call the food and service "first class."

Ernie's Mexican | ▽ 21 | 18 | 21 | $24 |

North Hollywood | 4410 Lankershim Blvd. (Moorpark St.) | 818-985-4654 | www.erniesnoho.com

A "family tradition" in the "same location for a million years" (actually, the past 60), this "solid" North Hollywood staple for "decent" Mexican grub serves up "basic", "old-style" tacos, burritos, margaritas and more for a "good price"; live entertainment on weekends adds sizzle, so "everyone leaves happy."

Euro Pane Bakery | 25 | 16 | 17 | $15 |

Pasadena | 345 E. Colorado Blvd. (Euclid Ave.) | 626-844-8804
Pasadena | 950 E. Colorado Blvd. (Mentor Ave.) | 626-577-1828

"Delectable pastries" ("try the fleur de sel macarons"), "glorious bread" and a signature egg salad sandwich are "invariably first-rate" at this "cute neighborhood bakery" and cafe duo offering "a little bit of Paris in Pasadena"; "lines can be long", service "slow" and seating tight, so "be ready to sit in close quarters" if you can score a table.

Eva Ⓜ Californian | 25 | 19 | 22 | $48 |

Beverly Boulevard | 7458 Beverly Blvd. (bet. Gardner & Vista Sts.) | 323-634-0700 | www.evarestaurantla.com

"Charming", "passionate" chef-owner Mark Gold "works magic" in the kitchen of this "tiny cottage" on Beverly Boulevard, preparing "amazingly fresh farm-to-table" Californian dishes in a "homey" atmosphere devoted to "neighborhood fine dining"; regulars also appreciate the "well-informed" service and call the "upscale" prices "reasonable", especially if you go for the family-style Sunday "feast."

Eveleigh ◐ American/European | 21 | 25 | 20 | $43 |

West Hollywood | 8752 W. Sunset Blvd. (Sherbourne Dr.) | 424-239-1630 | www.theeveleigh.com

It feels like a "*A Midsummer Night's Dream*" on the rustic, covered patio of restaurateur Nick Mathers' New American–European that will "transport you far away" from the Sunset Strip; small and large plates of "imaginative", "wholesome" cuisine and "terrific" cocktails are served with "no pretensions", and if a few find the food "unspectacular", the view adds a "dramatic" touch.

NEW exEat by Eatalian Cafe *Italian*

| - | - | - | I |

Gardena | 14842 Crenshaw Blvd. (bet. Marine Ave. & 147th St.) | 310-516-0121 | www.eataliancafe.com

This quirky sibling of Eatalian Cafe in Gardena is about a quarter of the size of the original, with a fraction of the gelatos, but it does offer a full Italian menu of affordable pizzas and pastas; housed in an airy, industrial space (in a seemingly empty shopping mall), it's an unexpected find in a neighborhood dominated by Korean BBQ houses and fast-food stands.

Extreme Pizza *Pizza*

| 22 | 14 | 19 | $18 |

NEW Culver City | 6000 Sepulveda Blvd. (Slauson Ave.) | 310-390-7788
Westwood | 1067 Glendon Ave. (Weyburn Ave.) | 310-295-2535
Long Beach | 21 The Paseo (S. Pine Ave.) | 562-901-9700
www.extremepizza.com

"The name says it all" at this often "crowded" "gourmet" pizza chain where you select "crazy high-quality toppings" among "lots of ingredient choices" with an "unusual" twist, or opt for one of the pies on the colorful menu; it's "better than average" and "wowing" at times, even if it strikes some as "a little spendy for pizza."

Fab Hot Dogs *Hot Dogs*

| 24 | 11 | 20 | $11 |

Reseda | Loehmann's Plaza | 19417 Victory Blvd. (Tampa Ave.) | 818-344-4336 | www.fabhotdogs.com

"Fab-tastic!" rave reviewers of this Reseda stand that elevates the basic frank "into another category", offering a "huge variety" of "delish dogs", sausages and burgers, recommended with "spicy relish", "tots and a drink on the side"; "there's no decor to speak of", but the "fair" prices, "friendly staff and quick service make it a pleasure."

Fabiolus Café *Italian*

| 22 | 18 | 23 | $26 |

Hollywood | 6270 W. Sunset Blvd. (Vine St.) | 323-467-2882 | www.fabiolus.org

The staff always makes you "feel special" and the "homemade pastas" and Northern Italian entrees are an "excellent value" at this "Hollywood favorite" for chowing down in the "ArcLight area"; it provides a "quieter start to the evening" than many, and guests also give props to its "good work in the community for the homeless."

Fabrocini's *Italian*

| 23 | 16 | 22 | $31 |

Mid-City | 2960 N. Beverly Glen Circle (N. Beverly Glen Blvd.) | 310-475-7404 | www.fabrocinibeverlyglen.com

"Homestyle" cooking "from grandma's kitchen" draws diners to this "neighborhood Italian" in a "charming location" on Beverly Glen Circle, "away from the traffic in the hills"; there are low tabs, "generous portions and no attitude", and even if the interior could use a "refresh", the patio beckons for "people-watching while enjoying a well-prepared meal."

Factor's Famous Deli *Deli*

| 20 | 15 | 20 | $23 |

Pico-Robertson | 9420 W. Pico Blvd. (Beverly Dr.) | 310-278-9175 | www.factorsdeli.com

"Order the lox and eggs with a bagel and be in heaven" at this Pico-Robertson "classic" supplying the "whole panoply of deli food", from "good-size sandwiches" to "delicious soups"; there's "helpful" service and "rarely a wait for a table", though some would like to see the place "spruced up."

Falafel King *Mideastern*

18 | 9 | 15 | $14

Santa Monica | Third St. Promenade | 1315 Third St. Promenade (Arizona Ave.) | 310-587-2551
Westwood | 1010 Broxton Ave. (bet. Kinross & Weyburn Aves.) | 310-208-4444

Loyalists of this "real-deal" Middle Eastern duo in Westwood and Santa Monica "can't get enough" of the falafel, shawarma and "killer" fried potatoes, with "just the right balance of ingredients overflowing your pita"; despite some claims that it's sliding into "mediocrity", most feel the "cheap eats" still "hit the mark."

Falafel Palace *Mediterranean/Mideastern*

∇ 23 | 11 | 20 | $12

Northridge | 9255 Reseda Blvd. (Prairie St.) | 818-993-0734 | www.falafelpalacenorthridge.com

An "always satisfying" "falafel shack" near Cal State Northridge, this little "joint" turns out "tasty" Med–Middle Eastern fare that stirs up "cravings"; sure, it's a "hole-in-the-wall", but customers agree "there's a reason it's been there forever."

Farfalla *Italian*

23 | 19 | 20 | $33

Encino | 16403 Ventura Blvd. (Hayvenhurst Ave.) | 818-380-0200 | www.farfallaencino.com
Westlake Village | 160 Promenade Way (Thousand Oaks Blvd.) | 805-497-2355 | www.farfallawestlakevillage.com

Farfalla Trattoria *Italian*

Los Feliz | 1978 Hillhurst Ave. (Finley Ave.) | 323-661-7365 | www.farfallatrattoria.com

Vinoteca Farfalla ● *Italian*

Glendale | 1968 Hillhurst Ave. (Finley Ave.) | 323-661-8070 | www.vinotecafarfalla.com

They're "in touch with their roots" and "really know how to cook" at these "bright", midpriced "neighborhood haunts" (including a Glendale wine bar) matching "terrific" Italian food with solid service; while the "busy" rooms do fill up, regulars like the "lively" atmosphere.

Farmer Boys ⊠Ⓜ *Burgers*

23 | 17 | 21 | $14

Downtown | 726 S. Alameda St. (E. 7th St.) | 213-228-8999 | www.farmerboysla.com

"Count on this place" for "fresh", "hearty" American eats (including "big burgers") that fit the bill when you're "in a pinch, on a budget" and it's "4 AM"; though skeptics liken it to "standard fast food" with "order-at-the-counter" service, those who dub it a Downtown "oasis" give it "two thumbs way up."

Farm of Beverly Hills *American*

19 | 18 | 18 | $30

Downtown | LA Live | 800 W. Olympic Blvd. (S. Figueroa St.) | 213-747-4555
Beverly Hills | 439 N. Beverly Dr. (S. Santa Monica Blvd.) | 310-273-5578
www.thefarmofbeverlyhills.com

The "home cooking" "meets expectations for the price" and desserts "steal the show" at these "decent" Americans; service varies and the brunch crowds can make it "difficult to get in", but otherwise it's "good for families", with "cute" "farmhouse decor" and "pleasant" patios.

Farmshop *American*

26 | 19 | 22 | $47

Santa Monica | Brentwood Country Mart | 225 26th St. (San Vicente Blvd.) | 310-566-2400 | www.farmshopla.com

This "knockout" Cal-American at the Brentwood County Mart "knows how to satisfy" with "delectable" market-driven breakfast, lunch and family-style dinners served in a "casual" "barnlike" setting; while some cite a "limited" menu and "breathtaking" prices, the "impeccably sourced" ingredients and "attention to detail" add up to "remarkable" meals; P.S. no dinner Monday–Tuesday.

Farm Stand *Eclectic*

21 | 16 | 19 | $28

El Segundo | 422 Main St. (Holly Ave.) | 310-640-3276 | www.farmstand.us

"Down-home" yet "unique" Eclectic dishes with a Mediterrean touch arrive at an "easy pace" at this "hidden" nook in El Segundo offering a number of "vegetarian and vegan options"; "understated" with "good bang for the buck", it's "very popular with locals" and a "treat" for newcomers.

Far Niente *Italian*

24 | 20 | 22 | $40

Glendale | 204½ N. Brand Blvd. (Wilson Ave.) | 818-242-3835 | www.farnienteristorante.net

"Superior food continues to reign" at this "classy" Northern Italian in Glendale inspired by flavors of the Cinque Terre, a "friendly place to bring an out-of-towner" or dine before heading to the Alex Theater next door; the room is "comfortable" and the prices "fair", so while service can be a bit inconsistent, it's "popular" for a reason.

Fat Dog ◐ *American*

▽ 22 | 17 | 23 | $24

West Hollywood | 801 N. Fairfax Ave. (Waring Ave.) | 323-951-0030
Montrose | 2265 Honolulu Ave. (Ocean view Blvd.) | 818-236-4810
www.thefatdogla.com

These "laid-back" canine-themed hangs in West Hollywood and Montrose with "excellent" service are beginning to build a neighborhood following with "oversized" dogs, burgers and other "solid" gastropub fare, plus "tasty" craft beer and cocktails; it's extra-economical during the "great happy hour", and pooch-owners "love" bringing their pups to hang out on the patio.

Father's Office *American*

24 | 17 | 15 | $24

Culver City | Helms Bldg. | 3229 Helms Ave. (bet. Venice & Washington Blvds.) | 310-736-2224
Santa Monica | 1018 Montana Ave. (bet. 10th & 11th Sts.) | 310-736-2224 ◐
www.fathersoffice.com

The "out-of-this-world" blue-cheese burger is "perfection" and the "fantastic" beer list "will never let you down" at this "affordable", "order-at-the-bar" American gastropub duo in Santa Monica and Culver City that continues to outdo newcomers on the "gourmet burger trend"; no menu substitutions (or ketchup) are allowed and "it's a royal pain to find a place to sit", so "expect to wait awhile"; P.S. must be 21 to enter.

Fat Spoon *Japanese*

▽ 18 | 14 | 21 | $18

Little Tokyo | 329 E. First St. (Judge John Aiso St.) | 213-621-7890 | www.fatspoonfood.com

Nestled in Downtown's Little Tokyo, this unconventional "little spot" (sharing an owner with Lazy Ox Canteen) whips up an assortment of

	FOOD	DECOR	SERVICE	COST

Japanese curries, pastas, salads and a few whimsical side dishes in an open kitchen; though a few feel it's "strange" and "so-so", others "enjoy everything", including the daily specials.

Feast from the East *Asian*   23 | 11 | 19 | $15

West LA | 1949 Westwood Blvd. (bet. La Grange & Missouri Aves.) | 310-475-0400 | www.ffte.com

For 30 years, customers have been returning to this "terrific" West LA Asian for "the best Chinese chicken salad this side of Hong Kong" (with dressing that's "practically an industry unto itself") and sesame wings that "run a close second"; it's not so much "a place for dining" due to the lack of atmosphere, but a hit for "fast", "inexpensive" takeout.

Federal Bar ● *American*   21 | 22 | 19 | $23

North Hollywood | 5303 Lankershim Blvd. (Weddington St.) | 818-980-2555 | www.thefederalbar.com

"Style and substance" make a strong showing at this "decently priced" North Hollywood gastropub that's a "hot new scene" in an "early-20th-century bank building" with a club upstairs and a "loud" crowd rolling in "late"; it "seems to be more about the atmosphere", but the menu's "all-around good" and "getting better."

Fig *American/French*   23 | 23 | 22 | $48

Santa Monica | Fairmont Miramar Hotel & Bungalows | 101 Wilshire Blvd. (Ocean Ave.) | 310-319-3111 | www.figsantamonica.com

"Creative, but not over-the-top" French–New American dishes are "packed with flavor" using "selections from the local farmer's market" at this "warm-weather favorite" with "intelligent" service at Santa Monica's "pretty" Fairmont Miramar Hotel; early-goers tout the "Fig at Five" happy hour as a "tremendous" bargain, and the "attractive poolside setting" has a "definite hideaway feel", encouraging you to "relax and enjoy."

Fig & Olive *Mediterranean*   23 | 26 | 22 | $55

Melrose | 8490 Melrose Pl. (La Cienega Blvd.) | 310-360-9100 | www.figandolive.com

This "gorgeous", "vibrant" West Hollywood entry "does everything right", as evidenced by the "phenomenal" Med cuisine, the "knowledgeable" staff and the "über-trendy" crowds "packed to the rafters" of the "modern", "airy" space; a few insist it's "overpriced" and "overrated", but most agree it's "utterly satisfying."

Figaro Bistrot *French*   23 | 24 | 19 | $33

Los Feliz | 1802 N. Vermont Ave. (Melbourne Ave.) | 323-662-1587 | www.figarobistrot.com

The "closest thing to a visit to Paris" in Los Feliz – from the "sidewalk dining" to the vintage decor to the "authentic wait for service" – this "truly French" bistro is a "best-kept secret" for savoring the "classics" in a "wonderful atmosphere"; some swear by the "to-die-for" pastries ("breakfast is the best bet"), while others advise everything's "plentiful for the price" at happy hour.

NEW FigOly *Californian/Italian*   - | - | - | E

Downtown | Luxe City Center Hotel | 1020 S. Figueroa St. (Olympic Ave.) | 213-743-7600 | www.figoly.com

Named for its intersection (Figueroa and Olympic), this Downtown Cal-Italian in the newly remodeled Luxe City Center Hotel serves pricey pastas, housemade charcuterie and wood-fired mains; the dining room – decked out with a chrome chandelier and floor-to-ceiling wine cellar – opens via glass stairway to an expansive patio, making it an upscale destination before an event at nearby Staples Center or Nokia Theater.

Fins Continental/Seafood

| 25 | 20 | 24 | $42 |

Westlake Village | Westlake Plaza | 982 S. Westlake Blvd. (bet. Agoura & Townsgate Rds.) | 805-494-6494 | www.finsinc.com

"A find for fish", this "cozy", "accommodating" Westlake Village Continental specializes in "delicious" seafood as well as updated gastropub fare from a chef who's "not afraid to create interesting dishes"; while it can get "pricey", it has "all the makings" of a fine evening out, including "live music on the weekends."

Firefly ● American

| 22 | 23 | 20 | $38 |

Studio City | 11720 Ventura Blvd. (Colfax Ave.) | 818-762-1833 | www.fireflystudiocity.com

"Surrounded by candlelight" on the "divine" patio, "trendy" diners bask in the "romantic" ambiance or join the "cool" bar scene at this Studio City New American as they nibble on "tasty" "Californian-foodie dishes"; meanwhile, dissenters say the cooking "varies" too much for the cost, and "wish" the servers could be "more present."

Firefly Bistro Ⓜ American

| ▽ 21 | 20 | 20 | $40 |

South Pasadena | 1009 El Centro St. (Meridian Ave.) | 626-441-2443 | www.eatatfirefly.com

The "pleasing" menu "changes with the seasons" at this midpriced New American in South Pasadena, a "tented venue" that delights with an "outdoor feel" and frequent live music (Wednesday–Thursday and during Sunday brunch); an "attentive (but not intrusive)" staff adds to the "breezy" mood.

Firenze Osteria Italian

| 22 | 20 | 21 | $43 |

North Hollywood | 4212 Lankershim Blvd. (Valley Spring Ln.) | 818-760-7081 | www.firenzeosteria.com

Locals feel "lucky" to have this trattoria from *Top Chef* contestant Fabio Viviani in North Hollywood, providing "generous portions" of "gourmet yet approachable" Italian in an "energetic" setting with "ok" service; less satisfied surveyors feel it's "overpriced" and wish they could "turn down the noise."

First & Hope Ⓜ American

| 18 | 21 | 17 | $47 |

Downtown | 710 W. First St. (Hope St.) | 213-617-8555 | www.firstandhope.com

An "easy walk to Disney Hall and the Music Center", this "swellegant" Downtown American with an "attractive" atmosphere for "pre-show dinner and drinks" stirs up mixed reviews, with some calling it "surprisingly good" and "offbeat", and others citing a costly, "too-cute" menu that changes but "never succeeds"; on the plus side, "they'll get you out before curtain" and the occasional live piano is "entertaining."

Fishbar ● Seafood

| 23 | 18 | 21 | $29 |

Manhattan Beach | 3801 Highland Ave. (38th Pl.) | 310-796-0200 | www.fishbarmb.com

Customers give "kudos" to this new "local hangout" in Manhattan Beach offering "simple but delicious" seafood (mesquite-grilled skewers, the "best clam chowder") from "plenty of fresh fish options" while it "rocks" a "casual" "sports-bar atmosphere"; the staff does a "wonderful job", prices are "amazingly fair" and weekend breakfast boasts a "fabulous" Bloody Mary ("you can't go wrong with shrimp, bacon and asparagus in your drink"), so it's a "welcome surprise."

Fish Grill *Seafood*   24 | 16 | 20 | $20

Beverly Boulevard | 7226 Beverly Blvd. (bet. Alta Vista Blvd. & Formosa Ave.) | 323-937-7162
Pico-Robertson | 9618 W. Pico Blvd. (Beverwil Dr.) | 310-860-1182
Brentwood | 12013 Wilshire Blvd. (bet. Bundy Dr. & Saltair Ave.) | 310-479-1800
Malibu | 22935 PCH (Malibu Pier) | 310-456-8585
www.fishgrill.com

"Nothing but the freshest", "wonderful kosher seafood" comes "fast" and "flavorful" off the grill at this "deli-style" mini-chain offering "unexpected" delights (like "awesome" fish tacos) for a "bargain"; even if the locales lend themselves to "takeout", the Malibu patio is a "hot spot by the pier" ("who knew?"); P.S. closed Friday after 2:30 PM and Saturday, and there's no alcohol or shellfish.

Fish King *Seafood*   25 | 11 | 22 | $19

Glendale | 722 N. Glendale Ave. (Monterey Rd.) | 818-244-2161 | www.fishkingseafood.com

This "popular" Glendale "fish market/cafe" is considered a "rare find" where "they'll cook up a plate" of "premium" seafood for "almost nothing"; if you don't mind the deli-style setting you can "dine in and watch the circus" of customers "choosing from more kinds of fish than they've ever seen in one place", but many take their orders to go.

555 East *Steak*   26 | 23 | 24 | $51

Long Beach | 555 E. Ocean Blvd. (bet. Atlantic & Linden Aves.) | 562-437-0626 | www.555east.com

"Steaks and ambiance" come together in "winning" fashion at this Long Beach bastion of "old-time elegance" proffering "remarkable" cuts in a "classic", "über-masculine" space replete with wood, brass and marble; factor in an "awesome" wine list and servers who "go out of their way to please", and reviewers "highly recommended" it as a "place to celebrate and splurge."

Five Guys *Burgers*   21 | 14 | 19 | $12

Carson | South Bay Pavilion | 20700 Avalon Blvd. (Del Amo Blvd.) | 310-515-7700
Cerritos | Cerritos Promenade | 11461 South St. (bet. Gridley Rd. & Jersey Ave.) | 562-809-0055
Culver City | Westfield Culver City | 6000 Sepulveda Blvd. (Slauson Ave.) | 310-391-0603
www.fiveguys.com

Fans throw a "high five" to this East Coast fast-food transplant turning out burgers that "taste like something you'd grill on a summer day in the backyard" served with "lots of toppings", "jazzed-up fries" and "free peanuts while you wait" ("a nice touch"); detractors "don't get all the hype", although "quick" service and "not-that-expensive" tabs keep them perpetually "busy."

	FOOD	DECOR	SERVICE	COST

Flavor of India *Indian*
22 | **20** | **20** | **$24**

West Hollywood | 9045 Santa Monica Blvd. (Nemo St.) |
310-274-1715
Burbank | 161 E. Orange Grove Ave. (bet. 1st St. & San Fernando Blvd.) |
818-558-1199
www.theflavorofindia.com

Eaters "on the hunt" for Indian food give props to this "refreshing"
West Hollywood and Burbank pair for its "consistently tasty" dishes
"cooked to the level of spiciness requested"; "pleasant" and "affordable" with "considerate" service, it's a "reliable staple" for many.

Fleming's Prime
Steakhouse & Wine Bar *Steak*
25 | **23** | **25** | **$59**

Downtown | LA Live | 800 W. Olympic Blvd. (Figueroa St.) |
213-745-9911
El Segundo | Atrium Court | 2301 Rosecrans Ave. (Douglas St.) |
310-643-6911
Woodland Hills | 6373 Topanga Canyon Blvd. (Victory Blvd.) |
818-346-1005
www.flemingssteakhouse.com

Carnivores call this steakhouse chain a "genuine top-tier" choice for
"flavorful" cuts, a "terrific" wine list and "tremendous" service provided in "plush" surroundings; it works for "business or pleasure"
among a "jovial crowd", and while it's certainly "expensive", you "can't
beat the price" for happy hour – "if you can find a place at the bar."

Flore Vegan Cuisine *Vegan*
▽ **21** | **16** | **21** | **$19**

Silver Lake | 3818 W. Sunset Blvd. (Hyperion Ave.) | 323-953-0611 |
www.florevegan.com

"A vegan lover's dream" where both "your body and wallet will be
happy", this Silver Laker "satisfies" with its "delicious", "imaginative
and varied" dishes proffered by a "friendly" crew; the "quaint" space
with flea-market stylings is on the "spare" side, but comfortable
enough to stay for the "well-made" desserts.

Flying Pig Truck ⊠🀫 *Asian/Pacific Rim*
22 | **15** | **19** | **$10**

Location varies; see website | 714-234-5107 |
www.flyingpigtruck.com

"Marvelous" Asian–Pacific Rim combos that "burst with flavor" have
Angelenos traversing the town for this mobile maker of "just-right"
buns and tacos with "unique" fillings like tamarind duck and braised
pork belly, plus toppings with a little "crunch"; sure, "having to chase
a truck" can be "annoying" – but fortunately a new Little Tokyo cafe
provides a stay-put option.

Fogo de Chão *Brazilian/Steak*
25 | **23** | **25** | **$63**

Beverly Hills | 133 N. La Cienega Blvd. (bet. Clifton Way & Wilshire Blvd.) |
310-289-7755 | www.fogodechao.com

"Bring on the beef" at this Brazilian steakhouse chain link with "style
and pizzazz" in Beverly Hills, where endless skewers of "tender"
"prime cuts" arrive via "outstanding" "continuous tableside service"
by "gaucho chefs", and it's easy to "fall for" the "huge" "gourmet"
salad bar too; yes, the cost is "substantial", but the "all-you-can-eat
aspect makes it an unparalleled experience" – just be sure to "bring a
grizzly bear's appetite."

Follow Your Heart Cafe *Vegetarian*   22 | 14 | 19 | $18

Canoga Park | 21825 Sherman Way (Vassar Ave.) | 818-348-3240 |
www.followyourheart.com

"One of the originals" when it comes to veggie vittles, this Canoga Parker
nestled in a health food market is "as granola as you can get" with its
"straight-out-of-the-'70s" looks and "wholesome" menu offering a number of "vegan options"; most find it "surprisingly good" and "reasonably
priced", and appreciate its "independent, pro-community" spirit.

Food *American*   24 | 17 | 20 | $18

Rancho Park | 10571 W. Pico Blvd. (Prosser Ave.) | 310-441-7770 |
www.food-la.com

Grab "soul-satisfying breakfasts and lunches" "among the locals" – and
even "spot a celeb once in a while" – at this "inviting" contemporary
American cafe that's "strong on sandwiches, pastries" and "personable" service in Rancho Park; there's limited indoor and outdoor seating, but the "lovely" deli case provides tempting take-out options.

Food + Lab *Californian*   23 | 18 | 17 | $19

Silver Lake | 3206 W. Sunset Blvd. (Descano Dr.) | 323-661-2666
West Hollywood | 7253 Santa Monica Blvd. (bet. Formosa Ave. &
Poinsettia Dr.) | 323-851-7120
www.foodlabcatering.com

Admirers "absolutely love" these West Hollywood and Silver Lake cafes whose Austrian-influenced Californian fare includes "high-quality"
sandwiches, salads and "perfectly cooked" omelets; they're small and
"cool" with some outdoor seating, though they're "not the cheapest"
and a few find the service "too laid-back."

Forage ⊠Ⓜ *Californian*   26 | 16 | 20 | $20

Silver Lake | 3823 W. Sunset Blvd. (bet. Hyperion & Lucille Aves.) |
323-663-6885 | www.foragela.com

"Amazingly fresh" ingredients from "local sources" go into the "rotating menu" of "savory" dishes (with vegan options) and appealing desserts at this "tiny" Silver Lake Californian that's a "lifesaver in the
neighborhood", even if it is "a little pricey"; "order at the counter" and
then "hope that there'll be an empty table somewhere, indoors or
outside" – or simply take your meal to go.

Ford's Filling Station *American*   21 | 18 | 20 | $39

Culver City | 9531 Culver Blvd. (bet. Cardiff & Watseka Aves.) |
310-202-1470 | www.fordsfillingstation.net

"Drop by for drinks and a nibble" at this "cool", "loud" Culver City gastropub from Harrison's son, Ben, featuring an "inventive", midpriced
American menu focusing on "glorified bar food" like housemade charcuterie and an "outstanding burger" backed by "terrific cocktails" and
craft beers; service earns mixed marks and some call it "pricey for
what you get", but the "rustic" space is "always busy" with a "young,
vibrant crowd" nonetheless.

Formosa Cafe ❶ *Asian*   16 | 22 | 17 | $29

West Hollywood | 7156 Santa Monica Blvd. (N. Formosa Ave.) |
323-850-9050

"A slice of LA history", this "vintage" WeHo Asian opened in 1939 and
still has the aura of an "old movie-star hangout", complete with signed

photos on the walls from its famous former clientele; the menu isn't highly regarded, but most go for the drinks, the "cool" ambiance and the "nostalgia" factor.

Foundry on Melrose *American*

| 24 | 20 | 22 | $50 |

Melrose | 7465 Melrose Ave. (bet. Gardner & Vista Sts.) | 323-651-0915 | www.thefoundryonmelrose.com

Grilled cheese "fit for foodies" leads the lineup at this "feel-good" Melrose New American where chef-owner Eric Greenspan turns out a "unique, audacious" menu with specials that "will knock your socks off"; live blues and jazz often dominates the lounge up front, and in back is a patio that's "wonderful for a date", and though it's not inexpensive, the no-corkage fee for BYO keeps the costs down.

Foxy's Restaurant *Southwestern*

| 21 | 17 | 21 | $19 |

Glendale | 206 W. Colorado St. (S. Central Ave.) | 818-246-0244 | www.foxysglendale.com

It's a "throwback to a simpler time" at this "sparkling clean", '60s-era Glendale Southwestern where "breakfast is the best", "drinks get refilled after you've taken one sip" and the staff sometimes "sings while working the cash register"; even if some call it "typical coffee-shop decor and fare", "there's usually a line of people waiting" on the weekends.

Fraîche *French/Italian*

| 21 | 20 | 19 | $45 |

Santa Monica | 312 Wilshire Blvd. (3rd St. Promenade) | 310-451-7482 | www.fraicherestaurantla.com

Diners find "delicious" French-Italian in a "relaxed", "industrial-style" room with a "bistro atmosphere" at this Santa Monica spin-off that's survived the shuttered Culver City original; service gets mixed marks, but the "bustling", "bargain" happy hour (with "top-rate" pizzas) is the main draw for many, and it now lasts all night Sunday–Thursday.

Frascati *Italian*

| 23 | 20 | 21 | $41 |

Rolling Hills Estates | Promenade on the Peninsula | 550 Deep Valley Dr. (Crossfield Dr.) | Rolling Hills | 310-541-8800 | www.frascatiristorante.net

South Bay denizens say *bravissimo!* to this Northern Italian in Rolling Hills Estates that's a "dependable favorite" for "flavorful, well-presented" dishes in a "busy, but not frenzied" old-world setting; it's "a tad expensive", but "professional" service helps support the bill.

⬛NEW⬛ Freddy Smalls Bar & Kitchen ⬤🅕 *American*

| ▽ 26 | 24 | 24 | $31 |

West LA | 11520 W. Pico Blvd. (Gateway Blvd.) | 310-479-3000 | www.freddysmalls.com

"Adventurous foodies" will delight in the "innovative" American fare ("try the bacon cashews") at this "hip but welcoming" new West LA "neighborhood bar and kitchen" by owner Jeff Weinstein (The Counter) and chef Charlie Parker; with its "vintage" design, "nicely curated cocktail menu" and "jagged" but "cool" music selection, the "tiny" room feels like "stepping into a speakeasy", so it's "excellent for dates."

Fred 62 ⬤ *Diner*

| 19 | 18 | 19 | $21 |

Los Feliz | 1850 N. Vermont Ave. (bet. Franklin & Prospect Aves.) | 323-667-0062 | www.fred62.com

"Plenty casual", this round-the-clock, "nifty neighborhood joint" with "retro decor" in Los Feliz offers a "wide selection" of "modern" takes on diner staples to satisfy "late-night cravings" and "breakfast-sandwich" needs; a few call the food "hit-or-miss", but the "super-chill" service and "reasonable" tabs go over well with an "interesting cross-section of people", including the "tight-jeans and liberal-arts-degree" set.

French Crêpe Co. *French* | 23 | 16 | 20 | $15 |

Fairfax | Farmers Mkt. | 6333 W. Third St. (Fairfax Ave.) | 323-934-3113
Hollywood | Hollywood & Highland Ctr. | 6801 Hollywood Blvd. (Highland Ave.) | 323-960-0933
Burbank | 108 E. Palm Ave. (First St.) | 818-846-0566
www.frenchcrepe.com

These French counter-service triplets in Burbank, Hollywood and the Farmers Market cook up "wonderful" crêpes of "all types from sweet to savory" and other "well-prepared", low-cost dishes; they're "definitely not Paris", but worthwhile "if you're in a pinch and need a crêpe fix."

Frida *Mexican* | 20 | 19 | 20 | $34 |

Beverly Hills | 236 S. Beverly Dr. (bet. Charleville Blvd. & Gregory Way) | 310-278-7666
Glendale | Americana at Brand | 750 Americana Way (bet. Brand Blvd. & Central Ave.) | 818-551-1666
Melrose | 7217 Melrose Ave. (Formosa Ave.) | 323-549-4666
Santa Monica | Brentwood Country Mart | 225 26th St. (San Vicente Blvd.) | 310-395-9666
www.fridarestaurant.com

"Refreshing", "higher-end" Mex dishes are served with "style" at this "gourmet", "mini-chain" with a "contemporary" touch; there's a "lively" "after-work" scene in Beverly Hills and Glendale, while the taquerias on Melrose and in the Brentwood Country Mart are best for on-the-go bites.

Frisco's *American* | ▽ 21 | 25 | 22 | $20 |

Long Beach | 4750 E. Los Coyotes Diagonal (bet. N. Park Ave. & Ximeno Ave.) | 562-498-3663
Rowland Heights | 18065 Gale Ave. (Fullerton Rd.) | 626-913-3663
www.friscos.com

"Gals on roller skates" "wheel in plates groaning with deep-fried bar food" at these "colorful", "gimmicky" '50s-style diners in Long Beach and Rowland Heights, where the affordable American grub is "ok but nothing you can't get at your local burger joint", so "go for the atmosphere, service" and "fun entertainment."

Fritto Misto *Italian* | 22 | 15 | 21 | $24 |

Santa Monica | 601 Colorado Ave. (6th St.) | 310-458-2829
Hermosa Beach | 316 Pier Ave. (Monterey Blvd.) | 310-318-6098

"Create-your-own-pasta" plates "hit the spot" (and fit your "budget") at these "family-friendly" Hermosa Beach and Santa Monica Italians where "customization never tasted so good" – and the various options accommodate even the "most complicated diets"; the spaces are "simple and clean" (decorated with tabletops made from wine crates) and the service "helpful", but "expect a long wait" on weekend nights.

Fromin's Deli *Deli* | 17 | 11 | 18 | $21 |

Santa Monica | 1832 Wilshire Blvd. (bet. 18th & 19th Sts.) | 310-829-5443 | www.frominsdeli.com

Guests flash back to "grandma's kitchen" at this slightly "frumpy" but "reliable" deli in Santa Monica dishing up "old-fashioned, stick-to-your-ribs" faves like potato pancakes and corned beef sandwiches set down by a "no-nonsense" staff; some say it's "second-tier" and "more expensive" than it should be, though dinner specials help keep the bill in check.

Frysmith ☒Ⓜ *American* | 23 | 17 | 21 | $9

Location varies; see website | 818-371-6814 | www.eatfrysmith.com
Tater connoisseurs are "mildly stalking" this truck for "crisp", "gourmet fries" covered with "outstanding toppings" ("delicious" kimchi, "amazing" rajas) that add up to a "whole meal"; "you may hate yourself a little" afterward, but "it's worth every minute of penance at the gym."

Fuego at the Maya *Mexican/Pan-Latin* | ▽ 23 | 28 | 24 | $41

Long Beach | Hotel Maya | 700 Queensway Dr. (Harbor Scenic Dr.) | 562-481-3910 | www.fuegolongbeach.com
Boasting a "beautiful deck" looking out to the waterfront and Downtown Long Beach, this "exquisitely decorated" Mexican–Pan-Latin at the Hotel Maya is "great for apps" and other "scrumptious" seafood-focused fare, as well as an "incredible selection of tequila"; Sunday brunch is a "blast" too, so while a few find the prices "steep for what you get", night or day it's the place to "impress a date."

🆕 Fukuburger ● *Burgers* | 24 | 22 | 21 | $17

Hollywood | 1634 N. Cahuegna Blvd. (Hollywood Blvd.) | 323-464-3858 | www.fukuburger.com
"Savory" Japanese-style burgers are the cornerstone of this "decently priced" Hollywood patty purveyor with a striking look accentuated by bright-red picnic tables and funky lighting orbs; the "trendy, helpful" staff also shuttles a "wide selection of beer" and sake bombs, making for a "fun" time (and fans even "like how the name insults you right off the bat").

Full House ● *Chinese/Seafood* | 22 | 10 | 16 | $22

Chinatown | 963 N. Hill St. (College St.) | 213-617-8382
A "hole-in-the-wall" that's "been here forever" (since the early '80s), this C-towner is a "tradition" "embraced" by locals who love the "quality" Chinese with seafood specialties; it's seriously low on ambiance, but "fast", "reasonable" and "open late", so you can usually "make it" after a night out.

Fundamental LA Ⓜ *American/Sandwiches* | ▽ 23 | 18 | 21 | $18

Westwood | 1303 Westwood Blvd. (Wellworth Ave.) | 310-444-7581 | www.fundamental-la.com
Folks with a "fine-dining" pedigree turn out some of the "most creative sandwiches in the city" as well as other "innovative" American eats at this "casual" Westwood place set up for group dining at long wooden tables in a slim, whitewashed room; "fresh churros", "homemade cream soda" and "elegant" wine flights are other pluses, and the "good vibe" keeps guests "going back" too.

Furaibo Restaurant *Japanese* | 23 | 15 | 19 | $24

West LA | 2068 Sawtelle Blvd. (Mississippi Ave.) | 310-444-1432
Dubbed the "ultimate bar snack", the "fried chicken wings are little flavor bombs" and the other Japanese tapas are "delicious" too at this

"busy" West LA izakaya where groups go to chow down for "cheap" and "drink up"; there's not much to the "wood-furnished" room and the waits are "long", but it's "definitely an adventure" for the uninitiated and "awesome" for regulars.

Gaby's *Mediterranean*   20 | 11 | 17 | $17
Culver City | 12219 Jefferson Blvd. (S. Centinela Ave.) | 310-306-9058
Culver City | 2901 La Cienega Blvd. (W. Washington Blvd.) | 310-202-8122
Gaby's Mediterranean *Mediterranean*
Marina del Rey | 20 Washington Blvd. (Speedway) | 310-821-9721
Palms | 10445 Venice Blvd. (Motor Ave.) | 310-559-1808 ●
Gaby's Express *Mediterranean*
Marina del Rey | 3216 Washington Blvd. (S. Lincoln Blvd.) | 310-823-7299
www.gabysexpress.com
"Get your hummus on" at this "solid" Med chain that proves "healthy doesn't have to be boring" with "fresh", "tasty" eats like kebabs and rotisserie chicken topped with an "addictive" garlic sauce, plus a "wide variety" of meze; sure, some of the locations "could use a makeover", but it's "quick", "affordable" and "convenient" for eat-in or takeout, and "cops love it" too.

Gaffey Street Diner *Diner*   21 | 13 | 20 | $17
San Pedro | 247 N. Gaffey St. (1st St.) | 310-548-6964 |
www.gaffeystreetdiner.com
"Humongous", "kick-ass" breakfasts – with items like "softball-sized biscuits" smothered in "homemade" gravy – and "tasty" lunches are a real "value" at this "simple, tidy" daytime San Pedro diner with "courteous, efficient" service; "if you're looking for atmosphere, you're in the wrong place", but if you like "local hangouts" you're in for a treat.

Gale's Ⓜ *Italian*   23 | 17 | 23 | $33
Pasadena | 452 S. Fair Oaks Ave. (bet. California & Del Mar Blvds.) |
626-432-6705 | www.galesrestaurant.com
The "warm" staff greets you "like a long-lost friend" at this "informal, family-friendly" Italian in Pasadena prized for its "lovingly prepared" "traditional" fare; "fair prices" and a "jovial" (some say "loud") atmosphere mean most "can't wait to go back."

Galletto Bar & Grill ● *Brazilian/Italian*   23 | 20 | 21 | $37
Westlake Village | Westlake Plaza | 982 S. Westlake Blvd. (bet. Agoura & Townsgate Rds.) | 805-449-4300 | www.gallettobarandgrill.com
Live music and lots of caipirinhas create a festive atmosphere at this upscale-casual Westlake Villager offering an "extensive" Brazilian-Italian menu of steaks and pastas; critics call the food and service only "ok" for the price, although many agree it's nonetheless an appealing "change of pace."

The Galley *Seafood/Steak*   20 | 19 | 22 | $39
Santa Monica | 2442 Main St. (bet. Hollister Ave. & Ocean Park Blvd.) |
310-452-1934 | www.thegalleyrestaurant.net
"An oldie but a goodie", this "one-of-a-kind" Santa Monica surf 'n' turfer with a "kitschy", nautical-themed setting opened in 1934 and is "still full of character (and characters)"; most find the fare merely "decent", but the drinks are "stiff" and there's "tons of charm" in the "warm" atmosphere, while the happy-hour pricing is "very reasonable" too.

Gaucho Grill *Argentinean/Steak*   21 | 19 | 21 | $27

Brentwood | 11754 San Vicente Blvd. (Gorham Ave.) | 310-447-7898 |
www.gauchobrentwood.com
Long Beach | 200 Pine Ave. (E. B'way) | 562-590-5000 |
www.gauchogrillusa.com

"If you like meat" and "don't want to spend a bundle", head to these
"easy" Argentinean grills in Brentwood and Long Beach for "large portions" of "reliable" steaks, chicken and fish dressed up with chimichurri
sauce; they're "nothing too fancy", but "comfortable" enough, and
wallet-watchers insist the "lunch specials alone make it worth a visit."

Geisha House ● *Japanese*   22 | 24 | 19 | $42

Hollywood | 6633 Hollywood Blvd. (Cherokee Ave.) | 323-460-6300 |
www.dolcegroup.com

It's all about "atmosphere" at this "dark, sexy" Hollywood nightspot
with a "cool" futuristic-Tokyo decor; although the drinks are "pretty" and
"tasty", many find the Japanese fare and sushi "meh for the price" and
the service merely "ok" – it's a "club", "not a fine-dining experience."

Genwa *Korean*   ▽ 25 | 23 | 26 | $36

Koreatown | 5115 Wilshire Blvd. (Orange Dr.) | 323-549-0760 |
www.genwakoreanbbq.com

"Korean BBQ novices and pros" alike get "grilling suggestions" galore
from the "friendly" staff at this "superb" spot in K-town where the
meat quality is "outstanding" and the "variety of side dishes" is "really
over the top"; plus, thanks to "excellent ventilation" in the contempo
setting, you'll leave with "no smoky smell on your clothes."

⧄ Geoffrey's *Californian*   22 | 27 | 22 | $61

Malibu | 27400 PCH (4 mi. north of Malibu Canyon Rd.) | 310-457-1519 |
www.geoffreysmalibu.com

It's like a "mini-vacation" at this "enchaining" Malibu restaurant boasting
"sweeping views of the Pacific" and an "incredibly romantic" setting
where "you may even catch a glimpse of your favorite star"; even if it
doesn't quite live up to the "grand" ambiance, many find the Californian
fare and service "pretty darn good" too (especially at brunch), although
for many it's "too expensive for anything but a special occasion."

George's Greek Café *Greek*   24 | 19 | 24 | $24

Lakewood | 5252 Faculty Ave. (Candlewood St.) | 562-529-5800
Long Beach | 135 Pine Ave. (bet. B'way & 1st St.) | 562-437-1184
Long Beach | 5316 E. Second St. (Pomona Ave.) | 562-433-1755
www.georgesgreekcafe.com

"Get your Greek on" at this "festive", "easy-on-the-wallet" Hellenic
mini-chain where the "wonderful" eats come in ample portions and
servers "treat you like family"; the blue-and-white checkered tablecloths
and paintings of Greece lend an "evocative", "old-world" feel, and weekly
live music and belly dancing add to the ambiance.

⧄ Getty Center,   23 | 27 | 24 | $45
Restaurant at the Ⓜ *Californian*

Brentwood | Getty Ctr. | 1200 Getty Center Dr. (Sepulveda Blvd.) |
310-440-6810 | www.getty.edu

"A feast for the eyes" awaits at this "sophisticated" aerie atop the Getty
Center in the Brentwood hills matching "one of the prettiest views" in

town with "original", "artistic" Californian cuisine proffered by an "excellent" staff; it's "not inexpensive", but "what a wonderful way to spend a day"; P.S. dinner is only served on Saturdays, or on Fridays in summer.

Gina Lee's Bistro ⓜ Asian/Californian
| 25 | 17 | 24 | $39 |

Redondo Beach | Riviera Plaza | 211 Palos Verdes Blvd. (bet. Catalina Ave. & PCH) | 310-375-4462

"Creative", "beautifully presented" Cal-Asian dishes shine at this Redondo Beach "strip-mall treasure" by owners Gina and Scott Lee, who "take food seriously" and "really care" about their customers; the "fairly priced" wine list also impresses, and while the "loud" digs "could be better", most call it a "delightful dining experience" nonetheless; P.S. "go for the bento box."

Gingergrass Vietnamese
| 23 | 17 | 20 | $24 |

Silver Lake | 2396 Glendale Blvd. (Brier Ave.) | 323-644-1600 | www.gingergrass.com

"Tasty" noodle bowls and other "California-ized" Vietnamese dishes win a following for their "simple, clean flavors" at this Silver Lake locale with "fantastic prices"; service is "prompt", and while the "crowded" room doesn't stand out, "you're there for the food, not the scenery."

Gin Sushi Japanese
| ▽ 23 | 17 | 19 | $25 |

Pasadena | 3589 E. Colorado Blvd. (N. Lotus Ave.) | 626-440-9611 | www.ginsushi.com

"Excellent sushi" and "surprisingly affordable" prices make a "rare" combo at this tiny Japanese where the chef himself is a "Pasadena institution"; it's nothing "too fancy" but "many regulars" say they "always enjoy coming here."

Giorgio Baldi ⓜ Italian
| 25 | 19 | 20 | $82 |

Santa Monica | 114 W. Channel Rd. (PCH) | 310-573-1660 | www.giorgiobaldi.us

Some of the "best Italian west of Roma" attracts an elite clientele to this "high-class" Santa Monican serving "luxurious pastas" (some "with truffles") and other "wonderful" specialties; a few critics find fault with the staff "attitude" and call the "cramped tables" a drawback – unless you're seated near any of the "movie stars that fill the room", willing to pay the "beyond expensive" tabs; P.S. its namesake has passed away ("R.I.P. Giorgio"), but his family is still at the helm.

Giovanni Italian
| 22 | 16 | 21 | $34 |

Woodland Hills | 21801 Ventura Blvd. (Topanga Canyon Blvd.) | 818-884-0243 | www.giovanniristorante.com

"Well-prepared", "generous" plates of "homestyle" Italian food come with "family"-oriented hospitality and "fair" prices at this Woodland Hills staple; while some say the "simple" decor lacks "charm", others find the "friendly owner" keeps it a "warm neigborhood place."

ⓩ Gjelina ● American
| 26 | 21 | 19 | $46 |

Venice | 1429 Abbot Kinney Blvd. (bet. California & Milwood Aves.) | 310-450-1429 | www.gjelina.com

"Glorious" small plates, "beautifully crafted" pizzas and a "killer wine list" (not to mention the "holy grail" butterscotch pot de crème) earn an "animated scene" at chef/co-owner Travis Lett's "outstanding" New American in Venice, leading "arty" "Westsiders with money" to land "coveted reservations" or else crowd into "cool communal tables"; while the "pretentiously casual" service, "inflexible" kitchen and "noisy, cramped" interior get knocked, the "patio is a pleasure", further heightening the "intoxicating" experience.

⚋ Gjelina Take Away *American*
27 | 14 | 18 | $22

Venice | 1429 Abbot Kinney Blvd. (bet. California & Milwood Aves.) | 310-450-1429 | www.gjelina.com

"You'll never forget the pork belly sandwich" say those who swear by this Venice take-out spin-off offering the same "tremendous" food as Gjelina (including "excellent pizzas") without the need for "month-in-advance" reservations; it's "a little expensive for lunch every day" and service can be "slow", but reviewers recommend it "if you don't mind sitting on milk crates."

Gladstones Malibu *Seafood*
18 | 21 | 18 | $43

Pacific Palisades | 17300 PCH (Sunset Blvd.) | 310-454-3474 | www.gladstones.com

Gladstone's *Seafood*

Long Beach | 330 S. Pine Ave. (S. Pine Ave.) | 562-432-8588 | www.gladstoneslongbeach.com

The "marvelous view of the ocean" trumps everything else at these separately owned Pacific Palisades and Long Beach venues serving "average but plentiful" seafood to an "overwhelming klatch of tourists"; inconsistent service and "high prices" are common complaints.

Gloria's Cafe *Mexican/Salvadoran*
23 | 15 | 21 | $18

Culver City | 10227 Venice Blvd. (Vinton Ave.) | 310-838-0963 | www.gloriascafela.com

"Pupusas are a must" at this "family-run" Salvadoran-Mexican "neighborhood find" in Culver City, offering "quality food on a budget" as well as service that's "remarkable for a strip-mall joint"; "good, healthy portions" are another plus for the "happy" clientele.

Go Burger *Burgers*
22 | 18 | 20 | $21

Hollywood | 6290 W. Sunset Blvd. (Vine St.) | 323-327-9355 | www.goburger.com

An "inspired" menu of "flavorful" burgers, "duck fat fries and spiked shakes" makes this BLT offshoot with a "happening" Hollywood atmosphere "one of the better" upscale patty-slingers around; a "diligent" staff keeps up the pace, so despite costs for the "convenient" location, it's filled with "locals day and night."

Golden Deli *Vietnamese*
25 | 12 | 17 | $15

San Gabriel | Las Tunas Plaza | 815 W. Las Tunas Dr. (Mission Dr.) | 626-308-0803 | www.thegoldendeli.com

"Wildly popular for a reason", this San Gabriel Vietnamese has been setting the "standard" since 1981, delivering "fool-proof delicious" dishes, particularly the "don't-miss" spring rolls and "rich, piping-hot" bowls of pho; it's "not fancy" but "friendly" – just expect to wait on a "line out the door."

Golden Dragon Restaurant *Chinese*
21 | 16 | 18 | $22

Chinatown | 960 N. Broadway (W. College St.) | 213-626-2039

The "dumplings are to die for" at this "inexpensive" C-town Chinese, a Sunday-brunch staple offering a "fresh, varied" menu of "authentic" dim sum – "you want it, they got it"; the food beats out the service and old-fashioned decor that "could use a pick-me-up."

Golden State ⓜ *Burgers* 26 | 14 | 22 | $19

Fairfax | 426 N. Fairfax Ave. (bet. Oakwood & Rosewood Aves.) | 323-782-8331 | www.thegoldenstatecafe.com

Go for the "revelatory", "amazingly made" burgers and "keep the pig-out ball rolling" with sweet potato fries and Coke floats at this "tiny" Fairfax storefront where the "cool owners and staff" also "know their beer"; despite "standing in line" for counter service and "waiting for tables to open up", diehards dub it the "hands-down best" around; P.S. Let's Be Frank hot dogs are on the menu too.

Gonpachi *Japanese* 20 | 25 | 21 | $47

Torrance | Miyako Hybrid Hotel | 21381 S. Western Ave. (bet. 213th & 214th Sts.) | 310-320-6700 | www.miyakohybridhotel.com

Diners encounter a "slice of Japan in Torrance" at this "refreshing" hotel locale serving "delicious" soba noodles and sushi in a "beautiful", "hip" setting; "helpful" servers enhance it as an "asset" to the area, even if it can get "expensive" for dinner (lunch is more "reasonable").

Good Girl Dinette ⓜ *Vietnamese* ▽ 24 | 20 | 23 | $18

Highland Park | 110 N. Ave. 56 (Figueroa St.) | 323-257-8980 | www.goodgirlfoods.com

The "unique fusion" of Vietnamese and American "comfort food with a kick" gets a "thumbs-up" at this Highland Park "local" with "the charm of a small diner"; though it's not "traditional" or speedy enough for some, it's a "cheap" go-to for the "hipster" set.

Good Stuff *American* 21 | 14 | 20 | $17

West LA | 11903 W. Olympic Blvd. (Bundy Dr.) | 310-477-9011
El Segundo | 131 W. Grand Ave. (Main St.) | 310-647-9997
Hermosa Beach | 1286 The Strand (Pier Ave.) | 310-374-2334
Redondo Beach | 1617 S. PCH (Elena Ave.) | 310-316-0262
www.eatgoodstuff.com

Even if it's "not for foodies", sold surveyors say "you'll be surprised at how good" the American fare is at this longtime quartet delivering "healthy choices" and "value"; there's "no money wasted on decor", but with its "eclectic atmosphere", "low-key vibe" and "consistent" service, it's a "favorite" for breakfast and lunch, especially among "families."

The Gorbals ◗🅧 *Eclectic* 22 | 17 | 20 | $38

Downtown | Alexandria Hotel | 501 S. Spring St. (5th St.) | 213-488-3408 | www.thegorbalsla.com

Top Chef winner Ilan Hall offers "original" "Scottish-Jewish" small plates with "a sense of humor" – like "brilliant" bacon-wrapped matzo balls – and "spot-on" cocktails at this "hip" Downtown Eclectic set in "wildly weird and wonderful" "basement-chic" digs in an old hotel; factor in "laid-back" service and pricing and it's a perfect "conversation starter" and "date spot for the semi-adventurous."

Gordon Biersch *Pub Food* 19 | 20 | 20 | $26

Burbank | 145 S. San Fernando Blvd. (Angeleno) | 818-569-5240 | www.gordonbiersch.com

"Stick to the beer" and the "easy stuff" ("excellent garlic fries") at this American brew pub in Burbank serving "bar grub at its chain-iest" in a "comfortable" atmosphere that works for "happy hour" with a "large group" or just "watching sports"; there's "friendly" service too, though the operation feels too "generic" to some.

Gordon Ramsay   *Californian/French* | 24 | 24 | 23 | $83 |

West Hollywood | London West Hollywood | 1020 N. San Vicente Blvd. (Sunset Blvd.) | 310-358-7788 | www.thelondonwesthollywood.com

"Exceptional" Californian-French cuisine and "fantastic" wine pairings make for an "outstanding meal" at this "destination" in the London West Hollywood (where Ramsay acts as a consultant); the "serene" setting may not be "something to get excited about", and a few pooh-pooh "small portions" and "fussy" leanings, but most agree the "beautiful" service supports the highly "expensive" tabs.

NEW Gottsui ● *Japanese* | - | - | - | I |

West LA | 2119 Sawtelle Blvd. (bet. Mississippi Ave. & W. Olympic Blvd.) | 310-478-0521 | www.gottsui-usa.com

Lovers of Japanese "street food" dig this "great new place" in West LA specializing in "delicious" okonomiyaki (savory grilled pancakes) and yakisoba (Japanese fried noodles) in a minimalist black-and-white setting; "be prepared to wait" and pay slightly "high" prices for the "small" savories, but it's "easier than going to Toyko."

Grand Lux Cafe   *Eclectic* | 21 | 23 | 21 | $28 |

Beverly Hills | Beverly Ctr. | 121 N. La Cienega Blvd. (bet. Beverly Blvd. & 3rd St.) | 310-855-1122 | www.grandluxcafe.com

A "slightly upscale version of the Cheesecake Factory" with the vibe of a "Vegas hotel", this "busy", "whimsical"-looking offshoot in Beverly Hills serves "portions that can feed a small country" from an "extensive", "dependable" Eclectic menu; though not exactly "nuanced", it's "reasonably priced" with solid service, so "satisfied" customers say it's "not bad for a chain."

Granville Cafe   *American* | 21 | 21 | 21 | $24 |

Burbank | 121 N. San Fernando Blvd. (bet. E. Olive & E. Orange Grove Aves.) | 818-848-4726
Glendale | Americana at Brand | 807 Americana Way (Brand Blvd.) | 818-550-0472
www.granvillecafe.com

For "for a night out" or an "amazing" breakfast, these "upscale" yet casual twins in Burbank and Glendale – lauded for "moderate" prices – serve up "solid" (some say "generic") American "comfort food" to diners of all ages in a homey, bistro-style environment; the "energetic" staff "treats everyone like family", and for voyeurs, the patios offer "great people-watching" too.

Great Greek   *Greek* | 23 | 19 | 23 | $30 |

Sherman Oaks | 13362 Ventura Blvd. (bet. Dixie Canyon & Nagle Aves.) | 818-905-5250 | www.greatgreek.com

"*Opa!*" shout fans of this "boisterous" Sherman Oaks taverna "straight out of *Never on Sunday*", which plates "abundant" portions of "authentic" Greek delicacies in a "party atmosphere" ("be prepared to join a line dance"); philosophical types find the photo-bedecked digs "crazy loud", but with "no shortage of hospitality" and fair prices, it's "as close to Athens as you'll get" in SoCal.

Greenblatt's Deli & Fine Wines ● *Deli* | 19 | 12 | 17 | $24

Hollywood | 8017 W. Sunset Blvd. (Laurel Ave.) | 323-656-0606 | www.greenblattsdeli.com

"You can't go wrong" with a "generous" pastrami sandwich and a "nice bottle of red" at this Hollywood deli and "impressive" attached wine shop; kvetchers lament "slow" service amid the "old-school", two-floor setting, though late hours (till 2 AM) can be a godsend.

Green Field Churrascaria *Brazilian* | 23 | 20 | 22 | $36

Long Beach | 5305 E. PCH (Anaheim St.) | 562-597-0906
West Covina | 381 N. Azusa Ave. (bet. Rowland & Workman Aves.) | 626-966-2300
www.greenfieldchurrascaria.com

"Bring your appetite" to these "enormous", family-friendly churrascarias in Long Beach and West Covina, an all-you-can-eat Brazilian "meatfest" where you're plied with an "incredible variety" of *carne* "till you beg for mercy", plus an "abundant" salad-bar buffet; count in "excellent" service and "colorful" surroundings, and beef eaters make it clear – "you can't beat the price."

Greenleaf Gourmet Chopshop 🗷 *American* | 22 | 15 | 19 | $15

Beverly Hills | 9671 Wilshire Blvd. (Bedford Dr.) | 310-246-0756
Century City | 1888 Century Park E. (Constellation Blvd.) | 424-239-8700
www.greenleafchopshop.com

Pleasing "even non-vegetarians", these Beverly Hills and Century City saladeers let customers build their own leafy creations, in addition to spinning out other "fresh" and "healthy" American eats; pleasant service and modern, bright-green settings make them "welcome" for lunch, though a few tree-shruggers gripe "who knew greens could cost that much?"

Green Street Restaurant *American* | 22 | 17 | 20 | $25

Pasadena | 146 Shoppers Ln. (Cordova St.) | 626-577-7170 | www.greenstreetrestaurant.com

Pasadena families and "ladies who lunch" frequent this casual American "mainstay" for its "generous" portions of "comfort-food" standards, including a "still-tops" Dianne salad and "delish" zucchini bread; quibblers sniff at "spotty" service and a "plain" interior, but a "delightful" patio and "fair prices" entrench it as a "local institution."

Green Street Tavern *Californian* | 24 | 19 | 22 | $37

Pasadena | 69 W. Green St. (bet. De Lacey & Fair Oaks Aves.) | 626-229-9961 | www.greenstreettavern.net

"Tucked away on Green Street" is this "charming" Pasadena "treasure", which offers "sophisticated", "reasonably priced" Californian cuisine with an "eclectic" European flair – plus a "glorious" wine list – in a "cozy" yet "urbane" atmosphere; coupled with its "warm hospitality" and brunch menu, fans wish it could remain a "best-kept secret."

Griddle Cafe *American* | 25 | 15 | 21 | $19

Hollywood | 7916 W. Sunset Blvd. (bet. Fairfax & Hayworth Aves.) | 323-874-0377 | www.thegriddlecafe.com

"Hubcap-sized" pancakes in myriad "over-the-top" combinations and other "amazing" treats "drive lines of locals and tourists" to this "gold standard" of American breakfast spots, right in the heart of Hollywood; the "hip", "urban" space, enhanced by a "gorgeous" staff, is often "extremely busy" (particularly on weekends), so regulars suggest "arriving early" to avoid a "long wait."

The Grilled Cheese Truck *Sandwiches*

24 | 15 | 20 | $10

Location varies; see website | www.thegrilledcheesetruck.com

It "ain't your mother's grilled cheese" at this "top-tier" truck turning out "incredible, gourmet" sammies in "novel" combos like the "genius" mac and rib accompanied by shots of tomato soup and tater tots to perpetual "lines" of followers; sure, some say you can "make them at home for half the price", but it works for a "comfort-food fix" on the run.

Grill 'Em All Truck 🗷 Ⓜ ✍ *Burgers*

26 | 16 | 21 | $13

Location varies; see website | 323-252-5603 | www.grillemalltruck.com

"Bitchin'", "super-clever flavor combos" – such as the "gotta-try" Molly Hatchet (with "sausage gravy, bacon and maple") and other "gooey extravanzas" – "hit the lights and shatter the bulbs" at this "rock 'n' roll–themed" burgermobile; the "smiling" crew gets a definite "thumbs-up" despite "long lines", so it's one to "follow for sure."

The Grill on Hollywood *American*

24 | 24 | 25 | $52

Hollywood | Hollywood & Highland Ctr. | 6801 Hollywood Blvd. (Highland Ave.) | 323-856-5530

The Grill on the Alley Westlake *American*

Thousand Oaks | Promenade at Westlake | 120 Promenade Way (Thousand Oaks Blvd.) | 805-418-1760
www.thegrill.com

"Excellent" steaks, chops and other American standards are elevated by a "stellar" staff at these "elegant" Hollywood and Westlake offshoots of The Grill on the Alley in Beverly Hills deemed a worthy "splurge"; they're "fabulous places to take out-of-towners or celebrate a special occasion", or try the "fantastic" happy hours for lower-cost bites and burgers.

The Grill on the Alley *American*

25 | 23 | 25 | $61

Beverly Hills | 9560 Dayton Way (bet. Camden & Rodeo Drs.) | 310-276-0615 | www.thegrill.com

"Feel like a movie mogul" at this "snapshot of old LA" in Beverly Hills, where nearly "impeccable", "expensive" steaks, chops and seafood are served up in a "clubby, high-end scene" full of "industry types" ready to "close the next deal"; there's "pampering" service that "treats you like a regular", although "snagging a table is not so easy" at lunch, so some try it during the "quieter" dinner hours.

Grissini 🗷 *Italian*

23 | 22 | 23 | $36

Agoura Hills | Agoura Hills Town Ctr. | 30125 Agoura Rd. (Reyes Adobe Rd.) | 818-735-9711 | www.grissiniristoranteitaliano.com

With countless variations of "mix-and-match" pastas enthralling diners, this "authentic", shopping center–located Italian "gem" in Agoura Hills is "always a delight", offering pizzas and other "delicious" fare in a candlelit, frescoed setting; the "charming" owner wins over fans as well, and though some say meals can get "a bit pricey", most have a "memorable" experience.

	FOOD	DECOR	SERVICE	COST

Grub *American*

| 24 | 20 | 23 | $19 |

Hollywood | 911 N. Seward St. (bet. Romaine St. & Willoughby Ave.) | 323-461-3663 | www.grub-la.com

"They really have something special" cooking inside this "charming" former bungalow on a residential block in Hollywood, where former *Top Chef* contestant Betty Fraser cooks up "quirky" yet "homey" American eats – including a grilled-cheese-and-tomato-soup combo that may "transport you to mother's kitchen" – at modest prices; grubsters also dig the "excellent" brunch, "personable" staff and "lovely" patio, which make the experience like "hanging out at a friend's house."

Guelaguetza *Mexican*

| 24 | 15 | 20 | $24 |

Koreatown | 3014 W. Olympic Blvd. (Normandie Ave.) | 213-427-0608
Lynwood | 11215 Long Beach Blvd. (Beechwood Ave.) | 310-884-9234
www.guelaguetzarestaurante.com

The black mole's "to die for" at these "definitive" Mexican spots in Koreatown and Lynwood, where families dig into "big", "value"-oriented portions of "authentic" Oaxacan cuisine; a staff that "likes to help" and traditional decor accented with live music create an ambiance that's "full of life" – remember, "you're in flavortown."

Guido's *Italian*

| 22 | 20 | 23 | $43 |

Malibu | 3874 Cross Creek Rd. (PCH) | 310-456-1979 | www.guidosmalibu.com
West LA | 11980 Santa Monica Blvd. (Bundy Dr.) | 310-820-6649 | www.guidosla.com

"Take a walk down memory lane" at this "dependable" Italian duo, where the "impeccable", tux-clad waiters "fuss over you" like in "the good old days"; the "traditional" cuisine – served in an "intimate" (some say "dated") West LA location featuring red booths and a fireplace, and in a natural light–enhanced Malibu site – entices locals, though some warn of "sticker shock" come tab time.

Gulfstream *American/Seafood*

| 23 | 22 | 23 | $40 |

Century City | Westfield Century City Shopping Ctr. | 10250 Santa Monica Blvd. (bet. Ave. of the Stars & Century Park W.) | 310-553-3636 | www.hillstone.com

Surveyors deem this "fishy sibling of Houston's" "another success story" from the Hillstone group, with "fresh", "honest" American seafood luring businessfolk to its upscale Century City and Newport Beach outposts; a "knowledgeable" staff, "slick" setting and prices that are "reasonable" for the quality keep these spots "busy", despite some complaints about "noise" and "waits."

Gumbo Pot *Cajun*

| 20 | 10 | 15 | $16 |

Fairfax | Farmers Mkt. | 6333 W. Third St. (Fairfax Ave.) | 323-933-0358 | www.thegumbopotla.com

This "super-casual" stall in the Fairfax Farmers Market is the "real deal", churning out gumbo, beignets and other "classic Cajun" treats that are so good, "you think you're in the Big Easy"; sure, critics fret over chow that's "nothing memorable" while citing "passable" outside seating, but for a "quick", inexpensive bite, it "hits the spot."

Gus's BBQ *BBQ*

20 | 18 | 21 | $27

South Pasadena | 808 Fair Oaks Ave. (bet. Hope & Mission Sts.) |
626-799-3251 | www.gussbbq.com

"Cholesterol and calories be damned" say 'cueheads of this "friendly"
South Pasadena joint, a mainstay since 1946 for "solid" BBQ staples
such as pulled pork and beer-braised brisket, along with "rich sauces";
the "spiffy" nostalgic-meets-modern space makes for a "lively", family-
oriented atmosphere, and while rib-sticklers sniff "it's not Texas or
Memphis", with such moderate prices, "it'll do."

Gusto ⓜ *Italian*

- | - | - | M

Third Street | 8432 W. Third St. (bet. La Cienega Blvd. & Orlando Ave.) |
323-782-1778 | www.gusto-la.com

Chef Vic Casanova (ex Culina at the Four Seasons Beverly Hills) is behind this narrow Beverly Center–adjacent storefront serving a rustic,
midpriced menu he describes as 'free-range Italian' – think salt cod
croquettes, exotically shaped pastas and beef-heart tartare; add the
unfussy space featuring exposed-beam ceilings and a simple red-
white-and-wood aesthetic to the fast-growing list of eateries making
Third Street the next Mid-City Restaurant Row.

Gyu-Kaku *Japanese*

22 | 19 | 19 | $32

Beverly Hills | 163 N. La Cienega Blvd. (Clifton Way) |
310-659-5760
West LA | 10925 W. Pico Blvd. (bet. Veteran Ave. & Westwood Blvd.) |
310-234-8641
Torrance | Cross Road Plaza | 24631 Crenshaw Blvd. (Skypark Dr.) |
310-325-1437
Pasadena | 70 W. Green St. (De Lacey Ave.) | 626-405-4842
Canoga Park | Westfield Topanga Ctr. | 6600 Topanga Canyon Blvd.
(Victory Blvd.) | 818-888-4030
Sherman Oaks | 14457 Ventura Blvd. (Van Nuys Blvd.) | 818-501-5400
www.gyu-kaku.com

The "novelty" of "DIY" tabletop grilling intrigues adventurers at this
"festive" Japanese yakiniku chain, where families, friends and first
dates cook their own "scrumptious" meats in an Asian-themed setting; meanwhile, some grumble about the "hit-or-miss" staff serving
"small", "pricey" portions, though "bargains" may be found during
regular happy hours.

Habit Burger Grill *Burgers*

23 | 16 | 21 | $11

Norwalk | 12401 Norwalk Blvd. (bet. Crewe St. & Imperial Hwy.) |
562-863-3061
El Segundo | 311 N. Sepulveda Blvd. (E. Grand Ave.) |
310-524-9016
Burbank | 103 E. Alameda Ave. (bet. Flower St. & San Fernando Blvd.) |
818-260-0083
Encino | 17132 Ventura Blvd. (Balboa Blvd.) | 818-783-6162
Glendale | 249 N. Glendale Ave. (E. California Ave.) | 818-246-6095
Northridge | 9215 Reseda Blvd. (bet. Nordhoff & Plummer Sts.) |
818-993-7113
Sherman Oaks | 14622 Ventura Blvd. (Cedros Ave.) |
818-386-0995
Woodland Hills | 22651 Ventura Blvd. (Ponce Ave.) | 818-225-2231
La Verne | 1608 Foothill Blvd. (bet. B St. & Wheeler Ave.) |
909-593-1640

(continued)

Habit Burger Grill

Valencia | 25948 McBean Pkwy. (Del Monte Dr.) | 661-291-1575
www.habitburger.com
Additional locations throughout Southern California

Habitués of this "gourmet fast-food" burger chain with sites throughout California are "addicted" to the "juicy" charbroiled patties and "crisp" fries; "thoughtful" service, "casual" decor and "easy-on-the-wallet" prices offer an "alternative" to the rest of the quick-bite pack, and while claustrophobes mutter about "crowds", fans are "never disappointed."

Hakata Ramen Shinsengumi ❶ *Japanese*   25 | 15 | 20 | $14

Gardena | 2015 W. Redondo Beach Blvd. (Gramercy Pl.) | 310-329-1335 | www.shinsengumigroup.com

"Outstanding" ramen awaits at this inexpensive Japanese "dive" in Gardena, where servers help you "customize" your noodles before they're "cooked to perfection"; pundits cite the "casual" atmosphere where you may have to "yell across the table" to be heard and say to "expect a wait", but overall, it "feels like Tokyo."

🄯 Hamasaku 🄯 *Japanese*   28 | 19 | 24 | $67

West LA | 11043 Santa Monica Blvd. (Sepulveda Blvd.) | 310-479-7636 | www.hamasakula.com

"Memorable enough to be your last meal", the "innovative" rolls named for celebs and "fresh" sushi (plus omakase) star at this "high-class" West LA Japanese in an unassuming strip mall; the "gracious" host treats everyone – from plebs to Hollywood luminaries – "like a VIP" in the upscale, homey space, but note that "the check will get your attention."

Hama Sushi *Japanese*   25 | 17 | 22 | $35

Venice | 213 Windward Ave. (Main St.) | 310-396-8783 | www.hamasushi.com

"Traditional", "inventive" rolls, "no-nonsense" sushi and other Japanese classics "keep 'em coming back" to this longtime Venice "hole-in-the-wall", a popular "local hang" that attracts ichthyophiles for its "friendly" "group vibe" and "reasonable" prices, including happy-hour deals; a patio's also on hand for those seeking more subdued dining.

Hamburger Hamlet *Diner*   19 | 17 | 19 | $24

Pasadena | 214 S. Lake Ave. (Cordova St.) | 626-449-8520
Sherman Oaks | 4419 Van Nuys Blvd. (Moorpark St.) | 818-784-1183
www.hamletrestaurants.com

For "a bit of old LA", locals patronize these "classic" diners in Pasadena and Sherman Oaks, a "standby" for "moderately priced" American munchies; doubters, however, say it's "not what it was", finding the dark-wood setting "outdated" and the service "adequate", though for nostalgia it remains "tried-and-true."

Hamburger Mary's *Diner*   18 | 17 | 18 | $23

West Hollywood | 8288 Santa Monica Blvd. (Sweetzer Ave.) | 323-654-3800 | www.hamburgermarysweho.com
Long Beach | 740 E. Broadway (Alamitos Ave.) | 562-436-7900 | www.hamburgermaryslb.com ❶

"If you're in a campy mood", these diner-style "hangouts" in WeHo and Long Beach can be a "blast", with bingo nights, karaoke and drag shows complementing "delicious" cocktails in "casual" digs; as for the American menu, most find it just "ok" ("food – what food?") and service is "hit-or-miss", but for "kitsch"-seekers, "it's the spot for you."

NEW Hannosuke �}M *Japanese*

| – | – | – | I |

Mar Vista | Mitsuwa Market | 3760 S. Centinela Ave. (Venice Blvd.) | 310-398-2113 | www.hannosuke.com

The busy Mitsuwa Market in Mar Vista hosts the first American outpost of this hugely popular Tokyo tempura specialist, which offers just two options, both wallet-friendly: tempura (fried fish and vegetables over rice) or eel donburi; local foodies and Japanese expats alike queue up for a taste of the freshly fried treat.

Harold & Belle's *Creole*

| 25 | 18 | 20 | $35 |

Mid-City | 2920 W. Jefferson Blvd. (bet. 9th & 10th Aves.) | 323-735-3376 | www.haroldandbellesrestaurant.com

You'd "have to drive to Louisiana to do better" than the "home cookin'" – think étouffée and gumbo – of this "old-school" Creole in Mid-City, where locals enjoy "humongous" portions and authentic "Southern hospitality" in a warm, comfortable space; regular jazz nights add luster, though some point to prices that are "steep" for what you get.

Z Hatfield's *American*

| 27 | 25 | 26 | $72 |

Melrose | 6703 Melrose Ave. (Citrus Ave.) | 323-935-2977 | www.hatfieldsrestaurant.com

"Simply perfection", this "marvelous" Melrose New American from husband-and-wife team Quinn and Karen Hatfield provides "ambrosial" locavore cuisine (including an "extraordinary" tasting menu) to those "serious about food"; "impeccable" service (you "never feel rushed") and a "soothing" contemporary setting enchant too, and while some may blink at the "sky-high" prices, it's a place that "shouldn't be missed."

NEW Haven Gastropub +Brewery ● *American*

| 22 | 21 | 21 | $27 |

Pasadena | 42 S. De Lacey Ave. (Mc Cormick Alley) | 626-768-9555 | www.havengastropub.com

"Fab" "calorie-unfriendly menus" of "innovative pub-style" fare and a rotating selection of "obscure" beers endear Pasadena patrons to this midrange gastropub with a modern feel; service is solid and it's open late, however, it's "always packed" and some say the "college-campus" crowd can get "noisy" and "spoil your appetite."

Heroes and Legends *Pub Food*

| 23 | 22 | 22 | $22 |

Claremont | 131 N. Yale Ave. (bet. W. 1st & W. 2nd Sts.) | 909-621-6712

"Beer nuts" adore the "abundant" brew selection at this "locals' gathering hole" in Claremont, which dishes out "huge" portions of "moderately priced" pub grub in a "loud", "lively" sports-bar environment; a "mega-friendly" vibe prevails despite the "busy" scene.

Hide Sushi M⌿ *Japanese*

| 24 | 12 | 20 | $32 |

West LA | 2040 Sawtelle Blvd. (bet. La Grange & Mississippi Aves.) | 310-477-7242 | www.hidesushi.com

You won't find "exotic or fancy rolls" at this Japanese "hole-in-the-wall" in West LA, which slices up "generous" cuts of "straightforward", "quality" sushi at "bargain" prices; the "sweet" staff moves things along, but surveyors say the "tiny", "bare-bones" space can get "crowded" – a trade-off when you want "the real thing"; P.S. cash only.

Hirosuke *Japanese* 23 | 14 | 20 | $35

Encino | Plaza de Oro | 17237 Ventura Blvd. (Louise & Amestoy Aves.) | 818-788-7548

"Dependable" sushi and "excellent" specialty rolls may be had at this Encino Japanese, a local fixture for its "fresh", "reasonably priced" finned fare and accommodating service; the casual setting is often "busy" with loyal regulars, who like its "consistency" – no small feat for a neighborhood spot.

❷ Hirozen ⧉ *Japanese* 27 | 16 | 22 | $41

Beverly Boulevard | 8385 Beverly Blvd. (bet. Kings Rd. & Orlando Ave.) | West Hollywood | 323-653-0470 | www.hirozen.com

"Serious, enthusiastic eaters" swoon over the "delectable sushi" (including selections "you rarely see" elsewhere) prepared with "imagination, elegance and an element of wit" by "caring" chef-owner Hiro Obayashi at this "incredible" Beverly Boulevard find "embedded in an unassuming strip mall"; it's "too small to linger" and there's "no atmosphere", but "who cares?" – the omakase's available at "different price ranges", so "your taste buds and wallet will thank you."

Hof's Hut *American/Eclectic* 21 | 17 | 22 | $20

Long Beach | 2147 N. Bellflower Blvd. (Stearns St.) | 562-597-5811
Long Beach | 4251 Long Beach Blvd. (bet. Countryclub Ln. & San Antonio Dr.) | 562-424-0390
Long Beach | 6257 E. Second St. (bet. Marina Dr. & Pacific Coasy Hwy.) | 562-598-4070
Torrance | 23635 Crenshaw Blvd. (236th Pl.) | 310-325-0470
www.hofshut.com

"Take a gentle step back in time" to this "old-fashioned" SoCal chain that's "two cuts above" a diner, turning out "hearty" portions of "affordable" Eclectic-American "down-home cooking"; with a "pleasant" atmosphere and "helpful" staff that makes sure "you're comfortable", it's a top "family choice."

Holdren's Steaks & Seafood *Seafood/Steak* 22 | 20 | 22 | $45

Thousand Oaks | 1714 Newbury Rd. (bet. Hillcrest Dr. & Ventu Park Rds.) | 805-498-1314 | www.holdrens.com

"Reasonably priced" steaks and "specials every day but Saturday" mean you'll find a wait "even on a weeknight" at this "dark", saloon-inspired duo in Thousand Oaks and Santa Barbara; generally "attentive" service is a plus, though critics call it "cramped and noisy" with "hit-or-miss" cooking, adding they just don't "understand the fuss."

Hole in the Wall Burger Joint *Burgers* 24 | 11 | 18 | $14

NEW **West Hollywood** | 7998 Santa Monica Blvd. (Laurel Ave.) | 323-654-0484
West LA | 11058 Santa Monica Blvd. (Bentley Ave.) | 310-312-7013 ⧉ www.holeinthewallburgerjoint.com

"Juicy" patties "cooked to perfection", "housemade condiments" and "killer buns" ("get the pretzel") draw young Angelenos to these inexpensive, "funky" burger stands in West LA and West Hollywood; they're run by the "nicest owners" who are "serious" about food (and deliver "large portions"), so "who cares" if they're "not comfy" enough to linger?

	FOOD	DECOR	SERVICE	COST

Home *Eclectic*

20 | 20 | 19 | $20

Los Feliz | 1760 Hillhurst Ave. (Kingswell Ave.) | 323-665-4663 |
www.homelosfeliz.com

Silver Lake | 2500 Riverside Dr. (Fletcher Dr.) | 323-665-0211 |
www.homesilverlake.com

It "feels like mama's cooking" at these "two-of-a-kind" "faves" with a
"hipster vibe" in Los Feliz and Silver Lake, where an "engaged" staff
serves up "huge quantities" of "homey" Eclectic "comfort food" from an
"affordable" menu; just be sure to "get there early" if you'd like a "romantic" booth on the "fabulous" patio, or the "wait can be interminable."

Homeboy Diner ⑤ *Sandwiches*

▽ 21 | 14 | 21 | $17

Downtown | LA City Hall | 200 N. Spring St. (W. 1st St.) | 323-526-1254 |
www.homeboy-industries.org

Homegirl Café ⑤ Ⓜ *American/Mexican*

Chinatown | 130 W. Bruno St. (Alameda St..) | 213-617-0380 |
www.homegirlcafe.org

Pegged as the "best-tasting gang-abatement program ever", the bright
Homeboy Diner stand inside City Hall offers "quality" soups, salads and
sandwiches, while Chinatown's Homegirl Café augments the menu with
tacos and other American-Mex fare – some of it sourced through the or-
ganization's own gardens – as part of a project supporting at-risk youth;
it all adds up to a "fast", low-cost lunch and service is "genuine as you
can get", so fans say "keep it going" and fuel the "success stories."

Honda-Ya *Japanese*

24 | 19 | 20 | $27

Little Tokyo | Mitsuwa Shopping Ctr. | 333 S. Alameda St. (3rd St.) |
213-625-1184 ◑

City of Industry | 17200 Railroad St. (Azusa Ave.) | 626-964-6777
www.izakayahondaya.com

"Mix and match all night long" from the menu "like a phone book" at
these "addicting" izakayas in Little Tokyo and the City of Industry, where
the "well-priced" "pub-style plates", yakitori skewers and sushi come
with plenty of sake, beer and "old-school" atmosphere; the staff aptly
handles the "busy" scene, plus it's "open late, a rarity" for these parts.

Hop Li *Chinese/Seafood*

19 | 13 | 17 | $22

Chinatown | 526 Alpine St. (Hill St.) | 213-680-3939

Pico-Robertson | 10974 W. Pico Blvd. (Veteran Ave.) | 310-441-3708

West LA | 11901 Santa Monica Blvd. (Armacost Ave.) | 310-268-2463

Arcadia | 855 S. Baldwin Ave. (bet. Fairview Ave. & W. Huntington Dr.) |
626-445-3188 ◑

www.hoplirestaurant.com

"Multigenerational families chow down with gusto" at these Cantonese
"standbys" proffering a "lengthy" menu of "classic seafood" dishes
and other "tasty", "typical" fare; while service and decor "won't win
any prizes" and some find the eats "uninspired", supporters say the
"reasonable" tabs and "bargain" lunches "continue to please."

Hop Woo *Chinese*

20 | 11 | 16 | $21

Chinatown | 845 N. Broadway (bet. Alpine & College Sts.) | 213-617-3038 ◑

West LA | 11110 W. Olympic Blvd. (Sepulveda Blvd.) | 310-575-3668

www.hopwoo.com

"Terrific" Peking duck stands out at this Chinatown and West LA duo
abounding in the "authentic flavors" of "Chinese home cookin'"; it's an

"unbelievable value at lunch", though many prefer "quick delivery" to facing the "iffy" service and decor of "plastic kitsch."

Hostaria del Piccolo   *Italian*   26 | 24 | 25 | $39

Santa Monica | 606 Broadway (6th St.) | 310-393-6633 | www.hostariadelpiccolo.com

"Fabulous" pizzas "like you'd get in Italy" and other "inspired" cooking (including gluten-free selections) keep the crowds coming to this "stylish", "more-casual" "sister to Piccolo" in Santa Monica; service is "knowledgeable" and "kid-friendly" and the tabs are moderate, so the only negative is the "noise", "but the delicious food almost makes it tolerable" and the "charming" patio also offers some relief.

🄿 Hot's Cantina   *Eclectic*   27 | 20 | 22 | $26

Northridge | 18673 Devonshire St. (Reseda Blvd.) | 818-368-0123 | www.hotscantina.com

🄿 Hot's Kitchen   *Eclectic*

Hermosa Beach | 844 Hermosa Ave. (8th St.) | 310-318-2939 | www.hotskitchen.com

"Portions are small, but the taste is huge" at this "high-quality" hang adjacent to the Hermosa Beach Pier, a spin-off of the Northridge original, turning out "inventive, delicious" tacos ("including alligator, duck and crawfish") and other "creative" Eclectic eats in an open-air setting; though it "isn't cheap", the "wonderful energy", "fast service" and lots of "craft beers on tap" work for the surf crowd.

House Café   *Eclectic*   21 | 17 | 20 | $30

Beverly Boulevard | 8114 Beverly Blvd. (Crescent Heights Blvd.) | 323-655-5553 | www.housecafe.com

One of the "best-kept secrets" on Beverly Boulevard, this "small", "informal" bistro by Bruce Marder (Capo) "fares well" among "bigger names in the neighborhood" by offering "tasty", thoughtfully sourced Eclectic food, including breakfast all day, to please "unstuffy people"; "quality" service and specials provide added "value for the money."

Houston's   *American*   24 | 23 | 23 | $38

Santa Monica | 202 Wilshire Blvd. (2nd St.) | 310-576-7558
Manhattan Beach | 1550-A Rosecrans Ave. (bet. Aviation & Sepulveda Blvds.) | 310-643-7211
Pasadena | 320 S. Arroyo Pkwy. (Del Mar Blvd.) | 626-577-6001
www.hillstone.com

"As non-chainy as the chains get", this "reliable, grown-up" national franchise "gets everything right" with midpriced American eats (like "messy, tender" ribs and "delicious" spinach-artichoke dip) in "cool, clubby" surroundings with a "top-rate" bar scene; "rapid, tag-team service" is a plus, but "reservations are a must if you don't like to wait."

Huckleberry Café & Bakery   *American*   23 | 15 | 16 | $22

Santa Monica | 1014 Wilshire Blvd. (bet. 10th & 11th Sts.) | 310-451-2311 | www.huckleberrycafe.com

Diners "dream" of the "outstanding" breakfasts and "dangerous" sweets at this cafeteria-style American "morning haunt" and kin to Rustic Canyon in Santa Monica; despite "horrific" lines, sometimes "snobby" service and "pricey-for-a-bakery" tabs, "crowds of pretty people" agree it's "worth it"; P.S. closes at 5 PM on weekends.

	FOOD	DECOR	SERVICE	COST

Hudson House ● *American*

23	18	19	$26

Redondo Beach | 514 N. PCH (Beryl St.) | 310-798-9183 |
www.hudsonhousebar.com

"Quirky, delicious" dishes like the signature pretzel-bun burger and "an impressive array of beers and ales" keep this "lively", "inviting" gastropub in Redondo Beach "hopping" with a "mix of locals in sandals and hipsters in skinny jeans"; factor in "good-value" prices (especially at happy hour), and "the only downside is the noise."

Hugo's *Californian*

22	16	20	$26

West Hollywood | 8401 Santa Monica Blvd. (bet. Kings Rd. & Orlando Ave.) | 323-654-3993
Studio City | 12851 Riverside Dr. (Coldwater Canyon Ave.) | 818-761-8985
www.hugosrestaurant.com

"Organic before it was trendy", these "popular" all-day sibs in Studio City and West Hollywood "cheerfully accommodate every conceivable weirdo dietary restriction" with "fresh", "flavorful" Cal–New American cuisine that "will make you feel healthier than a yoga class"; service can be "scatterbrained" and some "don't get the raves", but the "casual" quarters are often "an absolute zoo", especially during brunch.

Hummus Bar ● *Mideastern*

22	14	18	$23

Tarzana | 18743 Ventura Blvd. (Burbank Blvd.) | 818-344-6606 |
www.hummusbargrill.com

You get "a lot of food for the price" at this Tarzana Middle Eastern doing justice to its namesake with "yummy hummus" joined by "perfectly spiced skewers", "warm bread" and "fresh salads"; "efficient" service and "crowded", basic setting are in keeping with the "low cost."

Hungry Cat *Seafood*

24	19	21	$49

Hollywood | 1535 N. Vine St. (bet. Selma Ave. & Sunset Blvd.) | 323-462-2155
Santa Monica | 100 W. Channel Rd. (PCH) | 310-459-3337
www.thehungrycat.com

"Luscious" seafood, including "glistening" raw-bar selections, plus "sublime burgers" by chef-owner David Lentz are "the cat's meow" at these "hip" "foodie" destinations in LA and Santa Barbara also famed for "exquisite cocktails" made with fresh juices, all served in "minimal" digs; "crowded" conditions, "maddening" acoustics and "moderately high" bills are drawbacks, but on the whole, most find eating here "one of the best decisions you can make."

Hurry Curry of Tokyo *Japanese*

21	15	20	$15

West LA | 2131 Sawtelle Blvd. (Mississippi Ave.) | 310-473-1640 |
www.hurrycurryoftokyo.com

Customers commend the Japanese "guilty pleasures" at this casual West LA spot specializing in "quite good" curries and cutlets; the surroundings are humble, but service is "fast" and the prices low, and the "novelty" alone is worth it to many.

Il Cielo *Italian*

23	26	23	$58

Beverly Hills | 9018 Burton Way (bet. Almont & Wetherly Drs.) | 310-276-9990 | www.ilcielo.com

"Wedding proposals are a common sight" at this "gorgeous" Beverly Hills Italian that's "the definition of lovely" with a "twinkle-lit" garden and a "top-notch", "conventional" Northern Italian menu; a few find service "needs to be better" for the prices, but for a "special summer evening", it's hard to beat.

Il Covo *Italian*   21 | 25 | 20 | $52

West Hollywood | 8700 W. Third St. (Hamel Rd.) | 310-858-0020 | www.Ilcovo.com

"A secret garden in the midst of West Hollywood's chaos", this "romantic" Italian from New York restaurateur/hotelier Sean MacPherson seduces guests with its "cozy", Tuscan-inspired surroundings and "good, not stellar" food and service; even if prices are on the high side, it's all so "beautiful", many are willing to "go just for the atmosphere."

Il Fornaio *Italian*   22 | 21 | 22 | $35

Beverly Hills | 301 N. Beverly Dr. (Dayton Way) | 310-550-8330
Santa Monica | 1551 Ocean Ave. (Colorado Ave.) | 310-451-7800
Manhattan Beach | Manhattan Gateway Shopping Ctr. |
1800 Rosecrans Ave. (Aviation Blvd.) | 310-725-9555
Pasadena | One Colorado | 24 W. Union St. (Fair Oaks Ave.) | 626-683-9797
www.ilfornaio.com

"True to its name, the bread is marvelous" at this "trustworthy" Italian chain also proffering "affordable" pizzas and pastas, plus monthly regional menus that "keep things interesting" in "pleasant", "business-casual" settings; "considerate" service adds to the "consistent" experience, and even if some find it all a little "run of the mill", it's certainly "serviceable", "especially for lunch."

Il Forno *Italian*   23 | 18 | 23 | $31

Santa Monica | 2901 Ocean Park Blvd. (bet. 29th & 30th Sts.) |
310-450-1241 | www.ilfornocaffe.com

"Delicious, unpretentious" Northern Italian cuisine is the forte of this "well-kept secret" in Santa Monica where both the "accommodating" staff and "simple" recipes come "straight from The Boot"; add in "affordable" prices and an "easy", "no-attitude" atmosphere and it's exactly "what a neighborhood trattoria should be."

Il Forno Caldo *Italian*   22 | 19 | 20 | $33

Beverly Hills | 9705 Little Santa Monica Blvd. (Roxbury Dr.) | 310-777-0040 | www.ilfornocaldo.com

"Cute, cozy and pretty inexpensive for Beverly Hills" sums up this Italian "sleeper" favored by locals for its "good, basic" eats proffered by a "pleasant" staff; with a "quiet", "old-fashioned" setting, it's "nothing fancy", but regulars have "no complaints" and say you always "feel you've gotten your money's worth."

Il Grano Ⓩ *Italian*   25 | 21 | 23 | $59

West LA | 11359 Santa Monica Blvd. (Purdue Ave.) | 310-477-7886 | www.ilgrano.com

"Everything is spot-on" at this "upscale" "undiscovered gem" in West LA, where chef-owner Salvatore Marino crafts "extraordinary" Italian highlighting "superb" seafood (like "great crudo") and other "fresh" ingredients (he "literally feeds patrons from his own garden"); the "low-key" atmosphere is "special without being stuffy", so in the whole it comes "highly recommended for an elegant evening"; P.S. the all-tomato menu in summer "should not be missed."

Il Moro *Italian*
22 | 22 | 22 | $46

West LA | 11400 W. Olympic Blvd. (Purdue Ave.) | 310-575-3530 |
www.ilmoro.com

"Ask for a table outside and you'll feel like you left West LA" proclaim proponents of this "elegant" "business-lunch" "favorite" "hidden
in an office tower", but boasting a "lovely garden" for "well-prepared"
Italian cuisine and mains; "capable" service is another plus, and while
critics complain of "expensive" prices, others cheer the happy hour
with complimentary apps.

Il Pastaio *Italian*
26 | 18 | 22 | $46

Beverly Hills | 400 N. Cañon Dr. (Brighton Way) | 310-205-5444 |
www.giacominodrago.com

An "elite clientele" comes in "droves" to this "vibrant" Drago Brother
Italian that's "Beverly Hills at its most Beverly Hillsish" with a "see-
and-be-seen" crowd tucking into "exquisite" "homemade pastas" and
other "fabulous" fare on the patio; indeed, it's "on the expensive side",
but after a few visits the "staff knows you by name" and the "jam-
packed" setting means "you might actually rub elbows with an A-lister."

Il Piccolino ⧉ *Italian*
24 | 20 | 24 | $60

West Hollywood | 350 N. Robertson Blvd. (Rosewood Ave.) |
310-659-2220 | www.ilpiccolinorestaurant.com

"Industry heavyweights" favor this "buzzy" West Hollywood Italian
known for "exemplary" Italian (including exceptional Dover sole and
roast chicken) and "real drinks" served in a "charming", "private" garden patio setting; service is "first-rate", although a few mere mortals
feel "blown away" by the bills.

Il Tiramisù Ristorante & Bar Ⓜ *Italian*
24 | 20 | 24 | $37

Sherman Oaks | 13705 Ventura Blvd. (Woodman Ave.) | 818-986-2640 |
www.il-tiramisu.com

Father-and-son owners Ivo and Peter "make you feel at home" at this
"neighborhood jewel" in Sherman Oaks presenting "showstopping"
Northern Italian fare in a "quaint" setting decorated with white tablecloths and terra-cotta floors; prices are "reasonable" for the area, and
the "monthly wine dinners are a real bargain."

Il Tramezzino *Italian*
23 | 14 | 20 | $21

Beverly Hills | 454 N. Cañon Dr. (Santa Monica Blvd.) | 310-273-0501
Studio City | 13031 Ventura Blvd. (bet. Coldwater Canyon Ave. &
Valley Vista Blvd.) | 818-784-2244
Tarzana | 18636 Ventura Blvd. (Yolanda Ave.) | 818-996-8726
www.iltram.com

"Wonderful" soups, salads and panini make for "quick", "healthy" eating at this "casual" Italian trio that's "reasonably priced" too; "friendly
waiters" provide "smooth", "swift" service in a "down-to-earth" setting with "delightful" outdoor dining, although many "sandwich lovers" "take it to go."

India's Tandoori *Indian*
23 | 16 | 20 | $22

Mid-Wilshire | 5468 Wilshire Blvd. (bet. Cochran & Dunsmuir Aves.) |
323-936-2050 | www.indiastandoori.net
Hawthorne | 4850 W. Rosecrans Ave. (bet. Inglewood & Shoup Aves.) |
310-675-5533 | www.indiastandoorilax.net

(continued)

India's Tandoori

West LA | 11819 Wilshire Blvd. (Granville Ave.) | 310-268-9100 | www.indias-tandoori.com

"Curry, curry, curry!" cry patrons "thrilled with the prices" and the "tasty" grub at this trio of Indians known for its "large portions", "great value" and noteworthy lunch buffet; although most "have no problem" with the service or modest decor, many rely on them for takeout.

NEW Industriel Urban Farm Cuisine *French*

| - | - | - | M |

Downtown | 609 S. Grand Ave. (bet. 6th St. & Wilshire Blvd.) | 213-488-8020 | www.industrielfarm.com

The cooking runs from French rustic creations like poutine served with rib-eye to the requisite pork sandwiches and an offal combo plate of tongue, cheek and marrow, served in a Downtown space dominated by Depression Era photos of rawboned farmers, bottles of preserved vegetables and packing crates piled on one wall; there's even a mobile made of 287 plastic honey bears, adding to the eclectic mix.

Z NEW Ink *American/Eclectic*

| 26 | 21 | 24 | $65 |

West Hollywood | 8360 Melrose Ave. (N. Kings Rd.) | 323-651-5866 | www.mvink.com

Heavily inked *Top Chef* winner Michael Voltaggio is "working magic" in the kitchen of his "exciting" Melrose restaurant featuring "clever", "exquisitely plated" and "obscenely tasty" New American–Eclectic creations and "killer cocktails" in a "chic", understated setting; service can sometimes have "attitude", and a few find it "doesn't live up to the hype", but it's a magnet for "big-spending young foodies" nonetheless – "book early"; P.S. next door is Ink Sack, selling offbeat sandwiches.

Z Inn of the Seventh Ray *Californian*

| 21 | 27 | 22 | $42 |

Topanga | 128 Old Topanga Canyon Rd. (Topanga Canyon Blvd.) | 310-455-1311 | www.innoftheseventhray.com

It's "like stepping into a fairy tale" at this "enchanting" Topanga "hippie hang" from 1975 channeling a "true Cali vibe" with a "wonderful woodland setting" and Californian cuisine "with an emphasis on fresh, in-season, organic" ingredients; even if some find the service and "pricey" fare "uneven", it's still an "unforgettable" experience – where else can you "hear frogs in the creek" while you dine?

Z In-N-Out Burger ❷ *Burgers*

| 26 | 16 | 23 | $10 |

Hollywood | 7009 W. Sunset Blvd. (Orange Dr.)
Culver City | 13425 W. Washington Blvd. (bet. Glencoe & Walnut Aves.)
Palms | 9245 W. Venice Blvd. (Canfield Ave.)
Westwood | 922 Gayley Ave. (Levering Ave.)
Westchester | 9149 S. Sepulveda Blvd. (bet. 92nd St. & Westchester Pkwy.)
North Hollywood | 5864 Lankershim Blvd. (bet. Califa & Emelita Sts.)
Sherman Oaks | 4444 Van Nuys Blvd. (Moorpark St.)
Studio City | 3640 Cahuenga Blvd. (Fredonia Dr.)
Van Nuys | 7930 Van Nuys Blvd. (bet. Blythe & Michaels Sts.)
Woodland Hills | 19920 Ventura Blvd. (bet. Oakdale & Penfield Aves.)
800-786-1000 | www.in-n-out.com
Additional locations throughout Southern California

"The double-double animal style is the eighth wonder of the world" proclaims the "fanatical following" of this "iconic" SoCal burger chain – once again voted LA's top Bang for the Buck – perfecting "what fast food should be" with "simple", "mind-blowing" patties and "real shakes" served in bright "vintage" settings manned by a "smiling", "organized" team; "no visit to LA is complete without a stop", now "if only there were a way to make the lines shorter."

Iroha ● *Japanese* | 25 | 20 | 23 | $42

Studio City | 12953 Ventura Blvd. (bet. Coldwater Canyon & Ethel Aves.) | 818-990-9559

"Superlative", "innovative" sushi plus a "quaint" setting that's "like being in a little tucked away house in Japan" makes this Studio City charmer the ultimate "date-night spot"; service is "fast, friendly" and "if you dream up a roll, they'll execute it with ease", although if you "sit at the bar the chefs will tell you what's best."

Irori *Japanese* | ▽ 26 | 22 | 24 | $37

Marina del Rey | 4371 Glencoe Ave. (Mindanao Way) | 310-822-3700

"Enter and leave your shoes at the door" of this midpriced Marina del Rey Japanese nook serving "amazing" "traditional" fare in an "intimate" setting with "sunken tables"; whether the concept is "uncomfortable" or "cool" is debatable, but all agree "they make you feel right at home."

Itzik Hagadol *Israeli* | 21 | 13 | 20 | $28

Encino | 17201 Ventura Blvd. (Louise Ave.) | 818-784-4080 | www.itzikhagadol.com

"Straight from Tel Aviv", this Encino offshoot of an Israeli grill shop delivers an "authentic eating experience" via "tasty skewers", an "amazing array" of salads and "puffy, warm laffa bread", all at "affordable" prices; "curt" service and minimal decor don't seem to deter the crowds – it's always "jumping" and "you won't leave hungry" either.

The Ivy *Californian* | 22 | 23 | 21 | $60

West Hollywood | 113 N. Robertson Blvd (bet. Beverly Blvd. & 3rd St.) | 310-274-8303 | www.theivyrestaurant.com

"The paparazzi are always camped out in front" of this WeHo "classic" that still attracts plenty of "celebs looking to be seen" for "enjoyable" Cal cuisine; it's "expensive" and service can be uneven, "but the ambiance is really what you're going for", so settle at a table in the "charming" farmhouse space and "keep your eyes peeled for the somebodies."

Ivy at the Shore *Californian* | 22 | 22 | 22 | $63

Santa Monica | 1535 Ocean Ave. (bet. B'way & Colorado Ave.) | 310-393-3113 | www.theivyrestaurant.com

"A little more relaxed than its West Hollywood sister", this Santa Monica Californian is a "haven for the well-heeled, expense-account and upcale-tourist sets" with "simple" fare served in a "pleasant" seaside setting; some say service can be "arrogant", and it certainly isn't cheap, but the "star sightings will make everything else meaningless."

Izaka-ya by Katsu-ya *Japanese* | 26 | 18 | 22 | $41

Third Street | 8420 W. Third St. (bet. La Cienega Blvd. & Orlando Ave.) | 323-782-9536

Manhattan Beach | 1133 Highland Ave. (Center Pl.) | 310-796-1888 | www.katsu-yagroup.com

Boasting "all the deliciousness of Katsuya" "without the pretense", these Third Street and Manhattan Beach izakayas offer "inspired modern Japanese" bar food and "revelatory" sushi plus signatures like spicy tuna and crispy rice from chef-owner Katsuya Uechi; acoustics can be "loud enough to wake the fish on your plate" and service can be "rushed", but with relatively "low" pricing, it "won't disappoint."

Jack n' Jill's American | 20 | 16 | 18 | $23 |

Beverly Hills | 342 N. Beverly Dr. (bet. Brighton & Dayton Ways) | 310-247-4500
Santa Monica | 510 Santa Monica Blvd. (5th St.) | 310-656-1501
www.eatatjacknjills.com

"Oversized" portions of "well-prepared" eggs and pancakes along with "a little bit of everything" at lunch make this "upscale diner" duo in Beverly Hills and Santa Monica a "cute place for a casual meal"; the spaces are "bright" and "energetic", and though some complain there's "too many kids, what do you expect from a place called Jack n' Jill's?"

Jaipur Cuisine of India Indian | 22 | 16 | 20 | $24 |

West LA | 10916 W. Pico Blvd. (bet. Veteran Ave. & Westwood Blvd.) | 310-470-4994 | www.jaipurcuisineofindia.com

"Zingy", "well-seasoned" Indian – offered à la carte or in an "amazing lunch buffet" – makes this long-standing West LA eatery the "spot of choice" for many; the setting is modest and "service varies", but it's often "crowded" nonetheless.

James' Beach American | 21 | 20 | 21 | $38 |

Venice | 60 N. Venice Blvd. (Pacific Ave.) | 310-823-5396 | www.jamesbeach.com

"Awesome" fish tacos are the highlight at this "beachy", "casual" canteen in Venice, where the "clever" American menu and "well-mixed" cocktails offer "good value for the money"; it's often quite the "scene", with a "cool" crowd "packed like sardines", but outdoor seating eases the crush, as does a "super-friendly" staff.

Jar American | 25 | 23 | 23 | $59 |

Beverly Boulevard | 8225 Beverly Blvd. (Harper Ave.) | West Hollywood | 323-655-6566 | www.thejar.com

Devotees "dream about the pot roast" ("perfect on a blustery day") and "top-end" steaks at chef-owner Suzanne Tracht's "sleek, modern" Beverly Boulevard American offering "delicious", "haute" takes on "comfort food" evoking "the way dining used to be"; the decor is "like you just stepped into *Mad Men*" and service is "thoughtful", so most don't mind the "splurge"-worthy tabs.

Javan Persian | 22 | 17 | 19 | $26 |

West LA | 11500 Santa Monica Blvd. (Butler Ave.) | 310-207-5555 | www.javanrestaurant.com

"The kebabs are some kind of wonderful" at this West LA Persian also presenting "flavorful" stews on "crispy rice" and other "brilliant" items that "won't break your wallet"; service is "attentive", "if occasionally harried" and the atmosphere is "vibrant", so "what's not to like?"

Jer-ne American | ▽ 19 | 23 | 20 | $62 |

Marina del Rey | Ritz-Carlton, Marina Del Rey | 4375 Admiralty Way (Lincoln Blvd.) | 310-574-4333 | www.ritzcarlton.com

"Eat on the terrace and enjoy the view of the harbor" at this luxurious "special-occasion" New American nestled in the Marina del Rey Ritz-

Carlton; opinions on the menu with Cal and Spanish touches are mixed, but "fine cocktails and wine" plus "accommodating" service mean that for some, "the only disappointment is the bill."

Jerry's Famous Deli *Deli*   18 | 15 | 17 | $24

West Hollywood | 8701 Beverly Blvd. (San Vicente Blvd.) | 310-289-1811 ◐
Marina del Rey | 13181 Mindanao Way (bet. Glencoe Ave. & Lincoln Blvd.) | 310-821-6626 ◐
Westwood | 10925 Weyburn Ave. (bet. Broxton Ave. & Westwood Blvd.) | 310-208-3354
Encino | 16650 Ventura Blvd. (Petit Ave.) | 818-906-1800
Woodland Hills | 21857 Ventura Blvd. (bet. Canoga Ave. & Topanga Canyon Blvd.) | 818-340-0810 ◐
www.jerrysfamousdeli.com

There's "something for everyone" at this SoCal chain that's an "old standby for Jewish deli food" with "gigantic" sandwiches and "huge bowls of matzo-ball soup" served in "typical" "NYC"-style digs; critics call it "ordinary" with almost "too much food", but it sure "hits the spot" late at night.

Jinky's *Diner*   20 | 14 | 19 | $18

Santa Monica | 1447 Second St. (bet. B'way & Santa Monica Blvd.) | 310-917-3311
Sherman Oaks | 14120 Ventura Blvd. (Stansbury Ave.) | 818-981-2250
Studio City | 4000 Colfax Ave. (Ventura Blvd.) | 818-308-8418
Agoura Hills | 29001 Canwood St. (Kanan Rd.) | 818-575-4216
www.jinkys.com

Early birds go bonkers for the "big bountiful breakfasts" from a "huge menu" at this "popular", "kid-friendly" Southwestern-American mini-chain that's "everything a neighborhood coffee shop should be"; it also doubles as a "lunch spot" with "homey" digs, "bang-for-the-buck" tabs and a staff that "aims to please."

Jin Patisserie Ⓜ *Bakery*   23 | 19 | 18 | $22

Venice | 1202 Abbot Kinney Blvd. (Aragon Ct.) | 310-399-8801 | www.jinpatisserie.com

A "lovely garden hideaway" right off Abbot Kinney, this "serene" Venice tea shop is a "quaint" stop for "high-priced and high-quality" "dainty pastries", "delicate macarons" and light French lunchtime fare; even if service can be "uneven", most find it a "nice soothing escape."

JiRaffe Ⓧ *American/French*   26 | 22 | 25 | $58

Santa Monica | 502 Santa Monica Blvd. (5th St.) | 310-917-6671 | www.jirafferestaurant.com

For "simple, elegant food just blocks from the beach", try this Santa Monica "classic" from Raphael Lunetta that "continues to delight" with "delectable", market-driven French–New American cuisine served in a "lovely, civilized" space with a "quiet" balcony; the staff is "nothing short of amazing", so although it's "pricey", prix fixe specials "make it affordable" and most "gladly go back."

❷ Jitlada *Thai*   27 | 12 | 16 | $31

East Hollywood | 5233½ W. Sunset Blvd. (bet. Harvard Blvd. & Kingsley Dr.) | 323-667-9809 | www.jitlada.com

"Completely fearless in pushing the envelope in spiciness", this Southern Thai "favorite" in an East Hollywood strip mall "entertains the most

	FOOD	DECOR	SERVICE	COST

adventurous foodie" with Jazz Singsanong's "robust menu" full of "vibrant" flavors ("the mussels are a must"); "tight" digs, "long" waits and "flaky, but sweet, service" are no matter to connoisseurs who call it one of the "best in the U.S."

Joan's on Third Cafe *American* | 24 | 17 | 17 | $24 |

Third Street | 8350 W. Third St. (bet. Fairfax Ave. & La Cienega Blvd.) | 323-655-2285 | www.joansonthird.com

A "dizzying selection" of "delicious", "sophisticated" salads, sandwiches and desserts awaits at this "wildly popular" "eat in/take out", "gourmet" American bakery on Third Street, a "favorite splurge" for picnics; the "bright, open" space with "casual outdoor seating" is "always packed with celebs and beautiful people", who don't mind the "lines and limited seating", nor the somewhat "slow" counter service.

Jody Maroni's *Hot Dogs* | 20 | 9 | 16 | $11 |

Venice | 2011 Ocean Front Walk (20th Pl.) | 310-822-5639
Universal City | Universal CityWalk | 1000 Universal Studios Blvd. (off Rte. 101) | 818-622-5639
www.jodymaroni.com

"They know their links" at these sausage stands serving up "tasty", inexpensive dogs and wursts that come "loaded with onions and peppers"; there's no indoor seating, but the Venice original provides a "ringside seat at the boardwalk", and you can even order delivery from the beach.

☒ Joe's ⓜ *Californian/French* | 26 | 22 | 24 | $56 |

Venice | 1023 Abbot Kinney Blvd. (bet. B'way St. & Westminster Aves.) | 310-399-5811 | www.joesrestaurant.com

"The grandaddy of Abbot Kinney", this longtime Venice standout "hasn't missed a beat in all these years" thanks to Joe Miller's "ambitious", "endlessly inventive" seasonal Cal-French menu that has "foodies falling over each other to praise" and a "no-pretense" setting that's "just the right blend of trendy and quiet"; service is "congenial", and even if prices are "somewhat steep", the "prix fixe lunch is a steal."

Joe's Pizza *Pizza* | 24 | 11 | 18 | $14 |

Hollywood | 6504 Hollywood Blvd. (Cahuenga Blvd.) | 323-467-9500 | www.joespizza.it
West Hollywood | 8539 W. Sunset Blvd. (Alta Loma Rd.) | 310-358-0900 | www.joespizza.it ◐
Santa Monica | 111 Broadway (Ocean Ave.) | 310-395-9222 | www.joespizza.com ◐

"As close as you can get to real NYC pizza", these "no-frills", independently operated outlets in Santa Monica, Hollywood and West Hollywood offer delicious, "crispy-crust" slices and pies that fans find "every bit as good" as their Big Apple counterparts; they're open "late", service is speedy and delivery is a plus, so in all, "you can't beat it."

Joey's ☒ⓜ *BBQ* | 26 | 20 | 25 | $21 |

Pomona | 117 W. Second St. (Garey Ave.) | 909-865-0699 | www.joeysbbq.com

"Get along, little doggies!" holler would-be wranglers who savor the "fall-off-the-bone" ribs, smoked meats and fixin's at these modestly priced Chino, Pomona and Upland American 'cue joints; "better-than-average" service also hits the spot, and while some city slickers note the "cowboy" decor "isn't fancy", for many longtime regulars, it's a "family favorite."

Johnnie's New York Pizzeria *Pizza*

20 | 13 | 18 | $17

Downtown | California Plaza | 350 S. Grand Ave. (W. 4th St.) |
213-613-9972 Ⓢ

Downtown | City Nat'l Plaza | 505 S. Flower St. (bet. 5th & 6th Sts.) |
213-489-9002 Ⓢ

Mid-Wilshire | Wilshire | 3183 Wilshire Blvd. (S. Vermont Ave.) |
213-385-3100

Mid-Wilshire | Museum Park Sq. | 5757 Wilshire Blvd. (S. Curson Ave.) |
323-904-4880

Carson | 1000 E. Victoria St. (bet. Avalon Blvd. & Central Ave.) |
310-516-2077

Century City | Fox Apts. | 10251 Santa Monica Blvd. (Century Park W.) |
310-553-1188

Santa Monica | Third St. Promenade | 1444 Third St. Promenade
(Santa Monica Blvd.) | 310-395-9062

Venice | Hoyt Plaza | 2805 Abbot Kinney Blvd. (Washington Blvd.) |
310-821-1224

West LA | 11676 Olympic Blvd. (Schumacher Dr.) | 310-477-2111

Glendale | 138 N. Brand Blvd. (Wilson Ave.) | 818-546-1091
www.johnniesnypizza.com
Additional locations throughout Southern California

Perhaps it's "not New York", but the "big pizzas" with "lotsa toppings"
still "rock" at this "casual" chain that certainly "satisfies in a pinch";
the decor score speaks for itself, but service is "quick" and it's "good
for delivery" too.

Johnnie's Pastrami ●⇄ *Diner*

22 | 11 | 19 | $16

Culver City | 4017 Sepulveda Blvd. (bet. Washington Blvd. &
Washington Pl.) | 310-397-6654 | www.johnniespastrami.com

"Legendary" is the "fat, juicy pastrami sandwich" – "packed with
meat" and "worth every penny" – at this "longtime Culver City landmark" dating back to the '50s with little jukeboxes at each booth and
"old-school service" by "worldly waitresses"; there's little in the way
of frills, but it's a "rare" "late-night guilty pleasure."

Johnny Rebs' *BBQ*

25 | 21 | 24 | $24

Bellflower | 16639 Bellflower Blvd. (Flower St.) | 562-866-6455

Long Beach | 4663 Long Beach Blvd. (bet. 46th & 47th Sts.) | 562-423-7327
www.johnnyrebs.com

"When you need a rib fix", try these Southern BBQ joints in Bellflower
and Long Beach dishing out "down-home" "roadhouse grub", from
"nicely smoked" meats slathered in "tangy" sauce to "honest" plates
of biscuits and gravy, plus country breakfasts offered every day;
"prices are competitive", while the "super-relaxed", "shotgun-shack"
atmosphere with peanut shells on the floor is made "warm" and
"friendly" by a "cheerful" staff.

John O'Groats *American*

20 | 14 | 20 | $21

Rancho Park | 10516 W. Pico Blvd. (bet. Beverly Glen Blvd. & Overland Ave.) |
310-204-0692

Encino | 16120 Ventura Blvd. (bet. Libbit Ave. & Woodley Park Ln.) |
818-501-2366
www.ogroatsrestaurant.com

"Join the breakfast crowd" at these "neighborhood favorites" in Encino
and Rancho Park known for "simple", "old-fashioned" Americana
("thick bacon" and "oh those biscuits") with a handful of "healthy"

tems thrown into the mix; "affable" service and moderate tabs mean
t's "filled with regulars" and especially "jammed" on weekends, although "dinner is less crowded."

Josie ⓜ American
26 | 24 | 25 | $63

Santa Monica | 2424 Pico Blvd. (25th St.) | 310-581-9888 |
www.josierestaurant.com

"A culinary oasis off the beaten path", this Santa Monica New American
"does it right" with "deft and delicious", "market-inspired" cuisine
from Josie Le Balch's set down in a "refined" setting; yes, it's "expensive", but a "first-rate" staff provides "impeccable" service and it's a
"rare find" – a place to go "when you want to be a grown-up."

JR's BBQ ⓩ BBQ
▽ 25 | 14 | 20 | $20

Culver City | 3055 S. La Cienega Blvd. (Blackwelder St.) | 310-837-6838 |
www.jrs-bbq.com

The "smells are tantalizing" at this Culver City BBQer run by a "terrific" mother-and-son team and turning out "authentic" eats like brisket and mac 'n' cheese; "don't look for atmosphere", but the vibe's
"friendly" and prices are a pittance; P.S. the housemade BBQ sauce is
also for sale.

Julienne ⓩ French
26 | 23 | 22 | $26

San Marino | 2651 Mission St. (bet. El Molino & Los Robles Aves.) |
626-441-2299 | www.juliennetogo.com

"It's not just for ladies who lunch" insist fans of this bistro in San Marino
that draws a "crowd" with "splendid breakfasts" and other "top-quality"
French cuisine capped by "divine" desserts in a "lovely" indoor-outdoor
space; an "exceptionally friendly" staff complements the "charming"
setting, but to escape the "waits", many opt for takeout from the adjoining cafe/market; P.S. the rosemary currant bread is "a legend."

Junior's Deli
16 | 12 | 17 | $22

West LA | 2379 Westwood Blvd. (W. Pico Blvd.) | 310-475-5771 |
www.jrsdeli.com

"All the old standbys" like matzo-ball soup, knishes and corned beef
are here at this longtime Jewish-style deli/bakery in West LA that surveyors call "decent" but "unremarkable" and "priced on the high end";
decor may be "dated" and the "service can vary dramatically", but it's
"full of regulars" nonetheless.

Kabuki Japanese
22 | 20 | 20 | $27

Hollywood | 1545 N. Vine St. (bet. Selma Ave. & Sunset Blvd.) |
323-464-6003
Westchester | Howard Hughes Center | 6081 Center Dr.
(bet. Howard Hughes Pkwy. & Sepulvda Blvd.) | 310-641-5524
Pasadena | 3539 E. Foothill Blvd. (bet. Halstead St. & Rosemead Blvd.) |
626-351-8963
Pasadena | 88 W. Colorado Blvd. (bet. De Lacey & Pasadena Aves.) |
626-568-9310
Burbank | 201 N. San Fernando Blvd. (Orange Grove Ave.) | 818-843-7999
Woodland Hills | 20940 Ventura Blvd. (bet. Paralta & Serrania Aves.) |
818-704-8700
www.kabukirestaurants.com

"Nothing extraordinary, but always reliable" is the word on this "bargain" Japanese sushi chain churning out "respectable" renditions of

"the standard hits and a few surprises" with "Westernized" twists and "great deals" at happy hour; even though they're usually "bustling", "service is fast but not rushed" and they're "kid-friendly" too.

☑ Katana ● *Japanese*

27 | 27 | 24 | $62

West Hollywood | 8439 W. Sunset Blvd. (bet. La Cienega Blvd. & Sweetzer Ave.) | 323-650-8585 | www.katanarobata.com

"Beautiful people" dig the "see-and-be-seen" "scene" at this Sunset Strip Japanese where you can "grab a seat on the patio and watch the action" while nibbling on "fab", "diverse" sushi and yakitori that "never disappoint"; sure, it's "getting up in years", but service from the "actor/model" staff is solid and "it's still a reliable option to wow out-of-town guests."

Kate Mantilini *American*

20 | 19 | 20 | $36

Beverly Hills | 9101 Wilshire Blvd. (Doheny Dr.) | 310-278-3699 ●
Woodland Hills | 5921 Owensmouth Ave. (Califa St.) | 818-348-1095
www.katemantilini.biz

A "glamorous" take on the coffee shop, this Beverly Hills comfort-fooder delivers a "solid" "all-American" bill of fare and "great martinis" to "industry types" and "lots of head-swivelers looking for stars", from morning till late; the newer Woodland Hills outpost is equally "reliable" with "consistently fine" service, although many insist both are "pricey for what you get."

☑ Katsu-ya *Japanese*

27 | 15 | 20 | $43

Encino | 16542 Ventura Blvd. (Hayvenhurst Ave.) | 818-788-2396
Studio City | 11680 Ventura Blvd. (Colfax Ave.) | 818-985-6976
www.katsu-yagroup.com

A "trailblazer for modern sushi", chef-owner Katsuya Uechi's Studio City "original" and its Encino offshoot are famed for "exquisite" "rock-star" sushi and "innovative chalkboard specials" ("the spicy tuna on crispy rice continues to be a revelation"); sure, "you'll have to wait", service can be "rushed" and the settings could "use a face-lift", but even so, most find it's one of the "best for the price" and the food surpasses any "hassle."

Katsuya *Japanese*

25 | 24 | 21 | $56

Downtown | L.A. Live | 800 W. Olympic Blvd. (Figueroa St.) | 213-747-9797 Ⓜ
Hollywood | 6300 Hollywood Blvd. (Vine St.) | 323-871-8777 ●
Brentwood | 11777 San Vicente Blvd. (bet. Gorham & Montana Aves.) | 310-207-8744
Glendale | Americana at Brand | 702 Americana Way (bet. Brand Blvd. & Central Ave.) | 818-244-5900
www.sbe.com

For sushi with a side of "glitz", try these "cooly elegant" Japanese "hot spots" attracting "A-listers" and other "eye candy" for "amazing" sushi, "fun drinks" and "kicked-up", "not-so-authentic" dishes from Katsuya Uechi like baked crabs rolls and spicy tuna on crispy rice ("a must"); on the downside are "loud" acoustics, "hefty prices" and occasional "attitude" from the staff, but "where else are you going to go pre-clubbing?"

Kay 'n Dave's *Mexican*

19 | 16 | 20 | $23

Culver City | 9341 Culver Blvd. (S. Canfield Ave.) | 310-558-8100

(continued)

Kay 'n Dave's

Pacific Palisades | 15246 W. Sunset Blvd. (bet. Monument St. & Swarthmore Ave.) | 310-459-8118
Santa Monica | 262 26th St. (bet. Georgina Ave. & San Vicente Blvd.) | 310-260-1355
www.kayndaves.com

"Wholesome Mexican" with a "healthy" bent is the thing at these "economically priced" cantinas where "you can gorge or go minimal" in a "casual, laid-back" setting; purists pan the "bland" eats, although it's "great for kids and families" and a "reliable" bet for takeout.

Kendall's Brasserie *French* | 20 | 22 | 22 | $48 |

Downtown | Dorothy Chandler Pavilion | 135 N. Grand Ave. (bet. 1st & Temple Sts.) | 213-972-7322 | www.patinagroup.com

"Concertgoers" rely on this "busy" Patina group bistro Downtown for its efficient servers who handle the pre-performance rush "without fuss or confusion"; critics claim that the "pricey", "traditional" French menu could use a "change up", but most maintain that "convenience" and its "charming" "Parisian" atmosphere more than compensate.

🆕 Killer Cafe *American* | – | – | – | M |

Marina del Rey | 4213 Admiralty Way (Promenade Way) | 310-578-2250 | www.killershrimp.com

This harborside breakfast-and-brunch sibling of Killer Shrimp in Marina del Ray offers crustacean-heavy omelets, Benedicts, Bloodys and more on its midpriced American menu; snag a seat at the expansive waterfront patio or fill up on the wallet-friendly portions indoors, while million-dollar sailboats drift by the floor-to-ceiling windows.

🆕 Killer Shrimp *Seafood* | 21 | 17 | 20 | $26 |

Marina del Rey | 4211 Admiralty Way (Promenade Way) | 310-578-2293 | www.killershrimp.com

"They're back!" exclaim fans of the "spicy", "satsfying" peel 'n' eat shrimp headlining the expanded menu at this "lively" Marina seafooder now reopened after a three-year hiatus; service gets mixed reviews and frequent happy hours in the "ample" bar area keep "noise levels high", but water views from the deck are a plus, so most are "thankful" that it's "on the map" again.

Kincaid's *Seafood/Steak* | 22 | 24 | 21 | $42 |

Redondo Beach | Redondo Beach Pier | 500 Fisherman's Wharf (Torrance Blvd.) | 310-318-6080 | www.kincaids.com

"Beautiful" ocean views are the main motivation for dining at this upmarket Redondo surf 'n' turfer prized by "romantics" for date night as well as "locals" with out-of-town guests; the menu is deemed somewhat "hit-or-miss" and service is likewise "sporadic", but the "great happy hour" makes it a "terrific" bet near the pier for drinks and apps.

King's Burgers *Burgers* | 24 | 14 | 20 | $21 |

Northridge | 9345 Reseda Blvd. (Plummer St.) | 818-885-6456

"Who would've thunk a divey-looking burger joint would have such amazing sushi?" ask admirers of this offbeat Northridge "classic" turning out "high-quality" fish at a small counter in back; tabs are "a bit pricey" for "a place that looks like an old Carl's Jr.", but it's a "local favorite" and "a must" for intrepid eaters nonetheless; P.S. the patties are "all right" too, but the raw stuff is the main draw.

King's Fish House *Seafood*
23 | 20 | 22 | $35

Long Beach | 100 W. Broadway Ave. (bet. Pacific & Pine Aves.) | 562-432-7463
Calabasas | Commons at Calabasas | 4798 Commons Way (Calabasas Rd.) | 818-225-1979
www.kingsfishhouse.com

A "fine assortment of fresh fish" – including oysters and sushi – is the hook at these SoCal seafood houses set in "comfy", "casual" digs with "pleasant" patio seating; they're "reasonably priced" and happily "accommodate" kids, so many consider them "good for the whole family" and "buzzy" enough for just grown-ups.

King's Hawaiian Bakery &
Restaurant *Hawaiian*
22 | 19 | 22 | $19

Torrance | 2808 Sepulveda Blvd. (bet. Crenshaw & Hawthorne Blvds.) | 310-530-0050 | www.kingshawaiianrestaurants.com

"Hawaiian expats" "longing for home" turn to this Torrance standby for "homestyle" eats with "island flavor", including standout breakfasts and "awesome" sweets like the signature pastel Paradise Cake that will "ruin you for all other cakes"; expect a "family-friendly" setting and wallet-friendly bills.

Kings Road Cafe *American*
18 | 13 | 17 | $21

West Hollywood | 8361 Beverly Blvd. (Kings Rd.) | 323-655-9044
Studio City | 12401 Ventura Blvd. (Whitsett Ave.) | 818-985-3600
www.kingsroadcafe.com

"Feel the LA buzz" at these WeHo and Studio City hangouts drawing "loyal regulars" and industry "wannabes talking loudly on their cell phones" for a "so-so" all-day American menu bested by the "tastiest coffee in town" roasted in-house and poured by "serious" baristas; acoustics inside get "noisy", but sidewalk tables provide relief – either way, "plan for a wait on the weekends."

King Taco *Mexican*
24 | 12 | 19 | $12

Chinatown | 1951 S. San Pedro St. (bet. Washington Blvd. & 21st St.) | 213-747-3176
Downtown | 4504 E. Third St. (S. Ford Blvd.) | 323-264-4067
Downtown | 645 E. Washington Blvd. (S. San Pedro St.) | 213-747-9915 ◗
Lincoln Heights | 2904 N. Broadway (Griffin Ave.) | 323-222-8500
Mid-City | 1118 Cypress Ave. (bet. Loosmore St. & Roseview Ave.) | 323-223-2595 ◗
Mid-City | 2020 W. Pico Blvd. (S. Alvarado St.) | 213-384-8115
Boyle Heights | 2400 E. Cesar Chavez Ave. (N. Soto St.) | 323-264-3940 ◗
East LA | 4300 E. Olympic Blvd. (S. Downey Rd.) | 323-264-9051 ◗
Baldwin Park | 14318 Ramona Blvd. (bet. Maine & Pacific Aves.) | 626-962-5995 ◗
El Monte | 3900 N. Peck Rd. (Forest Grove St.) | 626-350-5698
www.kingtaco.com
Additional locations throughout Southern California

"Fast-Mex at its finest", this chain provides "cheap, filling" tacos and burritos that convince customers to "dive in head first and throw the LDL out the window"; service is "quick and to the point", so even if decor "isn't much", it still "hits the spot", especially "after a night of partying."

Kitchen 24 *American*

| 21 | 20 | 19 | $22 |

Hollywood | 1608 N. Cahuenga Blvd. (bet. Hollywood Blvd. & Selma Ave.) | 323-465-2424 ●

NEW **West Hollywood** | 8575 Santa Monica Blvd. (bet. La Cienaga & San Vicente Blvds.) | 424-777-0959 ●
www.kitchen24.info

"Open whenever you need it", this 24/7 duo in WeHo and Hollywood's Cahuenga Corridor turn out "elevated" American "diner food" – like cocktails and disco fries – for "hipsters" galore, especially after the bars close; the "good-looking staff" and "modern" digs are appealing, but the "club-volume" music isn't for everyone, though, and a few say it's best for "hanging out" "if the quality of food is not your number one priority."

Kitchen Faire 🖾 *American*

| – | – | – | I |

Downtown | 512 W. Sixth St. (bet. Grand Ave. & Olive St.) | 213-347-0211 | www.kitchenfaire.com

This farm-to-table American brings creative, affordable lunchtime offerings like ahi sandwiches, couscous salads and fresh juices (like cucumber) to Downtown LA; the fast-casual space stays sleek with barn wood and white tile, though takeout is the norm.

☑ Kiwami *Japanese*

| 28 | 19 | 24 | $52 |

Studio City | 11920 Ventura Blvd. (Carpenter Ave.) | 818-763-3910 | www.katsu-yagroup.com

An "upscale version" of sibling Katsu-ya, this Studio City "jewel" impresses guests with "sublime" sushi, sashimi and "beautifully prepared" small plates; the vibe is "cool" without being "trendy", and though bills can be "painfully high" – especially for the hard-to-reserve private omakase with Katsuya himself – it's regarded as one of "the best" in town.

Kogi Korean BBQ-to-Go ●⇥ *Korean/Mexican*

| 26 | 15 | 20 | $10 |

Location varies; see website | 323-315-0253 | www.kogibbq.com

Redefining the "roach coach" and jump-starting the food-truck craze, Roy Choi's "brilliant" Korean-Mex truck continues to be a magnet for "addicts" who "track Twitter" and "drive miles" to chase down their "fix" of "transcendental" tacos and "crave-worthy" kimchi quesadillas doled out by a "cool" crew; though the "hoopla" has "died down" a wee bit, it's still "a must-try for any dedicated foodie"; P.S. chef Choi's chow also shows up at the Alibi Room, A-Frame, Chego! and Sunny Spot.

Koi *Japanese*

| 25 | 25 | 23 | $65 |

West Hollywood | 730 N. La Cienega Blvd. (bet. Melrose Pl. & Waring Ave.) | 310-659-9449 | www.koirestaurant.com

"Showbiz sushi" could be the nickname of this "architecturally gorgeous" WeHo Japanese where "fresh fish" and other "tasty little morsels" are presented amid a "glam" scene rife with a "parade of erstwhile actresses showing up to gain attention"; critics call it "snooty" and "overpriced", but if you're into the "Hollywood" thing, you have to "go at least once."

Kravings *Brazilian*

| 23 | 22 | 22 | $58 |

Tarzana | 18663 Ventura Blvd. (Yolanda Ave.) | 818-881-7111 | www.kravingsfusion.com

"Handsome men with swords of meat" proffer an array of cuts "cooked to perfection" at this all-you-can-eat rodizio in Tarzana, which does

"Brazilian with a twist" of Med and Indian flavors plus an ample salad bar buffet; clubby red-and-black decor and frequent live (and "loud") music add to the "enjoyable" atmosphere, so even if it's a little "expensive", most call it a "refreshing" change of pace.

Kyochon ● *Korean* | 22 | 12 | 15 | $15 |

Koreatown | Serrano Marketplace | 3833 W. Sixth St. (Serrano Ave.) | 213-739-9292 | www.kyochon.us

"Crispy, spicy" Korean chicken wings doused in "seriously addictive" sauces are the thing at this K-town joint that's a "weekly lunch stop" for some; on the downside are "unbearable waits" that would try the "patience of a saint" and bills some deem "a bit pricey" for the fare, but most keep "coming back" nonetheless.

K-Zo *Japanese* | 26 | 20 | 23 | $47 |

Culver City | 9240 Culver Blvd. (Washington Blvd.) | 310-202-8890 | www.k-zo.com

"Easily rivaling the big names", this "under-the-radar" "jewel" in Culver City turns out "exquisite", "perfectly proportioned" sushi and "innovative" Japanese tapas courtesy of "gifted" chef Keizo Ishiba; it's "expensive", but service is "attentive", and many find the "delectable" omakase well worth the "splurge."

NEW Lab Brewing Co. *American/Eclectic*   ∇ | 22 | 22 | 20 | $29 |

Agoura Hills | 30105 Agoura Rd. (Reyes Adobe Rd.) | 818-735-0091 | www.labbrewingco.com

"Beer, food and music" come together at this "fun" Agoura Hills entry where the low-cost American-Eclectic menu featuring burgers and "interesting" small plates offers "something for everyone" and there are dozens of brews on tap to wash it all down; live blues and rock on weekends boosts the "cool" atmosphere, so most leave "satisfied."

Label's Table *Sandwiches* | 24 | 11 | 18 | $17 |

Century City | 9226 W. Pico Blvd. (bet. Cardiff Ave. & Glenvilla Dr.) | 310-276-0388 ✏
Woodland Hills | 23311 Mulholland Dr. (Calabasas Rd.) | 818-222-1044 | www.labelstabledeli.com

"Pastrami from heaven" and other sandwiches that "can't be beat" lure locals to this venerable Century City and Woodland Hills duo deemed one of "the best" kosher-style delis in town; the settings aren't fancy, but service is swift, bills are low and there's always takeout.

La Boheme *Californian* | 21 | 24 | 21 | $50 |

West Hollywood | 8400 Santa Monica Blvd. (Orlando Ave.) | 323-848-2360 | www.boheme.globaldiningca.com

With decor that's like *The Phantom of the Opera* on steroids", this West Hollywood "destination" "shines" for "romantic" gatherings in its "magnificent" space with indoor and outdoor fireplaces; in comparison to the setting, some find the Californian cuisine only "fair", although "friendly" service, "reasonable" prices and a "vibrant happy hour" win over many.

La Botte *Italian* | 24 | 21 | 23 | $60 |

Santa Monica | 620 Santa Monica Blvd. (7th St.) | 310-576-3072 | www.labottesantamonica.com

"A wizard in the kitchen and a charmer on the floor", chef-owner Stefano De Lorenzo "dazzles" guests with "exceptional" Italian cuisine, "fantastic" wines and "charming" service at this "inviting" Santa Monican; it's "pricey", but the ambiance is "quiet and refined", so it's the "perfect place to treat someone special."

La Bottega Marino *Italian*   21 | 14 | 19 | $28

Hancock Park | Larchmont Vill. | 203 N. Larchmont Blvd. (bet. Beverly Blvd. & 1st St.) | 323-962-1325
West LA | 11363 Santa Monica Blvd. (Purdue Ave.) | 310-477-7777
www.labottegausa.com

"One of the best-kept secrets" in town, this family-run trattoria/deli duo from Mario and Salvatore Marino (Il Grano) is held dear for "old-fashioned" Italian served in way-"casual" settings; service can be "spotty", but the bills are low, so many rely on it for takeout.

La Bruschetta Ristorante *Italian*   23 | 20 | 25 | $43

Westwood | 1621 Westwood Blvd. (bet. Massachusetts & Ohio Aves.) | 310-477-1052 | www.lbwestwood.com

A "local favorite", this "inviting" Westwood Italian is esteemed for "consistently good, traditional" fare and "stellar service" led by "welcoming" chef-owner Angelo Peloni, who seems to "know all his patrons"; prices are "affordable" and the "quiet, civilized" ambiance makes it "easy to hear tablemates", making it a "rare and wonderful option in LA."

La Cabanita *Mexican*   24 | 16 | 20 | $21

Montrose | 3447 N. Verdugo Rd. (Ocean View Blvd.) | 818-957-2711
The "wonderful, authentic" regional Mexican cuisine inspires a "cult-like following" at this long-established Montrose cantina famed for "complex" moles and other "interesting" items "you don't often see"; it's "a little noisy" and some encounter "occasional breakdowns in service", but factor in "peerless margaritas" and "reasonable prices" and it's clear why the crowds keep coming.

La Crêperie Cafe *French*   24 | 23 | 22 | $26

Long Beach | 130 Pine Ave. (Broadway) | 562-437-8648
Long Beach | 4911 E. Second St. (bet. Argonne & St. Joseph Aves.) | 562-434-8499
www.lacreperiecafe.net

Francophiles fawn over these "very bohemian" Long Beach cafes offering a "wonderful assortment" of "delicious", "proper" sweet and savory crêpes as well as other affordable French fare like the "must-have" garlic fries; they can get "pretty packed" and "noisy", but sidewalk seating is a plus, "and the prices aren't bad either."

La Dijonaise Café et Boulangerie *French*   20 | 16 | 18 | $22

Culver City | Helms Bldg. | 8703 Washington Blvd. (Helms Ave.) | 310-287-2770 | www.ladijonaise.com

This "cute cafe" in Culver City's Helms Bakery complex is a find for "basic", "low-cost" French fare and pastries ("oh those Napoleons!") in "large, pleasantly airy" digs with a patio; a few detect a little "attitude" amongst staffers, but otherwise it's a "reliable" "neighborhood" option.

La Dolce Vita 🗷 *Italian*   24 | 21 | 23 | $57

Beverly Hills | 9785 Little Santa Monica Blvd. (Wilshire Blvd.) | 310-278-1845 | www.ladolcevitabeverlyhills.com

"Reminiscent of an earlier LA era", this "old-school" Beverly Hills Italian proffers traditional steaks and pastas in an "intimate" "tryst"-worthy setting anchored by dark-red circular leather booths; opinions on service are mixed ("perfect" vs. "unfriendly"), and some complain about pricing, but most agree it's still a "classy" package.

La Frite *French* | 19 | 16 | 21 | $30 |

Sherman Oaks | 15013 Ventura Blvd. (Lemona Ave.) | 818-990-1791
Woodland Hills | 22616 Ventura Blvd. (bet. Fallbrook & Sale Aves.) | 818-225-1331
www.lafritecafe.com

A bit of "Paris" in the valley, these French sibs are "old standards" serving a much-"loved" onion soup, "huge" salads and other mid-priced bistro items in "lively" digs; opinions are still mixed, however, since Gordon Ramsay made over the Sherman Oaks decor and menu ("a mixed bag") and some say the Woodland Hills interior could use some "freshening", but they remain "crowded" nonetheless.

NEW Lago d'Argento Pizzeria ● *Italian* | - | - | - | I |

Silver Lake | 2609 N. Hyperion Ave. (Evans St.) | 323-300-5500 | www.pizzerialago.com

Pizza rules at this zany Silver Lake Italian from the team behind the nightlife-y Barbarella and Bugatta, with an inexpensive, kid-friendly menu of pies, plus salads and pasta sides for the table; the cartoonish room is full of chalkboard walls with 'Bread' and 'Oil' writ large, a graphic reminder of what you're eating at the big red booths.

La Grande Orange Café *Californian* | 21 | 22 | 19 | $31 |

Pasadena | 260 S. Raymond Ave. (Del Mar Blvd.) | 626-356-4444 | www.lgostationcafe.com

The restored Del Mar train depot in Pasadena makes the "unique" setting for this "vibrant", "crowded" Californian serving "enormous", well-priced portions to families, happy-hour hounds and locals taking advantage of "neighborhood night" deals and the patio; the less-impressed say it's "overrated" and draws "too many kids", but it's a "reliable" bet for most; P.S. the deviled eggs and red-velvet cake are favorites.

Lala's *Argentinean/Steak* | 23 | 18 | 21 | $25 |

West Hollywood | 7229 Melrose Ave. (Doheny Dr.) | 323-934-6838 Ⓢ Ⓜ
Studio City | 11935 Ventura Blvd. (Radford Ave.) | 818-623-4477
www.lalasgrill.com

For "down-home meat and potatoes done Argentine style", try this steakhouse duo on Melrose and in Studio City where the "generous", "flavorful" cuts and "fair prices" make it the ultimate "feel-good meal"; though the surroundings are "nothing fancy", the patios are appealing "especially on warm nights" and "sensual desserts" smothered in dulce de leche "close the deal."

L.A. Market *Californian* | 21 | 20 | 21 | $44 |

Downtown | JW Marriott at LA Live | 900 W. Olympic Blvd. (Figueroa St.) | 213-765-8600 | www.lalivemarriott.com

"Great before a game", this Cal-American by chef Kerry Simon in the atrium lobby of Downtown's JW Marriott at LA Live doles out "creative", midpriced takes on American classics, from "gourmet" burgers and meatball pizza to Hostess cupcakes; the smart, "mod" decor and "lively" atmosphere work well for "large groups", although under-whelmed critics call it "average in every way."

LAMILL Coffee Boutique *Californian*   22 | 22 | 18 | $24

Silver Lake | 1636 Silver Lake Blvd. (Effie St.) | 323-663-4441 | www.lamillcoffee.com

"Obsessive" caffeine lovers hail this Silver Lake lounge – aka the "PhD of coffee houses" – for its "attentively brewed" java and "innovative", all-day Californian menu served in a "hipster-chic" setting; critics con-tend it's all a bit "silly" with "expensive" tabs and a "snooty" staff, but defenders insist "it's a splurge that's worth it", adding that there's al-ways the hope of "seeing Jake Gyllenhaal" drink an $8 hand drip.

Lamonica's NY Pizza ● *Pizza*   24 | 10 | 16 | $12

Westwood | 1066 Gayley Ave. (bet. Kinross & Weyburn Aves.) | 310-208-8671 | www.lamonicasnypizza.com

"A slice of NY near UCLA", this inexpensive Westwood pizzeria has been vending "true", "tasty" Gotham-style pies with dough flown in from Brooklyn for more than 30 years; naysayers complain about stale decor, saying the "hole-in-the-wall" digs done up like a subway station need an update, but "New Yawkers feel right at home."

Lamppost Pizza *Pizza*   22 | 15 | 18 | $21

Torrance | 2955 E. Rolling Hills Rd. (Fallenleaf Dr.) | 310-325-4864 | www.lamppost-backstreet.com
El Monte | 4368 Peck Rd. (bet. Killian St. & Lambert Ave.) | 626-444-2631 | www.lamppostpizza.com
Moorpark | 530 E. Los Angeles Ave. (bet. Miller Pkwy. & Spring Rd.) | 805-529-6220 | www.lamppostpizza.com
Westlake Village | 1145 Lindero Canyon Rd. (bet. Kanan & Lakeview Canyon Rds.) | 818-879-2195 | www.lamppostpizza.com
Santa Clarita | 27661 Bouquet Canyon Rd. (Haskell Canyon Rd.) | 661-297-7092 | www.lamppostpizzascv.com

"Gooey" "thick-crust" pies pull crowds into this set of "family-friendly" pizzerias catering to both "little-league team parties" and "grown-ups" "hanging out with friends" over a beer; on the downside, the surrounds could use some sprucing and service gets mixed reviews, leading some to rely on "fast takeout."

NEW L&E Oyster Bar ⊠ *Seafood*   - | - | - | M

Silver Lake | 1637 Silver Lake Blvd. (bet. Berkeley Ave. & Effie St.) | 323-660-2255 | www.leoysterbar.com

Showing due "respect for the mollusk", this Silver Lake start-up special-izes in smoked, raw, steamed, fried and grilled variations on the oyster plus a "small" mostly seafood menu; the "tiny" digs done up vintage style with tufted booths are "not for the claustrophobic", but amiable staffers are a positive, so overall it's a welcome addition to the neighborhood.

Langer's Deli ⊠ *Deli*   26 | 13 | 20 | $21

Downtown | 704 S. Alvarado St. (7th St.) | 213-483-8050 | www.langersdeli.com

"Even the proudest New Yorkers" sing the praises of the truly "epic" No. 19 sandwich – "exquisite" "hand-carved" pastrami piled high on "stellar" double-baked rye – at this Downtown LA "landmark" from 1947; it's "old-school" all the way, from the Naugahyde booths to the "saucy waitresses "who won't hesitate to let you know if you made a poor effort at finishing your meal", and there's even curb-side pickup if you're in a rush – "now that's a deli!"; P.S. closes at 4 PM daily, closed Sundays.

La Paella ☒ *Spanish*

23 | 20 | 24 | $42

Beverly Hills | 476 S. San Vicente Blvd. (bet. La Cienega & Wilshire Blvds.) | 323-951-0745 | www.usalapaella.com

A bit of "Spain" awaits in the form of "authentic" paellas, "terrific tapas" and sangria at this "quaint", midpriced Beverly Hills "hide-away"; "charming" surroundings and a "gracious" staff further the "charm" – "for a romantic night, you can't do better."

La Parolaccia Osteria Italiana *Italian*

25 | 19 | 23 | $30

Long Beach | 2945 E. Broadway (Orizaba Ave.) | 562-438-1235
Claremont | 201 N. Indian Hill (2nd St.) | 909-624-1516
www.laparolacciausa.com

"*Delizioso*" Neapolitan pizza, "standout" pastas and other "tradi-tional", moderately priced Italiana are on offer at this "lively" duo in Long Beach and Claremont; "engaging" staffers set a "friendly" tone and the "comfortable" vibe is pure "neighborhood trattoria", so though even if some aren't "overly impressed", defenders declare they're "never disappointed."

La Paz *Mexican*

24 | 21 | 24 | $27

Calabasas | 4505 Las Virgenes Rd. (Agoura Rd.) | 818-880-8076

"Don't question it, just do it" urge fans tucking into the "authentic" Yucatán-style seafood dishes ("try the whole fish in garlic") offered alongside more typical Mexican fare at this Calabasas "tradition" also known for massive lunch buffet "spreads"; add in a "friendly" staff and many varieties of tequila and it's clear why many say it "rocks."

La Pergola *Italian*

25 | 22 | 25 | $40

Sherman Oaks | 15005 Ventura Blvd. (bet. Lemona & Noble Aves.) | 818-905-8402 | www.lapergolaristorante.net

"Vegetables from the back garden" go into "wonderful" pastas and other "well-priced" Italian dishes at this perennial "favorite" in Sherman Oaks tended by what some call the "nicest staff in town"; antique pot-tery and other "authentic Tuscan" touches add to the "warm", "charm-ing" atmosphere, so many consider it the "Valley's best-kept secret"; P.S. "don't miss the stuffed zucchini flowers in season."

La Provence *French*

22 | 19 | 19 | $24

Brentwood | Brentwood Gdns. | 11677 San Vicente Blvd. (bet. Barrington & Darlington Aves.) | 310-442-1144
La Provence Patisserie & Cafe *French*
Beverly Hills | 8950 W. Olympic Blvd. (bet. S. Doheny Dr. & S. Robertson Blvd.) | 310-888-8833
www.laprovencecafe.com

"Ooh-la-la", these "unstuffy" French sibs are finds for "reasonably priced" "casual" bistro eats as well as "beautiful" pastries offered in somewhat "nondescript" digs that garner an edge from assorted chandeliers and antiques for sale; the Beverly Hills locale is breakfast and lunch only, while the Brentwood branch offers steak frites and the like at dinner and also boasts an outdoor terrace that's an "oasis" on a sunny day.

	FOOD	DECOR	SERVICE	COST

Larchmont Bungalow *American*   `21` `18` `17` `$21`

Hancock Park | 107 N. Larchmont Blvd. (Beverly Blvd.) | 323-461-1528 | www.larchmontbungalow.com

"Very cozy", this "cute" converted home in the heart of Larchmont Village proffers an all-day American menu with "yummy" savories, "sinful" desserts and a notable breakfast with red-and-blue velvet pancakes that are "a decadent treat"; critics complain that it's a touch "overpriced" and "service can be slow", but it usually fits the bill for a "casual" bite.

Larchmont Grill *American*   `26` `23` `25` `$45`

Hollywood | 5750 Melrose Ave. (Lucerne Blvd.) | 323-464-4277 | www.larchmontgrill.com

It's "not fancy or exotic", but this Hollywood grill turns out "classic" American fare that's "sensational" nonetheless in a "charming" Craftsman setting that "feels like you're dining in a friend's home"; "gracious" service, midrange tabs and a "relaxing" atmosphere mean most "never have a bad meal here"; P.S. Tuesday's half-price wine night and Sunday's prix fixe special add value

NEW Larder at Maple Drive 🗷 *Eclectic*   `-` `-` `-` `l`

Beverly Hills | 349 N. Maple Dr. (3rd St.) | 310-248-3779 | www.thelarderattavern.com

Chef Suzanne Goin and sommelier Caroline Styne (A.O.C., Lucques) join together again for this casual breakfast-and-lunch Eclectic in the courtyard of a technology-heavy office complex in the Beverly Hills Business District; order your croissants, chopped salad or a ficelle filled with burrata or Iowa ham at the counter, and then dine outside in the sun or under umbrellas should it be rude enough to rain.

Lares ❶ *Mexican*   `22` `18` `22` `$25`

Santa Monica | 2909 Pico Blvd. (29th St.) | 310-829-4559 | www.lares-restaurant.com

For over 40 years, Santa Monicans have been relying on this "festive", family-run "neighborhood Mexican" for "flavorful", "traditional" eats for breakfast, lunch and dinner in "colorful" digs with live mariachi; it's always "packed" because prices are "reasonable", and insiders insist it "seems kid-friendly too, but maybe that's the margaritas talking."

NEW Larry's ❶ *American*   ∇ `24` `21` `20` `$31`

Venice | 24 Windward Ave. (Speedway) | 310-399-2700 | www.larrysvenice.com

"The essence of what a gastropub should be", this boardwalk-adjacent Venice hang from the folks behind Waterloo & City is a "great place to grab a drink, a bite and unwind" with lots of "tasty", "creative" small plates, burgers and heartier fare meeting up with an "excellent selection of craft beers" on tap; with moderate prices and a "comfortable" patio, many call it a "welcome addition" to the area; P.S. it's named for local artist Larry Bell and displays some of his work.

Larsen's Steakhouse *Steak*   `25` `25` `25` `$59`

Encino | Encino Pl. | 16101 Ventura Blvd. (Woodley Ave.) | 818-386-9500 | www.larsensteakhouse.com

Locals "love" having this Encino chophouse "just down the street" with "excellent" steaks and "accommodating" service, which saves them from driving over the hill for a "special evening"; "live piano music is a real plus" in the "dark" wood-and-stone surroundings, so though it's "a bit pricey", consensus is it's "worth it."

La Salsa *Mexican*

| 19 | 12 | 18 | $13 |

Downtown | 445 S. Figueroa St. (W. 5th St.) | 213-683-8815
Brentwood | 11740 San Vicente Blvd. (Gorham Ave.) | 310-826-7337
Malibu | 22800 PCH (Sweetwater Canyon Dr.) | 310-317-9466
Santa Monica | Third St. Promenade | 1401 Third St. Promenade (Santa Monica Blvd.) | 310-587-0755
www.lasalsa.com

"Go for a quickie" to this "healthy, fresh-Mex" chainlet churning out "tasty" fish tacos and "overstuffed burritos" dressed up with a variety of different salsas; perhaps there's "more authentic fare elsewhere", but most agree it's "high quality" at a "super value", and provides speedy takeout too.

La Scala ☒ *Italian*

| 22 | 19 | 21 | $39 |

Beverly Hills | 434 N. Cañon Dr. (bet. Brighton Way & Santa Monica Blvd.) | 310-275-0579

La Scala Presto ☒ *Italian*

Brentwood | 11740 San Vicente Blvd. (bet. Barrington & Gorham Aves.) | 310-826-6100
www.lascalabeverlyhills.com

The chopped salad is "legendary" ("everyone orders it in some fashion or another") at these "charming" Italians in Beverly Hills and Brentwood also luring "ladies who lunch" with other "reliable", "nothing-complicated" fare; expect "civilized" settings, "cordial" service and moderate prices; P.S. it's "great for takeaway" too.

Lascari's Deli *Deli*

| 23 | 19 | 23 | $20 |

Whittier | 14104 Lambert Rd. (bet. Calmada & Gunn Aves.) | 562-698-5899
Whittier | 16255 Whittier Blvd. (Bagardus Ave.) | 562-943-1113
www.lascarisdeli.com

"You can get almost anything" at these Italian delis churning out "solid", "red-sauce" pastas and overstuffed sandwiches from a "varied" menu; seating and service vary by locale, but "quick" takeout and low prices are a constant.

La Serenata de Garibaldi *Mexican/Seafood*

| 23 | 18 | 21 | $30 |

Boyle Heights | 1842 E. First St. (bet. Boyle Ave. & State St.) | 323-265-2887

La Serenata Gourmet *Mexican/Seafood*

West LA | 10924 W. Pico Blvd. (bet. Veteran Ave. & Westwood Blvd.) | 310-441-9667
www.laserenataonline.com

The "amazing", "inspired" Mexican dishes go "way beyond standard south-of-the-border fare" at this "classy" pair that's "especially good for seafood"; both locales boast an "upscale" ambiance and "friendly" service, but the "warm, pretty" hacienda-style setting at the Boyle Heights original is a "festive" favorite for "rehearsal dinners and parties."

Las Fuentes Mexican *Mexican*

| ▽ 24 | 17 | 19 | $15 |

Reseda | 18415 Vanowen St. (Reseda Blvd.) | 818-708-3344 | www.lasfuentesusa.com

Some of the "best Mexican food in the Valley" turns up at this long-time Reseda "favorite" where "you can't go wrong" choosing among the "amazing", "authentic" fare like tacos and tortas dished out in a "bright, happy" setting decorated with folk art; prices are low and the staff "makes you feel like home", so the only downside is it's often "packed."

La Vecchia Cucina *Italian*   26 | 20 | 24 | $39

Santa Monica | 2654 Main St. (bet. Hill St. & Ocean Park Blvd.) | 310-399-7979 | www.lavecchiacucina.com

Locals "love the vibe" at this Santa Monica neighborhood "find" where all of the "bustle", "noise" and "garlic aroma emanating throughout" give it the feel of a "real Italian cafe"; expect "top-notch" standards and pizzas proffered by a "helpful" crew, while affordable prices also explain why it's "always a pleasure."

Lawry's Carvery *American*   22 | 15 | 18 | $21

Downtown | LA Live | 1011 S. Figueroa St. (Olympic Blvd.) | 213-222-2212 | www.lawrysonline.com

"Lawry's lite" in Downtown's LA Live offers "mouthwatering" sandwiches made with the chain's signature prime rib plus salads and other items served up "quick", fast-food style; it's a convenient option before a game or concert, and "interesting people-watching" from the sidewalk patio helps make up for the "noisy", "food-court" setting.

☑ Lawry's The Prime Rib *Steak*   26 | 24 | 26 | $56

Beverly Hills | 100 N. La Cienega Blvd. (bet. Beverly Blvd. & 3rd St.) | 310-652-2827 | www.lawrysonline.com

"A throwback to the old days", this "tony" circa-1938 Beverly Hills "staple" remains a "favorite" with the "juiciest prime rib imaginable" proffered "in grand style" by uniformed servers who "roll big silver carts" around the dining room and carve the beef tableside; the "formal" surroundings may feel "dated, but that's part of the charm", and though it's "expensive", for most it just "proves you get what you pay for"; P.S. "leave room for the hot-fudge sundaes for dessert."

Lazy Dog Cafe *Eclectic*   22 | 23 | 22 | $22

Torrance | Del Amo Fashion Ctr. | 3525 W. Carson St. (bet. Hawthorne Blvd. & Madrona Ave.) | 310-921-6080

Thousand Oaks | 172 W. Hillcrest Dr. (bet. McCloud Ave. & Wilbur Rd.) | 805-449-5206

Valencia | 24201 Valencia Blvd. (Magic Mountain Pkwy.) | 661-253-9996 ◑
www.lazydogcafe.com

"Geared to please", this "easygoing" So Cal mini-chain appeals to "families", big groups and "man's best friend" – who's welcome to "join the feast" outside on the patios – with an Eclectic, "everything-under-the-sun" menu served by an "energetic" team; the somewhat "noisy" digs are done up with a "cute" dog motif, and though some find it all a bit "lacking", others insist its "deservedly popular."

Lazy Ox Canteen ◑ *Eclectic*   25 | 17 | 21 | $41

Little Tokyo | 241 S. San Pedro St. (bet. 2nd & 3rd Sts.) | 213-626-5299 | www.lazyoxcanteen.com

A "foodie paradise", this "exhilarating" little spot in Little Tokyo "wows" with an ever-"evolving" Eclectic menu featuring "amazing" "out-of-the-box" small plates based on "unique" seasonal ingredients and "all things pig", plus a "great burger"; prices are "moderate", servers are "informed" and the the vibe is "cool", even if the "ear-splitting" music could "scare off anyone over 28."

Le Chêne *French* ▽ 26 | 24 | 24 | $56

Saugus | 12625 Sierra Hwy. (bet. Sierra Vallejo Rd. & Steele Ave.) | 661-251-4315 | www.lechene.com

You might need a "GPS" to find this "out-of-the-way" Saugus spot featuring "exquisite" classic French fare and game served by a "fantastic" staff in a "romantic setting" that resembles a "country estate" (complete with "beautiful" grounds); though a few find the food and decor "could use a refresh", most say it still fits the bill for "special occasions."

Lee's Sandwiches *Sandwiches* 21 | 13 | 18 | $9

Artesia | Artesia Oasis Plaza | 18001 Pioneer Blvd. (bet. Ashworth & 178th Sts.) | 562-809-6869
NEW **Long Beach** | 6598 Cherry Ave. (Artesia Blvd.) | 562-728-1088
NEW **Pasadena** | 766 E. Colorado Blvd. (Lake Ave.) | 626-796-1908
Alhambra | 1289 E. Valley Blvd. (S. Vega St.) | 626-282-5589
West Covina | 1465 Plaza Dr. (Sunset Ave.) | 626-338-1888
Monterey Park | 500 N. Atlantic Blvd. (Hellman Ave.) | 626-457-8188
Rosemead | 8779 Valley Blvd. (Muscatel Ave.) | 626-291-2688 ⊭
Rowland Heights | 18194 Colima Rd. (bet. Fullerton & Larkvane Rd.) | 626-810-8887 ⊭
www.leesandwiches.com
Additional locations throughout Southern California

For a lesson in "banh mi 101", visit this SoCal chainlet putting out countless iterations of "tasty, filling" Vietnamese sandwiches on "hot, fresh baguettes" plus smoothies in surprising flavors like avocado and "great iced coffee" that could "keep you awake for days"; there's "no ambiance" and the counter-style service can be "lacking", but "when you're hungry and on a budget, this is the place."

∄ Leila's ⓜ *Californian* 27 | 20 | 25 | $53

Oak Park | Oak Park Plaza | 706 Lindero Canyon Rd. (Kanan Rd.) | 818-707-6939 | www.leilasrestaurant.com

"A local gem" in an Oak Park shopping center, this "little-known" Californian is "worthy of a spot" alongside the big guns thanks to its "terrific" "original" small and large plates plus a "well-crafted" wine list; the service is "attentive" and the earth-toned decor is, well, "comfortable" enough, rounding out a "wonderful", "pricey" experience that is "worth seeking it out.

Lemonade *Californian* 22 | 15 | 17 | $18

Downtown | MOCA | 250 S. Grand Ave. (bet. 2nd & 3rd Sts.) | 213-628-0200
Downtown | Ronald Tutor Student Campus Ctr. | 3607 Trousdale Pkwy. (34th St.) | 213-821-3482 🖻
Downtown | 505 S. Flower St. (bet. 5th & 6th Sts.) | 213-488-0299 🖻
West Hollywood | 9001 Beverly Blvd. (Almont Dr.) | 310-247-2500
Venice | 1661 Abbot Kinney Blvd. (Venice Blvd.) | 310-452-6200
www.lemonadela.com

"Needless to say, the lemonades are terrific" at this "budget"-priced SoCal chainlet also vending a "huge selection" of "fresh, healthy" salads, soups and other "inspired" Californian-casual fare plus "fab" desserts, all dished out cafeteria-style; the "cool, contemporary" digs have a "relaxed" vibe, however, lunch can draw "quite a crowd."

Lemon Moon ⌗ *Californian/Mediterranean*   21 | 16 | 18 | $24

West LA | Westside Media Ctr. | 12200 W. Olympic Blvd. (Bundy Dr.) | 310-442-9191 | www.lemonmoon.com

"Delicious cafeteria food, who knew?" ask incredulous fans of this "posh" West LA counter-service spot from Josiah Citrin and Raphael Lunetta turning out "tasty" Cal-Med sandwiches and "salads galore"; the "casual" industrial setup is spare, but includes "lovely" outdoor seating and fair prices, so most only "wish they were open for dinner."

Le Pain Quotidien *Bakery*   22 | 18 | 18 | $20

Beverly Hills | 320 S. Robertson Blvd. (bet. Burton Way & 3rd St.) | 310-858-7270
West Hollywood | 8607 Melrose Ave. (Westbourne Dr.) | 310-854-3700
Beverly Hills | 9630 S. Santa Monica Blvd. (bet. Bedford & Camden Drs.) | 310-859-1100
Brentwood | Barrington Ct. | 11702 Barrington Ct. (Barrington Ave.) | 310-476-0969
Brentwood | 13050 San Vicente Blvd. (26th St.) | 310-393-8909
Santa Monica | 316 Santa Monica Blvd. (bet. 3rd & 4th Sts.) | 310-393-6800
Westwood | 1055 Broxton Ave. (bet. Kinross & Weyburn Aves.) | 310-824-7900
Manhattan Beach | Metlox Plaza | 451 Manhattan Beach Blvd. (bet. Morningside & Valley Drs.) | 310-546-6411
Pasadena | 88 W. Colorado Blvd. (De Lacey Ave.) | 626-396-0814
Studio City | 13045 Ventura Blvd. (bet. Coldwater Canyon Ave. & Valley Vista Blvd.) | 818-986-1929
www.lepainquotidien.com
Additional locations throughout Southern California

"Amazing bread" is at the center of this well-priced Belgian bakery chain offering mostly organic "fresh, healthy" daytime fare, from "lovely" open-faced sandwiches and "sweet little salads" to "quality" pastries; service tends to be "a bit European", but the "inviting" atmosphere redeems with a "charming", "rustic" space perfect for a meeting or a post-exercise bite.

Le Petit Bistro ☻ *French*   25 | 20 | 24 | $40

West Hollywood | 631 N. La Cienega Blvd. (Melrose Ave.) | 310-289-9797 | www.lepetitbistro.us

"When there's no time to jet to Paris for the weekend", this WeHo bistro offers "considerable charm" in its "delicious", "bargain"-priced French fare, "pleasant" service and relatively "understated" setting; no wonder it's a "favorite" for "date night" and "still going strong" after close to 20 years.

Le Petit Cafe ⌗ *French*   24 | 18 | 21 | $38

Santa Monica | 2842 Colorado Ave. (bet. Stewart & Yale Sts.) | 310-829-6792 | www.lepetitcafebonjour.com

"*Petite* in size, *grande* in fare", this *très* "adorable" Santa Monica bistro charms locals with "down-home" traditional French cuisine served in a "lovely" space adorned with Provençal pastels; some say "they squeeze you in like sardines" and service can be "spotty", but "reasonable prices" compensate.

Le Petit Greek *Greek*

23 | 17 | 23 | $34

Hancock Park | 127 N. Larchmont Blvd. (bet. Beverly Blvd. & 1st St.) | 323-464-5160 | www.lepetitgreek.com

"Wonderful", "classic" Greek fare at a "fair value" keeps regulars coming back to this family-run Hancock Park Hellenic manned by a "pleasant" crew; inside is pretty, but it's especially "lovely to sit outside in the summer" at the tables overlooking Larchmont Boulevard.

Le Petit Restaurant *French*

24 | 20 | 22 | $39

Sherman Oaks | 13360 Ventura Blvd. (bet. Dixie Canyon & Nagle Aves.) | 818-501-7999 | www.lepetitrestaurant.net

A "lovely" "secret in the Valley", this Sherman Oaks bistro is "always a delight" thanks to its *delicieux*, "affordable" French standards ferried by a "warm" staff; add in an "unpretentious, comfortable" Parisian-style setting and you really "can't go wrong" here; P.S. look for lobster specials on Monday and Tuesday nights.

L'Epicerie *French*

21 | 17 | 19 | $31

Culver City | 9900 Culver Blvd. (Duquesne Ave.) | 310-815-1600 | www.lepiceriemarket.com

A "delightful stop" in Culver City, this restaurant/bar/market hybrid covers all the bases with City Bean coffee and pastries for the latte-and-laptop crowd, wine at happy hour and "perennial French favorites" for dinner, along with a full selection of imported groceries; "helpful" staffers maintain a "chill" vibe, while prices are "a bargain for the Westside."

Le Sanglier French Restaurant Ⓜ *French*

24 | 23 | 23 | $66

Tarzana | 5522 Crebs Ave. (Ventura Blvd.) | 818-345-0470 | www.lesanglierrestaurant.com

Recalling a time when "French food was king and the 405 moved at the speed limit", this circa-1970 Tarzana standby serves "traditional" Gallic fare in a "dark, romantic" "country-style" setting; true, it's "expensive" and critics contend "it should be better for the money you spend", but "it's a gem for people living in the San Fernando Valley."

Les Sisters Southern
Kitchen Ⓜ *Southern*

25 | 10 | 20 | $19

Chatsworth | 21818 Devonshire St. (bet. Jordan & Vassar Aves.) | 818-998-0755 | www.lessisters.com

Devotees "dream of the collard greens" at this Chatsworth Southern specializing in "down-home classics" ("all the stuff you know you shouldn't be eating") like "stupendous po' boys" and BBQ plus some "scrumptious" Cajun-Creole items that "remind you of New Orleans"; there's no alcohol, no BYO and the setting are "not much to look at", but prices are low and the mood's so "inviting" that "eating here is like visiting those Louisiana relatives you didn't know you had."

Let's Be Frank Ⓜ⊅ *Hot Dogs*

19 | 12 | 19 | $9

Culver City | Helms Ave. (National Blvd.) | 888-233-7265 | www.letsbefrankdogs.com

"I'll be frank, I love the dogs!" proclaims a fan of the "superior-quality" links crafted from all-natural meats and "gourmet" condiments at this red trailer parked daytimes Wednesday–Sunday at Culver City's

Helms Bakery Complex, and most Thursday nights outside Silverlake Wine; critics growl that they're "overhyped", but most are won over by the "decent" prices.

Lilly's French Cafe & Bar *French*
19 | 19 | 17 | $36

Venice | 1031 Abbot Kinney Blvd. (bet. B'way St. & Westminster Aves.) | 310-314-0004 | www.lillysfrenchcafe.com

"Very Gallic" through and through, this "civilized" Abbot Kinney bistro delivers "solid" French standards in an "inviting" "indoor/outdoor garden setting"; though prices are "reasonable", some surveyors complain about "inconsistent" fare and "indifferent" service from the expat staff.

NEW Limani Taverna *Greek*
- | - | - | M

San Pedro | 301 W. Sixth St. (S. Centre St.) | 310-833-3033

In the sprawling San Pedro space that was home to Papadakis Taverna, this cozy newcomer serves the same classic, moderately priced Athenian cuisine that's drawn crowds for so long – think lamb, seafood and gyros, all washed down with retsina and cries of *'Opa!'*; the Hellenic banquet-hall aesthetic is pure fun, even more so with the live entertainment on weekends.

Literati Bar & Grill *Californian/Eclectic*
18 | 17 | 17 | $25

West LA | 12081 Wilshire Blvd. (S. Bundy Dr.) | 310-479-3400

Literati Cafe *Californian/Eclectic*
West LA | 12081 Wilshire Blvd. (S. Bundy Dr.) | 310-231-7484 www.literaticafe.com

"Venture capitalists and screenwriters" "fueled by lattes" fill up this "neighborhood destination", an "atmospheric" West LA cafe serving "simple" Cal-Eclectic fare, pastries and "huge cups of coffee" in a high-ceilinged space adorned with photos of authors; the more "formal" bar and grill next door offers a varied menu that includes wine, beer and cocktails.

NEW Little Bear ● *Belgian*
∇ 18 | 19 | 22 | $28

Downtown | 1855 Industrial St. (bet. Mateo & Mill Sts.) | 213-622-8100 | www.littlebearla.com

This Downtown gastropub from Andrew Guerrero and Ryan Sweeney "hidden" away in the Industrial District sets itself apart with a "focus on Belgian" beers, with almost 20 rotating taps of obscure brews; the menu mixes of-the-moment LA fare like a burger made with grass-fed beef, stilton cheese and truffle oil with "interesting" stapes of the Low Country, such as gougères and carbonnade de flamande.

Little Dom's *Italian*
23 | 21 | 21 | $37

Los Feliz | 2128 Hillhurst Ave. (Avocado St.) | 323-661-0055

Deli at Little Dom's *Italian*
Los Feliz | 2128 Hillhurst Ave. (Avocado St.) | 323-661-0088 www.littledoms.com

This "hipster heaven" in Los Feliz is "always packed" thanks to "freakin'-good" thin-crust pizzas and other Italiana offered in a "cozy, romantic" setting with a bar scene by night and a "deliciously decadent" breakfast in the morn; the setting with an attached deli is like a "flashback to 1956 Mulberry Street", but while "service is usually solid", some say they could lose the "attitude."

	FOOD	DECOR	SERVICE	COST

Little Door *Mediterranean*
| 24 | 25 | 22 | $58 |

Third Street | 8164 W. Third St. (bet. Kilkea Dr. & La Jolla Ave.) | 323-951-1210 | www.thelittledoor.com

Fans heart this Third Street charmer with a candlelit "country-house" interior and a "magical garden" deemed "one of the most romantic" in LA; the service is "gracious" and the Med menu is "quite good", although bills are "on the pricey side", even for such an "enchanting" experience.

NEW Livello *Eclectic*
| - | - | - | E |

Beverly Hills | L'Ermitage Beverly Hills | 9291 Burton Way (bet. Foothill Rd. & Maple Dr.) | 310-385-5302 | www.lermitagebh.com

The Beverly Hills L'Ermitage Hotel is home to this new stunner serving an "ambitious", expensive Eclectic menu showcasing a mix of Italian, European and Asian dishes; it's all served in a strikingly "beautiful" indoor-outdoor space that features a dramatic fountain and a fireplace.

Lobsta Truck 🅂🅼 *Seafood*
| 23 | 12 | 19 | $16 |

Location varies; see website | www.lobstatruck.com

Even "fussy New Englanders" "love" this roaming seafooder and its "amazing" lobster and crab rolls full of "large chunks of buttery, fresh", "succulent" crustacean and served alongside "chowdah" and whoopie pies; lines can be long, but they "fly by fast", although a few report a little "sticker shock" with the bill.

The Lobster *Seafood*
| 25 | 24 | 23 | $57 |

Santa Monica | 1602 Ocean Ave. (Colorado Ave.) | 310-458-9294 | www.thelobster.com

With a "fabulous" location at the Santa Monica Pier, this seafood mainstay offers "stunning views" of the Pacific plus "terrific" lobster "prepared a zillion ways" and other "market-fresh" dishes; "expensive" tabs and a "loud, crowded" space are drawbacks, but the "wow" factor is high, especially for a "special occasion."

Locanda del Lago *Italian*
| 24 | 24 | 24 | $47 |

Santa Monica | 231 Arizona Ave. (2nd St.) | 310-451-3525 | www.lagosantamonica.com

A "welcoming" "escape" from the "tourist hot zone" of Santa Monica's Third Street Promenade, this expensive Northern Italian specializes in "amazing", "authentic" dishes of the Lake Como region served along an "extensive" wine list; add in a "cozy atmosphere" and "down-home Italian hospitality" and it's an "all-around wonderful experience."

Locanda Positano *Italian*
| 25 | 19 | 23 | $50 |

Marina del Rey | 4059 Lincoln Blvd. (Washington Blvd.) | 310-526-3887 | www.locandapositano.com

This "little jewel" in Marina del Rey "practically defines the term charming" with "exquisite, authentic" Italian cuisine and "fine wines" delivered by "swoon-worthy" accented waiters in a "tiny", "romantic" space; indeed, it's "pricey", but cheaper than "a trip to Italy."

Locanda Veneta *Italian*
| 25 | 20 | 23 | $50 |

Third Street | 8638 W. Third St. (Willaman Dr.) | 310-274-1893 | www.locandaveneta.net

Ever "inviting", this 25-year-old Third Street Italian is "still tops" for fans when it comes to "fantastic" Venetian fare like noteworthy cala-

FOOD | DECOR | SERVICE | COST

mari and risotto dishes; the "romantic" setting can be "cramped" and tabs daunting, but the "amazing food and service" enhanced with a "celeb sighting" or two make it one of the city's "little gems."

The Loft *Hawaiian*
20 | 15 | 18 | $19

Cerritos | 20157 Pioneer Blvd. (Del Amo Blvd.) | 562-402-3538
Torrance | 2210 W. Artesia Blvd. (Van Ness Ave.) | 310-217-1000
Torrance | 23305 Hawthorne Blvd. (Lomita Blvd.) | 310-375-4051
www.thelofthawaii.com

For "solid" Hawaiian "grub" like island-style fried chicken and bacon-fried rice, look no further than this casual chain putting out all the standards at a "reasonable price"; there's "not much" happening decor-wise, and some feel the fare's only "so-so", but service is "fast and friendly" and most "swear by" it for an "authentic" bite.

Lomo Arigato 🍴 *Japanese/Peruvian*
22 | 17 | 21 | $10

Location varies; see website | www.lomoarigato.com

"The cooks give quite a show" at this Peruvian-Japanese truck cooking up "truly addictive" renditions of lomo saltado and other "tasty" eats over "fiery flames and smoke"; the vibe's "friendly", and prices aren't bad either; P.S. for extra "kick" don't be shy with the "amazing" *aji* sauce.

L'Opera *Italian*
25 | 24 | 24 | $49

Long Beach | Historic Clock Tower | 101 Pine Ave. (bet. Alta Way & 1st St.) | 562-491-0066 | www.lopera.com

For a "special-occasion" spot or a "high-end business lunch", Long Beachers tout this Northern Italian for its "excellent" homemade pastas and other "rich" Italiana served by a "spot-on" crew; it's all set in the "wonderful" Historic Clock Tower building from 1902 making for a "truly memorable" setting that justifies the upmarket tabs.

Los Arroyos *Mexican*
24 | 18 | 21 | $23

Camarillo | Promenade at Camarillo Premium Outlets | 630 Ventura Blvd. (S. Las Posas Rd.) | 805-987-4000 | www.losarroyos.net

"Always crowded", this Mexican "comfort-food" chainlet churns out "fresh", "authentic" eats in "informal", "family-friendly"environs decorated with traditional south-of-the-border touches; prices are a "good value" too, so "the only bummer is that you pay for chips."

Los Balcones del Peru *Peruvian*
▽ 23 | 17 | 21 | $24

Hollywood | 1360 N. Vine St. (De Longpre Ave.) | 323-871-9600

"Legit Peruvian" cuisine is served up in a "convenient" Hollywood locale right around the corner from The ArcLight at this unassuming spot specializing in ceviche, lomo saltado and other well-priced fare; "caring" service and a "neighborhood feel" make up for ambiance that's otherwise "lacking."

Los Toros *Mexican*
23 | 19 | 20 | $20

Chatsworth | 21743 Devonshire St. (bet. De Soto Ave. & Topanga Canyon Blvd.) | 818-882-3080 | www.lostoros.com

"Generous" helpings of "real-deal" Mexican fare are the draw at this el cheapo Chatsworth "institution", especially "loved" by "lively locals" for its "exceptional" margaritas and famous bean dip; murals, tiles and festive streamers make the huge space "feel fun", and so does the staff that welcomes you "like family" even when the crowds are "overflowing at happy hour and dinner."

Lotería! Grill *Mexican* | 23 | 15 | 18 | $24

Fairfax | Farmers Mkt. | 6333 W. Third St. (Fairfax Ave.) | 323-930-2211
Hollywood | 6627 Hollywood Blvd. (bet. Cherokee & Whitley Aves.) | 323-465-2500
NEW Santa Monica | 1251 Third St. Promenade (Arizona Ave.) | 310-393-2700
Studio City | 12050 Ventura Blvd. (Laurel Canyon Blvd.) | 818-508-5300
NEW Westlake Village | 180 Promenade Way (Thousand Oaks Blvd.) | 805-379-1800
www.loteriagrill.com

"Bright and lively" describes both the scene and the eats at Jimmy Shaw's "colorful" chain of "well-priced" Mexicanos – born as a stand in the Farmers Market – crafting "surprising, delicious" spins on regional specialties; the staff is "friendly" across the board, but only the full-service sit-down branches offer "strong margaritas" and full tequila bars.

Louise's Trattoria *Californian/Italian* | 20 | 18 | 21 | $26

Hancock Park | 232 N. Larchmont Blvd. (Beverly Blvd.) | 323-962-9510
Los Feliz | 4500 Los Feliz Blvd. (Hillhurst Ave.) | 323-667-0777
Santa Monica | 1008 Montana Ave. (10th St.) | 310-394-8888
Santa Monica | 264 26th St. (San Vicente Blvd.) | 310-451-5001
West LA | 10645 W. Pico Blvd. (bet. Manning & Pelham Aves.) | 310-475-6084
Pasadena | 2-8 E. Colorado Blvd. (S. Fair Oaks Ave.) | 626-568-3030
www.louises.com

"Reliable, but not exciting" Cal-Italian fare gets a lift from the "addictive" complimentary focaccia at this "comfortable" SoCal chain offering just "enough choices to keep your interest" and "friendly" service; critics who are "not terribly impressed" claim "nothing stands out" except for the budget-friendly bills.

Lucille's Smokehouse Bar-B-Que *BBQ* | 24 | 22 | 22 | $30

Cerritos | 11338 South St. (Gridley Rd.) | 562-916-7427
Culver City | Westfield Culver City | 6000 Sepulveda Blvd. (Slauson Ave.) | 310-390-1227
Long Beach | 4828 E. Second St. (bet. Park & St. Joseph Aves.) | 562-434-7427
Long Beach | Long Beach Towne Ctr. | 7411 Carson St. (Nectar Ave.) | 562-938-7427
Torrance | Del Amo Fashion Ctr. | 21420 Hawthorne Blvd. (Carson St.) | 310-370-7427
www.lucillesbbq.com

"Come hungry" to this "down-home" BBQ chain, a meat-eater's "heaven" that entices with "messy", "generous" portions of "tasty" 'cue and "cute" Southern-themed rooms filled with the "sweet smell of barbecue sauce and smoke"; critics beef about "overpriced tabs", but it's "plenty filling", with "friendly" service to boot.

☑ Lucques *Californian/Mediterranean* | 27 | 25 | 26 | $66

West Hollywood | 8474 Melrose Ave. (La Cienega Blvd.) | 323-655-6277 |
www.lucques.com

"Take pride in being a local" at this "casually masterful" Cal-Med in WeHo where the "brilliant" Suzanne Goin (A.O.C.) "does wonders" crafting "thoughtful, seasonal" cuisine, complemented by a "smart wine list" and "gracious" service; set in an "old carriage house" with an "ivy-lined courtyard", it's "pleasurable" all around and "well worth the cost" – plus the "value" prix fixe Sunday Supper is still a "big hit."

	FOOD	DECOR	SERVICE	COST

LudoBites *Asian/French* | 26 | 16 | 23 | $48 |

Location varies; see website | www.ludobites.com

"Getting a reservation is like winning the lottery" at this pricey pop-up from chef Ludo Lefebvre where "lucky and perseverant" patrons are rewarded with "fantastic, whimsical" Asian-French cuisine with molecular touches; the location varies each time so naturally decor "varies" and there can be "hits and misses" with the food too, but "it's sure to be a meal you talk about even if every dish doesn't strike your fancy."

LudoTruck *Eclectic* | 24 | 15 | 19 | $13 |

Location varies; see website | 213-973-8839 | www.foodtrucks.com/ludotruck

"Mind-blowing" fried chicken is the main attraction at this truck by Burgundy-born chef Ludo Lefebvre (LudoBites), where the *Provençal pepittes* are accompanied by honey-lavender biscuits and "spicy, kickin' slaw"; perhaps it's a little "expensive" for "glorified chicken nuggets" and the "waits" can be trying, but most "love it anyway."

Luggage Room Pizzeria *Pizza* | 23 | 16 | 17 | $24 |

Pasadena | 260 S. Raymond Ave. (Del Mar Blvd.) | 626-356-4440 | www.theluggageroom.com

Set in the luggage room of Pasadena's historic (circa 1934) Del Mar Train Station, this "casual" offshoot of the neighboring La Grande Orange offers a "limited" lineup of "boutique" thin-crust pizzas with "unexpected toppings" capped off with gelato for dessert; service can be "uneven" and it "gets a bit loud when it's packed", but most don't seem to mind.

Lukshon *Asian* | 25 | 24 | 23 | $47 |

Culver City | Helms Bldg. | 3239 Helms Ave. (bet. Venice & Washington Blvds.) | 310-202-6808 | www.lukshon.com

Chef Sang Yoon (of Father's Office fame) earns kudos for his "highly original", "habit-forming" Southeast Asian small plates on a mid-priced menu "worth working your way through" at this "epicurean delight" inside Culver City's Helms Bakery; factor in "accommodating" service and a "gorgeous" "modern" setup with an open kitchen and patio, and it's "enjoyable" all around.

Lulu's Cafe *American* | 23 | 19 | 24 | $21 |

West Hollywood | 7149 Beverly Blvd. (N. Detroit St) | 323-938-6095 | www.luluscafelosangeles.com

This busy corner cafe in West Hollywood is a "good choice" for "well-prepared" American comfort food with a few surprises (think ahi tuna burgers and breakfast pasta) served morning to night at a "reasonable" cost; the small interior can be "noisy", so those in the know nab a seat on the sidewalk and try to ignore the traffic.

Lulu's Restaurant *American* | ▽ 22 | 16 | 23 | $21 |

Van Nuys | 16900 Roscoe Blvd. (Balboa Blvd.) | 818-988-0707 | www.lulusrestaurant.com

At this long-standing Van Nuys "local", dining is done the old-school way with servers who "always get your order right" setting down "no-frills", low-cost American comfort food like burgers and seafood; the "coffee-shop" decor "is not much to look at", but the adjacent bar provides "a great hangout" if you like karaoke or watching a game.

Luna Park *American*

21 | 18 | 20 | $35

La Brea | 672 S. La Brea Ave. (Wilshire Blvd.) | 323-934-2110 | www.lunaparkla.com

Specialty cocktails, fondue and make-your-own s'mores ("a must") are the signatures of this "funky" La Brea American serving a well-priced menu that's "strong on comfort food"; "attentive service" and "dark", semi-private booths make it an "excellent date-night sort of place."

Lupe's *Mexican*

22 | 18 | 22 | $18

Thousand Oaks | 1710 E. Thousand Oaks Blvd. (Civic Arts Plaza) | 805-495-3573 | www.lupesmexicanrestaurant.menutoeat.com

"Delivering the goods for 60 years", this casual, family-run cantina in Thousand Oaks turns out "homestyle" Mex fare for not a lot of pesos; some say "it has more nostalgia value than culinary", but "friendly" service keeps locals "returning again and again"; P.S. beer and wine only.

Lure Fish House *Seafood*

24 | 24 | 24 | $32

Camarillo | 259 W. Ventura Blvd. (S. Las Posas Rd.) | 805-388-5556 | www.lurefishhouse.com

"Definitely a keeper" declare fans of this well-priced Camarillo seafooder featuring "a wide array" of "fresh", locally caught fin fare that's "well prepared and pleasantly served" with local wines and fruity cocktails; the modern-nautical space with an oyster bar and patio has an "inviting ambiance", just prepare for "mobs on Saturday night" since they don't take reservations; P.S. happy hour is also popular.

Madame Chou Chou Ⓜ *French*

∇ 21 | 17 | 20 | $41

Santa Monica | 2518 Main St. (Norman Pl.) | 310-392-2509 | www.madamechouchou.com

Quite the *"très chic"* "find" on Main Street, this midpriced Santa Monica bistro purveys "creative" French fare and homemade pastries in an "intimate" setting with a patio; service can be "lacking", but even so, regulars count on it as "the kind of place where you can sit and relax with friends."

Madeo *Italian*

26 | 20 | 24 | $67

West Hollywood | 8897 Beverly Blvd. (Swall Dr.) | 310-859-4903

"If you can get past the paparazzi", this "clubby", "celeb-loaded" Northern Italian in West Hollywood offers "excellent" "old-school" dishes (the Bolognese is a highlight) at "eye-popping" prices; many surveyors suggest there's "major attitude if you're not a heavy hitter", but it still "packs them in" each night nonetheless.

Maggiano's Little Italy *Italian*

22 | 22 | 22 | $33

Fairfax | The Grove | 189 The Grove Dr. (bet. Beverly Blvd. & 3rd St.) | 323-965-9665

Woodland Hills | Westfield Promenade | 6100 Topanga Canyon Blvd. (bet. Erwin & Oxnard Sts.) | 818-887-3777
www.maggianos.com

"Family-style is the way to go" at this perpetually "packed" Italian chain sending out "generous proportions" of "old-style" fare that's "not anything that would send you into rapture, but it gets you full"; the "crowded, noisy" settings are kid-friendly "with a New York flavor", while "courteous" service and "moderate prices" make it a "can't lose" with a large group.

	FOOD	DECOR	SERVICE	COST

Maison Akira ☒ French/Japanese — 27 | 23 | 25 | $60

Pasadena | 713 E. Green St. (bet. El Molino & Oak Knoll Aves.) | 626-796-9501 | www.maisonakira.com

Akira Hirose is still at "the top of his game" at this Pasadena "classic" where "intriguing" French-Japanese dishes that are "uniformly superb" and "worth every penny" are served by a "professional" team; the "quiet, intimate" atmosphere's "a little staid" (and "lost in the 1980s") for some, although it remains "great for special occasions or if you're going to the nearby Pasadena Playhouse."

NEW Maison Giraud French — 24 | 18 | 18 | $44

Pacific Palisades | 1032 Swarthmore Ave. (Monument St.) | 310-459-7561 | www.maison-giraud.com

The menu is classic French at this "great addition" to the Palisades, an all-day bakery and restaurant from chef Alain Giraud purveying "buttery, flaky croissants", "wonderful pastries", "approachable" entrees and a "genius" chocolate soufflé for dessert in a sun-dappled space with floor-to-ceiling windows; a few fuss over service that's too "leisurely", "noisy" acoustics and "pricey" bills, but "all is forgiven because of chef Giraud's menu."

Malbec Argentinean/Steak — 23 | 20 | 22 | $36

Pasadena | 1001 E. Green St. (S. Catalina Ave.) | 626-683-0550
Toluca Lake | 10151 Riverside Dr. (Forman Ave.) | 818-762-4860
www.malbeccuisine.com

"Excellent cuts of meat" await at this Argentinean duo known for its "generous portions" at "fair prices" and "long list of red wines" from South America (including plenty of Malbecs, natch); the "dark" "romantic" settings and "attentive service" earn plaudits, although the "busy" weekends are "too noisy" for some.

Malibu Seafood Seafood — 25 | 14 | 18 | $21

Malibu | 25653 PCH (bet. Corral Canyon & Malibu Canyon Rds.) | 310-456-6298 | www.malibuseafood.com

"Bring your own wine and tablecloth" and "take in the ocean breezes" at this "no-frills" seafood shack on the PCH in Malibu serving up affordable, "fresh, cooked-to-order" fare on three patios with "killer" views; it gets "crowded", but a "seriously organized ordering system" keeps the "long lines" moving; P.S. the "tasty clam chowder and excellent fish 'n' chips are easy pleasers."

Malo Mexican — 23 | 21 | 19 | $28

Silver Lake | 4326 W. Sunset Blvd. (Fountain Ave.) | 323-664-1011 | www.malorestaurant.com

"Muy bueno" say late-night "hipsters" of this dark, "trendy" Silver Lake Mexican known as much for its "cool vibe" as its unusual "chewy chips", "fabulous" salsa flights and "creative" tacos that may be "a bit gringo" but are "decent" nonetheless; "fantastic margaritas" from the attached tequila bar take the edge off servers "with attitude"; P.S. happy hour is also popular.

Mama D's Italian — 22 | 14 | 23 | $26

Hermosa Beach | 1031 Hermosa Ave. (bet. Pier Ave. & 10th St.) | 310-379-6262

(continued)

(continued)
Mama D's
Manhattan Beach | 1125 Manhattan Ave. (Manhattan Beach Blvd.) | 310-546-1492
www.mamadsrestaurant.com
"Homey" describes these "archetypal family-friendly Italians" in Hermosa and Manhattan Beach moving "cheap and voluminous" platters of "home cooking" plus "irresistible" garlic bread while you wait; despite the fact that you'll be "packed in like sardines" at traditional red-checkered tables, they're nonetheless "popular" with "locals" who "go back again and again."

Mama Terano *Italian*   22 | 12 | 24 | $28
Rolling Hills Estates | 815 Deep Valley Dr. (Roxcove Dr.) | Rolling Hills | 310-377-5757 | www.mamaterano.com
Robert Bell (Chez Mélange, Bouzy) relies on "grandmama's recipes from the old world" at this Rolling Hills Estates Italian putting out "delicious" pastas, flatbread pizzas and the like for "unusually reasonable" sums; service is "attentive", and it's often "crowded like a neighborhood bistro should be."

Mandarin Deli *Chinese*   22 | 11 | 16 | $18
Northridge | 9305 Reseda Blvd. (Prairie St.) | 818-993-0122
Mandarin Noodle House ⊅ *Chinese*
Monterey Park | 701 W. Garvey Ave. (Chandler Ave.) | 626-570-9795
"Steaming bowls of soup", "chewy handmade noodles" and "juicy, tender dumplings" are the hallmarks of these inexpensive Chinese "comfort-food" stops in Monterey Park and Northridge; the atmosphere's on the "stark" side, but at least a "friendly" staff "gets [you] in and out quickly."

M & M Soul Food *Soul Food*   25 | 18 | 21 | $30
Carson | 335 E. Albertoni St. (bet. Avalon Blvd. & S. Main St.) | 310-324-5317
When you have a hankering for "real soul food, cooked from scratch", this Carson standby hits the spot with "huge portions" of fried chicken, catfish and other "amazing" eats at a reasonable price; it "feels like home" with "friendly" staffers and a "down-home" atmosphere, although "long waits" are sometimes part of the package.

Manhattan Beach BrewCo ● *American*   21 | 18 | 20 | $24
Manhattan Beach | 124 Manhattan Beach Blvd. (Manhattan Ave.) | 310-798-2744 | www.brewcomb.com
"Crowded and noisy", this Manhattan Beach sports bar is "a great place to grab a bite after a day at the beach" with an affordable American menu starring a "tasty burger" that's "worth every calorie", plus a wide range of draft beers; there's no outdoor seating, but the modern exterior features a garage-door front, and there are plenty of TVs showing the game.

NEW Manna *Korean*   ▽ 18 | 12 | 16 | $24
Downtown | 333 S. Alameda St. (3rd. St.) | 323-733-8516 | www.mannakoreanrestaurant.com
"All-you-can-eat deliciousness" is yours at this "loud, smoky" Korean BBQ joint Downtown, where diners "stuff themselves to the gills" with midpriced galbi and other sear-it-yourself meats plus shabu-shabu

FOOD | DECOR | SERVICE | COST

served at mostly outdoor tables; on birthdays they'll "douse you with champagne", so for a "fun party atmosphere", it's just the ticket.

Maria's Italian Kitchen *Italian*   20 | 16 | 20 | $23

Downtown | 615 Flower St. (bet. W. 6th St. & Wilshire Blvd.) | 213-623-4777
Brentwood | 11723 Barrington Ct. (S. Barrington Ave.) | 310-476-6112
West LA | 10761 W. Pico Blvd. (Malcolm Ave.) | 310-441-3663
Pasadena | Hastings Ranch Shopping Ctr. | 3537 E. Foothill Blvd.
(Rosemead Blvd.) | 626-351-2080
Encino | 16608 Ventura Blvd. (Rubio Ave.) | 818-783-2920
Northridge | 9161 Reseda Blvd. (bet. Dearborn & Nordhoff Sts.) |
818-341-5114
Sherman Oaks | 13353 Ventura Blvd. (bet. Dixie Canyon & Fulton Aves.) |
818-906-0783
Woodland Hills | El Camino Shopping Ctr. | 23331 Mulholland Dr.
(Deseret Dr.) | 818-225-0586
Agoura Hills | Ralph's Shopping Ctr. | 29035 Thousand Oaks Blvd.
(Kanan Rd.) | 818-865-8999
www.mariasitaliankitchen.com
"Red-sauce lovers unite" over "generous portions" of Italian "comfort food" at this "homey" "no-frills chain" that "feels like a mom and pop" to some with its "red-checked tablecloth decor"; sure, "service varies" and some find the food only "so-so", but "reasonable prices keep 'em coming back" for more.

Marino 🗷 *Italian*   26 | 20 | 26 | $47

Hollywood | 6001 Melrose Ave. (Wilcox Ave.) | 323-466-8812 |
www.marinorestaurant.net
"It feels like you're visiting friends" at this longtime family-run Italian in Hollywood that turns out "marvelous", "homestyle" Italian with "no pretense" in a "lovely" updated setting; it's not cheap, but the "comfortable", "quiet" ambiance makes it a "local treasure."

Mario's Peruvian & Seafood *Peruvian*   26 | 9 | 18 | $20

Hollywood | 5786 Melrose Ave. (Vine St.) | 323-466-4181
"It's all about the ceviche" and "addictive" pollo saltado at this Hollywood Peruvian that often hosts "lines out the door" for its inexpensive eats; even if the "decor has all the personality of a DMV", most have "no complaints"; P.S. it's also "terrific for takeout."

Marix Tex Mex Café *Tex-Mex*   17 | 14 | 19 | $26

West Hollywood | 1108 N. Flores St. (Santa Monica Blvd.) | 323-656-8800

Marix Tex Mex Playa *Tex-Mex*

Santa Monica | 118 Entrada Dr. (PCH) | 310-459-8596
www.marixtexmex.com
"Killer margaritas" fuel the "lively" scene at these perpetually "packed" Tex-Mex twins where solid servers deliver "plentiful" portions of "passable" Mexican fare ("but who comes here for the food?"); the Santa Monica location is a post-"beach hang" with "kids on the loose", while WeHo's happy hour hosts "hot men" and "pretty people" on the patio.

Marmalade Café *American*   19 | 18 | 20 | $25

Fairfax | Farmers Mkt. | 6333 W. Third St. (Fairfax Ave.) | 323-954-0088
Rolling Hills Estates | Avenue of the Peninsula Mall | 550 Deep Valley Dr.
(Drybank Dr.) | Rolling Hills | 310-544-6700

(continued)

(continued)
Marmalade Café

Malibu | 3894 Cross Creek Rd. (PCH) | 310-317-4242
Santa Monica | 710 Montana Ave. (7th St.) | 310-395-9196
El Segundo | Plaza El Segundo | 2014 E. Park Pl. (Rosecrans Ave.) |
310-648-7200
Calabasas | Commons at Calabasas | 4783 Commons Way (Calabasas Rd.) |
818-225-9092
Sherman Oaks | 14910 Ventura Blvd. (Kester Ave.) | 818-905-8872
Westlake Village | Promenade at Westlake | 140 Promenade Way
(Thousand Oaks Blvd.) | 805-370-1331
www.marmaladecafe.com

"A step up from a coffee shop", this SoCal chain offers a "varied menu" of American "comfort food" "with a Californian touch", including "particularly good breakfasts"; some say the food's "just ok", but with "cute" "shabby-chic" settings, a "pleasant staff" and "fair" prices, it certainly works "in a pinch."

Marouch Ⓜ *Lebanese*　　▽ 29 | 19 | 23 | $27

East Hollywood | 4905 Santa Monica Blvd. (Edgemont St.) | 323-662-9325 |
www.marouchrestaurant.com

"Intense, creamy baba ghanoush" and "tasty" kebabs are just a few of the "authentic" affordable treats at this East Hollywood eatery considered to be "the best Lebanese" in LA; just "ignore the setting" in a nondescript mini-mall and let the "helpful staff" guide you through "the wonderful daily specials" – whatever it is "it's bound to be delicious."

Marrakesh *Moroccan*　　22 | 25 | 25 | $41

Studio City | 13003 Ventura Blvd. (Coldwater Canyon Ave.) |
818-788-6354 | www.marrakeshdining.com

For "something different", Valley dwellers look no further than this Studio City Moroccan that's "authentic in all aspects", from the traditional decor (mosaics, arches) to the "well-prepared" feasts served by a staff that "takes care of you"; with live music and belly dancers, prepare to "kick back" for a few hours to get the "total experience."

☒ Mar'sel Ⓜ *Californian*　　26 | 28 | 25 | $63

Rancho Palos Verdes | Terranea Resort | 6610 Palos Verdes Dr. S.
(Hawthorne Blvd.) | 310-265-2780 | www.terraneamarsel.com

Set in the "world-class" Terranea Resort, this Californian "should be on every romantic's bucket list" with its "breathtaking" ocean views from its perch atop Rancho Palos Verdes; the cuisine's as "stunning" as the setting, with "fabulous" fare made with ingredients picked straight from the chef's garden, while the service is what "you would expect at a luxury resort", and so are the prices.

Marston's *American*　　21 | 17 | 19 | $22

Pasadena | 151 E. Walnut St. (bet. Marengo & Raymond Aves.) |
626-796-2459
Valencia | 24011 Newhall Ranch Rd. (McBean Pkwy.) | 661-253-9910 Ⓜ
www.marstonsrestaurant.com

"Breakfasts are the bomb" at this Pasadena "institution" (and its newer Valencia spin-off) where "fresh, tasty" American fare comes served in a "quaint" "old-fashioned cottage" by a "personable" crew; just know, "it's mobbed on weekends", so "come early" or try it for lunch.

Martha's 22nd St. Grill *American*

25 | 19 | 23 | $18

Hermosa Beach | 25 22nd St. (bet. Beach Dr. & Hermosa Ave.) | 310-376-7786

"Sit on the patio and watch the world go by" at this Hermosa Beach American known for its "bountiful breakfasts" and other "solid" fare from a menu styled with a "California nod to vegetarians"; with "great service", water views ("you can hear the waves crashing") and afford-able tabs, it's no surprise the "crowds line up on sunny days."

Masa *Pizza*

24 | 18 | 23 | $34

Echo Park | 1800 W. Sunset Blvd. (Lemoyne St.) | 213-989-1558 | www.masaofechopark.com

"If you're hankering for deep dish" this late-night Echo Park pizzeria is considered one of "the best this side of Chicago" for "true" pies fash-ioned with "buttery-soft dough" and authentic toppings; a "friendly" staff and a "casual, festive" setting make up for long waits (pies are baked to order) and prices that can feel on the high side for the genre.

Mastro's Steakhouse *Steak*

27 | 25 | 26 | $79

Beverly Hills | 246 N. Cañon Dr. (bet. Clifton & Dayton Ways) | 310-888-8782

Thousand Oaks | 2087 E. Thousand Oaks Blvd. (bet. Conejo School Rd. & Los Feliz Dr.) | 805-418-1811

www.mastrosrestaurants.com

It's "power scene" central at these "flashy" chophouses attracting a "glamorous" crowd with "spectacular beef", "decadent seafood plat-ters", "large martinis" and a "sinful" warm butter cake for dessert; "plush doesn't begin to describe" the "supper-club" setting (with a piano player and a "big bar scene") tended by an "attentive", "well-versed" staff, so "if you've got the big bucks", you're in for a "memorable" evening.

☑ Matsuhisa *Japanese*

28 | 19 | 24 | $87

Beverly Hills | 129 N. La Cienega Blvd. (bet. Clifton Way & Wilshire Blvd.) | 310-659-9639 | www.nobumatsuhisa.com

"Impeccable in all respects", this Japanese "temple" from Nobu Matsuhisa – his first and some say "his best" – showcases his "stupen-dous sashimi with Peruvian flavors" employing "melt-in-your-mouth fresh" fish as well as other "tantalizing" creations; the "tranquil" setting is the most "low-key" in the Nobu empire, with a "professional" staff and a "comfortably modest" ambiance – just don't expect modest prices.

Matteo's Ⓜ *Italian*

21 | 22 | 23 | $51

West LA | 2321 Westwood Blvd. (bet. Pico Blvd. & Tennessee Ave.) | 310-475-4521 | www.matteosla.com

This "iconic" circa-1963 Rat Pack "hangout" in West LA has an "old-school" setting but a "new-school" "pricey" menu featuring "novel takes on modern Italian cuisine" delivered by a "delightful" staff; though the decor's been freshened up, the "classic" feel remains, and you can still nab a seat in Frank Sinatra's corner booth (station eight).

NEW Maximiliano *Italian*

∇ 25 | 21 | 25 | $30

Highland Park | 5930 York Blvd. (N. Figueroa St.) | 323-739-6125 | www.maximilianohp.com

Chef Andre Guerrero of The Oinkster makes Highland Park locals "happy" with his "happening" red sauce-intensive Italian serving "solid" midpriced fare like pork chops and meatballs; "well-trained" servers preside over a "trendy, yet comfortable" setting featuring an open-beam ceiling, spaghetti-themed wall art and a massive pizza oven in the open kitchen, while accessible pricing completes the package.

Maxwell's Cafe *Diner* ▽ 20 | 12 | 18 | $17
Venice | 13329 W. Washington Blvd. (Walgrove Ave.) | 310-306-7829 | www.novelcafe.com
"You can't beat it for down-home breakfasts and lunches" declare fans of this "funky", "friendly" neighborhood "staple" in Venice known for its "generous" helpings of inexpensive Americana dished out in a "cute" setting decked out with knickknacks; critics call it "nothing special", but expect "long lines" on weekends nonetheless.

☑ M.B. Post *American* 28 | 23 | 24 | $46
Manhattan Beach | 1142 Manhattan Ave. (Manhattan Beach Blvd.) | 310-545-5405 | www.eatmbpost.com
The "innovative small plates" come out "fast and furious" at this New American "hot spot" in Manhattan Beach where chef David LeFevre (ex Water Grill) creates a true "foodie experience" with his "amazing" locavore fare; it's housed in a former post office with exposed rafters and reclaimed wood lending a "cool vibe" – just remember to "bring earplugs", your premium plastic and start with the biscuits.

M Café de Chaya *Vegetarian* 22 | 16 | 20 | $21
Melrose | 7119 Melrose Ave. (La Brea Ave.) | 323-525-0588
Beverly Hills | 9433 Brighton Way (Beverly Dr.) | 310-858-8459
www.mcafedechaya.com
"A score for vegans and omnivores alike", these Melrose and Beverly Hills macrobiotics make "healthy food that actually tastes good" with enough "tempting" fare that "even your most food-phobic friend will be happy"; servers are helpful in making suggestions and the spare settings boast "lots of celeb sightings too", so fans only "wish it were a bit cheaper."

McCormick & Schmick's *Seafood* 22 | 22 | 22 | $43
Downtown | US Bank Tower | 633 W. Fifth St. (Grand Ave.) | 213-629-1929
Beverly Hills | Two Rodeo | 206 N. Rodeo Dr. (Wilshire Blvd.) | 310-859-0434
El Segundo | 2101 Rosecrans Ave. (Parkway Dr.) | 310-416-1123
Pasadena | 111 N. Los Robles Ave. (Bet. Union & Walnut Sts.) | 626-405-0064
www.mccormickandschmicks.com
Ever "dependable", this "enjoyable", "high-end" seafood chain offers "quality" "traditional" fare in a "clubby" setting that's "great for a business lunch"; prices aren't cheap, but "happy hour is a steal" with deals on drinks and appetizers.

McKenna's on the Bay *Seafood/Steak* 21 | 24 | 22 | $43
Long Beach | 190 Marina Dr. (PCH) | 562-342-9411 | www.mckennasonthebay.com
"Sit outside and watch the boats come and go" at this Long Beach entry overlooking Alamitos Bay purveying "good catch of the day" and other surf 'n' turf items in a "relaxing" milieu; some say the "incredible" scenery is tempered by "indifferent food at dear prices", although

the "lively" bar scene and a patio that's "perfect for lunch on a sunny day" redeem it for many.

Mediterraneo *Mediterranean*   22 | 19 | 22 | $32

Hermosa Beach | 73 Pier Ave. (Hermosa Ave.) | 310-318-2666 | www.mediterraneohb.com

"Pretend you're on vacation" at this Hermosa Beach eatery on the pier, where you can sample "tasty" Med tapas that are "fun to share" and "pitchers of sangria" while "enjoying the lovely weather and the never-ending parade of beachy hipsters"; service is "friendly", prices are manageable and "if you can make happy hour, all the better!"

Mediterraneo *Mediterranean*   21 | 23 | 21 | $40

Westlake Village | 32037 Agoura Rd. (Lakeview Canyon Rd.) | 818-889-9105 | www.med-rest.com

The "charming patio" with water views may be the "highlight" at this Westlake Village Mediterranean whose upscale-modern decor creates an equally "pleasant atmosphere" indoors; most find the "varied" menu "well prepared", if "a bit pricey", although "attentive service" takes the sting off, and happy-hour specials at the bar bring some relief.

Meet French Bistro *French*   24 | 19 | 23 | $37

Culver City | 9727 Culver Blvd. (Duquesne Ave.) | 310-815-8222 | www.meetrestaurantla.com

Channeling the "Champs-Élysées", this "cute, little" sidewalk cafe in Culver City "out-Frenches" the rest with bistro fare so "authentic" "you can tell the recipes are out of someone's grandmother's kitchen"; with "warm" service and "reasonable tariffs", it's a "winner" all around; P.S. it's also a "mussel-lover's heaven" on Tuesdays and Wednesdays.

🔲 Mélisse 🔳🅼 *American/French*   28 | 26 | 27 | $120

Santa Monica | 1104 Wilshire Blvd. (11th St.) | 310-395-0881 | www.melisse.com

Admirers insist it "doesn't get any better" than this "stunning" Santa Monica French–New American from Josiah Citrin known for its "impeccable" prix fixe menus based on the seasons, "deep wine list" and "seamless service" that's "pampering without being obsequious"; it also features a "civilized" atmosphere "where your ears are not assaulted by the noise level", so even if some call it "just a bit outdated", the majority deems it "well worth the pennies."

Mel's Drive-In *American*   18 | 19 | 19 | $17

Hollywood | 1650 N. Highland Ave. (Hollywood Blvd.) | 323-465-2111
West Hollywood | 8585 W. Sunset Blvd. (Londonderry Pl.) | 310-854-7200 ●
Sherman Oaks | 14846 Ventura Blvd. (Kester Ave.) | 818-990-6357 ●
www.melsdrive-in.com

"True Americana, from the jukeboxes to the burgers", this "fun" throwback chain caters to kids and "nostalgic" types with "reliable" updated American eats at "decent prices"; detractors call it "touristy" and "nothing special", but even they concede that the late-night hours "rock around the clock."

Melting Pot *Fondue*   23 | 21 | 21 | $51

Torrance | 21525 Hawthorne Blvd. (Carson St.) | 310-316-7500
(continued)

(continued)

Melting Pot

Pasadena | 88 W. Colorado Blvd. (bet. De Lacey & Pasadena Aves.) | 626-792-1941

Westlake Village | 3685 E. Thousand Oaks Blvd. (bet. Duesenberg Dr. & Westlake Blvd.) | 805-370-8802

www.meltingpot.com

"Return to the '70s" via this "fun", "unique" chain inducing "food co-mas" with a variety of fondue, from "gooey melted cheese" to chocolate pots worth "saving room for"; though the "dark", "romantic" setting works for a "special" night out, foes find the fare "overpriced" and "mediocre", and wonder if "once may be enough."

Mendocino Farms *Sandwiches*   25 | 16 | 22 | $15

Downtown | California Plaza | 300 S. Grand Ave. (W. 4th St.) | 213-620-1114 🖂

Downtown | Citibank Bldg. | 444 S. Flower St. (5th St.) | 213-627-3262 🖂

NEW **Fairfax** | 175 S. Fairfax Ave. (3rd St.) | 323-934-4261

NEW **West Hollywood** | 7100 Santa Monica Blvd. (La Brea Ave.) | 323-512-2700

Marina del Rey | 4724 Admiralty Way (PCH) | 310-822-2300

www.mendocinofarms.com

"Awesome, inventive sandwiches" stuffed with ultra-"fresh" locally sourced ingredients lure "obsessed" fans to this "eco-conscious" fast-casual chainlet famed for its "life-changing" pork-belly banh mi and "impressive vegan selections"; lunch brings "lines out the door", but the staff "keeps things moving" and "could they be any friendlier?"

NEW Mercado *Mexican*   - | - | - | M

Santa Monica | 1416 Fourth St. (Santa Monica Blvd.) | 310-526-7121 | www.mercadosantamonica.com

This sibling of Yxta Cocina in Santa Monica offers an upmarket Mexican menu of Niman Ranch carne asada and Jidori chicken in a chipotle sauce; it's all served in a whitewashed space with high ceilings, long, distressed wood tables and a bar pouring more than 70 tequilas.

NEW Mercato di Vetro *Italian*   ∇ 26 | 24 | 23 | $49

West Hollywood | 9077 Santa Monica Blvd. (N. Doheny Dr.) | 310-859-8369 | www.sbe.com

This "hip" Italian from Sam Nazarian's SBE Group brings a taste of la dolce vita to West Hollywood with a moderately priced Italian menu including pizzas and vino-friendly nibbles served to a "beautiful" crowd at a counter surrounding the antipasti bar or at polished wood tables; it's a total "scene", so "go early or take earplugs" if you want to avoid the din; P.S. there's also a mercato where you can buy oils, pastas and more.

Mezze *Mediterranean*   24 | 21 | 22 | $49

West Hollywood | 401 N. La Cienega Blvd. (bet. Beverly Blvd. & Rosewood Ave.) | 310-657-4103 | www.mezzela.com

"All I can say is 'yum'" sums up this "sensational" WeHo restaurant from Micah Wexler (ex Craft) whipping up "idiosyncratic, intelligent" "delicacies" "perfect for sharing" using "traditional ingredients from all over the Mediterranean in brilliant combinations"; the "beautiful" "sunwashed" tiled space feels like "a night out in Marrakesh", while "gracious" service makes the somewhat "dear prices" easier to handle.

	FOOD	DECOR	SERVICE	COST

Miceli's *Italian*   20 | 22 | 21 | $28

Hollywood | 1646 N. Las Palmas Ave. (Hollywood Blvd.) | 323-466-3438
Universal City | 3655 Cahuenga Blvd. W. (Fredonia Dr.) | 323-851-3344
www.micelisrestaurant.com

"The singing waiters are a kick" at this "corny", "old-school" Hollywood haunt and its Universal City sib slinging "saucy" inexpensive Italiana and "gooey" pizzas in "dark", moody digs that "would make Tony Soprano and his gang very comfortable"; those who are "not super-thrilled" about the menu or service say it lives off its "novelty", while defenders insist "a glass of wine will make the food more than tolerable."

☑ Michael's on Naples Ristorante *Italian*   28 | 25 | 26 | $56

Long Beach | 5620 E. Second St. (Ravenna Dr.) | 562-439-7080 |
www.michaelsonnaples.com

Locals "can't come up with enough superlatives" for this "rare" Long Beach "treasure", an Italian "fine-dining" destination for "exquisite" market-driven dishes elevated by "wonderful wines" and "on-point" service; indeed, it's "pricey", but the "romantic" setting is "perfect for a special occasion" and "viewing the sunset from the rooftop bar" is a treat.

☑ Michael's Pizzeria *Pizza*   28 | 20 | 24 | $23

Long Beach | 5616 E. Second St. (Ravenna Dr.) | 562-987-4000 |
www.michaelspizzeria.com

An offshoot of the venerable Michael's on Naples, this "fabulous" Long Beach pizzeria loads up its "heavenly", "authentic" Neapolitan pies with "fresh", homemade mozz, plus more "creative" items like clams, egg and baby artichokes; with "excellent service" and "modest prices", the "simple", "noisy" setting is easily excused.

Michael's Restaurant ☒ *Californian*   25 | 26 | 26 | $67

Santa Monica | 1147 Third St. (bet. California Ave. & Wilshire Blvd.) | 310-451-0843 | www.michaelssantamonica.com

This longtime "icon" of SoCal cuisine in Santa Monica "hasn't lost its touch", still impressing well-heeled guests with "sensational" seasonal fare from Michael McCarty and "exquisite", "professional" service offered in an art-filled dining room or on a "transporting" patio ("one of the most beautiful on the Westside"); indeed, it's "quite expensive", but "still very good for a special evening."

Mijares *Mexican*   20 | 18 | 21 | $22

Pasadena | 145 Palmetto Dr. (S. Pasadena Ave.) | 626-792-2763
Pasadena | 1806 E. Washington Blvd. (N. Allen Ave.) |
626-794-6674
www.mijaresrestaurant.com

"A truly old-school temple of Cal-Mex cuisine", this Pasadena standby has been serving "solid", "gringo-friendly" eats and "strong margaritas" at "bargain prices" since 1920; add in a "comfy" bar and "beautiful" patio and it's undeniably "popular"; P.S. the small Washington Boulevard outpost is best for takeout.

Mike & Anne's Ⓜ *American*   21 | 18 | 18 | $35

South Pasadena | 1040 Mission St. (Fairview Ave.) | 626-799-7199 |
www.mikeandannes.com

Both the "beautiful" twinkle-lit patio overlooking a garden and the well-priced New American "classics with a modern touch" are a "breath of fresh air" at this South Pasadena standby that's especially "enjoyable" on "warm summer evenings"; perhaps "service can be unreliable and curt when it gets busy", but on the whole it's a "nice, neighborhood spot."

Milk *Sandwiches* | 22 | 13 | 17 | $13 |

Mid-City | 7290 Beverly Blvd. (Poinsettia Pl.) | 323-939-6455 | www.themilkshop.com

The name says it all at this pint-sized purveyor of "melty" milky treats in Mid-City, where "fabulous shakes" and "amazing" ice creams share menu space with less-acclaimed sandwiches and other "decent" quick-bite fare at moderate cost; the setting and service aren't much to speak of, but "there are a handful of tables and some outdoor seating perfect for a sunny day."

Milky Way *Californian/Kosher* | ∇ 21 | 21 | 25 | $31 |

Pico-Robertson | 9108 W. Pico Blvd. (Doheny Dr.) | 310-859-0004

"Chatty" owner Leah Adler (aka Steven Spielberg's mom) "greets you at the door" of this "lovely, little" Pico-Robertson Cal-kosher putting out dairy "comfort food" "at its finest" like blintzes, salads and pastas; a few find the eats "unremarkable", but the "welcoming" service, "homey", "comfortable" ambiance and prices deemed "very reasonable by LA standards" mean "you'll leave satisfied."

NEW Milo & Olive *American* | 25 | 17 | 20 | $30 |

Santa Monica | 2723 Wilshire Blvd. (Harvard St.) | 310-453-6776 | www.miloandolive.com

"Another winner" from the folks behind Huckleberry and Rustic Canyon, this "instant hot spot" in Santa Monica features a "finely curated" array of near-"perfect" "gourmet" pizzas, affordable "market-inspired" New American small plates and "fabulous" breads and sweets (including vegan and gluten-free goodies); given the "long waits" for a seat at the "cramped" communal tables, fans "only wish is that it were twice the size" – luckily it's "great for takeout."

Mi Piace ● *Californian/Italian* | 22 | 21 | 19 | $33 |

Pasadena | 25 E. Colorado Blvd. (bet. Fair Oaks & Raymond Aves.) | 626-795-3131 | www.mipiace.com

This "classy" Californian-Italian in Old Town Pasadena is a find for an "excellent variety" of "crave-worthy carbs" (for instance, their standout bread basket and gnocchi), plus other "tasty" fare served in a "modern" setting completed with stellar "people-watching" from the patio; true, service is "hit-or-miss" and "the tables are so close together you can partake in your neighbors conversation", but "value" prices compensate.

The Misfit ● *Eclectic* | 22 | 24 | 21 | $34 |

Santa Monica | 225 Santa Monica Blvd. (2nd St.) | 310-656-9800 | www.themisfitrestaurant.com

This "cool" Santa Monica gastropub resembling "a high-end library" is a "fun" place to graze on Eclectic small plates ("a little of this, a little of that") with "expertly mixed" cocktails to wash it all down; factor in "fair prices" and "prompt" service, and consensus is it's a "great addition to the neighborhood"; P.S. the "free chocolate chip cookies with sea salt are the perfect ending."

	FOOD	DECOR	SERVICE	COST

Mistral *French*

26 | 23 | 25 | $54

Sherman Oaks | 13422 Ventura Blvd. (bet. Dixie Canyon & Greenbush Aves.) | 818-981-6650 | www.mistralrestaurant.net

"They go out of their way to make you feel special" at this "quaint" Sherman Oaks mainstay and "neighborhood favorite" for 25 years that's "like a trip to Paris" with "wonderful" French bistro standards and an "elegant" wood-paneled room adorned with artwork and chandeliers; yes, it's "expensive", but regulars report they've "never had a bad meal here"; P.S. "reservations are a must."

NEW Mo-Chica ● ☒ *Peruvian*

24 | 8 | 16 | $26

Downtown | 514 W. Seventh St. (bet. Grand Ave. & Olive St.) | 213-622-3744 | www.mo-chica.com

What began as a stand in Downtown's Mercado La Paloma has grown to a full-service sit-down restaurant where Ricardo Zarate whips up "intriguing, but accessible", "delicious" Peruvian fare like "daily ceviches and other splendors" deemed a "revelation"; there's a full bar pouring pisco cocktails and a hip graffiti look, but best of all, the prices are still relatively "cheap."

Modo Mio Cucina Rustica *Italian*

23 | 20 | 24 | $39

Pacific Palisades | 15200 W. Sunset Blvd. (La Cruz Dr.) | 310-459-0979 | www.modomiocucinarustica.com

A "solid" bet in Pacific Palisades, this "inviting" trattoria dishes out "moderately priced", "hearty" Italian in "warm" white-tablecloth environs; with "wonderful", "professional service" and a "relaxing" vibe, it's no wonder some call it the "perfect neighborhood restaurant."

2 NEW Mohawk Bend ● *Eclectic*

24 | 27 | 21 | $28

Echo Park | 2141 W. Sunset Blvd. (N. Alvarado St.) | 213-483-2337 | www.mohawk.la

"Vegans and carnivores coexist" at this "hip" Echo Park gastropub spotlighting "inventive", well-priced Eclectic plates, plus an "unparalleled" beer selection (the "knowledgeable staff" knows its brews too); it's situated in a "magnificent" "beautifully converted" movie theater with worn brick walls and a spacious patio with an immense fireplace making for a "charming" milieu for "hanging out", day or night.

Momed *Mediterranean*

22 | 15 | 19 | $23

Beverly Hills | 233 S. Beverly Dr. (bet. Charleville Blvd. & Gregory Way) | 310-270-4444 | www.atmomed.com

The name of this Bev Hills marketplace and deli is short for 'modern Mediterranean', and diners dig the "updated", "fresh", "healthy" takes on the standards like dips, meze and wraps served up "fast"; given such "great value", the all-white digs are frequently "crowded" – luckily it's also "good for takeout."

Monsieur Marcel *French*

21 | 15 | 19 | $31

Fairfax | Farmers Mkt. | 6333 W. Third St. (Fairfax Ave.) | 323-939-7792
Santa Monica | Third St. Promenade | 1260 Third St. Promenade (Arizona Ave.) | 310-587-1166
www.mrmarcel.com

"A taste of the Left Bank" can be found at these "pleasant" "cozy bistros" tucked into the Farmers Market (with an adjacent gourmet market) and in Santa Monica, where locals linger over "simple" French fare and "nicely priced wines"; added perks are "prompt service" and "great people-watching" at both branches.

Monsoon Cafe *Asian*

21 | **24** | **21** | **$31**

Santa Monica | Third St. Promenade | 1212 Third St. Promenade (Arizona Ave.) | 310-576-9996 | www.globaldiningca.com

"See and be seen" at this "date"-worthy Pan-Asian on The Promenade in Santa Monica with a massive space decked out like a "colonial mansion" with semi-private booths and serving a "broad", "dependable" array of eats and "exotic" cocktails; service is "hit-or-miss", but pricing's affordable and it boasts one of "the sexiest happy hours in town."

Monte Alban *Mexican*

23 | **15** | **20** | **$20**

West LA | 11929 Santa Monica Blvd. (Brockton Ave.) | 310-444-7736 | www.montealbanrestaurante.com

Amigos "savor every bite" of the "authentic" Oaxacan dishes like "wonderfully complex moles" at this strip-mall "gem" in West LA where the "servers work hard to take care of their patrons"; Mexican murals add a "cheerful" note to the plain storefront setting, though watch out, "it can get mobbed on the weekends – a testament to the food" and the modest prices.

Monty's Steakhouse *Steak*

22 | **20** | **23** | **$61**

Woodland Hills | 5371 Topanga Canyon Blvd. (Ventura Blvd.) | 818-716-9736 | www.montysprimesteakandseafood.com

"Gargantuan steaks" and "strong drinks" headline the "manly" menu at this Woodland Hills steakhouse, a "Valley mainstay" for over 22 years tended by a "friendly, pro" staff; its fans adore the "old-school feel" with large Naugahyde booths, although critics call it simply "outdated" and "not a very good value", either.

Moonshadows *American*

21 | **24** | **19** | **$44**

Malibu | 20356 PCH (bet. Big Rock Dr. & Las Flores Canyon Rd.) | 310-456-3010 | www.moonshadowsmalibu.com

"Bring a ring – the answer will be yes" insist admirers of this ultra-"romantic" Malibu New American perched over the Pacific and offering "stunning views"; given such an "amazing" setting, many find the "pricey" food to be "an afterthought", but sipping "strong drinks" on the tiki-themed patio is always "a delight."

Morels French Steakhouse & Bistro *French/Steak*

20 | **22** | **21** | **$61**

Fairfax | The Grove | 189 The Grove Dr. (bet. Beverly Blvd. & 3rd St.) | 323-965-9595 | www.mcchgroup.com

Bringing moules mariniere and filet mignon to the masses is this pricey French steakhouse and bistro in The Grove offering "good" eats, an upscale setting and some mighty-fine "people-watching" from the outdoor patio on ground level and balcony up above; some call the food and service "hit-and-miss", although a chef change may remedy that.

More Than Waffles *American*

23 | **14** | **22** | **$16**

Encino | 17200 Ventura Blvd. (bet. Amestoy & Louise Aves.) | 818-789-5937 | www.morethanwaffles.com

"Light, crisp" Belgian waffles are "served a gazillion ways" at this "bang-for-the-buck" breakfast entry in Encino also offering "terrific" omelets and other American daytime fare that fans happily "scarf down"; it's "jammed on weekends", but staffers "try hard to please", and there's often even free coffee while you wait.

🆕 Morinoya 🗷 *Japanese*

| – | – | – | M |

West LA | 11301 W. Olympic Blvd. (Sawtelle Blvd.) | 310-473-3960 | www.restaurant-morinoya.com

This elegant-looking, modestly priced West LA Japanese izakaya is a peaceful destination for small dishes and sake – little tastes like whitefish carpaccio or mini hot pots; the master behind it all is chef Takayuki 'Mori' Morishita, a three-decade veteran of the LA sushi wars who presides over the refined room with hanging banners and subtle framed art.

🛛 Mori Sushi 🗷 *Japanese*

| 27 | 17 | 24 | $88 |

West LA | 11500 W. Pico Blvd. (Gateway Blvd.) | 310-479-3939

The omakase is an "incredible experience" at this "high-quality, traditional" West LA Japanese that wows with "delicate, delectable sushi" crafted with specially grown rice and served by an "efficient, courteous" crew on handcrafted ceramics; a few find prices "out of line" with the "understated", "casual" surroundings, but the majority insists "it's an experience that you won't soon forget."

Morton's The Steakhouse *Steak*

| 26 | 24 | 26 | $70 |

Downtown | Seventh and Fig | 735 S. Figueroa St. (bet. 7th & 8th Sts.) | 213-553-4566
Beverly Hills | 435 S. La Cienega Blvd. (Colgate Ave.) | 310-246-1501
Burbank | The Pinnacle | 3400 W. Olive Ave. (Lima St.) | 818-238-0424
Woodland Hills | Warner Ctr. | 6250 Canoga Ave. (bet. Erwin St. & Victory Blvd.) | 818-703-7272
www.mortons.com

This "classic" chophouse chain is a "first choice" for many, thanks to its "fabulous" steaks, "superior" sides and "excellent wines" served in "sophisticated", "men's club" settings; bills can be "astronomically high", but with almost "embarrassingly attentive" service, most agree it's "worth it" for special occasions.

Mo's *American*

| 19 | 15 | 19 | $23 |

Burbank | 4301 W. Riverside Dr. (N. Rose St.) | 818-845-3009 | www.eatatmos.com

Burbank's answer to *Cheers* is this "friendly" American with its "inexpensive" array of "comforting" fare that's "dependable", even if it "won't set the world on fire"; the setting's "plain", and "dark", but it's a nexus for "media moguls' power breakfasts" nonetheless.

🛛 Mosto Enoteca *Italian*

| 27 | 19 | 26 | $49 |

Marina del Rey | Marina Connection | 517 Washington Blvd. (Via Marina) | 310-821-3035 | www.mostoenoteca.com

A "real sleeper" "hidden" in a Marina del Rey strip mall, this "fine" dinner-only Italian is a find for "genuine" "handmade pastas like grandma would make" to go with an impressive wine list; it can be "expensive", but pays off with "polished" service and a "romantic" vibe.

Mozza to Go *Pizza*

| 26 | 17 | 21 | $34 |

West Hollywood | 6610 Melrose Ave. (Highland Ave.) | 323-297-1130 | www.mozza2go.com

"When you can't get in" to Pizzeria Mozza, this West Hollywood annex is an "amazing" "fallback" offering "easy access" to Mario Batali and

Nancy Silverton's "exceptional" pizzas, "crispy, fennel-laden porchetta", lasagna and such "without the crazy waits" or reservation hassle; counter service is "efficient" too, and even if it's not cheap, the delivery service could "change [your] life", so put it "on speed dial"; P.S. there's also a small on-site market that's "superb for upscale picnics."

Mr. Chow ● *Chinese*　24 | 22 | 23 | $73

Beverly Hills | 344 N. Camden Dr. (bet. Brighton Way & Dayton Way) | 310-278-9911 | www.mrchow.com

It's "celebrity-spotting central" at this "hip", "legendary" Beverly Hills Chinese, a "high-energy" haunt ("an elegant zoo") where both stars and "normal folks" tuck into "refined" fare served in a "chic" black-and-white setting graced with original Warhols; fans call it a "must-go at least once" just to "see what the hullabaloo is all about", although many find both the "super-high" prices and the "snooty" service a little "over the top."

M Street Kitchen *American*　21 | 18 | 19 | $25

Santa Monica | 2000 N. Main St. (Pico Blvd.) | 310-396-9145 | www.mstreetkitchen.com

This "vibrant" neighborhood American in Santa Monica dishes up a "fine, but not memorable" "comfort-food" menu morning, noon and night; "affordable" tabs, a "laid-back" staff and a pet-friendly patio keep it "buzzing" with a "great vibe."

Mucho Ultima Mexicana *Mexican*　26 | 24 | 24 | $36

Manhattan Beach | 903 Manhattan Ave. (9th St.) | 310-374-4422 | www.muchomb.com

A "young, hip" crowd digs the "modern Mexican" cuisine and potent margaritas made from an "extensive" array of tequilas at this "high-end" cantina in Manhattan Beach; the "beautiful" "dimly" lit orange-and-red room may be "perfect for a date", although many favor it for the "happening bar scene" that runs late into the night.

Mulberry Street Pizzeria *Pizza*　23 | 12 | 19 | $16

Beverly Hills | 240 S. Beverly Dr. (bet. Charleville Blvd. & Gregory Way) | 310-247-8100
Beverly Hills | 347 N. Cañon Dr. (bet. Brighton & Dayton Ways) | 310-247-8998
Encino | 17040 Ventura Blvd. (Oak Park Ave.) | 818-906-8881
Sherman Oaks | 15136 Ventura Blvd. (Columbus & Noble Aves.) | 818-784-8880
www.mulberrypizzeria.com

For "real-deal" New York pizza, it's hard to beat this "no-frills" Italian chain offering "monstrously huge" slices and pies with "crispy crusts and chewy, stretchy cheese" served in "nothing-fancy" digs with "copies of the *NY Post* laying around"; with "appropriate attitude" from the counter staff, it "feels like you're back in the city" – "fold your slice in half and *mangia*."

Musashi *Japanese*　25 | 20 | 22 | $27

Northridge | 9046 Tampa Ave. (Nordhoff St.) | 818-701-7041 | www.musashirestaurant.com

This Northridge Japanese is "well-rounded" to say the least, offering "fresh" sushi, tempura-laden platters and "fun" communal teppanyaki tables with meats cooked up "Benihana"-style right before your eyes; the casual, "comfortable" setting can be "quiet" or "boisterous" depending on the crowd, but "friendly" service and "reasonable prices" are constants.

Musha *Japanese*   23 | 15 | 19 | $37

Santa Monica | 424 Wilshire Blvd. (bet. 4th & 5th Sts.) | 310-576-6330 ◐
Torrance | 1725 W. Carson St. (Western Ave.) | 310-787-7344
www.musha.us

Musha Izakaya *Japanese*

NEW Pasadena | 58 E. Colorado Blvd. (S. Raymond Ave.) | 626-576-6330
"Innovative and different", this "small-plates Japanese" trio is "fun for groups" with an "adventurous" array of well-priced dishes ("you can't go without trying the risotto served in a Parmesan wheel the size of a table drum"); expect "cheerful service" and a "noisy", "vibrant" atmosphere that "feels like you're in Tokyo."

Musso & Frank Grill 🚫Ⓜ️ *American*   23 | 23 | 23 | $43

Hollywood | 6667 Hollywood Blvd. (bet. Cherokee & Las Palmas Aves.) | 323-467-7788 | www.mussoandfrank.com
A "landmark" dating back to 1919, this "LA classic" is Hollywood's oldest restaurant ("the waiters may also be the oldest") where "you can almost imagine Faulkner and Fitzgerald guzzling" martinis amid the "nostalgic" dark-wood-and-red-booth setting; the Traditional American "steak and potatoes" menu is a little "pricey", but the service from "old pros" is "admirable", and fans say it's a "must-visit for the history" alone.

Z Nanbankan *Japanese*   27 | 16 | 23 | $38

West LA | 11330 Santa Monica Blvd. (Corinth Ave.) | 310-478-1591 | www.nanbankan.com
A "fantastic find" for "skewer cooking over a real charcoal grill", this "tiny" Santa Monica Japanese offers "little robata bites so tasty and reasonable, you can graze through many dishes and come away with change in your pocket"; the "welcoming" chefs "foster a party atmosphere" (it's also a "total date-night spot"), so "sit at the counter and make some new friends."

Napa Valley Grille *Californian*   19 | 22 | 20 | $41

Westwood | 1100 Glendon Ave. (Lindbrook Dr.) | 310-824-3322 | www.napavalleygrille.com
It's like a road trip to "wine country" at this "sophisticated", "yuppie" Westwood mainstay offering "an aging but appealing" Cal menu incorporating "fresh, local produce" and "great wines (no surprise)"; the mood is conducive to "quiet conversation" and service is "attentive" too, although some find it "a tad overpriced" for food that's "dependable, but nothing too exciting."

Naples Rib Co. *BBQ*   26 | 19 | 23 | $33

Long Beach | 5800 E. Second St. (Campo Walk) | 562-439-7427 | www.ribcompany.com
"Rockin' ribs" and other "meaty, tender" 'cue in helpings so "ample" "you can skip the appetizer" make this Long Beach stop a "go-to" for "lots of food for little money"; it's not fancy, but both the service and the woody dining room are "pleasant" enough, and takeout is also popular.

	FOOD	DECOR	SERVICE	COST

Natalee Thai *Thai*
21 | 17 | 19 | $23

Beverly Hills | 998 S. Robertson Blvd. (W. Olympic Blvd.) | 310-855-9380
Palms | 10101 Venice Blvd. (Clarington Ave.) | 310-202-7003
www.nataleethai.com

This "sleek" Thai twosome in Beverly Hills and Palms provides "spicy", "well-prepared" dishes along with cocktails in "fun", "noisy" environs deemed "upscale" for the genre, although at fairly "reasonable" prices; it's often "bustling" and servers move the "crowds" quickly, however, some customers complain about the "hurried" pace

Nate 'n Al *Deli*
20 | 12 | 18 | $25

Beverly Hills | 414 N. Beverly Dr. (bet. Brighton Way & Santa Monica Blvd.) | 310-274-0101
NEW LAX | LA Int'l Airport, Terminal 2 | 209 World Way (Sepulveda Blvd.) | 310-646-4680 ●
www.natenal.com

"Eat *bubbala* eat!" at this "classic Jewish deli" in Beverly Hills and its LAX satellite, an area "institution" that's "close to the hearts" of aficionados of "juicy" pastrami, chopped liver and other "comfort foods" "washed down with Dr. Browns"; "you don't go for the ambiance, because there isn't any", but service is "entertaining" and in all, it's "one of the last" of its kind; P.S. there's "usually a Larry King sighting" at breakfast.

Native Foods Café *Vegan*
25 | 17 | 22 | $17

Culver City | 9343 Culver Blvd. (Canfield Ave.) | 310-559-3601
Santa Monica | 2901 Ocean Park Blvd. (bet. 29th & 30th Sts.) | 310-450-3666
Westwood | 1114 Gayley Ave. (Wilshire Blvd.) | 310-209-1055
www.nativefoods.com

Even "carnivores dig" the meat-free eats at this growing Californian-Eclectic vegan chain churning out "evolved hippie food", from "gorgeous salads" and "fake chicken wings" to "desserts that are a blessing to lactose-intolerant people everywhere"; the setups are rather "basic", but there's "fast", "friendly" counter service and it's "not too expensive" either.

Nawab of India *Indian*
24 | 17 | 22 | $32

Santa Monica | 1621 Wilshire Blvd. (bet. 16th & 17th Sts.) | 310-829-1106 | www.nawabindia.com

A "favorite curry house" of many, this "reliable" Santa Monica Indian lures locals with "fresh", "fabulous" masalas and vindaloos that vary in heat "from mild to wow"; some find it a little "expensive" for the genre, but service is "amiable", the space is relatively "elegant" and there's a "bargain" lunch buffet too.

NBC Seafood *Chinese/Seafood*
21 | 14 | 16 | $23

Monterey Park | 404 S. Atlantic Blvd. (bet. Harding & Newmark Aves.) | 626-282-2323 | www.nbcrestaurant.com

For decades this Monterey Park Chinese banquet hall has been a "popular" pick for "solid", "authentic" dim sum rolled out on carts and Cantonese seafood; although some complain of "bare-bones service" and say the "decor has seen better days", it's still good for groups, so "go hungry", "get there early" and enjoy.

Neptune's Net *Seafood*

20 | 13 | 14 | $21

Malibu | 42505 PCH (Yerba Buena Rd.) | 310-457-3095 |
www.neptunesnet.com

"A seaside vacation and lunch all in one", this Malibu shack is a find
for "super-fresh" fish and "beers galore" served at picnic tables overlooking the ocean; it's a "favorite" for "tourists, bikers and locals", even
if service comes with "attitude" and a few find it a bit "overpriced" too;
P.S. hours can be erratic, so call ahead.

New Capital Seafood ⚫ *Seafood*

23 | 16 | 15 | $20

San Gabriel | 140 W. Valley Blvd. (S. Del Mar Ave.) | 626-288-1899
"It gets crowded quickly – that's how you know it's good" pronounce
fans of this cavernous San Gabriel seafooder hawking "high-quality"
"flavorful" dim sum and Cantonese shellfish for "cheap"; just "go
early, especially on weekends", and know that service is "fast" once
you're seated; P.S. it's open till 1 AM.

New Moon *Chinese*

24 | 20 | 22 | $24

Downtown | 102 W. Ninth St. (Main St.) | 213-624-0186 🛇
Montrose | 2138 Verdugo Blvd. (Clifton Pl.) | 818-249-4393
Valencia | Gateway Vill. | 28281 Newhall Ranch Rd. (Rye Canyon Rd.) |
661-257-4321
www.newmoonrestaurants.com

Furnishing "fresh", "updated" Chinese "for the American palate", this
trio "doesn't disappoint" with "wonderful" food (notably the "excellent"
soup and shrimp dishes) served by a "prompt" staff; "spacious" contemporary digs and a "varied, tempting drinks menu" make Montrose and
Valencia "a little more upscale" than the Downtown original.

Newport Seafood *Chinese/Seafood*

27 | 17 | 19 | $34

Rowland Heights | 18441 Colima Rd. (bet. Batson & Jellick Aves.) |
626-839-1239
San Gabriel | 518 W. Las Tunas Dr. (Santa Anita St.) | 626-289-5998
www.newportseafood.com

"Simply spectacular" seafood awaits at this Chinese duo moored in San
Gabriel and Rowland Heights incorporating Vietnamese, Cambodian
and Thai influences into the "fresh" fare, including the "must-have"
house special lobster "plucked fresh from the tanks" ("it's on every table"); with "fast, friendly" service and relatively "reasonable prices",
it's no wonder it draws "hordes of people every night."

NEW Next Door by Josie Ⓜ *American*

25 | 22 | 23 | $34

Santa Monica | 2420 Pico Blvd. (25th St.) | 310-581-4201 |
www.nextdoorbyjosie.com

"Craft cocktails and delicious bites, both large and small", attract "hip
foodies" to this "casual" Santa Monica sib of the venerable Josie's offering a less-expensive taste of Josie Le Balch's "imaginative" market-
driven New American menu; the mood is "friendly", but the "small"
footprint means it's "always crowded", but "worth the wait."

Nick & Stef's Steakhouse *Steak*

24 | 22 | 23 | $62

Downtown | Wells Fargo Ctr. | 330 S. Hope St. (bet. 3rd & 4th Sts.) |
213-680-0330 | www.patinagroup.com

"They know their steak" at this "luxurious" Downtown chophouse
from the Patina Group known for its "top-notch" beef dry-aged in an

"impressive glass-ensconced meat locker" and a "prompt" staff accustomed to "client lunches" and curtain calls (there's a free shuttle to the Music Center); many are "enamored" with the "elegant" vibe, less so the "à la carte" pricing.

Nickel Diner Ⓜ *Diner* | 23 | 18 | 21 | $20 |

Downtown | 524 S. Main St. (bet. 5th & 6th Sts.) | 213-623-8301 | www.nickeldiner.com

The "decadent" desserts – like housemade Pop Tarts and bacon-maple donuts – inspire "OMGs" at this "affordable" Downtown diner offering "clever twists" on American "comfort food" in a "tiny" vintage-inspired setting on the edge of Skid Row; the "staff's a little quirky", but that's part of the charm.

Nic's ❶Ⓧ *American* | 23 | 22 | 23 | $46 |

Beverly Hills | 453 N. Cañon Dr. (bet. Brighton Way & Santa Monica Blvd.) | 310-550-5707 | www.nicsbeverlyhills.com

"An unending list of vodkas" keeps the mood "fun" – especially for those who don "faux fur to brave the VodBox" (a walk-in exhibition freezer) – at this Beverly Hills boîte offering a "solid" New American menu; with "warm" hospitality and a "classy" vibe, many find it "expensive", but well "worth the price", and there's also a "superior" happy hour with deals on martinis, wines and small plates.

9021Pho *Vietnamese* | 22 | 19 | 21 | $23 |

Beverly Hills | 490 N. Beverly Dr. (Santa Monica Blvd.) | 310-275-5277
Westlake Village | 30990 Russell Ranch Rd. (Lindero Canyon Rd.) | 818-597-1902
www.9021pho.com

"Making bellies happy", this "welcoming" Vietnamese duo ladles out "big bowls" of "flavorful" noodle soups in a "bright" yet "sparse" Beverly Hills locale and more expansive Westlake Villager with two patios; though a few sticklers suggest it's made "for the masses", fans of the whole package declare it's "cheap" and "wonderpho"; P.S. a new Glendale Galleria location is planned for fall 2012.

Nishimura Ⓧ *Japanese* | ▽ 29 | 24 | 24 | $125 |

West Hollywood | 8684 Melrose Ave. (San Vicente Blvd.) | 310-659-4770

This "traditional" West Hollywood Japanese is a standard-bearer for "simple", "sublime" sushi and sashimi from "perfectionist" chef Hiro Nishimura, available à la carte or in an omakase; the entrance, hidden in a small garden, leads into a minimalist interior where no-rush service prevails, but watch out for the way-"expensive" bills.

N/Naka ⓍⓂ *Japanese* | ▽ 25 | 22 | 26 | $137 |

Palms | 3455 S. Overland Ave. (Palms Blvd.) | 310-836-6252 | www.n-naka.com

This omakase-only, ultrapricey Japanese on an industrial strip of Overland Avenue presents "perfectly crafted", "fascinating" feasts deemed "a delightful extravagance"; at the helm is chef Niki Nakayama – one of LA's few female Japanese culinarians – who uses "fabulous quality" ingredients, including veggies from the restaurant's organic garden, and oversees attentive service in the modern setting, making it an absolute "must for foodies."

Nobu Los Angeles *Japanese*

26 | 24 | 23 | $87

West Hollywood | 903 N. La Cienega Blvd. (bet. Santa Monica Blvd. & Sherwood Dr.) | 310-657-5711 | www.noburestaurants.com

"After all these years" "it's hard to top" the "exceptional" Peruvian-accented delicacies and "top-grade", "melt-in-your-mouth" sushi and sashimi from Nobu Matsuhisa at this West Hollywood Japanese where the "cutting-edge" David Rockwell–designed dining rooms are "swarming with elegant people", celebs and "wanna-be-seens"; service is usually "professional", but just know you're "paying a premium for the name."

❷ Nobu Malibu *Japanese*

27 | 21 | 25 | $86

Malibu | Malibu Country Mart | 22706 Pacific Coast Hwy. (Malibu Pier) | 310-317-9140 | www.noburestaurants.com

Though it's "much more low-key" than its West Hollywood sibling, Nobu Matsuhisa's Malibu Japanese still features "sublime", "novel" sushi and "delicious" Peruvian-inflected signatures that "have been copied at so many restaurants they almost sound pedestrian", delivered by a "stellar" staff; its locale right on the beach is "elegant" and "star-studded", just "take out a second mortgage before you go."

Noé *American*

21 | 23 | 22 | $54

Downtown | Omni Los Angeles Hotel | 251 S. Olive St. (3rd St.) | 213-356-4100 | www.noerestaurant.com

"Surprisingly good for a hotel restaurant" is the finding on this "pleasant pre-theater" stop in the Omni Downtown, where pricey New American fare is "creatively prepared" with Japanese flourishes in a "quiet, contemporary setting" adorned with "tasteful art"; it earns extra "points for being an overachiever" with a "lovely staff" and an "excellent late-night bar."

Noir Food & Wine *Eclectic*

24 | 19 | 22 | $43

Pasadena | 40 N. Mentor Ave. (Colorado Blvd.) | 626-795-7199 | www.noirfoodandwine.com

"You'll try wine you've never even heard of" at this "teeny" "hideaway" in Pasadena from Claud Beltran that "charms" locals with "terrific", "interesting" Eclectic small plates and "well-curated" vino pairings proffered by a "knowledgeable" staff; it's popular for pre-theater dining (Boston Court is nearby), even if a few lament the "small portions, big prices."

Nom Nom Truck 🅱🍴 *Vietnamese*

21 | 11 | 18 | $12

Location varies; see website | 323-639-3817 | www.nomnomtruck.com

The fusion-Vietnamese fare is particularly "nom-worthy" at this "cute" food truck with the monster mascot, which metes out "tasty" banh mi and tacos to "giant crowds" of devoted fans (aka "nomsters"); it's manned by the same "friendly" folks from when they appeared on Food Network's *Great Food Truck Race*, and prices are "incredibly low", so "chow down."

🆕 Nong La Cafe Ⓜ *Vietnamese*

– | – | – | I

West LA | 2055 Sawtelle Blvd. (Mississippi Ave.) | 310-268-1881 | www.nonglacafe.com

Adding to the Asian mix on Sawtelle Boulevard, this Vietnamese entry offers a menu built around Saigon favorites like hot steaming bowls of pho and chunky banh mi sandwiches; it's all served in a casually stylish space with reclaimed wood tables and chairs.

Nonna ☒ *Italian* ▽ 23 | 21 | 23 | $53

West Hollywood | 9255 W. Sunset Blvd. (bet. Doheny & Sierra Drs.) | 310-270-4455 | www.nonnaofitaly.com

"A restaurant for grown-ups", this "warm", "beautiful" West Hollywood trattoria puts out "excellent" "classical" Italian cuisine, including "crispy-crust" pizzas with a menu "varied enough to inspire repeat dining"; it's not inexpensive, but service is "welcoming", there's pleasant sidewalk seating and it's often "easy to get a table" too.

Noodle World *Asian* 19 | 13 | 16 | $14

Westwood | 1118 Westwood Blvd. (Lindbrook Dr.) | 310-208-0777
Pasadena | 24 W. Colorado Blvd. (bet. De Lacey & Fair Oaks Aves.) | 626-585-5885
San Marino | 932 Huntington Dr. (Chelsea Rd.) | 626-300-1010
Alhambra | 700 W. Valley Blvd. (bet. 7th & 8th Sts.) | 626-293-8800 ●⊅
www.noodleworld.com

"All kinds of noodle dishes from different cultures" are offered at "bang-for-your-buck" prices at this Asian chainlet that may not be "authentic", but which sates cravings with a "huge assortment" of slurp-worthy, globe-trotting dishes, from pad Thai to lo mein to ramen; most are too busy eating to notice uneven service and casual decor "that could be better."

Nook Bistro *American* 24 | 19 | 24 | $36

West LA | Plaza West | 11628 Santa Monica Blvd. (Barry Ave.) | 310-207-5160 | www.nookbistro.com

"Hidden away in a strip mall", this Santa Monica "gem" is "well worth the search" thanks to "wholesome", "delicious" American cooking that puts "interesting" Eclectic "twists on old classics"; a "well-curated wine selection" and "attentive servers" make for a near-"perfect neighborhood spot", with a "minimal", "noisy" space as the only setback.

Noshi Sushi Ⓜ *Japanese* 24 | 13 | 19 | $30

Koreatown | 4430 Beverly Blvd. (N. Hobart Blvd.) | 323-469-3458 | www.noshisushila.com

In a "highly unlikely Koreatown location" dwells this "popular" Japanese "delivering better-than-expected" sushi and sashimi for a "reasonable price"; there's "no fancy rolls", just "large portions" of "basic" "quality fish" that come out "fast" and furious in no-frills digs – for sushi-philes, "it's one of the best values in town."

Nyala Ethiopian *Ethiopian* 25 | 19 | 20 | $25

Mid-Wilshire | 1076 S. Fairfax Ave. (bet. Olympic Blvd. & Whitworth Dr.) | 323-936-5918 | www.nyala-la.com

"Terrific Ethiopian food" awaits at this "festive" art-filled find, in Mid-Wilshire's Little Ethiopia, known for its stews, which patrons scoop up using "excellent" injera bread; "gracious" service and "reasonable prices" also help explain why it's one of "the best in town", and "a great place for the uninitiated" to get an introduction to the cuisine.

Obika Mozzarella *Italian* 23 | 18 | 20 | $30

Beverly Boulevard | Beverly Ctr. | 8500 Beverly Blvd. (La Cienega Blvd.) | 310-652-2088

(continued)

Obika Mozzarella
Century City | Westfield Century City Shopping Ctr. |
10250 Santa Monica Blvd. (Ave. of the Stars) | 310-556-2452 |
www.obika.it

"You can't go wrong with a menu based on cheese" say formaggio fans
who frequent this Italian duo for its "tender, fresh" mozzarella and meats
"flown in from Italy", along with "simple" pizza, panini and pasta; with
"courteous" service and mod decor, it's an "interesting concept" for a
mall even if some call it a tad "expensive" for a "shopping break."

Ocean Ave. Seafood   *Seafood*   24 | 22 | 22 | $51
Santa Monica | 1401 Ocean Ave. (Santa Monica Blvd.) | 310-394-5669 |
www.oceanave.com

"Go hungry", "ask for a table near the windows" and "order the oyster
platter" advise afishionados tucking into a "broad" variety of "delicious", "high-quality" fin fare at this "busy" Santa Monica seafooder
across from the ocean and "handy to the Promenade"; service is "efficient", and although most consider it a "reliable" "beachfront" bet, a
few critics note it "should be better for the price."

The Ocean Park Omelette Parlor   *American*   20 | 18 | 19 | $18
Santa Monica | 2732 Main St. (bet. Ashland Ave. & Hill St.) |
310-399-7892 | www.theomeletteparlor.com

A "staple for breakfast" in Santa Monica, this "cute, little" parlor proffers "excellent omelets" and "generous" helpings of other American
breakfast and lunch items deemed "not innovative", but "solid"; "be
prepared to wait on weekends", but "quick service", "great prices" and
"comfortable seating" compensate.

Ocean Seafood   *Chinese/Seafood*   23 | 16 | 17 | $25
Chinatown | 750 N. Hill St. (bet. Alpine & Ord Sts.) | 213-687-3088 |
www.oceansf.com

There's "dim sum and then some" at this "cavernous" Downtown
Chinese, where the "authentic" fare from "marvelous" dumplings to
"heavenly" seafood is rolled out by servers willing "to explain what everything is"; some find the tabs "high compared to others" in the area,
but the "decent" decor with chandeliers and artwork makes up for it.

Ocean Star   *Chinese*   22 | 15 | 19 | $24
Monterey Park | 145 N. Atlantic Blvd. (bet. Emerson & Garvey Aves.) |
626-308-2128 | www.oceanstarrestaurant.com

"Darn-good dim sum" for just a small sum is the verdict on this "gigantic"
Monterey Park Chinese that rolls out a seemingly "endless" array of "authentic" treats "fresh and hot"; despite a "chaotic" setting, service is
generally "attentive", even as the space keeps "hustling and bustling."

Ocean Tava   *Indian*   ▽ 24 | 21 | 21 | $23
Redondo Beach | 1212 S. PCH (Ave. E) | 310-540-2240 |
www.oceantava.com

Redondo Beach locals are all aglow about the "incredible" flavors at
this "fantastic, neighborhood" Indian, where the "reasonably priced"
dishes can be tailored "to the degree of spiciness that you want"; servers who "take care of their guests", patio seating with ocean views plus
a bargain lunch buffet more than make up for the strip-mall location.

	FOOD	DECOR	SERVICE	COST

Octopus *Japanese*

| 20 | 18 | 21 | $25 |

Downtown | 729 W. Seventh St. (S. Flower St.) | 213-402-1500
Long Beach | 200 Pine Ave. (B'way) | 562-901-2100
Burbank | 227 E. Palm Ave. (N. San Fernando Blvd.) | 818-556-6622
Encino | 16733 Ventura Blvd. (La Maida St.) | 818-380-0855
Glendale | 112 N. Maryland Ave. (bet. B'way & Wilson Ave.) | 818-500-8788
www.octopusrestaurant.com

The "amazing" twice-daily happy hours are the "reasons to come" to this "bargain" Japanese chain churning out "generous" slabs of "fresh" fish and "big", "creative" rolls; expect "quick", "friendly" service, a "spacious", "modern" setting and a "young" crowd.

Off Vine *Californian*

| 22 | 22 | 23 | $38 |

Hollywood | 6263 Leland Way (bet. El Centro Ave. & Vine St.) | 323-962-1900 | www.offvine.com

You might almost "forget you're in the heart of Hollywood" as you sit on the "charming" front porch of this "adorable" Craftsman cottage dispensing "homey" Cal-American cuisine with "gourmet" touches; "efficient, friendly servers" and "surprisingly reasonable prices" (including an "affordable" wine list) make it "perfect for pre- or post-ArcLight" dates; it's also "marvelous for brunch."

The Oinkster *BBQ*

| 22 | 13 | 17 | $14 |

Eagle Rock | 2005 Colorado Blvd. (Shearin Ave.) | 323-255-6465 | www.oinkster.com

"A hip crowd" queues up for "amazing" pastrami and "bacon-laden, cheese-tastic burgers", plus pulled pork and other "messy, delicious" sandwiches matched with "serious craft beers" at this "slow fast-food" Eagle Rock BBQ joint from Andre Guerrero; although regulars report "long lines" and "slow service", prices are a "deal", and the retro "diner" decor with a pleasant patio makes it a "fun place."

Old Tony's *Italian/Seafood*

| 23 | 23 | 25 | $39 |

Redondo Beach | 210 Fishermans Wharf (Coral Way) | 310-374-1442 | www.oldtonys.com

"Old-school Redondo Beach" lives on at this "friendly" Italian seafooder that's been reeling 'em in since 1952 with "famous mai tais" and "excellent" eats offered against a picturesque backdrop of "beautiful" ocean views; with weekend entertainment, late hours and "reasonable pricing", fans say "you gotta love it."

Olio Pizzeria & Cafe *Italian*

| 24 | 15 | 19 | $22 |

Third Street | 8075 W. Third St. (Crescent Heights Blvd.) | 323-930-9490 | www.pizzeriaolio.com

Chef-owner Bradford Kent "seemingly slaves over each individual pie" at this rustic "little" Italian on Third Street where the "incredible pizzas" coming out of the wood-burning oven are made with "only the freshest in-season ingredients"; service can be "spotty", and with only a few seats inside and out, many "opt for takeout."

Oliva *Italian*

| 21 | 19 | 21 | $34 |

Sherman Oaks | 4449 Van Nuys Blvd. (Moorpark St.) | 818-789-4490 | www.olivarestaurant.com

They "treat you like *famiglia*" at this Sherman Oaks local "full of happy people" tucking into "solid" pastas, risotto and Northern Italian spe-

cialties ("a well-stocked bar" helps the mood too); some say the muraled dining room "lost some of its charm" with a recent expansion,
but "value" pricing keeps it "packed every night."

Olive & Thyme Café Market 🗷 *Eclectic* | 22 | 21 | 18 | $22 |

Burbank | 4013 Riverside Dr. (Pass Ave.) | 818-557-1560 |
www.oliveandthyme.com

"A rare stylish treat" in "chain-happy Burbank", this "cute", "high-end"
cafe and market brings "delightful" Eclectic fare like sandwiches, salads, "amazing cheeses" and other "temptations" – plus Intelligentsia
coffee – to a "media" crowd; the whitewashed setting stocked with
gourmet goodies can feel "cramped", but many get it to go.

Oliverio *Italian* | ▽ 28 | 24 | 25 | $40 |

Beverly Hills | Avalon Hotel | 9400 W. Olympic Blvd. (S. Beverly Dr.) |
310-277-5221 | www.avalonbeverlyhills.com

"Poolside dining" is de rigueur at this "retro-cool" Beverly Hills Italian
in the Avalon Hotel, where the design by Kelly Wearstler evokes "Miami
minus the humidity"; it serves an "excellent", wide-spanning menu and
"amazing drinks" that taste extra "fabulous" if you're lucky enough to
dine in one of the "wonderful cabanas."

Ombra Ristorante 🗷 *Italian* | 21 | 16 | 21 | $44 |

Studio City | 3737 Cahuenga Blvd. (Lankershim Blvd.) | 818-985-7337 |
www.ombrala.com

This "much-needed" Venetian Italian in Studio City turns out "delicious,
distinctive" Italian specialties – including standout handmade pastas –
at moderate prices in "lively", "casual" digs; a handful finds the fare
"overrated", but service is "charming" and the low corkage fee "is a
plus", so on the whole, it's a "satisfying" stop.

🗷 Omino Sushi *Japanese* | 27 | 15 | 24 | $38 |

Chatsworth | 20957 Devonshire St. (De Soto Ave.) | 818-709-8822 |
www.ominosushi.com

A "star" in the San Fernando Valley, this "hidden gem" is cherished by
Chatsworth denizens for its "top-flight sushi" and other "interesting"
Japanese "delicacies" served in a small, minimalist setting; add in a
"sweet" staff and prices reasonable for the quality, and admirers insist
that in the area "nothing else comes close."

O-Nami *Japanese* | 21 | 16 | 20 | $33 |

Torrance | 1925 W. Carson St. (Cabrillo Ave.) | 310-787-1632 |
www.onamitorrance.com

"Come hungry because you will leave stuffed" for not too much money
at this "huge" all-you-can-eat Japanese buffet spanning everything
from sushi to kalbi and crab legs in casual digs; "wonderful" service
keeps the masses moving through, just remember "you gotta be quick
when they drop off the lobster tails."

🆕 One Eyed Gypsy 🗷🅜 *Eclectic* | - | - | - | M |

Downtown | 901 E. First St. (Vignes St.) | 626-340-3529 |
www.one-eyedgypsy.com

On the menu at this midpriced Downtown Eclectic are a pulled pork
sandwich, individual pizzas, corn dogs and sliders, accompanied by
cocktails like Clown's Cup and Voodoo Doll; the digs have a 1930s
carny vibe, complete with a mechanical fortune teller, Skee-Ball ma-

chines and a Love-o-Meter, along with a small stage hosting jugglers, musicians and burlesque dancers.

☑ 101 Coffee Shop ● *Diner*

| 23 | 21 | 22 | $27 |

Hollywood | 6145 Franklin Ave. (Gower St.) | 323-467-1175 | www.the101coffeeshop.com

"Diner kitsch in its highest form" serves as a "hipster", "celebrity" and "tourist" magnet at this "late-night" Hollywood hang – voted LA's Most Popular restaurant – that dishes up plentiful portions of "spot-on" American coffee-shop eats, plus some "mean" java and "amazing" milkshakes at "fair prices"; an "enthusiastic" staff keeps it "vibrant", so it's "always hopping" whether curing "hangovers" in the morning or "getting them started" in the first place.

☑ 101 Noodle Express *Chinese*

| 23 | 18 | 20 | $21 |

Culver City | Westfield Culver City | 6000 Sepulveda Blvd. (Slauson Ave.) | 310-397-2060
Arcadia | 1025 S. Baldwin Ave. (Arcadia Ave.) | 626-446-8855 ⊞
Alhambra | 1408 E. Valley Blvd. (bet. New Ave. & Vega St.) | 626-300-8654 ●⊞
www.101noodleexpress.com

Offering a "basic course in noodle-ology", this "no-muss, no-fuss" Sino trio dishes up "awesome" soups and dumplings as well as a "gotta-get-it" beef roll (picture a "Chinese burrito") served at a "prompt" pace; the settings vary, but most don't mind given the "generous" servings of "wonderfully cheap" eats.

One Pico *Mediterranean*

| 24 | 26 | 24 | $55 |

Santa Monica | Shutters on the Beach | 1 Pico Blvd. (Ocean Ave.) | 310-587-1717 | www.shuttersonthebeach.com

"Stunning views over the ocean" qualify this Santa Monica hotel dining room as "one of the top places for taking visitors", and the Med menu is quite "tasty" too; with a "classy, but not stuffy", setting perfect for "lingering" and "attentive" service, most don't mind a little "overspending"; P.S. it's also "excellent" for Sunday brunch.

Open Sesame *Lebanese*

| 25 | 20 | 21 | $24 |

Long Beach | 5201 E. Second St. (Nieto Ave.) | 562-621-1698
Long Beach | 5215 E. Second St. (bet. Corona & Nieto Aves.) | 562-621-1698
Manhattan Beach | 2640 N. Sepulveda Blvd. (bet. Marine Ave. & 27th St.) | 310-545-1600
www.opensesamegrill.com

"Always crowded", but "ohhhh the food" rave Med mavens who devour "perfectly prepared kebabs", "wonderful" signature fried potatoes and other "fairly priced" "garlic-infused" Lebanese eats at this bargain trio with a "cute name"; the "funky" setups with murals and throw pillows are a "welcome change" for fast-casual, as is "helpful, courteous" service.

Original Pancake House *American*

| 25 | 15 | 22 | $16 |

Redondo Beach | 1756 S. PCH (bet. Palos Verdes Blvd. & Paseo De Las Delicias) | 310-543-9875 | www.walkerbros.net

"Come hungry" to this popular American chain featuring a "near-infinite" selection of "ginormous" pancakes (the Dutch apple are "out of this world") and other "carb-loaded" breakfast items set down in "cheerful" country digs; it's often "packed to the rafters", but an "efficient" team handles the crowds and always "keeps your coffee cup full", while "good-value" pricing furthers the good vibes.

Original Pantry Cafe ● ♥ *Diner*
20 | 13 | 20 | $20

Downtown | 877 S. Figueroa St. (W. 9th St.) | 213-972-9279 | www.pantrycafe.com

"LA history" is served up on a plate at this "ancient" (circa 1924) Downtown diner owned by former mayor Richard Riordan that dishes out "huge portions" of "homestyle" eats to an "an amazing mix of power brokers, cops, construction workers, tourists and bums" 24 hours a day; with a "snappy staff, "bargain" pricing and a constant "line winding down the street", regulars bet "it will outlive us all."

Original Red Onion *Mexican*
22 | 21 | 23 | $25

Rolling Hills Estates | 736 Silver Spur Rd. (Crenshaw Blvd.) | Rolling Hills | 310-377-5660 | www.originalredonion.com

Bottomless bowls of "crispy chips" and other "typical" south-of-the-border eats hit the spot at this "popular" Rolling Hills Mexican "tradition" beloved for its "bargain" prices and "family-friendly atmosphere"; detractors may call the food "dull", but "faithful" fans find the whole package is "comfortable like a favorite pair of house slippers."

Original Roadhouse Grill *Steak*
23 | 20 | 22 | $28

Long Beach | 7391 Carson Blvd. (Norwalk Blvd.) | 562-377-5952
Whittier | 15156 Whittier Blvd. (bet. Cole Rd. & Scott Ave.) | 562-945-7796
www.originalroadhousegrill.com

For "A-ok" steaks, ribs and burgers without the "fancy" trappings or high prices, this chophouse duo in Long Beach and Whittier "delivers as expected" – large platters of mesquite-grilled proteins ferried by a "wonderful" crew; with a knotty-wood roadhouse aesthetic and a jukebox playing country tunes, it's "just a plain fun place to go."

Ortega 120 *Mexican*
22 | 21 | 19 | $27

Redondo Beach | 1814 S. PCH (bet. Palos Verdes Blvd. & Prospect Ave.) | 310-792-4120 | www.ortega120.com

"Elegant, authentic Mexican" cuisine keeps customers coming to this "modern" Redondo Beach cantina famed for its "creative" "twists" on tradition like ahi poke tacos; the art-filled digs are "loud and busy", the service "spotty" and the bill might set you back, but most agree the "incredible" margaritas will ease the pain.

NEW Osteria Drago *Italian*
- | - | - | E

West Hollywood | 8741 W. Sunset Blvd. (Holloway Dr.) | 310-657-1182 | www.osteriadrago.com

The ubiquitous Drago brothers hit the Sunset Strip with this pricey modern Italian, whose flashy menu matches the celeb-heavy crowd clustered inside; the sun-washed space boasts floor-to-ceiling windows, wainscoting on the ceiling and Milanese pottery in nooks on the wall.

Osteria La Buca M *Italian*
23 | 20 | 21 | $42

Hollywood | 5210 Melrose Ave. (Wilton Pl.) | 323-462-1900 | www.osterialabuca.com

Devotees "dream about the carbonara" and other "comfort food" "made with love" at this "charming" Hollywood Italian that's "surprisingly affordable" too; despite some ownership, decor and menu changes over the years, it's frequently "crowded" with a "nice, neighborhood" feel and fittingly affable service.

Osteria Latini *Italian*

| 26 | 20 | 24 | $45 |

Brentwood | 11712 San Vicente Blvd. (bet. Barrington & Gorham Aves.) | 310-826-9222 | www.osterialatini.com

Despite "heavy competition" in Brentwood, admirers insist this "gem" is still "the Italian that Italians go to" for "amazing", "authentic" fare and "charming" hospitality from "attentive" owner Paolo Pasio; if you mind "tight" quarters and "eavesdropping" on your neighbors, "better to go during the week" when it's less crowded.

Osteria Mamma *Italian*

| 25 | 17 | 22 | $36 |

Hollywood | 5732 Melrose Ave. (Lucerne Blvd.) | 323-284-7060 | www.osteriamamma.com

"Mamma Loredana puts a lot of love" into her "fantastic, homemade" fare at this "true" Italian trattoria in Hollywood where the gnocchi, pastas and other "heavenly" treats are some of "the best this side of Napoli"; perhaps the modest decor "leaves a bit to be desired", but "everyone's treated like family" and moderate prices seal the deal.

⊿ Osteria Mozza *Italian*

| 27 | 23 | 24 | $68 |

Hollywood | 6602 Melrose Ave. (Highland Ave.) | 323-297-0100 | www.osteriamozza.com

"If you manage to score a reservation, you're in for a treat" at this "exquisite" Hollywood Italian from Nancy Silverton and Mario Batali that's "pure indulgence", from the "ethereal, unforgettable" pastas to the "luscious, milky-fresh" cheese at the mozzarella bar to the "sublime" desserts "even carb-phobe friends" enjoy; given the "fabulous" food, most don't mind if the "sophisticated", "star-studded" setting is "noisy" or the "knowledgeable" staff sometimes "snooty", but as for the bill – "start saving your paychecks."

Outback Steakhouse *Steak*

| 23 | 21 | 23 | $31 |

Norwalk | 12850 Norwalk Blvd. (5 Fwy.) | 562-863-8908
Lakewood | 5305 Clark Ave. (Candlewood St.) | 562-634-0353
Torrance | Del Amo Fashion Ctr. | 21880 Hawthorne Blvd. (bet. W. Carson St. & W. Sepulveda Blvd.) | 310-793-5555
Arcadia | 166 E. Huntington Dr. (N. 2nd Ave.) | 626-447-6435
Burbank | Empire Ctr. | 1761 N. Victory Pl. (W. Empire Ave.) | 818-567-2717
Northridge | 18711 Devonshire St. (Reseda Blvd.) | 818-366-2341
City of Industry | Puente Hills Mall | 1418 S. Azusa Ave. (Colima Rd.) | 626-810-6765
Covina | 1476 N. Azusa Ave. (Arrow Hwy.) | 626-812-0488
Thousand Oaks | 137 E. Thousand Oaks Blvd. (N. Moorpark Rd.) | 805-381-1590
Valencia | 25261 The Old Rd. (Chiquella Ln.) | 661-287-9630
www.outback.com
Additional locations throughout Southern California

Perhaps it's "not gourmet", but this "enjoyable" chain is a source for "serious steaks" and other "solid-all-around" grub (like the "addictive" bloomin' onion) "without having to refinance your home"; cynics call it "average at best", but the "kitschy", "Aussie"-themed digs draw "crazy crowds" nonetheless.

NEW Outpost ● *American*

| - | - | - | I |

Hollywood | 1624 N. Cahuenga Blvd. (Hollywood Blvd.) | 323-464-7678 | www.outposthollywood.com

This Western-themed gastropub offers a menu of $10-and-under options like pulled pork sandwiches and oversized burgers, served by girls-next-door in Daisy Dukes; the atmosphere is pure Hollywood kitsch, with longhorn skulls, saddles and TV screens on the walls, and there's a massive wooden bar issuing giant cocktails served in glass boots.

Overland Cafe *Eclectic*

| 19 | 14 | 19 | $19 |

Culver City | 3601 Overland Ave. (Chamock Rd.) | 310-559-9999 | www.overlandcafe.com

Weekend brunch is "the bomb" with all-you-can-drink champagne at this all-day Culver City Eclectic offering all sorts of "hearty" "comfort food" in a "relaxed" setting; critics call it "nothing spectacular", but a "nice beer selection" and "incredible prices quickly help you forget" any shortcomings.

Ozumo *Japanese*

| 23 | 25 | 21 | $47 |

Santa Monica | Dining Deck, Santa Monica Pl. | 395 Santa Monica Pl. (3rd St. Promenade) | 424-214-5130 | www.ozumosantamonica.com

Set in a "cool" silk- and bamboo-laden dining room, this offshoot of a Bay Area Japanese chain housed inside Santa Monica Place dispenses "elaborate" sushi and sashimi plates to go with an "amazing" sake selection; although an "underwhelmed" contingent calls the food and service "mediocre" given the "kinda pricey" bills, it still draws the crowds come happy hour.

Pace *Italian*

| 25 | 25 | 23 | $47 |

Laurel Canyon | 2100 Laurel Canyon Blvd. (Kirkwood Dr.) | 323-654-8583 | www.peaceinthecanyon.com

"Tucked up in the hills" of Laurel Canyon, this "super-cute" Italian pulls a "beautiful crowd" for "excellent" Italian pizzas and pastas with an organic bent served in a "romantic", twinkle-lit setting with "atmosphere to spare"; though some grumble it's a little "pricey", service is "attentive" and it's a "great date spot if you want to get cozy."

Paco's Tacos *Mexican*

| 21 | 15 | 21 | $21 |

Mar Vista | 4141 S. Centinela Ave. (bet. Culver & Washington Blvds.) | 310-391-9616

Westchester | 6212 Manchester Blvd. (bet. La Tijera & Sepulveda Blvds.) | 310-645-8692

www.pacoscantina.com

"Heavenly, buttery tortillas made by a cute *abuela*" add a "special" touch to the otherwise "solid" eats at this affordable Mexican duo in Mar Vista and Westchester also appreciated for its "pretty-darn-good margaritas"; it follows through with "efficient" service and an atmosphere that "feels like Cinco de Mayo", just know "there's always a wait."

Padri *Italian*

| 22 | 23 | 21 | $39 |

Agoura Hills | 29008 Agoura Rd. (Cornell Rd.) | 818-865-3700 | www.padrirestaurant.net

"Charming" Tuscan farmhouse decor creates a "romantic" mood at this midpriced Italian in Agoura Hills where an "attentive" staff proffers "authentic", "homestyle" fare (osso buco is a standout) in the "cozy" interior or out on the patio; although it's "quiet" early on, the adjoining martini bar hosts live music and "the Friday night scene is great spectator sport."

Palermo *Italian*

| 23 | 20 | 24 | $22 |

Los Feliz | 1858 N. Vermont Ave. (bet. Franklin & Russell Aves.) | 323-663-1178 | www.palermorestaurant.net

"Go right for the pizza, baby" and the "incredible garlic bread" at this "unfussy", "old-world" Los Feliz Italian boasting "hearty" red-sauce feasts and "one of the friendliest owners in the SoCal area"; "it's as much about the atmosphere as it is the food", and the "cheap prices" don't hurt either.

NEW Palikitchen *American*

| - | - | - | I |

West Hollywood | Palihotel | 7950 Melrose Ave. (N. Doheny Dr.) | 323-272-4588 | www.pali-hotel.com

This breakfast-and-lunch sibling of The Hall in WeHo's Palihotel features a casual menu of toasted sandwiches and salads from consulting chef Brendan Collins (Waterloo & City); the counter-service space is decorated with plenty of knickknacks, and there's also a long communal table that's a "great place to hang out."

The Palm *Steak*

| 25 | 22 | 25 | $69 |

Downtown | 1100 S. Flower St. (11th St.) | 213-763-4600
West Hollywood | 9001 Santa Monica Blvd. (bet. Doheny Dr. & Robertson Blvd.) | 310-550-8811
www.thepalm.com

"A well-deserved classic", this "convivial", "old-fashioned" chophouse chain – aka "home of the giant lobsters" – impresses guests with "excellent" surf 'n' turf and "perfect martinis" served in a setting chockfull of "character"; service is "top-notch" too, so even if "it can get pricey fast", you "always leave feeling like a million bucks."

Palmeri *Italian*

| 26 | 23 | 25 | $50 |

Brentwood | 11650 San Vicente Blvd. (bet. Barrington & Darlington Aves.) | 310-442-8446 | www.palmeriristorante.com

A "foodie haven" on "Brentwood's Italian row", this "excellent, neighborhood" ristorante is beloved for "talented" chef Ottavio Palmeri's "original", "fabulous" Sicilian-influenced recipes like "wonderful" salt-crusted branzino; "warm, welcoming" service "makes the cost worth it", so the only drawback is that it's "a bit noisy on a crowded Saturday night."

NEW Palmilla Cocina y Tequila *Mexican*

| - | - | - | M |

Hermosa Beach | 39 Pier Ave. (Beach Dr.) | 310-374-4440 | www.palmillarestaurant.com

This "upscale" Hermosa Beach Mexican offers "unique" regional specialties like carnitas Michoacán, camarones Veracruz and Baja-style fish in a bar-intensive space that claims one of the largest tequila collections in town; the eccentric setting features lamps that cast a mysterious glow, walls of pebbled glass and exotic swirly plasterwork on the walls.

Palms Thai ❶ *Thai*

| 23 | 16 | 21 | $20 |

East Hollywood | 5900 Hollywood Blvd. (Bronson Ave.) | 323-462-5073 | www.palmsthai.com

The "crooning Elvis" impersonator may be MIA, but admirers of this "late-night" East Hollywood Thai are undeterred, thanks to its "delectable" "authentic" eats with some "wild" offerings like deer with peppercorns; service is "fast, but not terribly attentive" and the "simple" setup lends it "a get-in-and-get-out feel" – that said, the "prices can't be beat."

Palomino *American*
21 | 21 | 20 | $37

Westwood | 10877 Wilshire Blvd. (Glendon Ave.) | 310-208-1960 | www.palomino.com

The "happening" bar scene and "all-day happy hours" are the main draws at this Westwood New American whose more "relaxed, elegant" dining room is also a "go-to for business lunches" and pretheater dinners thanks to servers who "understand tight schedules"; some say you're "paying more for mood than the food", although the Med-influenced menu is "very good" too.

Panda Inn *Chinese*
24 | 21 | 22 | $26

Ontario | 3223 E. Centrelake Dr. (Guasti Rd.) | 909-390-2888
Pasadena | 3488 E. Foothill Blvd. (bet. Rosemead Blvd. & Sierra Madre Villa Ave.) | 626-793-7300
Glendale | 111 E. Wilson Ave. (Brand Blvd.) | 818-502-1234
www.pandainn.com

"It may be Americanized Chinese, but it still hits the mark" swear habitués of these upscale progenitors of Panda Express presenting "well-prepared" Mandarin cuisine like honey-walnut shrimp and other "recipes lost in time from the 1970s"; if the red-and-orange-hued setting is "comfortable but not memorable", at least service is "polite" and "prices won't break the bank" either.

Panini Cafe *Italian/Mediterranean*
22 | 17 | 21 | $20

Downtown | 600 W. Ninth St. (bet. Flower & Hope Sts.) | 213-489-4200
Beverly Hills | 9601 Santa Monica Blvd. (Camden Dr.) | 310-247-8300
Westwood | 10861 Lindbrook Dr. (bet. Glendon & Tverton Aves.) | 310-443-2100 ♥
Woodland Hills | 21000 Victory Blvd. (Independence Ave.) | 818-992-3330
www.mypaninicafe.com

"Value"-seekers rely on this "casual" all-day Italian-Med chain for "fresh", "filling" and "plentiful" kebab platters, salads, wraps and "tasty" panini; the settings are nothing fancy, but service is usually "friendly" and it's "great for takeout" too.

Panzanella *Italian*
25 | 23 | 25 | $52

Sherman Oaks | 14928 Ventura Blvd. (bet. Sepulveda & Van Nuys Blvds.) | 818-784-4400 | www.giacominodrago.com

"It's one of the Drago brothers' restaurants, so you can't go wrong" assert admirers of this "high-end" Sherman Oaks Italian built around a "wonderful" selection of "traditional" Sicilian dishes and wines; "excellent service" and a setting suited to "special occasions" (including an "intimate wine cellar") make it easy to take the "expensive" tabs.

Papa Cristo's Ⓜ *Greek*
23 | 12 | 19 | $19

Mid-City | 2771 W. Pico Blvd. (Normandie Ave.) | 323-737-2970 | www.papacristos.com

"The mother lode of Greek authenticity", this "quirky" Mid-City Hellenic market and eatery has been going strong for 65 years with "generous" servings of "simple" fare served off paper plates and lots of "delicacies" available to go; it "looks like a hole-in-the-wall, but has a lot of charm and character" (Papa himself "can often be seen roaming the tables"), while already "affordable" pricing is enhanced by live bouzouki Thursdays–Sundays.

Papaya King ● *Hot Dogs*
18 | 10 | 19 | $11

Hollywood | 1645 Wilcox Ave. (Hollywood Blvd.) | 323-871-8799 | www.papayaking.com

"A decent facsimile" of the NYC original, this late-night Hollywood hot dog counter courtesy of Sam Nazarian serves up Big Apple signatures like "snappy franks" and tropical drinks at recession-friendly prices; "fast" service is a plus, although "disappointed" expats call it "not as good" as its precursor.

Paradise Cove *American/Seafood*
19 | 22 | 19 | $33

Malibu | 28128 PCH (Paradise Cove Rd.) | 310-457-2503 | www.paradisecovemalibu.com

"Even Matthew McConaughey–spotters need to eat" joke patrons of this surfside Malibu seafooder by Gladstone's founder Bob Morris set on a "fantastic" stretch of beachfront real estate; expect "enormous portions" of "elevated bar food" and fruity drinks ("nothing says SoCal" like "drinking out of a pineapple"), and even if some call the service "inconsistent" and the fare "mediocre and overpriced", "where else can you dig your toes in the sand and eat?"

The Parish *British*
- | - | - | M

Downtown | 840 S. Spring St. (9th St.) | 213-225-2400 | www.theparishla.com

Casey Lane (Tasting Kitchen) heads for Downtown's Gallery Row for this British-accented, midpriced gastropub with heady fare and house-cured meats, plus a food-friendly beer menu; the airy space features exposed ductwork above and polished wood and ornate wallpaper below.

The Park *American*
25 | 17 | 23 | $27

Echo Park | 1400 W. Sunset Blvd. (Douglas St.) | 213-482-9209 | www.thepark1400sunset.com

A "neighborhood" mainstay with "lots of personality", this Echo Park eatery is a "go-to" for "inventive" Americana – plus $5 burgers on Wednesdays – in a simple bistro setting; add in way-"reasonable" prices and "inviting" hospitality, and insiders insist "once you find it, you'll be back over and over again."

Parker's Lighthouse *Seafood*
23 | 24 | 23 | $39

Long Beach | 435 Shoreline Village Dr. (E. Shoreline Dr.) | 562-432-6500 | www.parkerslighthouse.com

"You won't find a better view" in Long Beach say fans of this seafooder overlooking the Queen Mary and the harbor, where "excellent" surf 'n' turf is set down by "professional" servers; a few find it "too expensive for what you get", but "the location can't be beat", especially at happy hour.

Park's Barbeque ● *Korean*
25 | 14 | 19 | $37

Koreatown | 955 S. Vermont Ave. (bet. Olympic Blvd. & San Marino St.) | 213-380-1717 | www.parksbbq.com

Devotees "dream about the galbi" at this perpetually "packed" K-Town grill known for its "premium" BBQ meats (including Wagyu) and "amazing array of banchan" offered in a "slick", "not-too-smoky" setting; yes, it's "one of the more expensive" in the genre, but consensus is it's also "one of the best."

	FOOD	DECOR	SERVICE	COST

Parkway Grill *Californian*
26 | 26 | 25 | $53

Pasadena | 510 S. Arroyo Pkwy. (bet. California & Del Mar Blvds.) | 626-795-1001 | www.theparkwaygrill.com

"Quintessentially Pasadena", this "longtime favorite" from the Smith Brothers "still draws a crowd" with "simple" Cal cuisine like "top-notch steaks" "done perfectly", plus "elegant" "old-school" service and a "lovely" art-filled dining room with "fireplaces ablaze"; factor in Friday night jazz, and it's a "first-rate experience" – and "a classy place to impress those picky in-laws" – that's "well worth the cost."

Pasta Pomodoro *Italian*
21 | 18 | 20 | $24

West Hollywood | West Hollywood Gateway Ctr. | 7100 Santa Monica Blvd. (bet. Formosa & La Brea Aves.) | 323-969-8000
Manhattan Beach | 401 Manhattan Beach Blvd. (N. Morningside Dr.) | 310-545-5401
www.pastapomodoro.com

"Nicely done for a chain", this casual Italian rolls out "reasonably priced" pastas, pizzas and other "consistent" (if "uninspired") eats in contempo settings; they're often "loud" and you can "expect to see strollers", but the staff "handles children well" and "great value" compensates.

Pastina Ⓢ *Italian*
24 | 19 | 24 | $40

West LA | 2260 Westwood Blvd. (bet. Tennessee Ave. & W. Olympic Blvds.) | 310-441-4655 | www.pastina.net

Exuding "family-run warmth", this "old-school" "frequent favorite" in Westwood offers "excellent" Southern Italian fare – including a nightly prix fixe – at prices that "won't break you"; add in a "quiet", "pleasant" atmosphere and it's "like you're eating in your own dining room", but with "attentive" service and white tablecloths.

❷ Patina Ⓢ Ⓜ *American/Californian*
27 | 26 | 27 | $91

Downtown | Walt Disney Concert Hall | 141 S. Grand Ave. (2nd St.) | 213-972-3331 | www.patinarestaurant.com

"Splendid in every way", this Patina Group flagship in the "stunning" Walt Disney Concert Hall is a nexus for "refined" New American-Californian dishes ("some traditional, some avant-garde"), "impeccable" service and a "quiet", "luxurious" atmosphere; expect "serious food with serious prices", but for "fine dining before a show", "you can't get much better than this."

Patrick's Roadhouse *Diner*
∇ 19 | 18 | 17 | $26

Santa Monica | 106 Entrada Dr. (PCH) | 310-459-4544 | www.patricksroadhouse.info

"Pretty good" breakfasts top the menu of "ok" diner food at this "atmospheric" 1970s-era American "right off the beach" in Santa Monica that's known for its "quirky" setup with antiques "hanging from the ceiling" and peek-a-boo ocean view; "don't expect lightning-fast service" or much more than "average" eats – for most "the best thing about it" is the "funky" ambiance.

Paul Martin's American Bistro *American*
22 | 23 | 22 | $39

El Segundo | 2361 Rosecrans Ave. (bet. Aviation Blvd. & Redondo Ave.) | 310-643-9300 | www.paulmartinsamericanbistro.com

"Local" and "organic" are the watchwords at this "pleasant" "eco"-American chain link from Paul Fleming (P.F. Chang's, Fleming's) turning out "fresh" takes on the classics like fish tacos and burgers abetted by California-centric wines, "cozy" Napa-inspired decor and "welcoming, informative" staff; prices can be a sticking point, but then "sustainability ain't cheap."

Pearl Dragon *Asian*
21 | 19 | 20 | $35

Pacific Palisades | 15229 W. Sunset Blvd. (Swarthmore Ave.) | 310-459-9790 | www.thepearldragon.com
"Quite the happening bar and grill" in the Palisades, this midpriced Pan-Asian "locals' place" entices with "well-executed" sushi and burgers and "sensational cocktails" in a candlelit setting; since it features "one of the few full bars in the area", it's often busy, so some say "distracted" service and "loud" acoustics come with the territory.

Pecorino *Italian*
25 | 22 | 24 | $50

Brentwood | 11604 San Vicente Blvd. (bet. Darlington & Mayfield Aves.) | 310-571-3800 | www.pecorinorestaurant.com
Flying somewhat "under the radar", this "high-end" eatery wins "neighborhood" hearts with "authentic Italian" fare, a "warm, receptive" staff and a cozy space with exposed brick and a beamed ceiling; its "tiny" dimensions can mean "little privacy" and lots of "noise", but *amici* insist it's "one of the finest" on Brentwood's Restaurant Row.

☑ The Penthouse *American*
22 | 27 | 21 | $53

Santa Monica | Huntley Santa Monica Beach Hotel | 1111 Second St. (Wilshire Blvd.) | 310-394-5454 | www.thehuntleyhotel.com
The setting just "exudes sexiness" at this "chic" Santa Monica stunner atop the Huntley Beach Hotel boasting "spectacular" panoramic views of the ocean framed by "immaculate" "billowy white curtains"; the "creative" New American menu "doesn't disappoint" either, but with such a "vibrant bar scene", it's really all about the mingling here; P.S. brunch is also popular.

Peppone *Italian*
22 | 20 | 22 | $58

Brentwood | 11628 Barrington Ct. (Barrington Ave.) | 310-476-7379 | www.peppone.com
"Old-school" all the way, this "been-there-forever" Brentwood Italian "hasn't changed" in years, with "authentic", "consistently good" food like osso buco and calf's liver delivered by a "professional" staff that coddles the "regulars"; some call it "too expensive and too clubby", although it remains a "favorite of many."

☑ Perch ●☑ *French*
18 | 27 | 18 | $44

Downtown | 448 S. Hill St. (W. 5th St.) | 213-802-1770 | www.perchla.com
"Above the chaos of Pershing Square", this multilevel rooftop French provides "soaring views of Downtown" along with updated Gallic grub – in small and large plates – in a setting "reminiscent of a supper club from the big-band days", with live music; several call the food and service only "so-so", although defenders insist it's a "perfect spot" for dates or drinks.

Pete's Cafe & Bar ● *American*
21 | 20 | 21 | $31

Downtown | 400 S. Main St. (4th St.) | 213-617-1000 | www.petescafe.com
There's a "cool Downtown vibe" at this atmospheric American in LA's historic bank district that "satisfies" with "classic" bites like burgers, "addictive" blue-cheese fries and other "solid" midpriced fare ("keep

it simple and you can't go wrong"); it's "popular" thanks to a "comfortable, easy" ambiance that's "not too intimidating or precious", and "even when they're crowded, service isn't rushed"; added perks are a pooch-friendly patio and late-night hours.

Petros *Greek* — 25 | 21 | 21 | $46

Manhattan Beach | Metlox Plaza | 451 Manhattan Beach Blvd. (bet. Morningside & Valley Drs.) | 310-545-4100 | www.petrosrestaurant.com

This "fashionable", "upscale" Hellenic in Manhattan Beach "never fails to please" with its "refined", "lighter-style California-Greek" cuisine that's "a cut above" plus "refreshing cocktails" proffered by an "upbeat" staff; it's set in a "cool" Santorini-inspired space, although some loyalists only wish it "wasn't so loud."

Petrossian Paris *French* — 24 | 21 | 24 | $57

West Hollywood | 321 N. Robertson Blvd. (Rosewood Ave.) | 310-271-0576 | www.petrossian.com

"Fantastic caviar" and flutes of champagne "make the time slip away" at this "wonderfully decadent" Beverly Hills boutique offering delicacies to go along with an "enjoyable", abbreviated French menu; the setting's *très chic* and servers "try hard to please", just remember "it's easy to run up the price quickly."

P.F. Chang's China Bistro *Chinese* — 22 | 22 | 22 | $32

Beverly Hills | Beverly Ctr. | 121 N. La Cienega Blvd. (bet. Beverly Blvd. & 3rd St.) | 310-854-6467

Santa Monica | 326 Wilshire Blvd. (4th St.) | 310-395-1912

El Segundo | 2041 Rosecrans Ave. (Nash St.) | 310-607-9062

Long Beach | 340 S. Pine Ave. (Shoreline Dr.) | 562-308-1025

Torrance | Del Amo Fashion Ctr. | 3525 W. Carson St. (bet. Hawthorne Blvd. & Madrona Ave.) | 310-793-0590

Pasadena | Paseo Colorado | 260 E. Colorado Blvd. (bet. Los Robles & Marengo Aves.) | 626-356-9760

Burbank | Burbank Town Ctr. | 201 E. Magnolia Blvd. (bet. N. 1st & N. 3rd Sts.) | 818-391-1070

Sherman Oaks | Sherman Oaks Galleria | 15301 Ventura Blvd. (Sepulveda Blvd.) | 818-784-1694

Woodland Hills | Promenade at Woodland Hills | 21821 Oxnard St. (Topanga Canyon Blvd.) | 818-340-0491

Thousand Oaks | 2250 E. Thousand Oaks Blvd. (Conejo School Rd.) | 805-277-5915

www.pfchangs.com

Additional locations throughout Southern California

Families swarm to this midpriced Chinese chain that plates "inventive" (some say "Americanized") eats, like its signature lettuce wraps plus gluten-free and vegan selections, in an "airy" setting "right out of the movies"; though cantankerous types feel they're "shouting at their dinner partners" and quibble with "commercial" fare and just -"ok" service, it's always "crowded" nonetheless.

Philippe the Original ⊄ *Sandwiches* — 24 | 15 | 19 | $14

Chinatown | 1001 N. Alameda St. (Ord St.) | 213-628-3781 | www.philippes.com

An "LA icon", this circa-1908 "legend" in Chinatown – purported inventor of the French dip – is famed for its "glorious" sandwiches ("double-dipped is the way to go") served in "old-style deli" digs with long communal tables and sawdust-covered floors; "don't be intimidated by the crazy cattle corral they call a line" – counter service is "quick", so "don't miss it."

Phillips Bar-B-Que *BBQ*

26 | 9 | 19 | $19

Leimert Park | 4307 Leimert Blvd. (43rd St.) | 323-292-7613 🏂
Mid-City | 2619 Crenshaw Blvd. (Adams Blvd.) | 323-731-4772 Ⓜ
Inglewood | 1517 Centinela Ave. (bet. Beach Ave. & Cedar St.) | 310-412-7135 🏂

Fans are in "rib heaven" at this BBQ mini-chain plying "addictive", "fall-off-the-bone" 'cue along with "all the trimmings"; the "no-frills" settings are basically for takeout only (with some outdoor seating at the Mid-City locale), but service is "warm" and prices are a solid "value"; P.S. don't miss the signature spicy sauce.

Pho Café ●⊅ *Vietnamese*

▽ 25 | 14 | 21 | $15

Silver Lake | 2841 W. Sunset Blvd. (Silver Lake Blvd.) | 213-413-0888

"Silver Lake twentysomethings" hunker down over "plentiful" bowls of "hot, steaming" pho at this "hipster" Vietnamese tucked in a "nondescript strip mall"; there's "no sign", but it's "always packed" because it works for a "quick, cheap and delicious" meal; P.S. cash only.

Phoenix ● *Chinese*

21 | 14 | 16 | $14

Arcadia | 1108 S. Baldwin Ave. (Arcadia Ave.) | 626-446-7668
South Pasadena | 456 Fair Oaks Ave. (State St.) | 626-403-1828
San Gabriel | 712 W. Las Tunas Dr. (S. Mission Dr.) | 626-289-9888

Phoenix Dessert ● *Chinese*

Alhambra | 220 E. Valley Blvd. (bet. S. Chapel Ave. & S. Montery St.) | 626-299-1918
www.phoenixfoodboutique.com

High school–aged fans flock to this fast-casual Chinese chain for "wondrous", "weird-sounding" tapioca drinks, "tasty" bubble teas, sweets and other "cheap" eats; the settings are spare, but "quick" service and "reasonable" tabs are enticements.

Pho 79 *Vietnamese*

24 | 12 | 17 | $13

Alhambra | 29 S. Garfield Ave. (Main St.) | 626-289-0239

The "holy grail of pho" awaits at this Alhambra Vietnamese purveying "satisfying" noodle soups with "rich, flavorful" broth and other "fresh, appealing" South Asian specialties; service is "abrupt" and the setting's "not pretty", but the food's "cheap", so it's "always busy", especially on weekends.

Pho Show ● *Vietnamese*

21 | 15 | 20 | $13

Culver City | 4349 Sepulveda Blvd. (Culver Blvd.) | 310-398-5200 | www.phoshow.net

"Get your pho on" at this "casual" Vietnamese in Culver City that "satisfies cravings" with "huge portions" of "delicious noodles" and other "basic" Pan-Asian eats; "don't expect glamour or first-class service", but the "comfortable" atmosphere makes it a "welcome" stop in the neighborhood"; P.S. "drinkers rejoice" – they're open till 2 AM every night.

Pho So 1 *Vietnamese*

26 | 11 | 19 | $13

Gardena | 1749 W. Redondo Beach Blvd. (Western Ave.) | 310-329-7365

(continued)

Pho So 1

Reseda | 7231 Reseda Blvd. (bet. Sherman Way & Wyandotte St.) |
818-996-6515
Van Nuys | 6450 Sepulveda Blvd. (Victory Blvd.) | 818-989-6377
Simi Valley | 2837 Cochran St. (Sycamore Dr.) | 805-306-1868
www.phoso1.com
This no-frills Vietnamese mini-chain "is one of the best" for "wonderful" pho "rich in spices and beefy goodness" served up "quick"; the
strip-mall settings aren't fancy, but "generous" portions at "excellent"
prices keep locals coming back.

Picanha Churrascaria *Brazilian*   21 | 15 | 19 | $36

Burbank | 269 E. Palm Ave. (bet. San Fernando Blvd. & 3rd St.) |
818-972-2100 | www.picanharestaurant.com
You "have to like meat" to appreciate this Burbank and Cathedral City
Brazilian duo where an "awesome variety" of "fantastically filling" rotisserie items are carved tableside by roving waiters who "don't stop
serving until you put your stop sign up"; gaucho-themed decor and
caipirinhas complete the package, and while some find it too "expensive", others maintain it's "worth it."

Picca ⊠ *Japanese/Peruvian*   25 | 22 | 22 | $53

Century City | 9575 W. Pico Blvd. (Edris Dr.) | 310-277-0133 |
www.piccaperu.com
The "foodie darling of the moment", this "hip", "upscale" Century City
entry from Ricardo Zarate (Mo-Chica) delivers an "amazing experience" via "bold", "inventive" Peruvian-Japanese small plates "unlike
anything you've ever tried" and "phenomenal" cocktails; you "can't go
wrong following waiters' recommendations", so "the only negative is
the noise level"; P.S. upstairs is quieter.

⊠ Piccolo *Italian*   28 | 25 | 26 | $67

Venice | 5 Dudley Ave. (Spdwy.) | 310-314-3222 | www.piccolovenice.com
Surveyors say it "doesn't get much better" than this "quaint" Venice
hideaway just "steps from the beach" serving "delectable", "refined"
Venetian fare that "rivals the best in Italy"; prices are a "splurge", but
with an exceedingly "knowledgeable" staff and "romantic" setting,
"what's not to love?"

Piccolo Paradiso *Italian*   24 | 20 | 24 | $51

Beverly Hills | 150 S. Beverly Dr. (bet. Charleville & Wilshire Blvds.) |
310-271-0030 | www.giacominodrago.com
"The locals fill the tables night after night" at this neighborhood Italian
from Giacomino Drago serving "wonderful" fare in an "unassuming"
storefront in Beverly Hills; so maybe it's not cheap, and it can "get noisy
on weekends", but "warm" service makes it "always a pleasure."

Pico Kosher Deli *Deli*   24 | 15 | 18 | $18

Century City | 8826 W. Pico Blvd. (S. Robertson Blvd.) | 310-273-9381 |
www.pkdla.com
"Delicious" pastrami and corned beef are the specialties at this "old-
style" Jewish deli on Pico's Kosher Corridor; perhaps the way-"casual"
digs and "gruff" service "leave a lot to be desired", so those in the know
opt to "take it home to enjoy."

Pie 'N Burger ⊄ *Diner*
22 | 11 | 20 | $16

Pasadena | 913 E. California Blvd. (Lake Ave.) | 626-795-1123 |
www.pienburger.com

"What the name says is what you get" at this Pasadena "classic" that's
been putting out "juicy" griddled burgers, "heavenly" pies and "superior" shakes and malts since 1963; the decor "hasn't been updated
since Jimmy Carter was in office" and service "runs the gamut from
accommodating to hostile", but true fans cheer that "it still delivers."

Pig 'n Whistle ● *Continental*
19 | 21 | 19 | $23

Hollywood | 6714 Hollywood Blvd. (N. McCadden Pl.) | 323-463-0000

There's "lots of character" at this "historic" "old-style Hollywood" pub
dating back to 1927 that's "aimed at the tourist crowd"; yet while the
"cool, classic" setting has "so much potential", detractors decry the
"overpriced", "so-so" Continental fare and "weak drinks", saying "it's
sad such an icon isn't better."

🆕 The Pikey ● *Pub Food*
- | - | - | M

Hollywood | 7617 W. Sunset Blvd. (Stanley Ave.) | 323-850-5400 |
www.thepikeyla.com

Hearty pub food plus inventive cocktails crafted from an extensive list
of spirits (absinthe, anyone?) make this well-priced Hollywood newcomer a happy-hour crowd-pleaser; tiled floors, dark wooden booths
and cheery servers in suspenders add to the authentic English
watering-hole feel.

Pink's Famous Chili Dogs ●⊄ *Hot Dogs*
23 | 12 | 18 | $12

La Brea | 709 N. La Brea Ave. (Melrose Ave.) | 323-931-7954 |
www.pinkshollywood.com

"Beyond iconic", this "legendary", late-night La Brea hot dog stand is
a go-to for "delicious", "classic" dogs "that go 'snap' with each bite",
and if you top them with chili, cheese and bacon, "you have all the major food groups covered"; "parking is a nightmare", "the lines are insane" and there's "too many tourists", but die-hard fans still say "you
have to go at least once"; P.S. "BYO Pepto."

Pink Taco *Mexican*
18 | 20 | 18 | $26

West Hollywood | 8225 Sunset Blvd. (bet. Harper Ave. & Havenhurst Dr.) |
323-380-7474
Century City | Westfield Century City Shopping Ctr. |
10250 Santa Monica Blvd. (bet. Ave. of the Stars & Century Park W.) |
310-789-1000
www.pinktaco.com

"Delightfully tacky", these "trendy", "truly LA" stops in Century
City and West Hollywood are where an "eye-candy" crowd downs
"strong" margaritas in a setting that's "too loud and too dark" for
many; as for the food, perhaps "it's not Mexican, but it's edible", and
service can be "unenthusiastic", but the "rowdy" happy hour keeps the
crowds coming back.

Pita Kitchen *Mideastern*
24 | 6 | 18 | $14

Sherman Oaks | 14500 Ventura Blvd. (Van Nuys Blvd.) | 818-990-7006 |
www.thepitakitchen.com

It's all about "terrific value" at this Middle Eastern "hole-in-the-wall"
in Sherman Oaks offering "large portions" of "cheap", "amazing" ke-

babs, "terrific" hummus and "yummy sandwiches"; just ignore the "nonexistent" decor, or grab a seat on the sidewalk.

Pitfire Artisan Pizza *Pizza*   23 | 17 | 19 | $19

Downtown | 108 W. Second St. (Main St.) | 213-808-1200
West Hollywood | 801 N. Fairfax Ave. (bet. Waring & Willoughby Aves.) | 323-544-6240
Culver City | 12924 W. Washington Blvd. (Beethoven St.) | 424-835-4088
West LA | 2018 Westwood Blvd. (La Grange Ave.) | 310-481-9860
North Hollywood | 5211 Lankershim Blvd. (Magnolia Blvd.) | 818-980-2949
www.pitfirepizza.com

It's "kid central" at this "popular" chainlet specializing in "paper-thin" "crusty-edged" pizzas with "interesting toppings", "delicious" salads and other "market-fresh", "Californiaized" Italian fare brought by an "enthusiastic" staff; an "excellent tap selection" keeps the atmosphere "lively" till late, and there's also a bargain no-corkage policy; P.S. the outdoor fire pit at the North Hollywood locale is a "nice touch."

🄯 Pizzeria Mozza ◐ *Pizza*   27 | 20 | 22 | $40

Hollywood | 641 N. Highland Ave. (Highland & Melrose Aves.) | 323-297-0101 | www.pizzeriamozza.com

"If heaven opened up a pizza spot" it might just look like this Nancy Silverton and Mario Batali effort in Hollywood and Newport Beach putting out "sublime" pies, "unique" antipasti, "obscure Italian meats" and other "delicacies" plus a butterscotch budino dessert "fit for a last meal"; service can be uneven, the tables are "so tightly placed that you might eat your neighbor's pizza by mistake" and "loud doesn't even begin the describe" the acoustics, "but ah, that food!"; P.S. reservations are a must, or try for a seat at the bar.

Pizzicotto *Italian*   23 | 18 | 21 | $36

Brentwood | 11758 San Vicente Blvd. (bet. Gorham & Montana Aves.) | 310-442-7188 | www.pizzicottorestaurant.com

Brentwood locals fill up this "rustic Italian" "neighborhood favorite" offering "simple", "authentic" pastas, pizzas and salads in a "homey" "Tuscan" setting; moderate pricing and "friendly" service make for "crowded" conditions, but "upstairs is more relaxing."

🆕 Plan Check ◐ *American*   ∇ 19 | 18 | 18 | $27

West LA | 1800 Sawtelle Blvd. (Nebraska Ave.) | 310-288-6500 | www.plancheckbar.com

Situated at the north end of West LA's Little Osaka strip, this "hip" New American newcomer offers many craft beers, mixology exotica and a casual, well-priced menu with the likes of fried chicken and a Wagyu beef burger complete with their signature ketchup leather; the room features an open truss ceiling and an open kitchen, and there's an outdoor patio in front.

Plate 38 *Eclectic*   22 | 15 | 18 | $27

Pasadena | 2361 E. Colorado Blvd. (Sierra Madre Blvd.) | 626-793-7100 | www.plate38.com

Surveyors say they're "pleasantly surprised" by the "sophisticated" Eclectic gastropub fare like truffle burgers and fried Cornish game hen coming out of this otherwise "unassuming" Pasadena cafe set in

	FOOD	DECOR	SERVICE	COST

modern-industrial digs with counter service by day and table service at night; some find the food and hospitality only "so-so", but "great value" compensates.

Playa *Latin*　　　　　25 | 23 | 23 | $49

Beverly Boulevard | 7360 Beverly Blvd. (bet. Fairfax & La Brea Aves.) | 323-933-5300 | www.playarivera.com

"A winner" from "culinary rock star" John Sedlar, this Beverly Boulevard Pan-Latin serves "sensational", "clever" small plates and "terrific cocktails" in a "fun, flirty" setting that's an "informal, less expensive version of Rivera"; service is "knowledgeable" too, so the "insanely loud" acoustics are the only drawback; P.S. "the brunch is an undiscovered treasure."

Polo Lounge ● *Californian/Continental*　22 | 26 | 25 | $63

Beverly Hills | Beverly Hills Hotel | 9641 W. Sunset Blvd. (bet. Crescent Dr. & Hartford Way) | 310-887-2777 | www.beverlyhillshotel.com

"Quintessential Beverly Hills", this art deco "landmark" provides "perfect" celeb-watching in a "classy", "old-style" setting that "makes you want to dress up and be pampered"; the Cal-Continental cuisine is "predictable, but well prepared" and "served with the highest level of professionalism", so even though it's "expensive, expensive, expensive", "who can resist?"; P.S. "the patio is a delight for lunch."

Poquito Más *Mexican*　　　23 | 14 | 20 | $13

West Hollywood | 8555 W. Sunset Blvd. (Londonderry Pl.) | 310-652-7008
Santa Monica | 2025 Wilshire Blvd. (bet. 20th & 21st Sts.) | 310-828-1700
West LA | 2215 Westwood Blvd. (Olympic Blvd.) | 310-474-1998
Burbank | 2635 W. Olive Ave. (Naomi St.) | 818-563-2252
Chatsworth | 9229 Winnetka Ave. (Prairie St.) | 818-775-1555
North Hollywood | 10651 Magnolia Blvd. (Cartwright Ave.) | 818-994-8226
Sherman Oaks | 13924 Ventura Blvd. (Colbath Ave.) | 818-981-7500
Studio City | 3701 Cahuenga Blvd. (bet. Lankershim Blvd. & Regal Pl.) | 818-760-8226 ●
Woodland Hills | 21049 Ventura Blvd. (Alhama Dr.) | 818-887-2007
www.poquitomas.com

"The freshly made tortillas keep you coming back" to this "quality" Mex – one of the "best of the gringo-burrito chains" – that also pleases with its "fresh" salsa bar and complimentary tortilla soup on rainy days; the "fast-food" settings are often crammed with "noisy kids", but with "quick" service and "inexpensive" tabs, it's a "blessing" for many.

Porta Via *Californian*　　　22 | 20 | 23 | $39

Beverly Hills | 424 N. Cañon Dr. (bet. Brighton Way & Santa Monica Blvd.) | 310-274-6534 | www.portaviabh.com

A "home away from home" for Beverly Hills locals, this all-day Californian offers "dependable" fare based on organic ingredients, "warm" hospitality and an "understated, elegant" ambiance; the ample patio is a perk, and it remains an "inexpensive alternative to some of the pricier fare" nearby; P.S. picky eaters and dieters rejoice "they accommodate any and all requests."

Portillo's Hot Dogs *Hot Dogs*　25 | 22 | 21 | $14

Moreno Valley | 12840 Day St. (Gateway Dr.) | 951-653-1000 | www.portillos.com

"Authentic Chicago-style" dogs and "juicy" Italian beef sandwiches bring back "happy memories" for displaced Windy City folks at these Buena

Park and Moreno Valley chain imports done up in a "cute", "retro" style evoking the gangster era; the line can get "long", but service is generally "efficient", and the "affordable" pricing makes it family-friendly too.

Porto's Bakery *Bakery/Cuban*
26 | 18 | 21 | $15

Downey | 8233 Firestone Blvd. (bet. Downey & Paramount Aves.) | 562-862-8888
Burbank | 3614 W. Magnolia Blvd. (Hollywood Way) | 818-846-9100
Glendale | 315 N. Brand Blvd. (bet. California Ave. & Lexington Dr.) | 818-956-5996
www.portosbakery.com

"An immense selection of sweets", cheese rolls, "amazing" potato balls and "delicious" sandwiches lie in store at this "legendary" Cuban bakery trio where devotees are "dumbfounded at how much deliciousness you get for how little money"; it's "always mobbed, but they know how to move 'em in and move 'em out", and although the vibe is "cheery", you "definitely don't come for the ambiance."

🆕 Post & Beam *American*
∇ 26 | 25 | 25 | $38

Mid-City | Baldwin Hills Crenshaw Plaza | 3767 Santa Rosalia Dr. (Stocker St.) | 323-299-5599 | www.postandbeamla.com

Peripatetic, dreadlocked chef Govind Armstrong (of the now-shuttered Table 8) heads for the chain restaurant-heavy Baldwin Hills Crenshaw Plaza, where he's teamed up with Brad Johnson (formerly of BLT Steak) for this midpriced New American serving the likes of short ribs, beer-brined pork chops and pizzas; early samplers say it shows "great potential" with a patio for "evening summer hangouts" and a full bar with a small-plates menu that's perfect after work.

Prado *Caribbean*
∇ 23 | 19 | 23 | $32

Hancock Park | 244 N. Larchmont Blvd. (bet. Beverly Blvd. & 1st St.) | 323-467-3871 | www.pradola.com

"There's something for everyone" at this "charming" little "mainstay" in Hancock Park offering "tasty, well-prepared" Caribbean-inspired cuisine like crab cakes, corn chowder and combo plates for over 20 years; service is "more than accommodating" and prices are "reasonable", and an appealingly "quiet", "laid-back" dining room seals the deal.

Primitivo Wine Bistro *Mediterranean*
21 | 20 | 21 | $44

Venice | 1025 Abbot Kinney Blvd. (bet. B'way St. & Westminster Aves.) | 310-396-5353 | www.primitivowinebistro.com

"Taste away" at this "fun" little tapas stop with a "cool Venice vibe" known for its varied Med small plates ("bacon-wrapped dates anyone?"), "fantastic wine selection" and happy-hour specials; the "dark" digs can be "great for romance", but tables are "so close it's like [you're] eating dinner with the couple at the next table"; P.S. the patio provides extra elbow room.

Prosecco 🈂 *Italian*
25 | 23 | 25 | $39

Toluca Lake | 10144 Riverside Dr. (bet. Forman & Talofa Aves.) | 818-505-0930 | www.proseccotrattoria.com

"Don't change a thing" plead fans of this Toluca Lake "gem" where "exceptional" Northern Italian fare comes at "moderate" prices; the "cozy" space is often "crowded", but "accommodating" waiters "who fawn over you" compensate, and many find it so "pleasant" "you hate to leave."

❷ Providence *American/Seafood* | 28 | 26 | 28 | $104 |

Hollywood | 5955 Melrose Ave. (Cole Ave.) | 323-460-4170 | www.providencela.com

"Everything is exquisite" at this "world-class" fine-dining destination in Hollywood, where Michael Cimarusti turns out "amazing, innovative" seafood dishes like "delectable works of art" in a "luxurious" setting that's an "oasis of tranquility"; factor in "superb", "knowledgeable" service – fittingly rated tops in the LA Survey – plus a "fantastic" cheese platter wheeled tableside and it adds up to "a delightful gastronomic experience", albeit one that "doesn't come cheap"; P.S. the six-course dessert tasting menu will "blow your mind."

NEW P'tit Soleil *Quebecois* | – | – | – | I |

Westwood | 1386 Westwood Blvd. (Wilkins Ave.) | 310-441-5384 | www.soleilwestwood.com

This French-Canadian lounge in Westwood specializes in no less than 10 versions of poutine, the gut-busting Québécois french fry/cheese/gravy favorite; the minimalist space – adjacent to the more formal Soleil – has bare-brick walls, a long zinc bar, and maple leaf and fleur de lis paintings on the walls.

R+D Kitchen *American* | 22 | 20 | 21 | $33 |

Santa Monica | 1323 Montana Ave. (bet. Euclid & 14th Sts.) | 310-395-3314 | www.hillstone.com

This "rock-solid" Santa Monica American from the Houston's group is "always hopping" with a "good-looking" crowd there for "thick, juicy" burgers, "great salads", "refreshing" cocktails and a "lively" bar scene; a few find the no-reservations policy and subsequent "waits" "maddening", but "professional" service, "excellent value" and a "cool" setting with an open-air feel make up for it.

NEW Racion Ⓜ *Spanish* | – | – | – | M |

Pasadena | 119 W. Green St. (De Lacey Ave.) | 626-396-3090 | www.racionrestaurant.com

This "exciting newcomer" in a narrow storefront in Pasadena is earning kudos for its well-priced Spanish tapas menu rounded out with authentic Basque specialties; the space is minimal and the vibe informal with a bar that can be used as a stopover for a quick bite and a glass of Txakolina.

Raffi's Place *Mideastern* | 26 | 17 | 20 | $28 |

Glendale | 211 E. Broadway (Maryland Ave.) | 818-240-7411 | www.raffisplace.com

"The king" of kebabs, this "popular" Glendale Middle Eastern offers "huge" helpings of "perfectly grilled" meats, fish and poultry and "authentic" stews; the landscaped patio offers "great atmosphere", while solid service plus "reasonable" prices ensure it's always "crowded."

Ramen Jinya *Japanese* | 24 | 15 | 19 | $19 |

NEW **West LA** | 2208 Sawtelle Blvd. (Olympic Blvd.) | 310-481-0977
Studio City | Studio City Place | 11239 Ventura Blvd. (Tujunga Ave.) | 818-980-3977
www.jinya-ramenbar.com

"Acolytes line up" outside these Studio City and West LA ramen joints for "rich" "umami-bomb" broth full of "fatty porky goodness", "superb" noodles and Japanese accompaniments ("don't miss the gyoza"); the settings aren't much, but a "friendly" staff and low prices compensate, and most find they "hit the spot" anytime.

Ramenya ⊅ *Japanese* | 21 | 10 | 20 | $14 |

West LA | 11555 W. Olympic Blvd. (Colby Ave.) | 310-575-9337 | www.ramenya-usa.com

"Popular for lunch", this West LA Japanese offers a "wide selection" of "very good" ramen served in bowls so big "you can dunk your head in"; the white-walled setting with fluorescent lighting isn't exactly romantic, but with such "low prices", "you really can't go wrong"; P.S. cash only.

Ramen Yamadaya *Japanese* | 23 | 13 | 19 | $15 |

Westwood | 1248 Westwood Blvd. (Ashton Ave.) | 310-474-1600
Torrance | 3118 W. 182nd St. (Crenshaw Blvd.) | 310-380-5555
NEW Sherman Oaks | 15030 Ventura Blvd. (Noble Ave.) | 818-501-1115
NEW Culver City | 11172 Washington Blvd. (Sepulveda Blvd.) | 310-815-8776
www.ramen-yamadaya.com

"Happy people slurping up noodles and broth" fill the tables at this Japanese chainlet known for "robust" pork-based ramen soups full of "complex flavor profiles" with "lots of options" for customization; decor is nonexistent, but brisk, "friendly" service and "reasonable" prices mean most could "eat here every day."

☑ Raphael *American* | 25 | 27 | 23 | $58 |

Studio City | 11616 Ventura Blvd. (Colfax Ave.) | 818-505-3337 | www.raphaelonventura.com

The "Valley's dining cognoscenti" cram in to this Studio City American where chef Adam Horton prepares "exciting", "well-conceived" small plates that pair with "amazing" wines; it features a "gorgeous" (some say "gaudy") interior with a "quiet" vibe making it "well worth a visit", even if a few call it "expensive for the neighborhood."

RA Sushi *Japanese* | 23 | 22 | 21 | $28 |

Torrance | Del Amo Fashion Ctr. | 3525 W. Carson St. (bet. Hawthorne Blvd. & Madrona Ave.) | 310-370-6700 | www.rasushi.com

"Great happy-hour" specials on maki rolls and appetizers are the main draw at this Torrance link in a Japanese chain from Benihana set in "hip" digs deemed "nicer than one would expect in a mall"; however, even with "amazing prices", many find the fare "run-of-the-mill."

Rattler's Bar-B-Que *BBQ* | 25 | 23 | 24 | $22 |

Santa Clarita | 26495 Golden Valley Rd. (Golden Triangle Rd.) | 661-251-4195 | www.rattlersbbq.com

The "tender" tri-tip "never disappoints" at this casual Santa Clarita BBQer where folks have their fill of babyback ribs, pulled pork and "out-of-this-world" gratis garlic rolls, plus selections from the "fantastic" salad bar; prices are good and service is "friendly and quick", so it's a "keeper", especially for families; P.S. designated parking for to-go orders makes takeout a breeze.

The Raymond Ⓜ *Californian* | 25 | 26 | 25 | $53 |

Pasadena | 1250 S. Fair Oaks Ave. (Columbia St.) | 626-441-3136 | www.theraymond.com

There's "charm all over" this longtime Californian in Pasadena, from the "romantic" Craftsman setting with a patio to the vintage bar from

1886; "thoughtfully prepared" steaks, seafood and such are complemented by "delightful" service making it just right for a "special occasion" if you can abide the "high" prices.

Ray's & Stark Bar *Mediterranean*
| 24 | 22 | 21 | $49 |

Mid-Wilshire | LACMA | 5905 Wilshire Blvd. (S. Fairfax Ave.) | 323-857-6180 | www.patinagroup.com

"A perfect compliment" to LACMA, this somewhat "pricey" museum-restaurant "destination" is a find for "ambitious" Med dishes that are "artworks in and of themselves" set down in a "magnificent", "light-filled" setting by a "charming" staff; there's also a "beautiful outdoor lounge" that's "great for people-watching" with a "light bite and crazy cocktail", which is named after the late movie producer Ray Stark (*Steel Magnolias, The Way We Were*).

Real Food Daily *Vegan*
| 23 | 18 | 21 | $26 |

West Hollywood | 414 N. La Cienega Blvd. (Oakwood Ave.) | 310-289-9910
Santa Monica | 514-516 Santa Monica Blvd. (5th St.) | 310-451-7544
NEW **Pasadena** | 899 E. Del Mar Blvd. (Lake Ave.) | 626-844-8900
www.realfood.com

You'll "feel healthier just walking in" to this "vegan paradise", a moderately priced chainlet in Pasadena, Santa Monica and West Hollywood serving a "diverse" lineup of "surprisingly tasty" meat-free eats to a "beautiful" crowd sprinkled with celebrities; the atmosphere's "a tad New-Age-y" for some, and the staff can swing from "super-friendly" to "indifferent", but it's inevitably "packed."

Reddi Chick BBQ ⬚ *BBQ*
| 20 | 7 | 17 | $13 |

Santa Monica | Brentwood Country Mart | 225 26th St. (San Vicente Blvd.) | 310-393-5238 | www.brentwoodcountrymart.com

Westsiders "love sitting around the fire pit and munching on delish chicken" at this "beloved" BBQ "landmark" in the old-fashioned Brentwood Country Mart featuring "finger-licking good" rotisserie birds, "tenders that are actually tender" and "mouthwatering fries"; prices are a bargain, and the setting with umbrella-topped communal tables is "great for young kids and star sightings."

Red Medicine ● *Vietnamese*
| 23 | 18 | 20 | $53 |

Beverly Hills | 8400 Wilshire Blvd. (Gale Dr.) | 323-651-5500 | www.redmedicinela.com

"Awaken your senses" at this "exciting" Vietnamese fusion in Beverly Hills where chef Jordan Kahn presents "wild, esoteric" dishes that "look like they came straight out of a food magazine"; all comes served against a "simple" backdrop with "amazing" cocktails, although a few take issue with "spotty" service, "noisy" acoustics and a bill that can "add up fast."

⬚ Red O *Mexican*
| 25 | 27 | 22 | $58 |

Melrose | 8155 Melrose Ave. (Kilkea Dr.) | 323-655-5009 | www.redorestaurant.com

A "stunning", "over-the-top" clublike space forms the backdrop for this "fancy" Melrose Mexican featuring "highly original", "memorable" cuisine from celebrity chef Rick Bayless plus "perfectly concocted" margaritas made from an "extensive tequila selection" ("the cucumber margs rock"); on the downside is somewhat "pretentious" front-of-the-house service, and those that don't get the "hype" say "o stands for overrated."

redwhite+bluezz *American*   23 | 21 | 22 | $40

Pasadena | 70 S. Raymond Ave. (Green St.) | 626-792-4441 | www.redwhitebluezz.com

"Come for the music, stay for the food" at this Pasadena jazz venue offering "delicious small dishes" as well as heartier midpriced American fare matched with "great wine flights"; solid service and a "lovely ambiance" enhanced by all those "talented" musicians complete the package; P.S. "you can't beat the happy hour", either.

Reel Inn *Seafood*   22 | 15 | 16 | $25

Malibu | 18661 PCH (Topanga Canyon Blvd.) | 310-456-8221 | www.reelinnmalibu.com

"One of the few classic fish shacks left", this "funky" "favorite" in Malibu proffers "delicious" "fresh seafood" in way-"informal" digs with surf decor and picnic tables out back; the counter service can be hit-or-miss, but many still find it "perfect after a day at the beach."

Restaurant at The Standard ● *Eclectic*   19 | 24 | 18 | $45

Downtown | The Standard Downtown LA | 550 S. Flower St. (6th St.) | 213-892-8080
West Hollywood | The Standard | 8300 W. Sunset Blvd. (Sweetzer Ave.) | 323-650-9090
www.standardhotel.com

"Hip food for hip folks" sums up these "cool" 24/7 hotel mainstays at The Standard Downtown and in West Hollywood, where the Eclectic menu of dressed-up comfort fare takes a backseat to the "fun" scene; prices are moderate and service is "pleasant" enough, but no surprise, they get "loud" during peak hours.

Ribs USA *BBQ*   23 | 11 | 19 | $24

Burbank | 2711 W. Olive Ave. (N. Naomi St.) | 818-841-8872 | www.ribsusa.com

Diners get "down and dirty" with "stick-to-your-ribs" ribs and other "messy", meaty eats at this old-fashioned Burbank BBQ; some call the food "hit-or-miss", but it's wallet-friendly and the "nothing fancy" atmosphere can be lots of "fun."

Rive Gauche Cafe Ⓜ *French*   21 | 22 | 23 | $40

Sherman Oaks | 14106 Ventura Blvd. (Hazeltine Ave.) | 818-990-3573 | www.rivegauchecafeandlounge.com

If it's romance you seek, Sherman Oaks natives say this "quaint", "charming" French bistro makes for a "wonderful date-night destination" with its "beautiful garden" outside and a fireplace making things "cozy" inside; the atmosphere's "quiet" and both the service and the "traditional" fare are "consistently good" too, making it an "old reliable" for an older crowd.

Rivera *Pan-Latin*   26 | 24 | 23 | $60

Downtown | Met Lofts | 1050 S. Flower St. (11 St.) | 213-749-1460 | www.riverarestaurant.com

"A knockout every time", this Downtown Pan-Latin from "genius" chef John Sedlar presents "playful", "high-concept, beautifully executed" dishes that "look like art and taste like heaven" alongside "brilliant" cocktails in a "chic" dining room; service "always pleases" too, and although some complain the multiple menus are "confusing" and that it "needs to tone down the noise", most consider it a "privilege" "worth the high prices."

Riviera Restaurant & Lounge *Italian*   25 | 22 | 24 | $49

Calabasas | 23683 Calabasas Rd. (Park Granada) | 818-224-2163 | www.rivieracalabasas.com

There's "always something new to try" at this "enjoyable" upmarket Calabasas Italian that's "a perfect choice when you don't want to take chances on service or food", with "excellent" fare that's "nothing too crazy" and "attentive" treatment; despite the strip-mall locale, there's a "lively" bar, a "cozy" dining area and "you can almost always get a table."

Road to Seoul *Korean/BBQ*   ▽ 24 | 17 | 19 | $21

Mid-City | 1230 S. Western Ave. (W. Pico Blvd.) | 323-731-9292

At this all-you-can-eat Mid-City Korean, expect "endless" BBQ options and kimchi at "fantastic" prices offering some of the "best bang for your buck" in town; service is often "excellent" too, but the trade-off is a no-frills setting that can be "loud and smoky."

Robin's Woodfire BBQ & Grill Ⓜ *BBQ*   23 | 19 | 20 | $20

Pasadena | 395 N. Rosemead Blvd. (bet. E. Foothill Blvd. & Sierra Madre Villa Ave.) | 626-351-8885 | www.robinsbbq.com

You can "smell the smoke a block away" at this "down-home" Pasadena BBQer dishing out "heaping" helpings of "fabulous" meats doused in "gooey, sticky" sauce sided with "tangy coleslaw" that's studded with blue cheese; service is "friendly and fast", and nightly specials (kids under 12 eat free after 4 PM) plus a "fun" roadhouse setting make it fit for families.

The Rockefeller *American*   ▽ 19 | 21 | 19 | $31

Hermosa Beach | 422 Pier Ave. (Cypress Ave.) | 310-372-8467 | www.eatrockefeller.com

This midpriced Hermosa Beach gastropub plys patrons with an "ever-evolving" American menu featuring shareable plates, oysters and interesting beers and wines in a "noisy" rustic-meets-modern setting packed with twentysomethings; though the concept is a "nice change" for the area, some suggest "the execution hasn't been perfected yet."

Röckenwagner Bakery Cafe *Bakery*   20 | 14 | 17 | $19

Santa Monica | 311 Arizona Ave. (3rd St. Promenade) | 310-394-4267 | www.rockenwagner.com

The "fantastic" pretzel bread gets top billing at Hans Röckenwagner's bakery/cafe on the Third Street Promenade also putting out "cute, little sandwiches", salads, pastries and other well-priced daytime Cal cuisine; expect "helpful" (if "not that friendly") service and a no-nonsense contemporary setting that caters to the grab-and-go crowd.

Rock'n Fish *Seafood*   22 | 20 | 21 | $35

Downtown | LA Live | 800 W. Olympic Blvd. (Figueroa St.) | 213-748-4020 | www.rocknfishlalive.com

Manhattan Beach | 120 Manhattan Beach Blvd. (bet. Manhattan Ave. & Ocean Dr.) | 310-379-9900 | www.rocknfishmb.com

"The navy grog is a must" (warning: "lightweights beware") at these "hip, happening" seafooders known for a "nice variety" of "awesome" "fresh fish" and oak-grilled steaks at a "good value"; regulars report it's "tough to get a seat and kind of noisy", but most are "never disapppointed" nonetheless.

⊠ RockSugar Pan Asian Kitchen *Asian* | 22 | 27 | 23 | $36 |

Century City | Westfield Century City Shopping Ctr. | 10250 Santa Monica Blvd. (bet. Ave. of the Stars & Century Park W.) | 310-552-9988 | www.rocksugarpanasiankitchen.com

Prepare for "sensory overload" at this Cheesecake Factory off-shoot in the Westfield Century City Shopping Center where the "over-the-top", "Asian Disneyland" decor is "a spectacle to behold"; the Pan-Asian fare is "surprisingly good" too, not to mention "perfect for sharing", and it comes "well served" with "fabulous drinks", so even if some say it's "a little on the expensive side", it's still "well worth checking out."

Roll 'n Rye Deli *Deli* | 17 | 12 | 19 | $20 |

Culver City | Studio Village Shopping Ctr. | 10990 W. Jefferson Blvd. (Sepulveda Blvd.) | 310-390-3497 | www.rollnrye.com

Culver City locals craving "Jewish comfort food" head to this "friendly" "New York-style" deli for "prescription-strength matzo ball soup", "decent" sandwiches and such served in a space that's like "stepping back four or five decades"; critics complain it's "past its prime", plus "at these prices you shouldn't have to ask for more pickles."

Rosa Mexicano *Mexican* | 21 | 21 | 21 | $39 |

Downtown | LA Live | 800 W. Olympic Blvd. (Figueroa St.) | 213-746-0001

Sunset Strip | 8570 W. Sunset Blvd. (Alta Loma Rd.) | West Hollywood | 310-657-4991

www.rosamexicano.com

"*Dios mio*", the tableside guacamole is "to die for" and the margaritas are "strong" at these upscale Mexican chain imports from NYC set in "eye-catching" digs in Downtown's LA Live and on the Sunset Strip; consensus is the other fare on the "extensive, creative" menu is "reliable" enough, and while prices are "not so *bueno*" for everyone, "happy hour is justifiably popular and a bargain."

⊠ Roscoe's House of Chicken 'n Waffles *Soul Food* | 24 | 14 | 20 | $20 |

Hollywood | 1514 N. Gower St. (bet. Hollywood & Sunset Blvds.) | 323-466-7453 ◗

Mid-City | 106 W. Manchester Ave. (Main St.) | 323-752-6211

Mid-City | 5006 W. Pico Blvd: (Mansfield Ave.) | 323-934-4405 ◗

Long Beach | 730 E. Broadway (bet. Alamitos & Atlantic Aves.) | 562-437-8355

Pasadena | 830 N. Lake Ave. (bet. Mountain St. & Orange Grove Blvd.) | 626-791-4890

www.roscoeschickenandwaffles.com

"The perfect blend of salty and sweet" awaits in the "sublime" signature dish at this "legendary" soul-food chain that "sets the standard" matching "succulent" fried chicken with "light, fluffy" waffles for a pairing that "goes together better than peanut butter and jelly"; the "old-school" digs are "not much to look at" and service can be "so-so", but even so, it "doesn't disappoint"; P.S. "prepare for a wait, especially after church on Sundays."

Rose Cafe *Californian*
21 | 20 | 20 | $22

Venice | 220 Rose Ave. (Hampton Dr.) | 310-399-0711 | www.rosecafe.com
Brunch-seekers "just love" the "inviting" patio at this otherwise "unassuming", moderately priced daytime spot that's "just a short walk away from hectic Venice Beach"; it serves a "healthy", "varied" Cal menu via sit-down service as well as "a nice selection of pick-and-choose" deli items available to go.

Rosti *Italian*
18 | 14 | 19 | $25

Santa Monica | 931 Montana Ave. (10th St.) | 310-393-3236
NEW Calabasas | 23663 Calabasas Rd. (Park Granada) |
818-591-2211 Ⓢ Ⓜ
Encino | 16350 Ventura Blvd. (bet. Noeline & Libbit Aves.) | 818-995-7179
www.rostituscankitchen.com
The "*perfecto*" brick-pressed chicken is the standout at this "inexpensive" chainlet specializing in "Americanized" takes on "rustic Italian food" like thin-crust pizzas, grilled salmon and panini; the vibe is "family-friendly", but some find the service and ambiance only "so-so", making it a "go-to for takeout."

Ⓩ The Royce Ⓢ Ⓜ *American*
24 | 27 | 26 | $75

Pasadena | Langham Huntington | 1401 S. Oak Knoll Ave. (Huntington Cir.) | 626-585-6410 | www.theroycela.com
Chef David Féau "brings some life to the hotel dining scene" with his "adventurous", "beautifully presented" New American cuisine at this "stunning" modern space at the Langham in Pasadena; "tremendous" wines and "top-notch" service elevate the experience, and although it's pricey, "for a night you'll never forget, sit at the chef's table and get the tasting menu."

Roy's *Hawaiian*
25 | 23 | 23 | $51

Downtown | 800 S. Figueroa St. (8th St.) | 213-488-4994
Pasadena | 641 E. Colorado Blvd. (El Molino Ave.) | 626-356-4066
Woodland Hills | 6363 Topanga Canyon Blvd. (Victory Blvd.) | 818-888-4801
www.roysrestaurant.com
For a "special occasion" or "date night", Roy Yamaguchi's "upscale" chain in "elegant", "tropical" digs is "always a treat" thanks to "delish", "creative" Hawaiian fusion fare capped by an "unbelievable" chocolate soufflé; service is "smooth" and "astonishingly kid-friendly", so even if a few find it a little spendy, it remains a "favorite"; P.S. the $35 three-course prix fixe dinner is a "real bargain."

R23 Ⓢ *Japanese*
25 | 21 | 21 | $53

Downtown | 923 E. Second St. (bet. Garey & Vignes Sts.) | 213-687-7178 | www.r23.com
"If you can find it", this "arty" Japanese in a "funky" Downtown warehouse showcases "fantastic" sushi and "seasonal creations" served on handcrafted ceramics in an "edgy" room complete with Frank Gehry chairs and a skyline view; you might have to "pay an arm and a leg", but service is solid and most find the "quality" is worth it.

Ruby's *Diner*
21 | 21 | 21 | $19

Rolling Hills Estates | Avenue of the Peninsula Mall | 550 Deep Valley Dr. (Drybank Dr.) | Rolling Hills | 310-544-7829
Long Beach | Long Beach Mktpl. | 6405 E. PCH (2nd St.) | 562-596-1914

(continued)

Ruby's

Redondo Beach | 245 N. Harbor Dr. (Portofino Way) | 310-376-7829

Woodland Hills | Westfield Promenade | 6100 Topanga Canyon Blvd. (bet. Erwin & Oxnard Sts.) | 818-340-7829

Whittier | Whittwood Mall | 10109 Whittwood Dr. (Cullen St.) | 562-947-7829

LAX | LA Int'l Airport, Terminal 6 | 1 World Way (Sepulveda Blvd.) | 310-646-2480

www.rubys.com

"Put up your ponytail" and "roll down your socks" to fit in at this chain of "nifty-'50s" diners where "perky" "costumed" servers serve up "yummy, sloppy burgers", malts and other "classic" fare at "rock-bottom prices"; the "casual" setup is especially "handy" for families, so "be prepared to be surrounded by kids."

Rush Street *American*   18 | 18 | 17 | $28

Culver City | 9546 Washington Blvd. (Irving Pl.) | 310-837-9546 | www.rushstreetculvercity.com

"Always hopping", this Culver City lounge is a "good meetup spot" thanks to its "all-American" "comfort-food" menu, "nicely curated" cocktail list and "jumping" bar scene; it's all "too loud and too young" for some, although the patio is slightly more sedate.

Rustic Canyon *Californian/Mediterranean*   25 | 19 | 22 | $48

Santa Monica | 1119 Wilshire Blvd. (11th St.) | 310-393-7050 | www.rusticcanyonwinebar.com

"It's like eating from the farm without the work" at this Santa Monica Cal-Med matching "phenomenal" farm-to-table small plates ("wonderful fried cauliflower") with "interesting wines" in a "stylish, yet casual" setting; servers are "knowledgeable" too, but "it's a little pricey" and along with the "well-heeled" crowds come "noisy" acoustics; P.S. the "fantastic" burger is a standout.

Rustico *Italian*   26 | 20 | 26 | $45

Westlake Village | 1125 Lindero Canyon Rd. (Lakeview Canyon Rd.) | 818-889-0191 | www.rustico-restaurant.com

A "go-to" in Westlake Village, this "lovely neighborhood Italian" is a find for "delicious" dishes cooked up in a wood-burning oven and set down by a "personable", "professional" staff that offers "great recommendations"; yes, it's set in a strip mall, but it's "priced better" than many and most find it a "delight" nonetheless.

Ruth's Chris Steak House *Steak*   27 | 24 | 26 | $68

Beverly Hills | 224 S. Beverly Dr. (bet. Charleville Blvd. & Gregory Way) | 310-859-8744

Pasadena | 369 E. Colorado Blvd. (Euclid Ave.) | 626-583-8122

Woodland Hills | Westfield Promenade | 6100 Topanga Canyon Blvd. (bet. Erwin & Oxnard Sts.) | 818-227-9505

www.ruthschris.com

"Flavorful steaks still sizzling on your plate" are the thing at this up-market chophouse chain also known for its "standout" sides, "nice wines" and "big martinis" served by a "knowledgeable" staff in "plush" surroundings; a few find it "a bit formulaic", but at least "you can depend on a great meal every time."

Rutts *Hawaiian*

22 | 12 | 19 | $13

Culver City | 12114 W. Washington Blvd. (bet. Grand View Blvd. & Lindblade Dr.) | 310-398-6326 | www.ruttscafe.com

"It's not much to look at", but this Hawaiian "hole-in-the-wall" in Culver City offers an "expansive menu" of "tasty" traditional breakfast items and plate lunches, from the omeletlike royales to spam; "cheap" prices keep it especially "crazy busy" during Sunday brunch.

☒ Saam at The Bazaar by José Andrés ☒ ☒ *Eclectic*

27 | 26 | 26 | $130

Beverly Hills | SLS at Beverly Hills | 465 S. La Cienega Blvd. (Clifton Way) | 310-246-5545 | www.thebazaar.com

"You'll swear you've died and gone to foodie heaven" at this Eclectic tasting room at The Bazaar in Beverly Hills showcasing an "unparalleled" 22-course tasting menu from José Andrés featuring "playful", "crazy-delicious" plates that "will create converts out of even the most staunch modernist cuisine skeptics"; the "chic, private" setting is "more intimate" than its sib and topped off with "exquisite" service that takes the sting out of the "splurge"-worthy bills.

☒ Saddle Peak Lodge ☒ *American*

26 | 28 | 26 | $69

Calabasas | 419 Cold Canyon Rd. (Piuma Rd.) | 818-222-3888 | www.saddlepeaklodge.com

"Nestled in the mountains", this "one-of-a-kind" New American is "worth the trek" to Calabasas thanks to its "wonderfully prepared" game, "nice wines" and "superior" service in a "magical", "transporting" setting decked out like a "huntsman lodge"; in sum, it's "the go-to place for a special occasion, especially if someone else is picking up the tab."

NEW Sadie Kitchen & Lounge ☒ ☒ *American*

_ | _ | _ | M

Hollywood | 1638 N. Las Palmas Ave. (Hollywood Blvd.) | 323-467-0200 | www.sadiela.com

Early samplers say this sleek, upscale Hollywood newcomer is "a great addition" to the area with a market-driven American menu and interesting hand-crafted cocktails; the handsome setting includes a cozy, wood-lined bar, and the airy courtyard is sure to be packed come summertime.

Safire *American*

26 | 25 | 25 | $34

Camarillo | 4850 Santa Rosa Rd. (bet. Ventura Fwy. & Verdugo Way) | 805-389-1227 | www.safirebistro.com

"Excellent all around" proclaim regulars of this Camarillo bistro that "delivers the goods" with "top-drawer" New American fare like miso-glazed sea bass and wet-aged rib-eye and "excellent" service; it's "a little pricey" for the area, but it's "nicer" than most too, with a handsome, "upscale" dining room and outdoor cabanas around a fire pit; P.S. there's also live music on weekends.

Saladang *Thai*

24 | 19 | 20 | $25

Pasadena | 363 S. Fair Oaks Ave. (bet. California & Del Mar Blvds.) | 626-793-8123

Saladang Song *Thai*

Pasadena | 383 S. Fair Oaks Ave. (bet. California & Del Mar Blvds.) | 626-793-5200

"Busy for a reason", these Pasadena Thais are praised for their "delicious", if "Americanized", fare presented by a "gracious" staff "at very reasonable prices"; Saladang is set in a "modern concrete set-ting" while the younger Saladang Song is equally "austere", but boasts a "serene" patio that's "great on a warm evening" as well as a menu that's somewhat "more adventurous" than its elder's.

Salt Creek Grille *Steak*

20 | 21 | 20 | $35

El Segundo | Plaza El Segundo | 2015 E. Park Pl. (Rosecrans Ave.) | 310-335-9288

Valencia | Valencia Town Ctr. | 24415 Town Center Dr. (McBean Pkwy.) | 661-222-9999

www.saltcreekgrille.com

These "comfortable" chophouse chain links in El Segundo and Valencia are fallbacks for "casual" dining with "decent" steaks served in "lively" environs with live music on weekends; critics call the food "uninspired" and "overpriced", but happy hour by the fire pits is a lot of "fun."

Salt's Cure *American*

25 | 19 | 21 | $38

Hollywood | 7494 Santa Monica Blvd. (Vista St.) | 323-850-7258 | www.saltscure.com

"Adventurous eaters" are "madly in love" with this "brilliant" locavore American in Hollywood, where everything on the midpriced meat-heavy menu is butchered and made in-house, from the "legendary" ba-con and sausages to "fine" smoked fish and a "chicken-liver pudding so good you'll want to rub it on your body"; the "dedicated" staff "can tell you the origins of all of the ingredients" too, so even if the space is a tad "too crowded", on the whole you "won't be disappointed."

Sammy's Woodfired Pizza *Pizza*

21 | 16 | 20 | $22

El Segundo | Plaza El Segundo | 780 S. Sepulveda Blvd. (Rosecrans Ave.) | 310-335-9999 | www.sammyspizza.com

There's "something for everyone" at this casual El Segundo outpost of a San Diego–based 'healthy' pizza-and-more chain known for "inter-esting" concoctions like the popular Brie and truffle oil pie; ample "portions make sharing easy", which keeps the cost down and makes for a "great family night out"; P.S. save room for the "marvel-ous" hot-fudge sundae.

Samosa House *Indian*

21 | 12 | 16 | $12

Culver City | 11510 W. Washington Blvd. (Berryman Ave.) | 310-398-6766

Samosa House East *Indian*

Culver City | 10700 Washington Blvd. (Overland Ave.) | 310-559-6350 www.samosahouse.net

"Watch Bollywood videos while you eat" at these Indian pit stops in Culver City, where "affordable", "filling" vegetarian platters are served with garlic naan "fresh out of the tandoori"; the order-at-the-steamtable digs are "colorful", if nothing fancy, and the original location further west on 11510 W. Washington Boulevard doubles as a grocery store.

⊠ Sam's by the Beach Ⓜ *Californian/Mediterranean*

26 | 22 | 26 | $55

Santa Monica | 108 W. Channel Rd. (PCH) | 310-230-9100 | www.samsbythebeach.com

"A quaint find" just off PCH in Santa Monica, this Cal-Med "treasure" delivers "inventive fare crafted from the freshest ingredients" in an "intimate" setting that "really pushes the romance factor"; "impeccable" service led by "hands-on" owner Sam is "free of LA attitude", so "if budget was no concern" devotees declare they'd "go every night."

Sam Woo *Chinese*   21 | 12 | 15 | $19

Chinatown | 803 N. Broadway (bet. Alpine & College Sts.) | 213-687-7238 ●⇺

Cerritos | 19008 Pioneer Blvd. (South St.) | 562-865-7278 ●

Van Nuys | Signature Plaza | 6450 Sepulveda Blvd. (Victory Blvd.) | 818-988-6813 ⇺

Alhambra | 514 W. Valley Blvd. (bet. 5th & 6th Sts.) | 626-281-0038 ●⇺

San Gabriel | 140 W. Valley Blvd. (Manley Dr.) | 626-572-8418 ●⇺

San Gabriel | 425 S. California St. (Agostino Rd.) | 626-287-6528 ⇺

San Gabriel | 937 E. Las Tunas Dr. (bet. Angelus & Earle Aves.) | 626-286-3118 ●⇺

"Peking duck done right" and other "honest", "Cantonese-style comfort food" comes at "unbeatable" prices at this "no-frills" Chinese BBQ chainlet; "the decor isn't much" and service is of the "eat and leave" variety, but takeout is "easy" and it often hits the spot late at night.

Sanamluang Cafe *Thai*   23 | 10 | 17 | $16

East Hollywood | 5176 Hollywood Blvd. (Kingsley Dr.) | 323-660-8006 ●⇺

North Hollywood | 12980 Sherman Way (bet. Coldwater Canyon & Ethel Aves.) | 818-764-1180

www.sanamluangcafe.menutoeat.com

When "it's 2 AM and you need that Thai fix", this East Hollywood "hole-in-the-wall" with a North Hollywood offshoot is "open after the clubs close" offering "filling", "flavorful" grub; perhaps service is "meh" and decor "needs help" but the "cops, hipsters and locals" that cram in don't seem to care.

Santa Monica Seafood Café *Seafood*   26 | 16 | 20 | $31

Santa Monica | 1000 Wilshire Blvd. (10th St.) | 310-393-5244 | www.santamonicaseafood.com

"The seafood's so fresh it's like a slap in the face" at this Santa Monica market-cum-cafe selling an "impeccable" selection of fish retail while also serving "top-flight" "straightforward" fare, including a "great cioppino" and "fantastic crab"; it's certainly "not a glamorous place", but service is "friendly" and if it's usually "loud and crowded", it's because "you can't get better for the price."

Santouka Ramen ⇺ *Japanese*   24 | 8 | 13 | $12

Mar Vista | Mitsuwa Market | 3760 S. Centinela Ave. (Venice Blvd.) | 310-391-1101 | www.santouka.co.jp

Santouka Ramen Torrance ⇺ *Japanese*

Torrance | 21515 S. Western Ave. (Mullin Ave.) | 310-212-1101

"Noodle addicts" "worship" this Japan-born chain of ramen shops for its "heavenly" broth and "meltingly tender" pork; the "no-nonsense" supermarket settings are "not the most atmospheric", but you can't beat it for a "cheap, fast and tasty" bite; P.S. cash only.

Savory *American*   26 | 21 | 21 | $48

Malibu | Point Dume Vill. | 29169 Heathercliff Rd. (PCH) | 310-589-8997 | www.savorymalibu.com

"It's about time Malibu got a restaurant that's worth going to" proclaim fans of this New American "gem" from chef Paul Shoemaker (ex Bastide, Providence) turning out "truly terrific", "creative" seasonal small and large plates in a "sleek, modern" setting that makes up for the strip-mall locale; most "love it", even if a few complain of "spotty", "snobby" service and "expensive" bills.

Scarpetta *Italian*　24 | 25 | 23 | $65

Beverly Hills | Montage Beverly Hills | 225 N. Cañon Dr. (bet. Clifton & Dayton Way) | 310-860-7970 | www.scottconant.com

The "humble" $24 spaghetti dish "is all it's cracked up to be" at this "expensive" Beverly Hills Italian from NYC, where Scott Conant's "fabulous" food is served in a "beautiful", "modern" setting with a patio affording primo people-watching; service is "pleasant" too, although a "let-down" contingent calls it "disappointing after all the hype."

Sea Empress *Chinese*　22 | 15 | 18 | $26

Gardena | Pacific Sq. | 1636 W. Redondo Beach Blvd. (bet. Normandie & Western Aves.) | 310-538-6868

Fans say "it's hard not to stop every cart" at this Gardena dim-sum mainstay rolling out "solid" Chinese nibbles and "fantastic seafood"; the space is "huge", but the prices are so "reasonable" that "it's worth putting up with the noise and the crowds."

Sea Harbour *Chinese/Seafood*　26 | 18 | 18 | $29

Rosemead | 3939 Rosemead Blvd. (Valley Blvd.) | 626-288-3939

"Arrive early" because "there's always a line" at this relatively "high-end" Rosemead Chinese banquet hall, a "venerable" source for "sublime" dim sum served without the carts and Cantonese seafood at dinner; service can be "borderline rude, but with dumplings like these, who cares?"

NEW Seoul House of Tofu *Korean*　- | - | - | M

West LA | 2101 Sawtelle Blvd. (Mississippi Ave.) | 310-444-9988 | www.seoultofuhouse.com

This oversized Sawtelle Boulevard Korean may be the fanciest option on the Asian-lined West LA street, offering a moderately priced menu of 13 varieties of bubbling soon tofu stew along with Korean classics like bulgogi, galbi and bibimbop; the spacious, glass-accented dining room offers views of locals bustling around the surrounding mini-mall.

NEW Settebello *Pizza*　▽ 24 | 17 | 22 | $24

Pasadena | 625 E. Colorado Blvd. (El Molino Ave.) | 626-765-9550 | www.settebello.net

This affordable pizzeria chainlet (with branches in Salt Lake City and Las Vegas) arrives in Pasadena, boasting "authentic Neapolitan pizza" "done simply and well" the old-fashioned way – first by hand, and then in a wood-burning oven; a "welcoming" vibe and "ample seating" looking out onto Colorado Boulevard makes it "a perfect place to relax" and enjoy a casual bite.

17th Street Cafe *Californian*　21 | 18 | 21 | $26

Santa Monica | 1610 Montana Ave. (16th St.) | 310-453-2771 | www.seventeenthstreetcafe.com

"When promenading on Montana", Santa Monicans turn to this "neighborhood fixture" for Cal fare like "delicious" salads served in a "light, airy" room that manages to feel both "restful" and "upbeat", rounded out by "lovely" service and "people-watching"; though some dub the food "standard, not special", most are pleased by the "positive difference" the new owners are making, "keeping the favorites and adding new creative dishes", all for "decent" prices.

71 Palm Ⓩ *American/French*   25 | 23 | 23 | $49

Ventura | 71 N. Palm St. (bet. Main & Poli Sts.) | 805-653-7222 | www.71palm.com

"Magnificent" French-American fare by chef-owner Didier Poirier keeps "longtime customers" coming back to this "quaint" Craftsman cottage in Downtown Ventura that's "peaceful" and "intimate" with seating by the fireplace and "friendly" service; though "a tad expensive", it's well suited to "date nights" and "special occasions."

Shabu Shabu House Ⓜ *Japanese*   23 | 11 | 16 | $22

Little Tokyo | 127 Japanese Village Plaza Mall (bet. 1st & 2nd Sts.) | 213-680-3890

Cook-it-yourself types tout the "masterful version" of the eponymous dish at this budget Little Tokyo Japanese where the "delicious" meats, sauces and condiments can be had for "bargain-basement prices"; decor isn't a strong suit, and it's always "busy", so prepare to "wait."

The Shack *Burgers*   20 | 13 | 17 | $17

Playa del Rey | 185 Culver Blvd. (Vista del Mar) | 310-823-6222 | www.the-shacks.com
Santa Monica | 2518 Wilshire Blvd. (26th St.) | 310-449-1171 | www.theshacksm.com

"Big, juicy" burgers – like the signature Shackburger topped with a Louisiana hot link – and lots of "cold beer" are the draws at these "laid-back" beach "dives" in Playa del Rey and Santa Monica; there's "no frills and no fancy sides", just a "nice staff, sandy locals" and lots of TVs for Philadelphia sports fans on weekends.

Shaherzad *Persian*   23 | 17 | 20 | $27

Westwood | 1422 Westwood Blvd. (bet. Santa Monica & Wilshire Blvds.) | 310-470-9131 | www.shaherzadrestaurant.com

Go for "anything lamb" at this Westwood Persian known for its "wonderful kebabs" and other "authentic" eats accompanied by "warm, fresh bread coming from the oven"; service can be "aloof" and "don't expect a luxury atmosphere", but low prices for "huge portions" mean for most it "never fails."

Shamshiri Grill *Persian*   24 | 18 | 20 | $25

Westwood | 1712 Westwood Blvd. (Santa Monica Blvd.) | 310-474-1410 | www.sshamshiri.com

"One of the highlights of Little Teheran" in Westwood, this "welcoming" Persian "shines" with "fresh, hot bread", stews and kebabs dished out in "enormous" portions ("few leave without a Styrofoam container in their hand"); service veers from "welcoming" to attitudinal, but the "bargain" prices get no complaints.

Shin-Sen-Gumi Yakitori *Japanese*   25 | 15 | 23 | $23

Gardena | 18517 S. Western Ave. (W. 185th St.) | 310-715-1588
Shin-Sen-Gumi Yakitori Shabu-Shabu *Japanese*
Monterey Park | 111 N. Atlantic Blvd. (Garvey Ave.) | 626-943-7956 | www.shinsengumiusa.com

"A gastronomic ride from start to finish", these Gardena and Monterey Park grills serve some of "the best yakitori" around and other "A+",

	FOOD	DECOR	SERVICE	COST

"authentic" Japanese items; prices are "low" while the tavern-style settings and "warm, loud" welcome from the staff transport you to "Tokyo without the jet lag."

☒ Shiro ⓜ *French/Japanese* 27 | 21 | 28 | $56

South Pasadena | 1505 Mission St. (bet. Fair Oaks & Mound Aves.) | 626-799-4774 | www.restaurantshiro.com

The sizzling catfish is still a "must" at this longtime "gem" in South Pasadena serving "creative", "spot-on" French-Japanese cuisine that's "a little pricey but so worth it"; its understated setting isn't its strong point, but service is always "warm and wonderful" and it's "totally enjoyable if you are blind to the decor"; P.S. open Wednesdays–Sundays only.

NEW Short Order *Burgers* 18 | 16 | 17 | $25

Fairfax | Farmers Mkt. | 6333 W. Third St. (Fairfax Ave.) | 323-761-7970 | www.shortorderla.com

Nancy Silverton teamed with the late Amy Pressman for this burger joint in the Fairfax Farmers Market, where the offerings include "messy" burgers made with grass-fed beef, "shameful and delicious" milkshakes and "interesting sides" served in an airy space with a few tables inside and additional seating on heated patios; though the mood's "fun", "disappointed" diners say the food "falls short" and it's "expensive for what you get."

Sidecar Restaurant ⓜ *American* 23 | 19 | 23 | $39

Ventura | 3029 E. Main St. (bet. Mills & Telegraph Rds.) | 805-653-7433 | www.thesidecarrestaurant.com

Housed in a refurbished 1910 Pullman car, this "warm, friendly" Ventura American from chef-owner Tim Kilcoyne offers an "excellent" seasonal menu and well-made cocktails in a "classic" setting; though it's not cheap, some call it "the best deal in town for a higher-end meal"; P.S. grilled cheese and jazz night on Tuesdays "is a must."

Simmzy's *American* 23 | 18 | 20 | $25

NEW Long Beach | 5271 E. Second St. (Laverne Ave.) | 562-439-5590
Manhattan Beach | 229 Manhattan Beach Blvd. (Highland Ave.) | 310-546-1201
www.simmzys.com

"Grab a beer and a burger" at these "loud, crowded" entries in Long Beach and Manhattan Beach matching accessible American fare with a "rotating selection" of craft brews in a "terrific location" just blocks from the water; prices are low, so "get there early" or be prepared for a "long wait."

Simon LA *American* 21 | 24 | 21 | $51

West Hollywood | Sofitel LA | 8555 Beverly Blvd. (bet. La Cienega & San Vicente Blvds.) | 310-278-5444 | www.simonlarestaurant.com

"Modern" twists on "comfort food" come courtesy of *Iron Chef* champ Kerry Simon at this "casual" spot in West Hollywood's Sofitel catering to a somewhat "hip" crowd with New American plates for nibbling capped by "unique" desserts like a homemade Kit Kat bar; a patio and fire pit are added appeals, although foes find the food "mediocre", the service "amateurish" and say it's "expensive" to boot.

	FOOD	DECOR	SERVICE	COST

⛫ Sir Winston's *Californian/Continental*   `26` `28` `26` `$58`

Long Beach | Queen Mary | 1126 Queens Hwy. (Harbor Scenic Dr.) | 562-499-1657 | www.queenmary.com

Where regulars "go to dine, not just eat", this "top-flight" Cal-Continental anchored on the original Queen Mary ocean liner in Long Beach – voted tops for Decor in LA – is "like a trip back in time", having charmed guests with its "perfect" coastal views and "elegant", romantic room for decades; the "excellent" cuisine and "second-to-none" service make it a "special" place where you "take someone you want to impress", just "bring a fat wallet."

Sisley Italian Kitchen *Italian*   `20` `19` `21` `$30`

Sherman Oaks | 15300 Ventura Blvd. (Sepulveda Blvd.) | 818-905-8444
Valencia | Valencia Town Ctr. | 24201 Valencia Blvd. (McBean Pkwy.) | 661-287-4444
www.sisleykitchen.com

A "locals' place", this Sherman Oaks and Valencia pair purvey "large portions" of "old-school" Italian at "a fair price" in "family-friendly" environs with "prompt" service; consensus is it's "tasty" but "nothing spectacular", though it certainly works "in a pinch."

The Six *American*   `22` `16` `19` `$31`

Rancho Park | 10668 W. Pico Blvd. (Pelham Ave.) | 310-837-6662
Studio City | 12650 Ventura Blvd. (Fairway Ave.) | 818-761-2319 Ⓢ Ⓜ
www.thesixrestaurant.com

These numerically obsessed Rancho Park and Studio City Americans have a "creative" menu built around the number six (e.g. six apps, six entrees) as well as pizza and burgers, all at a "good price"; a "cool atmosphere" and a "friendly" staff make each a "neighborhood hangout."

Sky Room *American*   `25` `27` `24` `$61`

Long Beach | Historic Breakers Bldg. | 40 S. Locust Ave. (Ocean Blvd.) | 562-983-2703 | www.theskyroom.com

"Step back into another era" at this "ritzy" 1920s-style entry atop Long Beach's historic Breakers Building New American boasting "eye-candy" views of the ocean and servers "standing by for your every whim"; the New American cuisine is "pretty good" too, and live entertainment and dancing are weekend perks.

Slaw Dogs *Hot Dogs*   `22` `13` `21` `$13`

Pasadena | 720 N. Lake Ave. (Orange Grove Blvd.) | 626-808-9777
Woodland Hills | 19801 Ventura Blvd. (Corbin Ave.) | 818-887-8882
NEW Duarte | 1355 Huntington Dr. (Buena Vista St.) | 626-358-8898
www.theslawdogs.com

"The king of dogs" according to fans, this "awesome" concept elevates the humble frank to "a whole new level" with its "extensive menu" of "cleverly crafted" offerings with "untraditional" toppings like kimchi and truffle oil; service is "quick" and the picnic-seating setting's "unpretentious", although some quibble with the somewhat "steep" prices.

Smitty's Grill *American*   `22` `21` `22` `$42`

Pasadena | 110 S. Lake Ave. (bet. Cordova & Green Sts.) | 626-792-9999 | www.smittysgrill.com

"Right out of *Mad Men*", this "dark, classy" Pasadena American from the Smith brothers (Arroyo Chop House, Parkway Grill) serves "solid" "comfort-food classics" like steaks and chicken pot pie in a "lively", "noisy" setting with a "beautiful bar"; service is "welcoming" too, so even if the bills are "a little costly", most "return again and again."

Smoke City Market *BBQ*

▽ 24 | 12 | 16 | $22

Van Nuys | 5242 Van Nuys Blvd. (bet. Magnolia Blvd. & Weddington St.) | 818-855-1280 | www.smokecitymarket.com

"True Texas-style" 'cue is the specialty of this Van Nuys young 'un that's roping in customers with "heavily smoked", "tender" brisket, "notable sides" and Shiner Bock on tap; even if some call it "a little on the pricey side" for such a "casual" setting, consensus is it's "a real treat and a great addition for LA BBQ lovers."

Smoke House *Steak*

22 | 19 | 22 | $40

Burbank | 4420 W. Lakeside Dr. (Barham Blvd.) | 818-845-3731 | www.smokehouse1946.com

"An institution for the studio set", this "legendary" Burbank steakhouse "hasn't changed a bit" since 1946 and "continues to shine" with "strong" martinis and "addictive", "mysteriously Day-Glo orange garlic bread" tendered alongside "decent" cuts; it's "sorta pricey", but most find it worth it thanks to the "entertaining" servers and overall "old-school charm."

Soleil Westwood *Canadian/French*

21 | 18 | 23 | $33

Westwood | 1386 Westwood Blvd. (Wilkins Ave.) | 310-441-5384 | www.soleilwestwood.com

"Affable host Luc Alarie greets guests with a smile" at his "quaint" Westwood bistro with a "dependable" French-Canadian menu featuring poutine in a dozen variations served in a "quiet" space that "feels like home"; a "low corkage fee", all-you-can-eat mussels on Wednesdays and "great" wine-tasting dinners all make it a highly "affordable" option.

🆕 Soleto Trattoria & Pizza Bar *Italian*

- | - | - | M

Downtown | 801 S. Figueroa St. (8th St.) | 213-622-3255 | www.soletorestaurant.com

Conveniently situated a short walk from Staples and Nokia, this moderately priced Southern Italian is the first pasta and pizza concept from the team behind Sushi Roku and Boa; the space has an exhibition-style pizza kitchen, bare-brick walls and a garden patio surrounded by the skyscrapers of Downtown LA; it's also open late enough to catch a bite after seeing the Lakers or the Clippers just down the street.

Sol y Luna *Mexican*

22 | 20 | 20 | $27

Tarzana | 19601 Ventura Blvd. (Melvin Ave.) | 818-343-8488 | www.solylunausa.com

"No need to make a run for the border" thanks to this "solid", sit-down Tarzana Mexican famed for its tableside guac, "excellent margaritas" and carne asada that could "make a vegetarian switch teams"; the folk art-adorned digs are "festive", but the "jet-engine roar of the crowds" can "make it impossible to talk, let alone think."

Son of a Gun *Seafood*

25 | 17 | 22 | $47

Third Street | 8370 W. Third St. (bet. Kings Rd. & Orlando Ave.) | 323-782-9033 | www.sonofagunrestaurant.com

A "deliciously fishy" concept from the chef dudes behind Animal, this "buzzy" Third Street seafooder draws "salivating" fans with its "mouthwatering" midpriced menu, featuring "stunning standouts" like a "dyn-o-mite" fried-chicken sandwich and "not-to-be-missed" shrimp toast served in a "packed" setting with a "Hemingwayesque, *Old Man and the Sea* thing going on"; "reservations are a pain", but you can expect a staff that's "at your beck and call" and an overall "good-time vibe."

Soot Bull Jeep *Korean*   25 | 10 | 17 | $34

Koreatown | 3136 W. Eighth St. (Catalina St.) | 213-387-3865
"Be ready to get smoked" at this "popular" DIY Koreatown "dive" where "delish" "flavorful meats" are cooked up over charcoal grills, which "makes all the difference" to aficionados; just ignore the "old-cafeteria" decor, "wear disposable clothes" and focus on the "real-deal", inexpensive eats.

Sor Tino *Italian*   23 | 20 | 23 | $41

Brentwood | 908 S. Barrington Ave. (San Vicente Blvd.) | 310-442-8466
A "reliable neighborhood trattoria", this "cozy" Brentwood spot from Agostino Sciandri (Ago) delivers "authentic", "rustic" fare via a "gracious" crew; a "lovely patio" and "reasonable prices" seal the deal.

Sotto ⓜ *Pizza*   22 | 19 | 20 | $44

Century City | 9575 W. Pico Blvd. (bet. Beverwil & S. Beverly Drs.) | 310-277-0210 | www.sottorestaurant.com
A "culinary wonder" in Century City, this "dark", "trendy" "basement boîte" offers "gorgeously charred pizzas" and "really different, fantastic" Italian fare crafted from local, sustainable ingredients and complemented by "inspired" cocktails; some say it has "a few kinks to work out" with food and service and it's "a bit expensive", but on the whole, most are "thankful to have it in the neighborhood"; P.S. "definitely try the meatballs."

South Beverly Grill *American*   22 | 22 | 23 | $38

Beverly Hills | 122 S. Beverly Dr. (bet. Charleville & Wilshire Blvds.) | 310-550-0242 | www.hillstone.com
This "upmarket Houston's" from the group behind that chain (as well as Bandera and R+D Kitchen) hosts a well-heeled Beverly Hills crowd for "expertly prepared" American comfort food at "relatively reasonable" prices; it boasts "attentive" service and a "swanky, comfortable" setting, while the adjacent Honor Bar has "live jazz and great hamburgers."

Spaghetti Eddie's *Italian*   24 | 22 | 24 | $21

Glendora | 946 S. Grand Ave. (W. Baseline Rd.) | 626-963-0267 | www.spaghettieddies.com
"Everyone knows everyone else" at this "family-friendly" Glendora Italian that's been putting out pizzas and "huge portions" of "wonderful" red-sauce fare since 1985; all comes reasonably priced and "promptly served" in an informal, "busy" setting where large booths and dim lighting create a cozy atmosphere.

☒ Spago *Californian*   27 | 25 | 26 | $80

Beverly Hills | 176 N. Cañon Dr. (Wilshire Blvd.) | 310-385-0880 | www.wolfgangpuck.com
"What's left to say" about this "quintessential LA" hub in Beverly Hills – "the jewel in the crown" of the Wolfgang Puck empire – that's "going strong after all these years" turning out "knock-your-socks-off"

Californian cuisine in a "glamorous", "glittering" setting sprinkled with "aging celebs", "power producers and socialites"; "everyone gets treated royally" and "with a little luck, you can get a handshake from the man himself" – in sum, there's "no finer place" to "impress", as long as you can handle the "sky-high" tabs; P.S. as we went to press Spago was closed for a remodel and menu revamp.

Spark Woodfire Grill *American* 22 | 19 | 22 | $37

Studio City | 11801 Ventura Blvd. (bet. Carpenter & Colfax Aves.) | 818-623-8883 | www.sparkwoodfiregrill.com

For an "easy", "reliable" meal, try this "sophisticated, casual" American in Studio City where "hearty" grill fare is dished out in "cozy", "comfortable" environs; though it's "a tad loud", "decent" prices and "accommodating" service make it a worthy "neighborhood standby."

Spice Table ☒ *Asian* 25 | 21 | 23 | $35

Little Tokyo | 114 S. Central Ave. (E. 1st St.) | 213-620-1840 | www.thespicetable.com

"Super-delicious", "fun-to-share" Southeast Asian plates await at this "charming find" in Little Tokyo, where the "unusual" menu pays homage to Singapore and Vietnam, the respective culinary heritages of chef-owner Bryant Ng (ex Pizzeria Mozza) and his wife, Kim; "interesting" craft beers, "friendly service" and a "stylish" brick-walled setting complete the "low-key" (and relatively low priced) experience.

Spitz *Turkish* 23 | 18 | 19 | $14

Eagle Rock | 2506 Colorado Blvd. (College View Ave.) | 323-257-5600

Spitz Little Tokyo *Turkish*

Little Tokyo | 371 E. Second St. (Central Ave.) | 213-613-0101 | www.eatatspitz.com

This "nifty" "Turkish fast-food" duo in Eagle Rock and Little Tokyo is a "favorite" source for "yummy" "street-cart" eats like wraps, sandwiches and doner kebabs ("get them zesty-style"), plus "delicious" gelato; look for wallet-friendly prices, a "cool", "laid-back" setting and a full bar at the Little Tokyo locale.

Spumoni *Italian* 21 | 17 | 22 | $24

Santa Monica | 713 Montana Ave. (7th St.) | 310-393-2944
Sherman Oaks | 14533 Ventura Blvd. (bet. Van Nuys Blvd. & Vesper Ave.) | 818-981-7218
Stevenson Ranch | 24917 Pico Canyon Rd. (The Old Rd.) | 661-799-0360

Spumoni Brentwood *Italian*

Brentwood | 11714 San Vicente Blvd. (Barrington Ave.) | 310-207-6700 | www.spumonirestaurants.com

"Marathoners could do their carbo-loading" at this "reliable" Italian chainlet where "well-prepared" pizzas and pastas are dished out by a "friendly" crew in "casual" digs; despite some gripes about only "so-so" food and service, "inexpensive" tabs make it a "neighborhood standby."

Square One Dining *American* ▽ 23 | 15 | 18 | $21

East Hollywood | 4854 Fountain Ave. (bet. Berendo & Catalina Sts.) | 323-661-1109 | www.squareonedining.com

"A happy, sunny place both inside and out", this well-priced East Hollywood American is known for its "amazing breakfasts" and brunches crafted from "fresh, tasty ingredients" ("they can even make a kale salad taste delicious – quite a feat"); the vibe is low-key and a seat on the patio can "make your day", but know that weekends are "busy."

The Stand Hot Dogs
| 19 | 14 | 16 | $13 |

Century City | 2000 Ave. of the Stars (Constellation Blvd.) | 310-785-0400 🛇
Westwood | 1116 Westwood Blvd. (Kinross Ave.) | 310-443-0400
Encino | 17000 Ventura Blvd. (Balboa Blvd.) | 818-788-2700
Woodland Hills | Warner Ctr. | 5780 Canoga Ave. (Burbank Blvd.) | 818-710-0400
www.thestandlink.com

"Custom" hot dogs "dressed the way you like", "big burgers" and other Americana bring out the crowds at this counter-service chainlet where free pickles "make the waits less painful"; while the inside dining areas are rather "pedestrian", it's "always a picnic" outside at wooden tables with benches, making it "great for a group with kids."

Stanley's Californian
| 20 | 16 | 20 | $25 |

Sherman Oaks | 13817 Ventura Blvd. (bet. Mammoth & Matillja Aves.) | 818-986-4623 | www.stanleys83.com

You "can't go wrong with the Chinese chicken salad" at this "steady-eddie" Sherman Oaks "institution" offering a "well-rounded", "fair-priced" array of "basic", "healthy" Cal cuisine; though some say "it's not what it was" in the 1980s, it boasts a "cute patio", a "lively bar area" and regulars report there's "almost never a wait" for a table.

Stefan's at L.A. Farm Eclectic
| 22 | 21 | 20 | $50 |

Santa Monica | 3000 W. Olympic Blvd. (Stewart St.) | 310-449-4000 | www.stefansatlafarm.com

Top Chef finalist Stefan Richter presents "funky" "riffs on classic comfort food" like tater tots, s'mores and lollipops at this Santa Monica Eclectic whose modern space transforms from a "bustling lunch place" into a "relaxing" dinner destination with outdoor fire pits; the service varies widely ("friendly" vs. "slow" and "inattentive"), while prices hover on the expensive end.

Stella Rossa Pizza Bar ❶ Pizza
| 25 | 20 | 20 | $26 |

Santa Monica | 2000 N. Main St. (bet. Bay St. & Bicknell Ave.) | 310-396-9250 | www.stellarossapizzabar.com

At this Santa Monica pizzeria adjacent to M Street Kitchen, "hipsters" devour "artfully crafted" pies employing "unique toppings" like burrata, black truffles and housemade sausage on a "crisp, light" crust plus "fresh salads", small plates and "decent wines", all at a "fair price"; it's a "fun", "buzzy" place with "professional" service, but "the noise level can be hard on conversation" and the "no-reservations policy makes it a tough table."

Stinking Rose Italian
| 23 | 22 | 22 | $38 |

Beverly Hills | 55 N. La Cienega Blvd. (Wilshire Blvd.) | 310-652-7673 | www.thestinkingrose.com

"There's garlic, garlic and more garlic" – even in the ice cream – at this "fun" midpriced Beverly Hills Italian providing a "fragrant night out" with "tasty" eats delivered by a "helpful" staff in a "quirky" "boudoir-like atmosphere with exotic rich reds and booths in curtains"; critics call it an "interesting concept" with "mediocre" results, though many find it worth it for the "novelty" – just "bring mints."

STK ◗ *Steak*   25 | 25 | 23 | $71

West Hollywood | 755 N. La Cienega Blvd. (Waring Ave.) | 310-659-3535 | www.stkhouse.com

"Fantastic steaks", "amazing" truffle fries and "celeb sightings" go together at this "loud", "sexy" West Hollywood chophouse for "beautiful people" with modern looks and an "amazing" DJ spinning most nights; service is usually "polished" too, so in spite of the "high prices", most call it a "whole lot of fun."

Stonefire Grill *BBQ*   23 | 17 | 20 | $20

Pasadena | 473 N. Rosemead Blvd. (Greenhill Rd.) | 626-921-1255
Chatsworth | Pacific Theater Ctr. | 9229 Winnetka Ave. (Prairie St.) | 818-534-3364
West Hills | Fallbrook Ctr. | 6405 Fallbrook Ave. (Victory Blvd.) | 818-887-4145
Thousand Oaks | Paseo Mktpl. | 3635 E. Thousand Oaks Blvd. (Auburn Ave.) | 805-413-0300
Valencia | Cinema Park Plaza | 23300 Cinema Dr.
(bet. Bouquet Canyon Rd. & Valencia Blvd.) | 661-799-8282
www.stonefiregrill.com

"There's something for everyone" at this "meaty", "value"-minded BBQ chain deemed a "dependable" bet for "grilled delights" in "ample" helpings like "yummy" tri-tip, chicken and ribs, plus "surprisingly good" salads; the "busy", "casual" settings are counter service–only, but "you can feed a family of four for cheap" and it also makes "excellent takeout when no one wants to cook."

NEW Strand House 🅼 *American*   21 | 26 | 22 | $53

Manhattan Beach | 117 Manhattan Beach Blvd. (Manhattan Ave.) | 310-545-7470 | www.thestrandhousemb.com

"Pretend you're part of the 1% and live like a millionaire" at this "upscale" multistory New American just a few feet from the Manhattan Beach Pier boasting "world-class views", "especially at sunset"; the menu – conceived by a team led by Neal Fraser (Grace, BLD) – presents an "excellent assortment" from charcuterie and cheese to pork chops and exotic pizzas, although some call it " too expensive for what it is."

Street *Eclectic*   25 | 20 | 24 | $44

Hollywood | 742 N. Highland Ave. (Melrose Ave.) | 323-203-0500 | www.eatatstreet.com

"It really does feel like you're walking the streets of a foreign city" at this "delightful" global Eclectic in Hollywood from Susan Feniger (Border Grill) delivering "lots of little bites from all over" that are "fun to share" in the "cool" space with a "great patio"; servers are "knowledgeable" and "guide you to the perfect dishes" too, so just "go with an open mind and an open wallet"; P.S. "the Kaya toast is the must-have" and the cocktails "rock" too.

Sugarfish by Sushi Nozawa *Japanese*   26 | 20 | 22 | $41

NEW Downtown | 600 W. Seventh St. (Grand Ave.) | 213-627-3000
Brentwood | 11640 San Vicente Blvd. (bet. Darlington & Mayfield Aves.) | 310-820-4477

(continued)

(continued)

Sugarfish by Sushi Nozawa

Marina del Rey | The Waterside | 4722¼ Admiralty Way (Mindanao Way) | 310-306-6300
Santa Monica | 1345 Second St. (Santa Monica Blvd.) | 310-393-3338
www.sugarfishsushi.com

"The 'trust me' omakase lives on forever" at this Japanese chain-in-the-making from "master" Kazunori Nozawa (of the "late, great Sushi Nozawa") famed for its "butter-soft", "top-grade" fish on "warm, vinegary rice" that will "spoil you for the rest" offered in "brilliant" set menus or à la carte; the settings are "modern", service is "prompt" (some say "rushed") and the prices are "surprisingly affordable", so fans keep "coming back."

Sunnin *Lebanese*   24 | 13 | 18 | $22

Westwood | 1776 Westwood Blvd. (Santa Monica Blvd.) | 310-475-3358 | www.sunnin.com

"First-rate" kebabs and other "traditional", "homestyle" dishes with "exquisite spicing" plus "lots of vegetarian options" make this inexpensive Lebanese in Westwood "worth regular visits"; the crew of servers is "friendly" and "ultraquick", and though the large, informal space is essentially devoid of ambiance, it's a "go-to" spot for many.

🆕 Sunny Spot *Eclectic*   ▽ 22 | 20 | 21 | $36

Marina del Rey | 822 Washington Blvd. (Abbot Kinney Blvd.) | 310-448-8884 | www.sunnyspotvenice.com

Kogi BBQ truck maven Roy Choi has transformed Marina del Rey's Beechwood into this "trendy" midpriced 'roadside cookshop' with a "tasty" Eclectic menu featuring "big, bold-flavored" dishes like jerk chicken wings, grilled shrimp and a standout burger ; the "noisy" space is decked out with "bright and flowery" fabrics, island colors and a bar wrapped in burlap featuring a "top-notch cocktail menu."

Super Mex *Mexican*   23 | 17 | 23 | $15

Lakewood | 5254 Faculty Ave. (Candlewood St.) | 562-408-1048
Long Beach | 4711 E. Second St. (Roycroft Ave.) | 562-439-4489
Long Beach | 732 E. First St. (1st St.) | 562-436-0707
www.supermex.com

There's "cheesy everything" at this "down-home" Cal-Mex chain churning out "tried-and-true" dishes in "plentiful" portions; a "family-friendly" vibe prevails with a "thoughtful" staff and "fast" service, and "the price is right" too.

Sushi Dan ❶ *Japanese*   21 | 15 | 18 | $29

Hollywood | 8000 W. Sunset Blvd. (N. Crescent Heights Blvd.) | 323-848-8583 | www.sushidanla.com

Behind a "deceivingly generic facade" in a Sunset Boulevard mini-mall, this "solid" Hollywood Japanese is "popular with minor TV stars" thanks to its "huge menu" of "fresh, flavorful" sushi and "Americanized" rolls at fair prices; perhaps the setting could "use a makeover", but multiple big-screens and a "sports-bar" ambiance provide ample distraction and the constant "crowds" don't seem to mind anyhow.

Sushi Gen 🈂 *Japanese*

26 | 18 | 22 | $46

Little Tokyo | 422 E. Second St. (bet. Alameda St. & Central Ave.) | 213-617-0552

"Simplicity" rules at this Little Tokyo Japanese "stalwart" where "superb", "super-fresh" slabs of fish are fashioned into "fine pieces of art" and the prices are very "fair" for the quality; both service and decor are understated, but "be prepared to wait unless you come at off hours"; P.S. lunch offers "unbelievable deals."

🈂 Sushi Masu Ⓜ *Japanese*

27 | 16 | 25 | $47

West LA | 1911 Westwood Blvd. (bet. La Grange & Missouri Aves.) | 310-446-4368

"Lots of loyal regulars" count on this West LA Japanese, a "quiet, neighborhood" "gem" for "fresh, delish", "expertly prepared" sushi at an "ideal cost/quality ratio"; though the simple space is "not fancy", chef Hiroshi Masuko is an "engaging host" who "makes you feel at home"; P.S. "sit at the bar" if you can.

Sushi Roku *Japanese*

23 | 22 | 21 | $51

Third Street | 8445 W. Third St. (bet. Croft Ave. & La Cienega Blvd.) | 323-655-6767

Santa Monica | 1401 Ocean Ave. (Santa Monica Blvd.) | 310-458-4771

Pasadena | One Colorado | 33 Miller Alley (Fair Oaks Ave.) | 626-683-3000

www.sushiroku.com

"See and be seen" at this "rollicking" Japanese trio where a "cool" staff proffers "innovative", "expensive" sushi and "fun" drinks in a "chic" Asian setting"; waits can be a hassle" and critics claim it's "better suited to tourists than serious aficionados", but it's still a "favorite" for many.

🈂 Sushi Sasabune 🈂 *Japanese*

27 | 16 | 22 | $69

West LA | 12400 Wilshire Blvd. (Centinela Ave.) | 310-268-8380 | www.trustmesushi.com

🈂 Sushi-Don Sasabune Express *Japanese*

Pacific Palisades | 970 Monument St. (bet. Bashford St. & Sunset Blvd.) | 310-454-6710 | www.sushidonppl.com

"Impeccably fresh", "exquisite" fish is served in "traditional" preparations (aka no California rolls) at this "expensive" West LA Japanese stalwart and its takeout-focused Pacific Palisades offshoot that purists proclaim offers one of "the best omakases on the Westside"; perhaps service could use "more flexibility" and the settings aren't much to speak of, but it comes "highly recommended" nonetheless.

Sushi Sushi 🈂Ⓜ *Japanese*

▽ 27 | 19 | 24 | $55

Beverly Hills | 326½ S. Beverly Dr. (bet. Gregory Way & Olympic Blvd.) | 310-277-1165 | www.sushisushibh.com

Loyalists insist this "small, refined" Beverly Hills Japanese is "a winner" for its "creative", "top-quality" sushi, with a "first-class omakase" from chef Hiroshige Yamada; the only downside is that the creations are "a bit on the pricey side" in contrast with the rather nondescript setting.

🈂 Sushi Zo 🈂 *Japanese*

28 | 15 | 20 | $116

West LA | 9824 National Blvd. (bet. Castle Heights Ave. & Shelby Dr.) | 310-842-3977

"Beautiful little morsels" of "extraordinary, melt-in-your-mouth" sushi appeal to "purists" at this ultra-"expensive", omakase-only Japanese "indulgence" in West LA set in "spartan" digs; service can feel "rushed" (and "too strict with requests"), but even that does "not detract from the exquisite experience."

Susina Bakery & Cafe *Bakery*

24 | 21 | 21 | $17

Beverly Boulevard | 7122 Beverly Blvd. (La Brea Ave.) | 323-934-7900 | www.susinabakery.com

"A vision of decadence" with rows upon rows of "gorgeous" cakes and tarts, this Beverly Boulevard bakery/cafe also purveys "fantastic coffee" along with "good" sandwiches, salads, omelets and such; service is "professional", the setting's "quaint" and "at night, it becomes a bit of a de facto office for the local scenesters."

☑ Suzanne's Cuisine *French/Italian*

27 | 24 | 24 | $41

Ojai | 502 W. Ojai Ave. (Bristol Ave.) | 805-640-1961 | www.suzannescuisine.com

Chef Suzanne Roll whips up an "imaginative locavore menu with fresh produce from [her] own garden" at this "superlative", midpriced French-Italian in Ojai that's "always a treat" for fans; service is "excellent" and the "low-key" setting's "quite lovely" too, especially on the "peaceful" patio at lunch – "what could be better?"

Sweet Lady Jane *Bakery*

23 | 16 | 18 | $19

Melrose | 8360 Melrose Ave. (bet. Kings Rd. & Orlando Ave.) | 323-653-7145
Santa Monica | 1631 Montana Ave. (bet. 16th & 17th Sts.) | 310-254-9499
www.sweetladyjane.com

For "gorgeous", "decadent" pastries, birthday cakes and pies that "taste as good as they look", patrons pop into this "expensive, but worth it" Melrose and Santa Monica bakery/cafe duo that also serves "fab" sandwiches and salads washed down with "strong, delicious java"; although some grumble about "ornery" service and limited seating, most are "grateful to have this top-notch [spot], so no real complaints."

Swingers ● *Diner*

20 | 18 | 20 | $17

Beverly Boulevard | Beverly Laurel Motor Hotel | 8020 Beverly Blvd. (Laurel Ave.) | 323-653-5858
Santa Monica | 802 Broadway (Lincoln Blvd.) | 310-393-9793
www.swingersdiner.com

Boasting "the perfect LA vibe", these "hip", "rock 'n' roll" coffee shops on Beverly Boulevard and in Santa Monica sling all the "old standards" plus other inexpensive items "leaning toward the healthier side" and "lots of vegetarian options" too; sure, the service often comes "without a smile" and some say it's "all style and no substance", but for the "late-night munchies", it's hard to beat.

Tagine Ⓜ *Moroccan*

▽ 24 | 21 | 24 | $50

Beverly Hills | 132 N. Robertson Blvd. (Wilshire Blvd.) | 310-360-7535 | www.taginebeverlyhills.com

At this "dark", "cozy" Beverly Hills Moroccan co-owned by chef Ben Benameur and actor Ryan Gosling, the "delicious" dishes include "authentic tagines and couscous" offered à la carte or in a multicourse tasting menu that's "a treat"; although it's not inexpensive, "attentive" service and an "intimate, romantic atmosphere" with plush banquettes make it well-tailored to "dates."

	FOOD	DECOR	SERVICE	COST

Taiko ◪ *Japanese* | 24 | 19 | 22 | $33 |

Brentwood | Brentwood Gdns. | 11677 San Vicente Blvd. (bet. Barrington & Darlington Aves.) | 310-207-7782

An "unusually extensive" Japanese menu featuring "amazing" udon and soba "hits the spot every time" at this "economical" eatery in Brentwood that's "popular" with the college crowd and "kid-friendly" too; the decor is sparse, but pleasant, and service is generally "pretty good", so most are "never disappointed."

Taix *French* | 21 | 20 | 25 | $33 |

Echo Park | 1911 W. Sunset Blvd. (Glendale Blvd.) | 213-484-1265 | www.taixfrench.com

"However you pronounce it, it's been in Echo Park forever", and the "charming" staff enhances the "old-world" atmosphere at this "excellent-value" French from 1927 featuring reliable bistro "staples" accompanied by tureens of soup; though some pan the "dated" decor, others find the "few wrinkles" it has acquired "add character" and make this family-owned "institution" "better than expected."

🗷 Takami Sushi & Robata *Japanese* | 24 | 27 | 23 | $47 |

Downtown | 811 Wilshire Blvd. (bet. Figueroa & Flower Sts.) | 213-236-9600 | www.takamisushi.com

Perched on the 21st floor of a Downtown skyscraper, this "fancy" Japanese "has it all": "gorgeous" 360-degree views of the city and "amazing" sushi and cocktails served by a "friendly" staff in a contemporary setting; despite somewhat high prices many find it a "wonderful place to treat yourself."

Takao *Japanese* | 27 | 15 | 23 | $67 |

Brentwood | 11656 San Vicente Blvd. (bet. Barrington & Darlington Aves.) | 310-207-8636 | www.takaobrentwood.com

This "quietly elegant" Japanese in Brentwood delivers "fabulous, high-quality" fare via an "exceptional" omakase, "wonderful sushi" and other "unique" dishes; perhaps the "understated" setting won't win any awards, but the staff is "charming and helpful", and "if you're willing to spend, you can have a first-rate experience."

Take a Bao *Asian* | 19 | 12 | 17 | $16 |

Century City | Westfield Century City Shopping Ctr. | 10250 Santa Monica Blvd. (bet. Ave. of the Stars & Century Park W.) | 310-551-1100

NEW **Studio City** | 11838 Ventura Blvd. (Carpenter Ave.) | 818-691-7223 www.takeabao.com

For a "quick", "low-priced" bite, customers turn to this duo in Century City and Studio City offering Pan-Asian noodles, salads and "unique takes" on the bao that are "not really authentic", but "tasty" nonetheless; the counter staff is "courteous", although some find the concept "disappointing", insisting "the name is cuter than the rest."

Talésai *Thai* | 23 | 17 | 22 | $34 |

West Hollywood | 9043 W. Sunset Blvd. (Doheny Dr.) | 310-275-9724 | www.talesai.com

Studio City | 11744 Ventura Blvd. (bet. Colfax Ave. & Laurel Canyon Blvd.) | 818-753-1001 | www.talesairestaurant.com ▨

(continued)

(continued)

Café Talésai *Thai*

Beverly Hills | 9198 W. Olympic Blvd. (Palm Dr.) | 310-271-9345 | www.cafetalesai.com

Night + Market *Thai*

West Hollywood | 9041 W. Sunset Blvd (bet. Doheny & Wetherly Drs.) | 310-275-9724 | www.nightmarketla.com

"More people should know" about these "hidden" Thai "treasures" and their "wide variety" of "sophisticated" takes on the standards "artfully prepared" and served in "upscale, hip" surroundings by a "helpful" staff; Night + Market is their latest low-cost venture, an "interesting concept" that brings a meat-centric menu of Thai street food to Sunset.

Tam O'Shanter Inn *Scottish*   23 | 25 | 24 | $41

Atwater Village | 2980 Los Feliz Blvd. (Boyce Ave.) | 323-664-0228 | www.lawrysonline.com

If you "come in a tartan kilt you'll feel at home" at this 90-year-old Scottish scion of the Lawry's chain in Atwater Village, housed in a "quaint" pub where "friendly" plaid-clad waiters proffer "classic" prime rib and the like; it's "not cheap eats", but the "quality has remained high" so "you always come out satisfied."

Tanino *Italian*   22 | 23 | 23 | $50

Westwood | 1043 Westwood Blvd. (bet. Kinross & Weyburn Aves.) | 310-208-0444 | www.tanino.com

Set in a "romantic" Florentine-style building (circa 1929) with antique chandeliers and high ceilings, this Westwood Italian from Tanino Drago is a "reliable" pre-theater pick for "well-prepared" cuisine served by a staff that "always seems happy to see you"; though some regulars grouse about "pricey" bills, its "convenient" proximity to the UCLA campus and the Geffen Playhouse keeps it "extremely busy."

Tanzore *Indian*   ▽ 23 | 24 | 23 | $40

Beverly Hills | 50 N. La Cienega Blvd. (Wilshire Blvd.) | 310-652-3838 | www.tanzore.com

For "upscale Indian" in a "lovely", "color-saturated" setting, try this Beverly Hills respite, an "excellent" option for "standard curries" as well as other "flavorful", "specialty" items; a usually "attentive" staff helps make up for some complaints about "pricey" bills for "small portions."

NEW Tar & Roses *Eclectic*   ▽ 23 | 22 | 24 | $51

Santa Monica | 602 Santa Monica Blvd. (6th St.) | 310-587-0700 | www.tarandroses.com

Chef Andrew Kirschner (Joe's, Wilshire) is behind this "trendy" Santa Monica Eclectic pulling in a "beautiful" "LA" crowd with "interesting", "delicious" dishes built around his blazing wood-burning oven; service is "accommodating", but the rustic digs made from reclaimed and rough-hewn materials are frequently "packed", so prepare for "waits" and a "high noise level" "made more tolerable by the food."

Tara's Himalayan *Asian*   23 | 17 | 22 | $21

Culver City | 10855 Venice Blvd. (Midvale Ave.) | 310-836-9696 | www.tarashimalayancuisine.com

"Who knew yak could taste so good?" ask incredulous guests of this "wonderful" Culver City Tibetan-Nepalese providing a "delicious deviation" from the usual with stews, momos (dumplings) and other "different and exotic" dishes accompanied by "milky herbed tea", all at way-"reasonable" prices; the staff "couldn't be more helpful" with recommendations, and the space, while casual, "feels like home."

Taste *American*   22 | 20 | 22 | $35

West Hollywood | 8454 Melrose Ave. (La Cienega Blvd.) |
323-852-6888

Taste at the Palisades *American*

Pacific Palisades | 538 Palisades Dr. (Sunset Blvd.) | 310-459-9808
www.ilovetaste.com

This pair of "comfortable neighborhood spots" can be relied on for "simple", "well-prepared" New Americana (the mac 'n' cheese is "pure heaven") in "low-key" settings in Pacific Palisades and West Hollywood; factor in "relaxed" service and "affordable prices" – plus prix fixe specials and half-price wine nights – and it's a "sure thing."

Taste of India *Indian*   22 | 17 | 20 | $23

Sherman Oaks | 13903 Ventura Blvd. (Stern Ave.) | 818-501-5550
Woodland Hills | 21833 Ventura Blvd. (Topanga Canyon Blvd.) |
818-999-0600
www.tasteofindiala.com

These Indian sibs in Woodland Hills and Sherman Oaks are an "excellent value" for "authentic" dishes, particularly those served up as lunch specials or on the weekend champagne buffet; although the settings "don't look like much from the outside", the staff is "pleasant" and allies attest "you won't be disappointed."

Tasting Kitchen ● *Mediterranean*   26 | 22 | 21 | $55

Venice | 1633 Abbot Kinney Blvd. (Venice Blvd.) | 310-392-6644 |
www.thetastingkitchen.com

"Everything is amazing, even down to the bread and butter" at this "cool", upscale Venice Med that's "packed elbow to elbow with beautiful people" tucking into "wonderful, creative" dishes elevated by "great wines" and some of "the best mixed cocktails west of the 405"; you'll need to deal with "so-so" service, "loud" acoustics and "difficult-to-get reservations", but even so, it's worth "every bit of trouble"; P.S. "for those on a budget, the front room is lovely for brunch on weekends."

NEW Tatsu Ramen ● *Japanese*   - | - | - | I

West LA | 2123 Sawtelle Blvd. (bet. Olympic Blvd. & Mississippi Ave.) |
310-684-2889 | www.tatsuramen.com

Little Osaka may have to be renamed Ramen Row, as yet another noodle shop has opened, this one featuring a brightly lit modernist space with a long counter and an iPad ordering system; there are just two choices of ramen – with meat and without – but you can add extras and toppings, and drink options include beer and sake.

Tavern *Californian/Mediterranean*   24 | 25 | 22 | $53

Brentwood | 11648 San Vicente Blvd. (bet. Barrington & Darlington Aves.) |
310-806-6464 | www.tavernla.com

Lucques and A.O.C. team Suzanne Goin and Caroline Styne "have another winner" in this "neighborhood favorite" attracting "foodies and A-listers" with "scrumptious" Cal-Med fare and "suave cocktails" served in a "bright, beautiful" space that defines "elegance in Brentwood";

while it's "fairly expensive", it pays off with "graceful" service, and budget-conscious types can try a "luscious" burger at the bar, the "lovely brunch" or the "casual" Larder cafe, offering "light meals" and gourmet goodies at cheaper prices.

Taverna Tony *Greek*

| 22 | 21 | 22 | $45 |

Malibu | Malibu Country Mart | 23410 Civic Center Way (Cross Creek Rd.) | 310-317-9667 | www.tavernatony.com

"Malibu locals hang out" at this "hospitable" Greek moving "huge portions" of "flavorful" eats like moussaka and spanakopita in a "celebratory" setting with belly dancers and live music that "can get quite noisy"; it's not cheap and some find the food and service "hit-or-miss", but it "can't be beat on a warm summer evening" if you "sit outside" with a glass of wine.

Taylor's Steak House *Steak*

| 24 | 21 | 23 | $42 |

Koreatown | 3361 W. Eighth St. (Ardmore Ave.) | 213-382-8449
La Cañada Flintridge | 901 Foothill Blvd. (Beulah Dr.) | 818-790-7668
www.taylorssteakhouse.com

"Steaks and drinks are done right" at this "thoroughly charming, old-school" steakhouse duo in Koreatown and La Cañada Flintridge set in "clubby", vintage digs like something "out of Mike Hammer detective novels"; with a "pleasant" staff, "quiet" atmosphere and "reasonable" tabs, it's "always a treat."

Tea Station *Taiwanese/Tearoom*

| 19 | 17 | 16 | $13 |

Hacienda Heights | 1637 Azusa Ave. (bet. Colima Rd. & Pepper Brook Way) | 626-913-7450
Artesia | 11688 South St. (bet. Gridley Rd. & Pioneer Blvd.) | 562-860-7089 ☽
Gardena | 1610 W. Redondo Beach Blvd. (La Salle Ave.) | 310-515-2989 ☽
Alhambra | 560 W. Main St. (Atlantic Blvd.) | 626-289-7389 ☽
Rowland Heights | 18558 Gale Ave. (Fullerton Rd.) | 626-839-2588 ☽
San Gabriel | 158 W. Valley Blvd. (Abbot Ave.) | 626-288-3785 ☽
Temple City | 9578 E. Las Tunas Dr. (Temple City Blvd.) | 626-291-5688 ☽
www.teastation.us

"The name says it all" at this "cheap", cheerful Taiwanese chain famed for its bubble teas and shaved ice, plus "modern" (some say "mediocre") Chinese eats and tea-flavored snacks; the "generic" settings aren't much, but counter service is "efficient" and since "you can take your time", it's a "great place to hang out"; P.S. it's also a popular destination after dinner at one of the nearby seafood palaces.

Tender Greens *American*

| 23 | 17 | 19 | $18 |

Hollywood | 6290 W. Sunset Blvd. (Vine St.) | 323-382-0380
West Hollywood | 8759 Santa Monica Blvd. (Hancock Ave.) | 310-358-1919
Culver City | 9523 Culver Blvd. (bet. Cardiff & Watseka Aves.) | 310-842-8300
Pasadena | 621 E. Colorado Blvd. (bet. El Molino & Madison Aves.) | 626-405-1511
www.tendergreensfood.com

"It's easy eating green" thanks to this "virtuous, semi-fast food" chainlet – a "smart concept" – turning out "mix-and-match" salads, sandwiches and platters crafted from "exceptionally fresh" "high-quality" organic ingredients; "long lines are the norm, but they move fast", while the cafeteria settings are augmented by "pleasant outdoor seating" at all locales.

Terroni *Italian*
23 | 21 | 19 | $34

Beverly Boulevard | 7605 Beverly Blvd. (Curson Ave.) | 323-954-0300 | www.terroni.ca

"Fabulous pasta done right" brings in a "young industry crowd" to this "scene-y" Beverly Boulevard Southern Italian – an outpost of a Toronto mini-chain – also purveying "first-rate" pizzas; despite some gripes about service, "pricey" tabs and an "ear-splitting noise level", on the whole, fans insist "they nail it."

Teru Sushi *Japanese*
23 | 19 | 20 | $37

Studio City | 11940 Ventura Blvd. (bet. Carpenter Ave. & Laurel Canyon Blvd.) | 818-763-6201 | www.terusushi.com

"Still reliable" is the word on this midpriced Japanese stalwart in Studio City, "one of the originals on sushi row" turning out "fresh" fish and "playfully named special rolls" for a neighborhood crowd; some surveyors say it's "not as good as some of its competition" nearby, but the chefs are "friendly" and the "attractive" landscaped patio is a plus.

Thai Dishes *Thai*
20 | 14 | 18 | $22

Malibu | 22333 PCH (Carbon Mesa Rd.) | 310-456-6592
Santa Monica | 123 Broadway (2nd St.) | 310-394-6189 | www.thaidishessantamonica.com
Santa Monica | 1910 Wilshire Blvd. (19th St.) | 310-828-5634
Inglewood | 11934 Aviation Blvd. (W. 119th Pl.) | 310-643-6199 | www.thaidishestogo.com [S]
LAX | 6234 W. Manchester Ave. (bet. Sepulveda Blvd. & Truxton Ave.) | 310-342-0046
Manhattan Beach | 1015 N. Sepulveda Blvd. (bet. 10th & 11th Sts.) | 310-546-4147
Valencia | 23328 Valencia Blvd. (Cinema Dr.) | 661-253-3663 | www.thaidishescv.com

This "venerable" Thai chain is a "reliable" pick for "unimaginative, but well-prepared" curries and noodles priced for "those on a budget"; the service is "fair", but the atmosphere, while "family-friendly", has little to speak of in the ambiance department, so many "get it for takeout."

Think Bistro *American/French*
▽ 24 | 21 | 26 | $27

San Pedro | 1420A W. 25th St. (S. Western Ave.) | 310-548-4797 | www.thinkbistro.com

This dressier cousin of Think Café in San Pedro offers moderately priced French-American items like bouillabaisse and veal chops dished in "generous" helpings in an open, airy space; servers "accommodate your every whim", it's open late and live music every Sunday is a plus.

Think Café *American/Eclectic*
▽ 23 | 20 | 23 | $25

San Pedro | 302 W. Fifth St. (S. Center St.) | 310-519-3662

"Casual" dining in Downtown San Pedro comes via this "homey" all-day spot with an American-Eclectic menu featuring breakfast fare, sandwiches, salads and heartier items at dinner; solid service, decent prices and music on the weekends keep it "crowded."

1321 Downtown Taproom Bistro *American* 22 | 21 | 20 | $27

Torrance | 1321 Sartori Ave. (Marcelina Ave.) | 310-618-1321
Banging out "reliable" American "bar food" that pairs well with an "excellent craft-beer selection" tended by a "knowledgeable" staff, this "upscale-casual" Torrance arrival is "just what Downtown needed"; it's a "little on the noisy side" – what with big-screen TVs and all – but the experience "won't leave your wallet tapped out" so "local" loyalists say "thumbs-up."

31Ten Lounge 🅂Ⓜ *Eclectic* 22 | 23 | 20 | $48

Santa Monica | 3110 Main St. (Navy St.) | 310-450-5522 | www.31tenlounge.com
Bringing a "Hollywood feel" to a generally "laid-back area", this "exciting" Santa Monica Eclectic establishment draws quite a "trendy" clientele for "dinner, dancing" and cocktails in an indoor/outdoor lounge decked out with "romantic" cabanas and a fire pit; while not the main attraction, bites ranging from "great thin-crust pizza" to tacos to steak help fuel the party – though be ready to "dish out the dough" for a "happening" night; P.S. it's open Thursday-Saturday till 2 AM.

3 Square Cafe + Bakery *Sandwiches* 24 | 19 | 21 | $24

Venice | 1121 Abbot Kinney Blvd. (bet. San Juan & Westminster Aves.) | 310-399-6504 | www.rockenwagner.com
"Hans still rocks" attest acolytes of chef Röckenwagner and his "cool" cafe/bakery in Venice serving "Germanesque" breakfasts, "tantalizing" pretzel burgers, "mini-sandwiches" and "neat" pastries in a "sleek" space where patrons can "watch the Abbot Kinney world go by"; some say it's a "long" wait for "nothing extraordinary", but most surveyors dig it for "something LA and different" that's "not too pricey."

Thyme Café *Sandwiches* 25 | 19 | 21 | $22

Santa Monica | 1630 Ocean Park Blvd. (bet. 17th & 16th Sts.) | 310-399-8800 | www.thymecafeandmarket.com
"Fresh, tasty and inspired" sandwiches, salads and other "gourmet treats" like muffins, cookies and cupcakes make for some "amazing takeout" at this "lovely, little" well-priced cafe and marketplace "away from all the hoopla" in Santa Monica; a "pleasant welcome" and an "attractive" rustic-modern setting with a patio make it equally pleasant for eating in.

Tierra Sur at Herzog
Wine Cellars *Kosher/Mediterranean* ▽ 28 | 23 | 25 | $55

Oxnard | Herzog Wine Cellars | 3201 Camino Del Sol (Del Norte St.) | 805-983-1560 | www.herzogwinecellars.com
At this "unique" "upscale" kosher establishment in Oxnard's Herzog winery, chef Todd Aarons puts out "fabulous", "original" dairy-free Mediterranean cuisine matched with "excellent wines" (tours and tastings are also available); service is "excellent" and the "lovely ambiance" is "great for a date", especially if you sit on the terrace; P.S. hours are limited, so call ahead.

Tinga *Mexican*
24 | 18 | 19 | $18

La Brea | 142 S. La Brea Ave. (First St.) | 323-954-9566 |
www.tingabuena.com

"Gourmet tacos" and other "tasty", "interesting" Mex eats – like cochinita pibil "with a kick" and a dirty horchata with a double-shot of
espresso – garner "rave reviews" at this counter-service "gem" on La
Brea; cheery, "casual" environs with a communal table and midlevel
pricing make it a "solid" bet all around.

Tin Roof Bistro *American*
24 | 21 | 22 | $34

Manhattan Beach | Manhattan Vill. | 3500 N. Sepulveda Blvd. (bet. Marine &
Rosecrans Aves.) | 310-939-0900 | www.tinroofbistro.com

A South Bay "favorite", this upscale Manhattan Beach cousin of
Simmzy's features a "dynamite" New American menu with spicy tuna
spring rolls and "fabulous burgers" – all "totally affordable" – plus "impressive" wines and cocktails and a "reasonable corkage policy"; inside
is "convivial" with a "noisy", "crowded bar scene", while the "charming patio" presents a more "relaxed atmosphere" with a bocce court.

Tito's Tacos ⊅ *Mexican*
23 | 8 | 17 | $10

Culver City | 11222 Washington Pl. (Sepulveda Blvd.) | 310-391-5780 |
www.titostacos.com

"The long lines don't lie" at this inexpensive circa-1959 Culver City
Mexican, a "local treasure" beloved for its "unbelievably fresh and
delicious" "crispy-style" tacos and "heavenly" burritos; "you don't
go for the ambiance" and "seating can be challenging", so "be patient,
or get takeout."

Tlapazola Grill *Mexican*
24 | 15 | 23 | $31

Venice | 636 N. Venice Blvd. (Abbot Kinney Blvd.) | 310-822-7561 |
www.tlapazolagrill.com

West LA | 11676 Gateway Blvd. (bet. Barrington Ave. & Pearl Pl.) |
310-477-1577 | www.tlapazola.com Ⓜ

It's "not your garden-variety Mexican" at this separately owned pair in
Venice and West LA lauded for "superb Oaxacan cooking" like "transporting" moles and other "wonderful" dishes with "interesting twists"
plus "unbeatable margaritas" that "pack a wallop"; the setting's "casual
and relaxed", the staff "couldn't be nicer" and prices aren't bad either.

Toast *American*
19 | 16 | 17 | $22

Third Street | 8221 W. Third St. (S. Harper Ave.) | 323-655-5018 |
www.toastbakerycafe.net

"Quite a scene", this breakfast and brunch mainstay on Third Street
hosts the "*US* magazine crowd" for "original spins on breakfast burritos,
benedicts, big salads" and other "fresh" American fare at a "fair price";
"expect a wait" – especially for a coveted sidewalk table – and don't be
surprised if the staffers seem "more concerned with their hair and
next audition than refilling your cup"; P.S. "lines disappear" at dinner.

Tofu Ya *Korean*
21 | 10 | 17 | $16

West LA | 2021 Sawtelle Blvd. (La Grange Ave.) | 310-473-2627 |
www.tofuyabbq.com

This West LA Korean is a "cheap, cheerful" stop for "fill-your-belly"
"comfort-food" standards like "spicy, bubbling hot tofu soup", bulgogi
and bibimbop at "economical" prices; there's "zero ambiance", but it's

frequently "packed" with "workers during lunch and hipsters in the evening" and takeout is popular too.

Toi ● *Thai*

▽ 21 | 22 | 20 | $20

West Hollywood | 7505 1/2 Sunset Blvd. (N. Gardner St.) | 323-874-8062 | www.toirockinthaifood.com

Set amid a cluster of guitar shops in West Hollywood, this "cool", little spot offers an "awesome", "extensive" Thai menu in a "fun" space that's a veritable "shrine" to rock 'n' roll; "inexpensive" prices and late hours (till 4 AM) make it a "go-to" for many.

Tomato Pie *Pizza*

24 | 14 | 20 | $14

Melrose | 7751 Melrose Ave. (N. Genesee Ave.) | 323-653-9993
Silver Lake | 2457 Hyperion Ave. (Tracy St.) | 323-661-6474
www.tomatopiepizzajoint.com

Some of the "best NY-style pies" around turn up at this Silver Lake and Melrose twosome that "does it right" with "crisp-crusted pizza" ("you gotta get the Grandma") plus subs, salads and other Italiana; seating is limited, but delivery is a perk and the low prices will make you positively "nostalgic."

Tom Bergin's ● *Irish*

- | - | - | M

Mid-City | 840 S. Fairfax Ave. (Wilshire Blvd.) | 323-936-7151 | www.tombergins.com

Dating back to 1936, this venerable Mid-City Irish pub has restored its original wood paneling, the horseshoe bar and the cathedral ceiling (its autographed shamrocks remain); it's also introduced a new mixology-driven cocktail list and a midpriced menu of reconceived Irish pub grub like deep-fried chicken skins with blue cheese dressing and a serious bid for corned-beef greatness.

Tommy's ●◒ *Burgers/Hot Dogs*

25 | 11 | 21 | $10

Downtown | 2575 W. Beverly Blvd. (bet. Coronado St. & Rampart Blvd.) | 213-389-9060 | www.originaltommys.com

"They don't make 'em like this anymore" declare devotees of this 1940s Downtown "shack", an "LA classic" famed for its "sloppy", "delightfully disgusting" chili-burgers and hot dogs served 24/7 and especially cherished "after a night of drinking"; there's "long lines" and little seating, but for most that's "part of the charm."

Tops *American*

24 | 13 | 19 | $13

Pasadena | 3838 E. Colorado Blvd. (Merlon Ave.) | 626-449-4412 | www.theoriginaltops.com

A Pasadena mainstay since 1952, this affordable neighborhood spot slings "great, greasy-spoon" American fare in "hearty" helpings, starring a standout burger; the vibrant, fast-casual setup is a true throwback with "polite" service and a drive-thru window.

Torafuku Japanese Restaurant *Japanese*

▽ 22 | 16 | 19 | $42

West LA | 10914 W. Pico Blvd. (Westwood Blvd.) | 310-470-0014 | www.torafuku-usa.com

At this West LA outpost of a Tokyo-based chain, the menu offers "unique" Japanese specialties like *kamado* (iron-pot) rice – which arrives "fragrant" and "piping hot" – as well as grilled items and sushi in a sleek, minimalist setting; it's not inexpensive, but service is professional and lunch and happy-hour specials provide some relief.

	FOOD	DECOR	SERVICE	COST

NEW Tortilla Republic Ⓜ *Mexican* | - | - | - | M

West Hollywood | 616 N. Robertson Blvd. (Melrose Ave.) |
310-657-9888 | www.tortillarepublic.com

The original location of this chic West Hollywood Mexican grill and margarita bar is in Hawaii, but the modern, moderately priced menu trans-
lates just fine on the mainland: duck-confit tacos and hibiscus flower
enchiladas join an impressive selection of bespoke margaritas; the dramatic space is outfitted with dangling white ropes, softly lit lanterns and
glittering mirrors, with a fine view of the crowds on Robertson Boulevard.

Toscana *Italian* | 26 | 19 | 23 | $54

Brentwood | 11633 San Vicente Blvd. (Darlington Ave.) | 310-820-2448 |
www.toscanabrentwood.com

"A real showbiz hangout", this "star-studded" Brentwood trattoria
"maintains it standards" year after year with "delicious", "rustic"
Tuscan cuisine and "lovely" service that "couldn't be more friendly despite the 1% crowd"; it's too "loud", "crowded" and "expensive" for
some, but for "special occasions", many find it an "absolutely delight";
P.S. Bar Toscana next door has lower-priced nibbles and drinks.

Toscanova *Italian* | 19 | 20 | 20 | $37

Century City | Westfield Century City Shopping Ctr. |
10250 Santa Monica Blvd. (bet. Ave. of the Stars & Century Park W.) |
310-551-0499

Calabasas | 4799 Commons Way (Calabasas Rd.) | 818-225-0499
www.toscanova.com

A "dependable" "respite" in the Westfield Century City Shopping Center,
this Italian from Agostino Sciandri (Ago) provides "consistent" fare in
a contempo setting with a "lovely" patio; perhaps it's "not terribly authentic" and some find it "pricey", but the staff's "accommodating"
making for a "comfortable" stop; P.S. the Calabasas branch is new.

NEW Towne *American* | - | - | - | M

Downtown | 705 W. Ninth St. (bet. Figueroa & Flower Sts.) |
213-623-2366 | www.towne-la-com

The owners of Old Pasadena's Mi Piace head Downtown with this
sprawling New American a block from Staples, with a team of chefs
who've worked under David Burke and Scott Conant turning out moderately priced, quirky spins on comfort-food classics; the modern red-
and-white dining room has an open kitchen, billowing white curtains
to partition different dining areas and leather ceilings.

Trader Vic's *Polynesian* | 19 | 22 | 21 | $45

Downtown | LA Live | 800 W. Olympic Blvd. (S. Figueroa St.) |
213-785-3330 | www.tradervicsla.com

Trader Vic's Lounge ◗ *Polynesian*

Beverly Hills | Beverly Hilton | 9876 Wilshire Blvd. (Santa Monica Blvd.) |
310-285-1300 | www.tradervics.com

"More tikis!" clamor fans of this "transformed" Beverly Hills poolside
lounge and Downtown location in LA Live, where the "kitschy" islands-
themed setting, "tasty" Polynesian eats and "rummy drinks" – including "killer mai tais" – plus "excellent" service leave "nostalgic" fans
feeling "like celebrities"; lei-abouts point to "overpriced", "mediocre"
munchies, noting it's "not what it was", but because it's a "classic",
"you have to go here at least once."

	FOOD	DECOR	SERVICE	COST

Tra Di Noi *Italian*

| 24 | 21 | 23 | $45 |

Malibu | Malibu Country Mart | 3835 Cross Creek Rd. (bet. Civic Ctr. Way & PCH) | 310-456-0169 | www.tradinoimalibu.com

"The stars come out to eat" at this "warm, welcoming" "slice of Italy in Malibu" offering "enjoyable" pastas, risottos and entrees at prices deemed moderate for the area; although it's set in a shopping mall, the dining room is modern and "comfortable" and it's "particularly pleasant to eat outdoors in good weather."

Trastevere *Italian*

| 21 | 20 | 20 | $33 |

Hollywood | Hollywood & Highland Ctr. | 6801 Hollywood Blvd. (Highland Ave.) | 323-962-3261
Santa Monica | Third St. Promenade | 1360 Third St. Promenade (Santa Monica Blvd.) | 310-319-1985
www.trastevereristorante.com

"It's wonderful to sit outside on a warm summer night" at these "energetic", "touristy" Italians whose prime locales in the heart of Hollywood and Santa Monica provide ideal "people-watching"; opinions on the food – pastas, wood-fired pizzas, fish and meat – range from "good" to "underwhelming", but at least service is solid and the prices are "fair."

Trattoria Neapolis *Italian*

| - | - | - | M |

Pasadena | 336 S. Lake Ave. (Del Mar Ave.) | 626-792-3000 | www.trattorianeapolis.com

This casually elegant Italian on Pasadena's busiest shopping street offers a familiar menu of midpriced Boot favorites, along with an extensive and eclectic cocktail, beer and wine list; the space boasts a streetside patio, long bar and an upstairs mezzanine for those seeking a bit more privacy; P.S. the gelato is made in-house daily.

Traxx ⓩ *American*

| 21 | 22 | 21 | $42 |

Downtown | Union Station | 800 N. Alameda St. (bet. Cesar Chavez Ave. & Rte. 101) | 213-625-1999 | www.traxxrestaurant.com

A "well-kept secret", this "unique" destination in Downtown's "beautiful" art deco Union Station provides "satisfying" New American fare in a "memorable" setting with a "fabulous garden in summer"; the staff is "professional and takes care of you without hovering", so even though some call it "a bit pricey", it's a "fun alternative" in the area.

Tres by José Andrés *Eclectic*

| ▽ 29 | 27 | 24 | $53 |

Beverly Grove | SLS at Beverly Hills | 465 S. La Cienega Blvd. (Clifton Way) | 310-246-5551

Situated off the lobby of the *très soigne* SLS at Beverly Hills, this breakfast, lunch, afternoon tea, dinner and brunch sibling of The Bazaar shares the same elegant-quirky Philippe Starck decor, but is more family-friendly with a "fun" menu that runs the gamut from granola to molecular mac 'n' cheese; prices suit the upmarket setting, while exceptional service flatters an environment ripe with movers and shakers.

The Tripel *Eclectic*

| ▽ 24 | 20 | 24 | $27 |

Playa del Rey | 333 Culver Blvd. (Pershing Dr.) | 310-821-0333 | www.thetripel.com

Husband-and-wife chefs Nick Roberts and Brooke Williamson of Hudson House are behind this retro-modern, beach-adjacent gastropub in Play del Rey, where a "knowledgeable" crew proffers "unique" Eclectic eats (exotic burgers, crispy frogs' legs) and lots of microbrews in "trendy" environs; prices are decent too, but the space is "tiny" and "seating is communal and limited, so come early."

True Food Kitchen *Health Food* | 23 | 21 | 21 | $30 |

Santa Monica | Dining Deck, Santa Monica Pl. | 395 Santa Monica Pl. (3rd St. Promenade) | 310-593-8300 | www.truefoodkitchen.com
"See and be seen" at these "healthy hot spots" in Santa Monica and Newport Beach from wellness guru Dr. Andrew Weil featuring providing "guilt-free eating" with "fabulous, flavorful" organic New American items, fresh-squeezed juices and even cocktails all deemed "a bit pricey", but worth it for the "variety"; service is "friendly, but sporadic", but a "bright, modern" setting with pleasant patio seating compensates.

Truxton's *American* | 21 | 16 | 22 | $24 |

Westchester | 8611 Truxton Ave. (Manchester Ave.) | 310-417-8789 | www.truxtonsamericanbistro.com
"A local favorite since it opened", this "family-friendly" American in Westchester near LAX offers a "something-for-everyone" menu of "creative" comfort food in a modern, warehouselike space; the noise level can be "a little much", but with low prices, most call it a "great place to grab a bite when you don't feel like cooking."

NEW Tsujita LA ● *Japanese* | ▽ 26 | 19 | 21 | $30 |

West LA | 2057 Sawtelle Blvd. (Mississippi Ave.) | 310-231-7373 | www.tsujita-la.com
Offering "Japan in a bowl with every sip", this "spectacular" noodle shop in West LA (a branch of a Tokyo original) brings "ramen to a whole other level" with its "amazing" specialty *tsukemen* served cool with a dipping sauce; perhaps the dinner menu of sashimi and small plates "doesn't quite match up" to the soups, but with a sleek compact setting and moderate prices, most find it "well worth" the trip; P.S. ramen served at lunch only, and waits are the norm.

Tuk Tuk Thai *Thai* | 22 | 17 | 21 | $25 |

Pico-Robertson | 8875 W. Pico Blvd. (bet. Doheny Dr. & Robertson Blvd.) | 310-860-1872 | www.tuktukla.com
A "cute" "little oasis" for Thai-food lovers in Pico-Robertson, this "neighborhood place" whips up "wonderfully fresh" recipes with "a few surprises" along with fruity cocktails; an "attentive" staff and affordable prices – plus lunch and happy-hour specials – keep it tried-and-true.

☑ Tuscany Il Ristorante *Italian* | 26 | 23 | 26 | $52 |

Westlake Village | Westlake Plaza | 968 S. Westlake Blvd. (bet. Agoura & Townsgate Rds.) | 805-495-2768 | www.tuscany-restaurant.com
"Culinary perfection in a strip mall" turns up at this "polished", "high-end" ristorante in Westlake Village purveying "superb" Italian including stellar veal chops and pumpkin ravioli; the service "is as good as anywhere in Beverly Hills" too, so the only downside is that the "pricey menu keeps visits to a minimum" for some.

Tutti Mangia Italian Grill *Italian* | 24 | 24 | 24 | $43 |

Claremont | 102 Harvard Ave. (1st St.) | 909-625-4669 | www.tuttimangia.com
A "gem" in Claremont, this upmarket Italian earns high marks across the board for its "fantastic", "classic" fare – including a standout roast

chicken – "romantic" ambiance and "lovely" staff; although critics call it "too expensive", the majority maintains it "never disappoints."

25 Degrees ● *Burgers*　　24 | 22 | 22 | $32

Hollywood | Roosevelt Hotel | 7000 Hollywood Blvd. (Orange Dr.) | 323-785-7244 | www.25degreesrestaurant.com

"Decadent" burgers "kick buns" at this "hip" 24/7 hamburger joint in Hollywood's Roosevelt Hotel that's also sought out for "wonderful" sweet-potato fries and Guinness milkshakes; with bordello-style red-flocked wallpaper, the "groovy" setting completes your "rock 'n' roll midnight snack", so most are willing to put up with "infernal waits", "high noise levels" and "add-ons" that up the price; P.S. locations in Downtown, Glendale and Studio City are in the works.

2117 Ⓜ *Asian/European*　　23 | 16 | 21 | $36

West LA | 2117 Sawtelle Blvd. (bet. Mississippi Ave. & W. Olympic Blvd.) | 310-477-1617 | www.restaurant2117.com

"Masterful" chef Hideyo Mitsuno fuses European and Japanese traditions with "sophisticated", sometimes "spectacular" results according to acolytes of this "little-known" West LA "find" that stands out among neighboring "strip-mall noodle shops"; it "won't win any prizes for ambiance" and service can be "inconsistent", but it provides real "value for your dollar" (see the prix fixe) while "surpassing" many of its peers.

22nd St. Landing Ⓜ *Seafood*　　24 | 21 | 21 | $31

San Pedro | 141 W. 22nd St. (Harbor Blvd.) | 310-548-4400 | www.22ndstlandingrestaurant.com

"Fantastic marina views" are accompanied by "excellent", "straight-forward" seafood at this open harbor setting in San Pedro that's a prime "place to celebrate"; the "festive atmosphere", "competent" service and "comfortable" prices are all pluses, and if it's a little "old-school" in feel, that's part of the "charm."

26 Beach *Californian*　　24 | 20 | 22 | $31

Venice | 3100 Washington Blvd. (Lincoln Blvd.) | 310-823-7526 | www.26beach.com

"Locals" are "hooked" on this Venice Californian flipping "out-of-this-world" burgers on house-baked buns, "flavorful, filling" salads and "insane" French-toast combos for brunch in a "quirky", "dollhouse"-like space flowing out to a "delightful" patio; given the "fair prices" for "gigantic" plates, most find it an "old faithful that never disappoints."

Twohey's *American*　　19 | 16 | 21 | $16

Alhambra | 1224 N. Atlantic Blvd. (Huntington Dr.) | 626-284-7387 | www.twoheys.com

"A classic", this "popular" circa-1943 diner in Alhambra is considered a "cut above" with its "big menu" of "hearty" Americana where the "burgers and hot-fudge sundaes reign supreme"; a few find it's "not what it used to be", but the "fun" retro setting and low prices make it a "pleasantly reliable" place to take the kids.

208 Rodeo *American*　　24 | 23 | 22 | $43

Beverly Hills | Two Rodeo | 208 Via Rodeo Dr. (Wilshire Blvd.) | 310-275-2428 | www.208rodeo.com

Shoppers on Rodeo Drive find a perfect perch for "people-watching" and "being seen" at this New American delivering "enjoyable" "up-

"scale" fare (with "great recommendations" from the staff); you may meet some "nice tourists and locals" while leisurely lunching on the patio, so the "location" and "vibe" win out for most.

Typhoon *Asian* 21 | 22 | 21 | $39

Santa Monica | Santa Monica Airport | 3221 Donald Douglas Loop S. (Airport Ave.) | 310-390-6565 | www.typhoon.biz

"Eat the weirdest thing you can if only for the bragging rights" at this midpriced Pan-Asian at the Santa Monica Airport featuring an "adventurous" bill of fare that includes "exotic" specialties like crickets and scorpions as well as more conventional items like fried catfish; it's especially "fantastic at sunset" ("it's also nice to watch the planes take off"), and the weekly live jazz alone makes it "worth it."

Ugo an Italian Cafe *Italian* 19 | 17 | 20 | $26

Culver City | 3865 Cardiff Ave. (Culver Blvd.) | 310-204-1222

Café Ugo *Italian*

Santa Monica | Santa Monica Pl. | 315 Colorado Ave. (4th St.) | 310-394-2014
www.cafeugo.com

For "laid-back, affordable meals" of pasta and pizza capped with "inspired" gelato, Culver City denizens "squeeze into" this "casual" Italian that boasts a "pleasant staff", outdoor seating and a wine bar next door; though the kiosk in Santa Monica is "nothing special foodwise" (they don't have a kitchen), locals love it for a "gelato and espresso after a movie."

🅩 Umami Burger *Burgers* 23 | 16 | 18 | $21

NEW Fairfax | The Grove | 189 The Grove Dr. (bet. Beverly Blvd. & 3rd St.) | 323-954-8626 ◗

Hollywood | 1520 N. Cahuenga Blvd. (bet. Selma Ave. & Sunset Blvd.) | 323-469-3100

Hollywood | 4655 Hollywood Blvd. (Vermont Ave.) | 323-669-3922

Mid-Wilshire | 850 S. La Brea Ave. (bet. 8th & 9th Sts.) | 323-931-3000

Santa Monica | Fred Segal | 500 Broadway (5th St.) | 310-451-1300

NEW Hermosa Beach | 1040 Hermosa Ave. (bet. Pier Ave. & 10th St.) | 310-214-8626

North Hollywood | 12159 Ventura Blvd. (bet. Laurel Canyon Blvd. & Vantage Ave.) | 818-286-9004 ◗
www.umamiburger.com

"Believe the hype" pronounce the many fans of this "gourmet" hamburger "empire" where "mind-bending" patties are served on "sweet, buttery buns" with "equally amazing" sides like truffle fries and tempura onion rings; all arrives in a "stylish" space, so even if downsides can include "waits", "bored" service and portions that are "small for the price", the food provides a "life-changing" experience that's "all it's cracked up to be"; P.S. the cheesy tater tots are an "off-the-menu secret."

NEW Umamicatessen ◗ *Eclectic* ▽ 23 | 20 | 18 | $29

Downtown | 852 S. Broadway (Bet. 8th & 9th Sts.) | 213-413-8626 | www.umami.com

This "hipster" food hall spin-off of famed Umami Burger is set in a massive Downtown LA space offering a pleasantly "schizophrenic" menu of Eclectic eats, from the signature "juicy" Umami burger, pork dishes from Chris Cosentino's Pigg, kosher-style deli fare from The Cure and artisanal java from Spring for Coffee, all ordered at the table off of one menu; the high-ceilinged room has a "fun, loud vibe", and there's a long bar issuing serious mixology concoctions.

Uncle Bill's Pancake House   *Diner* | 23 | 15 | 19 | $16 |

Manhattan Beach | 1305 Highland Ave. (13th St.) | 310-545-5177
The "perfect lazy brunch spot", this "cute, homey" Manhattan Beach nook is an area "institution" thanks to its "delicious", "old-fashioned" omelets and pancakes offered at a "great value"; though the line can be "longer than Disneyland's" on weekends, it "moves pretty well", and besides, most agree the eats and ocean views from the patio are so "worth the wait."

Uncle Darrow's   *Cajun/Creole* | 21 | 13 | 20 | $20 |

Marina del Rey | 2560 S. Lincoln Blvd. (W. Washington Blvd.) | 310-306-4862 | www.uncledarrows.com
"When you want a little Cajun to spice up your day", try this "little corner of Louisiana" in Marina del Rey where the catfish and po' boys are "guaranteed to pique your taste buds"; although many opt for takeout, the vibe is "pleasant" in the casual space and prices "won't break the bank."

Upper West   *American* | 21 | 18 | 19 | $34 |

Santa Monica | 3321 W. Pico Blvd. (33rd St.) | 310-586-1111 | www.theupperwest.com
A "neighborhood hot spot", this "fun" Santa Monica New American is a find for "satisfying, high-end bar food" and market-based specials supported by cocktails and a "nice selection of wines by the glass"; if you can get past the "high decibels", you'll find an "unpretentious" vibe, moderate prices and "super" happy-hour specials.

Upstairs 2 🅂🅼 *Mediterranean* | 24 | 20 | 24 | $47 |

West LA | Wine House | 2311 Cotner Ave. (bet. Pico & W. Olympic Blvds.) | 310-231-0316 | www.upstairs2.com
Though it's "off the radar", fans tout this "cozy" tapas stop above a West LA wine emporium offering "unique", "tasty" Med-influenced small plates "that ain't so small" alongside "fabulous wines" in "intelligent" pairings; with "knowledgeable", "unpretentious" service and "reasonable prices", "what more could you want?"

🅩 Urasawa 🅂🅼 *Japanese* | 28 | 25 | 27 | $488 |

Beverly Hills | 218 N. Rodeo Dr. (Wilshire Blvd.) | 310-247-8939
"Every dish is a work of art and a labor of love" at Hiro Urasawa's Beverly Hills Japanese – LA's No. 1 for Food – where the "sublime" omakase-only feasts are prepared by the "maestro" himself with the "utmost attention to detail" in a "tranquil" setting; service is "impeccable" too, so "put it on your bucket list", but "be ready to fork over your car payment" for the "once-in-a-lifetime treat."

Urth Caffé   *American* | 22 | 18 | 18 | $20 |

Downtown | 451 S. Hewitt St. (5th St.) | 213-797-4534 ●
West Hollywood | 8565 Melrose Ave. (bet. Westbourne & Westmount Drs.) | 310-659-0628 ●
Beverly Hills | 267 S. Beverly Dr. (Gregory Way) | 310-205-9311 ●
Santa Monica | 2327 Main St. (Hollister Ave.) | 310-314-7040
www.urthcaffe.com
"Such a scene", this "quintessential LA" coffee-shop chain attracts a "gorgeous" crowd with "amazing Spanish lattes", "healthy juices",

"gargantuan salads" and other "fresh" American fare, plus "decadent" desserts that are "hard to resist"; the patio seating makes it a "go-to for breakfast or lunch on a sunny day", even if the perpetual crowds "make you wonder, 'shouldn't these people be at work or something?'"

NEW Ushuaia Argentinean Steakhouse *Argentinean/Steak*

- | - | - | E

Santa Monica | 2628 Wilshire Blvd. (Princeton St.) | 310-315-5457 | www.ushuaiasteakhouse.com

Named after Argentina's southernmost city, this relative newcomer in Santa Monica serves a moderately priced menu of traditional grilled meats with spicy sauces and South American wines; the vibe is steakhouse-cozy, with cork ceilings and handsome wood furnishings befitting the upper-end prices.

U-Zen *Japanese*

24 | 14 | 24 | $39

West LA | 11951 Santa Monica Blvd. (Brockton Ave.) | 310-477-1390 | www.u-zenrestaurant.com

"Been here forever and still terrific", this West LA Japanese is a source for "ample cuts" of "fresh" fish (the "toro is tops") at "reasonable prices"; chef-owner Masaru Mizokami and his "accommodating" crew create a "welcoming" atmosphere, and just about all agree it's "one of the best in town."

ⓩ Valentino ⓩ *Italian*

26 | 24 | 26 | $74

Santa Monica | 3115 Pico Blvd. (bet. 31st & 32nd Sts.) | 310-829-4313 | www.valentinorestaurants.com

"Still fabulous" is the word on this "legendary" Santa Monica Northern Italian that "sets the bar high and delivers" "marvelous" food matched with "remarkable wines" from a cellar that's "without peer"; "A+" service led by "ever-gracious" owner Piero Selvaggio and a "dressy" setting make for a "memorable meal", but "wowee" is it "expensive"; P.S. the small-plates menu at the Vin Bar is a "more affordable" option.

Valentino's *Pizza*

23 | 11 | 20 | $21

Manhattan Beach | 975 N. Aviation Blvd. (10th St.) | 310-318-5959 | www.valentinospizza.net

"Large slices" of "New York–style pizza" with "abundant cheese and great sauce" are the thing at these "cheap" mostly "take-out joints", where the "incredible" sausage rolls also get a shout-out; don't expect much in the way of decor, but "easy" takeaway and delivery is a plus.

Valley Inn Restaurant *American*

21 | 19 | 23 | $35

Sherman Oaks | 4557 Sherman Oaks Ave. (Dickens St.) | 818-784-1163 | www.valleyinndining.com

"A throwback to the 1950s", this Sherman Oaks "old-timer" attracts a "loyal following" with the "time-honored formula of friendly service" and "classic" American "comfort food" like prime rib and fried chicken ("stick to the basics"); its "older" clientele also appreciates the "comfy" setting with over-stuffed booths and "fair prices."

Vegan Glory *Vegan*

22 | 14 | 20 | $18

Beverly Boulevard | 8393 Beverly Blvd. (Orlando Ave.) | 323-653-4900 | www.veganglory.com

"Who knew vegan food could taste this good?" ask fans of the "fresh" "flavorful options" at this "affordable" Asian eatery on Beverly Boulevard known for its "excellent fake meats"; service is "quick", but some find the fluorescent-lit strip-mall location best suited for takeout.

Veggie Grill *Vegan*

23 | 18 | 21 | $16

Fairfax | Farmers Mkt. | 110 S. Fairfax Ave. (3rd St.) | 323-933-3997
West Hollywood | 8000 W. Sunset Blvd. (Laurel Ave.) | 323-822-7575
Santa Monica | 2025 Wilshire Blvd. (bet. 20th & 21st Sts.) | 310-829-1155
El Segundo | Plaza El Segundo | 720 S. Allied Way (Rocrans Ave.) |
310-535-0025
Torrance | 2533 PCH (Skyline Dr.) | 310-325-6689
www.veggiegrill.com

"Surprisingly tasty", "guilt-free" vegan eats – including "delicious" faux-chicken sandwiches, "craveable kale" and sweet potato fries – make this fast-casual chain a "go-to" for a "skinny yoga types"; the service is "fast and friendly" and the look is "simple, clean and modern", making it a "great place to meet for cheap."

Vermont *American*

22 | 22 | 22 | $41

Los Feliz | 1714 N. Vermont Ave. (Prospect Ave.) | 323-661-6163 |
www.vermontkitchenandbar.com

"Always a pleasure", this "lovely" neighborhood fixture in Los Feliz is "great for a date" thanks to its "robust", "tasty" New American cuisine offered in "pretty", "romantic" surroundings with lots of exposed brick and a patio; service is "accommodating" too, and those who find it a touch pricey say "go for drinks."

Versailles *Cuban*

23 | 12 | 20 | $21

Mid-City | 1415 S. La Cienega Blvd. (Pico Blvd.) | 310-289-0392
Palms | 10319 Venice Blvd. (Motor Ave.) | 310-558-3168
Manhattan Beach | 1000 N. Sepulveda Blvd. (10th St.) | 310-937-6829
Encino | 17410 Ventura Blvd. (bet. Louise & White Oak Aves.) |
818-906-0756
www.versaillescuban.com

"The garlic chicken is heaven" at this "high-energy" Cuban chain beloved by many for its "soul-satisfying" fare that "tastes like *abuela's* in the kitchen"; service is "welcoming" despite the "barren", "cafeteria-style" setting, and prices are a downright "bargain", so it "hits the spot" every time; P.S. "bring Tic Tacs!"

Vertical Wine Bistro ● Ⓜ *Eclectic/Mediterranean*

21 | 24 | 21 | $42

Pasadena | 70 N. Raymond Ave. (Union St.) | 626-795-3999 |
www.verticalwinebistro.com

There's "always a vibrant crowd" at this "'in' place" for oenophiles in Pasadena owned by movie producer Gale Anne Hurd, where "tasty", "approachable" Eclectic-Med small plates are matched with "amazing wines" and a "good selection of flights" in a "stylish, modern" setting; though some caution that the tabs can "add up", happy hour offers one of the "best deals in town."

Via Alloro *Italian*

22 | 21 | 21 | $47

Beverly Hills | 301 N. Cañon Dr. (Dayton Way) | 310-275-2900 |
www.viaalloro.com

An upmarket "Italian sports bar", this Beverly Hills standby from the Drago brothers "gets it right" for fans with "great food" from a "wonderful" staff in a "relaxing" atmosphere; those who want to avoid the TVs inside can opt for some stellar "people-watching on the patio."

Via Veneto *Italian*

26 | 22 | 22 | $63

Santa Monica | 3009 Main St. (bet. Marine St. & Pier Ave.) | 310-399-1843 | www.viaveneto.us

"Every bite's a dream" at this Santa Monica Italian laying out an "amazing", "authentic" array of pastas and roasts in a setting that's "noisy, happy and full of life"; service is "attentive" too, so while it's "pricey", most find the overall atmosphere "so charming" that it's "worth it."

Vibrato Grill 🅜 *American/Steak*

23 | 26 | 23 | $65

Bel-Air | 2930 N. Beverly Glen Circle (Beverly Glen Blvd.) | 310-474-9400 | www.vibratogrilljazz.com

This "old-fashioned supper club" in Bel-Air co-owned by trumpet great Herb Alpert is an "elegant place" with "real-life chanteuses and jazz singers" performing while you tuck into "better-than-expected" American steakhouse fare in a "lovely" setting with a "thriving bar scene"; it's "expensive", but "interesting for a change of pace."

Villa Blanca *Mediterranean*

19 | 24 | 20 | $45

Beverly Hills | 9601 Brighton Way (N. Camden Dr.) | 310-859-7600 | www.villablancarestaurant.com

"The people-watching is amusing" to say the least at this "air-kissing" "ladies lunch" spot owned by Real Housewife of Beverly Hills Lisa Vanderpump-Todd and her husband, Ken, whose "pristine" all-white space "feels like you've escaped to Miami or St. Tropez for the afternoon", save for the fact that "everyone is looking for cameras and hoping to be on TV"; it's "quite buzzy", even if critics call the upmarket Med menu "overpriced" and "mediocre", the staff "pleasant, but ditzy" and the "style-over-substance" scene "kind of silly."

Village Pizzeria *Pizza*

25 | 14 | 20 | $17

Hancock Park | 131 N. Larchmont Blvd. (bet. Beverly Blvd. & 1st St.) | 323-465-5566

Hollywood | 6363 Yucca St. (bet. Cahuenga Blvd. & Ivar St.) | 323-790-0763 www.villagepizzeria.net

Totally "legit" "New York–style" pizza pleases the masses at this inexpensive quick-bite pair in Hollywood and Hancock Park whose "crust has just the right balance of crispy and chewy"; sure, some could "do without the attitude" from the counter staff, but the Big Apple decor "is a hoot", and most are content to just "indulge in a slice" – "fold it in half, shove it in your mouth and be happy."

Villetta *Italian*

21 | 24 | 21 | $68

Santa Monica | 246 26th St. (San Vicente Blvd.) | 310-394-8455 | www.villetta.us

"For lunch the garden can't be beat" at this "vibrant" Santa Monica Italian set in a historic building, purveying a varied lineup of pizzas, pastas, fish and chops; however, despite the "cozy" setting, many find the food and service "inconsistent", especially given the "steep" pricing.

Vincenti 🅩 *Italian*

27 | 25 | 25 | $71

Brentwood | 11930 San Vicente Blvd. (bet. Bundy Dr. & Montana Ave.) | 310-207-0127 | www.vincentiristorante.com

"A star among the many Italian options in Brentwood", this "top-notch" entry matches its "superb" cuisine "prepared with minimal fuss" with "excellent" wines in an "inviting", "elegant" atmosphere;

FOOD | DECOR | SERVICE | COST

yes, it's "expensive", but there's "wonderful hospitality", making it the "perfect spot for a special quiet dinner."

Vince's Spaghetti *Italian*   24 | 18 | 23 | $19

Ontario | 1206 W. Holt Blvd. (N. Mountain Ave.) | 909-986-7074 | www.vincesspaghettirestaurant.com

After nearly 70 years, pastaphiles are "still in love" with these "*benissimo*" Ontario, Rancho Cucamonga and Temecula Italians where "there's no such thing as too much cheese"; "generous" portions, "welcoming" service and "budget" prices mitigate what some call a "down-home" ambiance, though critics confess they'd "rather make spaghetti at home."

Vito *Italian*   23 | 21 | 24 | $43

Santa Monica | 2807 Ocean Park Blvd. (28th St.) | 310-450-4999 | www.vitorestaurant.com

"About as old-school Italian as you can get", this "romantic" Santa Monica hideaway is a "step back in time" where "wonderful" red-sauce fare is proffered by tuxedoed waiters who "make a mean tableside Caesar salad" and "even the diners look like a casting call for a 1950s movie"; though it's "a bit pricey", most find it "delightful" and are "thankful a place like this still exists."

Vito's *Pizza*   27 | 13 | 21 | $19

Beverly Hills | 846 N. La Cienega Blvd. (Waring Ave.) | 310-652-6859 | www.vitopizza.com

"A favorite for New York transplants", this Beverly Hills pizzeria puts out "authentic" 'za that's "a slice of heaven", along with sandwiches and pastas; although the setting's modest and it's "not a bargain", "Vito and the whole crew are amazing" and fans "leave well fed and entertained"; P.S. "save room for the knockout cannoli."

Vivoli Café & Trattoria *Italian*   22 | 16 | 21 | $33

West Hollywood | 7994 W. Sunset Blvd. (Laurel Ave.) | 323-656-5050
Westlake Village | North Ranch Mall | 3825 E. Thousand Oaks Blvd. (Westlake Blvd.) | 805-373-6060
www.vivolicafe.com

Surveyors throw a "thumbs-up" for these "cozy, little" "neighborhood favorites" in WeHo and Westlake Village, where "authentically Italian" homemade pastas and such come at "reasonable" prices; add in a "warm reception", and "the biggest challenge is to save room for dessert."

Wabi-Sabi *Japanese*   22 | 19 | 20 | $45

Venice | 1635 Abbot Kinney Blvd. (Venice Blvd.) | 310-314-2229 | www.wabisabisushi.com

"A longtime fixture on Abbot Kinney", this "trusty" Venice Japanese pulls in a "young" crowd with "fresh" "Cal-style" slabs and rolls plus "innovative" small plates washed down with "good" martinis at happy hour; with a "fun", "local vibe" and "sincere" service, it's a "reliable" bet in spite of the somewhat "expensive" tabs.

The Waffle *American*   21 | 17 | 19 | $19

Hollywood | 6255 W. Sunset Blvd. (bet. Argyle Ave. & Vine St.) | 323-465-6901 | www.thewafflehollywood.com

"Decadent" sweet and savory waffles lead the lineup at this "busy breakfast joint" in Hollywood that also "hits the spot" late at night;

FOOD | DECOR | SERVICE | COST

some say service "needs to get it together" and "execution is lacking" for the prices, but the retro space with dog-friendly patio is often "jumping" nonetheless.

Wahib's Middle East *Mideastern*
22 | 16 | 21 | $20

Alhambra | 910 E. Main St. (Granada Ave.) | 626-576-1048 | www.wahibmiddleeast.com

It's "worth a drive for pigging out" at the "great-value" lunch and dinner buffets at this Alhambra Middle Eastern, an area "institution" where it's easy to "over-indulge"; while the setting and service may be unremarkable, outdoor seating is a plus, and you can light up a hookah on the patio in the evening.

Wahoo's Fish Taco *Mexican/Seafood*
22 | 16 | 20 | $12

Hancock Park | 6258 Wilshire Blvd. (McCarthy Vista) | 323-933-2480
Santa Monica | 418 Wilshire Blvd. (4th St.) | 310-393-9125
Long Beach | 6449 E. PCH (bet. 2nd St. & Studebaker Rd.) | 562-430-7034
Manhattan Beach | 1129 Manhattan Ave. (Center Pl.) | 310-796-1044
Torrance | 3556 Torrance Blvd. (Amie Ave.) | 310-540-7725
Pasadena | 264 S. Lake Ave. (E. Del Mar Blvd.) | 626-449-2005
Burbank | 201 E. Magnolia Blvd. (N. 1st St.) | 818-843-3665
Santa Clarita | 24230 Valencia Blvd. (McBean Pkwy.) | 661-255-5138
www.wahoos.com

"It's not your average fast-food Mexican" at this "wholesome, healthy" SoCal chain putting out "fresh" grilled takes on fish and shrimp tacos plus other types of "surfer grub" crafted from "quality ingredients" in "busy", "beachy" digs; tabs are "cheap", so many "can count on it" for a "quick" bite.

Walter's *Eclectic*
21 | 18 | 21 | $24

Claremont | 310 N. Yale Ave. (Bonita Ave.) | 909-624-4914 | www.waltersrestaurant.biz

"Everyone can find something they like" at this "neighborhood favorite" "for budget-conscious diners in Claremont" boasting a "wildly varied" Eclectic menu peppered with "unusual" Afghan specialties at dinner; the mood's "friendly and comfortable" with patio seating that's especially "pleasant" and a "delightful" Sunday brunch buffet.

Warszawa Ⓜ *Polish*
23 | 19 | 22 | $36

Santa Monica | 1414 Lincoln Blvd. (Santa Monica Blvd.) | 310-393-8831 | www.warszawarestaurant.com

"It's old world" all the way at this "*gemütlich*" Santa Monica standby where "hearty", "authentic Polish" "delicacies" are "reasonably priced" and washed down with glasses of vodka; it's set in a "charming old house" with a "fun" outdoor lounge, all boosted by "warm" hospitality; P.S. "get the duck – it's fab."

🅩 Water Grill *Seafood*
27 | 25 | 26 | $65

Downtown | 544 S. Grand Ave. (bet. 5th & 6th Sts.) | 213-891-0900 | www.watergrill.com

"Still the king of seafood restaurants in LA", this Downtown "standout" has long been a source for "exquisite", "exceptionally fresh" fish and "extraordinary white wines" served by an "attentive" staff in a "nicely remodeled" "elegant" setting; it's known as "power-lunch" central, as you may "need an expense account budget" to handle the bill.

Waterloo & City ● *British*   24 | 20 | 22 | $42

Culver City | 12517 W. Washington Blvd. (Mildred Ave.) | 310-391-4222 | www.waterlooandcity.com

"LA meets London gastropub" at this "hip" Culver City "favorite" from "innovative chef" Brendan Collins spotlighting a "sophisticated" Modern British menu "heavy on meat" with "lots of surprises", elevated by "awesome" beers and a "nicely curated" cocktail list; prices are "reasonable", the servers are "savvy" and the space has a pleasantly "ramshackle feel", although it's frequently "jam-packed", so "noise is an issue."

Watermark on Main Ⓜ *American*   ▽ 24 | 27 | 24 | $43

Ventura | 598 E. Main St. (Chesnut St.) | 805-643-6800 | www.watermarkonmain.com

A "beautifully restored" bank building with mahogany woodwork and dramatic chandeliers is the setting for this "upscale" Ventura American providing "excellent" food and service; it's not inexpensive, but works for a "special evening", thanks in part to its noteworthy bar pouring "imaginative" cocktails and "wonderful" nightly live music.

Westside Tavern *Californian*   23 | 22 | 21 | $36

West LA | Westside Pavilion | 10850 W. Pico Blvd. (Westwood Blvd.) | 310-470-1539 | www.westsidetavernla.com

Groupies "go as much as possible" to this "attractive" Westside Pavilion "favorite" for "rock-solid, high-end pub food" featuring "modern", "seasonal" Californian items, from "amazing" flatbreads to "fantastic" cocktails; service is "pleasant" and prices relatively "affordable" too, so don't be surprised by the frequently "long waits"; P.S. it's especially "dependable before or after a movie."

Whale & Ale *Pub Food*   21 | 20 | 19 | $27

San Pedro | 327 W. Seventh St. (S. Centre St.) | 310-832-0363 | www.whaleandale.com

"If you want real fish 'n' chips", this "proper" San Pedro tavern is a "solid" bet with "authentic English pub grub" and "some great ales" on tap in a "charming" environment; moderate pricing and frequent live music make it a "fun place to hang out."

Whist *Californian*   22 | 25 | 21 | $52

Santa Monica | Viceroy Santa Monica | 1819 Ocean Ave. (Pico Blvd.) | 310-260-7500 | www.viceroysantamonica.com

"Celeb sightings abound" at this "beautiful, happening" enclave inside the glam Viceroy Santa Monica, where you can "sit poolside on a nice day" or even "splurge on a cabana" rental; some say both service and the upmarket, seasonal Cal menu can be "wildly inconsistent", although the "incredible" ambiance usually makes up for it.

Wienerschnitzel *Burgers/Hot Dogs*   20 | 14 | 20 | $8

Burbank | 3203 W. Alameda (W. Olive Ave.) | 818-841-1917
Diamond Bar | 23300 Sunset Crossing Rd. | 909-860-9011 Ⓢ Ⓜ
www.wienerschnitzel.com

"Families on a budget" favor the "cheap, cheap, cheap" chili-cheese dogs, fries and other similarly "satisfying", "fast" eats at this vintage chain with drive-thru at most locales; while it's often "convenient", antis allege "you get what you pay for."

Wilshire 🗷 *American* | 23 | 23 | 22 | $54 |

Santa Monica | 2454 Wilshire Blvd. (bet. Chelsea Ave. & 25th St.) | 310-586-1707 | www.wilshirerestaurant.com

"The scene is good, but the food's much better" at this "modern, trendy" Santa Monican helmed by chef Nyesha Arrington of *Top Chef*, who whips up "delicious" seasonal New American with "creative" touches elevated by "fantastic" cocktails; it's "expensive", but pays off with "engaging" service and an "elegant" atmosphere with a "lovely" patio (one of the "best in LA"), plus a "high-energy" bar that gets hopping late at night.

Wirtshaus 🌙 *German* | 20 | 16 | 19 | $24 |

La Brea | 345 N. La Brea Ave. (Oakwood Ave.) | 323-931-9291 | www.wirtshausla.com

Expect a "good variety of German deliciousness" at this "friendly", "low-key" La Brea "beer house" with a sheltered outdoor patio, a Ping-Pong table and a polished bar with a score of suds to choose from; foodwise, there's "epic platters" of wursts, "dreamy potatoes" and such, and with modest tabs, fans can think of no better place "to spend a Saturday afternoon."

Wokcano Restaurant 🌙 *Asian* | 22 | 23 | 22 | $30 |

Downtown | 800 W. Seventh St. (Flower St.) | 213-623-2288
West Hollywood | 8408 W. Third St. (bet. La Cienega Blvd. & Orlando Ave.) | 323-951-1122
Santa Monica | 1413 Fifth St. (bet. B'way St. & Santa Monica Blvd.) | 310-458-3080
Long Beach | 199 The Promenade N. (B'way) | 562-951-9652
Pasadena | 33 S. Fair Oaks Ave. (bet. Colorado Blvd. & Green St.) | 626-578-1818
Burbank | 150 S. San Fernando Blvd. (Angeleno Ave.) | 818-524-2288
Santa Clarita | Valencia Mall Shopping Ctr. | 24201 Valencia Blvd. (Town Center Dr.) | 661-288-1913
www.wokcanorestaurant.com

There's "lots of choices" on the Asian fusion menu at this "surprisingly cool" chain that's a "reliable option for upscale Chinese, sushi" and Thai at "nonupscale prices"; late hours, a full bar and DJs are perks at some locations, but some find the "Vegas" feel and "loud" '80s arena-rock soundtrack less than appealing; P.S. "the happy-hour specials are your friend."

🆕 Wolfgang Puck at | 25 | 24 | 25 | $87 |
Hotel Bel-Air *Californian/Mediterranean*

Bel-Air | Hotel Bel-Air | 701 Stone Canyon Rd. (Chalon Rd.) | 310-909-1644 | www.hotelbelair.com

"Dine with Oprah, Nancy Reagan" and other well-heeled types at this revamped dining room in the Hotel Bel-Air showcasing Wolfgang Puck's "amazing" ultrapricey Cal-Med fare backed by "unparalleled service with attention to every last detail"; although a few feel "the charm is gone" from the "classic" space since the redo, most still find the "beautiful", "secluded" setting a "real treat" that's perfect for a "special occasion."

	FOOD	DECOR	SERVICE	COST

Wolfgang Puck Bar & Grill *Californian* | 23 | 21 | 21 | $46 |

Downtown | LA Live | 800 W. Olympic Blvd. (Figueroa St.) | 213-748-9700 | www.wolfgangpuck.com

You can go "casual or fancy" at this Puck production in Downtown's LA Live doling out "Wolfgang-worthy" Cal cuisine, from burgers and "fancified pizzas" to almond-crusted salmon, in "lively", "modern" digs; service is usually "attentive", but it's "always crowded" – especially before an event at the Staples Center – so "reservations are a must."

Wolfgang Puck Express *Californian* | 21 | 16 | 18 | $26 |

Santa Monica | 1315 Third St. Promenade (bet. Arizona Ave. & Santa Monica Blvd.) | 310-576-4770
LAX | LA Int'l Airport, Terminal 2 | 209 World Way (bet. Sky & West Ways) | 310-215-5166

Wolfgang Puck LA Bistro *Californian*

Universal City | Universal CityWalk | 1000 Universal Studios Blvd. (Coral Dr.) | 818-985-9653
www.wolfgangpuck.com

These "convenient" "fast-food" outlets from Wolfgang Puck offer a "something-for-everyone" array of "light" Cal sandwiches and salads to shoppers, moviegoers and travelers at "decent prices"; even if many call the food "nothing special" and say they're "certainly not destinations on their own accord", it works if you're "on the go."

Wolfgang's Steakhouse *Steak* | 24 | 24 | 24 | $71 |

Beverly Hills | 445 N. Cañon Dr. (Santa Monica Blvd.) | 310-385-0640 | www.wolfgangssteakhouse.net

One of the "best steaks this side of the Williamsburg Bridge" turns up at this "Manhattan"-style chophouse in Beverly Hills from Peter Luger alum Wolfgang Zwiener, pulling a "sophisticated crowd" for "amazing porterhouses sliced right at your table" and other "excellent", "expensive" eats; a "manly", "upscale" ambiance and servers who "greet regulars and newbies alike with warm familiarity" complete the "old-school" package.

🆕 Wolfslair Biergarten ❶ *German* | - | - | - | M |

Hollywood | 1521 N. Vine St. (Sunset Blvd.) | 323-467-9653 | www.wolfslairla.com

Top Chef contestant Jamie Lauren reappears at this Hollywood beer and sausage shop, where the brews are Teutonic, and so is the sausage-heavy menu; it's the latest in an increasingly large number of bierhauses where the tables are shared, the beer is cold and the toppings for the wursts tend to be exotic.

Wood & Vine *American/French* | 23 | 25 | 23 | $39 |

Hollywood | Taft Bldg. | 6280 Hollywood Blvd. (bet. Argyle Ave. & Vine St.) | 323-334-3360 | www.woodandvine.com

This restaurant in the historic Taft Building in Hollywood takes its inspiration from the Golden Age, offering "amazing" classic cocktails and "tasty little plates" of American and French comfort fare – from chicken 'n' waffles to pork rillette – at "reasonable prices"; the "cool" "old-industrial" interior with tin ceilings and a "beautiful bar" opens onto a "rustic patio" with a "mellow" vibe, and "friendly" service seals the deal.

	FOOD	DECOR	SERVICE	COST

Wood Ranch BBQ & Grill *BBQ*

| 24 | 21 | 23 | $30 |

Fairfax | The Grove | 189 The Grove Dr. (bet. Beverly Blvd. & 3rd St.) | 323-937-6800

Cerritos | Cerritos Towne Ctr. | 12801 Towne Center Dr. (bet. Bloomfield & Shoemaker Aves.) | 562-865-0202

Arcadia | 400 S. Baldwin Ave. (Huntington Dr.) | 626-447-4745

Northridge | Northridge Fashion Ctr. | 9301 Tampa Ave. (bet. Nordhoff & Plummer Sts.) | 818-886-6464

Agoura Hills | Whizins Plaza | 5050 Cornell Rd. (Agoura Rd.) | 818-597-8900

Camarillo | 1101 E. Daily Dr. (Lantana St.) | 805-482-1202

Moorpark | 540 New Los Angeles Ave. (Spring Rd.) | 805-523-7253

Ventura | Pacific View Mall | 3449 E. Main St. (Mills Rd.) | 805-620-4500

Newhall | Valencia Mktpl. | 25580 The Old Rd. (bet. Constitution Ave. & McBean Pkwy.) | 661-222-9494

www.woodranch.com

"Always a crowd-pleaser", this "wildly popular" 'cue chain inspires "pig-outs" with "tender tri-tips" and other "meaty, flavorful" fare at "fair prices"; there's "prompt" table service and a "comfy", "family-friendly" setting, but "lines can be overwhelming", so many rely on the curbside takeout.

Woody's Bar-B-Que *BBQ*

| 27 | 13 | 22 | $20 |

Mid-City | 3446 W. Slauson Ave. (Crenshaw Blvd.) | 323-294-9443

Inglewood | 475 S. Market St. (bet. Hillcrest Blvd. & La Brea Ave.) | 310-672-4200 ⑤

www.woodysbarbquela.com

"Right up there" with the best BBQ in town, this "no-frills" duo doles out "delicious", "finger-licking" ribs "worth traveling to" Mid-City or Inglewood for; it's primarily takeout, but you'll "get in and get out" "fast", and "you can't beat the price."

⧉ WP24 *Chinese*

| 26 | 27 | 25 | $90 |

Downtown | Ritz-Carlton | 900 W. Olympic Blvd. (Figueroa St.) | 213-743-8824 | www.wolfgangpuck.com

"Heart-stopping views" from the 24th floor of Downtown's Ritz-Carlton set the stage for Wolfgang Puck's prix fixe menu of "brilliant", "ultra-luxe" Chinese cuisine that's totally "unique" served by a "precise" team; sure, the prices can seem "out of sight", but most insist it's "well worth the money" for such a "memorable" meal; P.S. budget-minders can opt for cocktails and small plates in the bar.

W's China Bistro *Chinese*

| 22 | 19 | 20 | $27 |

Redondo Beach | 1410 S. PCH (Ave. F) | 310-792-1600 | www.wschinabistro.com

It's "not your usual Chinese" at this Redondo eatery presenting "elevated" eats "with a California attitude" in a "casual, but well-designed" setting; service can be variable, but tabs are "reasonable", and on the whole you really "can't go wrong here"; P.S. happy hour has "great deals."

Wurstküche *European*

| 24 | 19 | 17 | $19 |

Downtown | 800 E. Third St. (Traction Ave.) | 213-687-4444 ◑

NEW Venice | 625 Lincoln Blvd. (bet. Sunset Ct. & Vernon Ave.) | 213-687-4444

www.wurstkucherestaurant.com

"Exactly what a modern bierhall should be", this Downtown-Venice duo dispenses "exotic tubular meat concoctions" (rattlesnake, rabbit and even vegan) and "crispy fries" with "dipping sauces galore", washed down with "fab", "unusual" Belgian and German brews in a "trendy", "loud" industrial setting with communal tables and DJs spinning; sure, the "cafeteria-style" service and "hipper-than-thou" vibe's not for everyone, but it's "fun" "with a group", and especially "packed" late at night.

Xi'an *Chinese*   22 | 18 | 20 | $36

Beverly Hills | 362 N. Cañon Dr. (bet. Brighton & Dayton Ways) | 310-275-3345 | www.xian90210.com

The "default Sunday night Chinese" for many Beverly Hills denizens, this longtime venue is a find for "fresh", "creative" takes on the classics with a "healthy", "Americanized" bent; with "moderate prices", "gracious" service and contemporary digs, most don't mind the "noisy" acoustics.

Xiomara ☒ *Californian*   21 | 23 | 24 | $46

Hollywood | 6101 Melrose Ave. (Seward St.) | 323-461-0601 | www.xiomararestaurant.com

Xiomara Ardolina turns out an "eclectic" array of "well-executed" Californian cuisine with Cuban touches at this "easygoing" spot in Hollywood; a "friendly staff", "jazzy" soundtrack and "cozy" Mediterranean-style setup create a "romantic" mood, and almost all agree it has one of "the best mojitos in town"; P.S. it's also a lunch mainstay near Paramount Studios.

Yabu *Japanese*   23 | 16 | 20 | $34

West Hollywood | 521 N. La Cienega Blvd. (bet. Melrose & Rosewood Aves.) | 310-854-0400
West LA | 11820 W. Pico Blvd. (bet. Barrington Ave. & Bundy Dr.) | 310-473-9757
www.yaburestaurant.com

"People rave about the soba", homemade tofu and other "Japanese delicacies" at this "real-deal" pair in West Hollywood and West LA also purveying "solid" sushi; the settings are "casual", but "gracious" servers offer "spot-on" recommendations, and prices are relatively modest given the "high-end" grub.

☒ Yamashiro *Asian/Californian*   22 | 27 | 23 | $47

Hollywood | 1999 N. Sycamore Ave. (Franklin Ave.) | 323-466-5125 | www.yamashirohollywood.com

"Enjoy the scenery from high in the Hollywood Hills" at this veteran Cal-Asian boasting a "tranquil" pagoda setting with "lush gardens" that "takes you back to Japan of the 1940s"; service "excels", and if many find the "lovely location" "upstages" the "pricey" sushi, at least "you can't beat it for drinks."

Yamato *Japanese*   21 | 20 | 21 | $29

Agoura Hills | 28700 Roadside Dr. (Liberty Canyon Rd.) | 818-706-7711
Yamato Westwood *Japanese*
Brentwood | 1099 Westwood Blvd. (Kinross Ave.) | 310-208-0100 | www.yamatorestaurants.com

These Japanese chain links in Agoura Hills and Brentwood are "popular hangouts" for "sushi fanatics on a budget", offering fare that many call "not the most amazing" but "worth it for the price"; Agoura Hills also features teppanyaki shows that "always delight" ("no one ever gets tired of an onion volcano!"), so even if the settings can be "a bit hectic", on the whole it's "fun for the whole family"; P.S. happy hour is especially "affordable."

Yang Chow *Chinese*   23 | 13 | 19 | $25

Chinatown | 819 N. Broadway (bet. Alpine & College Sts.) | 213-625-0811

Pasadena | 3777 E. Colorado Blvd. (Quigley Ave.) | 626-432-6868

Canoga Park | 6443 Topanga Canyon Blvd. (Victory Blvd.) | 818-347-2610

www.yangchow.com

The "famous" slippery shrimp alone are "worth the trip" to this "old-school" Chinese trio turning out "delish", "down-home" dishes that are "satisfying" and about "as authentic as chop suey"; digs are "drab", "crowded and noisy" and service can be "indifferent", but it remains the ultimate "guilty pleasure" for "nostalgic" fans nonetheless.

Yard House ● *American*   22 | 22 | 22 | $28

Downtown | LA Live | 800 W. Olympic Blvd. (bet. Figueroa & Georgia Sts.) | 213-745-9273

Long Beach | Shoreline Vill. | 401 Shoreline Village Dr. (Shoreline Dr.) | 562-628-0455

Pasadena | Paseo Colorado | 330 E. Colorado Blvd. (bet. Los Robles & Marengo Aves.) | 626-577-9273

www.yardhouse.com

"Tons of TVs and taps" pouring an "off-the-hook" beer selection foster the "sports-bar atmosphere" at this American tavern chain, a "fun place to watch a game" that also scores with "dependable comfort food" "above the pub standard" and one of the "best happy hours" around; sure, it's "always crowded" and "noisy", but you know "this ain't the place for scintillating conversation."

Yen Sushi & Sake Bar *Japanese*   23 | 21 | 21 | $30

Little Tokyo | California Market Ctr. | 110 E. Ninth St. (bet. Los Angeles & Main Sts.) | 213-627-9709 🗲

Pico-Robertson | 9618 W. Pico Blvd. (bet. Beverwil & Edris Drs.) | 310-278-0691

Brentwood | 11819 Wilshire Blvd. (bet. Granville & Westgate Aves.) | 310-996-1313

Long Beach | 4905 E. Second St. (bet. Argonne & St. Joseph Aves.) | 562-434-5757

Studio City | 12930 Ventura Blvd. (bet. Coldwater Canyon Ave. & Valley Vista Blvd.) | 818-907-6400

www.yenrestaurants.com

"Load up on sushi without breaking the bank" at this Japanese chain where the "big", "innovative" rolls are priced to move during the all-day happy hours; service is solid and the atmosphere's vaguely "hip", although many get it "to go."

Ye Olde King's Head *Pub Food*   18 | 18 | 20 | $28

Santa Monica | 116 Santa Monica Blvd. (bet. Ocean Ave. & 2nd St.) | 310-451-1402 | www.yeoldekingshead.com

"Brits and lovers of all things British" tuck into "filling" fare like fish 'n' chips at this "real-deal" Santa Monica pub (aka "Oxford on the Pacific") also featuring a "tremendous beer and ale selection", all "cheerfully served"; sure, some "can think of better places to eat", but with moderate prices, a "quaint, cozy" setting and football on the telly, it's a "sentimental favorite" for many.

Yuca's *Mexican*

25 | 9 | 22 | $11

Los Feliz | 2056 Hillhurst Ave. (bet. Ambrose Ave. & Price St.) | 323-662-1214 ⊠⊅

Los Feliz | 4666 Hollywood Blvd. (bet. Rodney Dr. & Vermont Ave.) | 323-661-0523

www.yucasla.com

"Tiny but amazing", this taco-shack duo in Los Feliz is famed for its "melt-in-your-mouth" cochinita pibil and "outrageous" carnitas as well as some of "the best cheapo burritos in town"; it's primarily take-out at both locales, but fans still call it "a must-visit" for anyone seeking a "real LA" experience.

Yxta Cocina Mexicana ⊠ *Mexican*

24 | 22 | 20 | $29

Downtown | 601 S. Central Ave. (6th St.) | 213-596-5579 | www.yxta.net

A "hidden oasis in a rough part of town", this "modern" Mexican Downtown "utilizes the freshest of ingredients" in its "terrific", "original" south-of-the-border fare; moderate pricing, "professional" service and an "energetic" vibe make it "well worth the trip to find it"; P.S. there's also a "fabulous happy hour" daily.

Zane's *Italian/Steak*

21 | 19 | 21 | $38

Hermosa Beach | 1150 Hermosa Ave. (Pier Ave.) | 310-374-7488 | www.zanesrestaurant.com

"Sophisticated yet economical", this "unpretentious" Hermosa Beach spot is a "solid" bet for "well-prepared" Italian steakhouse fare – including a "damn fine cioppino" – backed by a "comprehensive wine list" and "smart cocktails"; service is "attentive" and the "lively", "adult" setting provides "interesting people-watching" through plate-glass windows, and being within "walking distance to the beach for an after-dinner stroll" is a plus.

Zankou Chicken *Mediterranean*

23 | 9 | 16 | $14

East Hollywood | 5065 W. Sunset Blvd. (Normandie Ave.) | 323-665-7845 ◑

West LA | 1716 S. Sepulveda Blvd. (Santa Monica Blvd.) | 310-444-0550

Pasadena | 1296 E. Colorado Blvd. (bet. Chester & Holliston Aves.) | 626-405-1502

Burbank | 1001 N. San Fernando Blvd. (Walnut Ave.) | 818-238-0414

Glendale | 1415 E. Colorado Blvd. (Verdugo Rd.) | 818-244-1937

Glendale | 901 W. Glenoaks Blvd. (Highland Ave.) | 818-244-0492

North Hollywood | 10760 Riverside Dr. (Lankershim Blvd.) | 818-655-0469

Tarzana | 19598 Ventura Blvd. (bet. Corbin & Shirley Aves.) | 818-345-1200

Van Nuys | 5658 Sepulveda Blvd. (bet. Burbank Blvd. & Hatteras St.) | 818-781-0615

Montebello | Newmark Mall | 125 N. Montebello Blvd. (Whittier Blvd.) | 323-722-7200

www.zankouchicken.com

Additional locations throughout Southern California

Devotees "dream about" the "juicy, flavorful" rotisserie chicken at this "popular" Mediterranean fast-food chain cherished for its "glorious", "kick-ass" "garlic sauce of the gods" that will make you want to "buy a tub, take it home and put it on everything you eat for the next week";

"morose" service plus "over-bright fluorescent lighting" add up to "zero atmosphere, but who cares when the food rocks?"

Zazou *Mediterranean*

24 | 21 | 22 | $40

Redondo Beach | 1810 S. Catalina Ave. (Vista Del Mar) | 310-540-4884 | www.zazourestaurant.com

"Pretty restaurant, pretty food and pretty clientele" sums up this lively Redondo Beacher that "fills a niche" in the area with an "excellent" Med menu and "terrific" wines; it can get "crowded" and "noisy", however, "timely, considerate service" smoothes things over, as do the moderate bills.

Zeke's Smokehouse *BBQ*

21 | 17 | 20 | $22

Montrose | 2209 Honolulu Ave. (Montrose Ave.) | 818-957-7045 | www.zekessmokehouse.com

"Well-executed BBQ standards" are dressed up with "some of the zingiest sauces you can find" at this "solid" Montrose entry set in a contemporary Southern-themed space with a sidewalk patio; service is "happy and quick", although a few find prices "too high" for the genre.

Zelo Pizzeria *Pizza*

24 | 16 | 21 | $17

Arcadia | 328 E. Foothill Blvd. (bet. Northview & 5th Aves.) | 626-358-8298 | www.zelopizzeria.com

"Amazing, unusual pizzas" with "abundant toppings" (corn is a favorite) are the thing at this "funky neighborhood gathering place" in Arcadia that's also "easy for takeout"; it isn't fancy, but with "friendly" service and low prices for slices and pies, it's an area "favorite."

Zengo *Asian/Nuevo Latino*

23 | 23 | 22 | $40

Santa Monica | Dining Deck, Santa Monica Pl. | 395 Santa Monica Pl. (3rd St. Promenade) | 310-899-1000 | www.richardsandoval.com

Nibblers "love the menu" at Richard Sandoval's moderately expensive Asian–Nuevo Latino in Santa Monica Place, where there's "lots of choices" of "fun", "unique" small plates and "powerful" cocktails; the "hip" setting includes a "beautiful patio", and there's both an "epic" Sunday brunch and a "good happy hour."

Zephyr Vegetarian *Vegetarian*

▽ 25 | 20 | 22 | $22

Long Beach | 340 E. Fourth St. (E. Roble Way) | 562-435-7113

This Long Beach oasis for vegetarians and vegans produces casual fare like portobello burgers and tempeh Reubens that might fool even the staunchest carnivores; the earthy-meets-rustic vibe is just as inviting as the affable service and favorable prices.

Zin Bistro Americana *American*

23 | 23 | 23 | $43

Westlake Village | 32131 Lindero Canyon Rd. (Summershore Ln.) | 818-865-0095 | www.zinwestlake.com

Lauded for its "stunning" lakefront views, this Westlake Village bistro offers "very good" New Americana in a "relaxing, romantic" atmosphere; "if you're watching your pennies, try it for lunch", when the "lovely location" and "charming" staff are still intact.

Zip Fusion *Japanese/Korean*

▽ 22 | 18 | 21 | $23

Downtown | 744 E. Third St. (Rose St.) | 213-680-3770 | www.zipfusion.com

"Sushi lovers" on a budget make a beeline for the "stuff-your-face buffet" at this Japanese-Korean fusion chain where "you need to bring your appetite along to make it worth it"; there's outdoor seating, but otherwise the atmosphere is "nothing too impressive", and some say "customer service can use improvement" too.

Z Pizza *Pizza*

23 | 16 | 20 | $19

Hancock Park | 123 N. Larchmont Blvd. (bet. Beverly Blvd. & 3rd St.) | 323-466-6969 | www.stores.zpizza.com

West Hollywood | 8869 Santa Monica Blvd. (N. San Vicente Blvd.) | 310-360-1414 | www.stores.zpizza.com ◕

El Segundo | 829 N. Douglas St. (Imperial Hwy.) | 310-648-7919 | www.stores.zpizza.com

Long Beach | 4612 E. Second St. (Livingston Dr.) | 562-987-4500 | www.stores.zpizza.com

Long Beach | 5718 E. Seventh St. (Bellflower Blvd.) | 562-498-0778 | www.stores.zpizza.com

Burbank | 116 E. Palm Ave. (1st St.) | 818-840-8300 | www.zpizzaburbank.com

Thousand Oaks | 5776 Lindero Canyon Rd. (Thousand Oaks Blvd.) | 818-991-4999 | www.stores.zpizza.com

Valencia | 27015 McBean Pkwy. (Magic Mountain Pkwy.) | 661-259-5000 | www.stores.zpizza.com

Northridge | 19300 Rinaldi St. (Index St.) | 818-363-2600 | www.zpizza.com

"Picky eaters" appreciate this "healthy" "build-your-own" pizza chain where the "fresh", customizable options include organic veggies, vegan cheese, whole wheat and gluten-free crusts, along with "tasty" salads and sides; the settings and service make it ideal for "a quick bite or a casual dinner date", while "sane prices" seal the deal for takeout.

ORANGE COUNTY/ PALM SPRINGS/ SANTA BARBARA USEFUL LISTS*

---

* Restaurant locations are indicated by the following abbreviations:
Orange County=OC; Palm Springs & Environs=PS; and Santa
Barbara & Environs=SB. These lists include low vote places that do not
qualify for top lists.

Special Features

Listings cover the best in each category and include names, locations and Food ratings. Multi-location restaurants' features may vary by branch.

BREAKFAST

(See also Hotel Dining)

Ramos Hse. | **San Juan Cap/OC**	27
Old Vine | **Costa Mesa/OC**	26
Break of Dawn | **Laguna Hills/OC**	26
Original Pancake | **Temecula/PS**	25
Cajun Kitchen | **multi.**	24
Tupelo Junction | **SB**	23
Ruby's | **Riverside/PS**	21
Billy Reed's | **PS**	21
NEW Early Bird | **Fullerton/OC**	–
NEW Scarlet Begonia | **SB**	–

BRUNCH

Le Vallauris | **PS**	28
Ramos Hse. | **San Juan Cap/OC**	27
Gemmell's | **Dana Pt/OC**	26
Taps Fish Hse. | **multi.**	26
Tyler's Burgers | **PS**	26
Sage | **Newport Bch/OC**	25
Bayside | **Newport Bch/OC**	25
AnQi | **Costa Mesa/OC**	25
Anaheim White Hse. | **Anaheim/OC**	25
Stella Mare's | **SB**	25
Cava | **Montecito/SB**	25
Montecito | **Montecito/SB**	25
Hungry Cat | **SB**	24
Spencer's | **PS**	24
Melvyn's | **PS**	24
Carlitos Café | **SB**	24
Lucky's | **Montecito/SB**	24
Citrus City | **Corona/PS**	24
Bella Vista | **Montecito/SB**	23
Zin | **PS**	23
Adobe Grill | **La Quinta/PS**	23
Cheesecake Factory | **multi.**	23
Trio | **PS**	23
BJ's | **multi.**	23
Coast | **SB**	23
Castaway | **San Bern/PS**	22
Tropicale | **PS**	22
Holdren's | **SB**	22
3rd Corner | **Palm Desert/PS**	21
Las Casuelas | **Rancho Mirage/PS**	21
Chronic Tacos | **Rancho Cuca/PS**	21
Daily Grill | **Palm Desert/PS**	21
El Torito | **SB**	21
NEW Bistro Bleu | **Anaheim/OC**	–
NEW Scarlet Begonia | **SB**	–

BUFFET

(Check availability)

Taps Fish Hse. | **multi.**	26
Citrus City | **Corona/PS**	24
Bella Vista | **Montecito/SB**	23
Castaway | **San Bern/PS**	22
All India | **SB**	21
Las Casuelas | **Rancho Mirage/PS**	21
El Torito | **SB**	21
Picanha | **Cathedral City/PS**	21

BUSINESS DINING

Park Ave | **Stanton/OC**	28
Antonello | **Santa Ana/OC**	27
Mastro's | **Costa Mesa/OC**	27
Ruth's Chris | **Irvine/OC**	27
Cat/Custard Cup | **La Habra/OC**	26
Mr Stox | **Anaheim/OC**	26
Morton's | **multi.**	26
Mastro's Ocean | **Newport Coast/OC**	26
Bayside | **Newport Bch/OC**	25
Fleming's | **Newport Bch/OC**	25
Anaheim White Hse. | **Anaheim/OC**	25
21 Oceanfront | **Newport Bch/OC**	25
Ritz | **Newport Bch/OC**	25
China Palace/Pavilion | **SB**	23
Arnold Palmer's | **La Quinta/PS**	22
NEW Juliette | **Newport Bch/OC**	–

CELEBRITY CHEFS

Takashi Abe	
Bluefin | **Newport Coast/OC**	29
Franco Barone	
Il Barone | **Newport Bch/OC**	27
Mario Batali	
Pizzeria Mozza | **Newport Bch/OC**	27
Marc Cohen	
230 Forest Ave. | **Laguna Bch/OC**	25
Andrew Copley	
Copley's | **PS**	25
Florent Marneau	
Marché Moderne | **Costa Mesa/OC**	29
Rich Mead	
Sage | **Newport Bch/OC**	25
Pierre Pelech	
Chez Pierre | **Palm Desert/PS**	27
Alessandro Pirozzi	

Cucina Alessá | **multi.**	25
NEW Mare | **Laguna Bch/OC**	–
Amar Santana	
Broadway/Amar Santana | **Laguna Bch/OC**	26
Nancy Silverton	
Pizzeria Mozza | **Newport Bch/OC**	27
Andrew Sutton	
Napa Rose | **Anaheim/OC**	27
Roy Yamaguchi	
Roy's | **Rancho Mirage/PS**	25

CHILD-FRIENDLY

(Alternatives to the usual fast-food places; * children's menu available)

Alicia's* | **Brea/OC**	27
Original Fish Co.* | **Los Alamitos/OC**	27
Cheeky's | **PS**	26
La Super-Rica | **SB**	26
Angelo's Hamburgers* | **Anaheim/OC**	26
In-N-Out | **Laguna Niguel/OC**	26
Jerry's Wood-Fired Dogs* | **multi.**	24
Cheesecake Factory* | **Newport Bch/OC**	23
Brophy Bros. | **SB**	23
Louie's | **SB**	23
Cold Spring* | **SB**	22
Las Casuelas* | **PS**	21
Ruby's* | **multi.**	21
Billy Reed's* | **PS**	21
NEW Birba Pizza & Cocktails | **PS**	–
NEW Early Bird* | **Fullerton/OC**	–

DANCING

Melvyn's | **PS**	24
Arnold Palmer's | **La Quinta/PS**	22
Las Casuelas | **multi.**	21

ENTERTAINMENT

(Call for days and times of performances)

Le Vallauris | **PS**	28
Jillian's | **Palm Desert/PS**	27
Mario's Place | **Riverside/PS**	27
Mastro's | **Costa Mesa/OC**	27
Wally's Desert | **Rancho Mirage/PS**	26
Gemmell's | **Dana Pt/OC**	26
Cork Tree | **Palm Desert/PS**	26
Mr Stox | **Anaheim/OC**	26
Taps Fish Hse. | **Brea/OC**	26
Mastro's Ocean | **Newport Coast/OC**	26
Summit Hse. | **Fullerton/OC**	26

Andrea | **Newport Coast/OC**	25
Bayside | **Newport Bch/OC**	25
AnQi | **Costa Mesa/OC**	25
Anaheim White Hse. | **Anaheim/OC**	25
Stella Mare's | **SB**	25
Fresco Cafe | **SB**	25
Castelli's | **Palm Desert/PS**	25
Cava | **Montecito/SB**	25
21 Oceanfront | **Newport Bch/OC**	25
Ritz | **Newport Bch/OC**	25
Palace Grill | **SB**	24
Spencer's | **PS**	24
Melvyn's | **PS**	24
Carlitos Café | **SB**	24
Lucille's | **multi.**	24
Citrus City | **Corona/PS**	24
Zaytoon | **SB**	23
Adobe Grill | **La Quinta/PS**	23
3Thirty3 | **Newport Bch/OC**	23
Castaway | **San Bern/PS**	22
Los Olivos | **Los Olivos/SB**	22
Tropicale | **PS**	22
Arnold Palmer's | **La Quinta/PS**	22
Brewhouse | **SB**	22
Cold Spring | **SB**	22
Las Casuelas | **multi.**	21
Picanha | **Cathedral City/PS**	21
King's Hwy. | **PS**	–

FIREPLACES

Le Vallauris | **PS**	28
Napa Rose | **Anaheim/OC**	27
Ballard Inn | **Ballard/SB**	27
Studio | **Laguna Bch/OC**	27
Cafe Zoolu | **Laguna Bch/OC**	26
Cat/Custard Cup | **La Habra/OC**	26
Gemmell's | **Dana Pt/OC**	26
Mr Stox | **Anaheim/OC**	26
Summit Hse. | **Fullerton/OC**	26
Cuistot | **Palm Desert/PS**	25
AnQi | **Costa Mesa/OC**	25
LG's | **La Quinta/PS**	25
Anaheim White Hse. | **Anaheim/OC**	25
Stella Mare's | **SB**	25
Cava | **Montecito/SB**	25
Wine Cask | **SB**	25
Pelican Grill | **Newport Coast/OC**	25
Hitching Post | **Buellton/SB**	24
Blue Agave | **SB**	24
Lucky's | **Montecito/SB**	24
Bella Vista | **Montecito/SB**	23
Adobe Grill | **La Quinta/PS**	23
3Thirty3 | **Newport Bch/OC**	23
Plow & Angel | **Montecito/SB**	22

Los Olivos | **Los Olivos/SB**	22
Arnold Palmer's | **La Quinta/PS**	22
Cold Spring | **SB**	22
Las Casuelas | **La Quinta/PS**	21

GREEN/LOCAL/ORGANIC

Marché Moderne | **Costa Mesa/OC**	29
Downey's | **SB**	28
Julienne | **SB**	28
Park Ave | **Stanton/OC**	28
Ballard Inn | **Ballard/SB**	27
Cheeky's | **PS**	26
Old Vine | **Costa Mesa/OC**	26
Break of Dawn | **Laguna Hills/OC**	26
Opal | **SB**	26
Hungry Cat | **SB**	24
Zin | **PS**	23
NEW Birba Pizza & Cocktails | **PS**	–
NEW Early Bird | **Fullerton/OC**	–
NEW Juliette | **Newport Bch/OC**	–
NEW Scarlet Begonia | **SB**	–

HISTORIC PLACES

(Year opened; * building)

1800 | Tupelo Junction* | **SB**	23
1881 | Ramos Hse.* | **San Juan Cap/OC**	27
1886 | Cold Spring* | **SB**	22
1890 | Wine Cask* | **SB**	25
1893 | Plow & Angel* | **Montecito/SB**	22
1909 | Hitching Post* | **Casmalia/SB**	24
1920 | Montecito* | **Montecito/SB**	25
1923 | South of Nick's | **San Clemente/OC**	24
1927 | Bella Vista* | **Montecito/SB**	23
1930 | Hobbit* | **Orange/OC**	27
1930 | Las Casuelas* | **PS**	21
1947 | Copley's* | **PS**	25
1958 | Las Casuelas | **PS**	21
1960 | Castaway | **San Bern/PS**	22
1960 | Stella Mare's* | **SB**	25

HOTEL DINING

Ace Hotel	
King's Hwy. | **PS**	–
Ballard Inn	
Ballard Inn | **Ballard/SB**	27
Canary Hotel	
Coast | **SB**	23
Disneyland Hotel	
Steakhouse 55 | **Anaheim/OC**	27
Disney's Grand Californian	
Napa Rose | **Anaheim/OC**	27
Four Seasons, Biltmore	
Bella Vista | **Montecito/SB**	23
Holiday Inn	
NEW Mare | **Laguna Bch/OC**	–
Ingleside Inn	
Melvyn's | **PS**	24
La Quinta Resort & Club	
Adobe Grill | **La Quinta/PS**	23
Montage Laguna Bch.	
Studio | **Laguna Bch/OC**	27
Montecito Inn	
Montecito | **Montecito/SB**	25
Ritz-Carlton Laguna Beach	
enoSTEAK | **Dana Pt/OC**	–
San Ysidro Ranch	
Plow & Angel | **Montecito/SB**	22
The Resort at Pelican Hill	
Andrea | **Newport Coast/OC**	25
Upham Hotel	
Louie's | **SB**	23

LATE DINING

(Weekday closing hour)

Angelo's Hamburgers | 12 AM | **Anaheim/OC**	26
Broadway/Amar Santana | varies | **Laguna Bch/OC**	26
In-N-Out | varies | **multi.**	26
Hat | 1 AM | **Upland/PS**	25
Honda-Ya | 1:30 AM | **Fountain Vly/OC**	24
Blue Agave | 11:30 PM | **SB**	24
Zaytoon | varies | **SB**	23
BJ's | varies | **multi.**	23
3Thirty3 | 2 AM | **Newport Bch/OC**	23
Yard House | varies | **multi.**	22
El Gallo Giro | 24 hrs. | **Fontana**	22
3rd Corner | 12:45 AM | **Palm Desert/PS**	21
Lee's Sandwiches | 24 hrs. | **Garden Grove/OC**	21
Wienerschnitzel | 12 AM | **Orange/OC**	20
King's Hwy. | varies | **PS**	–
NEW Mare | varies | **Laguna Bch/OC**	–

NEWCOMERS

Pizzeria Mozza | **Newport Bch/OC**	27
Broadway/Amar Santana | **Laguna Bch/OC**	26
South of Nick's | **San Clemente/OC**	24
Birba Pizza & Cocktails | **PS**	–
Bistro Bleu | **Anaheim/OC**	–

Early Bird | **Fullerton/OC** ⌐
enoSTEAK | **Dana Pt/OC** ⌐
Juliette | **Newport Bch/OC** ⌐
Mare | **Laguna Bch/OC** ⌐
Scarlet Begonia | **SB** ⌐

OUTDOOR DINING

Marché Moderne |
  Costa Mesa/OC 29
Le Vallauris | **PS** 28
Park Ave | **Stanton/OC** 28
Ramos Hse. | **San Juan Cap/OC** 27
Studio | **Laguna Bch/OC** 27
Cheeky's | **PS** 26
Taps Fish Hse. | **Brea/OC** 26
Tyler's Burgers | **PS** 26
Sage | **Newport Bch/OC** 25
Bayside | **Newport Bch/OC** 25
Copley's | **PS** 25
Ritz | **Newport Bch/OC** 25
NEW Birba Pizza & Cocktails | **PS** ⌐
NEW Mare | **Laguna Bch/OC** ⌐

PARTIES/
PRIVATE ROOMS

(Restaurants charge less at off
times; call for capacity)
Park Ave | **Stanton/OC** 28
Napa Rose | **Anaheim/OC** 27
Studio | **Laguna Bch/OC** 27
Hobbit | **Orange/OC** 27
Antonello | **Santa Ana/OC** 27
Cat/Custard Cup | **La Habra/OC** 26
Mr Stox | **Anaheim/OC** 26
Taps Fish Hse. | **Brea/OC** 26
Summit Hse. | **Fullerton/OC** 26
Bayside | **Newport Bch/OC** 25
AnQi | **Costa Mesa/OC** 25
Fleming's | **Newport Bch/OC** 25
Anaheim White Hse. |
  Anaheim/OC 25
21 Oceanfront | **Newport Bch/OC** 25
Ritz | **Newport Bch/OC** 25

PEOPLE-WATCHING

Pizzeria Mozza | **Newport Bch/OC** 27
Mastro's Ocean |
  Newport Coast/OC 26
Arigato | **SB** 26
Tyler's Burgers | **PS** 26
Bayside | **Newport Bch/OC** 25
AnQi | **Costa Mesa/OC** 25
230 Forest Ave. |
  Laguna Bch/OC 25
Plow & Angel | **Montecito/SB** 22
NEW Birba Pizza & Cocktails | **PS** ⌐

King's Hwy. | **PS** ⌐
NEW Mare | **Laguna Bch/OC** ⌐

POWER SCENES

Marché Moderne |
  Costa Mesa/OC 29
Pizzeria Mozza |
  Newport Bch/OC 27
Studio | **Laguna Bch/OC** 27
Antonello | **Santa Ana/OC** 27
Mastro's | **Costa Mesa/OC** 27
Mr Stox | **Anaheim/OC** 26
Morton's | **multi.** 26
Mastro's Ocean |
  Newport Coast/OC 26
Bayside | **Newport Bch/OC** 25
Fleming's | **Newport Bch/OC** 25
Anaheim White Hse. |
  Anaheim/OC 25
21 Oceanfront |
  Newport Bch/OC 25
Ritz | **Newport Bch/OC** 25
Arnold Palmer's | **La Quinta/PS** 22
NEW Mare | **Laguna Bch/OC** ⌐

QUIET
CONVERSATION

Bluefin | **Newport Coast/OC** 29
Marché Moderne |
  Costa Mesa/OC 29
Basilic | **Newport Bch/OC** 28
Napa Rose | **Anaheim/OC** 27
Steakhouse 55 | **Anaheim/OC** 27
Ballard Inn | **Ballard/SB** 27
Studio | **Laguna Bch/OC** 27
Hobbit | **Orange/OC** 27
Antonello | **Santa Ana/OC** 27
Mastro's | **Costa Mesa/OC** 27
Mr Stox | **Anaheim/OC** 26
Morton's | **Anaheim/OC** 26
Summit Hse. | **Fullerton/OC** 26
Andrea | **Newport Coast/OC** 25
Anaheim White Hse. |
  Anaheim/OC 25
Ritz | **Newport Bch/OC** 25
Arnold Palmer's | **La Quinta/PS** 22
NEW Bistro Bleu | **Anaheim/OC** ⌐
enoSTEAK | **Dana Pt/OC** ⌐
NEW Scarlet Begonia | **SB** ⌐

RAW BARS

Taps Fish Hse. | **multi.** 26
Hungry Cat | **SB** 24
King's Fish | **multi.** 23
Coast | **SB** 23
Enterprise Fish | **SB** 21

ROMANTIC PLACES

Marché Moderne | **Costa Mesa/OC**	29
Basilic | **Newport Bch/OC**	28
Le Vallauris | **PS**	28
Napa Rose | **Anaheim/OC**	27
Steakhouse 55 | **Anaheim/OC**	27
Ballard Inn | **Ballard/SB**	27
Studio | **Laguna Bch/OC**	27
Hobbit | **Orange/OC**	27
Antonello | **Santa Ana/OC**	27
Mastro's | **Costa Mesa/OC**	27
Cat/Custard Cup | **La Habra/OC**	26
Mr Stox | **Anaheim/OC**	26
Leatherby's Café Rouge | **Costa Mesa/OC**	25
Anaheim White Hse. | **Anaheim/OC**	25
21 Oceanfront | **Newport Bch/OC**	25
Ritz | **Newport Bch/OC**	25
Plow & Angel | **Montecito/SB**	22
Arnold Palmer's | **La Quinta/PS**	22
enoSTEAK | **Dana Pt/OC**	-
NEW Scarlet Begonia | **SB**	-

SINGLES SCENES

Broadway/Amar Santana | **Laguna Bch/OC**	26
Bayside | **Newport Bch/OC**	25
Fleming's | **multi.**	25
3Thirty3 | **Newport Bch/OC**	23
Plow & Angel | **Montecito/SB**	22
NEW Mare | **Laguna Bch/OC**	-

SPECIAL OCCASIONS

Marché Moderne | **Costa Mesa/OC**	29
Downey's | **SB**	28
Le Vallauris | **PS**	28
Napa Rose | **Anaheim/OC**	27
Steakhouse 55 | **Anaheim/OC**	27
Johannes | **PS**	27
Studio | **Laguna Bch/OC**	27
Hobbit | **Orange/OC**	27
Antonello | **Santa Ana/OC**	27
Mastro's | **Costa Mesa/OC**	27
Wally's Desert | **Rancho Mirage/PS**	26
Morton's | **multi.**	26
Mastro's Ocean | **Newport Coast/OC**	26
Leatherby's Café Rouge | **Costa Mesa/OC**	25
Cuistot | **Palm Desert/PS**	25
Bayside | **Newport Bch/OC**	25
Fleming's | **Newport Bch/OC**	25

Anaheim White Hse. | **Anaheim/OC**

Anaheim White Hse. | **Anaheim/OC**	25
21 Oceanfront | **Newport Bch/OC**	25
Roy's | **Rancho Mirage/PS**	25
Arnold Palmer's | **La Quinta/PS**	22

TRANSPORTING EXPERIENCES

Bluefin | **Newport Coast/OC**	29
Marché Moderne | **Costa Mesa/OC**	29
Basilic | **Newport Bch/OC**	28
Studio | **Laguna Bch/OC**	27
Hobbit | **Orange/OC**	27
Mastro's Ocean | **Newport Coast/OC**	26

TRENDY

Bluefin | **Newport Coast/OC**	29
Marché Moderne | **Costa Mesa/OC**	29
Pizzeria Mozza | **Newport Bch/OC**	27
Cheeky's | **PS**	26
Broadway/Amar Santana | **Laguna Bch/OC**	26
Mastro's Ocean | **Newport Coast/OC**	26
NEW South of Nick's | **San Clemente/OC**	24
Hungry Cat | **SB**	24
3Thirty3 | **Newport Bch/OC**	23
NEW Birba Pizza & Cocktails | **PS**	-
NEW Juliette | **Newport Bch/OC**	-
King's Hwy. | **PS**	-
NEW Mare | **Laguna Bch/OC**	-

VIEWS

Bouchon | **SB**	27
Ballard Inn | **Ballard/SB**	27
Johannes | **PS**	27
Studio | **Laguna Bch/OC**	27
Mastro's Ocean | **Newport Coast/OC**	26
Summit Hse. | **Fullerton/OC**	26
Cuistot | **Palm Desert/PS**	25
Andrea | **Newport Coast/OC**	25
Stella Mare's | **SB**	25
Pacifica Seafood | **Palm Desert/PS**	25
21 Oceanfront | **Newport Bch/OC**	25
Pelican Grill | **Newport Coast/OC**	25
Bella Vista | **Montecito/SB**	23
Adobe Grill | **La Quinta/PS**	23
3Thirty3 | **Newport Bch/OC**	23
Castaway | **San Bern/PS**	22

Arnold Palmer's | **La Quinta/PS** 22
Brewhouse | **SB** 22

VISITORS ON EXPENSE ACCOUNT

Bluefin | **Newport Coast/OC** 29
Marché Moderne | **Costa Mesa/OC** 29
Downey's | **SB** 28
Le Vallauris | **PS** 28
Gabbi's | **Orange/OC** 28
Napa Rose | **Anaheim/OC** 27
Pizzeria Mozza | **Newport Bch/OC** 27
Johannes | **PS** 27
Studio | **Laguna Bch/OC** 27
Hobbit | **Orange/OC** 27
Antonello | **Santa Ana/OC** 27
Mastro's | **Costa Mesa/OC** 27
Wally's Desert | **Rancho Mirage/PS** 26
Mr Stox | **Anaheim/OC** 26
Morton's | **multi.** 26
Broadway/Amar Santana | **Laguna Bch/OC** 26
Mastro's Ocean | **Newport Coast/OC** 26
Summit Hse. | **Fullerton/OC** 26
Leatherby's Café Rouge | **Costa Mesa/OC** 25
Cuistot | **Palm Desert/PS** 25
Bayside | **Newport Bch/OC** 25
Fleming's | **Newport Bch/OC** 25
Anaheim White Hse. | **Anaheim/OC** 25
21 Oceanfront | **Newport Bch/OC** 25
Roy's | **Rancho Mirage/PS** 25
Arnold Palmer's | **La Quinta/PS** 22
enoSTEAK | **Dana Pt/OC** ⌐

WATERSIDE

Studio | **Laguna Bch/OC** 27
Mastro's Ocean | **Newport Coast/OC** 26

Stella Mare's | **SB** 25
21 Oceanfront | **Newport Bch/OC** 25
Bella Vista | **Montecito/SB** 23
Cheesecake Factory | **Rancho Mirage/PS** 23
King's Hwy. | **PS** ⌐

WINE BARS

Mario's Place | **Riverside/PS** 27
Olio | **SB** 25
Fleming's | **Newport Bch/OC** 25
Ca' Dario | **SB** 25
Market Broiler | **Riverside/PS** 25
Hungry Cat | **SB** 24
Los Olivos | **Los Olivos/SB** 22

WINNING WINE LISTS

Marché Moderne | **Costa Mesa/OC** 29
Le Vallauris | **PS** 28
Napa Rose | **Anaheim/OC** 27
Pizzeria Mozza | **Newport Bch/OC** 27
Studio | **Laguna Bch/OC** 27
Golden Truffle | **Costa Mesa/OC** 27
Hobbit | **Orange/OC** 27
Antonello | **Santa Ana/OC** 27
Mastro's | **Costa Mesa/OC** 27
Wally's Desert | **Rancho Mirage/PS** 26
Old Vine | **Costa Mesa/OC** 26
Mr Stox | **Anaheim/OC** 26
Walt's Wharf | **Seal Bch/OC** 25
Cuistot | **Palm Desert/PS** 25
Bayside | **Newport Bch/OC** 25
Fleming's | **Newport Bch/OC** 25
Anaheim White Hse. | **Anaheim/OC** 25
Ritz | **Newport Bch/OC** 25
Plow & Angel | **Montecito/SB** 22
Cold Spring | **SB** 22
NEW Juliette | **Newport Bch/OC** ⌐

Cuisines

Includes names, locations and Food ratings.

AMERICAN

Park Ave | **Stanton/OC**	28
Ramos Hse. | **San Juan Cap/OC**	27
Alicia's | **Brea/OC**	27
Cheeky's | **PS**	26
Cat/Custard Cup | **La Habra/OC**	26
Mr Stox | **Anaheim/OC**	26
Taps Fish Hse. | **multi.**	26
Broadway/Amar Santana | **Laguna Bch/OC**	26
Sage | **Newport Bch/OC**	25
Bayside | **Newport Bch/OC**	25
Copley's | **PS**	25
Original Pancake | **Temecula/PS**	25
Zin | **PS**	23
Cheesecake Factory | **multi.**	23
Trio | **PS**	23
BJ's | **multi.**	23
3Thirty3 | **Newport Bch/OC**	23
Yard House | **multi.**	22
Arnold Palmer's | **La Quinta/PS**	22
Brewhouse | **SB**	22
Cold Spring | **SB**	22
Sojourner Cafe | **SB**	21
Daily Grill | **Palm Desert/PS**	21
Ruby's | **multi.**	21
Billy Reed's | **PS**	21
East Beach Grill | **SB**	20
Marmalade | **SB**	19
NEW Early Bird | **Fullerton/OC**	-
NEW Juliette | **Newport Bch/OC**	-
King's Hwy. | **PS**	-
NEW Scarlet Begonia | **SB**	-

ASIAN

Roy's | **Rancho Mirage/PS**	25
Elephant Bar | **Irvine/OC**	22

BARBECUE

Blake's Place | **Anaheim/OC**	28
Joey's | **multi.**	26
Hitching Post | **multi.**	24
Wood Ranch | **Corona/PS**	24
Lucille's | **multi.**	24

BRAZILIAN

Picanha | **Cathedral City/PS**	21

BURGERS

Angelo's Hamburgers | **Anaheim/OC**	26
Tyler's Burgers | **PS**	26
In-N-Out | **multi.**	26
Hungry Cat | **SB**	24
Jerry's Wood-Fired Dogs | **multi.**	24
Wienerschnitzel | **Orange/OC**	20

CAJUN

Palace Grill | **SB**	24
Cajun Kitchen | **multi.**	24

CALIFORNIAN

Downey's | **SB**	28
Julienne | **SB**	28
Napa Rose | **Anaheim/OC**	27
Bouchon | **SB**	27
Studio | **Laguna Bch/OC**	27
Cafe Zoolu | **Laguna Bch/OC**	26
Cat/Custard Cup | **La Habra/OC**	26
Cork Tree | **Palm Desert/PS**	26
Opal | **SB**	26
Leatherby's Café Rouge | **Costa Mesa/OC**	25
Cuistot | **Palm Desert/PS**	25
Stella Mare's | **SB**	25
Montecito | **Montecito/SB**	25
230 Forest Ave. | **Laguna Bch/OC**	25
Wine Cask | **SB**	25
Pelican Grill | **Newport Coast/OC**	25
Citrus City | **Corona/PS**	24
Bella Vista | **Montecito/SB**	23
Seagrass | **SB**	23
Louie's | **SB**	23
Coast | **SB**	23
Arts & Letters | **SB**	22
Castaway | **San Bern/PS**	22
Plow & Angel | **Montecito/SB**	22
Los Olivos | **Los Olivos/SB**	22
Acqua Pazza | **Rancho Mirage/PS**	22
NEW Bistro Bleu | **Anaheim/OC**	-

CARIBBEAN

Golden Truffle | **Costa Mesa/OC**	27

CHINESE

China Palace/Pavilion | **SB**	23
P.F. Chang's | **multi.**	22

CONTINENTAL

Jillian's | **Palm Desert/PS**	27
Hobbit | **Orange/OC**	27
Wally's Desert | **Rancho Mirage/PS**	26

Gemmell's | **Dana Pt/OC** `26`
Summit Hse. | **Fullerton/OC** `26`
Ritz | **Newport Bch/OC** `25`
Melvyn's | **PS** `24`
Andersen's | **SB** `24`

CREOLE

Palace Grill | **SB** `24`

DELIS

Fresco Cafe | **SB** `25`

DINER

Angelo's Hamburgers |
  Anaheim/OC `26`
Original Pancake |
  Temecula/PS `25`
Ruby's | **multi.** `21`
Billy Reed's | **PS** `21`
NEW Early Bird | **Fullerton/OC** `-`

ECLECTIC

Johannes | **PS** `27`
Old Vine | **Costa Mesa/OC** `26`
Break of Dawn | **Laguna Hills/OC** `26`
Opal | **SB** `26`
Spencer's | **PS** `24`
Blue Agave | **SB** `24`
Cheesecake Factory |
  Riverside/PS `23`
Plow & Angel | **Montecito/SB** `22`
Wahoo's Fish Taco |
  Rancho Cuca/PS `22`
Tropicale | **PS** `22`
3rd Corner | **Palm Desert/PS** `21`
King's Hwy. | **PS** `-`

FRENCH

Marché Moderne |
  Costa Mesa/OC `29`
Basilic | **Newport Bch/OC** `28`
Downey's | **SB** `28`
Le Vallauris | **PS** `28`
Bouchon | **SB** `27`
Ballard Inn | **Ballard/SB** `27`
Studio | **Laguna Bch/OC** `27`
Golden Truffle |
  Costa Mesa/OC `27`
Hobbit | **Orange/OC** `27`
Gemmell's | **Dana Pt/OC** `26`
Cuistot | **Palm Desert/PS** `25`
Stella Mare's | **SB** `25`

FRENCH (BISTRO)

Julienne | **SB** `28`
Chez Pierre | **Palm Desert/PS** `27`
Zin | **PS** `23`
NEW Bistro Bleu | **Anaheim/OC** `-`

HAWAIIAN

Roy's | **Rancho Mirage/PS** `25`

HOT DOGS

Jerry's Wood-Fired Dogs | **multi.** `24`
Wienerschnitzel | **Orange/OC** `20`

INDIAN

All India | **SB** `21`

ITALIAN

(N=Northern; S=Southern)

Il Barone | **Newport Bch/OC** `27`
Mario's Place | **Riverside/PS** `27`
Antonello | **Santa Ana/OC** `27`
Cucina Alessá | **multi.** `25`
Andrea | **Newport Coast/OC** `25`
Olio | S | **SB** `25`
Ca' Dario | **SB** `25`
Anaheim White Hse. |
  Anaheim/OC `25`
Fresco Cafe | **SB** `25`
Castelli's | **Palm Desert/PS** `25`
Tratt. Grappolo | **Santa Ynez/SB** `24`
Vince's Spaghetti | **multi.** `24`
Tre Lune | **Montecito/SB** `23`
Pane e Vino | **Montecito/SB** `23`
Arnoldi's Cafe | **SB** `22`
NEW Mare | **Laguna Bch/OC** `-`

JAPANESE

(* sushi specialist)

Bluefin* | **Newport Coast/OC** `29`
Taiko* | **Irvine/OC** `26`
Arigato* | **SB** `26`
Zip Fusion* | **Corona/PS** `22`
Gyu-Kaku | **Rancho Cuca/PS** `22`

LEBANESE

Zaytoon | **SB** `23`

MEDITERRANEAN

Le Vallauris | **PS** `28`
Seagrass | **SB** `23`
Los Olivos | **Los Olivos/SB** `22`

MEXICAN

Gabbi's | **Orange/OC** `28`
La Sirena | **Laguna Bch/OC** `27`
La Super-Rica | **SB** `26`
El Farolito | **Placentia/OC** `26`
Taco Mesa | **multi.** `26`
NEW South of Nick's |
  San Clemente/OC `24`
Carlitos Café | **SB** `24`
Los Arroyos | **multi.** `24`
Adobe Grill | **La Quinta/PS** `23`

Wahoo's Fish Taco | **Rancho Cuca/PS** — 22

El Gallo Giro | **Fontana** — 22

Las Casuelas | **multi.** — 21

El Torito | **multi.** — 21

Acapulco | **multi.** — 20

PAN-LATIN

Cava | **Montecito/SB** — 25

PIZZA

Pizzeria Mozza | **Newport Bch/OC** — 27

Olio | **SB** — 25

Z Pizza | **multi.** — 23

Graziano's Pizza | **Corona/PS** — 23

BJ's | **Laguna Hills/OC** — 23

Cal. Pizza Kitchen | **multi.** — 22

Lamppost Pizza | **Corona/PS** — 22

NEW Birba Pizza & Cocktails | **PS** — –

PUB FOOD

BJ's | **multi.** — 23

SANDWICHES

(See also Delis)

Alicia's | **Brea/OC** — 27

Hat | **multi.** — 25

Lee's Sandwiches | **multi.** — 21

SEAFOOD

Original Fish Co. | **Los Alamitos/OC** — 27

Taps Fish Hse. | **multi.** — 26

Morton's | **multi.** — 26

Mastro's Ocean | **Newport Coast/OC** — 26

Tabu | **Laguna Bch/OC** — 26

Walt's Wharf | **Seal Bch/OC** — 25

Paçifica Seafood | **Palm Desert/PS** — 25

Market Broiler | **Riverside/PS** — 25

21 Oceanfront | **Newport Bch/OC** — 25

Hungry Cat | **SB** — 24

Seagrass | **SB** — 23

Brophy Bros. | **SB** — 23

King's Fish | **multi.** — 23

Coast | **SB** — 23

Arts & Letters | **SB** — 22

Holdren's | **SB** — 22

Enterprise Fish | **SB** — 21

SMALL PLATES

Marché Moderne | **French** | **Costa Mesa/OC** — 29

Old Vine | **Eclectic** | **Costa Mesa/OC** — 26

Broadway/Amar Santana | **Amer./Eclectic** | **Laguna Bch/OC** — 26

Sage | **Amer.** | **Newport Bch/OC** — 25

Honda-Ya Izakaya | **Japanese** | **Fullerton/OC** — 24

3Thirty3 | **Amer.** | **Newport Bch/OC** — 23

SOUTHERN

Lucille's | **multi.** — 24

Tupelo Junction | **SB** — 23

STEAKHOUSES

Steakhouse 55 | **Anaheim/OC** — 27

Mastro's | **Costa Mesa/OC** — 27

Ruth's Chris | **multi.** — 27

Morton's | **multi.** — 26

Mastro's Ocean | **Newport Coast/OC** — 26

Tabu | **Laguna Bch/OC** — 26

Fleming's | **multi.** — 25

LG's | **multi.** — 25

Chop Hse. | **multi.** — 24

Lucky's | **Montecito/SB** — 24

Outback | **San Bern/PS** — 23

Holdren's | **SB** — 22

Arnold Palmer's | **La Quinta/PS** — 22

enoSTEAK | **Dana Pt/OC** — –

SWISS

Basilic | **Newport Bch/OC** — 28

VEGETARIAN

(* vegan)

Sojourner Cafe* | **SB** — 21

VIETNAMESE

AnQi | **Costa Mesa/OC** — 25

Locations

Includes names, cuisines and Food ratings.

Orange County

ANAHEIM/ANAHEIM HILLS

Blake's Place | BBQ 28
Napa Rose | Cal. 27
Steakhouse 55 | Steak 27
Ruth's Chris | Steak 27
Mr Stox | Amer. 26
Angelo's Hamburgers | Diner 26
Morton's | Steak 26
Anaheim White Hse. | Italian 25
Cheesecake Factory | Amer. 23
NEW Bistro Bleu | Cal./French -

BREA

Alicia's | American/Continental 27
Taps Fish Hse. | Amer./Seafood 26
Lucille's | BBQ 24
Cheesecake Factory | Amer. 23
BJ's | Pub 23

COSTA MESA

Marché Moderne | French 29
Golden Truffle | Carib./French 27
Mastro's | Steak 27
Old Vine | Eclectic 26
Taco Mesa | Mex. 26
In-N-Out | Burgers 26
Leatherby's Café Rouge | Cal. 25
AnQi | Viet. 25
Acapulco | Mex. 20

DANA POINT

Gemmell's | Continental/French 26
enoSTEAK | Steak -

FOUNTAIN VALLEY

Honda-Ya | Japanese 24

FULLERTON

Summit Hse. | Continental 26
Honda-Ya Izakaya | Japanese 24
Lee's Sandwiches | Sandwiches 21
NEW Early Bird | Diner -

GARDEN GROVE

Lee's Sandwiches | Sandwiches 21

HUNTINGTON BEACH

In-N-Out | Burgers 26
Cucina Alessá | Italian 25
Cheesecake Factory | Amer. 23

Z Pizza | Pizza 23
BJ's | Pub 23
Lee's Sandwiches | Sandwiches 21

IRVINE

La Sirena | Mex. 27
Ruth's Chris | Steak 27
Taiko | Japanese 26
Jerry's Wood-Fired Dogs | Hot Dogs 24
Cheesecake Factory | Amer. 23
Elephant Bar | Asian 22
Lee's Sandwiches | Sandwiches 21

LADERA RANCH

Taco Mesa | Mex. 26
Jerry's Wood-Fired Dogs | Hot Dogs 24

LAGUNA BEACH

La Sirena | Mex. 27
Studio | Cal./French 27
Cafe Zoolu | Cal. 26
Broadway/Amar Santana | Amer./Eclectic 26
Tabu | Seafood/Steak 26
230 Forest Ave. | Cal. 25
BJ's | Pub 23
NEW Mare | Cal./Italian -

LAGUNA HILLS

Break of Dawn | Eclectic/Viet. 26
BJ's | Pub 23

LAGUNA NIGUEL

In-N-Out | Burgers 26

LA HABRA

Cat/Custard Cup | Amer./Cal. 26
Jerry's Wood-Fired Dogs | Hot Dogs 24

LAKE FOREST

Lucille's | BBQ 24

LOS ALAMITOS

Original Fish Co. | Seafood 27

MISSION VIEJO

Taco Mesa | Mex. 26
Cheesecake Factory | Amer. 23

NEWPORT BEACH

Basilic | French/Swiss 28
Il Barone | Italian 27

Pizzeria Mozza	*Pizza*	27
Sage	*Amer.*	25
Cucina Alessá	*Italian*	25
Bayside	*Amer.*	25
Fleming's	*Steak*	25
21 Oceanfront	*Seafood*	25
Ritz	*Continental*	25
Cheesecake Factory	*Amer.*	23
BJ's	*Pub*	23
3Thirty3	*Amer.*	23
NEW Juliette	*Amer.*	-

NEWPORT COAST

Bluefin	*Japanese*	29
Mastro's Ocean	*Seafood/Steak*	26
Andrea	*Italian*	25
Pelican Grill	*Cal.*	25

ORANGE

Gabbi's	*Mex.*	28
Hobbit	*Continental/French*	27
Taco Mesa	*Mex.*	26
Lucille's	*BBQ*	24
Wienerschnitzel	*Burgers/Hot Dogs*	20

PLACENTIA

El Farolito	*Mex.*	26

SAN CLEMENTE

NEW South of Nick's	*Mex.*	24

SAN JUAN CAPISTRANO

Ramos Hse.	*Amer.*	27

SANTA ANA

Antonello	*Italian*	27
Morton's	*Steak*	26
Jerry's Wood-Fired Dogs	*Hot Dogs*	24

SEAL BEACH

Walt's Wharf	*Seafood*	25

STANTON

Park Ave	*Amer.*	28
Acapulco	*Mex.*	20

TUSTIN

In-N-Out	*Burgers*	26
Lucille's	*BBQ*	24
Z Pizza	*Pizza*	23

Palm Springs & Environs

CATHEDRAL CITY

Picanha	*Brazilian*	21

CHINO

Joey's	*BBQ*	26
Lee's Sandwiches	*Sandwiches*	21

CORONA

Taps Fish Hse.	*Amer./Seafood*	26
In-N-Out	*Burgers*	26
Wood Ranch	*BBQ*	24
Citrus City	*Cal.*	24
Graziano's Pizza	*Pizza*	23
BJ's	*Pub*	23
King's Fish	*Seafood*	23
Zip Fusion	*Japanese/Korean*	22
Lamppost Pizza	*Pizza*	22
Chronic Tacos	*Mex.*	21

FONTANA

El Gallo Giro	*Mex.*	22

LA QUINTA

LG's	*Steak*	25
Adobe Grill	*Mex.*	23
Arnold Palmer's	*Steak*	22
Las Casuelas	*Mex.*	21

PALM DESERT

Jillian's	*Continental*	27
Chez Pierre	*French*	27
Ruth's Chris	*Steak*	27
Cork Tree	*Cal.*	26
Morton's	*Steak*	26
Cuistot	*Cal./French*	25
Castelli's	*Italian*	25
Pacifica Seafood	*Seafood*	25
Chop Hse.	*Steak*	24
Cal. Pizza Kitchen	*Pizza*	22
3rd Corner	*Eclectic*	21
Las Casuelas	*Mex.*	21
Daily Grill	*Amer.*	21

PALM SPRINGS

Le Vallauris	*French/Med.*	28
Johannes	*Eclectic*	27
Cheeky's	*Amer.*	26
Tyler's Burgers	*Burgers*	26
Copley's	*Amer.*	25
LG's	*Steak*	25
Chop Hse.	*Steak*	24
Spencer's	*Eclectic*	24
Melvyn's	*Continental*	24
Zin	*Amer./French*	23
Trio	*Amer.*	23
Tropicale	*Eclectic*	22
Cal. Pizza Kitchen	*Pizza*	22
Las Casuelas	*Mex.*	21
Ruby's	*Diner*	21

Billy Reed's | *Amer.* — 21

NEW Birba Pizza & Cocktails | *Pizza* — -

King's Hwy. | *Amer./Eclectic* — -

RANCHO CUCAMONGA

Fleming's | *Steak* — 25
Hat | *Sandwiches* — 25
Lucille's | *BBQ* — 24
Vince's Spaghetti | *Italian* — 24
Cheesecake Factory | *Amer.* — 23
BJ's | *Pub* — 23
King's Fish | *Seafood* — 23
Wahoo's Fish Taco | *Mex./Seafood* — 22
Yard House | *Amer.* — 22
Cal. Pizza Kitchen | *Pizza* — 22
P.F. Chang's | *Chinese* — 22
Gyu-Kaku | *Japanese* — 22
Chronic Tacos | *Mex.* — 21
El Torito | *Mex.* — 21

RANCHO MIRAGE

Wally's Desert | *Continental* — 26
Fleming's | *Steak* — 25
Roy's | *Hawaiian* — 25
Cheesecake Factory | *Amer.* — 23
Yard House | *Amer.* — 22
Acqua Pazza | *Cal.* — 22
P.F. Chang's | *Chinese* — 22
Las Casuelas | *Mex.* — 21

RIVERSIDE

Mario's Place | *Italian* — 27
In-N-Out | *Burgers* — 26
Market Broiler | *Seafood* — 25
Cheesecake Factory | *Amer.* — 23
Yard House | *Amer.* — 22
Cal. Pizza Kitchen | *Pizza* — 22
P.F. Chang's | *Chinese* — 22
Ruby's | *Diner* — 21

SAN BERNARDINO

Outback | *Steak* — 23
BJ's | *Pub* — 23
Castaway | *Cal.* — 22

TEMECULA

Original Pancake | *Amer.* — 25
Lucille's | *BBQ* — 24
Vince's Spaghetti | *Italian* — 24
BJ's | *Pub* — 23
Yard House | *Amer.* — 22
Cal. Pizza Kitchen | *Pizza* — 22
P.F. Chang's | *Chinese* — 22

UPLAND

Joey's | *BBQ* — 26
Hat | *Sandwiches* — 25

Santa Barbara & Environs

BALLARD

Ballard Inn | *French* — 27

BUELLTON

Hitching Post | *BBQ* — 24

CARPINTERIA

Cajun Kitchen | *Cajun* — 24

CASMALIA

Hitching Post | *BBQ* — 24

GOLETA

In-N-Out | *Burgers* — 26
Cajun Kitchen | *Cajun* — 24

LOS OLIVOS

Los Olivos | *Cal./Med.* — 22

MONTECITO

Cava | *Pan-Latin* — 25
Montecito | *Cal.* — 25
Los Arroyos | *Mex.* — 24
Lucky's | *Steak* — 24
Bella Vista | *Cal.* — 23
Tre Lune | *Italian* — 23
Pane e Vino | *Italian* — 23
Plow & Angel | *Cal./Eclectic* — 22

SANTA BARBARA

Downey's | *Cal./French* — 28
Julienne | *Cal.* — 28
Bouchon | *Cal./French* — 27
La Super-Rica | *Mex.* — 26
Arigato | *Japanese* — 26
Opal | *Cal./Eclectic* — 26
Olio | *Italian* — 25
Ca' Dario | *Italian* — 25
Stella Mare's | *Cal.* — 25
Fresco Cafe | *Deli* — 25
Wine Cask | *Cal.* — 25
Palace Grill | *Cajun/Creole* — 24
Hungry Cat | *Seafood* — 24
Cajun Kitchen | *Cajun* — 24
Carlitos Café | *Mex.* — 24
Los Arroyos | *Mex.* — 24
Andersen's | *Danish/Continental* — 24
Blue Agave | *Eclectic* — 24
Zaytoon | *Mideast.* — 23
Seagrass | *Cal.* — 23

OC/PS/SB

LOCATIONS

Brophy Bros.	Seafood	23	Cal. Pizza Kitchen	Pizza	22
China Palace/Pavilion	Chinese	23	Enterprise Fish	Seafood	21
Tupelo Junction	Southern	23	All India	Indian	21
Louie's	Cal.	23	Sojourner Cafe	Amer./Veg.	21
Coast	Cal./Seafood	23	El Torito	Mex.	21
Arts & Letters	Cal./Seafood	22	East Beach Grill	Amer.	20
Arnoldi's Cafe	Italian	22	Marmalade	Amer.	19
Holdren's	Seafood/Steak	22	**NEW** Scarlet Begonia	Amer.	–
Brewhouse	Amer.	22		
Cold Spring	Amer.	22		

SANTA YNEZ

Tratt. Grappolo | Italian — 24

ORANGE COUNTY RESTAURANT DIRECTORY

Most Popular

OC

1. Marché Moderne | *French*
2. Anaheim White House | *Italian*
3. 21 Oceanfront | *Seafood*
4. 3Thirty3 Waterfront | *American*
5. 230 Forest Avenue | *Californian*

OC CHAINS

1. Cheesecake Factory | *Amer.*
2. In-N-Out | *Burgers*
3. BJ's | *Pub Food*
4. Lucille's BBQ | *BBQ*
5. Black Angus | *Steak*

Top Food

29	Bluefin	*Japanese*
	Marché Moderne	*French*
28	Basilic	*French/Swiss*
	Blake's Place	*BBQ*
	Gabbi's Mexican	*Mexican*

	Park Ave	*American*
27	Il Barone	*Italian*
	La Sirena*	*Mexican*
	Napa Rose	*Californian*
	Ramos House	*American*

Top Decor

29	Studio
28	Pelican Grill
27	Andrea
	Broadway by Amar Santana
	AnQi by Crustacean

	Ritz
	Steakhouse 55*
	Leatherby's Café Rouge
	Summit House
26	Napa Rose

Top Service

29	Broadway by Amar Santana
28	Napa Rose
27	Studio
	Park Ave
	Marché Moderne

	Basilic
	Ritz*
26	Hobbit
	Bluefin
	Summit House

GOOD VALUES

Angelo's Hamburgers
Blake's Place
Break of Dawn
Early Bird
In-N-Out

Jerry's Dogs
Lee's Sandwiches
Taco Mesa
Wienerschnitzel
Z Pizza

Excludes places with low votes; * indicates a tie with restaurant above

	FOOD	DECOR	SERVICE	COST

Acapulco *Mexican*

20 | 20 | 21 | $23

Costa Mesa | 1262 SE Bristol St. (Newport Blvd.) | 714-754-6528
Stanton | 12765 Beach Blvd. (Acacia Ave.) | 714-895-4444
www.acapulcorestaurants.com

The margaritas take you "back to spring break in Cabo" at this "festive" Mexican chain putting out *"gigante"*, "traditional" plates for "cheap"; critics call the fare "forgettable" ("where's the spice?"), but "fast", "courteous" service makes it a "reliable" bet for "family or groups of all ages."

Alicia's ⏏Ⓜ *American/Continental*

27 | 19 | 23 | $14

Brea | 590 W. Central Ave. (Berry St.) | 714-990-4700 | www.aliciasinc.com

A "favorite" breakfast and lunch spot, this Brea American lays out an "excellent variety" of sandwiches, soups and "cookies with every meal" that make some "feel like a kid again"; peak times can be "noisy", but service is "friendly" and outdoor seating is like "having a picnic", plus the gift shop is "beautiful" too; P.S. open Wednesday–Saturday till 3 PM, take-out dinners can be ordered in advance.

Anaheim White House *Italian*

25 | 24 | 25 | $57

Anaheim | 887 S. Anaheim Blvd. (Vermont Ave.) | 714-772-1381 | www.anaheimwhitehouse.com

"The staff treats you like royalty" at this "regal" Anaheim landmark "just down the road from the land of Mickey and Donald", where chef-owner Bruno Serato is lauded for both his "beautifully prepared" Italian fare and community work with needy kids; critics may find the decor "dated" and "stuffy", but an "older clientele" appreciates the "formal" yet "festive" ambiance that makes it "great for celebrations."

Andrea *Italian*

25 | 27 | 26 | $67

Newport Coast | The Resort at Pelican Hill | 22701 Pelican Hill Rd. (Newport Coast Dr.) | 949-467-6800 | www.pelicanhill.com

"Stunning" views of the Pacific Ocean "set this fine Italian restaurant apart" say guests of this "gorgeous" Newport Coaster in the "high-end" Pelican Hill Resort, which also "impresses" with "fabulous" hand-made pasta and "impeccable" service; if a few find the whole package "over the top" and "overpriced", others sum up "sometimes you just want to pamper yourself."

Angelo's Hamburgers ●🝙 *Diner*

26 | 20 | 24 | $20

Anaheim | 511 S. State College Blvd. (E. Santa Ana St.) | 714-533-1401 | www.angeloshamburgers.com

Families and sports fans "get their fill" of "nice, big burgers", fries and shakes before heading to Angel Stadium at this "unique" Anaheim diner where "rollerskating" carhops "reminiscent of the '50s and '60s" deliver the goods; though "not the fanciest place in the world", prices are "fair" and the overall experience is "a lot of fun"; P.S. there's indoor seating and "ice-cold beer" too.

AnQi by Crustacean *Vietnamese*

25 | 27 | 23 | $52

Costa Mesa | Bloomingdale's at South Coast Plaza | 3333 S. Bristol St. (W. Sunflower Ave.) | 714-557-5679 | www.anqibistro.com

"Trendy" doesn't begin to describe the "sophisticated" digs at this Asian fusion–Vietnamese in Costa Mesa's South Coast Plaza, whose "chic" design employs a front-and-center catwalk; the "flavorful", "stylized" dishes (including tapas) take cues from sister eatery Crustacean in LA, most notably the garlic noodles, which are known to ignite "indescribable cravings" – though it costs "beaucoup bucks" to satiate them.

Antonello ☒ *Italian*　　　27 | 25 | 26 | $59

Santa Ana | South Coast Plaza | 3800 S. Plaza Dr. (Sunflower Ave.) | 714-751-7153 | www.antonello.com

"The pasta is always al dente to perfection" at this "slice of Italy" in South Coast Plaza, an "OC classic" that's long catered mostly to an "older crowd with high expectations" with "top-of-the-charts" fare, "exceptional" service and an "elegant" (some say a bit "stuffy") setting; indeed, it's "pricey, but worth it" "if you want to impress."

☑ Basilic ☒Ⓜ *French/Swiss*　　28 | 22 | 27 | $53

Newport Beach | 217 Marine Ave. (Park Ave.) | 949-673-0570 | www.basilicrestaurant.com

Intrepid eaters say "you'll never forget" the "superb", "pricey" French-Swiss fare that "deserves its reputation" at this "hard-to-find" Balboa Island "jewel box" by chef-owner Bernard Althaus; a "thoughtful" wine list, "wonderful" service and "quaint, romantic" ambiance are further assets, though since it only seats 24, "definitely make reservations"; P.S. "Raclette Night is a must-do."

Bayside *American*　　　25 | 23 | 23 | $51

Newport Beach | 900 Bayside Dr. (Marine Ave.) | 949-721-1222 | www.baysiderestaurant.com

"Delicious", "unique" New American plates matched with an "on-point" wine list have well-heeled locals charmed by this Newport Beacher; checks can be "expensive", but "wonderful" service and live entertainment in the "lovely" art-clad space create an ambiance that "makes you feel like a million bucks"; P.S. Sunday's champagne brunch is popular.

NEW Bistro Bleu ☒ *Californian/French*　　 - | - | - | I

Anaheim | 918 S. Magnolia Ave. (Ball Rd.) | 714-826-3590 | www.bistrobleudining.com

West Anaheim is an unlikely 'hood for a blue-hued Cal-French bistro, but chef-owner David Kessler (ex Pascal, The Cellar) targets value-minded Francophiles with classics that include moules frites and croque monsieur for prices not seen in a blue moon; time-pressed lunchers can get three courses and out the door in 30 minutes.

BJ's *Pub Food*　　　23 | 22 | 22 | $24

Brea | 600 Brea Mall (S. State College Blvd.) | 714-990-2095 ◗
Huntington Beach | 200 Main St. (Walnut Ave.) | 714-374-2224
Laguna Beach | 280 S. PCH (bet. Forest & Ocean Aves.) | 949-494-3802
Laguna Hills | 24032 El Toro Rd. (Paseo De Valencia) | 949-900-2670 ◗
Newport Beach | 106 Main St. (Balboa Blvd.) | 949-675-7560
www.bjsrestaurants.com
Additional locations throughout Southern California
See review in Los Angeles Directory.

☑ Blake's Place *BBQ*　　　28 | 19 | 25 | $15

Anaheim | 2905 E. Miraloma Ave. (Red Gum St.) | 714-630-8574 | www.blakesplacebbq.com

This "bustling local favorite" in Anaheim has an "IQ for BBQ" say carnivores who "crave" its "tender" brisket and ribs with "real wood-smoke pit flavor", slathered in "incredible" sauce and conveyed by an "on-the-ball" crew; those indulging off-site say it's "even better as take-out" and the catering's "well worth it."

⚡ Bluefin *Japanese*   29 | 23 | 26 | $53

Newport Coast | Crystal Cove Promenade | 7952 E. PCH (Reef Point Dr.) | 949-715-7373 | www.bluefinbyabe.com

"Way beyond a sushi bar", this "busy" Newport Coast Japanese – voted OC's No. 1 for Food – showcases chef-owner Takashi Abe's "phenom-enal" fish and other "yummy" creations for a mostly local clientele; the "fast" service and "fabulous", waterfall-enhanced modern decor make the most of the Crystal Cove Promenade space, and though some think it's "pricey", the omakase lunch is still a "deal."

Break of Dawn Ⓜ *Eclectic/Vietnamese*   26 | 18 | 21 | $22

Laguna Hills | 24351 Avenida de la Carlota (Los Alisos Blvd.) | 949-587-9418 | www.breakofdawnrestaurant.com

Housed in a Laguna Hills strip mall, chef-owner Dee Nguyen's "inven-tive" Eclectic-Vietnamese continues to astound devotees with "clever", "East-meets-West" twists on breakfast and lunch traditions – sausage and rice, French toast crème brûlée – plated in "huge" portions at "rea-sonable" prices; the "fast" service and casual, "sunny" digs also charm the frequent crowds of foodies, who merely "wish it was open for dinner."

⚡NEW Broadway by   26 | 27 | 29 | $57
Amar Santana ⬤ *American/Eclectic*

Laguna Beach | 328 Glenneyre St. (Forest Ave.) | 949-715-8234 | www.broadwaybyamarsantana.com

"Laguna Beach has a new star" in chef-owner Amar Santana's "swanky", Manhattan-themed New American–Eclectic "oasis" – rated tops for Service in OC – where an "impeccable" staff ferries tasting menus and small plates (plus "unique" cocktails and a Cal-heavy wine list) into the night while navigating a "lively" space featuring chef's-table seats overlooking the kitchen; costs are proportionate, and some cite a "noisy" scene, but to most, it's "raised the bar."

Cafe Zoolu Ⓜ *Californian*   26 | 15 | 23 | $43

Laguna Beach | 860 Glenneyre St. (bet. St. Anns Dr. & Thalia St.) | 949-494-6825 | www.cafezoolu.com

"Quirky doesn't begin to describe" this midpriced Californian "gem" in Laguna Beach, where "incredible" seafood (the charbroiled mesquite swordfish is the specialty) is served up by a "wonderful" staff in a "beachy" Polynesian setting; the portions are "huge", but the dining room is tiny, so "make reservations."

Cat & The Custard Cup Ⓜ *American/Californian*   26 | 25 | 25 | $51

La Habra | 800 E. Whittier Blvd. (Stonewood St.) | 562-694-3812 | www.catandcustardcup.com

Celebrants, longtime admirers and other Cat-oholics descend upon this "perennial neighborhood favorite" in La Habra for its "incredible" Cal-New American cuisine, served in a "heavenly", fireplace-furnished dining room echoing European "gentry" life; the "wonderful" staff remains "one step ahead of your needs", and although a few say it's "expensive", it's "worth every penny"; P.S. check out the "special" on-site wine shop.

	FOOD	DECOR	SERVICE	COST

Z Cheesecake Factory *American* — 23 | 22 | 22 | $28

Anaheim | Anaheim GardenWalk | 321 W. Katella Ave. (S. Clementine St.) | 714-533-7500
Brea | Brea Mall | 120 Brea Mall Way (E. Birch St.) | 714-255-0115
Huntington Beach | Bella Terra | 7871 Edinger Ave. (Beach Blvd.) | 714-889-1500
Irvine | Irvine Spectrum Ctr. | 71 Fortune Dr. (Enterprise Dr.) | 949-788-9998
Mission Viejo | Shops at Mission Viejo | 42 The Shops at Mission Viejo (Marguerite Pkwy.) | 949-364-6200
Newport Beach | Fashion Island | 1141 Newport Center Dr. (Santa Barbara Dr.) | 949-720-8333
www.thecheesecakefactory.com
See review in Los Angeles Directory.

Cucina Alessá *Italian* — 25 | 19 | 22 | $38

Huntington Beach | 520 Main St. (6th St.) | 714-969-2148
Newport Beach | 6700 W. PCH (Orange St.) | 949-645-2148
www.cucinaalessa.com

"You won't get better from anyone's Italian grandmother" at chef-owner Alessandro Pirozzi's Huntington Beach and Newport Beach Italian duo, where "perfect", well-priced pastas, plus thin-crust pizzas, draw frequent (and, to some, "noisy") crowds; also suiting diners are the "warm" staff and rustic space, and while churls quibble with "waits" and parking "issues", it's generally on diners' "return list."

NEW Early Bird *Diner* — - | - | - | I

Fullerton | Morningside Plaza | 1000B E. Bastanchury Rd. (Brea Blvd.) | 714-529-4100 | www.earlybirdoc.com

Joseph Mahon – of the enormously popular Burger Parlor pop-up – is behind this hip Fullerton diner slinging coffee-shop grub with a local, sustainable bent in a lofty, modern space; caffeine fiends note the rotating selection of fresh-roasted single-origin coffee; P.S. closes at 3 PM.

Elephant Bar *Asian* — 22 | 23 | 21 | $27

Irvine | 14346 Culver Dr. (Walnut Ave.) | 949-651-6087 | www.elephantbar.com
See review in Los Angeles Directory.

El Farolito *Mexican* — 26 | 14 | 22 | $15

Placentia | 201 S. Bradford Ave. (W. Center St.) | 714-993-7880 | www.elfarolitomex.com

It's "not fancy", but this family-owned Placentia hacienda provides "delicious", "authentic" Mexican fare like "extra-crispy carnitas" and some of the "best beans and rice this side of the border" for "reasonable prices"; the space is "small" and "busy", but a "great" staff keeps the crowds in check, and there's also always takeout.

NEW enoSTEAK ⑤Ⓜ *Steak* — - | - | - | VE

Dana Point | Ritz-Carlton Laguna Beach | 1 Ritz Carlton Dr. (South Coast Hwy.) | 949-240-5088 | www.ritzcarlton.com

This elegant steakhouse in the Laguna Ritz-Carlton serves a locavore menu built around Niman Ranch prime beef and a serious wine list (hence the name); those bottles double as decoration, with wine racks rising to the ceiling in the wood-paneled dining room, which is also filled with big spenders prepared to pay for the pleasure of a menu heavy on words like 'truffles' and 'duck fat.'

	FOOD	DECOR	SERVICE	COST

Fleming's Prime Steakhouse & Wine Bar *Steak*

| 25 | 23 | 25 | $59 |

Newport Beach | Fashion Island | 455 Newport Center Dr. (San Miguel Dr.) | 949-720-9633 | www.flemingssteakhouse.com
See review in Los Angeles Directory.

⊠ Gabbi's Mexican Kitchen *Mexican*

| 28 | 24 | 23 | $33 |

Orange | 141 S. Glassell St. (bet. Almond & Chapman Aves.) | 714-633-3038 | www.gabbipatrick.com

Those "in the know" head to this upmarket, "rustic" hacienda (with "no sign outside") for the "haute" side of Mexican cuisine in Old Town Orange, where the "next-level" plates by chef/co-owner Gabbi Patrick are not only "delightful" but "works of art", and the desserts are "delicious" too; long waits are "accurate indicators" of its popularity, and while it's slightly "pricey" for the genre, guests assure "you'll go away loving every bit."

Gemmell's *Continental/French*

| 26 | 21 | 25 | $44 |

Dana Point | 34471 Golden Lantern St. (Dana Point Harbor Dr.) | 949-234-0063 | www.gemmellsrestaurant.com

Chef-owner Byron Gemmell's "old-school" French-Continental "gem" brings a bit of the European "countryside" to Dana Point Harbor, offering "surprisingly good" dishes (like duck with caramelized banana rum) in a "homey", "romantic" setting; "professional" service is a plus, and though the menu hits expensive notes, the early-bird specials are a deal.

Golden Truffle ⊠Ⓜ *Caribbean/French*

| 27 | 14 | 24 | $43 |

Costa Mesa | 1767 Newport Blvd. (bet. 17th & 18th Sts.) | 949-645-9858 | www.goldentruffle.com

Spur-of-the-moment menus mean "you may not be sure what you're eating", but it's "always delicious" at this Costa Mesa star where "inventive" chef-owner Alan Greeley crafts "unique" French-Caribbean "masterpieces" (including some "crazy" creations that "work"); a casual, "relaxed" atmosphere provides a nice balance to the "off-the-charts" food, as does the "great service."

The Hobbit Ⓜ *Continental/French*

| 27 | 26 | 26 | $87 |

Orange | 2932 E. Chapman Ave. (Malena St.) | 714-997-1972 | www.hobbitrestaurant.com

"Not just dinner, an experience", this Orange fine-dining destination offers a seven-course "adventure" that begins with champagne and hors d'oeuvres in a "cool" wine cellar and follows through with "memorable" French-Continental plates from chef-owner Michael Philippi matched with "rare", divine" vinos; add in "impeccable" service and a "charming" setting in a "redone old house", and it's "expensive, of course", but it's "not an everyday thing"; P.S. reservations are a must, as there's only one seating a night (Wednesday–Sunday).

Honda-Ya *Japanese*

| 24 | 19 | 20 | $27 |

Fountain Valley | 18450 Brookhurst St. (Ellis Ave.) | 714-964-4629

Honda-Ya Izakaya *Japanese*

Fullerton | Target Ctr. | 2980 Yorba Linda Blvd. (Placentia Ave.) | 714-577-0401
www.izakayahondaya.com
See review in Los Angeles Directory.

	FOOD	DECOR	SERVICE	COST

Z Il Barone Ristorante 🖼 *Italian* `27` `22` `24` `$41`

Newport Beach | 4251 Martingale Way (Corinthian Way) | 949-955-2755 | www.ilbaroneristorante.com

The "chef's specials" alone are "well worth the drive" to this Newport Beach Italian where presiding couple chef Franco Barone and manager Donatella Barone treat guests to "superb", slightly "pricey" fare in a "lovely" ambiance; given the "warm, gracious hospitality" and "over-the-top" service, fans say it's "spot-on" when you're "celebrating."

Z In-N-Out Burger ● *Burgers* `26` `16` `23` `$10`

Costa Mesa | 594 W. 19th St. (bet. Anaheim & Maple Aves.)
Huntington Beach | 18062 Beach Blvd. (Talbert Ave.)
Laguna Niguel | 27380 La Paz Rd. (Avila Rd.)
Tustin | Tustin Mktpl. | 3020 El Camino Real (Jamboree Rd.)
800-786-1000 | www.in-n-out.com
Additional locations throughout Southern California
See review in Los Angeles Directory.

Jerry's Wood-Fired Dogs *Hot Dogs* `24` `17` `22` `$10`

Irvine | Irvine Market Pl. | 13786 Jamboree Rd. (El Camino Real) | 714-665-1480
Ladera Ranch | 1701 Corporate Dr. (Windmill Ave.) | 949-364-7080
La Habra | Westridge Plaza | 1360 S. Beach Blvd. (Imperial Hwy.) | 562-697-4644
Santa Ana | Ctr. on 17th | 2276 E. 17th St. (Tustin Ave.) | 714-245-0200
www.jerrysdogs.com

"Design your own dog" with "plenty of fixin's" at this "gourmet" frank chainlet also churning out burgers and "hot" housemade chips; prices are pleasing, and if the stainless steel–clad settings are far from fancy, it's still works for a "quick" bite "in a pinch."

NEW Juliette 🖼 *American* `-` `-` `-` `M`

Newport Beach | Plaza Newport | 1000 Bristol St. N. (Dove St.) | 949-752-5854 | www.juliettenb.com

After a sweeping remodel, the iconic Traditions by Pascal in Newport Beach is now a modern American bistro from the original owners of Old Towne Orange's Filling Station; it serves ambitious seasonal dishes – both small and large plates – plus interesting cocktails and beers in an upscale-casual space; diners can also pay a nominal corkage fee on bottles from the adjoining wine shop; P.S. meals feature Blue Bottle coffee from the famed San Francisco roaster.

Z La Sirena *Mexican* `27` `17` `22` `$18`

Irvine | 3931 Portola Pkwy. (Culver Dr.) | 714-508-8226
Laguna Beach | 30862 S. PCH (Beverly St.) | 949-499-2301

Z La Sirena Grill 🖼 *Mexican*

Laguna Beach | 347 Mermaid St. (Park Ave.) | 949-497-8226
www.lasirenagrill.com

"Eat without the guilt" at this casual "fresh-Mex" chainlet offering "bold takes" on the classics crafted from local, organic and sustainable ingredients like a "not-to-be-missed" blackened-salmon burrito; though the tabs are higher than the competition, allies appreciate the "quality" eats as well as the "friendly" crew that dishes it out; P.S. some locations have outdoor seating only.

Leatherby's Café Rouge Ⓜ *Californian*   25 | 27 | 24 | $64

Costa Mesa | Orange County Performing Arts Ctr. | 615 Town Center Dr. (Bristol St.) | 714-429-7640 | www.patinagroup.com

"Very convenient before the theater", this Patina Group venue inhabits a "stark", "coolly elegant" setting within the Segerstrom Concert Hall, where customers come for "beautifully presented" Californian cuisine; a few find food and service "less than expected" given the "expensive" prices, but it's sure "handy", and the prix fixe options are less pricey; P.S. the restaurant is closed on non-performance nights, so call ahead.

Lee's Sandwiches *Sandwiches*   21 | 13 | 18 | $9

Fullerton | Fullerton Town Ctr. | 1028 S. Harbor Blvd. (W. Hill Ave.) | 714-525-2989 ⊭
Garden Grove | 12905 Harbor Blvd. (Buaro St.) | 714-638-4268
NEW Huntington Beach | 16058 Goldenwest St. (Edinger Ave.) | 714-847-1588
Irvine | 4127 Campus Dr. (Bridge Rd.) | 949-509-9299
Garden Grove | 13991 Brookhurst St. (Westminister Ave.) | 714-636-2288 ●⊭
www.leesandwiches.com
See review in Los Angeles Directory.

Lucille's Smokehouse Bar-B-Que *BBQ*   24 | 22 | 22 | $30

Brea | 1639 E. Imperial Hwy. (N. Associated Rd.) | 714-990-4944
Lake Forest | Orchard at Saddleback | 23760 El Toro Rd. (Rockfield Blvd.) | 949-581-7427
Orange | 4050 W. Chapman Ave. (Lewis St.) | 714-634-1227
Tustin | The District | 2550 Park Ave. (bet. Barranca Pkwy. & Jamboree Rd.) | 714-259-1227
www.lucillesbbq.com
See review in Los Angeles Directory.

🅩 Marché Moderne *French*   29 | 25 | 27 | $61

Costa Mesa | South Coast Plaza | 3333 Bristol St. (Anton Blvd.) | 714-434-7900 | www.marchemoderne.net

"*C'est magnifique!*"exclaim fans of this "expensive" "gem" in South Coast Plaza (OC's Most Popular restaurant) featuring such "exquisite" French fare – from "decadent" classics to "inventive" small plates – that "you almost want a reverse gastric banding so you can eat the entire menu"; add in a "charming" staff and "gorgeous" setting with a patio and "a view of the Christian Louboutin store across the way", and "what more could you ask for?"; P.S. the three-course prix fixe lunch is a "flat-out steal."

NEW Mare Culinary   - | - | - | M

Lounge *Californian/Italian*
Laguna Beach | Holiday Inn | 696 S. PCH (Cleo St.) | 949-715-9581 | www.mareculinarylounge.com

Set in an unlikely spot inside the Laguna Beach Holiday Inn is this sultry new entry from chef-owner Alessandro Pirozzi of the thriving OC mini-empire that includes Alessa and Café Alessa; look for moderately priced creative Cal-Italian cuisine served from breakfast through late-night, with a menu that runs the gamut from oxtail tacos to salmon with champagne sauce.

Mastro's Ocean Club *Seafood/Steak*   26 | 26 | 23 | $78

Newport Coast | Crystal Cove Promenade | 8112 E. PCH (Reef Point Dr.) | 949-376-6990 | www.mastrosrestaurants.com

"If you're going to 'do it up', do it here" at this "flashy" "high-end" Crystal Cove chophouse where "excellent" steaks and seafood are paired with "appropriately old-school service and strong martinis" in luxe digs packed with "beautiful people"; it's a tad "superficial" to some, and "unless your bank account is in the six figures" it can be way "too expensive" to boot; P.S. don't miss the serious "pick-up action" at the bar.

Mastro's Steakhouse *Steak*   27 | 25 | 26 | $79

Costa Mesa | 633 Anton Blvd. (Park Center Dr.) | 714-546-7405 | www.mastrosrestaurants.com

See review in Los Angeles Directory.

Morton's The Steakhouse *Steak*   26 | 24 | 26 | $70

Anaheim | 1895 S. Harbor Blvd. (Convention Way) | 714-621-0101
Santa Ana | South Coast Plaza | 1641 W. Sunflower Ave. (bet. Bear & Bristol Sts.) | 714-444-4834
www.mortons.com

See review in Los Angeles Directory.

Mr Stox ⬛Ⓜ *American*   26 | 24 | 26 | $51

Anaheim | 1105 E. Katella Ave. (bet. Lewis St. & State College Blvd.) | 714-634-2994 | www.mrstox.com

An upscale "oasis in the fast-food desert around Disneyland", this Anaheim American establishment has long been a "classic" attracting "immaculately groomed gents with fat wallets" with "first-class" fare (lamb, prime rib) and "outstanding" wines served in a "supper-club" setting that oozes "old-world charm"; add in "wonderful" doting service, and it's easy to see why many call it "fabulous for a special evening out."

Ⓩ Napa Rose *Californian*   27 | 26 | 28 | $68

Anaheim | Disney's Grand Californian Hotel & Spa | 1600 S. Disneyland Dr. (bet. Ball Rd. & Katella Ave.) | 714-300-7170 | www.disneyland.com

An "elegant escape" within the Disneyland theme park, this "special-occasion" dining room spotlights Andrew Sutton's "breathtaking" seasonal Californian cuisine and "amazing" wines from "the best list within a walk of the Matterhorn"; the Craftsman-style setting boasts "exceptional" service and a surprisingly "kid-friendly" vibe – just "bring two checkbooks" to foot the bill.

Old Vine Café *Eclectic*   26 | 21 | 25 | $38

Costa Mesa | The Camp | 2937 Bristol St. (bet. Baker & Bear Sts.) | 714-545-1411 | www.oldvinecafe.com

Set inside the "hipster paradise" that is The Camp, this "cozy", mid-priced Costa Mesa Eclectic is best known for its "delectable" prix fixe wine-pairing dinners dished "without the high-end attitude" (à la carte small plates are available too); fans appreciate the "reasonable" prices and breezy Cal-style service, and say you'll always leave "stuffed, drunk and happy"; P.S. breakfast is "delicious", but do "expect to wait" for a table.

Original Fish Co. *Seafood*
27 | 21 | 24 | $38

Los Alamitos | 11061 Los Alamitos Blvd. (Katella Ave.) | 562-594-4553 | www.originalfishcompany.com

Though the clam chowder alone will incite "tears of joy", the "huge portions" of "tender, flaky" fish are also "worth the drive" to this perpetually "packed" Los Alamitos seafood palace; admittedly, the decor is "nothing special", but "efficient" servers with "big smiles" more than make up for it; P.S. there's also an on-site market vending the daily catch.

☑ Park Ave Ⓜ *American*
28 | 24 | 27 | $41

Stanton | 11200 Beach Blvd. (bet. Katella & Orangewood Aves.) | 714-901-4400 | www.parkavedining.com

A "gem" in Stanton, this "sophisticated" American from David Slay supplies "simple comfort food done perfectly", crafted from "fresh" ingredients from the "lovely" garden out back and matched with "phenomenal" cocktails; adding to the charm is the "swank" "midcentury Googie setting", "superb" hospitality and "reasonable" pricing.

☑ Pelican Grill *Californian*
25 | 28 | 25 | $56

Newport Coast | Pelican Hill Golf Club | 22800 S. Pelican Hill Rd. (Newport Coast Dr.) | 949-467-6800 | www.pelicanhill.com

A "beautiful" hilltop location with "outstanding water views" forms the backdrop for this "country-club casual" spot in Pelican Hill, a "sumptuous" "escape" featuring "first-class" Cal cuisine; add in "pleasant" service, and it's "never a disappointment", even if it's "pricey."

☑ Pizzeria Mozza *Pizza*
27 | 20 | 22 | $40

Newport Beach | 800 W. PCH (Dover Dr.) | 949-945-1126 | www.mozzarestaurantgroup.com

See review in Los Angeles Directory.

☑ Ramos House Café Ⓜ *American*
27 | 24 | 25 | $38

San Juan Capistrano | 31752 Los Rios St. (Ramos St.) | 949-443-1342 | www.ramoshouse.com

Set in a "beautiful" old cottage on the train tracks in Old San Juan Capistrano, this New American is a "treasure" serving "elaborate", "incredible" Southern-style lunches and brunches from chef John Q. Humphreys, along with massive Bloody Marys on the tree-shaded patio; "knowledgeable" service cements the "pleasurable", albeit "pricey", experience; P.S. the buttermilk biscuits alone are "worth the drive."

The Ritz Restaurant & Garden ⓈⓂ *Continental*
25 | 27 | 27 | $61

Newport Beach | 880 Newport Center Dr. (Santa Barbara Dr.) | 949-720-1800 | www.ritzrestaurant.com

Channeling an "old-fashioned supper club", this "opulent" Newport Beacher is a "special-occasion" standby with "superb", "traditional" Continental cuisine and martinis rolled out by an "excellent" tuxedoed staff; live piano Tuesday–Saturday completes the classy package.

Ruth's Chris Steak House *Steak*
27 | 24 | 26 | $68

Anaheim | 2041 S. Harbor Blvd. (bet. Katella & Orangewood Aves.) | 714-750-5466

Irvine | Park Pl. | 2961 Michelson Dr. (Carlson Ave.) | 949-252-8848 | www.ruthschris.com

See review in Los Angeles Directory.

ORANGE COUNTY

	FOOD	DECOR	SERVICE	COST

Sage *American* | 25 | 23 | 23 | $40 |

Newport Beach | Eastbluff Shopping Ctr. | 2531 Eastbluff Dr. (Vista del Sol) |
949-718-9650 | www.sagerestaurant.com

Chef-owner Rich Mead turns out "imaginative, well-executed" small
and large plates at this "low-key" American in Newport Beach that's
"hidden in a suburban strip mall", but well "worth the hunt"; "relaxed"
service and an "attractive" setting with a "beautiful patio great for
warmer evenings" ensure it's a "delight" all around.

NEW South of Nick's *Mexican* ▽ 24 | 24 | 24 | $32

San Clemente | 110 N. El Camino Real (Avenida Del Mar) |
949-481-4545 | www.thenicko.com

One of the latest additions to San Clemente is this sib of Nick's, a redo of a historic Spanish-tiled casita featuring "creative, modern" spins
on Mexican classics and a busy bar with an elite list of sipping tequilas; weekend breakfasts are welcome hangover fare.

Steakhouse 55 *Steak* | 27 | 27 | 26 | $45 |

Anaheim | Disneyland Hotel | 1150 W. Magic Way (Disneyland Dr.) |
714-781-3463 | www.disneyland.com

"Tucked away in the Disneyland Hotel", this "lovely" chophouse serves
"scrumptious" cuts that hit the spot after a "long day at the parks"; it's
"a little pricey", but the staff is "knowledgeable", the setting "elegant"
and "a break from children running around is a sigh of relief."

☑ Studio Ⓜ *Californian/French* | 27 | 29 | 27 | $102 |

Laguna Beach | Montage Laguna Bch. | 30801 S. PCH (Montage Dr.) |
949-715-6420 | www.studiolagunabeach.com

"Throw out the budget and splurge" at this cliff-top locale in the
Montage Laguna Beach resort, where "amazing" panoramas of the
sunset over the Pacific create a "romantic" backdrop ranked No. 1 for
Decor in Orange Conty; add in Craig Strong's "top-of-the-line" Cal-
New French cuisine, "exceptional" service and an "elegant" atmo-
sphere, and it "defines fine dining" to a T.

Summit House *Continental* | 26 | 27 | 26 | $55 |

Fullerton | 2000 E. Bastanchury Rd. (N. State College Blvd.) |
714-671-4111 | www.summithouse.com

Admirers "enamored" by the "never-ending" panoramas of city lights
at this "olde English–style" manor on a Fullerton hilltop, where "special occasions" are marked with "hearty" Continental creations like
"fantastic" prime rib and "melt-in-your-mouth" John Dory; expect
"exceptional" service, a "country-club feel" and fittingly "pricey" bills.

Tabu Grill *Seafood/Steak* | 26 | 22 | 24 | $62 |

Laguna Beach | 2892 S. PCH (bet. Hinkle & Nyes Pls.) | 949-494-7743 |
www.tabugrill.com

A "Laguna favorite", this "dark", "sophisticated" spot on the PCH serves
"exotic", "beautifully presented" surf 'n' turf fare prepared with Pacific
Rim influences that comes via a "top-notch" staff in an upscale tiki setting; a few find it a little "overpriced, but satisfying" nonetheless.

Taco Mesa *Mexican* | 26 | 15 | 21 | $13 |

Costa Mesa | 647 W. 19th St. (bet. Anaheim & Pomona Aves.) |
949-642-0629

(continued)

Taco Mesa

Ladera Ranch | Bridgepark Plaza | 27702 Crown Valley Pkwy.
(O'Neill Dr.) | 949-364-1957
Mission Viejo | Los Alisos Vill. | 22922 Los Alisos Blvd. (Trabuco Rd.) |
949-472-3144
Orange | Saddleback Shopping Ctr. | 3533 E. Chapman Ave.
(N. Prospect St.) | 714-633-3922
www.tacomesa.com

"Much better than your typical storefront Mexican", this "vividly painted" taqueria chain turns out "phenomenal", "healthier" menu choices and "unique specials" that are "full of flavor"; the digs are often "small" and the "made-to-order" eats may "take longer" than fast-food competitors, but "huge bang for the buck" compensates.

Taiko *Japanese*

26 | 19 | 23 | $30

Irvine | Arbor Vill. | 14775 Jeffrey Rd. (Walnut Ave.) | 949-559-7190
"Luscious" cuts of "über-fresh" fish attract "monster lines" to this Irvine Japanese that's "pretty reasonably priced for the portions and quality you get"; service is "polite" too, so just ignore the no-frills setting, "go early" and "bring a lot of patience to go with that appetite."

Taps Fish House & Brewery *American/Seafood*

26 | 25 | 25 | $37

Brea | 101 E. Imperial Hwy. (Brea Blvd.) | 714-257-0101 |
www.tapsbrea.com
An "impressive" array of craft beers meets up with "delicious fresh seafood" prepared with Cajun-Creole touches at this crowd-pleasing American seafood chain also known for its "fab oysters", "affordable happy hour" and "spectacular" Sunday brunch buffet; service is "attentive" too, but the casual digs are often so "slammed" and "loud" that some say you'll need to "bring your outside voice."

3Thirty3 Waterfront *American*

23 | 23 | 21 | $38

Newport Beach | 333 Bayside Dr. (PCH) | 949-673-8464 |
www.3thirty3nb.com
This "trendy" Newport Beacher is where "cougars", "sugar daddies" and young ones collide for "tasty" New American small plates and cocktails served against a backdrop of "knock-your-socks-off" waterfront vistas; some quibble about "slow" service and "loud" acoustics, but most don't mind since prices are moderate and it's mostly "about the scene."

21 Oceanfront *Seafood*

25 | 23 | 23 | $54

Newport Beach | 2100 W. Oceanfront (21st Pl.) | 949-673-2100 |
www.21oceanfront.com
"Gorgeous views" of the ocean set the scene at this lavish, long-established Newport Beach seafooder where "superb" servers ferry "fabulous" fish and steaks to a deep-pocketed crowd; although a few find fault with the "old-school" looks and "no-surprises" menu, on the whole most deem it "worth a try" for a "special occasion."

230 Forest Avenue *Californian*

25 | 20 | 22 | $42

Laguna Beach | 230 Forest Ave. (PCH) | 949-494-2545 |
www.230forestavenue.com
Chef-owner Marc Cohen's "lively" Californian in the heart of Laguna Beach is "frequented by locals" and tourists who come for the "unique",

"delicious" menu abetted by "top-notch" service and "great people-watching" in "trendy" surroundings; despite the "cramped quarters" ("be prepared to sit in the laps of the couple next to you"), "fair prices" make it a "winner."

Walt's Wharf *Seafood*

25	18	23	$36

Seal Beach | 201 Main St. (Central Ave.) | 562-598-4433 | www.waltswharf.com

"If the fish were any fresher, it would still be swimming" assert fans of this Seal Beach seafood "institution" near the pier, where prices for the "fresh, simply prepared" fare "won't break the bank"; even if the dining room could "use a face-lift", the vibe is "friendly" and window seats offer "superb" "people-watching", so it "never disappoints"; P.S. no reservations at dinner, so try lunch or "prepare to wait."

Wienerschnitzel ❶ *Burgers/Hot Dogs*

20	14	20	$8

Orange | 13011 Chapman Ave. (N. Hewes St.) | 714-621-0422 | www.wienerschnitzel.com

See review in Los Angeles Directory.

Z Pizza *Pizza*

23	16	20	$19

Huntington Beach | 10035 Adams Ave. (Brookhurst St.) | 714-968-8844
Huntington Beach | 19035 Golden West Ave. (bet. MacArthur Blvd. & Sunflower Ave.) | 714-536-3444
Tustin | 12932 Newport Ave. (Irvine Blvd.) | 714-734-9749
www.stores.zpizza.com

See review in Los Angeles Directory.

PALM SPRINGS/ SANTA BARBARA RESTAURANT DIRECTORY

Palm Springs & Environs

MOST POPULAR

❶ Las Casuelas/Casuelas | *Mex.*
❷ Acqua Pazza | *Cal.*
❸ 3rd Corner | *Eclectic*
❹ Le Vallauris | *French/Med.*
❺ Pacifica | *Seafood*

TOP FOOD

28 Le Vallauris | *French/Med.*
27 Jillian's | *Continental*
    Mario's Place | *Italian*
    Johannes | *Eclectic*
    Chez Pierre | *French*

TOP DECOR

27 Cuistot
    Le Vallauris
26 Tropicale
    Wally's Desert Turtle
    Jillian's

MOST POPULAR CHAINS

❶ Cheesecake Factory | *Amer.*
❷ In-N-Out | *Burgers*
❸ California Pizza | *Pizza*
❹ BJ's | *Pub Food*
❺ P.F. Chang's | *Chinese*

TOP SERVICE

28 Le Vallauris
27 Mario's Place
26 Ruth's Chris
    Jillian's
    Wally's Desert Turtle

BEST BUYS

1. In-N-Out
2. Lee's Sandwiches
3. Wahoo's Fish Tacos
4. El Gallo Giro
5. Chronic Tacos

Acqua Pazza *Californian*   22 | 21 | 20 | $30

Rancho Mirage | 71800 Hwy. 111 (Evening Star Dr.) | 760-862-9800 | www.acquapazzabistro.com

Enjoy meals "under the stars" on a "wonderful" waterside patio at this "unpretentious" Rancho Mirage Californian that may be known more for its "fantastic" all-day happy hour than its "reliable" bistro cuisine; detractors lament the "noisy" setting, but a "bargain" prix fixe menu, coupled with "spot-on" service, add up to "a lot of bang for the buck."

Adobe Grill *Mexican*   23 | 24 | 23 | $37

La Quinta | La Quinta Resort & Club | 49-499 Eisenhower Dr. (Avenida Fernando) | 760-564-5725 | www.laquintaresort.com

"Wonderful" patio dining awaits at this midpriced Mexican at the La Quinta Resort & Club (a former old-Hollywood hangout), where a "relaxing" hacienda setting and "gracious" service appeal to guests and locals alike; some may call it "resort Mexican", but regular mariachi music and margaritas served in handblown glassware "fit the mode."

Arnold Palmer's *Steak*   22 | 25 | 23 | $46

La Quinta | 78164 Ave. 52 (Washington St.) | 760-771-4653 | www.arnoldpalmersrestaurant.com

"Arnold Palmer fans" and "visiting golf addicts" will appreciate the memorabilia-covered walls and practice putting green at this La Quinta steakhouse ably staffed by a "pleasant" crew in a "relaxing" "resort"-like setting; despite some knocks that the "good", "home-style" American cuisine is perhaps "nothing extraordinary" for the price you pay, the "packed" house "shoots an eagle" as a "19th-hole hangout", complete with "middle-aged party action" as well as other nightly entertainment.

Billy Reed's *American*

| 21 | 18 | 21 | $28 |

Palm Springs | 1800 N. Palm Canyon Dr. (Hwy. 111) | 760-325-1946 | www.billyreedspalmsprings.com

"Step back in time" at this ersatz-Victorian coffee-shop "standby", which hashes out "enormous" portions of "down-home" (some say "pedestrian") American chow to an "older" Palm Springs crowd; sure, some feel the decor "needs updating" and consider the service "so-so", but "reasonable" prices and touches like a koi pond help it chug along.

NEW Birba Pizza & Cocktails 🅩 *Pizza*

| – | – | – | I |

Palm Springs | 622 N. Palm Canyon Dr. (Alejo Rd.) | 760-327-5678 | www.birbapalmsprings.com

This cheeky sib of Cheeky's offers traditional pizzas and small dishes, plus old-school cocktails, in a thoroughly modern space just off the center of the Palm Springs shopping district; seating is mostly outdoors on a shaded patio that's cooled by misters by day and thoroughly pleasant at night.

BJ's 🌑 *Pub Food*

| 23 | 22 | 22 | $24 |

Rancho Cucamonga | 11520 Fourth St. (Richmond Pl.) | 909-581-6750
San Bernardino | 1045 E. Harriman Pl. (Tippecanoe Ave.) | 909-380-7100
Temecula | 26500 Ynez Rd. (Overland Dr.) | 951-252-8370
Corona | Crossings at Corona | 2520 Tuscany St. (Grand Oaks) | 951-271-3610
www.bjsrestaurants.com
Additional locations throughout Southern California
See review in Los Angeles Directory.

California Pizza Kitchen *Pizza*

| 22 | 19 | 21 | $23 |

Rancho Cucamonga | Victoria Gdns. | 12517 N. Main St. (bet. Kew & Monet Aves.) | 909-899-8611
Riverside | Riverside Plaza | 3540 Riverside Plaza Dr. (Riverside Ave.) | 951-680-9362
Temecula | The Promenade in Temecula | 40820 Winchester Rd. (bet. Margarita & Ynez Rds.) | 951-296-0575
Palm Desert | Shops at El Paseo | 73080 El Paseo (bet. Hwy. 74 & Ocotillo Dr.) | 760-776-5036
Palm Springs | Desert Fashion Plaza | 123 N. Palm Canyon Dr. (bet. Amado Rd. & Tahquitz Canyon Way) | 760-322-6075
www.cpk.com
Additional locations throughout Southern California
See review in Los Angeles Directory.

Castaway *Californian*

| 22 | 25 | 22 | $41 |

San Bernardino | 670 Kendall Dr. (N. H St.) | 909-881-1502 | www.castawayrestaurant.com
See review in Los Angeles Directory.

Castelli's *Italian*

| 25 | 19 | 24 | $50 |

Palm Desert | 73098 Hwy. 111 (Monterey Ave.) | 760-773-3365 | www.castellis.cc

"Like a step into the 1940s", this "pricey" Palm Desert "treasure" frequented by "serious players" lands kudos for "dependable" cuisine that's like your "Italian grandmother's", plus "attentive" service in a Tuscan setting; often "crowded", it even has a "Sinatra-style" singing pianist who performs nightly.

Cheeky's *American*
26 | 19 | 24 | $22

Palm Springs | 622 N. Palm Canyon Dr. (bet. Grande Valmonte & Tamarisk Rd.) | 760-327-7595 | www.cheekysps.com

Surveyors have "one thing to say: bacon flight" when gauging the "innovative" breakfast and lunch options at this "funky" Palm Springs New American, which draws loyal locals to its small, patio-enhanced contemporary space; with a "friendly" staff and "reasonable prices", you can be sure there's "always a line."

☒ Cheesecake Factory *American*
23 | 22 | 22 | $28

Rancho Cucamonga | Victoria Gdns. | 12379 N. Main St. (bet. Monet & Monticello Aves.) | 909-463-3011

Rancho Mirage | The River | 71800 Hwy. 111 (Rancho Las Palmas Dr.) | 760-404-1400

Riverside | Galleria at Tyler | 3525 Tyler St. (bet. Indiana & Magnolia Aves.) | 951-352-4600

www.thecheesecakefactory.com

Additional locations throughout Southern California

See review in Los Angeles Directory.

☒ Chez Pierre Ⓜ *French*
27 | 17 | 24 | $49

Palm Desert | 44250 Town Center Way (Fred Waring Dr.) | 760-346-1818 | www.chezpierrebistro.com

For frogs' legs Provençal and other Gallic standards, this "real French bistro" in Palm Desert delivers chef Pierre Pelech's "knock-your-socks-off" renditions of classics, and he even takes the time to "chat" with his clientele; though the "plain" shopping-plaza locale can be disconcerting to some, and such quality doesn't come cheap, it's "reasonable for what you get" – especially if you opt for the $34 prix fixe.

Chop House *Steak*
24 | 22 | 24 | $55

Palm Desert | 74040 Hwy. 111 (Portola Ave.) | 760-779-9888

Palm Springs | 262 S. Palm Canyon Dr. (bet. Arenas & Baristo Rds.) | 760-320-4500

www.restaurantsofpalmsprings.com

"When you want your protein fix", try this "expensive" Palm Springs and Palm Desert steakhouse duo, where diners consume "large portions" of "perfectly cooked" meats, provided by a "solicitous" staff; some feel the "cozy", upscale-casual setting "isn't the fanciest", and others think "something's missing", but it can be "a good value" – especially "if someone else is paying."

Chronic Tacos Cantina *Mexican*
21 | 16 | 20 | $13

Rancho Cucamonga | 11920 Foothill Blvd. (Rochester Ave.) | 909-941-8226

Corona | 160 E. Ontario Ave. (S. Main St.) | 951-278-2643

www.chroniccantina.com

See review in Los Angeles Directory.

Citrus City Grille *Californian*
24 | 21 | 23 | $29

Corona | Promenade Shops at Dos Lagos | 2765 Lakeshore Dr. (Temescal Canyon Rd.) | 951-277-2888 | www.citruscitygrille.com

"Cheerful, noisy and good with kids", this Californian chain pumps out "flavorful" breakfasts, salads and other "simple", "consistent" eats well suited for a "casual bite"; even if the fare's not that "memorable", service is "polite", most branches boast patios and prices are "fair" too.

Copley's on Palm Canyon *American*

25 | 25 | 26 | $59

Palm Springs | 621 N. Palm Canyon Dr. (bet. Alejo & Tamarisk Rds.) | 760-327-9555 | www.copleyspalmsprings.com

"Fantasize about the days when movie stars ruled the roost" as you eat at this "special-occasion" Palm Springs New American, formerly Cary Grant's guesthouse, where chef Andrew Copley sends out "sophisticated" creations in the "romantic" hacienda-style room with patio seating; it's "expensive", but with "terrific" service, "what could be better?"; P.S. it's closed mid-July–September.

Cork Tree *Californian*

26 | 23 | 25 | $58

Palm Desert | Desert Springs Mktpl. | 74950 Country Club Dr. (Cook St.) | 760-779-0123 | www.thecorktree.com

"A rarity in the valley", this "imaginative" Palm Desert Californian, situated in a shopping plaza, "can compare with the best in Los Angeles", with "delicious" cuisine and "attentive" service; the "cozy", low-lit room also delights, as do the bar and patio, and though "expensive", many find it "worth every penny."

❷ Cuistot Ⓜ *Californian/French*

25 | 27 | 25 | $66

Palm Desert | 72595 El Paseo (Hwy. 111) | 760-340-1000 | www.cuistotrestaurant.com

This Palm Desert "homage to France" boasts a "grand" country-modern setting – voted No. 1 in Palm Springs for Decor – accented with fireplaces, making it an ideal "special-occasion" destination; it follows through with "first-class" eats, an "extraordinary" wine list and "professional" service – just know that such luxe can get "pricey."

Daily Grill *American*

21 | 19 | 21 | $32

Palm Desert | 73061 El Paseo (Monterey Ave.) | 760-779-9911 | www.dailygrill.com

See review in Los Angeles Directory.

El Gallo Giro *Mexican*

22 | 14 | 17 | $12

Fontana | 10161 Sierra Ave. (bet. Slover Ave. & Valley Blvd.) | 909-355-0273 | www.gallogiro.com

See review in Los Angeles Directory.

El Torito *Mexican*

21 | 20 | 21 | $24

Rancho Cucamonga | 12369 Foothill Blvd. (Day Creek Blvd.) | 909-463-9212 | www.eltorito.com
Additional locations throughout Southern California

See review in Los Angeles Directory.

Fleming's Prime Steakhouse & Wine Bar *Steak*

25 | 23 | 25 | $59

Rancho Cucamonga | Victoria Gdns. | 7905 Monet Ave. (bet. Foothill Blvd. & Victoria Gardens Ln.) | 909-463-0416
Rancho Mirage | The River | 71800 Hwy. 111 (Rancho Las Palmas Dr.) | 760-776-6685
www.flemingssteakhouse.com

See review in Los Angeles Directory.

Graziano's Pizza *Pizza*
23 | 20 | 21 | $23

Corona | 333 Magnolia Ave. (E. Ontario Ave.) | 951-734-8500 |
www.grazianoscorona.com

Get your "authentic Italian taste" at this Corona pizzeria, where
families and others dig the "wide variety" of pies and toppings presented at "affordable" prices in an informal space that includes an
arcade room as well as multiple TVs; not so comforting to detractors is service that "could be better", though for "ok" slices, it fills
an immediate need.

Gyu-Kaku *Japanese*
22 | 19 | 19 | $32

Rancho Cucamonga | Victoria Gdns. | 7893 Monet Ave. (Foothill Blvd.) |
909-899-4748 | www.gyu-kaku.com
See review in Los Angeles Directory.

⚡ In-N-Out Burger ● *Burgers*
26 | 16 | 23 | $10

Riverside | 6634 Clay St. (Van Buren Blvd.)
Riverside | 72265 Varner Rd. (Ramon Rd.)
Riverside | 7467 Indiana Ave. (Madison St.)
Corona | 2305 Compton Ave. (bet. Ontario Ave. & Taber St.)
Corona | 450 S. Auto Center Dr. (bet. Rte. 91 & Wardlow Rd.)
800-786-1000 | www.in-n-out.com
Additional locations throughout Southern California
See review in Los Angeles Directory.

⚡ Jillian's ☒ *Continental*
27 | 26 | 26 | $59

Palm Desert | 74155 El Paseo (Hwy. 111) | 760-776-8242 |
www.jilliansfinedining.com

A "top choice" for "classic" Continental cuisine, this Palm Desert
"charmer" remains a "favorite" for diners who enjoy "sensational"
meals served by a "gracious" staff in the "romantic" hacienda dining
rooms and courtyard; given the "pricey" bills and jacket-suggested
policy, some opt to "save it for a special treat"; P.S. hours vary by season, so call ahead.

Joey's *BBQ*
26 | 20 | 25 | $21

Upland | 1964 W. Foothill Blvd. (N. Central Ave.) | 909-982-2128
Chino | 3689 Riverside Dr. (End Ave.) | 909-628-1231
www.joeysbbq.com

"Get along, little doggies!" holler would-be wranglers who savor
the "fall-off-the-bone" ribs, smoked meats and fixin's at these
modestly priced Chino and Upland American 'cue joints; "better-
than-average" service also hits the spot, and while some city slickers note the "cowboy" decor "isn't fancy", for many longtime regulars,
it's a "family favorite."

⚡ Johannes ☒ *Eclectic*
27 | 18 | 23 | $55

Palm Springs | 196 S. Indian Canyon Dr. (Arenas Rd.) | 760-778-0017 |
www.johannesrestaurants.com

Chef-owner Johannes Bacher "knows how to please the palates" of admirers at this Palm Springs Eclectic "gem", purveying "unique" Austrian-
Asian cuisine, plus a "wonderful" wine list with "fabulous" half-bottle
selections; "warm" service also charms, and though the contemporary
decor may strike some as merely "pleasant", diners generally leave
"impressed"; P.S. the prix fixe menus are a "great value."

	FOOD	DECOR	SERVICE	COST

King's Fish House *Seafood* — 23 | 20 | 22 | $35

Rancho Cucamonga | Victoria Gdns. | 12427 N. Main St. (Monet Ave.) | 909-803-1280
Corona | Crossings at Corona | 2530 Tuscany St. (Grand Oaks) | 951-284-7900
www.kingsfishhouse.com
See review in Los Angeles Directory.

King's Highway ◐ *American/Eclectic* — - | - | - | M

Palm Springs | Ace Hotel | 701 E. Palm Canyon Dr. (bet. Calle Palo Fierro & S. Camino Real) | 760-325-9900 | www.acehotel.com
Mingle with the "hipsters" at this midpriced Palm Springs American-Eclectic, located at the trendy Ace Hotel in a former Denny's, where an "interesting", varied menu – offered nearly 'round the clock – and "laid-back" vibe (bolstered by creative cocktails) prevail; the modern, stone-walled setting features a patio and curiosities such as an ersatz elephant head, but pundits make clear that "the scene" is the thing.

Lamppost Pizza & — 22 | 15 | 18 | $21
Main Street Brewery 🗷🅼 *Pizza*

Corona | 300 N. Main St. (bet. Blaine & Harrison Sts.) | 951-371-1471 | www.lamppostpizzacorona.com
"Gooey" "thick-crust" pies pull crowds into this trio of "family-friendly" pizzerias catering to both "little-league team parties" and "grown-ups" "hanging out with friends" over a beer; on the downside, the surrounds could use some sprucing and service gets mixed reviews, leading some to rely on "fast takeout."

Las Casuelas *Mexican* — 21 | 22 | 22 | $26

Rancho Mirage | 70050 Hwy. 111 (bet. Country Club & Frank Sinatra Drs.) | 760-328-8844 | www.lascasuelasnuevas.com
La Quinta | 78480 Hwy. 111 (Washington St.) | 760-777-7715 | www.lascasuelasquinta.com
Palm Springs | 222 S. Palm Canyon Dr. (Arenas Rd.) | 760-325-2794 | www.lascasuelas.com
Palm Springs | 368 N. Palm Canyon Dr. (bet. Alejo & Amado Rds.) | 760-325-3213 | www.lascasuelas.com

Casuelas Café *Mexican*

Palm Desert | 73703 Hwy. 111 (San Luis Rey Ave.) | 760-568-0011 | www.casuelascafe.com
This family-owned Mexican chainlet – voted Palm Springs' Most Popular – is "always packed" thanks to "festive" patio settings, "potent" margaritas and "welcoming" service; perhaps the "American-ized" eats "won't win any awards for creativity", and some gripe about the "touristy" environs, but "fair" prices win out.

Lee's Sandwiches *Sandwiches* — 21 | 13 | 18 | $9

Chino | 3938 Grand Ave. (Pipeline Ave.) | 909-628-3999 | www.leesandwiches.com
See review in Los Angeles Directory.

🌠 Le Vallauris *French/Mediterranean* — 28 | 27 | 28 | $73

Palm Springs | 385 W. Tahquitz Canyon Way (Museum Dr.) | 760-325-5059 | www.levallauris.com
"An unforgettable evening amid trees and twinkling lights" awaits at this "magical", flower-filled French-Mediterranean, voted tops for

Food and Service in Palm Springs, where "exquisite" "old-world" cuisine, "personal" service and patio dining "set the standard"; sure, you may have to borrow "from your children's college fund" for the pleasure, but to many, "it's worth every dollar."

LG's Prime Steakhouse *Steak*   25 | 22 | 24 | $66

La Quinta | 78525 Hwy. 111 (Washington St.) | 760-771-9911
Palm Springs | 255 S. Palm Canyon Dr. (bet. Arenas & Baristo Rds.) | 760-416-1779
www.lgsprimesteakhouse.com

Co-owner Leon Greenberg may no longer be with us, but "the wow factor" still awes at these family-owned La Quinta and Palm Springs steakhouses supplying meat "so good, you think you're in heaven"; "welcoming" service and "clubby" rooms also gain accolades, and even if a few find it "overpriced", you'll still "leave with a smile."

Lucille's Smokehouse Bar-B-Que *BBQ*   24 | 22 | 22 | $30

Rancho Cucamonga | Victoria Gdns. | 12624 N. Main St. (Day Creek Blvd.) | 909-463-7427
Temecula | The Promenade in Temecula | 40748 Winchester Rd. (bet. Margarita & Ynez Rds.) | 951-719-7427
www.lucillesbbq.com

See review in Los Angeles Directory.

🄲 Mario's Place 🅂 *Italian*   27 | 25 | 27 | $52

Riverside | 3646 Mission Inn Ave. (Orange St.) | 951-684-7755 | www.mariosplace.com

"Let [chef] Leone Palagi be your guide" at this "classy", family-owned Riverside Italian, where "delicious" salads, pastas and meats "tempt the palate"; "top-notch" service and a "classy" patio-enhanced atmosphere beguile too, and while prices may be on the high side, it's still a spot "to impress someone"; P.S. late-night jazz entertains Fridays and Saturdays.

Melvyn's Restaurant *Continental*   24 | 24 | 24 | $48

Palm Springs | Ingleside Inn | 200 W. Ramon Rd. (S. Palm Canyon Dr.) | 760-325-2323 | www.inglesideinn.com

"You can feel the Sinatra vibe" at this nearly 40-year-old celeb "hangout" in Palm Springs' Spanish-style Ingleside Inn, where the "terrific", "retro" Continental food, "civilized" digs and a "first-rate" tux-clad staff earn plaudits; a nightly lounge pianist, small dance floor and prices that are "affordable" for such quality complete the "back-then" feel.

Morton's The Steakhouse *Steak*   26 | 24 | 26 | $70

Palm Desert | Desert Springs Mktpl. | 74880 Country Club Dr. (Cook St.) | 760-340-6865 | www.mortons.com
See review in Los Angeles Directory.

Original Pancake House *American*   25 | 15 | 22 | $16

Temecula | 41377 Margarita Rd. (Winchester Rd.) | 951-296-9016 | www.originalpancakehouse.com
See review in Los Angeles Directory.

Outback Steakhouse *Steak*   23 | 21 | 23 | $31

San Bernardino | 620 E. Hospitality Ln. (S. Waterman Ave.) | 909-890-0061 | www.outback.com
Additional locations throughout Southern California
See review in Los Angeles Directory.

	FOOD	DECOR	SERVICE	COST

Pacifica Seafood Restaurant *Seafood*   `25` `23` `24` `$46`
Palm Desert | The Gardens | 73505 El Paseo (San Pablo Ave.) |
760-674-8666 | www.pacificaseafoodrestaurant.com

"You'd think it was next to a pier" after sampling its "fresh, fresh, fresh"
seafood, yet this Palm Desert spot on El Paseo is well grounded, offering
"cool" patio dining with mountain views and an "out-of-sight" vodka selection, plus "friendly" service; perhaps the bills are "a bit high", but with
half-price wine nights and prix fixe specials, "what's not to like?"

P.F. Chang's China Bistro *Chinese*   `22` `22` `22` `$32`
Rancho Cucamonga | Victoria Gdns. | 7870 Monticello Ave. (S. Main St.) |
909-463-4095
Rancho Mirage | The River | 71800 Hwy. 111 (bet. Bob Hope &
Rancho Las Palmas Drs.) | 760-776-4912
Riverside | Galleria at Tyler | 3475 Tyler St. (bet. Indiana & Magnolia Aves.) |
951-689-4020
Temecula | 40762 Winchester Rd. (bet. Margarita & Ynez Rds.) |
951-296-6700
www.pfchangs.com
Additional locations throughout Southern California
See review in Los Angeles Directory.

Picanha Churrascaria Ⓜ *Brazilian*   `21` `15` `19` `$36`
Cathedral City | 68-510 Hwy. 111 (Cathedral Canyon Dr.) | 760-328-1818 |
www.picanharestaurant.com
See review in Los Angeles Directory.

Roy's *Hawaiian*   `25` `23` `23` `$51`
Rancho Mirage | 71959 Hwy. 111 (Bob Hope Dr.) | 760-340-9044 |
www.roysrestaurant.com
See review in Los Angeles Directory.

Ruby's *Diner*   `21` `21` `21` `$19`
Riverside | Galleria at Tyler | 1298 Galleria at Tyler (bet. Indiana &
Magnolia Aves.) | 951-359-7829
Palm Springs | 155 S. Palm Canyon Dr. (Arenas Rd.) | 760-406-7829
www.rubys.com
See review in Los Angeles Directory.

Ruth's Chris Steak House *Steak*   `27` `24` `26` `$68`
Palm Desert | 74740 Hwy. 111 (bet. Cook St. & Deep Canyon Rd.) |
760-779-1998 | www.ruthschris.com
See review in Los Angeles Directory.

Spencer's *Eclectic*   `24` `26` `24` `$51`
Palm Springs | 701 W. Baristo Rd. (S. Tahquitz Dr.) | 760-327-3446 |
www.spencersrestaurant.com

"Grab a table on the patio" at this "romantic" Palm Springs Eclectic "at
the foot of the San Jacinto Mountains" and savor "delicious" fare (including breakfast and Sunday brunch) and "excellent" service, accompanied by a pianist at lunch and dinner; it's "pricey" to some, but
"what a place."

Taps Fish House & Brewery *American/Seafood*   `26` `25` `25` `$37`
Corona | Promenade Shops at Dos Lagos | 2745 Lakeshore Dr.
(Temescal Canyon Rd.) | 951-277-5800 | www.tapsfishhouse.com
See review in Los Angeles Directory.

	FOOD	DECOR	SERVICE	COST

The 3rd Corner ✪ *Eclectic* | 21 | 20 | 21 | $32

Palm Desert | 73101 Hwy. 111 (Pines to Palms Hwy.) | 760-837-9600 | www.the3rdcorner.com

"Come for the wine, stay for the food" at this "interesting concept" – a Palm Desert vino shop/bistro where patrons choose bottles, then enjoy them alongside "tasty", "beautifully presented" Eclectic dishes; a "lovely patio", "swinging bar" and "sweet" service ensure a "pleasant time."

Trio *American* | 23 | 23 | 25 | $40

Palm Springs | 707 N. Palm Canyon Dr. (Merito Pl.) | 760-864-8746 | www.triopalmsprings.com

A "local favorite", this wallet-wise Palm Springs eatery known for its "enthusiastic" staff serves up "reliable" American cuisine in a "lively" modern space with a rotating collection of artwork for sale and a patio; factor in a "bargain" $19 daytime prix fixe, and it's a "can't-miss."

Tropicale Restaurant & Coral Seas Lounge *Eclectic* | 22 | 26 | 21 | $42

Palm Springs | 330 E. Amado Rd. (bet. Calle Encilia & Indian Canyon Dr.) | 760-866-1952 | www.thetropicale.com

"Swells" dig the "stylish, festive vibe" at this "reasonably priced" Palm Springs Eclectic, a 1950s-style spot marked by "colorful" "midcentury decor" and an "attention to detail"; a "varied", "well-prepared" menu, specialty cocktails and "solicitous" service also find favor, and you can bop to live jazz on Tuesdays, as well as chill on the patio.

Tyler's Burgers Ⓢ⇩ *Burgers* | 26 | 18 | 22 | $15

Palm Springs | 149 S. Indian Canyon Dr. (E. Tahquitz Canyon Way) | 760-325-2990 | www.tylersburgers.com

"A burger is a burger is a burger – except these are better" proclaim fans of this lunch-only, "value"-geared Palm Springs pattyist, almost as appreciated for its "fabulous" coleslaw and "iconic waitresses" as its beef; its "extremely casual" patio allows for prime people-watching, but it's "always busy", so regulars suggest "getting there early" to beat the "waits"; P.S. no credit cards.

Vince's Spaghetti *Italian* | 24 | 18 | 23 | $19

Rancho Cucamonga | 8241 Foothill Blvd. (Grove Ave.) | 909-981-1003
Temecula | 28145 Jefferson Ave. (Rancho California Rd.) | 951-587-2782
www.vincesspaghettiroute66.com
See review in Los Angeles Directory.

Wahoo's Fish Taco *Mexican/Seafood* | 22 | 16 | 20 | $12

Rancho Cucamonga | 11561 Foothill Blvd. (Mayten Ave.) | 909-948-6949 | www.wahoos.com
See review in Los Angeles Directory.

Wally's Desert Turtle *Continental* | 26 | 26 | 26 | $73

Rancho Mirage | 71775 Hwy. 111 (Rancho Las Palmas Dr.) | 760-568-9321 | www.wallys-desert-turtle.com

Regulars "don't show up without their diamonds" at this "stellar" Rancho Mirage "classic", which features "expertly prepared" Continental fare and "superb" service in a "stunning" art-laden mirrored room; though some call it "overpriced" and "stodgy" ("your grandmother would love it"), others say it's just right for that "special occasion."

	FOOD	DECOR	SERVICE	COST

Wood Ranch BBQ & Grill *BBQ*   24 | 21 | 23 | $30

Corona | Promenade Shops at Dos Lagos | 2785 Lakeshore Dr.
(Temescal Canyon Rd.) | 951-667-4200 | www.woodranch.com
See review in Los Angeles Directory.

Yard House *American*   22 | 22 | 22 | $28

Rancho Cucamonga | Victoria Gardens | 12473 N. Main St. (bet. Kew &
Monte Aves.) | 909-646-7116 ◑
Rancho Mirage | 71800 Hwy. 111 (bet. Bob Hope & Rancho Las Palmas Drs.) |
760-779-1415
Riverside | Galleria at Tyler | 3775 Tyler St. (bet. Indiana & Magnolia Aves.) |
951-688-9273 ◑
Temecula | The Promenade in Temecula | 40770 Winchester Rd.
(bet. Margarita & Ynez Rds.) | 951-296-3116 ◑
www.yardhouse.com
See review in Los Angeles Directory.

Zin *American/French*   23 | 21 | 21 | $53

Palm Springs | 198 S. Palm Canyon Dr. (Arenas Rd.) | 760-322-6300 |
www.zinamericanbistro.com
Surveyors say this farm-to-table Palm Springs bistro is an "excellent
choice", with "well-thought-out" American-French victuals and an
award-winning wine list; other perks are a contemporary room, "personal" service and prices deemed a "value" for the area; P.S. a recent
remodel added a patio and full bar.

Zip Fusion *Japanese/Korean*   ∇ 22 | 18 | 21 | $23

Corona | Crossings at Corona | 2560 Tuscany St. (Grand Oaks) |
951-272-2177 | www.zipfusion.com
See review in Los Angeles Directory.

Santa Barbara & Environs

MOST POPULAR

1 Hitching Post | *BBQ*
2 Brophy Bros. | *Seafood*
3 La Super-Rica | *Mexican*
4 Arigato Sushi | *Japanese*
5 Downey's | *Cal./French*

TOP FOOD

28 Downey's | *Cal./French*
Julienne | *Californian*
27 Bouchon | *Cal./French*
Ballard Inn | *French*
26 La Super-Rica | *Mexican*

TOP DECOR

25 Plow & Angel
Stella Mare's
Wine Cask
Coast
Bouchon

MOST POPULAR CHAINS

1 In-N-Out | *Burgers*
2 California Pizza | *Pizza*
3 Outback | *Steak*
4 El Torito | *Mexican*
5 Ruth's Chris | *Steak*

TOP SERVICE

27 Downey's
Bouchon
26 Ballard Inn
Opal Restaurant
25 Julienne

BEST BUYS

1. In-N-Out
2. Cajun Kitchen
3. Fresco Cafe
4. East Beach Grill
5. La Super-Rica

All India Cafe *Indian*

| 21 | 16 | 19 | $22 |

Santa Barbara | 431 State St. (bet. Gutierrez & Haley Sts.) | 805-882-1000 | www.allindiacafe.com
See review in Los Angeles Directory.

Andersen's *Danish/Continental*

| 24 | 20 | 23 | $22 |

Santa Barbara | 1106 State St. (E. Figueroa St.) | 805-962-5085 | www.andersenssantabarbara.com
For "a little bit of Europe in Santa Barbara", many head to this State Street bakery/restaurant where "generous", inexpensive breakfasts, "irrefutable" cakes and streudels and Danish-Continental dinners have delighted regulars since the mid-'70s; a staff that "loves what they do" and "charming old-world" decor please as well, even if a few fret that it's "not what it used to be."

Arigato Sushi *Japanese*

| 26 | 20 | 23 | $42 |

Santa Barbara | 1225 State St. (bet. Anapamu & Victoria Sts.) | 805-965-6074 | www.arigatosantabarbara.com
Diners "can't get enough" of this Santa Barbara Japanese's "fresh", "creative" sushi and rolls, evidenced by the "crowds" often filling the "lively" ("waaay toooo loud" to some) brick-walled room; nit-pickers grumble about "not-cheap" prices and a "bummer" no-reservations policy, but "come early" and "you won't be unhappy" with the food or service.

Arnoldi's Cafe *Italian*

| 22 | 20 | 22 | $26 |

Santa Barbara | 600 Olive St. (E. Cota St.) | 805-962-5394 | www.arnoldis.com
There's "nothing like" this "old-school" circa-1937 Santa Barbara Italian, where portions "big enough to provide lunch the next day", "warm" service and a "comfy" ambiance featuring patio bocce courts remind regulars of "a cafe in Italy"; wallet-friendly prices are an added perk.

	FOOD	DECOR	SERVICE	COST

Arts & Letters Cafe *Californian/Seafood*

| 22 | 23 | 23 | $29 |

Santa Barbara | Sullivan Goss, Amercian Art Gallery | 7 E. Anapamu St. (State St.) | 805-730-1463 | www.artsandletterscafe.com

Inside a Santa Barbara art gallery is this "hidden gem", a lunch-only Californian seafooder offering a "getaway" with an "exquisite" court-yard housing a fountain; combined with a staff that "remembers your name" and "delicious", easy-on-the-wallet specialties such as pump-kin soup, it's a local "treat."

☑ Ballard Inn & Restaurant Ⓜ *French*

| 27 | 22 | 26 | $52 |

Ballard | Ballard Inn | 2436 Baseline Ave. (bet. Alamo Pintado & Refugio Rds.) | 805-688-7770 | www.ballardinn.com

"In the heart of wine country", this "pricey" spot – stationed at a "quaint" Ballard inn – provides a "respite" from urban "hustle and bustle" with its "sophisticated", "Asian-influenced" French menu, accompanied by "lots of local wines"; "unpretentious" service and a "cozy", fireplace-enhanced room also sway locals who save it for "romantic celebrations."

Bella Vista *Californian*

| 23 | 23 | 24 | $60 |

Montecito | Four Seasons Resort, The Biltmore | 1260 Channel Dr. (bet. Hill & Olive Mill Rds.) | 805-565-8237 | www.fourseasons.com

"Watch the sunset" over the ocean from this terraced Californian, sit-uated at Montecito's Biltmore Four Seasons Resort, where a "classy" room, professional service and "solid" seasonal cuisine (including an "expensive" champagne-and-caviar Sunday brunch extravaganza) ex-ude "romance"; most deem it "amazing", though a small minority grouses "if only the food were as wonderful as the decor."

Blue Agave ❶ *Eclectic*

| 24 | 23 | 22 | $32 |

Santa Barbara | 20 E. Cota St. (State St.) | 805-899-4694 | www.blueagavesb.com

"Agave is all the rage" at this Downtown Santa Barbara Eclectic, named for its fine tequilas and "fairly priced" international menu emphasizing "locally grown" ingredients; the "loungey" digs featuring a bar, a smoking balcony (you can buy cigars on-site) and "secluded" velvet booths are ripe for "romance", especially given the "no-rush" staff – though some suggest it's "for drinkin', not eatin'."

☑ Bouchon *Californian/French*

| 27 | 25 | 27 | $57 |

Santa Barbara | 9 W. Victoria St. (bet. Chapala & State Sts.) | 805-730-1160 | www.bouchonsantabarbara.com

"Oh-so-popular", this Santa Barbara Cal-French "pioneer" proffers an "exceptional" menu using "farm-fresh" local and organic ingre-dients, paired with "fabulous" regional wines; "polished" service and a "relaxing" French country ambiance (including a "lovely" pa-tio) also win plaudits, and if the prices are high, most feel it's "worth every dollar."

Brewhouse *American*

| 22 | 19 | 23 | $28 |

Santa Barbara | 229 W. Montecito St. (Bath St.) | 805-884-4664 | www.brewhousesb.com

"Brew me up the good stuff!" exult proponents of this Santa Barbara American, which matches "sports-bar" eats with small-batch beers created in-house; daily happy hours, above-par service and a "cool" environment decorated with local artists' work please too, and you can't deny the "value"; P.S. there's live music weekly from Wednesday–Saturday.

Brophy Bros. Restaurant & Clam Bar *Seafood*

`23` `19` `21` `$29`

Santa Barbara | 119 Harbor Way (Shoreline Dr.) | 805-966-4418 | www.brophybros.com
See review in Los Angeles Directory.

Ca' Dario *Italian*

`25` `19` `22` `$43`

Santa Barbara | 37 E. Victoria St. (Anacapa St.) | 805-884-9419 | www.cadario.net

This "seriously good" Santa Barbara Italian delivers "terrific" pastas, meats and other midpriced standards, along with an extensive wine list (many available by the glass), to a mostly local clientele; some aren't inspired by the old-world-style digs and "noisy crowds", but with "helpful" service and a "great osso buco", "who needs conversation?"; P.S. reservations suggested.

Cajun Kitchen *Cajun*

`24` `16` `22` `$16`

Goleta | 6831 Hollister Ave. (Storke Rd.) | 805-571-1517
Carpinteria | 865 Linden Ave. (bet. 8th & 9th Sts.) | 805-684-6010
Santa Barbara | 1924 De La Vina St. (Mission St.) | 805-687-2062
Santa Barbara | 901 Chapala St. (W. Canon Perdido St.) | 805-965-1004
See review in Los Angeles Directory.

California Pizza Kitchen *Pizza*

`22` `19` `21` `$23`

Santa Barbara | Paseo Nuevo Mall | 719 Paseo Nuevo (De La Guerra St.) | 805-962-4648 | www.cpk.com
See review in Los Angeles Directory.

Carlitos Café y Cantina *Mexican*

`24` `22` `21` `$25`

Santa Barbara | 1324 State St. (bet. Sola & Victoria Sts.) | 805-962-7117 | www.carlitos.com

For "above-par" Mexican eats and margs, amigos head to this late-'70s Santa Barbara survivor well situated near the local theaters; adding to the appeal are decent service and a "comfortable" setting with a patio, plus live music Wednesday–Sunday, though some say prices are "a bit higher than one would expect" for a "good, not great" meal.

Cava *Pan-Latin*

`25` `24` `23` `$37`

Montecito | 1212 Coast Village Rd. (Olive Mill Rd.) | 805-969-8500 | www.cavarestaurant.com

"Sit outside on a sunny day" with a "fab marg" at this Carlitos Café sibling in Montecito, which serves "huge" portions of "delicate" Pan-Latin fare in a "warm" ambiance that "makes you feel like family"; while sticklers feel it's "overpriced", it remains a popular "favorite"; P.S. there's live music from Wednesdays–Saturdays.

China Pavilion *Chinese*

`23` `19` `20` `$27`

Santa Barbara | 1202 Chapala St. (Anapamu St.) | 805-560-6028 | www.china-pavilion.com

A "cut above the usual", this Santa Barbara eatery cooks up "delish", "reasonably priced" Chinese "favorites" in "pleasant" surroundings;

FOOD | DECOR | SERVICE | COST

the "fast" delivery makes it easier for some to ignore the "spotty" service – a moot point to fans who deem it a "solid choice."

Coast *Californian/Seafood* | 23 | 25 | 23 | $43 |

Santa Barbara | Canary Hotel | 31 W. Carrillo St. (Chapala St.) | 805-879-9100 | www.canarysantabarbara.com
See review in Los Angeles Directory.

Cold Spring Tavern *American* | 22 | 24 | 21 | $32 |

Santa Barbara | 5995 Stagecoach Rd. (Rte. 154) | 805-967-0066 | www.coldspringtavern.com

A "fascinating" crowd of "BMWs and bikers" frequents this circa-1886 "Old West–style saloon" in Santa Barbara, an antiques-filled former stagecoach stop in a "fairy tale" mountain setting; its local-wine selection and "wonderfully prepared" traditional American vittles (including game), plus "solicitous" service, fit both "princely and proletariat" budgets; P.S. the Saturday–Sunday tri-tip sandwich and music forays are a "must."

☑ Downey's Ⓜ *Californian/French* | 28 | 23 | 27 | $70 |

Santa Barbara | 1305 State St. (Victoria St.) | 805-966-5006 | www.downeyssb.com

A "legend" for 30 years, chef/co-owner John Downey's "divine" Cal-French – again rated tops for Food and Service in Santa Barbara – "never fails to entice" with its "exquisite" cuisine and "outstanding", "knowledgeable" service led by his wife Liz, whose paintings grace the "serene, elegant" room; it's "costly", but that hardly matters to its "older" clientele, who knows that while "trends come and go", this place "always delivers."

East Beach Grill *American* | 20 | 18 | 15 | $16 |

Santa Barbara | 1118 E. Cabrillo Blvd. (bet. Corona Del Mar & Ninos Dr.) | 805-965-8805

"Get some breakfast and a cup o' joe" at this wallet-wise spot "right along Santa Barbara beach", which dishes out "simple", "fast" American munchies to hungry landlubbers; its outdoor tables are "perfect" for watching the "boardwalk parade" of "bikers, dog walkers and tourists", and remember, "informality rules" – so "it's ok to dine in your swimsuit."

El Torito *Mexican* | 21 | 20 | 21 | $24 |

Santa Barbara | 29 E. Cabrillo Blvd. (State St.) | 805-963-1968 | www.eltorito.com
See review in Los Angeles Directory.

Enterprise Fish Co. *Seafood* | 21 | 19 | 20 | $35 |

Santa Barbara | 225 State St. (Montecido St.) | 805-962-3313 | www.enterprisefishco.com
See review in Los Angeles Directory.

Fresco Cafe ☒ *Deli* | 25 | 18 | 21 | $19 |

Santa Barbara | 3987 State St. (La Cumbre Rd.) | 805-967-6037 | www.frescosb.com

For "diner food kicked up a notch", visit this "reasonably priced" Santa Barbara Italian, where customers "queue up" to order "huge" portions of "superb" deli-style eats for patio lunching; the straightforward cafe decor complements the "harmonious" atmosphere, though regulars suggest staying ahead of the pack by going off-hours to avoid the "lines."

Z Hitching Post *BBQ* | 24 | 17 | 22 | $44 |

Buellton | 406 E. Rte. 246 (½ mi. east of Rte. 101) | 805-688-0676 | www.hitchingpost2.com
Casmalia | 3325 Point Sal Rd. (Santos St.) | 805-937-6151 | www.hitchingpost1.com

"You can't go wrong with a filet and a Pinot" at this midpriced BBQ duo in Buellton and Casmalia – voted Most Popular in Santa Barbara – famed for "outstanding" oak-grilled meats and "distinctive" house wines; the Buellton outpost may be the one with the celluloid cred ("*Sideways* brought me here"), but both boast "caring" service and "rustic", "wonderfully Western" digs – "you gotta go."

Holdren's Steaks & Seafood *Seafood/Steak* | 22 | 20 | 22 | $45 |

Santa Barbara | 512 State St. (Haley St.) | 805-965-3363 | www.holdrens.com
See review in Los Angeles Directory.

Hungry Cat *Seafood* | 24 | 19 | 21 | $49 |

Santa Barbara | 1134 Chapala St. (bet. Anapamu & Figueroa Sts.) | 805-884-4701 | www.thehungrycat.com
See review in Los Angeles Directory.

Z In-N-Out Burger ● *Burgers* | 26 | 16 | 23 | $10 |

Goleta | 4865 Calle Real (Turnpike Rd.) | 800-786-1000 | www.in-n-out.com
Additional locations throughout Southern California
See review in Los Angeles Directory.

Z Julienne Ⓜ *Californian* | 28 | 20 | 25 | $47 |

Santa Barbara | 138 E. Canon Perdido St. (Santa Barbara St.) | 805-845-6488 | www.restaurantjulienne.com
Nearly reaching culinary "perfection" is this husband-and-wife-owned storefront bistro in Santa Barbara, where "incredibly creative", locavore Californian fare (including housemade charcuterie) enchants foodies in a "simple" space with an open kitchen and chalkboard-written specials; "personal" service beguiles as well, and while it has been called "expensive", most surveyors agree that it's an "absolute joy."

Z La Super-Rica Taqueria ∌ *Mexican* | 26 | 8 | 16 | $16 |

Santa Barbara | 622 N. Milpas St. (Alphonse St.) | 805-963-4940
"Julia Child wasn't wrong" about this "classic" Santa Barbara taco stand, which sports "lines out the door" for its "*muy auténtico*", "made-from-scratch" Mexican bites, including "lovely" tortillas; *fanáticos* remain undaunted by the lack of table service, noting it's "worth putting up with" ambiance of the "paper-plate-and-plastic-fork" variety for such "legendary" chow and "unbelievably great value."

Los Arroyos *Mexican* | 24 | 18 | 21 | $23 |

Montecito | 1280 Coast Village Rd. (Olive Mill Rd.) | 805-969-9059
Santa Barbara | 14 W. Figueroa St. (bet. Chapala & State Sts.) | 805-962-5541
www.losarroyos.net
See review in Los Angeles Directory.

Los Olivos Cafe *Californian/Mediterranean*

22 | 20 | 21 | $31

Los Olivos | 2879 Grand Ave. (Alamo Pintado Ave.) | 805-688-7265 |
www.losolivoscafe.com

A "cameo in *Sideways*" continues to lure crowds to this "enchanting"
Los Olivos spot in wine country, where tastings-keen oenophiles sip
local vin from the "wonderful" cellar while nibbling the "solid", reasonably priced Cal-Med fare, all in a "casually elegant" setting; meanwhile, "perky" servers dispense "helpful" pairing advice, and
visitors sufficiently bedazzled can select vintages from the store's
wine wall to purchase.

Louie's *Californian*

23 | 22 | 24 | $39

Santa Barbara | Upham Hotel | 1404 De La Vina St. (Sola St.) |
805-963-7003 | www.louiessb.com

"Elegantly set" in the Victorian-age Upham Hotel, this still relatively "undiscovered" Santa Barbaran, helmed by a "sweet" staff,
cheers locals and visitors alike with "dependable", well-priced
Californian "classics" and area wines in a "soothing" bistro venue
featuring a wraparound veranda; it may be "small" and "off the
beaten track" to some, but "don't let that fool you" – advocates say
"it's worth looking for."

Lucky's *Steak*

24 | 23 | 23 | $72

Montecito | 1279 Coast Village Rd. (Olive Mill Rd.) | 805-565-7540 |
www.luckys-steakhouse.com

"Rich and beautiful" Montecito denizens "hobnob with celebs" at this
"super" carnivorium – owned by a Lucky Brand Jeans co-founder –
that's known for its "excellent" steaks and commensurate service; the
"upscale", photo-bedecked space and "lively bar scene" accentuate
the "buzzy" vibe, though critics warn you should "be prepared to fork
over your wallet" for the experience.

Marmalade Café *American*

19 | 18 | 20 | $25

Santa Barbara | La Cumbre Plaza | 3825 State St. (S. Hope Ave.) |
805-682-5246 | www.marmaladecafe.com

See review in Los Angeles Directory.

Montecito Cafe *Californian*

25 | 21 | 24 | $37

Montecito | Montecito Inn | 1295 Coast Village Rd. (Olive Mill Rd.) |
805-969-3392 | www.montecitocafe.com

Have a "Chaplin adventure" at this "always friendly" Montecito
Californian – housed in a "charming" 1920s inn built by the Little
Tramp himself – where "locals and out-of-towners" of all ages enjoy
"consistent", "delicious" cuisine served by a "helpful" staff in a bright
room; it's a "deal" for the quality, though some feel the concomitant
"noise level" may "limit conversation."

Olio e Limone *Italian*

25 | 21 | 23 | $44

Santa Barbara | 11 W. Victoria St. (bet. Chapala & State Sts.) |
805-899-2699 | www.olioelimone.com

Olio Pizzeria *Italian*

Santa Barbara | 11 W. Victoria St. (bet. Chapala & State Sts.) |
805-899-2699 | www.oliopizzeria.com

"Taste bud–tickling" Sicilian flavors culled from "fresh" ingredients,
along with an "extensive" wine list, are hallmarks of this "busy" Santa

Barbara Italian, a popular choice for "carefully crafted" food served by an "attentive" staff in a white-tableclothed room; budget-minders point to the somewhat high-"moola" cost, but it's in keeping with the "quality"; P.S. a more casual atmosphere – plus thin-crust pies – may be had at the next-door pizzeria.

Opal Restaurant & Bar *Californian/Eclectic*   26 | 22 | 26 | $34

Santa Barbara | 1325 State St. (Arlington Ave.) | 805-966-9676 | www.opalrestaurantandbar.com

You can "see all of Santa Barbara stroll by" if you snag a window table at this nearly 30-year-old bistro, a local "standby" for its "broad" Cal-Eclectic menu and "excellent" service; together with the specialty drinks, "comfortable" ambiance and "happening" vibe, you may think "there's a party going on" – though without the high cost of celebrating.

Palace Grill *Cajun/Creole*   24 | 19 | 23 | $37

Santa Barbara | 8 E. Cota St. (State St.) | 805-963-5000 | www.palacegrill.com

"What a wonderful world" it is at this affordable Santa Barbara "favorite", where locals go for "yummy" Cajun-Creole eats (including "amazing" free cornbread muffins) and jalapeño martinis; a staff that "treats you like family" and upbeat, "relaxing" environs – complete with live music – provide cheer too, making the frequent "long lines" bearable.

Pane e Vino *Italian*   23 | 21 | 23 | $37

Montecito | Upper Montecito Vill. | 1482 E. Valley Rd. (bet. Santa Angela Ln. & San Ysidro Rd.) | 805-969-9274 | www.panevinosb.com

"Imagine you're in Italy" on the romantic patio of this well-priced Montecito mainstay, which locals swear by for its "unpretentious" fare, including "*fantastico*" pastas and meats; supporters also make do with solid service and a "charming" trattoria ambiance, but they note "even if you just go for the patio, you won't be disappointed."

☑ Plow & Angel *Californian/Eclectic*   22 | 25 | 24 | $57

Montecito | San Ysidro Ranch | 900 San Ysidro Ln. (bet. Las Tunas Rd. & Mountain Dr.) | 805-565-1745 | www.sanysidroranch.com

For a "*très romantique*" evening, locals amble to this "magical" Montecito Cal-Eclectic – voted tops in Santa Barbara for Decor – at the "beautiful" San Ysidro Ranch, where a casual stone-walled interior with exposed beams, plus "outstanding" service, provide a "transporting" experience; the broad, "delicious" menu and "dreamy" 1,500-bottle wine list also satisfy – just know the bill can be "pricey."

🆕 Scarlet Begonia *American*   - | - | - | M

Santa Barbara | Victoria Court | 11 W. Victoria St. (State St.) | 805-770-2143 | www.scarlettbegonia.net

This casual Santa Barbara cafe offers breakfast and lunch only, in the retro Victoria Court shopping complex, with not one but two dog-friendly outdoor patios, and a menu of California-tinged Americana like smoked-salmon flatbread, chicken pot pie and cardamom-raisin French toast for breakfast; PS. the chef was at the highly rated Downey's for 10 years prior.

FOOD | DECOR | SERVICE | COST

Seagrass ⓜ *Californian*

| 23 | 23 | 25 | $64 |

Santa Barbara | 30 E. Ortega St. (bet. Anacapa & State Sts.) | 805-963-1012 | www.seagrassrestaurant.com

Offering "superb" service with "scrumptious" Mediterranean-influenced Californian cuisine, this "expensive" Santa Barbara boîte pulls in patrons with its "meticulously prepared" seafood and other "locavore"-oriented specialties; the "elegant", Cape Cod–style decor gratifies as well, even if a few have quibbles about the prices.

Sojourner Cafe *American/Vegetarian*

| 21 | 14 | 22 | $21 |

Santa Barbara | 134 E. Canon Perdido St. (Santa Barbara St.) | 805-965-7922 | www.sojournercafe.com

A taste of "hippie heaven" can be had at this longtime American-vegetarian in Santa Barbara, where a "mellow" staff doles out "healthy-feeling" organic meals and "rich" desserts in a "soothing" locale with sidewalk dining; the wallet-placating bills amplify the groovy feel, leaving most surveyors to concur it "hits the mark."

ⓩ Stella Mare's ⓜ *Californian*

| 25 | 25 | 25 | $43 |

Santa Barbara | 50 Los Patos Way (Cabrillo Blvd.) | 805-969-6705 | www.stellamares.com

There's much to "devour" at this "romantic", French-infused Californian in Santa Barbara; its "magnificent" waterside setting – a multiple-room layout with a working fireplace and terrace, plus an "airy" greenhouse overlooking a bird refuge – and "big-taste" cuisine dazzle diners, who also laud the "top-notch" service and prices that are "fair" for such luxury, especially when involving the "outstanding" prix fixe menus.

Trattoria Grappolo *Italian*

| 24 | 18 | 22 | $39 |

Santa Ynez | 3687 Sagunto St. (Meadowvale Rd.) | 805-688-6899 | www.trattoriagrappolo.com

"Mamma mia!" cry *paesani* of this "can't-miss" Italian "getaway" tucked away in Santa Ynez wine country, a "destination" showcasing "dang-good" "authentic" fare ("so enticing, we purchased the cookbook") and "friendly" service in a "tiny", oft-"busy" muraled space; with amenities such as a seat-equipped counter by the open kitchen and "reasonable" tabs, it's well ensconced as a "local favorite."

Tre Lune *Italian*

| 23 | 21 | 23 | $49 |

Montecito | 1151 Coast Village Rd. (bet. Butterfly Ln. & Middle Rd.) | 805-969-2646 | www.trelunesb.com

Montecito families flock to this "small" "neighborhood" Italian, where "stunning" breakfasts and the chance to dine among "Hollywood stars" – both past (via mounted photos) and present – draw crowds; the "energized" staff also creates "positive vibes", and while commensurate pricing and the need, as some put it, to "tune up your hearing aid" may be unavoidable, it remains something to "look forward to."

Tupelo Junction *Southern*

| 23 | 19 | 21 | $25 |

Santa Barbara | 1218 State St. (bet. Anapamu & Victoria Sts.) | 805-899-3100 | www.tupelojunction.com

"Comfort food" advocates claim "it doesn't get any better" than this "well-priced" Santa Barbara spot, a local "favorite" for "creative" Southern cooking meted out at breakfast, lunch and dinner; a "warm" staff and "casual", brick-walled digs fill out the experience, which admirers affirm "hits all the right notes."

Wine Cask *Californian*

25 | 25 | 24 | $59

Santa Barbara | 813 Anacapa St. (bet. Canon Perdido & De La Guerra Sts.) | 805-966-9463 | www.winecask.com

Business lunchers, tourists and locals "love" the extensive wine list at this Santa Barbara "institution", where the "seasonal" Californian food "shines" as much as the vin; housed in a late-19th-century building adorned with hand-stenciled ceilings, the "beautiful" setting also features "first-rate service", and while some call it "pricey", aficionados are positive this one comes out a "winner."

Zaytoon ◑ *Mideastern*

23 | 24 | 23 | $30

Santa Barbara | 209 E. Canon Perdido St. (Santa Barbara St.) | 805-963-1293 | www.zaytoon.com

Sit outdoors around the fire pit at this "delightful" Santa Barbara Lebanese, where there's "always positive energy" stemming from the "tasty", mildly priced Middle Eastern fare and "comfortable" ambiance; meze-maniacs also favor the "attentive" service, and with regular live entertainment (including belly dancing on Saturdays), it's easy to "love this place."